DE NIRO

DE NIRO

A Life

SHAWN LEVY

CROWN
ARCHETYPE
NEW YORK

All rights reserved.
Published in the United States by Crown Archetype, an imprint of the
Crown Publishing Group, a division of Random House LLC,
a Penguin Random House Company, New York.
www.crownpublishing.com

Crown Archetype and colophon is a registered trademark of
Random House LLC.

Grateful acknowledgment is made to the Harry Ransom Center at
The University of Texas at Austin for permission to use materials contained
in the Robert De Niro collection and the Paul Schrader collection.

Library of Congress Cataloging-in-Publication Data
Levy, Shawn.
De Niro / Shawn Levy. — First edition.
        pages   cm
1. De Niro, Robert. 2. Motion picture actors and actresses—United
States—Biography. I. Title.
PN2287.D37L47 2014
791.4302'8092—dc23
[B]   2014016798

ISBN 978-0-307-71678-1
eBook ISBN 978-0-307-71680-4

Printed in the United States of America

Book design by Lauren Dong
Jacket design by Christopher Brand
Jacket photography: Steve Schapiro/© Corbis

10 9 8 7 6 5 4 3 2 1

First Edition

For my sister, Jennifer, and her beautiful family

DE NIRO

INTRODUCTION

SPRING 2012, AND, AS FOR DECADES, THE ATTENTION OF THE world's film lovers is focused on the onetime fishing village of Cannes, France, and its annual film festival, one of the most prestigious and celebrated cultural events of the year.

On a muggy Friday evening, the air outside the famed Palais des Festivals is plangent with the hum of music written nearly thirty years prior for a movie about hunger, yearning, innocence, violence, crime, betrayal, and memory.

Once Upon a Time in America was an epic both in its creation (a dozen years of writing, eleven months of shooting) and in the vision of its director, Sergio Leone, whose preferred cut ran almost four and a half hours. The film premiered, slightly shorter than that, at Cannes in 1984 to a rapturous reception—a fifteen-minute standing ovation, one observer recalled. But its post-festival fate was a legendary catastrophe. Distributors hacked it almost in half and restructured the narrative, virtually ensuring negative reviews, tepid box office, and a kind of professional oblivion for Leone, who died five years later without directing another film. Over time, though, the movie grew in reputation—in part because of the posthumous stature of its director, in part because increasingly faithful versions of the original cut were released—and it came to be considered by some of its champions as the acme of its genre, the American gangster movie.

And so on this May evening twenty-eight years after its debut, a restored *Once Upon a Time in America*, twenty-five minutes longer than the version that first premiered at Cannes, will be shown in the very same theater where the original screened—as good an occasion as any for a typically deluxe Cannes gala.

In the dying daylight, with Ennio Morricone's luxurious and ghostly score on the PA system, the movie's star, Robert De Niro, climbs the legendary red carpet of the Palais to present the film.

De Niro has ample reason to feel nostalgic. Eight times previously he has visited Cannes in support of a film in which he appeared; twice his work garnered the festival's top prize, and just the previous year he served as president of the festival's jury. It has been, in many ways, a lifelong haunt.

And haunting too, surely, would be the absence of Leone, the reunions with his co-stars, some of whom he hadn't seen since they'd made the film together, and, of course, the spectacle of his younger self on-screen.

But De Niro has experienced all of that many times before, and he has accrued a reputation for stoicism and inscrutability, as well as a detached, even disinterested air about such proceedings.

Something pricks at him on this evening, though, unloosing feelings of the sort he usually reveals only within the strict confines of a movie role or in the hidden chambers of his private life. As he mounts the stairs, he has tears in his eyes, and photos will circulate of him standing in a tuxedo beside his wife with his face clenched in an effort to control his emotions.

Maybe it's the music, Gheorghe Zamfir's pan flute soaring sweetly and sadly over a mournful bed of strings.

Maybe it's the weather: stuffy, wet, thick.

Or maybe it's the knowledge that the chance to make a film like *Once Upon a Time in America* is exceedingly rare and impossible to duplicate once it is gone, the knowledge that movies, like life, can pass us by.

Such a sentiment would certainly mesh with the rueful themes and star-crossed history of Leone's film.

And it would serve, too, as an apt starting point for any discussion of the life and work of Robert De Niro.

WHEN HE BEGAN shooting *Once Upon a Time in America*, Robert De Niro was, almost without question, the most powerful and compelling actor in world cinema. This is an enormous claim, considering that such titans of screen acting as Al Pacino, Dustin Hoffman, Jack Nicholson, Jon Voight, Robert Duvall, and Gérard Depardieu were still ascendant at the time, and such older masters as Jack Lemmon, Paul Newman, Max von Sydow, Peter O'Toole, Michael Caine, Marcello Mastroianni, and even Laurence Olivier and (when he could be bothered) Marlon Brando were still in the game.

But the Robert De Niro of 1982 stood apart even amid such auspicious and accomplished company.

In the spring of 1981, he had won his second Oscar in six years for his role in *Raging Bull*, a performance that was immediately recognized as one of the greatest ever captured on film, built of astonishing physical transformations and raw, wrenching emotions. The previous decade had seen him rise quickly from career in shaggy independent films to the center of such landmark movies as *Mean Streets, The Godfather: Part II* (his first Oscar-winning role, in which he spoke almost entirely in a Sicilian dialect that he learned for the film), *Taxi Driver, 1900,* and *The Deer Hunter.* He worked with the cream of Hollywood's cohort of young Turk directors—Brian De Palma, Francis Ford Coppola, Michael Cimino, and especially Martin Scorsese, with whom he made five films in ten years—as well as with Bernardo Bertolucci and Elia Kazan. His pair of Academy Awards had been accompanied by two additional Oscar nominations, four BAFTA nominations, and a combined seven prizes from the top critics groups across the nation.

He was a master chameleon and an astonishing risk taker, diving as deeply into his roles as any Method actor ever had and coming through them stronger, bolder, better. He had a supernatural, mysterious air and conveyed danger, poetry, sex, loneliness, daring, intensity, surprise, and thrills. He was as exciting a screen actor as had been seen since the heydays of Brando and James Dean. His name on a movie marquee was a galvanizing draw. And at age thirty-eight, he was just getting started.

But thirty years later it could be hard sometimes to see De Niro's early glories through what had become the muddle of his later career.

The shift was gradual. For more than a decade after *Once Upon a Time* he continued to appear in high-quality projects with notable collaborators: *Brazil, The Mission, Angel Heart, The Untouchables, Midnight Run, We're No Angels, Mad Dog and Glory, Heat, Wag the Dog, Jackie Brown, Ronin*. He made three more movies with Martin Scorsese—*Goodfellas, Cape Fear, Casino*—and made his directorial debut with the tender and substantial *A Bronx Tale*. Over time, he gravitated toward smaller roles, working in ensembles or in cameos rather than carrying whole films, but he continued to be recognized by his peers, receiving Oscar nominations for *Awakenings* and *Cape Fear*. And he continued to be one of American cinema's most watched, imitated, and respected actors.

He didn't, however, have a real blockbuster hit until 1999, when the outright comedy *Analyze This* became the first film of his career to gross more than $100 million (by comparison, Arnold Schwarzenegger and John Travolta—and, more to the point, Dustin Hoffman and Jack Nicholson—had each reaped that sum at least five times by then). It was a clever movie, making comic hay of De Niro's tough-guy aura and giving him the chance to demonstrate a funny bone that he'd shown as far back as the 1960s but had long suppressed under his serious Method-actor veneer. The following year, De Niro appeared in *Meet the Parents*, a comedy that was neither as clever as *Analyze This* nor as carefully built around his on-screen persona; naturally, it was an even bigger box office hit. And it presented De Niro anew—for audiences and moviemakers—in a way that would muddy his public image and threaten the impact of his legacy.

Two *Parents* sequels would follow, culminating in a trilogy that took in more than $1.2 billion at the box office globally and accounted for three of the four highest-grossing films De Niro ever made. And they were, relatively, the highlights of his career in the 2000s and 2010s. In that era, he shared billing with the likes of Eddie Murphy, Edward Burns, Cuba Gooding Jr., and Dakota Fanning, as well as James Franco and Bradley Cooper before either of the latter two proved a solid talent. He appeared in action movies that the distributors hid from the critical press until opening day (one such, *Righteous Kill*, co-starred Al Pacino), and he worked with directors of finite gifts and dubious reputation.

He'd had misfires in the 1970s and '80s—*New York, New York, Falling in Love, Stanley and Iris*—but it had always been clear that they'd been made with superior collaborators and with an idea, perhaps unrealized, of quality at their heart. But the films he made after the first *Parents* and *Analyze* films were of another breed: make-work, work-for-hire, paycheck jobs, call them what you will. He was capable of moments of inspiration, but by and large, the De Niro of the twenty-first century erased much of the goodwill—and, indeed, awe—accrued by the younger De Niro. "How does he do it?" was the most common question asked about his gifts early in his career: later it would be replaced with "What happened?"

In 2012 there was a brief upswing—a grounded and unflattering performance as a self-styled literary genius (and sometime taxi driver) hobbled by mental illness in *Being Flynn* and, miracle of miracles, a wrenching and savvy turn as a neurotic gambler trying to connect with his troubled adult son in *Silver Linings Playbook*, which earned him his first Oscar nomination in twenty-one years. But he quickly followed those up with the sort of wheel-spinning and money-grabbing stuff that had marked his work of the previous decade. If the old De Niro had reemerged, he hadn't, seemingly, decided to stick around.

AND YET IN other ways, the qualities of application, focus, and doggedness that marked the work of his younger days were still salient as De Niro turned seventy. While his choice of acting roles in the 2000s and '10s may have seemed dubious, his working life *away* from the movie set had expanded in scope and had come to define him in dimensions having nothing to do with acting. He regularly produced films and TV shows and even theatrical works; some of them, such as *We Will Rock You*, a stage celebration of the music of Queen, turned out to be enormously profitable. He continued to pursue directing, spending years to make the quietly tense and credible 2006 spy saga *The Good Shepherd*. He amassed a real estate and restaurant empire, starting in New York and spreading around the world, by 2014 elevating his net worth to an estimated $310 million. And he raised second and third sets of kids following up on the pair of children he'd sired and adopted in the 1970s.

Most visible, and perhaps most significant, was his investment since the early 1990s in the economic and cultural renaissance of lower Manhattan, his birthplace and the site of so much of his most memorable screen work. He was one of the first high-profile residents of the community known as Tribeca (for "Triangle below Canal") and came to be a significant investor in the infrastructure of the neighborhood, which once was filled with small industries and warehouses but, after De Niro committed himself to its development, became an enclave of pricey apartments, chic restaurants, trendy boutiques and night spots, and cultural and tourist activity. He built a film center in the neighborhood, a block of offices suited to production companies and their ancillaries; he opened restaurants; and he provided Tribeca with a draw and an identity, even if the community was not always entirely willing. After the devastation of the 9/11 attacks on the nearby World Trade Center, De Niro and his associates created the Tribeca Film Festival, an event specifically geared toward celebrating independent film in a way that would bring vitality and attention to the neighborhood. He was a bona fide New York icon, both on and off the screen.

And *icon* is an entirely fitting term for a man of such secret depths. From virtually the first time reporters came to him to ask questions, De Niro scurried away like a wild animal. Though toward those who asked, he was respectful and apologetic through his clumsiness, he was determined to share, reveal, or explain next to nothing about his private life or his working methods. At first it was a seemingly playful thing—the new Brando acting much like the old one with the press. And when he did talk, the content was generally so bland and nonspecific that there was almost a comic air to it. In time, though, his reticence was discussed in darker tones as a pathology, a form of control, even a lack of professionalism, and by the 1980s, his stardom cemented, it became a theme in discussions of the man and his work. Whole articles were written in major magazines about the very subject of De Niro's reluctance to be interviewed, about journalists' courtships of and rejections by the star, and about the lengths to which shopkeepers and restaurateurs in Tribeca were willing to go to help their neighbor protect his privacy. Whenever he finally did emerge—to discuss a new business venture or a charitable venture—he lacked the ease and depth that marked the talk of, say, his famously garrulous chum Martin Scorsese. And when in 2012 he dove into the rigors of his first modern Oscar campaign, there was an air of unreality about the whole thing: when had Robert De Niro become the sort of movie star who would appear on daytime TV and choke back tears while discussing his family life?

Or was it just who he was—a man of unusual emotional capacity who had learned almost from childhood to be self-contained, guarded, and chary, even as he made tremendous strides in the most public of all occupations, acting? In many regards, De Niro's early life and the strong identities of his parents marked him in ways that he never escaped and maybe never even tried to.

His father, also named Robert De Niro, was a highly respected but somewhat neglected painter of the post–World War II New York School; his mother, born Virginia Admiral and known by that name after the brief two-year marriage that produced her only child, was an independent businesswoman in the midst of bohemian Greenwich Village, active in progressive arts and political scenes but savvy, wary, and tough with a dollar.

From his father, with whom he never lived after about 1945 but with whom he was always close, De Niro learned the virtues of dogged work, self-criticism, and creative integrity; the elder De Niro's career was at its brightest in the 1950s, and as his commercial luster faded he held ferociously to his artistic vision and ideals, sometimes taking menial work to keep a meager roof over his head, but always maintaining a strong sense of purpose in pursuit of his aesthetic standards. From his mother, who possessed a firm ethic of Yankee thrift and caution and who built a one-woman typing service into a full printing business and, years before her son, a small real estate empire in lower Manhattan, De Niro learned financial acumen and strong senses of loyalty and territoriality. Both parents were creatures of powerful will: the senior De Niro was brutally hard on his own work, abandoning version after version of paintings until they met his criteria of worthiness, and Admiral was, in her son's formative years, a tireless worker and networker, connected to theatrical, literary, and artistic lights and sufficiently intent on carving her own way in life that she never remarried.

Together not even long enough to see their son out of diapers, De

Niro's parents maintained separate households (such as households were in their circles), and the boy not infrequently bounced between the two, often on his own, a silent observer of grown-up life with his nose in books, bereft of siblings and cousins and, often, playmates. It can't be any sort of surprise that a child raised among adults—and adults who were swimming determinedly against the current of mainstream postwar American ideas of normalcy—should turn out to be guarded, suspicious, leery.

And yet, for all his vaunted privacy and secrecy, De Niro would spend most of his adult life in the most public of professions, pursuing it at first with his parents' sense of zeal and toil, then with a ferocious thirst for work that outweighed even that of his coevals and peers Dustin Hoffman, Al Pacino, and Jack Nicholson. Only four of the years after 1968 failed to see a new film featuring De Niro, often in the lead, and often, especially in those first decades, revealing startling depths, abilities, and personality. In his performances—and in the frequently arduous effort he put into creating his performances—he opened himself up in ways that he was almost never willing to when in the presence of a journalist with a microphone. He never, as he once suggested he might, wrote a memoir, but his work—and the work that went into his work—stands as his autobiography.

AND WHO WAS he, this inscrutable, talented, and elusive man? What did he bring to the screen, and what did audiences take from him?

Start with the looks. He was always handsome, with the aspect of a slightly more rugged Alain Delon. But with just a little tweak of lighting he could be either appealing or ugly.

There was that mole, perched on the corner of his right cheekbone like an asterisk, a mark of jauntiness or irony, or even, when he was roused to anger, the sight on the end of a rifle barrel: unblinking, accusatory, immutable. When his face was lean, as it was generally, the mole was accentuated and defined, almost like a third eye; when he was heavy, it could seem like a scrap left on his cheek after a messy meal. It was so clearly visible that it almost threatened his handsomeness, which bordered on prettiness when he was young and developed into ruggedness as he aged. But he carried it so unconsciously that you felt as guilty noting it as if you were staring at someone's lazy eye.

A lot of actresses sported such moles—beauty marks—almost as if defying the audience to see them as faults: Marilyn Monroe, Marion Cotillard, Angelina Jolie, Madonna. And, too, there might have been a time, perhaps when he was a young actor, when De Niro was tempted to have the thing removed. (Actors have done far more to themselves in their struggles toward careers.) Fortunately, he never succumbed to such a vain impulse, and the mole became as much a part of his persona as his smile, in which his whole face seems to pucker in delight (he can grin and grimace at once, show delight and menace at the same time, offer a smile that's a threat or a scowl that embraces), or his enviable, ever-changing hair, always thick and pliant and wavy even as it turned gray, often long enough to make him look like a rocker, sometimes cut short for the sake of accuracy or even to shock.

His body, too, was a malleable thing, at times chiseled and fit, at times soft and homey, now and then genuinely rotund. Lots of actors changed their looks for parts with makeup, hairpieces, prosthetics; De Niro, more than once, changed his entire shape, his commitment to his roles so thoroughgoing as to make his journey *beneath* the skin immediately apparent, like a tattoo, *upon* the skin.

And that's just what could be *seen* of his actorly craft. His work, from his earliest days as a student actor to very near the present, was actually far deeper, more technical, and more immersive than was generally acknowledged or understood. For the first forty years of his acting career, De Niro dove into almost every role he took with fervent research on the page and, when possible, in person: brutally paring away at dialogue (his preference was always for showing rather than telling), having long colloquies with screenwriters, directors, and fellow actors, and being meticulous in the preparation of props and costumes.

From his earliest days, he was prone to keeping lists of questions to ask, items to acquire, skills to master—always with an eye toward presenting a character as realistically as possible. He learned to speak Neapolitan and Sicilian dialects, drive a cab, play the saxophone, box, customize a military uniform like an Army Ranger in Vietnam, toss a catcher's mask aside like a major league ballplayer, and speak like a native of the American South, Northeast, and Northwest.

He could drive directors and acting colleagues crazy with his obsessive focus on detail, but he learned to build a character from the outside in, to allow the inner life of the men he played to emerge through a firmly established air of external realism. Even very late in his career, when critics and audiences often accused him of taking any part for a paycheck or phoning in his performances, you could see him building real men out of specifically chosen items of clothing, props, habits, turns of speech, and mannerisms. In a very real sense he saw acting as work and playing a character as a moral act, and he would almost always make an effort to live up to his own professional and ethical standards and do right by the men he portrayed.

That discipline of building from the outside in made him an actor with whom directors had to exhibit patience. Very rarely was he fully ready to play a scene at its best in the first or second take. He had to steep himself in the emotion of the story, feel the energy of his fellow actors, mine himself for psychological and physical nuances. When he and his colleagues had sufficient bonds of trust to allow him to explore, he could create remarkable moments—real and convincing and seemingly unrehearsed. In the first decades of his movie career, working in lead roles on large films with powerful directors and the luxury of time, he was able to produce one remarkable performance after another in just this fashion. Later, when the scripts weren't as precise and the directors not so patient or capable, his performances could come to feel generic; you get the very strong sense that he was given fewer chances to play each scene in, say, *Meet the Parents* than he was in *Taxi Driver*. But by then, like so many actors with scores of memorable films behind them, he could rely on an audience's accrued trust and memory and affection to add the depth that maybe he himself couldn't bring to a character. Lots of actors, for instance, could have played the neurotic mobster in *Analyze This*; De Niro, arguably, was the only leading man in Hollywood who could bring decades of resonant performances as a hard man to the film's seriocomic psychodrama.

HE HAS LONG been a figure of great contradiction in the movie business, reticent with the press but willing to go on late-night talk shows and do sketch comedy—and particularly agreeable about taking part in things that made fun of his own legend and persona. He would mock himself on *Saturday Night Live* and on TV commercials, but he was unwilling to share even with an innocent anecdote in conversation with, say, David Letterman or Jay Leno; sometimes he would speak in monosyllables or—defiantly, comically—not at all. You might wonder why he bothered, and then you realized that his show of taciturn stubbornness was in some ways more real and true and memorable than any palaver he might've offered up. It couldn't have pleased the movie studios whose pictures he was supposed to be publicizing, but it stuck with you, and when he finally did at least *appear* to be opening up, such as in the Oscar campaign for 2012's *Silver Linings Playbook*, he was all the more impressive for finally revealing himself.

And if he never truly opened up as a private man, there would still be so much of him to savor: Johnny Boy Civello riffing on various neighborhood characters in *Mean Streets*; Vito Corleone blending the ways of the Old World and the New in *The Godfather, Part II*; Travis Bickle ticking like a human time bomb in *Taxi Driver*; Michael Vronsky surviving hell and burying it within himself in *The Deer Hunter*; Jake LaMotta visiting righteous punishment on boxing foes, family members, and chiefly himself in *Raging Bull*; Rupert Pupkin wheedling his way into showbiz, legally or otherwise, in *The King of Comedy*; the gangsters and killers and bad guys of *The Untouchables, Goodfellas, Cape Fear, Casino, Heat,* and *Analyze This*; the complex but decent heroes of *Bang the Drum Slowly, Midnight Run, Awakenings, A Bronx Tale, Wag the Dog, Ronin, Being Flynn,* and *Silver Linings Playbook.*

Though movie actors may never say a single thing about themselves, may never once willingly open the door to the truth of their hearts and minds, nevertheless—if they are good enough and last long enough—they eventually spill everything about themselves out into the world.

De Niro may have tried assiduously to keep from revealing who he

is, providing only hints and allusions in response to personal questions. Yet, every time he appears before us, no matter the costume, the voice, the name, the story, there he is, stark and plain before the world: a working man, a man of principle, a man of ideals—in short, a man in full, as clearly defined by the work he has done as by the life he has lived.

1

WE SOMETIMES THINK OF THE LIVES OF CELEBRITIES IN terms of how their work and their fame intersect with the chronologies of our own lives. We know, rationally, that famous people are born and grow up, find their craft and work at it just as the rest of us do. But somehow we still think of them as having begun to exist only when we first encountered them in a star-making film role, hit record, or athletic feat. In the thrall of a new star, we don't necessarily care about his or her parentage or upbringing or education. In our minds and hearts, and in the mind and heart of the larger culture, stars arrive fully formed.

But Robert De Niro's story, strictly speaking, begins well before he was introduced to the art of acting or performed his breakthrough movie roles, before his parents met or made their professional marks in the world. Indeed, it begins so far back that it seems almost impossible to connect the history of it with the familiar figure of the actor.

Only three times in his career did Robert De Niro portray a character from earlier than the twentieth century; nearly as rarely did he take on the role of a soldier, and just once that of a full-blooded nobleman. But the genealogy of this characteristically modern figure runs back through the centuries to, of all times and places, medieval France, where one of his ancestors, a cavalry officer, took part in the Roman conquests of Languedoc and Dauphine with sufficient valor to be named governor of those regions by the Roman emperor Conrad II.

Raphael del Poggio was born in Lucca, Italy, in 1011 and died, his surname recast into French as DuPuy, a general of the Roman cavalry and grand chamberlain of the Roman Empire, in 1062. He would be entombed on a marble table with his sword, spurs, and helmet, along with a copper plaque celebrating his deeds and honor.

The DuPuy family maintained noble status through centuries of governors and generals until the sixteenth century, when it turned to Protestantism, creating a Huguenot line that would, in time, bring the family out of favor with both secular and sacred authorities. In the late seventeenth century, French persecution of Protestants climaxed with the Edict of Fontainebleau, which virtually outlawed the DuPuys' religion and forced them to flee, first to Germany and then to Virginia, to which King William III had invited Protestant settlers.

The DuPuy line thrived in the New World, merging in 1829 with the Holton family, also of old colonial stock.* Fifty years later, one of the daughters of that union, Virginia Moseby Holton, would marry the Dutch immigrant Nicholas Admiraal, and their son, Donald, born in 1890, would be the maternal grandfather of the actor Robert De Niro.

IF THE IDEA of Robert De Niro descending from French courtiers and Crusaders and English colonists who fought off Native Americans sounds incongruous, perhaps it's because the other lines of his family, though less marked with incident, would shine so strongly in him, particularly the Irish-Italian blend. That nearly stereotypical alloy of immigrant stocks was produced in Syracuse, New York, in the latter part of the nineteenth century, after De Niro's paternal ancestors fled hunger and poverty in Ireland or Italy to make a new start in America.

Luigi and Rosanna Mercurio of Campobasso, in southeastern Italy, arrived in New York Harbor in 1886 with their daughter Angiolina, whose future husband, Giovanni Di Niro (as it was spelled in some documents), arrived in America the following year. Giovanni, known by the Americanized name John, was, like his father-in-law, a stonemason, and he and his bride set up their home in the Italian section of Syracuse. There they raised two boys and a girl; the middle of the three, Henry (or Enrico, as he was sometimes called on official docu-

---

* The Holtons descended from the Woodson family of Virginia, among whose descendants are Dolley Madison and Jesse James.

ments), born in 1897, would be the paternal grandfather of Robert De Niro.

Henry may have been born to a lineage of stonemasons, but he found softer work as a clerk at Weeks and Anderson, a Syracuse haberdashery. He put in a spell of military service near the end of World War I, but by 1920 he was living back in his father's house in Syracuse. Not long after, he married Helen O'Reilly, the twenty-one-year-old daughter of Dennis, a bookkeeper, and Mary O'Reilly.

Like the De Niros and Mercurios, the O'Reillys were descended from immigrants who left only vaporous traces in official records. Dennis and Mary (née Burns) were both born in upstate New York, but *their* parents—Edward and Margaret O'Reilly and John and Mary Burns, respectively—were born in Ireland and arrived in America amid a flood of immigrants with similar names and similarly ordinary backgrounds, virtually unnoted by history or officialdom. In 1964, the young Robert De Niro himself, a twenty-year-old high school dropout, would travel to Ireland on a backpacking tour partly intended as a search for his roots, only to find out just how obscure they were. As his father would later recollect, "He asked about his background. He'd hitchhiked around Ireland for two weeks, trying to find relatives, and couldn't. I said, 'My father's people come from a place called Campobasso, halfway between Naples and Rome,' so Bobby went there and met them."

THAT TRIP TO Europe wasn't merely a young man's lark or a genealogical quest. De Niro was inspired to go overseas in large part because his father had been living in France since the previous year, having gone there to, in a sense, reverse the trail of his immigrant grandparents and seek a new way of life and new avenues of work.

Robert Henry De Niro, to give him his full name, was the oldest of Henry and Helen's four children, born on May 3, 1922, barely a year after his parents wed. The household in which he was raised was slightly more genteel than those in which his parents lived as children: a freestanding house on Tipperary Hill, in the Irish enclave of Syracuse, valued at $9,000 and owned by Dennis O'Reilly, who lived there with them. To help pay their way, Henry and Helen both worked out-side the home. After his return from military service, Henry took what might be called soft white-collar jobs as a salesman, a wholesale grocer, a general-store keeper, and eventually a government health inspector. Helen, too, brought in an income, at least in 1930, when she identified herself for the federal census as a "traveling salesman"—likely of the door-to-door sort. In the way of such things, their children (John, Joan, and Elizabeth followed Robert at two-year intervals) would have been expected to progress even further along the path of Americanization and upward mobility.

But Robert Henry wasn't the sort who did what was expected. In fact, he lived in pursuit of impulses and dreams that his father couldn't quite fathom. From a very young age—five, according to family legend—the eldest of the De Niro children displayed remarkable gifts for drawing and painting. Years later, he was unable to explain his in-congruous absorption in making art—"I don't know," he said with a shrug, "I was very isolated." But his enthusiasm was encouraged by his parents and teachers, and he was allowed to take art classes at the Syra-cuse Museum of Fine Arts,* where he demonstrated such talent that he was quickly promoted from the children's program to the adult classes and then, at age twelve, granted use of a studio space of his own, a lair to which he would repair regularly after school to draw and paint in sol-itude. His teachers took sufficient interest in the boy and his gifts that he was encouraged to seek more rigorous and more modern schooling in art. In 1938, he was awarded a scholarship to study with the noted etcher, critic, and teacher Ralph Pearson in Gloucester, Massachusetts. For any number of reasons his parents didn't want him to go, and quar-rels resulted, but—with their blessing or without—he made his way to Gloucester.

There the teenage artist was able to immerse himself in whatever passions and interests caught his fancy. Instructed by Pearson on an an-chored coal barge that served as a floating classroom, he learned of con-temporary painting theories and techniques and had his eyes opened to a wider world of culture than he had experienced in Syracuse. De-

---

*   Now the Everson Museum of Art.

cades later, asked about a long-standing fascination with Greta Garbo, whose image he painted frequently over the years, he explained, "I was at an art school on a coal barge in Gloucester Harbor when I was 16, and after I read [*Anna Christie*] I made a model of the stage set."

When the summer session ended, De Niro returned to his father's house determined to go back out into the world to study, learn, experience, and, chief of all, paint. He was in Massachusetts the following summer to work with a new teacher, and it would mark the beginning of several key relationships in his young life.

His new master was Hans Hofmann, an expatriate artist and teacher from Germany who had thrived until the Nazis rose to power. He came to the States in 1932 and found work as an instructor at the famed Art Students League. Soon thereafter he opened his own school, or, rather, a pair of programs, one held during the traditional academic year in a space on 8th Street in Manhattan, the other, run in the summers, in Provincetown, the bohemian village on the tip of Cape Cod. In these two fabled settings, Hofmann's modernist ideas were introduced to a burgeoning generation of young American artists eager for something beyond the pictorialism that still ruled their own schools and museums.

In Hofmann, Robert De Niro found a truly fatherly artistic mentor, a widely respected artist who was as renowned for his teaching as for his actual work. Hofmann preached a blend of European modernist theory with an untamed American energy. He had strong ideas, but he wasn't doctrinaire, and he was open to free and expressive work of all sorts. He emphasized the spiritual element of art making, and he favored a dynamic color palette so long as there was what he called a "push-pull" between the elements of an abstract composition. Partly because of his choice of Manhattan as a home base and partly because of his catholic tastes and ideas, he was extremely influential, with such famed painters as Helen Frankenthaler, Red Grooms, Lee Krasner, Joan Mitchell, and Larry Rivers among his pupils. (Indeed, his influence as a teacher would come to outshine his own work so completely that it would later be noted in a review of a show of his works alongside some by his students, "Sometimes he seems major *despite* his painting.")

When De Niro showed up in Provincetown, barely seventeen years old, he was introduced not only to Hofmann's modern and liberal ideas and frame of mind but also to a variety of ways of life more unconventional than anything he had ever experienced. Provincetown was nearly as old as American history, the spot at the tippy-tip of Cape Cod where the *Mayflower's* Pilgrims had alighted before moving on to Plymouth. Since then, its natural beauty and cheap housing—and, perhaps chief of all, its isolation from the workaday world and its norms—made it a celebrated enclave of bohemians (including Eugene O'Neill, whose *Anna Christie*, so beloved by the young painter Robert De Niro, was set there). Cut off geographically from the rest of the world, it was a perfect place to experiment with sexuality, drugs and alcohol, and virtually any lifestyle variation that could be imagined.

Tennessee Williams, who lived in Provincetown during the summers as he cobbled together his playwriting career, would comment, "The whole lunatic fringe of Manhattan is already here." Painter Larry Rivers remembered the scene, which he entered a few years after De Niro as a student of Hofmann's: "Romping and bathing in the nude was a popular activity among the young . . . trying to get laid was the number one preoccupation. Number two on the list was getting happy, either with alcohol or pot. Number three was making art at Hofmann's and at home, and looking forward to the weekly crit show of student painting."

In those crit shows, held on Friday afternoons, Hofmann assessed his pupils' most recent output with often abstruse explanations and impulsive reactions that varied from the discouragingly dismissive to the enthusiastically complimentary. He would speak of the techniques and strategies of old masters and modern heroes, pronounce theoretical precepts, and cajole and wheedle and nurture in turn, all in a soft, highly accented voice that could confound students but nevertheless transfixed them. "We couldn't understand what the fuck he was talking about," recalled another student, Nick Carone, "but you felt your life was at stake with every word he uttered. The atmosphere worked on you; it was serious, you were serious, and therefore you were an artist."

De Niro made an immediate impression on his peers upon arriving in Provincetown. Albert Kresch, who first knew him as a fellow student of Hofmann's and then throughout their parallel lives as New York painters, recalled, "He was handsome, very elegant. Better-looking than his son, a couple of inches taller and his hair was fairer. He was poetic in the Byronic sense." In a picture taken during one of Hofmann's celebrated Friday critiques, De Niro stands out prominently: tall and lean, with a wavy head of fair hair, a cocky posture, and a face that resembled, to a point nearing twinship, that of his son when the younger De Niro was a newcomer to the screen nearly thirty years later. He looks as if he's paying attention; he also looks as if he already knows everything that's being said and is contemplating something far more interesting. Despite his air of seeming detachment, though, he was an earnest pupil and something of a teacher's pet, being named Hofmann's best student of 1939—an honor that, cheesy as it sounds, was highly coveted. He was a star.

At Hofmann's suggestion, the seventeen-year-old De Niro took the next major step in his development as an artist, applying to study at Black Mountain College, the experimental arts school near Asheville, North Carolina, where a litany of significant artists in virtually every field were attempting to change American arts and education in a single revolutionary swoop. Inspired by the pedagogical theories of John Dewey and the Bauhaus school in Germany, Black Mountain was designed to stress the centrality of arts to a fully rounded education and to the larger society. It was founded in 1933 and didn't survive a quarter century, but it had a huge impact on twentieth-century art. Buckminster Fuller built his first geodesic dome as a Black Mountain instructor, and Merce Cunningham, another faculty member, formed his first dance troupe there. Other teachers—often former students—included John Cage, Walter Gropius, Alfred Kazin, Willem de Kooning, and Charles Olson. Among the school's many celebrated alumni would be the painters Cy Twombly, Robert Rauschenberg, and Elaine de Kooning; the poets Robert Creeley, Ed Dorn, and Joel Oppenheimer; and the filmmaker Arthur Penn.

Granted a full scholarship, De Niro arrived at Black Mountain in the fall of 1939 and, as in Provincetown, found himself in a miraculous kind of place. Decades later, he would still regard the physical setting of the school as a standard of visual beauty, and the atmosphere of study and work was an exhilarating boil of ideas, passions, and challenges. De Niro was studying with another German expatriate, the painter, sculptor, and theoretician Josef Albers, a key figure in the development of the Bauhaus who had emigrated to America after the Nazis shut the school down in 1933. Partly through the good offices of the young architect Philip Johnson, Albers had been named head of the art department at Black Mountain, where he and his wife, Anni, a famed textile artist, established one of the nation's finest arts education programs.

Though one of the youngest students at the school, De Niro was lauded by Albers, who compared his work to that of the Italian painter and sculptor Amedeo Modigliani and the medieval German master Matthias Grunewald. When Albers took a sabbatical partly through the academic year, leaving the school without a full-time art teacher, he was concerned that De Niro would leave, and he tried to mitigate the situation by giving his young pupil the keys to his personal studio.

Despite this preferential treatment, De Niro bridled at Albers's instruction. Contrasting with Hans Hofmann's sensual aesthetic and fatherly tenor, Albers advocated a rigorous, cool, and precise approach to art, and he took issue with the young painter's somewhat lurid color palette, which he claimed was "too emotional." (As De Niro said years later, "A painting can't be too emotional. It can be controlled, but never too emotional.") "He found Albers to be too dogmatic and preferred Hans Hofmann," wrote a Black Mountain historian, adding the proviso that "stories of his conflicts with Albers are exaggerated." Indeed, De Niro himself declared that rather than quarrel with his teacher, he complied, at least in form, with his instruction: in school, he recalled, he "painted to please Albers, then went home and painted what I wanted." But he wasn't satisfied with the arrangement and determined to leave Black Mountain in the spring of 1939. "One day I just walked out," he remembered, "with only five dollars on me."

He didn't exactly wander the streets of North Carolina in penury. From Black Mountain he went to Hofmann's school in New York, then to the summer session in Provincetown. For the next few years he would migrate seasonally to wherever Hofmann was teaching, Provincetown or New York, maintaining his meager art student existence by doing odd jobs, including working for Hofmann as a classroom monitor and school manager. He hadn't yet celebrated his twentieth birthday, he was immersing himself not only in art but also in poetry (he was partial to the French Symbolists, a taste he would hold throughout his life), and he had a seemingly favorable future ahead of him, a star pupil who would no doubt become a well-known painter.

He was emerging as a young man, as well. From its earliest days as an arts colony, Provincetown had been a community in which homosexuality was treated with far more acceptance than in the larger American society. In the ordinary course of studying painting, working on his art, and making a living, De Niro met any number of gay men, closeted and not, and somewhere along the way he began to explore his sexuality with them. Among his acquaintances was Tennessee Williams, with whom De Niro worked as a waiter at Captain Jack's restaurant. Williams, older and far more daring than his young coworker, was gay, out, and unabashed, and De Niro surely noticed his fearlessness. Another acquaintance was Valeska Gert, an expatriate German dancer and actress who operated an illicit after-hours saloon and was, like Williams, unconcerned with hiding her sexuality.

De Niro, a teenager from a traditional working-class Catholic home, may have had a mature confidence in his artistic abilities, but he was reserved and quiet by nature. Though he may have been drawn toward men, his sexual activities, whatever they were, weren't conducted nearly as brashly and publicly as those of his friends—a lifelong habit, as it happens. He may have experimented with men and women, but he formed no acknowledged romantic attachments.

And then, like in the movies, he met a girl.

IN POINT OF fact, Virginia Holton Admiral wasn't a girl but a young woman of twenty-seven—a full seven years De Niro's senior. She had been born on February 4, 1915, to Donald Admiral, a descendant of those noble lines of French courtiers and English colonialists (with some Dutch mixed in), who had been born in Danville, Illinois, in 1890, and Alice Groman, who was born to German immigrants in Odebolt, Iowa, in 1887. The couple wed in Danville in 1913 and would have two daughters, Eleanor following Virginia by almost two years. Virginia came into the world in The Dalles, Oregon, a port town along the Columbia River, because Donald was pursuing work there as a grain dealer. By 1917, when he registered for the military draft (he never served), he had relocated his family back to the Midwest. And by the time the Admiral girls were still in their midteens, Donald and Alice had divorced and were living in separate households in Berkeley, California, where Alice worked as a public school teacher with specialties in English and Latin.

Virginia, blond, of smallish stature, and with a spunky personality, distinguished herself as a student and especially as an artist. As a teenager she was offered a chance to study painting in Paris but passed, preferring to attend the University of California near her Berkeley home. Even in the mid-1930s, Cal was noted as much for the radicalism of the campus culture as for the quality of education it offered, and Virginia embraced the former avidly, engaging herself in the Young People's Socialist League, a Trotskyite group that was in regular conflict with the far larger Stalinist organization, the Young Communists League. Along with her political activities, she pursued an interest in avant-garde literature, which brought her into contact with a clique that included the poets Robert Duncan and Mary and Lili Fabilli, sisters who were as ardent about politics and sexual liberty as they were about modern verse. Along with Admiral, the four formed a makeshift bohemian family, sharing housing and fostering each other's work. Various decisions that any of them made about work, art, love, and life were made in consultation with one another; for example, Duncan, an outlandish and openly gay young man, was apparently talked out of fulfilling his ROTC service by his housemates.*

After graduating with a degree in English, Admiral spent a short time studying painting at the Art Institute of Chicago, only to return to California and work on the Federal Art Project, with which Duncan was also involved, in Oakland. Together, they published a literary review, *Epitaph*, which existed under that name for but a single issue,

---

* Among the younger students who ran with the circle centered on Duncan was Pauline Kael, who looked with admiration upon Admiral and her friends. Decades later, Kael would experience a long, ambivalent relationship with Robert De Niro's film performances.

then reemerged as *Ritual* and later, under different editorship, as *The Experimental Review.* The pair dreamed bigger for themselves and schemed about ways to get to New York and the lives of personal liberation and intellectual stimulation that they imagined awaited them there. In the summer of 1940, Admiral made her way back east, putatively to study for a master's degree at Columbia University's Teachers College. Before the term began, she visited Duncan in Woodstock, in upstate New York, where he was living on a communal farm dedicated to personal liberty and artistic experimentation. Then she moved on to Maine to teach art at a summer camp before finally settling in Manhattan in the fall to begin school.

Or at least that was the idea. Admiral was living, in part, on money that her mother had borrowed from her grandfather, and she was supposed to find a room at International House, a dormitory on the Columbia campus that was considered a safe zone for unattached young women in the big, mean city. But her housing plans went the way of her academic career. Admiral began to live exactly the sort of bohemian existence that she, Duncan, the Fabillis, and their new friend Janet Thurman had dreamed of, renting a cold-water walk-up apartment facing Union Square on 14th Street, waiting tables in a Greenwich Village restaurant, visiting a psychotherapist (even among starving student artists, psychoanalysis was a fad), and focusing on her painting and writing. It was a fairy tale of the artistic life. Indeed, as Duncan would describe Admiral's flat in his journal, "This is our last nursery—this is today's, 1941's projection of a Berkeley Paradise."

A mottled account of Admiral's *vie bohème* would come courtesy of Anaïs Nin, the not-yet-famed writer who befriended Duncan in Woodstock and, in time, served as something of a mentor to him and his circle, calling them "les enfants terribles." Like so many other European leftists and aesthetes, Nin had migrated to the United States to flee the burgeoning war, bringing with her sophisticated and even radical ideas about art and life. She was an intense draw for Admiral and her friends, who had never, of course, met anyone like her, and she introduced them to a variety of new experiences and faces to which they might otherwise never have had access.

Nin taught Admiral, Duncan, and their set, particularly the young women, about writing, about nightlife, about sexual freedom, about behaving in empowered and assertive ways. But Nin was not entirely a beneficent presence in the lives of her new acolytes. For one thing, she felt wholly superior to Virginia and the other young women in her circle. As she wrote in her diary:

> *Virginia and her friends dress like schoolchildren. Baby shoes, little bows in their hair, little-girl dresses, little-boy clothes, orphan hats, schoolgirl short socks, they eat candy, sugar, ice cream. And some of the books they read are like schoolchildren's books: how to win friends, how to make love, how to do this or that.*

And when she described her visits to Admiral's loft on 14th Street, she was again condescending:

> *The place is cold, but the hallways and lofts are big and high-ceilinged and the only place possible and available to a painter. . . . There is a lavatory outside, running water and a washstand inside, and that is all. On weekends the heat is turned off. The enormous windows which give on the deafening traffic noise of Fourteenth Street have to be kept closed. There are nails on the walls for clothes, a Sterno burner for making coffee. We drink sour wine out of paper cups. . . . The setting is fit for* Crime and Punishment, *but the buoyancy of Virginia and Janet and their friends, lovers, is deceptive. It has the semblance of youth and gaiety. They are in their twenties. They joke, laugh, but this hides deep anxieties, deep fears, deep paralysis.*

For her part, Virginia would claim, years later, that she and her friends saw Nin as more of a sugar mama than an inspiration. Duncan was the only one among them truly smitten by Nin, both erotically and intellectually. But Admiral had other ideas. "My role," she told Nin's biographer Deirdre Bair, "was to string along with Anaïs as long as Robert felt as he did about her. We were just two kids from Berkeley, and as she took us to parties and fed us, well . . ."

There was, in fact, a frankly financial aspect to the relationship of Nin and Admiral. One of Admiral's moneymaking enterprises was working as a typist (among her clients was the poet Kenneth Patchen). As Nin was in the process of having her journals transcribed from longhand into typescript, it was natural the two should cut a deal. As Admiral remembered,

> When I first met Anaïs, she was having problems with the person typing her journals (at ten cents a page, sometimes margin-to-margin, on rice paper with a carbon in French, but not a bad price at the time). I said I would type some of them for nothing since I wanted to read them anyway. Later, when I ran out of money she paid me. . . . One night a week I would stay up and type one of the journals, making ten dollars, which was enough for me to live on. . . . The early journals were rather heartrending, but when she seduced John Erskine it seemed unduly unkind. At night, the journals that were not out being read or typed were locked in a huge safe.

In total, Admiral would type a full sixty volumes of Nin's diaries, the pages of which Nin then edited and returned to Admiral for retyping. After that they were again tucked away in a secure spot, awaiting their publication decades later.

Admiral told one of Nin's biographers that she found the material in these pages boring, but Nin claimed (in a later diary, which, like the previously quoted passages, Admiral wouldn't have seen until they appeared in a published volume),

> Virginia tells me she is enriched and liberated by my writing and our talks. There is an interesting interplay between Virginia and her analyst, and his comments on my work and our talks. . . . Virginia suddenly realized that she had never lived, loved, suffered or enjoyed.

It was true, in fact, that Nin inspired Admiral's circle to examine themselves in new ways, to submit to sessions of psychoanalysis and write about their inner lives. But it wasn't the only thing they did, and hers wasn't the only inspiration they heeded or sought. Admiral, for one, was still painting. In the fall of 1941 she enrolled in Hans Hofmann's New York school. And there she met Robert De Niro.

ON PAPER THEY had almost nothing in common: a blue-blooded, pre-*Mayflower* Presbyterian spitfire from California and a taciturn second-generation Irish-Italian American from Syracuse. He was considerably taller than her, and she, of course, was considerably older, especially given their relative youth. But in light of his sexual mercuriality and her comfort with a variety of lifestyles, there seemed to be an ease between them. Both were reckoned physically attractive by their peers. And they were among the most accomplished and praised of Hofmann's students, which surely established a kinship or a kind of sibling rivalry—whether sexual or not. According to a fellow student, painter Nell Blaine, "Virginia and De Niro were considered among the most talented, the most gifted of Hofmann's students. We talked about them with great respect. They left an aura." That alone might have formed the basis of their bond. But a photo taken in the 1940s shows Admiral regarding De Niro with evident affection as they sit beside each other at a casual gathering. There was real love there.

During the latter months of the academic year, De Niro moved in with Admiral, and when summer arrived, they made their way to Hofmann's Provincetown school together. When Hofmann headed back to New York at season's end, Admiral and De Niro chose to stay on for a time, and he went to work at a fishery to help keep their little household afloat. But there was another moneymaking scheme in the air: Nin had been in Provincetown as well, and she enlisted the help of her clutch of young bohemian friends in writing pornography that she sold to a private collector who paid her a buck a page, first for fully formed fictions, ultimately for juicy passages alone. Although she found the famously scandalous pages of Nin's diaries "boring," Admiral was game to try her hand at writing erotica. However, Nin deemed her initial effort "too satiric." De Niro, with his love of Verlaine and Rimbaud (as Nin remembered, he "wanted to hear all about life in Paris"), had been doing some writing of his own at the time, and he was at least willing to try to earn a dollar with a pen, even if it was smut for hire. But it wasn't his ideal medium. As he later remembered, "I was working in the fishery . . . and having a hard time with money. Anaïs Nin suggested I write some pornography at $1 a page. Thirty years ago that was a lot of money. . . . It was very hard work, so eventually I went back to the fishery." Additionally, the couple threw parties to help cover household expenses. "Every Friday night Bob and Virginia had a rent party," remembered Larry Rivers. "You danced, you drank, and you brought money."

There was some trauma between the pair that summer. One night De Niro revealed to Admiral that he'd been sexually intimate with Duncan, instigating a row loud enough to be heard in an adjacent studio. According to Nin, during a lull in their quarrel the two suddenly heard one of their neighbors addressing them through the thin wall: "I have been listening to you. I have been weighing all your arguments. I think that Virginia is absolutely fair and right and the behavior of Bob and Robert treacherous and ugly." (In another account, the unseen commentator declared that De Niro had behaved "like a real shit.") For the circumspect De Niro, this was an utter humiliation, at least as Nin imagined it in a diary:

> Bob was completely shocked that anyone should have heard his homosexual confession and passed judgment on him. He had to know who it was, who now knew so much about him and had judged him. He did not recognize the voice. . . . He rushed out into the town. He sat at bars. If anyone looked at him too intently, he felt it might be the one. He wanted to talk with him, explain himself, justify himself. Every face he saw now he imagined was the face of his accuser, of his judge. . . . The idea was unbearable to him. He walked with his shoulders bowed. He was silent. He looked haunted.

De Niro would struggle with depression and neurosis throughout his adult life, but this was the first time it became manifest to his friends.

Eventually the couple returned to New York for the winter. De

Niro found work waiting tables alongside Tennessee Williams at the Beggar's Bar, a celebrated Greenwich Village watering hole that their old Provincetown acquaintance, Valeska Gert, had opened. The jobs didn't last long—Williams's lover of the moment, another painter who was also working at the bar, apparently flipped out over the policy of pooling tips, leading Gert to rid herself of the troublesome lot of them.

Nin, too, was out of the picture, weary of dealing with Admiral's provincialism. She was out one evening with Admiral and De Niro and talking about the various great artists she had encountered since arriving in New York. "Virginia stopped me with a prim tone of voice," Nin wrote. "'I'm not interested in the unfamiliar. I like the familiar.' After this I kept away from them."

Money for such necessities as food, rent, and art materials was still scarce, but a bigger challenge faced them all that December when the United States entered the global war and the likes of nineteen-year-old Robert De Niro and twenty-two-year-old Robert Duncan would have been prime candidates for service. Duncan, the ROTC dropout, was eventually drafted and spent several weeks in boot camp before wrangling a discharge on the basis of his homosexuality. De Niro, who had begun a furtive and sporadic sexual relationship with Duncan, had another means of avoiding the war: not long after the attack on Pearl Harbor, he and Admiral were married.

THE FOLLOWING YEAR provided plenty of excitement for the newly-wed couple. For one thing, they began to experience some real—if modest—success in the world beyond Hofmann's classroom. Admiral sold a canvas to the Museum of Modern Art for the princely sum of $100 (about $1,350 in 2013 dollars) and then another to Peggy Guggenheim, who had arrived in New York and begun to acquire and exhibit the work of new young artists at her 57th Street gallery, Art of This Century. De Niro would later acknowledge how impressive these sales were: the young Admiral, he recalled years later, was "a *very good* painter." As he put it, "What she was doing then wasn't fashionable," he recalled, "and a woman painter had a harder time." Nell Blaine, another painter in Hofmann's classes, affirmed the rare stature that

Admiral—and De Niro alongside her—had attained: "Virginia was the only student I knew at that time to sell a painting to the Museum of Modern Art."

The couple had another important patron in Guggenheim's uncle, Solomon Guggenheim, who had begun to amass the collection that formed the basis of the famed Fifth Avenue museum that would eventually bear his name. At the time, the nascent institution was known inelegantly as the Museum of Non-Objective Painting, and as part of its mission it had begun to offer small stipends to promising young artists, including the cream of Hans Hofmann's school. Admiral and De Niro were granted $15 per month each by a foundation run by Guggenheim's mistress, Hilla Rebay (Baroness Hildegard Rebay von Ehrenwiesen), who further aided the young couple's fortunes by hiring De Niro as an information desk clerk and night watchman at the museum, a position that found him working alongside his chum Jackson Pollock.

These windfalls allowed Admiral and De Niro to move from the 14th Street loft into a pair of adjacent studios on Bleecker Street. Likely they needed the space as much for personal as artistic reasons: before the year was over, Admiral found herself pregnant. And on August 17, 1943, the child, destined to be their only one, was born. They chose Hans Hofmann to be the baby's godfather, a purely honorary title, as no baptism was intended. They named the boy Robert Anthony De Niro, but around the house they would always call him Bobby.

2

I T'S INEVITABLE, PROBABLY, THAT WE THINK OF ROBERT DE NIRO as a product of the tumult and color of Manhattan's Little Italy, as he first came to prominence in *Mean Streets* and *The Godfather, Part II*, both of which were set (and partly filmed) there.

But in fact his childhood was spent a few crucial blocks north on Bleecker Street and, later, 14th Street, and the milieu in which he was raised wasn't the stereotype of an Italian American household, with hordes of relatives, massive pasta dinners, and the twin rule of the Catholic Church and the Mafia. Rather, he was a child of Greenwich Village bohemia, more familiar with the aroma of paint thinner than that of marinara sauce, usually the only kid at the party, a living emblem of bourgeois normalcy and adult responsibility in a world given over to aesthetic exploration and escape from social taboos.

"Our standards were so pure, we treated with scorn any humdrum references to the personal," painter Nell Blaine remembered of the world she and the De Niros inhabited. "Concepts, ideas were exchanged. Anything less was a tasteless distraction." A baby in a painter's loft may not have been tasteless, but it certainly constituted a distraction. De Niro and Admiral were still scraping for money to pay for the basic things of life, and they were still doggedly pursuing their artistic ambitions. Additionally, the elder De Niro was himself only twenty-one years old when he became a father, a green age for a man struggling not only with his sexual identity but also with his commitment to a field of endeavor that was unlikely to afford him a family wage.

There was, however, the promise of the moment, a surge of activity in New York that would soon affirm the city as the capital of the international art world. The United States had joined the war, yes, but it was still thousands of miles from the battlefields, and the city had provided a safe haven for a great many of the artistic luminaries who had helped create the various strains of contemporary art in Europe during the previous decades. Combined with the energetic young American painters who had been raised on modern ideas and techniques invented in the Old World, it made for America's first truly energetic art scene. If you were doomed, by fate or choice, to be a starving artist, New York in the 1940s was a pretty promising place to do it.

Admiral's reputation continued to grow while Bobby was still in diapers. In 1944 she was among twenty-four painters and sculptors selected for Peggy Guggenheim's Spring Salon for Young Artists, providing what the *New York Times* critic Edward Alden Jewell called "a gay if rather scattered oil lyric." The following year, the Museum of Modern Art exhibited the canvas it had previously bought from her (Jewell saw in it "abstract lyricism" but once again found her work "rather scattered"). And then in 1946 she was afforded a show of her own at Art of This Century, exhibiting six paintings alongside a selection of works by the jazz critic and artist Rudi Blesh (Jewell, again, offered as much praise as not, describing her as "a not too tidy lyricist with an often pleasing color sense").

By then, though, De Niro had superseded Admiral in the general esteem of the art world. In late 1945 he had a canvas appear in the Fall Salon at Art of This Century. And in May 1946, at age twenty-four, he had a one-man show at the gallery, an astounding coup marking him as a true meteor. The show, billed as a "First Exhibition of Painting," consisted of ten canvases that were priced for sale at $100 to $600. The titles give an idea of the young artist's emerging aesthetic; three of the paintings bore allusive names ("Environs of Biskra," "Ubu Roi," "Abstraction"), but the rest were given representational titles that would have been familiar to a Renaissance master: "Portrait of a Young Man," "Fruits and Flowers," "Woman in Armchair," "Still Life with Flowers," and so forth. Combining a deep-seated respect for tradition with an urge toward modern expressivity, De Niro's work of the time depicted real objects and people and places but used the techniques of abstract art. A vase, say, might be indicated by two distinct elements: an energetic area of color that suggested the physical gesture that created it and a similarly energetic but more controlled outline, often thick, black, and composed of a single stroke. The influence of Matisse and the Fauvists was clear in the color and shapes, but there were bits of Cézanne, Cubism, the not yet defined school of Action painting, and classical representational art in it as well.

De Niro's maiden show was respectfully received and widely reviewed. In the *New York Times*, the omnipresent Edward Alden Jewell praised the painter's "stimulating audacity" and noted the connection to Fauvism, concluding, "Color is savagely brilliant; the primaries, set off by black." *ARTnews* described the work as consisting of "circular and oval shapes, warmly colored," arranged into "handsome, vaguely sexual patterns." And in a significant coup, the great and influential critic Clement Greenberg, writing in *The Nation*, declared De Niro an "important young artist" exhibiting "monumental effects rare in abstract art." He offered powerful praise for De Niro's technique: "The originality and force of his temperament demonstrate themselves under an iron control of the plastic elements." But he had some reservations that ran counter to the impression his fellow critics took away from the show: "Where De Niro usually goes wrong is with his hot, violent color. . . . It is as if De Niro wished to compensate himself for his restraint as a draftsman by self-indulgence and bombast in his color."

By any standard, this was a significant splash to make in the New York art world, especially at such a tender age. For a time, De Niro was spoken of alongside such peers as Jackson Pollock, Willem de Kooning, Robert Motherwell, and Franz Kline, few of whom had yet enjoyed a one-man show and all of whom were older than him, sometimes by decades.

As the Abstract Expressionists—and the critics who favored them—rose to prominence in the years after World War II, De Niro slowly drifted from his exalted position. In part this was due to temperament: as the excitement grew around the new school of New York painters, De Niro remained doggedly adherent to the combination of

classical subject matter and modern technique, of precise craft and expressive energy. Now and again he toyed with novelty, such as in his
canvas "Venice at Night Is a Negress in Love," in which he painted a
passage of prose onto the canvas in a concession to contemporary fads.
But such trendy gestures had little appeal for him. De Niro seemingly
could partake of trendy practices only if they were contained inside a
specific context—a single painting or a series executed to see through
a single idea. Otherwise he showed no great enthusiasm for them, and
they had no discernible echo in his larger aesthetic. As Abstract Expressionism grew in popularity and impact, he could even become
antagonistic toward the movement, or at least to its looming presence
over the practice of modern American art: "Contemporary abstract art
is a heap of confusion, hatred, and paranoia, with a good dose of pre-
tension," he remarked a few years later. "Rembrandt could have drip-
painted too, if he had wanted. I'd take Grandma Moses any day over
this frenzied lot. . . . With all their theories and manifestos they sound
like science fiction."

But there were personal reasons that may have led to his inability to turn his Art of This Century show into the launching pad for a
profitable career. By the time the show was presented, he and Virginia
Admiral had separated, whether due to his ambivalent sexuality, to friction arising from their competing art careers, to disagreement about
the financial exigencies of establishing a household suited for raising
a child, or (and this is least likely, as their later lives would bear out)
to simple personal incompatibility. After a brief initial period around
1945, when the separating couple quarreled over custody and the boy
was sent to Syracuse to spend time with his father's family, De Niro and
Admiral continued to live near each other and to raise their only child
more or less in harmony. She assumed the more active parenting role
by far, effectively maintaining full custody of the boy, and her husband
(they wouldn't officially divorce for more than a decade) would continue on his singular, focused, iconoclastic path, taking only nominal
financial responsibility for his child and, in fact, coming to depend on
the largesse of his ex-wife to support him and his career.

A maniacal perfectionist and committed aesthete, De Niro so

required freedom to pursue his work that he was willing to forgo ordinary standards of financial and physical comfort. "He is lean and brooding and he has frequently gone hungry for want of artistic compromising," *Newsweek* said of him. He continued to work as a museum guard (he held the position, at least part-time, for five years), then sometimes as a picture framer, painting instructor, janitor, or dishwasher, or doing other sorts of odd, menial jobs. Very occasionally he worked on commissions. And as his son later remembered, he lived in uninviting and obscure parts of lower Manhattan: "He had these dank lofts in NoHo and SoHo at a time when nobody wanted to live in those areas. (Often he was the only tenant who wanted to live in the building.)" His preferred mode of life at the time, he confessed, was to turn everything upside down, perhaps in order to keep from falling into habits or routines, perhaps to escape the psychological depression that could occasionally trouble him.

His housing situation was often so tenuous that De Niro depended on Admiral to look after his finished canvases, a decision that had unfortunate consequences a few years into their separation, as his son remembered: "When I was about five," he recalled, "I went to visit Macy's to see Santa Claus, and when I came home there was a huge fire in my mother's apartment, so some artwork was lost," the toll apparently including some of the canvases exhibited at Art of This Century and the companion piece to "Venice at Night." And because he kept artist's hours and lived in such bohemian circumstances, De Niro saw his son less and less regularly. The places in which he lived, in fact, seemed singularly unsuited environments for a child: "As a kid, I remember I'd visit him at his studio," the boy recalled years later. "We weren't living together. I was living with my mother, and it was nothing like his studio as you see it now. It was like a real studio, a total mess, and it stank of paint and turpentine."

Given his professional and personal circumstances, it was perhaps no surprise that De Niro didn't mount another solo show until 1951, when he had three exhibitions at the prestigious Charles Egan Gallery and acquired more admirers among the ranks of critics and cognoscenti. His work was especially well received in the prestigious pages of *ARTnews*, which dedicated dozens of reviews to him over the decades, almost all of them favorable. This was to some degree the doing of Thomas B. Hess, the influential critic for and, eventually, editor of the magazine, who began championing De Niro with that first Egan show: "He must now be ranked among the best of the younger artists to have emerged from anonymity."

Over the years, De Niro's work was celebrated by *ARTnews* critics such as Henry McBride and Frank O'Hara ("each show of his is an event") almost without reservation, even when other publications, particularly the *New York Times*, took a more measured approach to their praise or offered none at all. But even with influential boosters, De Niro's star was waning. The fashion of the moment—Action painting, Abstract Expressionism, the artist as bohemian hero expressing his inner angst on canvas and in daily life without regard to public norms or approval—was a far cry from the work that De Niro was doing and the type of life he preferred to live. As he matured, the elder De Niro expressed a variety of impulses and predilections, sometimes genuine eccentricity of the sort often associated with bohemians but just as often considered an affect or pose. He played tennis and chess, studied metapsychology, took singing lessons so as to be able to perform gospel music (albeit never in public), and taught himself French to the point at which he could not only read his beloved Symbolist poets but write verse in their language (he was fond of signing letters "Bob Verlaine De Niro"). He kept pets in his stream of studios and lofts: parrots, a Maltese named Napoleon, and even a rabbit. He ran regularly at a downtown YMCA, with "a kind of funny stride," according to a friend. And he cut a startling figure, per his longtime advocate Thomas B. Hess: "*tall, saturnine,* given to black trench coats, his face as sharp as a switchblade."

He was, said another acquaintance, "a lonely soul" with "an elegant mind," and he was almost pathologically private. If he had lovers—male or female—he rarely let the outside world see or know about them. ("I didn't know much about his social life other than what my mother would say," his son would later reveal. "I was never exposed to his sexuality, but my mother told me about it later. That was part of his 'thing,' and he kept it very quiet.") He held the highest aesthetic standards and could be caustic in dismissing the work—or way of life—of those he felt were not worthy, though this disdain could cost him professionally. As painter Al Kresch, who'd known him since their student days, put it, "Anyone he knew he had a falling-out with."

As his son confirmed, "He had a temper, but he was witty and caustic. Very sarcastic about certain things, especially other artists who he didn't respect. He also used to make fun of people who would put on false airs and speak with an affected accent. . . . He was self-centered and concerned about what he wanted to do, but I think when you're an artist you have to have that selfishness to be alone and create great things to your satisfaction." The poet Barbara Guest, who remembered him as "fiercely engaged with his work," depicted him as "alone in the tremendously cluttered place in which he painted . . . erratic, gloomy, untidy. . . . There was no social life of dinners. . . . There were many parties he did not attend. . . . 'Affability' is not a word that applied to Bob, nor is 'social.' He was given to acid comments about the art scene, with which I might add, he was thoroughly familiar." He apparently struggled with depression on and off throughout his life, and there are hints in some accounts that he was diagnosed with what would later be known as bipolar disorder.

But he was well liked in the small world he frequented. His longtime friend Dick Brewer described him as the "loneliest person I ever knew" but also "the *funniest* person I ever knew." "He had the air of someone with a long and complicated history," recalled Larry Rivers. "He was a kinetic dandy, he was Baudelaire in New York." De Niro would sometimes sport large rings and a gold bracelet on his right— that is, his painting—hand. The artist Jane Freilicher recollected him with fondness as a kind of art world ghost, "a lonely soul, turning up places . . . whistling 'La Vie en Rose' through his teeth," but also remembered a far lighter side to him: "Bob was a great dancer. He would whirl around and around until his movements had no relation to the music or anything. Squeamish women sort of pressed against the wall trying to hide from him."

Still, he was always deeply respected for his work, albeit within smaller and smaller circles: as a magazine article said of him in the mid-1970s, when his son's ascending fame brought him new attention, "De Niro did not spend much time at the Cedar Bar, but according to at least one informal survey taken there, his name was the name most often mentioned in answer to the question, 'Who, besides you, is good?'"

That respect surely derived in large part from De Niro's relentless, neurotic perfectionism. In 1958, as part of a series of profiles of painters at work, *ARTnews* sent Eleanor Munro to his studio to watch him fashion a series of paintings. These weren't his already well-known studies of Greta Garbo, based on movie stills but designed to recall classical paintings (told, in 1956, that an avant-garde artist in Manhattan had an obsession with her image, the reclusive star replied, "How nice"). Rather, the paintings Munro observed De Niro working on were scenes of the Crucifixion, a strange subject for a man who had abandoned Catholicism as a teen, poked around in Eastern religion and even Christian Science, and quarreled with his parents after they baptized little Bobby against his wishes. The cross at Calvary was a completely unfashionable subject, but one that persistently haunted De Niro throughout his career: one of his biggest sales to that point had been a Crucifixion purchased for $1,000 by Gloria Vanderbilt (then Mrs. Leopold Stokowski) and selected for her by art historian Meyer Schapiro; it would eventually hang in a Rosicrucian museum in California.

Munro's portrait of the artist at work, full of details about his technique, his influences (Bonnard, Ingres, Rousseau—but no contemporaries), and his self-critical dedication, gave a vivid impression of De Niro as his own most severe critic, chasing after an aesthetic vision that often only he could comprehend. "Book after book of these quick studies pile up," Munro wrote. "Most end up in the wastebasket. Perhaps ten out of a hundred, De Niro keeps on exhibition and for his own use."

Other observers confirmed the artist's unusual technique: "He liked to work a long time on a painting to get a composition," reported his friend Dick Brewer, "then wipe it out and paint it again in an hour." And his niece Jean De Niro provided the most vivid depiction of the artist at work, describing a modeling session from the 1960s:

> He was becoming somebody I didn't know. . . . Suddenly I wasn't his relative, only a model. . . . His face changed, he seemed to get

a little angry . . . it was like a seizure. . . . He'd draw a sketch,
he'd rip it up, draw another, rip it up . . . it wasn't an attack on
me but on making the picture. . . . [He was] painting almost right
on my body . . . yet everything on the canvas was controlled—
composition, shading, moods, nuances—contained.

STILL, FOR ALL his eccentricity, doggedness, and idiosyncrasy, for all
his absences and the uncomfortable circumstances that were his preferred mode of living, De Niro was by all reports a caring father. He
was, his son would remember, "affectionate . . . always touching and
hugging," and he enjoyed taking young Bobby to museums, gallery
openings, and especially movie theaters. "He did take me to the movies," Bobby recalled, "like *King Kong* and other black-and-white films
at the arthouses on 42nd Street." He took him as well to sit in occasionally on his teaching sessions, letting the youngster experiment alongside paying students. "He had a good sense of color," the elder De Niro
fondly remembered. But the relationship between father and son was
intermittent—"I would see him every few weeks," the son recalled—and
it didn't extend very deeply into the making of real art: "He even tried
to paint me many times when I was younger, but I wouldn't sit still."

The preponderance of the responsibility—emotional, financial,
practical—for raising the boy fell on Virginia Admiral, who found herself a single mother thousands of miles from her family and living in a
neighborhood filled with countercultural types for whom the postwar
baby boom and rise of suburbia were things to be read about in magazines and mocked in taverns and cafés. Almost inevitably, she withdrew from her very promising painting career to focus on the realities
of motherhood.

At first, like her estranged husband, she tried to earn money on
the fringes of the art world—framing pictures, doing decorative work
such as jewelry making, and so on. Before very long, she turned her
full energies to a pair of fields in which she had enjoyed some commercial success in the past: writing and, even more lucrative, typing.
As she had for Anaïs Nin, Admiral wrote sensational prose for a steady
per-page rate, always under pseudonyms, for a variety of pulpish true-

crime magazines—tales of sex, violence, aberrant psychology, and karmic doom. More reliably, she began soliciting work as a typist for manuscripts, a common service in an era before there was a computer in every writer's home. She had clients among her various literary acquaintances, and she expanded to include students at nearby New York University and the New School. It was a business she would run for decades, eventually expanding to include a small pool of typists (including her son) and her own printing machinery.

Always an extremely private person, particularly as her son gained fame—"I want to keep my life *my* life," she once told a reporter—she perhaps offered insight into herself and her values when she was asked about her son's secret for success and answered bluntly: "Will. Force of will." The steadying of her income stream allowed Admiral to seek out a more suitable home in which to raise her son. After leaving the twin studios on Bleecker Street (which were soon incorporated into the expanding Little Red School House, the first institution in New York City to fully embrace John Dewey's progressive pedagogical theories), Admiral found a place on Hudson Street and then, finally, a large two-bedroom apartment at 219 West 14th Street, a central location between Seventh and Eighth Avenues, just a few blocks from her first Manhattan loft. She grew her business over the years in that space (eventually it became so big that she moved it around the corner) and raised her son there; he was so attached to it, in fact, that he would eventually live there on his own and hold on to the place after moving out, using it for storage or giving friends a place to crash when they were between situations.

With a working mother and a father who was, for the purposes of day-to-day life, largely absent, the young De Niro was put in school as soon as possible, first at a nursery school at Greenwich House, then in the Little Red School House itself (housed in the very building in which, quite possibly, he had been conceived), then finally into the public school system, starting with P.S. 41 on West 11th Street.

School wasn't the only social outlet the young boy had, but it was the most significant. Given the offbeat nature of his household and his parents' immersion in work that demanded long hours in exchange for relatively little pay, he was left largely to his own devices. "He was never coddled," a family friend remembered years later, while another acquaintance recalled, "Bobby was out in the street a lot as a child. He wasn't being rebellious—that's just the way the cookie crumbled." During his elementary and middle school years, his mother tried a variety of ways to socialize him: he was sent to Syracuse to visit Henry and Helen De Niro during the summers, and he was once even shipped off to Boy Scout camp ("Don't picture me," he cautioned a journalist who was trying to imagine him in that environment. "I wasn't in it too long"). He was an avid reader, which only added to the air of isolation surrounding him, the only child of divorced parents living in bohemian lower Manhattan in the middle of the baby boom.

And then his mom found something that captured his imagination. Among Admiral's New School clients was Maria Ley-Piscator, yet another artist who had escaped Europe before the war and become an influential teacher in America. She was a Viennese dancer who in 1937 married the German theater director Erwin Piscator (Bertolt Brecht was a groomsman) and fled the Nazis two years later. In 1940, the Piscators were invited to establish a theatrical program at the New School, and they ran it together until Erwin was once again exiled by politics, having to return to Europe as a result of the McCarthyist crackdown on leftists. Maria kept the school afloat, and by 1953, when Admiral was doing typing and proofreading work for her, their Dramatic Workshop counted among its alumni Marlon Brando, Harry Belafonte, Rod Steiger, Walter Matthau, Bea Arthur, Elaine Stritch, and even Tennessee Williams, among many, many others.

Years later, the grown-up De Niro would remember that it was *his* idea to attend acting classes: his mother, he said, "knew that I wanted to go to acting school, so in exchange for [her] work, I began going on Saturdays. It was the biggest acting school in the city at that time." In fact, Admiral did work out a deal, trading tuition for typing and printing, and so in his tenth year, the young Robert De Niro was first exposed to the study of acting and took the stage in his very first role: the Cowardly Lion in a production of *The Wizard of Oz*.

"I was very nervous," De Niro remembered of that debut years later. "It was very exciting. I was a kid." But at that tender age, the urge to perform didn't stick. In the coming years, in fact, young De Niro was attracted less by life on the stage than by life on the streets. He wasn't a juvenile delinquent, exactly, but he had his moments. Some of it was just the usual reckless boyhood thrills: "We used to roller-skate," he remembered. "Not like these souped-up Rollerblades they have today. Roller skates with ball bearings. We'd hang on to the back of a truck and go for a ride for a couple of blocks until the streetlight turned red and the truck stopped. Then one day they changed the lights to a stagger system. Only we didn't know. All the lights changed up an avenue at intervals so you could go twenty or thirty blocks without stopping. Suddenly, I'm stuck on the back of one of these trucks, and after four blocks I'm realizing that the next light isn't going to turn red. The driver doesn't know you're on the back. You have no choice but to keep hanging on till he stops."

There were other, less dangerous kicks, like comic books and illicit cigarettes. And very rarely there were the sorts of things that could genuinely get you in hot water with the law, such as the time he was pinched for scrawling graffiti on a subway car at age fifteen. He would claim later on that he was only experimenting: "It wasn't anything serious with me. If I had continued in a certain way, it might have been, but that's not what I intended to do with my life."

Still, there was a certain comfort to be taken, surely, in belonging to some kind of group. With the benefit of his Italian surname, De Niro was able to blend in with a group of schoolmates from Little Italy—Kenmare Street, specifically—who promptly dubbed him "Bobby Milk" because of his pale complexion. He affected the clothing and behavior that his new pals favored, even starting to attend church with them, despite his parents' admonitions. These kids weren't actual criminals, but they liked to present themselves as such, and De Niro grew so familiar with their ways that a friend of Admiral's asked him to pose as a street thug for a *Glamour* magazine photo spread about wild youth; chubby, disheveled, and self-conscious, he wore jeans and a leather jacket and looked for all the world like a tiny Marlon Brando manqué.

One day, hanging around with his throng of wannabe tough guys in Washington Square Park, De Niro was surprised by the sudden appearance of his father, who assessed his son's peers and then declared out loud, "Get away from these hoods"—a cringe-inducing encounter in innumerable ways, not least of which was fear, as some of his pals were genuinely hard cases. (At the dawn of his fame, De Niro was extremely reticent about the company he kept as a young teen: "You better not say anything about that because those guys are still around and I wouldn't want to embarrass them," he told the *New York Times*; years later, he elaborated, "Some of them are no longer around. Some of them were killed. Some of them went into legitimate stuff: policeman, fireman. Just living their lives, y'know?")

To that point, father and son had enjoyed a comfortable if slightly remote relationship. "I would see him every few weeks," De Niro remembered, "or sometimes I'd run into him in the street and we'd talk. We had a connection, but it was not one of going out and playing baseball together." (As he put it another time, "We had what I suppose people would call an understanding; we were close in some ways but not in others.") But with typical teenage discomfort at the very existence of his parents, De Niro felt a kind of shame at the image his father cut with his wild hair, shabby artist's wardrobe, and erratic schedule: "Most people I knew didn't have 'creative' parents who lived in kind of grungy places and did odd jobs when they had to."

Life with Mom wasn't necessarily easier. In addition to running a makeshift business out of their home, Admiral continued to engage in artistic and, increasingly, political activities, and she had a private life of her own, dating and even living with men over the years during which she was raising her son. "Among the many who courted her favors," remembered Larry Rivers, "were [artist and critic] Manny Farber and [critic] Clement Greenberg, causing the first of many one-rounders between these two." Farber and Admiral had a relationship of several years' duration, not long after which Farber started writing about movies for *ARTnews* and eventually emerged as one of the most influential film critics in the latter half of the century.* As uncomfort-

---

* That Robert De Niro should be raised by a woman who was a kind of inspiration to the young Pauline Kael and have, for a time, Manny Farber as a principal male figure in his household is a truly astounding realization, especially given the significant praise with which each writer would greet the actor's early work. De Niro may have formed ambivalent relations with film critics later on, but two of the most famous and influential people ever to have that job figured, if only obliquely, in his family history and his youth.

able as he may have been with his father's unorthodox behavior, De Niro was rendered truly squeamish by his mother's grown-up life, even if it was comparatively ordinary. Years later, as a famous actor, he was approached by Farber at a Hollywood gathering; the writer said hello and then asked, "Do you remember me? I used to go out with your mother. You have unbelievable eyes. Just like your father. You're much more like your father than your mother." De Niro, visibly appalled, said nothing and soon fled the party.

Not surprisingly, the lack of an intact home and the lure of the streets took a toll on De Niro's academic performance. He had struggled through elementary school, so Admiral sent him to Elisabeth Irwin High School, an adjunct of the Little Red School House that included an intermediate school. As it was a private school and the young De Niro wasn't particularly keen on succeeding in it, his mother decided to forgo paying tuition and enrolled him at New York's famed (and public) High School of Music and Art, up in Harlem (where among his fellow students at the time would have been such diverse talents as Steven Bochco, Lola Falana, Billy Cobham, Carole Bayer Sager, Erica Jong, and the upperclassman Al Pacino). When *that* didn't work out, it was back to private education at the Rhodes School (where James Caan was then enrolled). "I had a bad high school scene," De Niro admitted later, particularly regretting his failure to hang on at Music and Art: "It was a good school. I should have stayed there." His mother, though, knew exactly what the problem was: "His idea of high school was just not to show up," she declared flatly.

HE WASN'T A troubled kid, exactly, but he was rudderless, and then an old urge resurfaced. He decided he would like to return to the Dramatic Workshop and resume his exploration of acting and the theater. Relieved to find her son interested in something positive—and, even more than that, something creative—Admiral once again made arrangements for him to attend classes.

This time he wouldn't be the Cowardly Lion. As he was attending classes in lieu of regular schooling, he was thrown in with the adults and was expected to study and learn not only the nuts and bolts of the acting profession but the theory behind it. Plus there was an emphasis on self-exploration and self-revelation that wasn't part of the children's classes. On the very first day, he encountered, albeit somewhat comically, the sort of thing he'd be facing—and fearing—in the months and years ahead. "I went in," he remembered, "and the director said to me, 'Vy do you vant to be an acteh?' I didn't know how to answer, so I didn't say anything. And he said, 'To express yourself!' And I said, 'Yeah, yeah, that's it. That's right.'"

He stayed at the school for a year, more or less. He picked up some very good habits there, such as a taste for reading, particularly books that might have some potential acting roles in them, whether in the form of monologues he might learn or actual parts he dreamed about one day playing. And he began a lifelong habit of acquiring pieces of wardrobe—hats, coats, props—that he would hold on to, in some cases, for decades, turning the 14th Street apartment he shared with his mother into a makeshift theatrical costume house. Having observed his father's affection for the tools of his trade and his mother's careful accumulation and operation of typewriters and printing presses in her business, he naturally appreciated the place of such objects as props and pieces of wardrobe in the acting trade.

But he still wasn't entirely comfortable with the idea of being an actor, of getting up in the morning, putting on makeup and a costume, and pretending to be someone else, often someone radically different—emotional, vulnerable, complex. At the Dramatic Workshop, there was an emphasis on performance that left him, one of the youngest members of the class, feeling particularly uneasy: "They had so many students in the class," he reflected later, "it was hard to get up; you had to try to overcome that." He was especially intimidated by the public performance aspect of acting. His Bobby Milk days weren't that far behind him, and the idea that some of the gang he'd briefly run with would perhaps see him onstage was mortifying. "You figured the kids would make fun if they came to a play that you were in," he confessed years later, "so I would never even think of having them come."

In time, his devotion to his classes waned, and he stopped attending the Dramatic Workshop altogether. But then he had an epiphany, or at least a bug landed in his ear, and he began to develop a new attitude toward acting. "When I was around 18," he remembered, "I was look-ing at a TV show—a soap opera or some weekly western—and I said if these actors are making a living at it, and they're not really that good, I can't do any worse than them. I wasn't thinking of getting a job on a western or any of that. When I got into it more seriously, I saw how far I could go, what you could do. That it wasn't what I thought it was when I was younger. But I remember saying that to myself, watching those black-and-white TV shows."

Somehow it clicked: acting was work, like painting or typing, and you could do it and make it pay and maybe even learn how to be good at it. The question that remained unanswered in his mind—and maybe even unasked—was how to get there from where he was.

3

IN APRIL 1961 SEVENTEEN-YEAR-OLD BOBBY DE NIRO MADE HIS way to Manhattan's Pier 90, at West 50th Street, where the fabled *Queen Mary* was docked and preparing to sail for Cherbourg and Southampton. In a cabin aboard the ship, friends were throwing a going-away party for his father. Bobby "Verlaine" De Niro, the Fauvist boulevardier from Syracuse, New York, the wunderkind of Provincetown and Black Mountain, was finally going to visit the land of Matisse and Rimbaud, heading to France with only a one-way ticket.

The mid-to-late 1950s had been relatively prosperous for the painter. His work wasn't selling for anything like the prices that the more famous Abstract Expressionists commanded—the Pollocks and Rothkos and De Koonings and Klines, who had superseded him commercially but still respected him and regarded him as a peer. But he was making a mark. Throughout the latter part of the decade, De Niro exhibited and sold his work regularly on 57th Street, then the heart of Manhattan's high-end gallery scene, and his paintings were shown at the Whitney Museum, the Jewish Museum, and the Institute of Contemporary Art in Boston. He received a handful of foundation grants and prizes, he regularly enjoyed positive reviews in the serious art press (and occasionally, and somewhat less enthusiastically, in the *New York Times*), and he had started to draw a following among private collectors, including Joseph Hirschhorn, who would eventually acquire some forty of his pieces. He wasn't rich, but since he still chose to live like "the poorest of the poor," as fellow artist Paul Resika put it, he didn't need much, and he added to his income by teaching, framing pictures, and taking other jobs, sometimes menial ones. What's more, with his son doing exactly what he himself had done a few decades earlier—namely, dropping out of school to pursue an interest in the arts—he felt comfortable leaving New York and living, as he always wanted to, in the land that had produced his favorite poets and painters.

Before leaving, he carefully divested himself of the physical aspects of his New York life, entrusting his paintings to Admiral and offering other belongings to friends in the manner of bequests. "He showed up at my Village cold-water flat," writer Barbara Guest remembered, "with a box containing his volumes of French poetry. He was going to Paris, he said, and asked me to take care of his books."

De Niro had maintained a good relationship with his son throughout the boy's teens. They still went to the movies together, and with Bobby attending acting school, their cinematic diet had acquired a new dimension. They took in Marlon Brando and Montgomery Clift and James Dean movies whenever they could—Bobby shared teachers with each of them, after all—and they also liked the new wave of kitchen-sink dramas coming out of England, such as *A Taste of Honey* and *Saturday Night and Sunday Morning*. (They were partial, too, to the Three Stooges and to silent Laurel and Hardy films.) The son may never have felt entirely connected to his father—"there was a certain wall between me and him that I wish had been broken"—but he knew he would miss him.

Too, as the younger De Niro still hadn't yet fully committed himself to his studies, he was frankly jealous of his father's ability to pick up and leave town. "I loved traveling and wanted to go to Europe," he remembered. "I tried to get a job in the Merchant Marine. But I had no clout, so I was fourth class. I couldn't move up the ladder." He finally saved up money and resorted to more mundane means: "I just wound up taking Icelandic Airlines." He began in Ireland, with an ultimately fruitless search for his roots. "I hitchhiked from Dublin to Galway," he remembered later, "and took the ferry out to the Aran Islands, and then I went down through the south. Slept in some fields, and people gave me blankets for sleeping outside—the caretakers of an estate. I had breakfast with them in the morning. They were very friendly."

He hitchhiked around a bit—it was the heyday of beatnik-style vagabonding throughout the Old World, which was still cheap and exotic by American standards—and he was keen on it. He made his way to Paris, where he caught up with his father, and then, encouraged by the idea that his relations in Campobasso would be easier to find, headed for Italy.

"I made him a sign in English and Italian: 'Student wants ride,'" his father remembered. "On Capri he met [actress] Michele Morgan and told her I was interested in doing her portrait. Trying to drum up business for me. But I wasn't interested in doing her portrait or anyone else's." In Venice, Bobby had a surprise when he visited Peggy Guggenheim's art collection at her Palazzo Venier dei Leoni and found a picture by Virginia Admiral hanging in the permanent collection. As his father recalled, "He was particularly proud that his mother made a breakthrough for recognition that eludes so many women in art." Eventually his money ran out, but not his taste for spur-of-the-moment travel and adventure. Before he settled on a way of life, he would feel the urge of the road again.

Back home, Bobby locked in on acting in a more profound way than he had before, chiefly by entrusting himself to the famed teacher Stella Adler, who professed her craft at the Stella Adler Conservatory of Acting.

And *professing* is exactly what Adler did. A grand dame of the theater, she dressed, spoke, and bore herself with a regal air, and her speech, whether recounting performances she'd seen onstage or critiquing student efforts in her classroom, could veer almost violently from poetic exaltation to lacerating dismissal. She insisted that her class greet her each day by calling out "Good morning, Miss Adler" in unison, and in later years she would end class by asking them if they loved her. "When you stand on stage you must have a sense that you are addressing the whole world," she wrote, "and that what you say is so important that the whole world must listen"—and by all accounts she comported herself as if she were *always* onstage.

If that seemed a bit much, Adler could back it up. The daughter of Jacob Adler, a titan of the Yiddish theater, she was one of the pivotal figures in the rise of Method acting as an American style, virtually from the day it began. Along with other fevered young New York theater people, she had been wowed by the Moscow Art Theatre when the company visited New York in the 1920s, and she had fallen under the influence of two of its members: Richard Boleslawski, who stayed on in the States to operate a school and repertory company called the American Laboratory Theatre, and Maria Ouspenskaya, who also stayed, mainly to perform but also to teach. Through them, like so many others in the New York theater, Adler had taken as her master the great actor, theoretician, and impresario Constantin Stanislavski, whose performances, lectures, and writings would become the core of the Method revolution in American acting.

Library shelves would one day groan with Stanislavski's works and myriad books about his "system," which was a rigorous and thorough approach to the problems and craft of acting. He hoped to rationalize the art by prescribing a litany of skills that actors should acquire and goals for which they should strive. Most radically, he proposed that acting was a psychological undertaking, rather than, as previous generations' performances indicated, a representational one. In opposition to old-style actors who adopted stances, attitudes, and inflections that revealed emotions in a kind of exaggerated dummy show, Stanislavski argued that actors should experience the emotions indicated by the playwright and express those emotions onstage as they would in real life. To enable actors to do this, he spoke of something he called "emotion memory," a practice of finding a correlation between the character's situation and the actor's own inner life and history. Stanislavski wasn't dogmatic about the practice of mining one's actual psyche or past—in fact, he feared it might evoke hysteria. And he acknowledged that there were outstanding actors who achieved similar effects without following his ideas. But taken as a whole, his theories amounted to a revolutionary reconsideration of the craft and intent of acting.

Adler, a voracious creature of the theater, was thoroughly taken with Stanislavski's system, both its theory and as it was practiced by the Moscow Art Theatre and American Laboratory Theatre. She relocated to Paris for a time in the 1930s, becoming the only American actor ever to study with Stanislavski himself. Upon her return, she was among the ardent modernists who created the Group Theatre, which was dedicated to translating the Russian director's theories of stagecraft, dramaturgy, and acting, into an American idiom; the remarkable roster of founders included Lee Strasberg, Cheryl Crawford, Sanford Meisner, John Garfield, and Franchot Tone, and above all Harold Clurman, the architect of this acting revolution (and incidentally, Adler's second husband). In time, the likes of Elia Kazan, Clifford Odets, and Lee J. Cobb would become involved in the Group Theatre, helping to form a pantheon of talents whose stage, film, and classroom work would give rise to a half century and more of American masterpieces.

In the 1940s, Adler taught occasionally at Erwin Piscator and Maria Ley-Piscator's Dramatic Workshop, but by the end of that decade she had all but retired from acting and opened a school of her own, where she espoused a philosophy of acting that was distinct from the Piscators' and from that of her Group Theatre colleague and pedagogical rival Lee Strasberg—and maybe even from that of Stanislavski himself.

For Strasberg, whose Actors Studio became the high temple of the Method, Stanislavski's "emotion memory" meant that actors must explicitly find a reality within themselves to express the situations presented by the script; focusing on the actual emotions of the men and women who were acting the roles of fictional people, he encouraged the use of what he called "sense memory," an ability to recall, on command, an emotional sensation in an actor's own life that corresponded to the one demanded by a scene.

For Adler, Stanislavski's words and deeds meant something quite different—and she loved citing the fact that she'd personally studied with the man as proof that she was correct. She understood the principal task of Stanislavskian acting to be an imaginative commingling of the actor with the text and with the human situations contained in it—not a mining of the self to fill the emotions of the scene with traces of one's own life, but an effort to picture oneself in the shoes of one's character and then behaving as one's character would.

"The play is not in the words," Adler declared in one of her most famous precepts, "it is in *you*." She stressed using the imagination to deepen and expand the meaning of a scene; focusing on action and interaction as a means of communicating; cultivating the actor's psyche, spirit, and personality beyond mere stagecraft; and, especially, interpreting the script—a sometimes technical means of inhabiting and absorbing the material to be performed. "Your talent is in your choice" was her other most famous dictum (and Robert De Niro's favorite). She taught actors to use the script and the world around them to create a performance, and not, as she thought Strasberg did, to psychoanalyze themselves and use what they'd found to make the script their own.

When Method actors Montgomery Clift and, more explosively, Marlon Brando broke into the Hollywood mainstream, Adler was lifted along with them. Brando was her most famous student (he surely relished the in-joke in his famous bellow "Stella!"), and she was immediately recognized as among the most important teachers of the newly dominant American acting style. At the time De Niro entered her class, Adler could count among her past and present students the likes of Warren Beatty, Anthony Quinn, Eva Marie Saint, Karl Malden, and Elaine Stritch. By the dawn of the 1960s, her class was the largest in New York, and students would come from literally all over the world, sometimes to be launched into stardom or at least a career, sometimes to suffer withering dismissal. (A sign posted outside the classroom cautioned, "Stella wants everyone to know that criticism in the theatre is not personal. Nothing in the theatre is personal.")

The young De Niro entered this emotional and artistic minefield possessed of a personal bent toward silence, observation, and nose-to-the-grindstone work that happened to mesh with Adler's ideas. If watching his mother and father at work had taught him anything, it was the value of application, self-scrutiny, doggedness. Art could, at least in part, result from elbow grease. He studied the modern classics with Adler: Chekhov, Odets, and of course his dad's old chum Tennessee Williams. He appreciated the nuts-and-bolts aspect of Adler's approach: "It was just a way of making people aware of character, style, period, and so on. People could sit down in a classroom as opposed to having to get up and demonstrate it. . . . In fact, that's a class I'd want to take again. It taught me that if you have a very balanced script, you can *take* from the script without putting anything into something that isn't there. That's what she would call fictionalizing—which is not real, there's no substance to it, it's not concrete." She made something elusive seem, to his way of thinking, rational.

The idea that acting was built of observation and imagination must have been particularly resonant for De Niro. After a childhood spent among adults, left alone with his books, permitted to go out by himself to play in the street, the only kid at the table or at the party, he was constantly observing the world. He was an outsider: as an only child, as a student, as a kid from Greenwich Village at a time when being from the Village was truly a remarkable thing. Somewhere along the way, his silence and watchfulness became a form of alchemy. He knew how to look at people and read them, and converting his research, as it were, into art by pretending to climb inside their skins must have seemed a challenge, yes, but also something like a game. "To totally submerge into another character," he explained, "and experience life through him, without having to risk the real-life consequences—well, it's a cheap way to do things you would never dare to do yourself."

Given his tendency to watch and emulate, one of the strangest things about De Niro is how little he seemed to partake of the counter-culture that was so vital in his community during his early twenties. He had grown up in one of the most bohemian and cosmopolitan neighborhoods on earth, with parents who were artists, and with as-pirations toward a career of his own in the arts. He was twenty when the Beatles arrived, and he turned twenty-four during the Summer of Love; he managed to avoid military service in the Vietnam era, but he never really, by his own confession, seemed to have a hippie or even countercultural moment. Not once, he would tell *Playboy,* did he take LSD, nor was he an active antiwar protester. If anything, his bearing in his first films would reveal a kind of old-fashioned straightness and normalcy: he wanted to be thought of, at some level, as an ordinary fellow—or at least that was one of the guises he wore most comfortably. (The mini-Mafioso act he could easily slip into was also tinged with manners and echoes of a cultural past.)

Reflecting on his early acting days in the heart of the 1960s, he confessed that there had been a gap between him and the momen-tous goings-on of the time. "It was an exciting time to grow up," he admitted. "Kind of bohemian. Things were happening. There were big changes. I wasn't really a part of it, though. I was more on the outside. *But by virtue of being an actor I was a good observer of it.*"

Silence, stillness, observation, imitation, performance: the keys to his art were already inside him, had been since childhood, and Adler's methodology, with its emphasis on imagination, choices, and the text helped him unlock it and put it powerfully to use.

More specifically, especially given the nature of his work in the decades after he studied with Adler, De Niro explained that he learned how to do the most chaotic form of acting—that is, improvisation—by employing the hard, detail-oriented techniques on which Adler focused:

I think disciplined studying is good because you learn how to be aware of what improvising is. That you're somewhere, you have to head someplace. And I think I got that from acting school because of what they tell you about action and tension and what's the meaning and reason for a scene, also character things, and not drawing on your personal experience directly but more on creating that situation that the play calls for and then, in turn, personalizing it, and, in turn, making it work for you.

If De Niro shone in Adler's class, he didn't exactly blind people. Thurman Scott, among those who would eventually inherit Adler's mantle as a New York teacher-actor-director, recalled, "I was the star at Stella's; Bobby was about eighth in the class." (Scott noted as well, without knowing many details of his classmate's upbringing, his suspicion that "Bobby had abandonment issues. I know the pain of being connected on a journey with someone and then have them say, 'You can't come.'")

There were aspects of studying with Adler that weren't appealing to De Niro. "How she behaved, her affectation, that whole side of her, I never cared for personally," he admitted. "But she made a lot of sense as a teacher. She had a very healthy approach toward acting and technique." He was aware that there were other ideas about acting, such as those Lee Strasberg was promulgating at the Actors Studio. But he knew that Adler was a great resource—and, as he remembered, "she had a great actor, Brando, with her." He would always credit her with his foundations as an actor, and he would talk far more willingly about her influence on his thinking and practice than he would about almost anything else in his professional history.

In MANY WAYS, he was just where he should have been. Still not twenty, with little to no performing experience since before he was a teen, he was far better-off in the classroom setting of Adler's Conservatory than at the Actors Studio, which focused on praxis and critique of a sort more suited to working actors. Besides, he wasn't yet convinced that he wanted to *be* a working actor. He briefly enrolled in the Delehanty Institute, a technical school that specialized in preparing students for civil service careers, with an eye toward possibly attending the Police Academy. And he still wanted to satisfy the urge to see the world that had been sparked by the visit to his father a few years earlier. That most of all was what prevented him from immersing himself fully in the business of acting.

"I was afraid that I could get wrapped up in it so much that I wouldn't have time to do what I wanted, like travel," he later confessed. He had put together enough money to return to Europe for an extended hitchhiking jaunt, months longer than the previous had lasted. He "hitched all over Europe," as he recalled—Scotland, Yugoslavia, Greece—and spent several weeks living in Paris. "I lived in hotels near the Odéon on the Left Bank," he said. "I finally found a hotel in Montmartre. I went to Alliance Française, met a lot of expatriates. The French are hard to meet."

A principal attraction of France was, of course, visiting his father, who had left Paris and had taken to living in a string of what he referred to as "places I could afford": farmhouses, barns, cottages, and airy flats in such pastoral settings as Baren (in the Midi-Pyrénées), Gravigny (in Upper Normandy), and, finally, Saint-Just-en-Chevalet (in the Rhône-Alpes), where Bobby caught up with him: "I hitchhiked to where he was living in Central France in the Loire Valley, and I stayed with him for a week."

At first the elder De Niro's accounts of life in the countryside had been positive. In a 1962 letter to his friend Dick Brewer he said: "I never expected such beauty when I came here. It's dazzling." By the time Bobby reached him, though, there was a different tenor to the man, and the son was troubled by what he found. His father hadn't fared well in isolation. There was some suggestion of a genuine mental crisis: a scholar of his work would claim that "his 'erratic' behavior, culminating in a nervous breakdown in Paris, was diagnosed as bipolar disorder, and he was one of the first people treated with lithium." Decades later, the son disputed that diagnosis: "He didn't have a breakdown, but something happened to him there in France."

He tried to help his father by encouraging him in his work. "I felt that he had lost some of his career momentum," he recalled. "At one point I was on the Left Bank and took his paintings with me to show to gallery owners to push for him and try to get his work seen. But nothing came of it." De Niro's name was unknown in Europe, and he had no champions in the French art press. He knew all that, but his son did not. "Bobby was very impressed with France," the painter recalled years later in New York, "and urged me to take my paintings to the Parisian galleries. But the market was here."

Initially the younger De Niro continued hitchhiking around the Continent. But he was disturbed by what he'd seen in his dad—perhaps especially by the widening gap between his mother's relatively stable life and the professionally and emotionally troubled penury of his father. He returned to France and took a firmer tone with his father: life abroad wasn't working out for him, and he needed to be in familiar surroundings and near people who could help support him, financially and otherwise. They struggled with each other, the son urging the father to return home, to no avail. (Recollecting the experience at separate times, both men would refer to it as a "nightmare.") He came back alone to his studies with Stella Adler, to his slow acclimation to the acting profession.

PRACTICAL SON OF practical folks, De Niro determined that if he was going to pursue acting, he was going to make money at it, and he set about becoming a professional in the disciplined way in which he'd seen his parents go about their work. He kept a keen eye on the bulletin boards at the Adler school, where small productions posted advertisements for auditions and other casting opportunities; he became a habitual reader of theatrical trade magazines—*Drama-Logue*, *Backstage*, *Show Business*, and such. More and more he seemed to have turned a corner and committed himself to a path.

Through a friend of a friend he learned about a role that had become available in a play being put on at Hunter College, a German Expressionist drama by Rolf Lauckner entitled *Cry in the Street* that involved three blind men accosting a woman on a New Year's Eve. An actor playing one of the blind men had dropped out—unlike the play, his gig driving a taxi paid actual money, and he couldn't afford to give it up—and De Niro presented himself to the show's director, Roberta Sklar, as a replacement.

Sklar was then a graduate student in theater at Hunter, and she had the good fortune to be able to draw on the pool of young New York actors in her casting. Her other key actors were Sylvester Ciraulo, who would have a long career as a soap opera actor under the name Michael Durrell, and a collegiate actor and aspiring novelist from North Dakota named Larry Woiwode. "Larry was serious about acting," remembered Sklar, "but De Niro was *serious*." All three actors, she said, treated the production with respect, doing research and thinking along with her about how to play a pack of three. "They spent time watching monkeys at the Central Park Zoo," she recalled, "and came back with bodily expressions they got from the animals." But De Niro, she said, went even further. "I knew he was sitting somewhere watching some old guys," she said. "He didn't mention it, but you knew from watching him that what he was doing had come from real observation of real life." (De Niro did mention to Woiwode that he'd spent some time watching blind men get around New York.)

De Niro's reticence about discussing his technique was, Sklar remembered, exactly who he was. "He was very polite," she said.

It almost felt old-fashioned, without feeling silly or false or posed. He was serious about doing things studiously. He was extremely genuine. I don't know what his goals were at the time, but what came through was his focus on the work he was doing. No distractions, no hurry. Very respectful even though it was just a college production. His goal didn't seem to be "I'm gonna be a star," but "I'm gonna be an actor and do this work." At the time, you had a lot of young Method actors in New York who put on a show, all the time, of their intention to act. But he wasn't a caricature of an actor. He was very real and very sincere.

Woiwode, too, found in the young De Niro a stage presence of evident power but one that could be dangerously raw as well. He wrote later, "He seems oblivious to an unwritten rule of the stage, which is never, no, never manhandle a fellow actor, especially his or her body, but do only what you must for things to look good out front. . . . Bob grabs hold so hard in our blind grapples he is, according to Syl, out of control, wholly internal, with no sense of ensemble work. . . . He *seems* eager to please but is a lightning rod attracting the emotions of any observers . . . a presence to work with or to back from, not a performer of mere skills."

Offstage, De Niro would present another aspect entirely, and it drew Woiwode in. De Niro liked to mention, casually but seeking to create an effect, that he was studying with Stella Adler, and he was especially proud of his father's name and work. He carried around novels in a battered leather briefcase he'd picked up overseas—he was taking a speed-reading class ("the same one JFK took")—and he was keen to seek out new books. Woiwode was halfheartedly committed to pursuing acting; he was far more serious about writing fiction and had the legendary *New Yorker* editor William Maxwell as a mentor. But he was sufficiently engaged by De Niro's personality and energy to stay connected to him, at least for a time.

"He's out to please, with an easy, unselfconscious smile," he later wrote of his new friend, "which can shift into one of such abandon it draws his hairline back—the grin of a young man secure in his new maturity. . . . Caught off guard, he looks entirely like himself yet different each time. . . . It's difficult talking to him, because any question moves him to another quadrant of character, if not a new character altogether—the chameleon nature."

When they met, De Niro was living in a small apartment on Irving Place, a few blocks from his mom's place, which was still the headquarters of her typing and printing business. Admiral supported her son with gifts of cash—Woiwode saw multiple $20 bills change hands—and seemed unconcerned with his lack of financial independence or his pursuit of an acting career. There was a young lady on the scene, whom De Niro referred to as "my French girlfriend." And there was an undercurrent of anxiety. Woiwode noted that Bobby would bring up his parents whenever he felt blue and would speak as if he felt personally responsible for their separation and owed it to them to keep them connected.

There were larks as well. De Niro and Woiwode would sit in bars and practice communicating only with facial gestures ("He can focus one eye directly on you," Woiwode recalled, "while the other goes blank"), or they would lure a friend into a fake séance in one of their apartments, moving the table surreptitiously and startling their unsuspecting chum. When Woiwode and his wife acquired a large car, a Bonneville convertible, De Niro donned some of his costumes and pretended to be their chauffeur, driving them from one of their regular haunts to another and clearing the crowd as if for visiting celebrities. They would go on auditions together, talk about acting and even writing (De Niro hinted that he was trying to compose a novel that would feature a starring role for himself), and drink in their apartments or at Jimmy Ray's bar, a showbiz haunt on Eighth Avenue in the theater district. They became real pals.

WITH A "diamond in the rough" such as De Niro in her cast, Rebecca Sklar had hopes for *Cry in the Street*, but she saw something remarkable during the show's brief run: the young actor who'd been so galvanizing in the rehearsal space shrank away onstage. "He was intensely engaging in rehearsal," she remembered. "Every word and move. But it didn't translate to the stage in a larger arena. I knew he was an extraordinary actor, and I expected a spectacular public performance. But it wasn't anything like the explosive energy of the smaller venue." Strangely, Sklar wasn't as disappointed as might be expected. Instead, she had an epiphany about acting. "I didn't think, 'Oh my God, he's letting me down,'" she said. "I thought, 'This guy belongs in movies.' He was the same, but it didn't come across on a stage."*

De Niro kept pursuing auditions and other opportunities advertised in the showbiz trades. He quickly found something else worth pursuing: a microbudget film being planned by a professor and two graduate students at Sarah Lawrence College in Bronxville, just a few miles north of Manhattan. "I had seen an advertisement in *Show Business*," he remembered years later. "I went into De Palma's studio for the audition and after that he called me."

But there was more to it than that. The De Palma in question was, of course, Brian De Palma, a twenty-three-year-old doctor's son and science prodigy from Philadelphia who had graduated from Columbia College in 1962 and enrolled, as one of Sarah Lawrence's first male students, in the graduate theater program with the intention of becoming a filmmaker. Along with his professor Wilford Leach (who would go on to win Tony Awards for directing *The Pirates of Penzance* and *The Mystery of Edwin Drood* in 1981 and 1986, respectively) and another theater student, Cynthia Munroe, De Palma shared writing, directing, editing, and producing credits on a film, a comedy set during a wedding weekend. And they had so few resources that they would consider almost anyone for a role.

This audition would be the start of De Niro's first important working relationship with a director—as well as a memorable moment for those there to witness it. De Palma would tell the story in a number of ways, but they boiled down to the same initial impression that Woiwode had: a quiet kid who could somehow amp himself up into a release of explosive power. "He was very mild, shy, self-effacing," De Palma said a decade or so later. "He asked if he could do a scene from acting class. He disappeared for fifteen minutes and returned doing a heavy Lee J. Cobb number." (In another account, De Palma changed actors but

---

* Two decades later, no longer involved with the theater, Sklar would see De Niro in the only Broadway performance of his career, in *Cuba and His Teddy Bear*, and she came away with the same impression: "I was right. He was brilliant in front of the camera, but it didn't come across the same way in the theater."

created a similar impression: "It was amazing. Suddenly, from this shy 19-year-old kid, came this Broderick Crawford–like character of such power and force it blasted us out of the room.")

Naturally, De Palma and company wanted a dynamo like this in their movie. But there was the matter of money—or, more precisely, the lack of it. When they called him back and offered De Niro the part, he was so excited that he misheard what he would be paid. "I thought I was getting $50 a week," he remembered. "But my mother, who signed the contract because I was underage, told me, 'You get $50 for the complete movie.'" Chicken feed, yes, but, for the first time, he would be paid for acting. He took the job.

Virtually every face on-screen in the film, eventually entitled *The Wedding Party*, would be a new one, and most of them would only be seen this one time. But there were others beside De Niro with significant futures in acting. William Finley, who would become a staple figure in De Palma films, made his feature debut, and the film also introduced two Sarah Lawrence students: Jill Clayburgh, who had a large role as the bride, and Jennifer Salt, daughter of the famed screenwriter Waldo Salt and a girl who would have been at the High School of Music and Art when De Niro breezed through the place, as a member of the wedding party.

In addition to his scanty fee, De Niro took some tutelage from the experience of making the film. He appeared in a workshop production of *La Ronde* at the college, and the professor overseeing it offered him some advice that he held on to. "There was a teacher who taught at Sarah Lawrence," he remembered, "and he said, 'Just go on instinct.' And it kind of frees you because you get distracted with 'What's my character? What's my motivation?' . . . You forget in life people don't behave that way. They just do what they're doing; there's no thought behind it."

He learned as well to keep an eye on shifty independent producers, who were just as likely to seek perks for themselves as the starving actors who nourished themselves at the crafts service table. In the prop list he composed for himself, De Niro noted a few items from his own costume collection that he wanted to use for the production, then added a note of caution: "Have certain things like rifle and fishing that would like to use; what's this about producer keeping stuff?"

His script for the shoot was marked up, in a fashion he would follow for the rest of his life, with all sorts of insights, reminders, questions, prompts, and instructions, much the way that Stella Adler's script analysis class had taught him. "I have a disrespect for things like people's clothes," he wrote of his character, Cecil, "so I keep touching people all the time, and the same with any and all objects . . . Keep looking at all the nice broads that pass. Think which is good for a lay and which is not . . . Use napkin and don't put it in lap but finish and throw it in plate on rest of food . . . I bought my suit for $25 at Smith's Bargain Hall." Tiny, seemingly inconsequential things, written in a crabbed hand, but they would be the sorts of pry bars he would use to open up the script and the role and climb inside.

The film that resulted from all of this work was a sporadically charming, overlong pastiche about an uncertain bridegroom who must work out whether, in fact, he'll go through with his wedding during a long weekend spent on an eastern seaboard island. Charlie (Charles Pfluger) arrives via ferry, accompanied by his groomsmen, Cecil (De Niro, billed as "Denero") and Alistair (William Finley), and finds himself cowed by the blue-blooded milieu in which his intended, Josephine (Clayburgh), has been raised. His chums tempt him to ditch the whole thing, but he chooses to stay on, only to develop cold feet all on his own before the fateful ceremony. Finally he submits, and the film ends with the pealing of wedding bells.

De Niro, his face still round with baby fat, his head crowned with a buzz cut, plays Cecil as an overassured jock, arriving at the island with gear for fishing, water skiing, hunting, and baseball, and speaking in the fusty, patrician manner of a man of far older years. There isn't enough written for Cecil to be made into an actual character, and a few of De Niro's scenes would be altered into incomprehensibility by the post-production decision to impart a vaguely druggy style to them, but he does convince in the role of a worldly and mature fellow, and there is nothing of the Greenwich Village bohemian boy or the Little Italy street kid in his performance. When the film was finally seen by

critics, he was one of three actors cited by *Variety* as "making any impression."*

THROUGHOUT THIS PERIOD of his son's nascent career, the elder Robert De Niro continued to live, however precariously, in France. His son
wrote to him regularly, entreating him to return home, to no avail.

As his friend Larry Woiwode suspected, the subject of his parents
was an extremely sensitive one for Bobby, and it could release a startling
and angry energy from him when he felt prodded. There was the incident of a watercolor painted by the elder De Niro entitled "The Actor."
Visiting De Niro's apartment—a new one, larger, on 14th Street, closer
yet to Admiral's place—Woiwode had expressed admiration for the picture. Months later, when Woiwode and his wife moved into their own
place in Brooklyn, De Niro and his sweetie of the moment (not the
French girl, but a waitress from Max's Kansas City) showed up with a
housewarming gift: "The Actor." Bashful and clumsy, Woiwode pro-
tested that it was too generous, saying, "Your dad gave it to you." But
Bobby assured him that wasn't the case: "I kind of took it from stuff
at Mom's! He's got hundreds. Oils! I like a lot of them better." After a
little while, and some drinks, Woiwode tried once again to beg off the
gift, and this time De Niro exploded: "It's not good enough for you?
You're too damn special or what?" He leapt up and, yanking his girlfriend by the arm, left the apartment.

Woiwode grabbed the painting and gave chase, hoping to make
amends. He caught up to them in the street and found De Niro in a
fury:

> *"You're giving it back?" he yells, and grabs my shirt and spins
> me so hard buttons pop and the watercolor flies the length of my*

---

* De Palma wouldn't finish editing *The Wedding Party* until 1966, and it wouldn't be
released until 1969, when he and De Niro had acquired a patina of indie film cred and
someone saw some commercial possibilities in it. Over the years, it was released on video
and DVD as a De Niro/Clayburgh film (in fact, they would almost never be on-screen
together in a single shot), and one bottom-feeding distributor billed it, with almost larcenous disingenuousness, as "De Palma!! De Niro!! De Clayburgh!! De Lovely!!" (De trop.)

arm. . . . He bends me backward over the pickets until I'm sure its spear points of steel will puncture my spine. [His girlfriend] screams, "Bobby, stop that! Stop! You're friends!" That does it; he lets go. . . . I accept the gift, I thank him, and it's over.[*]

IN EARLY 1965, the elder De Niro returned to New York, finally persuaded by his son that it was the only place in which he could restart his career. "I eventually convinced him to get on a plane," Bobby recalled. Having seen his father safely returned to Manhattan, the son made good on his promises to help him professionally. And there really were opportunities for the painter. Through his dealer, Virginia Zabriskie, he had sold forty-odd canvases from the past decade to Joseph Hirschhorn, and some of his newer works had sold as well. Zabriskie scheduled him for a one-man show in January 1965, his first exhibition since his return home, which would require him to produce a lot of work—just the thing to get him back into the swing of the city.

The elder De Niro had shipped canvases, materials, and personal belongings back from France, and his son enlisted Woiwode, their quarrel behind them, to help move his dad's effects from the shipping yard to his new studio. They stuffed everything they could into a rented truck and then found themselves with a few oversized canvases—erotic paintings of women—that wouldn't fit. So they dropped the top of Woiwode's Bonneville and rode into Soho with them, father and son balancing the paintings during the slow promenade.[†]

And there was another favor: would Woiwode permit his wife, Carole, then pregnant with their first child, to pose for the senior De Niro as he prepared work for the new show? At first Woiwode tried to stammer a demurral, but Bobby assured him that it was on the up-and-up—his own girlfriend would be posing, and *she* wouldn't be nude or

---

[*] Decades later, Woiwode still owned the painting.

[†] The 2012 film *Being Flynn*, in which De Niro played a wayward Manhattan father struggling with mental issues, included a version of this very scene, with De Niro enlisting the help of his son (played by Paul Dano) and his chums to fetch his belongings out of a storage unit.

anything. The Woiwodes discussed the matter and Carole agreed. As ever, De Niro was a frantic presence in his studio, punishing himself with his perfectionism, trashing efforts that didn't meet his high standards. "If they didn't fall right in the first strokes," Woiwode's wife told him of the watercolors De Niro was attempting, "he not only tore the sheet off, he balled it up, then tossed it across the room."

On the night of opening, the Woiwodes accompanied the two Robert De Niros to the gallery and were greeted by the appearance of yet another De Niro—Henry, the father of the painter, in town from Syracuse to see how *his* son's career was faring. Woiwode remembered him as "tall and heavyset, silver-haired, with a way of walking with his arms out from his sides, as if about to quick-draw on the louts he sees on the street, as he calls them."

After the show, they all went for dinner. Walking along the street, they came upon Bobby's girl's boss from Max's, who she'd been complaining had been forward with her, pawing at her and making lewd chat. Told who the man was, Bobby pounced on him, grabbing him by the collar, shoving him against a building, hitting him in the head, and warning him of worse: "You touch my girl one more time and I'll bust your ass, you fucking scumbag!" Eventually his father and grandfather pulled him off ("Bobby, you cannot do that in this city," Henry told him), and the groper, terrified and chastened, fled into the night.

4

S UDDENLY HE WAS DRIVEN.

He would audition for almost anything—plays, movies, student projects, commercials. He'd show up, always prepared, distribute head shots and clippings, and mention his experience and schooling if he thought it would matter. He made a job of going out to look for jobs, on his own, without an agent, tireless. "If you don't go, you never know" became his mantra, and he'd hold on to it for years, sharing it with other hustling wannabes, dispensing it as advice to newcomers once he'd ascended, passing it on to his own children as a family ethic.

He wasn't afraid to look for or ask about work anywhere. Tagging along to a literary party with Larry Woiwode, he peppered John Updike with questions about who owned the film rights to *Rabbit, Run.** He showed up for auditions in empty storefronts where potential directors conducted business sitting on flattened cardboard boxes on the floor. He tried out for student productions.

"I had an optimistic outlook," he remembered. "I sent out my resume and went to open calls. I felt like a gambler. If I didn't go, I would never know. I was never discouraged as long as I was acting. I read for a lot of things."

His resumes were a particular specialty. Because he had access to

---

* A few years later, he would write a letter to the novelist Paul Tyner, a collegiate acquaintance of Woiwode's, asking if he would recommend him to the prospective director of the screen adaptation of Tyner's novel *Shoot It*. The film wasn't made until 1974, as *Shoot It Black, Shoot It White*, with De Niro's onetime co-star Michael Moriarty in the lead role De Niro coveted.

unlimited typesetting and printing through his mother's business, he built a small library of head shots—single images and composites in the guises of various personae: cops, cabbies, beatniks, a hippie with a guitar, a Chekhovian man with glasses and suit, an Italian gangster with cape and goatee, even some with his hair apparently dyed blond, and beyond that a thick pile of photos of him in various suits, coats, and hats, with dark glasses, cigars, a pistol, and so on and so on, often two or four to a page, many, many pages' worth. "He had a portfolio in which he appeared as an 80-year-old man and in costumes of all kinds," recalled the famed casting director Marion Dougherty of his first appearances on her desk. "I had never in my life seen anything like that."

He was projecting an image of himself as a chameleonic sort of actor, not a leading man but somebody who could play a variety of offbeat types. And he had a healthy attitude toward the entire process. "I didn't have a problem with rejection," he said, "because when you go into an audition you're rejected already. There are hundreds of other actors. You're behind the eight ball when you go in."

He did, though, have a particular name he liked to drop when appearing at a casting session—not Stella Adler's, but that of his dad. "I'm Bob De Niro," he'd say, introducing himself. "I'm sure you've heard of my father." (Sometimes he'd even bring clippings of his dad's reviews or images of his work.) The New York arts world was relatively small, after all; one never could say for sure who might have heard of whom.

AND SO HE WENT on auditions, some successful, some not. He also expanded his studies, attending Raphael Kelly's speech class at the Shakespeare Studio and studying a bit with the acting teacher Luther James. In late 1964 he landed a walk-on part in a film called *Three Rooms in Manhattan*, directed by, of all people, the French master Marcel Carné, famed for *Les Enfants du Paradis*, *Le Quai des Brumes*, and other milestones of the pre–Nouvelle Vague French cinema. The story, about an older man obsessed to the point of criminality with a young woman, was adapted from a Georges Simenon novel; a few years earlier, René Clément had come close to filming it with Henry Fonda and Simone Signoret, and there had been previous rumors that

Federico Fellini would make it with Marcello Mastroianni and Jeanne Moreau. Carné, who had Maurice Ronet and Annie Girardot as his leads, was apparently quite the volcano on the set, excoriating the union crew for its slow pace and bridling against the efforts to give the film a slick American feel. (As it happened, the film never received a proper release in the United States, not even in New York.)

None of that likely mattered to De Niro. Visible in two separate sequences set in restaurants in the first half hour of the film, he got a couple of days' work and, in addition to the pay, some valuable insight into the business. "I remember a bunch of other young actors," he said, "hanging around, moaning and bitching, all made up, with pieces of tissue in their collars; it was the kind of thing you always hear about actors—where they're just silly or vain, complaining back and forth, walking around primping, not wanting to get the make-up on their shirts. . . . I didn't want to be around those people at all. I just walked in and walked out. I *was* nervous, though, just to say the line 'Gimme a drink.'"*

Without an American release, it was as if the film had never been made, but that would be a glorious fate compared to what happened to his next film. In 1965, attending an audition that was advertised at Stella Adler's Conservatory, he was cast in one of the two lead roles in a movie written and directed by the Argentine playwright and film-maker Norman C. Chaitin. Chaitin had enjoyed a little bit of critical and underworld success with *The Small Hours*, an independent film, made on a minuscule budget, about the life of a Manhattan ad executive who goes bohemian on a visit downtown ("The dolls and guys of Greenwich Village and the real gone pads where they get their kicks," read the movie poster for the film when it was rereleased in 1969 as *Flaming Desire*).

Chaitin's new film was an adaptation of his own play *Times Square Encounter*, about the accidental meeting of a woman and the son she gave up for adoption. Once again the director was working with his own money, with a skeletal crew, on borrowed locations at the Mayflower

---

* Department of small worlds: another walk-on role in the film, that of a waiter, was filled by Abe Vigoda, who, like De Niro, would later play a role in the *Godfather* saga.

Hotel near Lincoln Center and a nightclub on Central Park West; costumes and props were loaned by generous friends, and meals were provided by the director's wife. It was pure indie filmmaking. "The actors
weren't paid," Chaitin remembered. "Nobody was paid. I wasn't paid. I
did it with my own money."

De Niro, recommended for the job by Adler, got the lead role.
Playing his mother—although almost the exact same age as him—was
another Adler student, Dyanne Thorne,* who almost didn't make it
through the production alive. "They shot a scene of me in a shower,"
she remembered, "through a frosted door. The lights fell into the
shower, and there were sparks everywhere, but luckily I hadn't stepped
into it yet."

Even with the shadowy nudity of the shower scene, the film, according to Chaitin, was De Niro's. "The son's part is the most important,"
he said. "The scenes between him and the mother were very emotional. I wouldn't have finished the film if he wasn't talented."

But, in fact, he didn't *quite* finish it. After shooting and editing the
film, which had been retitled *Encounter*, Chaitin was called back to
Argentina because of an illness in his wife's family. He left the film at a
lab in New York so that they could finish the post-production work he'd
begun, instructing them to hold on to the negative—the only copy of
the film—until his return.

That return, alas, was nearly a decade later, and when he finally
made it back to New York, Chaitin found that the lab to which he'd en-
trusted his movie had gone out of business and nobody knew where its
unclaimed contents were stored—if, in fact, they were stored anywhere
at all. Nobody, in short, would ever see *Encounter*. "I think it would
have been a fine film," Thorne reckoned. "Everyone was excited about
it at the time, and we were all full of energy."

Chaitin spent years trying to track the movie down, then noticed
that a fellow who resembled his leading man had become a genuine
movie star and acting phenomenon. He confirmed that it was the same
guy by digging out a shooting script and finding the words "Close-up

---

* Thorne would go on to later fame in exploitation films such as *Ilsa: She Wolf of the
SS* and *Wanda, the Wicked Warden*.

on De Niro" scribbled on a page in his own handwriting. "He was a star from the beginning," the director said.

In the years following the shoot, De Niro mentioned his work in *Encounter* on his resumes. But, like the director, he never saw it. Chaitin, who continued to write plays and whose son, Gregory, became a famed mathematician, never made another film. But he could always boast a singular achievement, even if he didn't have the film footage to prove it. "I was smart enough to choose him for my movie," he said. "What I saw in him is what everyone else saw afterward. I feel honored that I was the first one to give De Niro a leading role. I'm very proud of that."

FOR THE NEXT YEAR, De Niro continued his litany of auditions, augmented by the occasional working (but almost never paying) gig: a role as The Sheriff in a production of Arthur Sanier's *God Wants What Man Wants* at the Bridge Theatre on St. Mark's Place; a part as The Poet, the narrator of a production of *The World of Günter Grass* that featured a similarly unknown Charles Durning (a *New York Times* review by Stanley Kauffmann praised Durning as "completely credible" and failed to single out De Niro from among a cast prone to "transparent staginess"). He was given the opportunity to read for the lead in Mike Nichols's *The Graduate*, one of only two unknowns to be offered that chance, but he was far too raw and didn't really get anywhere near it.

Keeping himself afloat financially could be a dicey thing, even with his mom supplementing his income. But, like his dad, he kept his overhead low (he rode a bike to save cab and subway fare), and he didn't mind living a little rough. "I had years where I didn't work," he admitted. "Unemployment, stuff like that. Typical, usual stuff. I was lucky in that there was always something that I would wind up doing from here to there. It kept me moving just enough. I had down periods, but not where you would give up and say, 'I've got to do something else.'"

Surely thoughts of doing something else crossed his mind in the summer of 1967, when he left New York in April for a spell of work at the Barn Dinner Theatre in Greensboro, North Carolina—not exactly the sort of promising journey that his father had made when, as a teenager, he undertook a nearly identical trip to nearby Black Mountain College.

The Barn was the second in what would become a small chain of regional theaters that specialized in bringing relatively recent big-town shows to smaller cities in the South. De Niro had been cast in a role originated on Broadway by Anthony Quinn in Sidney Michael's *Tchin-Tchin*: Caesario Grimaldi, a construction worker who tries to seduce the wife of a surgeon out of revenge for the surgeon's having seduced *his* wife after removing her appendix.

It was a lukewarm domestic farce, but the folks in Greensboro loved it—or at least they loved De Niro. "Acting Is Good in Barn Play," read the review in the *Greensboro Daily News*, which commented that "De Niro and [Faith] Stanfield are both exceptionally talented actors. They never once let the action falter."

De Niro, who was becoming something of a pack rat of materials from his working career, kept a cutting of that notice, as well as several others. And he wrote a letter to the *Daily Tarheel* at the nearby University of North Carolina asking for a copy of its review (and enclosing a dollar to cover the cost of the newspaper and postage).

It wasn't Broadway, but it did pay: $35 a week, plus $3 a day in expenses, and he was given a room to live in right on the premises of the Barn for the duration of his stay. It was actually a bit of fun, he recalled. The show was performed in a theater-in-the-round, with the novelty of the stage actually being lowered into the theater after dinner. "We'd serve the desserts," De Niro remembered, "and then go upstairs to prepare for the play, and then the stage would drop and we'd perform. I liked it."

A few months later he came back, this time to Charlotte and the brand-new Pineville Country Dinner Theater, which had opened to rival the Barn chain and advertised "Broadway plays with New York casts." In William Goodhart's *Generation*, De Niro, by all accounts, stole the show in the role of a kooky obstetrician helping a hippieish young couple navigate the wife's first pregnancy ("Those laughs the playwright didn't give him, he took anyway," wrote the *Orlando Evening Star*). The play ran for two weeks in August, during which time he also found work acting on a pair of local television commercials, one for Duke Power, one for BankAmericard. Upon returning home, De Niro was greeted with a personal letter from the president of the theater, F. W. (Bill) Lorick, who thanked him for his "fine job" and assured him, "The patrons enjoyed your work of acting very, very much."

In reflection, De Niro was fond of the gigs. "I got so many tips that I didn't worry about having no job," he joked later. He reckoned it was a better job than summer stock, at least in terms of his craft: "You rehearse next week's show while you're playing this week's. . . . At least you do the same play every night and you can learn something from it."

He was making distinctions, making sacrifices, taking pains, all for his work. He was serious. And, again, the example of his father's willingness to forgo the ordinary comforts and niceties of life to pursue a career was a comfort to him. "I did not have a Plan B," he remembered, adding, "I never got to the point of needing one. I did one thing, then the next. I was able to sustain myself." (Sometimes that meant working odd jobs, such as waiting at catered affairs; years later he remembered that he'd served Dustin Hoffman—who, of course, had gotten the part in *The Graduate* for which De Niro had read—at a Eugene McCarthy fund-raiser in New York on the night in June 1968 when Robert F. Kennedy was shot.)

He was becoming increasingly professional. He hired a telephone answering service (Orchard 5-4372, in case you needed to reach him), but he wasn't yet comfortable with the expense and hassle of professional representation—or perhaps he wasn't able to secure it. "I got my first jobs without an agent," he said. "Sent out my resume and pictures and showed up at auditions. When you're starting out, you really have to do it all by yourself. And you still end up having to make the decisions. I don't like people to make decisions for me."

In 1968 he was onstage in New York again in the National Theatre Company's production of *The Boor* by Anton Chekhov. And then he got an unexpected bit of good fortune: the kid director for whom he'd worked on that film at Sarah Lawrence a few years earlier (which nobody had yet seen) was making a quickie independent film, mostly improvised, right in New York, with a budget of more than $40,000. Two weeks of work, and better-paid. Plus this time, instead of a professor and another student sharing in all the filmmaking duties with him, the kid, Brian De Palma, would direct the film on his own and have as a producer and co-writer Charles Hirsch, a young talent scout for Universal Pictures who'd been sent to New York to find youth-oriented projects and fresh faces.

Hirsch understood the emerging American market for exploitation films with an arty edge. In the course of his talent search, he encountered De Palma, who was just finishing up a groovy little thriller entitled *Murder à la Mod* (which would be his first release, as *The Wedding Party* remained unfinished). They discussed making a film about American youth alienation with a Gallic twist, a Truffaut-inspired tale of a young man flailing at the world and his obsessions, which happened to mirror those of his creators: voyeurism, filmmaking, the Vietnam War, the John F. Kennedy assassination, and computer dating. A little sex, a little politics, a little slapstick, a little social satire—they could sell just the novelty of it, they thought.

In time, the pair realized they might be asking too much of an actor (and an audience) to bundle all of that up into one character's head, so they split their hero into three heroes, a comic troika like that in *The Wedding Party*. Hirsch approached his bosses at Universal with the script, but they passed. He and De Palma raised the money by soliciting friends and relatives, and they planned to shoot the film in a breakneck two weeks while Hirsch was on (paid) vacation from the studio. De Palma knew how to do things cheap: "The most expensive thing in *Greetings*," he later noted, "was the stock, and getting it processed." He telephoned Columbia University, which he'd attended as an undergrad, and asked if he could use the rehearsal space and costumes of the student troupe, the Columbia Players, and maybe audition a few of them for roles.

He wound up finding one of his leads there: Gerrit Graham, a French major from New York. As Graham remembered, he learned that "there was a scenario but no screenplay" and that he'd have to improvise his audition with the other aspirants, including De Niro. After they'd both been cast, they found themselves working in what for all of them was essentially an experimental fashion. "We just plunged in," said Hirsch, "because the only way to find out about making a film is to make a film." The movie was basically a series of episodes, each based on a scenario that was presented to the actors to flesh out with dialogue and action of their own invention, with De Palma and Hirsch serving as guides and ringmasters. "We improvised a situation, then we filmed the scene, looked at it, and learned again," De Niro remembered. "Then finally we shot the scene."

"It was all ad-lib," according to Graham, "and what struck me was that De Niro worked so incredibly hard on everything. Bob was analytical of every scene in a Method way—he had to know why this scene had to have this material, where we were going with that scene. . . . He was a real actor. He'd already committed himself to it, devoted his life to it." De Palma, too, noted De Niro's work ethic and intensity, but he saw something else as well: the actor's chameleonic power was evident in a way it hadn't been a few years earlier. "He showed up to shoot a scene," he remembered, "and I didn't recognize him. We had to hang a title card on him to remind the audience that they'd seen him earlier in the film. It was make-up and clothes, but it was more than that—he just inhabits a character and becomes different physically."

HE HAD MADE four movies, and he still had yet to see himself on-screen in anything. But he kept at it, and in the summer another indie filmmaker looking to break into the biz hired him. Jordan Leondopoulos had written and would direct a picture entitled *Sam's Song*, a European-influenced movie about a young filmmaker invited by some well-to-do old friends to spend a weekend on their Long Island estate, where he meets a mysterious girl and is drawn unwillingly into mind games, bed-hopping, and other pursuits of the idle and indifferent rich.

Like *The Wedding Party*, *Sam's Song* was a debut film shot on spec with a tiny budget, but it was more accomplished as a narrative and a portrait of human beings than *The Wedding Party* or even *Greetings*. The mustachioed De Niro plays Sam, an aspiring director working as an editor of TV documentaries, reading André Bazin's *What Is Cinema?*, living on a diet of Yoo-hoo and cheese slices, drifting through Manhattan in search of inspiration and opportunity. His college friends Andrew (Jered Mickey) and Erica (Jennifer Warren) are in a long-term relationship that's prospering, and they appreciate his artistic purity and his quirks. The atmosphere is staid and even bucolic—a weekend-at-a-country-house movie, complete with cocktail parties, gambols on the beach, and a cruise.

The plotting, though, is threadbare. On the drive to the Hamptons (which, strangely, takes them from Manhattan through Staten Island) Andrew notices Carol, a leggy blonde (Terrayne Crawford), driving in the same direction in her Porsche; when she turns up at a luncheon party, she and Sam cavort together, and Andrew becomes frankly and obviously jealous. The next day, aboard a friend's yacht, Andrew moves in on her (he literally takes Sam's place in her bed within minutes of Sam's vacating it), leading Erica to a drastic response.

It all moves stolidly and glumly, with a fair amount of pretense and opacity: for instance, when Sam and Carol discover a windmill on their promenade, he charges at it with a large log. "You cast yourself very well," she tells him. "You think I'm a dreamer?," he responds, as though wounded. Influences of the French New Wave and especially Michelangelo Antonioni permeate the film, but none of it feels digested.

De Niro, though, is given lots to do and plenty of chances to shine. In one set piece, he plays cops and robbers and acts out getting shot in a series of amusing slow-motion takes. Later on, Sam and Carol turn the lights of a bedroom on and off quickly and pull faces at each other, and De Niro displays rubbery comic energy. Now and again Sam is given to spouting movie quotes and clichés, a task that De Niro clearly relishes (He also displays his nude body twice, albeit never from the front.) If anybody had seen *Sam's Song* at the time or in the form in which Leondopoulos made it, De Niro surely would have been noticed. But that was not to be the film's fate. In fact, no one would see it for more than a decade: in 1980, with De Niro one of the biggest stars in movies, the film played a very brief run in New York. A few years later, Cannon Films, which then owned the rights, shot segments of a thriller about a tough guy looking for his brother and cut Leondopoulos's movie into their new footage, using it as, in effect, the backstory. The original was utterly bastardized (for instance, the United Farm Workers documentary that Sam is editing on a Moviola in the original is replaced in the Cannon film, almost comically, with soft-core porn); retitled *The Swap* (and later *Line of Fire*), the recut film briefly played a single theater in New York.

IF HE WAS DOOMED to make movies that nobody would see, at least he still had the theater. Like the burgeoning indie film movement, the experimental theater scene in New York meant that there was ample work for somebody who was more interested in gaining experience than in working for fame or wealth or even mere pay. De Niro may have felt like an onlooker in the political and cultural events of the 1960s, but he was willing to throw himself in with any number of avant-garde artists who were pursuing radical new directions in film and theater.

One of them was Ron Link, a celebrated off-Broadway director who was preparing a revival of a campy show he'd had a minor hit with the previous year: *Glamour, Glory and Gold: The Life and Legend of Nola Noonan, Goddess and Star.* The play was a pastiche of the life of a tragic actress of old Hollywood (Jean Harlow's name was often mentioned in reviews), cobbled together as a series of sketches and blackouts rather than as a sustained drama. The makeshift structure of the script may have been the result of its having been the work of a first-time playwright, a twenty-year-old drag queen named Jackie Curtis who was a rising star in the firmament of Andy Warhol's Factory scene. The original production in the fall of 1967 became a cult smash on the strength of the casting of Curtis and another of Warhol's superstars, the famed drag queen Candy Darling, in support of Melba La Rose Jr.—an actual woman—who tackled the lead. (Warhol came to the show and gave it a word-of-mouth review that was, coming from him, a rave: "For the first time, I wasn't bored.")

The Playwrites (*sic*) Workshop Club, which had produced the first version of the show, would do the show again, at the tiny Bastiano's Cellar Studio theater on Waverly Place where it had played before. This time, Link would go with a less gender-bending cast, with the actress Paula Shaw in the lead role and, as in the original, a small cast of male actors playing multiple roles. De Niro certainly didn't run with a Warholian crowd, but he heard about the play and auditioned, trying to sweeten his chances of being hired by offering to have the posters and programs for the show printed for free by his mom.

He got the part, or rather the *parts*, ten in all: Duke, Lefty, Vinny, Peter Billings, Leading Man, Irvin, Harold Minsky, G.I. Joe, Baby Leroy, and Grady Eagles, per his resume. It was the biggest thing he'd ever done and the greatest proof yet of the versatility and malleability that he hinted at in those composite shots he passed out along with his resumes. The play opened in August, providing De Niro with the first reviews of his fledgling career. They were very, very positive: "Robert DeNiro [sic] appears in no less than ten cameo characterizations and is a standout comic actor," said *Show Business*. "He's a master of the art of underplaying." The *Village Voice* concurred: "DeNiro [sic] made clean, distinct character statements in a series of parts which many actors would have fused into a general mush. DeNiro is new on the scene and deserves to be welcomed."

The run of the play was brief, but it was crucial in a number of ways. With it, De Niro had gotten his foot well in the door of experimental theater in New York, he had acquired his first significant positive press, and he had grabbed the attention of a young woman who would become a booster of his work and his career as well as briefly a romantic partner.

Sally Kirkland was a big-eyed, statuesque twenty-year-old blonde from Pennsylvania who had been born to a life completely different from De Niro's. Named after her mother, also Sally Kirkland, a Vassar grad who had been an influential fashion editor for *Vogue* and held the same position at *Life* for decades, the younger Sally had been raised on Philadelphia's Main Line and the Upper East Side of Manhattan as a debutante and society girl (Ted Koppel took her to his prom and stole a kiss). But she had chucked it all for an acting career and an offstage role as a scene-sweller in the Manhattan of the 1960s.

In the summer of 1968 she was preparing for a daring new role in Terrence McNally's *Sweet Eros*, a one-act play that called for extended nudity ("My mother was showing people what to put on," she liked to joke, "and I was showing them how to take it off"). Along with her roommate, another aspiring actress named Susan Tyrell, she took in De Niro's performance in *Glamour, Glory and Gold*, and, like the critics, was deeply impressed. "He was electrifying," she remembered, "totally different in each part. I went backstage and told him, 'You are the greatest actor since Brando, and you are going to be a huge star.' And after, Bobby would phone me and ask over and over again, 'Do you really think I'm any good? Do you really think I'm any good?'"

There was a romance between them, but there was also an acting partnership. Kirkland was a member of the Actors Studio, the holy temple of Method acting in which Lee Strasberg practiced the Stanislavski system as he understood it. She wanted De Niro to seek admission to the Studio, but he demurred: there was a rigorous vetting process consisting of two auditions, and he was wary of Strasberg after having listened to Adler rail against her rival's theories in her classes. Instead, they created a little Actors Studio of their own, working on scenes in De Niro's apartment, giving real vent to their theatrical passions, as Kirkland remembered, without any fear of exposure or critique. "We had so much rage and energy in us," she said. "We would go at each other, have knockdown fights—kitchen-sink-drama-style."

He showed her his cache of wardrobe pieces and props. "It was like going into a costume room backstage of a theater," she remembered. "He had every conceivable kind of getup imaginable—and the hats! Derbies, straw hats, caps, homburgs." And in exchange for her insight and connections, he offered some advice of his own. When she told him she'd been rejected for a part for which she was sure she had auditioned well, he counseled her, "You are giving away too much. Hold something back. Be mysterious. It's more seductive."

During their time together, De Niro was granted entrée to a slightly tonier crowd than he had known on his own, and while very few of his new acquaintances became friends or colleagues, one in particular became both, and a tremendous boon to him. Among those to whom Kirkland introduced him, during one of many actors' nights out at Jimmy Ray's, the saloon on Eighth Avenue in midtown Manhattan that served for decades as a clubhouse for young performers, was Shelley Winters, who would become his first truly powerful advocate.

Winters was acting royalty, with two Oscars on her mantle (famously, she once brought them along when asked by a director to audition for a film part, pulling them slowly out of her bag one at a time to make the case that she didn't need to read for him to prove herself). She'd been born Shirley Schrift in St. Louis in 1920 and raised from age three in Brooklyn. She'd pursued a theatrical career throughout her teens, and she became a starlet in the blond-bombshell mode in her early twenties, with a little work on Broadway and in Hollywood. She finally found a niche in a string of films in which she played fallen women and/or the discarded victims of awful men: *A Double Life, Winchester 73, A Place in the Sun, The Night of the Hunter, Lolita.* Throughout that period she remained a serious student of acting, working principally with Lee Strasberg and her Actors Studio peers. And in time her dedication to the craft resulted in those Academy Awards, for her supporting roles in *The Diary of Anne Frank* (1959) and *A Patch of Blue* (1965).

With her brassy manner, zaftig figure, and penchant for blunt honesty, Winters had a lot of Brooklyn and more than a little bit of Stella Adler in her, and she was well known for a private life as colorful as the figure she cut in the world. She'd been married and divorced three times by 1960 (her husbands had included the actors Vittorio Gassman and Anthony Franciosa), and among the men with whom she'd shared romances, however fleeting, were Errol Flynn, William Holden, Clark Gable, Burt Lancaster, Marlon Brando, and Sean Connery. In her forties she had let her sexpot veneer fade, a decision that seemed to free her from all sorts of formalities, and she became the flamboyant den mother and Auntie Mame of the young New York Method acting scene, holding court in bars and restaurants, anointing tiny productions by arriving (often loudly) to take them in, encouraging study and work, and pulling strings to help further careers when she could.

Kirkland, who was an unofficial goddaughter of Winters's, insisted that she see De Niro perform, and so Winters made her way down to Waverly Place and *Glamour, Glory and Gold.* Right away she knew she was seeing something special. "When he moved across the stage it was like lightning," she remembered. "Gave me tingles. I haven't felt or seen anything like that since the '40s, when I saw Brando in a four-performance flop."

Winters immediately welcomed De Niro into her graces, honoring the raw talent she saw but recognizing, too, his boyish combination of frailty, earnestness, and energy. Just a few years after meeting him, when he was beginning to merit attention in the newspapers for his film work, she gushed about him in a telephone interview with the *New York Times*:

> *I'm Bobby's* Italian *mama. Well . . . maybe I am his Jewish mama, but if I am, he's my Jewish son. Bobby needs somebody to watch over him; he doesn't even wear a coat in the wintertime. . . . Of course, he will never borrow, so you have to find ways of giving him money without letting him know you're giving it to him. . . . Bobby will never talk about what made him the way he is, but I suspect he must have been a lonely kid, that somewhere along the line he was brutalized.*

By the time those words were printed, De Niro was already accruing a reputation for reticence in his dealings with the press, so it would be easy to imagine him being cross with his stage mama for her effusion. But amid the embarrassing kvelling, Winters offered some astounding insight into De Niro's craft, something that she had noticed almost immediately upon meeting him and seeing him perform:

> *Sometimes Bobby gives the impression that he's dumb, that his mind is wiped out, because he doesn't say anything. But behind those slit eyes he's watching everything . . . He scares me. The things that he does with his body are truly frightening. He can blush or get white as a sheet in a second, and he could force his hair to curl on command if he wanted to.*

IN LATE 1968 Virginia Admiral hosted a private screening of *Greetings* at her loft on 14th Street, and soon movie audiences around the country would get a chance to see what it was that had so captivated Kirkland and Winters—or, rather, some of them would. *Greetings*, De Niro's second film with Brian De Palma, was released on a single screen in midtown Manhattan with an X rating attached—only the fifth ever imposed by the Motion Picture Association of America in the two years of its ratings system (and, in turn, the first film to have its rating appealed and the first to have its appeal fail).

Decades later it would be hard to imagine anyone being scandalized by the picture. It follows three young New Yorkers—Paul (Warden), Lloyd (Graham), and Jon Rubin (De Niro)—as they strive to avoid the draft* and to follow their peculiar muses: Paul's forays into computer dating, Lloyd's obsession with the death of John Kennedy, and Jon's fascination with pornography and especially voyeurism, which he combines into a new medium he calls "peep art." In a series of disjointed episodes that don't remotely amount to a plot, they cavort around Manhattan—the Central Park Zoo, a Bleecker Street coffeehouse, an Upper East Side bookshop, the Staten Island ferry— encountering kindred and hostile souls, preying on women, scheming up ways to trick the Selective Service into classifying them as unfit for the military. Among the curiosities is a conversation between Graham and the famed English artist Richard Hamilton, widely credited with the first Pop Art painting, about making abstract art out of ordinary photographs. And there are many bits shot on the streets of the city clearly without permits or production assistants to keep out the passersby: guerilla moments that impart a strong sense of time and place.

De Niro wears donnish little spectacles and, again, a mustache, and he speaks in a high-toned, nearly stilted diction, as if striving to rid his voice of any trace of a Noo Yawk upbringing (he doesn't always succeed). He chases a few women, first a shoplifter (Ruth Alda) whom he directs in one of his little voyeuristic fantasies, then a leggy beauty whom he follows through Central Park to the Whitney Museum, where he is accosted by Alan Garfield, who chats him up and sells him a pornographic 8 mm film (and, in a very long take, causes De Niro to collapse with genuine laughter). As the film isn't really a narrative but rather a series of vignettes, it's difficult to speak about an actual characterization, but De Niro reveals a droll comic sense, an easy loquaciousness, and a genuine versatility. He's called on to read aloud from a sex manual, to chat up girls, to behave like a right-wing fanatic

---

* De Palma himself was passed over in the draft because of his asthma.

(his draft board ruse is to make himself seem *too* eager to serve), to playact a scene in Vietnam. But his best moments are in the scene with Garfield as he continually tries to edge away from his interlocutor, dragging the newspaper he's resting his elbows on with each sideways move as though using it to keep himself clean. Graham's Dealey Plaza–obsessed bookstore clerk is perhaps more vividly rendered, but De Niro does many more things and does them well.

BILLED AS "an over-ground sex protest film," *Greetings* wasn't widely reviewed. The *New York Times* sent Howard Thompson, who called it "tired, tawdry and tattered" and said of the cast, "Of [Graham's] pals, Robert De Niro and Jonathan Warden, the latter gives at least some evidence of a little talent." Briefly, *Greetings* became a cause célèbre. New York documentarian William Bayer wrote a letter to the *Times* protesting Thompson's notice (and at least three times as long). And then it became truly celebrated, playing at the Berlin Film Festival that winter and sharing, with two other films, the prestigious Silver Bear prize.

On the strength of the profit their tiny film had generated, Hirsch and De Palma began thinking about a follow-up, another pastiche of provocative scenes combining a little sex, a little comedy, a touch of the avant-garde, a splash of social satire. The success of *Greetings* meant that the budget available to them had more than doubled, to upward of $100,000. (As a lark, during the dreaming-up phase, they referred to the new film as *Son of Greetings*.) And this time they would be more focused in their approach. Rather than scatter the hijinks among three actors, they would have one character provide the spine of the film. Perhaps out of sheer habit's sake, they referred to him by the name of one of the fellows from *Greetings*: Jon Rubin. And they wanted De Niro, the original Jon, to take on the role, the starring part in a feature film.

Once again they would be working from a script that was more a bunch of discrete scenarios than a classically structured drama. This time, though, they began working with De Niro on his scenes well before the production or even the rehearsals. He went over the various episodes with a typewriter, scissors, and adhesive tape, stitching together specific scenes sometimes down to the level of dialogue, so that it looked like a cross between a traditional script and a ransom note. He made notes to himself—lists of props and costumes he wanted to acquire, the names of secondhand stores where some of the stuff might be found, things to do with his hair, bits of physical business. He wrote about Jon Rubin's motivation, state of mind, and intent, and he encouraged himself in certain behaviors: "When walking always looking at girls in street." Most of all, he roused himself to the challenge of the role: "Do whole thing with complete *conviction* and *confidence*." De Palma and Hirsch felt the same way: they shot the picture in early 1969 and worked determinedly to release it before the end of the year.

DE NIRO, MEANWHILE, pressed forward however he could. He was onstage in April, back at Bastiano's Cellar Studio, in a Café Mama production of playwright Julie Bovasso's *Gloria and Esperanza*. In the summer he shot a commercial for American Motors. As Joey, a neighborhood kid all grown up and making good money as a CPA, he drives a new Ambassador to his mom and pop's shop and offers them a ride while his little brother and the others in the street all coo over the car's air-conditioning, which comes standard. It was recognizably him in every syllable and gesture—grand arm gestures, a second-generation Italian American accent, the soon-to-be-famous crinkle-faced smile. It wasn't a full part, of course, but he was charming, and he clearly relished the broadly drawn texture of it. It would vanish—like the Ambassador—until he became famous, when it would resurface on the Internet, the first performance in which the actor who would soon become known everywhere was wholly visible.*

But if you wanted to see him actually at work that summer, you'd have to go to Arkansas, of all places, where he was joining Shelley Winters on a new film project. On August 1, *Variety* reported that "Bob

---

* The same ad campaign featured Richard Dreyfuss and Herb Edelman hawking different AMC models.

Deniro [*sic*] has been cast by American International Pictures as one of Ma Barker's notorious sons in 'Bloody Mama.'" He had finally broken out of the arty New York scene and was stepping into some old-fashioned Hollywood trash. No one could say if it would be a good movie, but it would definitely get seen.

5

THAT TINY ANNOUNCEMENT IN VARIETY WAS PROOF THAT HIS career had begun to take shape. Here was an actor who had appeared on-screen only once, who hadn't been on Broadway or a TV show, and who was known just barely to aficionados of New York avant-garde theater, and yet his name was being dropped in a Hollywood trade paper as an addition to a film cast as if that were a fact worth noting.

This small but quite meaningful step was no doubt thanks to De Niro's having acquired his first agent, Richard Bauman, a former actor who ran a small New York office and would come to make a specialty of finding talent in the nooks of the city and helping launch it toward bigger things (he'd soon do the same for Bette Midler). Bauman not only would have negotiated De Niro's contract (still peanuts, causing Shelley Winters to make a stink when she found out about it) but also would have seeded the trade papers with the casting news. And he would've been a help in getting De Niro into the Screen Actors Guild and Actors' Equity, both of which he joined after shooting *Son of Greetings* (the title had changed to *Blue Manhattan* and then to *Confessions of a Peeping John*), which was still being edited. De Niro was unknown to the public, but he was becoming a commodity in the business.

For *Bloody Mama*, he would demonstrate to the greatest degree yet the extent to which he took his art, his career, and himself seriously. The film, about the famed Depression-era bandit Kate "Ma" Barker and her feral brood of sons, was built to capitalize on the excitement around *Bonnie and Clyde*, the 1967 film that had begun to bring some of the energies of exploitation movies and youthful rebellion into the

Hollywood mainstream. American International Pictures, the font of much of that grindhouse fare, had already hopped on the gangster bandwagon with an Al Capone film, *The St. Valentine's Day Massacre*, which actually beat *Bonnie and Clyde* into theaters. A script for a Ma Barker film was written that year, but it seemed overly violent in the wake of the Martin Luther King Jr. and Robert Kennedy slayings. In the spring of 1969, though, AIP still saw opportunity in the project, and director and co-producer Roger Corman, the wild, kindly uncle of American exploitation cinema, went off to Arkansas to direct. The cast would include Shelley Winters in the center, Corman regular Bruce Dern as a member of the gang, Diane Varsi as the gal of one of the Barker boys, and Don Stroud, Clint Kimbrough, and Robert Walden as three of Barker's sons; the fourth, the drug-and-candy-bar addict, Lloyd, would be played by De Niro.

He went out to Arkansas by car, though it's not clear that he drove (AMC commercial or no, there was some dispute about whether, as a Manhattan native, he knew how to at the time). He spent a few weeks poking around the Ozarks before the shoot getting to know the regional accents, asking locals to read his lines into a tape recorder, and learning the speech patterns so well that he served as an unofficial dialogue coach for the rest of the cast. He also helped Winters when she struggled with a scene in which she gave her four grown-up sons a bath. "I don't even know all of you," she told him when he asked why she was so nervous. "But Shelley, we're you're babies," he reminded her.

Before arriving in Arkansas, De Niro learned all he could about the physical reality of being an addict: hygiene, teeth, habits, diet (he became a Baby Ruth fiend during the shoot). He may have had eighth billing in the promotional materials that were being printed as the film was in production, but he worked on his part as if it were the key to the picture: going to the New York Public Library to read up on the Barkers and Alvin Karpis and to absorb photographs and music of the Ozarks in the 1930s, learning to roll his own cigarettes, filling the margins of his script with handwritten notes that dealt sometimes with minutiae ("blow nose with finger, wipe nose on sleeve") and sometimes with profundities ("The satisfaction I have when stoned is so much better than the life around us. That's a key for me"). His chief transformation was physical: always thin, he dropped twenty or thirty pounds to play Lloyd, even staying up all night before some of his scenes to achieve a hollow aspect, acquiring without the help of makeup a pallor over his skin and even some sores on his body. His Jewish mama was, naturally, alarmed: "I thought he was concentrating too much on externals—I mean, the things he did to his body!" But as De Niro reminded himself in a note in his script, Lloyd was not wholly of this earth: "I'm closer to God. Always alienated."

For all the pains he took, he nevertheless had bouts of self-doubt along the way. One night in Arkansas he confessed his anxiety to Winters, and she wrote him a note the next morning, telling him, "You have a marvelous *mind, instinct* and *talent.* Leave yourself *alone* and *GO.*" When he finally got himself together, he did so in a way that actually frightened her. Lloyd was the first of Ma Barker's boys to die, collapsing of an overdose by a lakeside, and De Niro chose to play the scene of his corpse being discovered even though he wouldn't be photographed in it. He crawled down into the shallow grave that Lloyd's brothers had dug for him and lay there to, he said, "help the actors . . . once they saw me like that, they were forced to deal with it." He stayed in character in the makeshift grave throughout lunch, he recalled, even though technically his character no longer existed. And he nearly got Winters to join him in his make-believe afterlife . . . in real life. "I walked over to the open grave," she remembered, "and got the shock of my life. 'Bobby,' I screamed, 'I don't believe this! You come out of that grave this minute!'"

The pace that Corman kept pleased him, and he was given additional bits of business as the film progressed, such as driving an old car down to a ferry landing, something that, he wrote in his script pages, was "fun to do." In fact, he noted many of his impressions of the production, writing on the very first day of shooting, August 12, that "Roger is brief, gets what he wants and goes on to the next take without much excessive shooting on each set-up." They were done in Arkansas, after twenty-six days of work, before the end of September.

The shoot didn't delight everyone. An Arkansas College professor and three of his students who'd been hired on as interns quit midway through to protest the explicit violence, nudity, and drug use. That sort of news would only help such a film, of course; if Brian De Palma was piquing the movie ratings board with satire and titillation, Corman and AIP were blasting at them with blood and bosoms. Before the film was released, it was advertised on the Sunset Strip with a billboard reading, "The family that slays together, stays together." Though it was a tremendously tone-deaf gesture just weeks after the arrest of Charles Manson and *his* "family" for the Tate-LaBianca murders and garnered much protest, AIP kept using the slogan to promote the film.

THE MARKETING OF *Bloody Mama* would be a typically splashy AIP affair, and De Niro would take part, traveling to a few select locations, including North Carolina, to promote the film with personal appearances, complete with replica tommy gun. But there was yet more work ahead of him: the film had barely wrapped when he was off to another job, appearing with the Theatre Company of Boston in December 1969 in a repertory presentation of three short plays: *The Basement* by Harold Pinter, *Captain Smith in His Glory* by David Freeman, and *Come and Go* by Samuel Beckett. It was only a five-night stand and only a regional theater, but it was an important gig: such talents as Dustin Hoffman, Jon Voight, and Robert Duvall, all of whom were emerging ahead of him, had been through the company in recent seasons, and artistic director David Wheeler would soon offer work to the likes of Al Pacino, Stockard Channing, and Blythe Danner. But De Niro felt that he was on the cusp of bigger things, with two films due in the spring, and he returned to New York after the run ended.

He was still looking for his next gig when *Bloody Mama* opened in March to a surprisingly serious reception. Normally a picture from AIP wouldn't get much attention, but the strange critical history of *Bonnie and Clyde* seemed to hover over the film. *Bonnie* had been panned in the *New York Times* and *Newsweek*, though *Newsweek* published a reevaluatory mea culpa by its lead movie critic, Joe Morgenstern, a mere week after he had slammed the film, and not long afterward the *Times* removed its lead movie critic, Bosley Crowther, from his beat. Then, just months before *Bloody Mama's* release, *Easy Rider* took the Cannes Film Festival, Hollywood, and the rest of the world by storm.

The film press knew there was something happening, something to do with youth and violence and drugs and cheap moviemaking and young stars, and—whether through chariness about their own positions or genuine enthusiasm for the work—they were increasingly willing to give a movie such as *Bloody Mama* a serious look.

In fact, they were kind to it. Howard Thompson of the *New York Times* specifically noted that he preferred it to *Bonnie and Clyde*, calling it "more honest and less pretentious" and deeming Winters "plain wonderful." (De Niro was cited among a number of cast members as "fine.") A few weeks later, in the same paper, Peter Schjeldahl compared *Bloody Mama* favorably to Corman's horror films, suggesting that Winters was in the role usually played by Vincent Price and her sons took the place of the monsters; he particularly praised the performances, naming Winters and De Niro among a few others and declaring that "Academy Awards have been given for far lesser efforts." But he argued, against the film's admirers, that its bloodshed was prurient rather than cathartic: "What's so honest about a violent film that doesn't leave one feeling uneasy?" he asked, echoing the sentiments of the censors who would briefly ban the film from release in France the following year.

De Niro, whose role was billed in the publicity materials as "the way-out pothead of Ma Barker's belligerent brood," was singled out for attention in *Film Quarterly*, where Joseph McBride referred to him as "the most interesting character" in the film, "compulsively pulling on Baby Ruth bars and emitting defenselessness." And the *Hollywood Reporter* declared him "rather good, given the limited dimensions of his junkie role." Not every critic went for the film—*Life* and especially the *Los Angeles Times* were hard on it—but De Niro was commended in every review that mentioned him.

The film is deeply lurid, with more occasions of incest, gang rape, sadism, jailhouse sex, and other outré behaviors than there are of bank robbery. Amid it all, De Niro truly stands out as Lloyd. At first he's just another of the unformed mob of brothers, talking in a childlike drawl and exciting himself to the point of glee over gunplay, fast driving, and his mother's brazenness. But before long he reveals himself as a glue-sniffer, twitching and singing hymns in a zonked-out stupor, and he finally becomes a flat-out junkie, shooting up in secret and bumping his way through the gang's hideout as though he can't see where he's going.

His most startling episode comes about midway through the film, when he meets a girl named Rembrandt (Pamela Dunlap) who swims up to him and shows herself off flirtatiously. At first Lloyd seems like a moron, his feet dangling in the water while still in socks and shoes. But soon he starts revealing things—"I take lots of dope. . . . Everything frightens me"—and forces himself upon her, explaining, "Sometimes I can make it, sometimes I can't." Her cries of protest draw the attention of Lloyd's brothers, and she winds up tied to a bed, gang-raped, killed, and dropped in the lake, Lloyd showing no more concern than if he'd been deprived of one of his Baby Ruth bars.

Lloyd's narcoleptic gaze, his skittishness, his seeming lack of a sense of self-preservation, his habit of falling into distracted singsong, and such deft little touches of character as wearing a fedora with the brim turned up (he'd do the same a few years later in *Mean Streets*, of course) and hiding his face behind a fan with a picture of Jesus on it when he thinks the kidnap victim can see him: it all makes for the first full-blooded and fully memorable role of De Niro's screen career. He may not have received top billing, but he was the most haunting thing in a surprisingly haunting bit of grindhouse.

WHILE *Bloody Mama* was still making its way incrementally around the country, the Brian De Palma movie that he'd filmed the previous year had made its debut. *Hi, Mom!*, as it was finally called, caused an even greater splash than *Greetings*, with which, not by accident, it shared the fate of having been slapped with an X rating by the MPAA—and then recut to get an R.

In many ways, it's a reprise of *Greetings*: episodic, concerned with sex and voyeurism and Vietnam, peppered with glimpses of unrehearsed New York street life, spiced with gratuitous nudity (male and female this time), alternately daring and jejune. Several bits of it are near remakes of sequences from the earlier film: an encounter with a pornographer (Alan Garfield once again, and once again memorable), a sequence near the Staten Island ferry (making, oddly, for a ferry scene in each De Palma/De Niro film), a (feigned) computer dating snafu, a travelogue of the sorts of places a squarish young New Yorker of the moment might frequent. (In one scene, De Niro is shown a porn film that actually consists of footage right out of *Greetings*.)

But there is an evolution, too. For one thing, the Jon Rubin of the earlier film has changed—and we are given to believe that the transformation has to do with his time in Vietnam, which was presented so crudely in *Greetings* that it almost seemed unreal. This fellow, who stares into the lens in freeze-frame during the title sequence, is clean-shaven and free of eyeglasses; De Niro's face has acquired a physical sharpness and confident openness that bespeak maturity. And he's more direct in his actions, agreeing in an early scene to rent a horrifyingly uninhabitable apartment at an exorbitant price (his old stage colleague Charles Durning is the slovenly landlord) simply because it affords him an optimal platform from which to make his "peep art" porn films.

Much of this opening portion of *Hi, Mom!* is given over to Rubin's seduction of a girl (Jennifer Salt) with whom he plans to film himself having sex, and De Niro once again dons meek peepers and adopts a slightly affected, class- and geography-neutral style of diction to play a likely beau for the lonely lass. There's a droll tenor to all of this, with De Niro playing at playing the nerd, the cuckold, and the neurotic, subtly gauging the girl's responses.

And then the movie changes rapidly. Rubin watches a TV segment about a new experimental play, *Be Black, Baby*, and auditions to perform in it, frightening the other actors with his full-blooded embodiment of a sadistic cop, barking epithets and wielding his baton with frightening vigor. Presently he abandons the theater of revolution for life as an urban guerrila, marrying the girl he had previously seduced, pretending to work at an insurance company, and all the while harboring plans to bring down an apartment tower (one he'd once spied upon) with a load of dynamite set off in the basement laundry room.

The sheer cheek and energy of the thing sold it. Two *New York Times* writers praised the film (though not, oddly, its star). Elsewhere, though, critics were particularly taken with De Niro's work: the *Los Angeles Her-*

ald Examiner praised De Niro and Jennifer Salt as "splendid natural actors," the *Los Angeles Times*'s Kevin Thomas singled De Niro out as "a handsome, likeable and very gifted improviser," *Variety* noted that "De Niro's character is really a series of separate acts, and he is very capable at each of them," and the *Hollywood Reporter*, referring to him as "Nero," compared him, in a way meant as praise, to Alan Alda. Only Stanley Kauffmann (who hadn't cared for him a few years earlier in *The World of Günter Grass*) demurred, saying in the *New Republic* that De Niro "was very good as part of a troika in the first picture but lacks the range and appeal to sustain a film more or less by himself."

He was, in fact, terrific. *Bloody Mama* showcased him in a single, deep characterization that brought out some of his chameleonic ability to adopt the affect of someone utterly unlike himself. But in *Hi, Mom!* he was virtuosic, playing at a series of variations on Jon Rubin: the calculating voyeur, the (mock) button-down insurance man, the (mock) menacing cop, the (mock) southern war veteran. It's a complete acting resume, as varied and committed as those composite head shots he used to carry around, with a buffet of character types on display. Traces of some of these characters would surface in many of his later roles: the doofusness, the ironic propriety, the temper. But those traits are fully available to him here.

WITH *Bloody Mama* and *Hi, Mom!* in theaters at the exact same time, De Niro appeared onstage in New York in a project that, though small, was a plum. After the assassinations of 1968, Shelley Winters had written a series of three one-act plays about societal unease in wartime, each featuring two actors, a man and a woman, with one playlet set during World War II, one during the Korean War, and one in the here and now of the Vietnam War. She presented it in a ten-performance benefit for the Actors Studio in April under the title "The Noisy Passenger." In that production, De Niro performed the final act, set in Laurel Canyon in the pre-Manson-family innocence of April 1969, about an actress (Diane Ladd) who has just won an Oscar and is rewarding herself with a druggy, sexy night with a cynically hippieish younger actor (rumormongers held that the situation closely echoed a relationship between Winters and her *Wild in the Streets* co-star Christopher Jones).

Winters spent the summer rewriting the script and presented it anew in the fall at off-off-Broadway's famed Actors Playhouse, with her entire original cast set to reprise their roles. This time the play, retitled *One Night Stands of a Noisy Passenger*, wasn't a benefit performance but a bona fide show, which would have to succeed at the box office as well as with critics. But on November 16, the very night the show was to open, off-Broadway actors and stage managers went on strike against the League of Off-Broadway Theaters and Producers. "As an actress," Winters told the *New York Times*, "I feel that certainly working conditions and salaries off Broadway should be improved. As a playwright, I feel helpless. I'm sort of in shock."

The opening was pushed back into late December, and half the cast had to drop out because of scheduling conflicts. Indeed, Winters herself wasn't in town for the opening: "How can a baby be born without its mother?" she wailed in the *Times*. It may not have mattered, though. The play was neither widely seen nor favorably reviewed. Most of the notices blamed the writing for the failings (Richard Watts Jr. of the *New York Post* called her a "simply dreadful dramatist"), although Clive Barnes of the *New York Times* gave the script a pass as "mildly convincing in a hysteric fashion."

De Niro, though, caused a small sensation. Wearing only boxer shorts and a kimono, with his hair long and shaggy, and revealing a (real) tattoo on his right bicep—a panther or puma in an angry crouch—he was, as Winters put it, "like watching sexual lightning on stage." She marveled that "every night was a different performance," which meant that Ladd had to be alert for such stunts as De Niro deciding one night, without warning, to light some candles on the set, inadvertently catching his leading lady's sleeve on fire. The *Village Voice* hailed his "stunning performance," and *Newsweek* called him "brilliant." The show, however, never ignited, and it ran a mere seven performances before closing.

For Winters, the experience was traumatic. "I've been clobbered and I'm in a daze," was her initial response. Years later, she remem-

bered it only slightly more fondly: "Bobby was acclaimed in every magazine and review," she said. "The play did pretty well, too. But it was
undercapitalized, and it didn't have time to find its audience. I was so
bitter . . . that I have not written another play, even though the theater
critics gave me great encouragement."

"Undercapitalized" is a nice way to put it; Winters herself invested
$2,250 in the play and was supported by a pack of angels that included
her attorney Jay Julien. De Niro may have been acclaimed, but he
earned a mere $100—a week's wages for the sole week of the produc-
tion. In fact, despite everything he was doing, money was still tight for
him. In September he did a stint on the soap opera *Search for Tomorrow*, playing a junkie being grilled by a commission investigating police
corruption; it was but a day's work, yet he took it seriously enough to
ask the director to change his character from a Korean War veteran to
a Vietnam veteran and to make a note on his script reminding himself
to play the scene as if the whole thing was a gas: "You're talking to the
commission and really getting your rocks off." And in December, just
before the brief run of *Noisy Passenger*, he did another day's work providing the voice-over for a radio ad for Vitalis Dry Control hair treatment ("The supernatural . . . for natural hair!"), earning a cool $102.

It was a measure of his combination of ambition, workaholism, and
genuine need that he took jobs in a soap opera and on a radio commercial. Again, following the example of his father, he kept himself
afloat financially, banging at the business doggedly, seeking edges and
advantages over other actors. He took to writing scripts for himself,
hoping to turn his ideas and his ever-growing store of experience into
a vehicle that would well and truly launch his career as a going enterprise. But he was still reliant on the world of young independent
filmmakers for work. And, fortunately, Richard Bauman was able to
drum it up for him.

THROUGH 1970 AND 1971, De Niro worked on three films, each slightly
larger in budget, each bringing him a step or two closer to the imprimatur of a proper movie studio, each capable of getting him seen by
a larger audience both within the business and out in the moviegoing

world. After nearly a decade of banging on the door, he was finally edging it open.

He was far from having established himself, though; he was still very near the bottom of a very tall ladder. Many icons of old Hollywood—including Marlon Brando, William Holden, and John Wayne, for Pete's sake—were still defining the business, while reigning superstars such as Paul Newman, Jack Lemmon, Sean Connery, Clint Eastwood, and Steve McQueen showed no signs of losing their appeal to audiences. A new generation was emerging: Robert Redford was already a star, Ryan O'Neal was almost there, and Elliott Gould seemed to have hit the zeitgeist just so. Dustin Hoffman and Jon Voight had turned serious acting study into movie careers that were blossoming after the stunning success of *Midnight Cowboy*; further ahead, Jack Nicholson had become an overnight star in *Easy Rider* a full decade after first breaking into the business. Other actors such as Gene Hackman, James Caan, Robert Duvall, and Donald Sutherland were turning long tenures as young journeymen into something like bona fide star careers. Even Al Pacino—who, with Hoffman, seemed the nearest thing to De Niro—was getting serious about film work.

De Niro, though quiet about it, had a competitive streak that impelled him to try to keep up. And so, between the Vitalis ads and the off-off-Broadway shows, Richard Bauman kept him busy on film sets. The parts weren't big, but the payoffs in exposure and subsequent new opportunities were real and rich. He appeared in a couple of movies that dealt with the hot-topic issue of drug abuse: *Jennifer on My Mind*, based on the novel *Heir* by Roger L. Simon, and *Born to Win*, screenwriter David Milton Scott's adaptation of his own off-Broadway one-act play, *Scraping Bottom*. The films were low-budget efforts, but they were within the studio system, sort of: United Artists, which backed them both, didn't have a physical plant in Los Angeles like other big-name distributors, but rather had a business plan based on collaborating with producers on independently made films. They had some huge hits (in the 1960s alone, they'd released the Oscar-winners *The Apartment*, *West Side Story*, *Tom Jones*, and *In the Heat of the Night*), but as they didn't have to maintain an actual production studio, they were flexible enough to finance and release smaller films and give new talent a try.

Such was the case with both of these films. *Jennifer* was directed by Noel Black, who'd had a small, cultish success a few years earlier with the thriller *Pretty Poison*; its screenwriter, Erich Segal, was just breaking huge with his hit novel and film *Love Story*, which hit theaters while *Jennifer* was still being made. *Born to Win* director Ivan Passer was the latest of a group of young East European directors (including Roman Polanski and Milos Forman) who were making headway in American movies. *Jennifer* starred the relatively unknown Michael Brandon and Tippy Walker as young lovers whose lives are controlled by their drug use; *Born* may have had an unproven writer and director, but it centered on the stalwart George Segal, already something of an au courant, if offbeat, screen star, as a hepcat turned junkie whose habit had forced him into a life of street crime.

Whatever promise the films had, they offered only limited opportunities for De Niro, whose roles were peripheral. In *Jennifer* he played, of all things, a cab driver, blasting around New York on a cocktail of drugs and rock music; in *Born*, he had a slightly larger role as a cop who gets pleasure from roughing up Segal's character. Living up to his reputation as a serious and hardworking actor, he put as much as he could into his roles, giving *Jennifer* a terrific jolt of comic energy in his brief appearance and delving deeply into the business of playing a cop in *Born*, annotating his script with notes about how to frisk suspects and how to bear himself with a properly steely mien: "Attitude: always cocky . . . act as if voice made of steel . . . I never trust anyone . . . doesn't matter how I *look* but that I *am* a cop."

But, serious and hardworking as he was, he was also a creature of the insular world of New York theater and movie actors, and he had to have noticed that Al Pacino, like him a recent alumnus of the Theatre Company of Boston, was also making a drug film—Jerry Schatzberg's *The Panic in Needle Park*—and he had to have noticed that Pacino was the lead. Yes, De Niro's career was starting to blossom, but he was getting second-shelf stuff compared to his peers.

THAT STATUS MUST have been abundantly clear to him when his next film opportunity arose. Along with half of Hollywood and every wannabe actor with an Italian American surname, he auditioned for a role—a number of roles, actually—in Paramount Pictures' upcoming adaptation of Mario Puzo's smash-hit novel, *The Godfather*. The studio had considered a number of accomplished directors for the job of helping Puzo get his epic novel to fit into the small vessel of a movie, including Hollywood veterans Richard Brooks, Fred Zinnemann, and Otto Preminger and foreign talents Sergio Leone and Costa-Gavras. They all turned the job down. And then production executives met with a thirty-year-old director who had made some nudie movies, a few indie films (including a horror picture, *Dementia 13*, for Roger Corman), and a flop Hollywood musical (*Finian's Rainbow*). He'd moved from LA to San Francisco and set up his own studio there, which made him an extreme long shot for the gig, but he'd also written the script for *Patton*, which had premiered in April 1970 and was doing fabulous box office (on its way to winning a haul of Oscars, including Best Picture and Best Adapted Screenplay). It was a gamble to give this kid such a hot property, but Robert Evans, the head of production at the studio, was a gambler, and he liked the fact that the guy was an Italian American. And so in September 1970 he hired Francis Ford Coppola to co-write and direct *The Godfather*.

The battles Coppola would wage in the coming months to get his preferred cast would become legendary. There was the war over Marlon Brando, who seemed happy to burn every useful bridge he had to Hollywood but who perked up at the thought of playing Mafia boss Vito Corleone. One of the biggest names in movies, Brando was forced to do several screen tests, some in full makeup, before he finally won the approval of the studio. An even bigger struggle was over Coppola's desire to cast Al Pacino in the role of Michael, Vito's son and reluctant successor. The studio saw no upside to having this unknown, broody actor in such a key role, and they demanded that Coppola test virtually every actor under forty in the business. Coppola's notes for the process would list a number of names for every key role in the film—joining De Niro and Pacino in the list were Dustin Hoffman, Martin Sheen, and Michael Parks—and many of these shot screen tests for the role. De Niro's was strong enough that Coppola tested him further for the role of Michael's hot-headed older brother, Sonny.

It was an impressive effort. Dressed in a dark sports coat and a pork-pie hat, with his shirt buttoned to the neck but not wearing a tie, his hair, worn fashionably long, held in place by bobby pins, he adopted a preening, sneering humor to read Sonny's warning to Michael about what it was like to shoot a man, spinning around and gesturing with crackles of energy, interjecting self-amused notes of disbelief ("Madonna mi!"), smiling with genuine menace as he tells his brother that he'll get "brains all over your nice new Ivy League suit," holding that last syllable with a musical hint of mockery. Coppola was dazzled—"spectacular," he called it, "Sonny as killer"—but he was realistic, too: "It was nothing you could ever sell."

Besides, James Caan, who'd also tested for Michael, was being cast by the studio as Sonny. So De Niro was penciled in as Connie Corleone's traitorous husband, Carlo Rizzi, only to see the role go to Gianni Russo, a Las Vegas TV show host who'd never acted but spent $2,000 on a screen test of himself and sent it the producers. Finally, he was offered the part of Paulie Gatto, errand boy and chauffeur to the capo Pete Clemenza (the guy who would utter the famous line "Leave the gun, take the cannoli"). A tiny part, but a big step. Naturally, he was excited.

And then he had his hopes dashed. Coppola finally won the Battle of Michael, getting his bosses to agree that Pacino was the right choice for the role. But Pacino was under contract to MGM—in fact, he was about to shoot a *different* Mafia picture for them. The two studios worked out a deal with a curious wrinkle. In exchange for letting Pacino go, MGM wanted Paramount to give an actor to replace him in *their* mob movie. Paramount agreed . . . and gave them De Niro.

THE GANG THAT COULDN'T SHOOT STRAIGHT was a 1969 novel by New York newspaperman Jimmy Breslin, who turned the recent Mafia wars within the Colombo family into a garish, ghoulish, and truly hilarious satire. The focus was the outcast crew of Crazy Joe Gallo, transformed in Breslin's hand to Kid Sally Palumbo, a chic and daring but not too clever mobster with aspirations to take over a crime family from the aged and wily gang boss Baccala. The novel lampooned mob rituals, mob families, the operatic religiosity of gangsters, the rococo aesthetics of Italian Americans, even the great Italian love of bicycle racing. The book was so clearly going to be a smash hit that Irwin Winkler and Robert Chartoff, talent agents who'd gotten into the producing biz and had such pictures as *Point Blank, They Shoot Horses, Don't They?*, and *The Strawberry Statement* to their credit, optioned it in February 1969, before its actual publication. They had big plans for the film, talking about hiring Marcello Mastroianni to play Kid Sally and Al Pacino to play the role of Mario, an Italian bicycle racer and petty thief visiting America as part of one of Kid Sally's moneymaking schemes. But Mastroianni still considered himself unprepared to appear in American movies, and Pacino, off to play Michael Corleone, was out. So the lead went to Jerry Orbach, a recent Tony Award winner for the musical *Promises, Promises*. And De Niro stepped in as Mario.

The film was set to shoot in and around New York in the spring of 1971, at exactly the same time that *The Godfather* was in front of the cameras in the same city, which had to sting. But De Niro dove into the work of his part with what would become famously characteristic commitment. His character was an Italian thief and con artist who comes to New York as a competitor in a multiday bicycle race but spends his time glomming everything he can—clothes, food, consumer goods, and, when wearing a stolen priest's suit, cash donations from sentimental Italian Americans who intended their money to benefit his (completely fictional) tiny parish back home.

Mario's part was written largely in broken English, and De Niro thought it sufficiently important to get the character's accent right that he asked the producers if they'd send him to Italy to study the language. They balked at the cost, but he went anyway, at his own expense, for a quick linguistic immersion. He spent his own money on some pieces of wardrobe as well, adding to the store of costumes in his 14th Street apartment. And, as ever, he made fastidious character notes in his script, describing Mario's shoplifting technique as a form of studied nonchalance: "I make believe I don't see where to pay or how. It's like something that doesn't concern me."

Among the things that Mario steals is the heart of Angela, the young sister of Kid Sally and the white sheep of her family, a college girl with no part in the Palumbos' life of crime. The role went to Leigh Taylor-Young, who had become famous when she had an affair with and then married her *Peyton Place* co-star Ryan O'Neal (who was married when they met) and had been in a number of flashy films, including *I Love You, Alice B. Toklas* and, with O'Neal, *The Big Bounce*. Like Orbach—and, indeed, like director James Goldstone and most of the key members of a cast that included Lionel Stander, Jo Van Fleet, and Herve Villechaize—Taylor-Young had no ethnic connection to the material, and she was a bit intimidated when De Niro showed up at rehearsals with an impeccable accent and a seemingly absolute connection to his character.

But she was put at ease when he suggested that they spend a day or two traveling around New York City in character, with her taking the lead as the local showing the sights to the out-of-towner. They visited a few famous spots, took the bus, and then, at De Niro's suggestion, tried their hand at a little shoplifting at Macy's in Herald Square, where they were promptly collared and turned over to the police. Explaining their actual intent, they urged the cops to phone the production office, where somebody vouched for them and secured their release. It was, finally, a comical incident, but one that drew the actors close; they had, Taylor-Young later revealed, a brief affair that ended with the production.

HE HAD THREE films coming out virtually simultaneously at the end of the year, but he kept working. In November, he took a role in one of a pair of one-act plays being staged by the Repertory Theater of Lincoln Center, which had just launched a series of workshop productions under the rubric "Explorations in the Forum." *Kool Aid*, as it was called, was composed of two works by Merle Molofsky, a former Miss Beatnik of 1959 who was studying playwriting at NYU with Jack Gelber, noted author of the famed drug world play *The Connection*, who would be directing.

As Molofsky remembered, Gelber was very excited that De Niro was going to be in one of the two short plays, *Three Zen Koans*. "He told me, 'I'm casting someone that no one has ever heard of yet,'" she said. "'He just finished shooting a film, and when it premieres he'll be one of the biggest stars in the world.'" Such was Gelber's certainty that the role in which he cast the gaunt, gangly De Niro was a character called Fat Boy. That surprised the playwright, who, Molofsky recalled, "always envisioned a fat actor. But it didn't matter. [De Niro] was rocksteady. He gave a beautiful performance, and he was hardworking, scrupulous, and attentive."

Also in the cast was Verna Bloom, a stage and television actress who had just appeared in the films *Medium Cool* and *The Hired Hand* and who was married to *Time* magazine film critic Jay Cocks. Bloom didn't care for the play, in particular for a plot line involving the junkies having gotten a noisy child high to keep her quiet. "I had a real problem with that," she remembered. And she wasn't overly impressed with her co-star. "He was just this guy at the time," she said. "He wasn't near showing us he was gonna be an icon. But he was fun." They stayed in touch after the show's five-performance run.

WHILE DE NIRO was in rehearsals for *Kool Aid* at Lincoln Center, *Born to Win* had its premiere in the very same location, during the New York Film Festival of October 1971. It made its way to commercial theaters at the end of the year, almost simultaneous with the short release of *Jennifer on My Mind*. In fact, neither film was very much noted at the time: the vogue for gritty tales of urban junkies was shortlived, and these films came near the end of it. De Niro, however, made a favorable impression in at least one. For *Jennifer*, his gypsy cab driver was virtually the only aspect of the film critics found worthy of praise: he was commended in *Time* and *Boxoffice*, and the *Hollywood Reporter* positively raved about him: "There is one memorable, original character in 'Jennifer on My Mind': Mardigan, or 'the gypsy cab driver,'" declared Craig Fisher, adding, "Apart from De Niro, there's not much that's memorable. . . . Watching it is like mainlining taffy."

There's little to say about his work in *Born to Win*, which has points of interest as a low-key film of its moment and milieu; De Niro's few scenes seem to have been shot in just a few days (three of his four appearances find him wearing the same costume), and aside from his habit of calling the sorry junkie he's roughing up "Baby," he leaves as little impression as any run-of-the-mill TV cop of the time.

He was more memorable in the far more forgettable *Jennifer on My Mind*, blasting into his single scene in a psychedelically painted purple taxi and greeting his fare with, "I think I should warn you, Mac: I'm pretty high." Sporting a goatee and wearing a silky bandana on his head (because, as he explains, "it's a gypsy cab"), he speaks in a nasal, stoned tenor that recalls Dennis Hopper, trying to get his passenger to drop his plans for a ride to Oyster Bay in favor of going back to the cabbie's house, getting even higher, and maybe having sex with his sister. No dice, comes the reply, provoking De Niro to sigh, "The gypsies lose again." (As, alas, did anyone who paid money to see the wan and insipid movie.)

Far splashier in all ways proved the release of *The Gang That Couldn't Shoot Straight*. Even before the release of the film of *The Godfather*, Mafia stories were in vogue, Breslin's book was well liked, and this was an MGM picture, with a guaranteed big release. Unfortunately, it's truly tone-deaf as a comedy. Goldstone handles the material cartoonishly, a choice driven home by the movie's posters and advertising, which were drawn by *Mad* magazine illustrator Jack Davis. The physical humor is leaden and repetitious, the tenor and staging are grotesque, the ethnic touches are offensively broad, the nods toward the hip far too square. Everyone overacts out of his or her shoes: Orbach with his idiotic Kid Sally, Stander with his guttural madman Baccala, the oversized Pierre Cardin executive turned actor Irving Selbst (who also appeared in *Born to Win*, oddly enough), and the dwarfish Villechaize, whose voice is dubbed so deep that if it were a hole he would have vanished in it. It's cacophonous and wearying. Only Jo Van Fleet, turning Kid Sally's bloodthirsty grandmother into a Grand Guignol Italian *mammarella*, affords any entertainment, and then chiefly because she's so insanely distinct from the shambles of a reality around her that she actually seems plausible.

But interspersed through the film is De Niro's Mario, a vivid, fresh, and thoroughly appealing character—larcenous, insincere, and crooked to the bone, but open-faced, wide-eyed, handsome, and amazingly gallant toward the girl he fancies. Mario steals everything he lays an eye or a finger upon, but he offers to pay for Angela's meals and taxi rides, he treats her with gentlemanly courtesy, and at the film's climax he makes a choice that proves ruinous for him but saves her from injustice at the hands of a desperate district attorney. He comes from poverty, explaining that he eats chipmunks and dandelions back home, and devours what he calls "American food"—pizza and Italian ices—with gusto. With his olive complexion enhanced by a tan, his hair grown out in a Prince Valiant bob, his body slender and springy, and an appreciation of the wonders of America crackling from his eyes, he's immensely appealing.

And, unlike almost anyone else in the film, he's comical without being cartoonish. He steals scenes by slipping around the set and literally stealing: ashtrays, peanuts, hotel towels, canapés, a priest's vestments, statues of saints, and so on. He makes such a lark of larceny that you forget that it's wrong. He kisses money. He hides things in his pockets that are actually meant to be taken gratis, as if thinking only stolen things have value. And when he poses as a priest and starts seeking donations for a nonexistent church back home, his mockery of sacraments and blessings and clerical manners is impeccable, at once a mirror image and a slight, knowing distortion. His broken English is good, his Neapolitan-accented Italian is fluent, his physicality is lively: he's easily the highlight of the film. Beside him, Taylor-Young, attempting to sound New Yorkish and feisty, is hapless. The film is De Niro's, stolen just as surely as Mario steals everything in the coldwater flat he rents.

The critical consensus was the same. The *New York Times* called the film a "tasteless mess"; *Newsweek* moaned about its "lamentable goings-on"; the genteel *Films and Filming* complained about "offensive gags that choke on themselves"; and in *Time*, De Niro's friend Jay Cocks wrote, "You don't have to be Italian to hate 'The Gang That Couldn't Shoot Straight.'" But to a one the reviews cited De Niro as a—if not *the*—saving grace of the enterprise: the *Los Angeles Times* praised his "raffish charm," *Variety* called him "particularly good," and various other outlets, perhaps taken by De Niro's impression of being taken with Taylor-Young, praised the young lovers as the film's highlight. It didn't matter, though. Even with the success of Breslin's novel behind it, the film sank at the box office.

AT THE END of the year, De Niro hovered in a strange place professionally and personally. He had made seven films, including one produced by and three released by major studios, receiving good reviews regularly. He had made an impact on the stage in experimental works of increasing visibility and reputation. He continued to network and audition and pitch himself relentlessly, augmenting the efforts of his agent with his own determined careerism. At age twenty-eight, he was supporting himself: living on his own in his childhood home on 14th Street, which had been passed to him by his mother, and finding steady work, no longer thinking of waiting tables, putting in stints at his mom's print shop, or enduring stretches on unemployment insurance. He had been involved in romances with a number of women, and he had done some traveling.

But he was far from set in his path or his ways, and his acting career in particular still seemed a tenuous thing. He had no reason to think things wouldn't continue to open up for him—but to date they hadn't opened up all that wide. Among his peers, he was proving something of a late bloomer.

If this all nagged at him, he didn't show it. The aspect he wore, particularly professionally, was quiet, focused, pointed. If he ever brooded about his situation, it was camouflaged by his characteristic reticence, so observers saw him chiefly as quiet and shy and not self-absorbed or moody. Besides, he was gradually, genuinely getting somewhere. He may not have been riding the same rocket as Dustin Hoffman or Al Pacino, but he was being sought after for work and commanding a little more money each time.

In December, though, he had nothing lined up as he made his way to a Christmas Eve party at the home of his *Kool Aid* co-star Verna Bloom and her husband, Jay Cocks. It was an annual event, with a crowd of film and theater folk always on hand.

Despite the holiday air, De Niro was in no mood to celebrate. He had been dating another member of the *Kool Aid* cast for a little while, and the two of them arrived at the party under a cloud. "They must've had a fight before getting to our place," Bloom said, "because he spent the evening not uttering one word—not to her, not to us."

De Niro knew a good number of folks at the party, none so well as Brian De Palma, who despite his friend's mood was very keen to introduce him to another guy at the party—another independent filmmaker, another young Turk looking to bust into the business, another native New Yorker, another misfit Italian American, a chum of Jay Cocks's.

His name was Martin Scorsese.

6

I said to him, "Hey! Didn't you use to hang around Hester Street?" Bobby didn't answer, just stared at me—he does not look at you, he considers you—so I stared back. Then I remembered: "It was Kenmare Street—the Kenmare gang." And Bobby goes, "Heh heh." I hadn't seen him in fourteen years.

—MARTIN SCORSESE, 1987

HISTORY AND LEGEND TELL US THAT JOHN FORD DISCOVered John Wayne running errands on a movie studio lot; that John Waters was introduced to Divine by a mutual friend while they waited for a school bus; that François Truffaut spoke with hundreds of kids before the unknown Jean-Pierre Léaud delivered an audition so good that parts of it wound up, raw, in *The 400 Blows*.

And from such a similarly humble instance of kismet came the decades-long relationship between the great director Martin Scorsese and his greatest acting asset and alter ego, Robert De Niro.

At the time, they were only slightly better known to each other than they were to the world at large. Scorsese, a voracious consumer of movies and an ambitious figure in the small world of New York independent film, somehow hadn't yet caught *Greetings* or *Hi, Mom!*, so he'd never actually seen De Niro act. But a vibe of familiarity fluttered inside him: he knew this guy from somewhere, and that somewhere turned out to be the streets.

De Niro, though, knew Scorsese—or at least his work. He'd seen and enjoyed his first picture, the student film *Who's That Knocking at My Door?*, which, like *The Wedding Party*, cost its maker several years of editing, financing, and additional shooting before its public premiere. But even though he acknowledged that he was, indeed, the Bobby Milk whom Scorsese recalled, he didn't have a similar flash of recognition. "I didn't *really* know him," he said years later. "I'd see him around. We remembered each other. Sometimes when we were kids, we'd meet at the dances at a place on 14th Street. . . . It was just an Italian American dance place. I saw Marty around there. We knew each other. Friends of his, from his group, sometimes would change over into our group. We had like a crossover of friends."

They chatted, appreciating their common bond: among all the film and theater people at the party, they were the only ones who'd grown up with some of the dirt of the downtown streets underneath their fingernails. Of course, Scorsese didn't know at that moment that the cagy, watchful De Niro was more of an observer of neighborhood life than a full-throttle participant in it, that he was an art-world brat, not some tough kid. And De Niro, likewise, didn't know if the compact fast talker in front of him, who seemed to have the energy to direct ten movies before the night was out, was a genuine Little Italy street guy. They chatted for a bit, then parted, each far too caught up in his own struggle to make headway in his nascent career to think much more of it.

AFTER THE HOLIDAYS, De Niro became engrossed in pursuing a particular film role, one for which he wasn't the fellow you'd first consider: a dimwitted baseball player from Georgia in *Bang the Drum Slowly*. The movie was an adaptation of a 1956 novel by Mark Harris that had been memorably performed as a live teleplay some fifteen years prior. That production had starred Paul Newman as Henry Wiggen, a hotshot pitcher for the fictional New York Mammoths, who finds himself saddled with the dumb, earnest catcher Bruce Pearson (played by Albert Salmi) as batterymate and roommate. Wiggen, the protagonist of no fewer than four novels by Harris, has ambitions beyond the baseball field—selling insurance, writing books, squeezing extra money out of the front office—but Pearson, only modestly talented as an athlete, is just happy to be able to play the game, even if his grip on a major league career is somewhat tenuous. Wiggen considers his teammate a rube, and not without reason: thinking he's in sync with teammates who tease Wiggen by calling him "Author," Pearson calls him "Arthur." But when Pearson reveals in confidence that he's suffering from Hodgkin's disease and wants to hide it from the manager so as not to risk his spot in the lineup, Wiggen surprises himself by doing the honorable thing: without asking for recompense or credit of any kind, he supports his catcher professionally and personally until he is too ill to continue playing, and then until his death. Ashamed at the memory of his early treatment of his friend, he ends by declaring, "From here on in, I rag nobody."

The 1956 broadcast created a stir, and there was immediate talk of bringing the story to the big screen or even the stage. Producer-director Josh Logan announced plans for a film version starring Newman; Broadway impresario David Merrick toyed with the notion of presenting it as a stage drama; and Harold Rome, who'd done the trick with *Destry Rides Again* and *I Can Get It for You Wholesale*, imagined it as a musical. But the opportunity to do something bigger with Harris's book fell finally to a showbiz neophyte, the Chicago civil rights lawyer Maurice Rosenfield, who along with his wife, Lois, had read and admired the novel and decided to invest their own money, which Rosenfield had made defending, among other clients, *Playboy* magazine and Lenny Bruce.

The Rosenfields were hands-on producers—it *was* their money—and they made choices in their own fashion and their own time. As director, they selected John Hancock, a tall, thirtyish Harvard grad who'd grown up playing football (and violin) in nearby Cicero, Illinois, and was emerging as a stage director and indie filmmaker. He had a low-budget horror movie to his credit—the deliciously titled *Let's Scare Jessica to Death*. But it was his Oscar-nominated live-action short film, *Sticky My Fingers, Fleet My Feet*, about out-of-shape businessmen who play touch football in Central Park, that caught the Rosenfields' attention when they saw it on TV. They hired him to direct the script that Harris was adapting from his own novel.

As grand as it might have sounded, the Rosenfields had barely enough money to mount something as big as a sports film, so they were extremely particular about every aspect of the project, especially the casting. They had the hunch that casting newcomers would be economical and impart a certain verisimilitude to the production, and so they threw a wide net, having the then-unknown James Woods, Tommy Lee Jones, and John Lithgow, among many others, read for them.

De Niro made his way to the suite at Manhattan's Warwick Hotel where the Rosenfields were meeting actors. At first he read for the Wiggen role, but then, perhaps encouraged by his ability to reproduce the southern accent he'd developed for *Bloody Mama*, they steered him toward Pearson. If they were enthusiastic, they didn't let on immediately. "I read for John Hancock seven times," De Niro remembered. "I read for him, the producer, the producer's wife. But that's okay. I wanted them to be sure about me." Besides, the drawn-out business allowed him to address a fundamental deficiency in his qualifications for the role: he didn't know how to play baseball.

In reflection, it makes some sense that a kid raised in lower Manhattan by parents immersed in the art world hadn't been a Little Leaguer, even if his boyhood did coincide with the fullest flush of baseball in New York City (he was in his early teens when the Dodgers and Giants left for California). Faced with the possibility of playing a ballplayer, he set about systematically teaching himself the game, reading and heavily annotating books on batting and, once he knew he'd play Pearson, catching; taking tutelage from City College baseball coach Del Bethel; watching and making notes on more than a dozen games, in person and on TV, paying fastidious attention not only to the actual competitive action ("Learn to slide!!!!" he reminded himself) but also to the little details of behavior exhibited by batters and catchers. He was careful, for instance, to note something not found in books, namely, the habitual demeanor of professional athletes: "I saw in every baseball game how relaxed the players were. I could just pick it up. I could practice in my room watching them do nothing." That might've sounded deprecatory, but he genuinely developed a taste for the game. "I used to think it was a pretty dull sport unless you were playing. But now I go once in a while to Yankee Stadium with some friends and sip beer and spend the day having a good time."

When he finally got the part after the dragged-out casting process ("after which, I thought I deserved it," he said), he dove further. He sought out the advice of some experts, including Jim Bouton, the former Yankees pitcher who'd published the pioneering tell-all book *Ball Four* the year before and was then breaking into TV sportscasting. "I told him to read a wonderful book called 'Ball Four,'" Bouton said later, "and spend two weeks riding the buses with some minor league team down South." In fact, De Niro visited major league spring training camps in Florida, giving him the opportunity to soak up the sort of details he found enlightening: physiques, habits, clothing, little insiderish ways of talking. He went to the Yankees' camp and spoke with the young catcher Thurman Munson. But he found that professional players weren't much interested in helping him. "I went down to Florida and hung around," he said, "but that wasn't so good. Baseball players are like stars in a way—it's always, 'Later, kid.'"

From there he went to Georgia, spending time in towns of the sort that Pearson would have been from, observing local codes of dress, demeanor, diet, work, leisure, and especially speech. "I wanted to listen to the way Georgians talk," he explained. "I carried a tape recorder around with me into bars, gas stations, and hotels. Most everyone was remarkably friendly. I told them I was an actor preparing for a role and even went so far as to ask a couple of guys if they'd mind reading lines from the script into my recorder." He got so chummy with a few of them, including a small-town mayor, that he would practice line readings on them: "They would correct me when I sounded too much like a New Yorker," he said. After getting an idea of how the locals dressed, he bought a few outfits from a general store, and he took careful notes about how folks drove, how they stood while fishing, how they fussed to make sure that their hair was just so ("always carry a comb," he noted).

He read at length about Hodgkin's disease and spoke with doctors to learn how it would affect his behavior, mood, and energy. (He eventually hit upon a technique of spinning himself around a few times before a shot in which he needed to appear ill: "It made me dizzy, a very similar thing that the character was feeling," he recalled.) He read books about the process of dying. He built up his leg muscles for all the squatting he'd have to do behind the plate; he ate a high-protein diet to give himself a more athletic build. He also learned how to chew tobacco—and made himself ill more than once in the effort. "He worked like a dog," his director, Hancock, said. "He got sick chewing that tobacco but kept it up until he finally could do it." ("I tried mixing a lot of other things together to get the same effect," De Niro explained. "I bought licorice and tea leaves. But nothing works like the real thing.")

The most important thing he did, though, was to find the reality of the character Bruce Pearson. Reminding himself that it was important "to show what's unlikeable about me," he sketched out a bit of business that would show the man's inner life: "I do all the opposite things that people do (or are called to do) in certain situations. Like smiling when [I] tell Arthur Mamma died." He would play the part with a dignity and solidity that weren't immediately obvious in the character: "I didn't try to play dumb. I just tried to play each scene for where it was. Some people are dumb but they're not dumb—I guess they're insensitive, but they're not insensitive to everything." Hancock had his own idea of how De Niro achieved the effect he sought. "He used stupid eyes," he said. "Most actors play a dumb characterization with a wide-eyed, bland look. Bobby really knew what stupid eyes are—you're watching carefully in hopes of finding out what's going on, but you don't want to get caught watching." Hancock emphasized that he was not saying his star wasn't intelligent: "Bobby is very smart," he said, and then added, "but he feels he's not." De Niro seemed to confirm his director's impression with a telling note he made on his script: "Don't hide behind Bruce, but be exposed within him."

Another young actor, Jon Cutler, served as De Niro's stand-in and lighting double on the film (something he would continue to do for several years), and he admitted later that he didn't reckon much of what he saw De Niro doing, until he figured out the proper way to look at it:

> I watched Bob at first off-camera from the sidelines. He was totally unimpressive. Then, later on during the scene where he sits on his bed, too weak to pull on his pants, I walked closer to the camera. Finally I was sitting under the camera, on the crab dolly. Crouch-

*ing under the lens, I discovered a fascinating fact. If I leaned my
head three feet away from the lens, I didn't see very much coming
out of De Niro. He looked boring. But if I stuck my head under
the lens, I was watching a genius. He was only brilliant when I sat
under the lens. Bob is a guy the camera loves.*

Since so much of *Bang the Drum Slowly* involved the actual sporting interplay of his cast, Hancock held baseball practice in Central
Park every day before they rehearsed their scenes. They did this for
three weeks, during which time a friend of novelist Mark Harris's visited the set and, astonished by De Niro's transformation, reported back
to the man who'd created Bruce Pearson, "He has death in his eyes."
De Niro developed a rapport with Michael Moriarty, who, playing the
pitcher Wiggen, was also more or less unknown at the time; the rest of
the cast included Vincent Gardenia, the thick-featured New York stage
actor, as the Mammoths' manager; comic Phil Foster in a key role as
a coach; and, in virtually his first filmed role, Danny Aiello in a small
part as a fellow player.* They shot game and locker room sequences in
Shea and Yankee Stadiums (the film had such a low budget that Hancock could afford only seventy-five extras at a time and had to re-create
crowd scenes by moving them all around the stadium), and they used
Clearwater, Florida, as the location for Bruce's hometown. By summer
the film was in the can and De Niro once again was scrambling for a
job. And then he heard from the guy he'd met at that Christmas party.

SOON AFTER THEIR fateful encounter in December, Martin Scorsese found himself hired by none other than Roger Corman to direct
a commercial feature film—Scorsese's first—and was sent off to, of all
places, rural Arkansas to film it. The original idea was for a sequel
to *Bloody Mama*, yet another made-on-the-cheap gangster movie set

---

* Aiello claimed later on that he was mystified when he learned that De Niro would
be playing one of the lead roles in the film. He had seen *The Gang That Couldn't Shoot
Straight* and thought, "He's an immigrant from Italy. How's he going to speak the language?"

in the Depression. Instead, in the way of the American International Pictures gristmill, it morphed into *Boxcar Bertha*, the based-on-truth story of a couple of radical labor organizers who fall into a romance while fighting the corrupt management of a railroad company. It was a quickie production, as could be expected, falling into Scorsese's lap in early 1972 and due out in theaters before summer. But it had a budget of about a half million dollars, it starred a couple of hot young actors in David Carradine and Barbara Hershey, and it was a real movie, not a student film.

Scorsese had moved to Los Angeles in 1971 to seek work opportunities, which was how he came to Corman's attention. But he had also discovered a friend and mentor in one of his idols, John Cassavetes, the broody actor who was slowly building a catalogue of independent films as a writer-director. Cassavetes had already seen *Who's That Knocking at My Door?*, Scorsese's student film that, in its shaggy, personality-driven storytelling, resembled one of the older director's films, and he'd expressed appreciation for it. Scorsese, pleased to have completed *Boxcar Bertha*, arranged for Cassavetes to see it in rough cut. When it was over, Cassavetes called him into his office and told him point-blank, "You just spent a whole year of your life making a piece of shit. It's a good picture, but you're better than the people who make this kind of movie." He asked if Scorsese had anything else in mind like *Who's That Knocking?*, a movie that he was *dying* to make.

Scorsese did. *Who's That Knocking?* had been filmed piecemeal over a few years and hadn't fully explored the territory in which it took place, a world of young men in Little Italy whose lives consisted of petty crime, boozy nights, furtive romances, and stymied ambitions, a kind of update of Federico Fellini's *I Vitelloni* in which the characters and textures mattered more than the plot. Scorsese and his writing buddy Mardik Martin had been noodling with a second take on the material, another film about young, aimless men from the neighborhood caught between the culture of their immediate environment and the larger world beyond, which was changing in ways that ignited their own ambivalences about tradition, religion, honor, obligation, friendship, and more. Smitten by pop music almost as much he was by the cinema, Scorsese had given it the working title *Season of the Witch*, after the ominous Donovan hit. He told Cassavetes about it, saying that it still needed rewrites, and Cassavetes encouraged him to focus on that instead of signing on to direct one of the other projects that Corman might offer him (indeed, there were a couple). And so, in a Los Angeles apartment, Scorsese set about remembering and reimagining the old neighborhood.

THE OLD NEIGHBORHOOD, in Scorsese's case, meant Elizabeth Street in Little Italy, where he lived from the age of seven or so. But, really, it might as well have been Polizzi Generosa or Cimmina, the hardscrabble towns near Palermo, Sicily, from which his family hailed—or, just as much, the make-believe world of the movies, whether on a gigantic movie screen or the little black-and-white TV in his family's apartment. By blood Scorsese was a product of ancient culture, manners, obsessions, and tastes, but by personality he was purely a creature of the here and now, as embodied by the art of cinema.

He'd been born in 1942 to Charlie and Catherine Scorsese, themselves the children of Sicilian immigrants, who had managed through hard work in New York's garment district to lift themselves out of the tenements of lower Manhattan to the relative comfort of Corona, Queens, where their sons, Frank and Marty, were born. But money troubles forced them back to Little Italy, a place that, as the young Scorsese experienced it, was as tribal and insular as the provincial towns from which his grandparents immigrated.

Scorsese was a sickly kid, asthmatic, and Frank, who was six years older, took special care to see that he wasn't hassled, that he was included in the goings-on in the street, and that he got to do his favorite thing of all—go to the movies in Times Square, where the young Scorsese ate up the massive images on the big screen. It was an all-consuming passion: he watched movies on TV (once a week, a local station broadcast a film in Italian, which he'd never miss), and he was obsessed with pictures of all sorts. Always bookish, he was drawn to religious study in part because of the art in his schoolbooks and in the churches, particularly at St. Patrick's Old Cathedral, where he served as an altar boy. He had a romantic fantasy of becoming a painter, and he drew page after page of illustrations of stories. But that wasn't anything he would have shared with the flashy kids in the streets, sawed-off little tough guys who acted like the gangsters that they saw around them or in the movies. Scorsese was a small, nervous kid—a nail-biter, a twitcher, a chatterbox—but he knew enough to keep quiet out in the neighborhood, watching, making mental notes, timing his comings and goings so as to avoid conflicts, keeping an eye on the doorways and corners when he was in public places such as restaurants. ("For a long time," he revealed, "wherever I went, I tried to sit with my back to the wall.")

Given his studious nature and his genuine affection for the pageantry and ritual of the Church, it seemed natural that he would think about a life in the priesthood, and in his teens he would go on retreats with other serious-minded boys from his school and even entered Cathedral Preparatory High School, a junior seminary in Manhattan. But he was distracted, he later joked, by the twin temptations of girls and rock-and-roll, and he lasted just a single year. Attending Cardinal Hayes High School in the Bronx, he had hopes of enrolling at Fordham University, a Jesuit school, but his grades were too low. Instead, he wound up at New York University, just a few blocks away from home but worlds apart from the insulated microcommunity of Little Italy.

For Charlie and Catherine Scorsese, the hardworking children of immigrants, having a son at NYU would have been an achievement—"I always looked at the NYU college buildings and I used to say, 'I hope some day one of my sons will go there,'" Charlie Scorsese remembered—but Marty wasn't on the path to a traditional white-collar profession. (Nor, for that matter, was his older brother, who became a printing press operator.) He had spoken at first of becoming an English major, with an eye toward teaching someday. But in reality, he hadn't chosen NYU because of its excellent literature programs or even its proximity to home. Indeed, the gulf between his home world and the school was so great that he'd only been on the campus once before matriculating there. Rather, he'd chosen it because he knew that they taught filmmaking. He had already started to tinker with 8 mm movies made with his friends, complete with storyboards and title cards. At NYU, if things went right, he'd get a real chance to make a real film.

DE NIRO   115

Almost right away, he found a mentor: Haig Manoogian, who taught a large lecture class in the history of cinema. Manoogian, who Scorsese remembered talked "even faster than me," began teaching filmmaking and film aesthetics at NYU soon after World War II, and he was famously ruthless on his classes, whittling the number of students down during their first years in the program until they were permitted to make films as juniors and seniors. Scorsese was sufficiently serious about his film studies to make sure not only that he survived the cullings but also that his scripts were among the few selected to be shot and that he got to direct them. His student short films and his academic record were good enough that after he graduated he was admitted to NYU's master's program in film. And that was where he began work on *Who's That Knocking?*, the film that impressed both Cassavetes and De Niro.

In the years between the first, short version of that student movie (which had been fleshed out to feature length in part with a dream sequence involving a nude girl at the behest of a distributor who explained that bare skin could get the film onto screens) and *Boxcar Bertha*, Scorsese had been banging mightily at the door of the movie biz. He made more shorts, including the prize-winning film *The Big Shave*; he worked as a camera operator on the stage at Woodstock, providing footage for Michael Wadleigh's hit documentary *Woodstock*, which he then helped edit; he got editing jobs on other musical films, including *Medicine Ball Caravan* and *Elvis on Tour*; he did production chores on some student films; he taught a little bit at NYU; he even got hired to direct a low-budget thriller, *The Honeymoon Killers*, only to find himself fired after a week for taking too much time and shooting footage that was too arty.* And, almost as an aside, he had married, had a daughter, divorced, and moved to Hollywood.

He had ideas for films, but there was never any money to make them. And he was becoming genuinely morose about his prospects. Around him, similarly young filmmakers such as Brian De Palma, Francis Ford Coppola, and George Lucas—all of whom he'd met in the course of his various professional sallies—were getting to make

---

* Let history note that Leonard Kastle, who wrote the script, replaced him, receiving the sole directorial credit of his career.

bigger films and, often, films of their own devising; he, on the other hand, was cutting together footage of Elvis Presley concerts and struggling with his asthma in the filthy air of Los Angeles. Unsurprisingly, the chance to direct *Boxcar Bertha* seemed like a lifeline to him. And when it was over and he had in a sense proven himself, he had, if Cassavetes was right, the chance to do the sort of thing he'd always wanted to do: a real movie of his own, from his own head and heart, filled with his own experiences and inspirations.

So he set about rewriting *Season of the Witch*, with the help of his girlfriend, Sandy Weintraub, the New York–born daughter of a Warner Bros. development executive. "The first version of the script," remembered Scorsese, "was steeped very much in the religious conflict," the desire of the main character to live a saintly life in the garb of a modern-day Little Italy wiseguy. But Weintraub had a different take on the material. "Sandy had heard all the stories I told about my childhood," he said, "and she wondered why things like that weren't in the script I had at that time. Well, they weren't because they didn't bear directly on the story. But Sandy convinced me to concentrate on the atmosphere." What emerged from the rewriting was a more elliptical and episodic script, with an emphasis on the seemingly unimportant textures and tangents rather than the putative plot line. "The studios complained," Scorsese said, "that the plot is constantly interrupted by digressions. I said, 'But that's what it's all about. The idea is to start out broad, and then to build and build like a pyramid to the explosion at the end.'"

The script, retitled *Mean Streets* at the suggestion of Jay Cocks, echoing a phrase from Raymond Chandler, dealt with a small knot of neighborhood friends, in particular Charlie and Johnny Boy. Charlie is semirespectable, connected to the Mafia through his uncle, ambitious for some sort of personal redemption and even for escape from Little Italy; Johnny Boy is a crazed hothead whose disrespect for traditional decorum and propriety is in part informed by the cultural upheavals of the time and, even more, by a strain of anarchy woven into his very being. Charlie is a variation on the lead character of *Who's That Knocking?*, a tormented soul who is eager to please, with a sense of greater things but also a timid streak that often holds him from taking action. Johnny Boy, however, was something new in Scorsese's work, a hellion

who doesn't care what people think of him and has no sense of embarrassment or fear of self-destruction. The other characters function
as foils or enablers of the plot, but the heart of the film is the interplay
of Charlie and Johnny Boy, two strong personalities—both of which, it
was clear to those who knew him, lived within Scorsese: "One is the
guilt-ridden nice guy who's basically a coward," said Mardik Martin.
"The other is a crazy doer who doesn't care how he destroys himself."

Scorsese had done just what John Cassavetes had counseled him to
and written something unique and personal and impassioned, something that he had no choice but to film. Naturally, it was turned down
all over Hollywood—except at, of all places, American International
Pictures, where Roger Corman was interested in it, in a fashion. The
taste for African American–themed crime films was emerging at the
box office, and Corman thought Scorsese's script could be reworked
to meet it. As Scorsese remembered, the producer told him, " 'If you
want to make *Mean Streets*, and if you're willing to swing a little'—
I'll never forget that phrase—'and make them all black, I'll give you
$150,000 and you can shoot it with a non-union crew in New York.' "
But for Scorsese the subject matter was too personal, the milieu too
specific. Even with a deal on the table in front of him, he wasn't willing
to "swing."

Scorsese related his frustrations to Verna Bloom, his New York actress pal who was in Los Angeles performing in a play. Bloom had an
inspiration: she'd recently met Jonathan Taplin, a young guy from the
music business who was looking at breaking into movies and seemed to
have a line on some money. She suggested that the two of them meet
and see if there was any common ground.

Though he had no personal connection to the material in Scorsese's script, Taplin had a feel for what the director was trying to do,
and he decided to go ahead and try to get the picture made. Rebuffed
by several Hollywood studios from which he tried to raise funding,
Taplin turned to what he referred to as "acquaintances" in his hometown, Cleveland, and managed to put together a budget of just under a
half million dollars, which was enormous by the standards of independent filmmaking but insufficient for the sort of on-location shooting
that Scorsese had in mind. Paul Rapp, who had handled production

management for him on *Boxcar Bertha*, told him point-blank: "You're gonna have to shoot it in Los Angeles." Scorsese panicked, but then figured out a plan: he'd film the absolutely essential things in New York on a breakneck schedule—four days at first, bumped up to six, then eight—then film all the interiors in LA. It would be a challenge, but it was a lifeline to an opportunity that seemed as if it might get away if he didn't seize it. Somehow, he figured, he would make it work.

Then there was the matter of casting. In the lead role of J.R. in *Who's That Knocking?*, Scorsese had cast a young actor named Harvey Keitel who had answered an ad calling for actors, as De Niro so often had, that the director had placed in the showbiz trade papers. He was slightly older than Scorsese, a Jewish kid from Brooklyn, an ex-Marine who made ends meet in the lean early days of his acting career by working as a court stenographer. Keitel and Scorsese had become chummy during the on-and-off production of the film, and as Keitel still hadn't made a name for himself, he would be available for another low-paying job. Indeed, throughout the process of conceiving and writing the film, Scorsese had always imagined it as the second of a trilogy about the J.R./Charlie character, and so that was naturally where he saw Keitel. But others involved in the production were carping at him to aim higher for his lead actor, and so the script was presented to Jon Voight with the idea that he'd play Charlie and Keitel would play Johnny Boy. Voight considered the role for a while, then backed out, meaning that Keitel was back to playing the lead. Scorsese then had to fill the other roles, and he immediately thought of the guy he'd met at Verna Bloom and Jay Cocks's Christmas party. He got the script to De Niro and told him he could have his pick of roles in it—except, of course, the role of Charlie.

DE NIRO HAD just finished playing a co-starring role in a studio film, and while *Bang the Drum Slowly* was taking a while to reach the screen, he felt that he was due for bigger things. He remembered Scorsese and *Who's That Knocking?* with fondness, and he knew Keitel from the acting trenches, but he had a more ambitious idea of his current stature in the business. He resisted Scorsese's overtures, holding out for the leading role, if not in this film, then in the next.* Then one day, walking through Greenwich Village, he bumped into Keitel. "He'd already been cast in the movie as Charlie," De Niro recalled. "I had done a couple of leads in movies before, so I said, 'Well, careerwise, I should be playing Charlie.' I didn't say it like a wiseass. I was saying it sincerely, but not in a way that was threatening to him. Then Harvey said, 'You know who you should play? Johnny Boy.' And that clicked." (As an aside, De Niro added, "Now I say to people, 'If you get a part, do it.'")

De Niro went to discuss the role with Scorsese and, as ever, came prepared with props—in this case, a small-brimmed fedora. Little did he know when he selected it from his closet that it would be the thing that nailed it for him. "I had never seen Bobby act when I cast him in *Mean Streets*," Scorsese remembered. "We just talked. He was wearing a hat and tilted it a certain way, saying he thought the character would wear it that way, and I hired him." (As he put it later, "When I saw that crazy hat, I knew he'd be perfect.")

The two had a subverbal understanding of one another. As Scorsese put it, describing their early collaborations, "Bobby and I were as close as Siamese twins emotionally. We were tied together for the good and the bad—for everything. . . . There are certain things we relate to emotionally that cannot be explained." De Niro, naturally, was equally unable to find words to explain their bond: "There's a connection, but it's hard for me to define." But whether De Niro was an alter ego for Scorsese or simply a vessel that the director could fill, if only intuitively, with what he needed for a given picture, he had found a perfect actor for the work he wanted to do. And De Niro had found a director who was willing to work with him in a way that felt familiar and comfortable, who accepted his groping process, his incessant questioning of details, his need to make every bit of work intimate in order to allow his energy to flow fully.

At work on *Mean Streets*, De Niro prepared his script with what had

---

*   A sign of his increasing ambition was that he was considering changing agents. He would soon leave Richard Bauman's one-man shop for the gigantic and storied William Morris Agency, which had offices all over the world and where he would be represented by Harry Ufland, a classic agent sort with sharp suits, a businesslike but schmoozy mien, a slew of connections—and a client list that included Martin Scorsese.

become his habitual meticulousness. He badgered Scorsese for more screen time for his character, partly out of ego, no doubt, but partly because he sensed that there would be real interest in the explosive personality: "Marty: I think (know) audience is gonna wanna see more of Johnny. From experience. I know," he wrote. He carefully totted up, as best he could, a list of Johnny Boy's debts and debtors, as well as an estimation of his salary in the menial job that Charlie's uncle had arranged for him; he made plans to buy a new hat for the role, to acquire a St. Christopher medal, and to walk through Little Italy to make notes on haircuts and wardrobe. He reminded himself to salt his dialogue with mild Italian oaths (*mingia, Madonna mi*) and with nervous interjections such as "yes, but" and "you know, but." And he made note of a key to Johnny Boy's identity: "I aspire to be a big shot, but am slipping from that mold."

In a way, this was the first truly comfortable role he'd played, a variation on the neighborhood kid who made good in that AMC Ambassador commercial from a few years prior: Italian American, effusive, emotional, overflowing with grand gestures. He wasn't, of course, made entirely from that cloth, but he'd seen enough of it to know how it should look. That brief episode in which he was Bobby Milk, his little fling with being a sawed-off wiseguy, would now serve as raw material for his creative work. As he revealed later, preparing to play Johnny Boy was "a question of remembering my boyhood, recalling all the gestures and characteristics of friends and neighbors."

Ironically, he was as close to the real thing as *Mean Streets* would have. In the other crucial parts, Scorsese had cast complete unknowns: David Proval, like Keitel a Jewish guy from Brooklyn, and Richard Romanus, of Lebanese descent, from a small town in Vermont, as, respectively, Tony the barkeeper and Michael the loan shark, the other members of Charlie's circle; and Amy Robinson, a Jewish girl from Jersey, as Teresa, Johnny Boy's cousin (and, in a key plot point, Charlie's on-the-sly girlfriend). He was making a movie about the insular ways of Little Italy, and he had only one full-blooded Italian actor—Cesare Danova, playing Charlie's mobbed-up uncle—in anything like a key role. But these quixotic casting decisions were nothing compared to the confident heedlessness with which he went about actually making the thing.

SHOOTING OF *Mean Streets* began with the New York portion, which included rehearsals, in October 1972. Most of the street action, a couple of shots involving the Empire State Building and St. Patrick's Old Cathedral, some of the interior hallway shots (the location scouts found nothing in LA that looked quite like the innards of a Lower East Side tenement), and, most crucially, the footage of the famed San Gennaro Feast on Mott Street were all filmed in hurried, guerilla fashion. People in Scorsese's old neighborhood didn't know exactly what to make of the shoot. Chary of the negative impression of Italian Americans created by *The Godfather*, they were alarmed to see the title *Mean Streets* on the production slate. And the feast presented nightmarish logistical obstacles for the tiny crew. For one thing, they endured terrific winds and rain during the shoot, along with massive crowds so choking the street that it could take a half hour to move a single block. "The neighborhood was just a sea of heads," Scorsese remembered. "We got caught in the middle of the crowd with the camera and we couldn't move and just about passed out, which was worse than Woodstock, and I know because I was on the stage there for four days." Too, filming the famously mobbed-up San Gennaro Feast without the permission of the shadowy powers who ran it was a real risk. Eventually, Scorsese said, the organizers billed him $5,000, a sum he borrowed from Francis Coppola and then repaid as soon as the film was bought by a distributor.

The Los Angeles portion of the shoot was just as fast and loose, taking barely three weeks. De Niro stayed at the Montecito Hotel in the middle of Hollywood and kept himself deep in his role, impressing the relative newcomer Romanus with his determination to play the part as he thought he could and never settle for a take that wasn't fully committed. The gulf between De Niro's full-blooded immersion and Romanus's inexperience became an issue in a scene in which Johnny Boy taunts Michael as a fool for lending him money. Romanus reacted instinctively by laughing—"I was saving face," he said—but De Niro became increasingly agitated with him, feeling Michael should be angry. As Scorsese later remembered, "They had got on each other's nerves to the point where they really wanted to kill each other."

The rapport between De Niro and Keitel was different. Both savored the use of improvised rehearsals to build scenes, and some of the best-remembered and most revealing moments in the film would result from their experiments before the cameras rolled: a late-night battle in the streets of Little Italy using garbage can lids as shields and the justly famous "Joey Clams" scene, a touch of Abbott and Costello, in the backroom of a bar. Remembering the advice of Sandy Weintraub that the atmosphere was at least as important as the storytelling, Scorsese kept adding little bits like these to the film as he and his actors invented them.

The strain of the shoot was evident on the director's hands: as production wore on, Scorsese took to wearing white cloth gloves to prevent himself from nibbling his fingernails down to bloody stubs. But he managed to get the film wrapped on schedule less than two weeks before Christmas. Editing took up the rest of the winter and much of the spring, after which he started to show a rough cut to such trusted friends as Brian De Palma and John Cassavetes. De Palma didn't care for the improvised moments, which didn't sway Scorsese to cut them, but he did make a successful case for the removal of material relating to Charlie's dabbling in academia by taking a class at NYU: "Literary reference—cut it *out!*" he shouted at a screening. Cassavetes didn't care for the bedroom scenes and the brief nudity, but Scorsese was unmoved. A final hurdle was presented by, of all people, John Wayne, who wouldn't let Scorsese use a clip from his film *Donovan's Reef* because *Mean Streets* would be released with an R rating; Scorsese settled instead for a sequence from *The Searchers* that didn't include Wayne.* By summer, Jonathan Taplin had had a chance to show the completed film to potential distributors and submit it to film festivals for a fall debut.

---

*   Similarly, Phil Spector was riled to learn that Scorsese had used "Be My Baby" on the soundtrack without prior clearance, only to be mollified by John Lennon, who argued for the quality of the film; Spector agreed not to sue, but did extract a handsome royalty fee.

The festivals were first to respond: both the Chicago International Festival (where *Who's That Knocking?* had debuted and been celebrated) and the New York Film Festival accepted it. But Taplin and Scorsese were having no luck with distributors, driving around Los Angeles with cans of 35 mm film, screening the movie at several studios and getting nowhere. Taplin, who'd failed to acquire financing from the studios the previous year, knew he had a quality product on his hands, but the lack of name stars, the strange environment of the film, and the shaggy storytelling made executives at the first studios he approached uneasy. Eventually they showed up in Burbank at Warner Bros., which had acquired a reputation as being a youthful, even hippieish studio, where end-of-the-day martinis in the executive suites had been replaced by joints, and such films as *Woodstock, Performance, THX 1138, McCabe and Mrs. Miller, Superfly, Deliverance,* and *Billy Jack* had found a home. There wasn't really a tenor of youth culture to *Mean Streets*—bohemian Greenwich Village and its drug scene are actually anathema to the main characters—but the impact the film had on the executives in the Warner screening room was real, and they bought the rights to it on the spot, perhaps thinking that they had just discovered their own streetwise answer to *The Godfather.*

One other person saw *Mean Streets* before it was entirely finished, in the spring of 1972: Francis Ford Coppola, who invited Scorsese to his San Francisco studio to screen it for him. Coppola, of course, hadn't found the right role for De Niro in *The Godfather,* and Paramount had even traded him away. Now, though, the through-the-roof critical and commercial success of that film encouraged Paramount to demand a sequel almost immediately. And, with that production looming, Coppola looked at *Mean Streets* with the hope of finding actors for the film.

As Scorsese remembered, Coppola's response was instantaneous: as soon as he saw what De Niro did with Johnny Boy, "immediately, he put him in *Godfather II.*"

7

H E HAD TESTED FOR MICHAEL, BUT, AS HE CORRECTLY RE-
membered, "Everybody tested for Michael. The whole fuckin'
city tested for Michael. Even Al tested for it, but everybody
knew that he had the part and that Francis wanted him."

He had tested for Sonny, and he was good, but in a way *too* good. "I
thought he was very magnetic and had a lot of style," Francis Coppola
recalled. "He seemed like a crazy kind of kid with a lot of energy."
Sonny was all those things, yes, but he was also an eldest son, a father, a
future boss; to play him would require at least an appearance of stabil-
ity. De Niro's take on the role was too, well, Johnny Boy.

Now, however, De Niro was being offered something truly extraordinary, a real challenge, and he could have it without having to go
through any readings or screen tests: not just a role in the sequel to a
film that, commercially and critically, was one of the biggest hits Hollywood had ever produced, but the role of the young Vito Corleone.
In essence, De Niro would be able to reverse-engineer the part that
Marlon Brando had immortalized just a year earlier.

Scorsese believed, not without reason, that it was the sight of De
Niro as Johnny Boy that cemented Coppola's decision. But in fact
Coppola had been sufficiently impressed by De Niro's tests for the first
Godfather that he had kept him in mind for future roles—not knowing,
ironically, that it would be a *past* role for which he would find the actor
best suited. "It kept rolling around in my head that in a funny way
De Niro's face reminded me of Vito Corleone," Coppola said. "Not of
Brando, but of the character he played, with the accentuated jaw, the
kind of funny smile. De Niro certainly is believable as being someone

in the Corleone family and possibly Al's father, as a young man." He noted, too, that underneath De Niro's wildness lay an aspect of his character that suited the role: "De Niro had a sort of stately bearing, as if he really was the young Vito who would grow into that older man who was Marlon Brando. . . . He had grace."

Paramount had famously tortured Coppola over his casting decisions the first time out, but eleven Academy Award nominations and three Oscars, including Best Picture, and a take of more than $100 million at the box office when that was an almost unimaginable sum had led them to believe he knew what he was doing, and they let him make his own choices on the sequel, more or less. De Niro was one of those choices: "I just decided that it would be him. Very early, I just made the decision, unilaterally, that he was right and that he could do it."

The director knew he was setting the actor up for a titanic task. "De Niro's assignment," he said in the press notes for the film, "is incredibly difficult when you consider that he's being asked to become a well-known character created by one of the most famous actors in the world in a role for which he received tremendous credit. To have the audacity to play him as a young man. To evoke that character without doing an imitation of him. And, in addition, to do it all in Sicilian, which he doesn't speak."

Oh, that. De Niro knew New York street Italian, and he had augmented his Italian American vocabulary with a bit of Neapolitan for *The Gang That Couldn't Shoot Straight*. But Sicilian, as he knew, was another thing entirely, and with the exception of a handful of lines, Vito Corleone's dialogue was entirely written in it. De Niro got the first chunk of script—131 draft pages—in early July 1973, and, seeing the challenge in front of him, he dove into the task of learning the language with characteristic fervor.

He enrolled at a Berlitz school in New York, getting high marks from his instructors. Then the studio found him a tutor, Romano Pianti, a Sicilian-born linguist who was working as a director for an Italian-language TV station in the United States. He supplied De Niro with books, including a dictionary of Italian hand gestures, and lots of one-on-one tutelage. It was a crash course in a difficult language, and De Niro respected the singularity of it. "Sicilian is something else," he said. "It is much more staccato, far less rhythmic than Neapolitan. It seems to be related to Greek. I took my tape recorder and talked to Sicilians in California and New York, and then I went to Sicily."

He visited Sicily in October 1973, when Coppola was shooting the Nevada scenes of the film. He stayed for a while with Pianti's family in Trapani, spent time in the towns of Scopello and Castellammare del Golfo, and then, most delicately, traveled to the now-famous village of Corleone, where he ventured alone in order to, as he had in Georgia before *Bang the Drum Slowly,* get a sense of how his lines should sound in the local manner of speech.

He didn't make a secret of his motives. "I was always up front about what I was doing," he said. "I feel it would be underhanded not to say anything. I'm just an actor doing my work. I've found people enjoy helping you and if they understand what you're looking for, you save a lot of time and unnecessary suspicion." But even that attitude could seem overly hopeful in Sicily and especially Corleone. "When I went into a bar, I was a little hesitant about mentioning the picture," he confessed, "because I didn't know what the reaction would be. But they seemed genuinely proud of *The Godfather* and complained because the picture wasn't filmed there."

When he returned and continued working with Pianti, the tutor was amazed at his pupil's progress: "If you'd asked me if it was possible that an actor master a language like Sicilian in such a short time," Pianti later commented, "I would have said, 'Never. Impossible.' But this De Niro has done it."

Coppola claimed that he was never in doubt that the man he'd chosen as young Vito could pull off this part of the role: "Bobby De Niro is such a unified, concentrated guy that I always had faith he could do it," he said. "Later I heard he'd been a terrible student in high school— which tells us something about positive motivation. Also, I always knew, and I'm sure he did too, that if it had turned out a disaster, I could always dub him with a Sicilian. Which, I suppose, tells us something more about motivation."

In fact, De Niro's proficiency in Sicilian became such that he did extensive rewrites of Coppola's dialogue, not only for his own character but also for all of the Sicilian-language scenes in the script, sometimes emphasizing little idioms and tics of pronunciation, sometimes ratcheting back speeches that he felt, after his exposure to the manners of Sicilians, were too forthright and direct. (This practice came to dominate virtually all of De Niro's work. Other actors might want to pump their parts up by adding dialogue; throughout his career, based on the evidence of scores of his working copies of scripts, he indulged the opposite impulse, paring and even slashing away at his own lines to make them less explicit, less verbal, less everything—subsuming actorly ego to the belief that he could do more with a gaze or a gesture than could be accomplished with words.)

Spending time among Sicilians had filled his head with many ideas for his portrayal of the young Vito Corleone. In particular, he found that he ought to augment his linguistic work with the practice of, in a word, silence. "The people are very wonderful to you, invite you into their homes. And yet, there's another side, another layer of logic that runs through the Sicilian communities," he said "They have a tremendous disrespect for authority. . . . The only people they trust are members of the immediate family. Ultimately, everyone else is a foreigner. Suspicion runs high. And although they are very cordial to you as a tourist, you are still aware of this. Sicilians have a way of watching without watching; they'll scrutinize you thoroughly and you don't even know it."

Reading through Puzo's novel and the various drafts of Coppola's script, De Niro continually took note of the stillness of his character, the way Vito would never let on what he was truly thinking, no matter the seeming triviality of the moment. "Never show how you feel cause you never know how things will turn out," he scribbled in the margins of the book, and "NEVER LET ANYONE KNOW THINKING. ALWAYS KEEP OFF GUARD. BE DOING ONE THING WHILE THINKING ANOTHER." In the script, he reminded himself to "give smile with mouth, not with eyes. Chilling smile." And, most revealingly, he underscored a moment in which Vito would like to react but doesn't with this note: "Think of my father here. Don't get too rash. Wait. Control yourself."

He also, of course, had to calibrate his performance to match

Brando's. The Don Corleone whom Brando had made world-famous had certain physical, vocal, and behavioral characteristics that De Niro would have to incorporate in his portrayal of the younger man in order to make the connection between the two credible to audiences. At first, he admitted, the character eluded him—"There's a peasant shrewdness which I haven't found yet," he said before traveling to Sicily. But then, having gotten a sense of the culture from which the man arose, he went about studying the specifics of Brando's performance. In a screening room at Paramount, Coppola's crew set up a videotape camera and filmed each of Brando's scenes so that De Niro could watch them again and again on his own. He did this at least a half dozen times, making detailed notes on Brando's gestures, facial expressions, and habits of speech: "lead a little with shoulders . . . head cocked . . . when thinking hand to chin . . . sly smile, sense of humor . . . raised eyebrows when making certain deliberate expressions . . . use back of fingers to scratch face . . . when point lift only forearm when want something . . . maybe should do more of chin sticking out. Esp. for smiling . . . Big thing is he is relaxed talker . . . Lets things happen. Let things happen."

He specifically assigned each of the characteristic gestures of Brando's he had identified to one or more of his own scenes, choosing a strategy of slowly revealing the future man in the nuanced behavior of the man of the past. As he said at the time, "It's like being a scientist or a technician. Audiences already know Vito Corleone. I watch him and I say, 'That's an interesting gesture. When could he have started to do that?' It's my job as an actor to find things I can make connections with. I must find things and figure out how can I use them, in what scenes can I use them to suggest what the older man will be like."

Besides the physical aspects, he also had to reveal the nascent pieces of the elder Vito's personality: his easy command, his purring warmth, his confidence, his charm. The character, as he saw it, had a feline quality, "an attitude of just about to *strike*," and should be played "perfectly still like a cat ready to STRIKE." Stillness and silence were, finally, his keys: "I listen. I'm a listener. I don't have to move to do a lot. . . . Talking is really not that important. . . . Don't just answer. Think . . . Really think, weigh." But there was another animal he had in mind, because he was playing someone who would soon be a killer of men: "Don't forget to get that serpent color."

In effect, the job in front of him was to take a prebuilt older man, project what he likely might have been like decades before, and bring that sketch to life. "I watched the tape," he said, "and I saw if I had done the part myself I would have done it differently. But I tried to connect him with me, how I could be him only younger. So I tried to speed up where he was slower, to get the rasp of his voice, only the beginning of the rasp. It was interesting. It was like a scientific problem."

He did the usual physical things that helped him prepare for a role: acquiring hats and other bits of wardrobe that were appropriate for the era of his performance (roughly 1918–23, when Vito would have been in his mid- to late twenties), then aging them to take off the store-bought sheen; finding old-time knives and change purses for Vito to carry, even though they might never appear in the film; and working closely with costumer Theadora Van Runkle to ensure that his wardrobe matched the research he had done in Sicily and in the New York Public Library. He visited Dick Smith, who had helped Brando devise his makeup in the first film, to settle on facial appearances: "The slicked-down hair seemed natural, that was how they wore it in those days. We decided to do a little with the cheeks, suggesting the padding that Brando used." (They also settled on a makeup scheme to hide the mole on his right cheekbone.) And he even went to Brando's Los Angeles dentist, Henry Dwork, to be fitted with a removable implant that would give him some of the facial and vocal appearance Brando had. "He made up a smaller piece," De Niro explained, "because my character was younger."

In early November he arrived in Los Angeles for thirteen days of shooting the interiors of Vito's Little Italy world: his apartment, his workplaces, various shops and theaters. In January he joined Coppola and the crew in New York, where production designer Dean Tavoularis had undertaken the mammoth task of converting East 6th Street between Avenues A and B on the Lower East Side into a remarkable semblance of it some fifty or sixty years prior; for three weeks De Niro was able to walk from his 14th Street apartment to the film set and go backward in time.* At the end of the month, he returned to Sicily for seven days of shooting. The last of his twenty-nine days of work on the film was February 4, and even though production would continue on into June, the workaholic Coppola was already editing, determined to have the film out in theaters by Christmas.

You would think that with *Bang the Drum Slowly* and *Mean Streets* ready to premiere and *The Godfather, Part II* due the following winter, De Niro could coast on his reputation for a little while. But his metabolism for work had escalated to a pace that wouldn't allow him to sit still. He formed a brief liaison with the screenwriter James Toback, who wanted De Niro for the title role in his script *The Gambler*, only to have director Karel Reisz dismiss the actor as too lightweight.† In June 1973, while studying the role of Vito Corleone, De Niro went onstage again briefly in playwright Julie Bovasso's off-Broadway comic romance *Schubert's Last Serenade*, playing a right-wing hard hat who saves a debutante from a spot of trouble on the street and then tries to romance her. The production, mounted by the Manhattan Theatre Club, ran barely a week at the Stage 73 space, and Bovasso watched appreciatively during rehearsals as De Niro used his increasingly renowned immersion techniques to find a way into his character. "He wanted to do one scene while chewing on breadsticks," she remembered. "Dubiously, I let him, and for three days I didn't hear a word of my play—it was all garbled up in breadsticks. But I could see something happening, he was making a connection with something, a kind of clown element. At dress rehearsal he showed up without the breadsticks. I said, 'Bobby, where are the breadsticks?' And he said simply, 'I don't need them any more.' " His performance was "gruff and a little confused," per the only review, which was in *Show Business*. That sum-

---

*   The makeover of the setting was so complete that the outdoor pay telephones were removed, and everyone on the set, De Niro included, had to use the handful of phones that were available inside stores along the block. Patient Old World Sicilian that he had become, at least temporarily, De Niro waited quietly in line along with extras and crew members for his turn to make a call.

†   Just a few years later, Toback would make his directorial debut with *Fingers*, by which time De Niro was too much of a heavyweight to headline a small film; the part went to Harvey Keitel.

mer he appeared in yet another production, a one-act entitled *Billy Bailey* that had an even shorter run at the American Place Theatre; De Niro played the sole character, and the show didn't garner a single review.) Nor did he need experimental theater anymore. Despite rumored possibilities now and then, he didn't perform in live theater again for more than a dozen years.

DURING ALL THIS, while he was figuring out Sicilian and fiddling with old hats and dental implants and a rasp in his voice, De Niro became famous. In August, as he was studying at Berlitz, *Bang the Drum Slowly* was released to reviews that were largely favorable for the film and almost entirely adulatory for De Niro and Michael Moriarty.

De Niro's Pearson builds on elements of Lloyd Barker—the accent, of course, and the feral passions and the dumb grin. But it's a fuller portrayal, a whole character with a variety of habits and longings and fears and relationships and attitudes, and it's genuinely moving, his most thoroughgoing performance yet on film.

Pearson isn't a great player—he still lacks in some rudiments of catching such as snapping the ball back to the pitcher, and his batting average usually hovers in the .250 range.* He's no good at ragging his teammates, or at the card games in which players and coaches engage outsiders to rob them of beer money. But he participates, when permitted, with the glee of a kid brother following the older boys' lead, even if he's not entirely sure what it's all about.

In fact, he's a rube. His greasy pompadour, piled high like meringue, makes him look like Woody Woodpecker or an Elvis imitator. He wears a smiley-face shirt under a white suit to go the ballpark on game day, and white socks with dark shoes when dressed more formally, and the belt on his pants is far too long for him, leaving a long line of slack flopping about. He pees in the hotel room sink; he chews

---

* It's worth noting here that De Niro only partly pulls off the masquerade of being a baseball player. He has the moves down when behind the plate and runs the bases with a professional (or at least semipro) vigor and intelligence. But he's utterly unconvincing at bat, swinging from the elbows with his laughably skinny arms.

tobacco and spits juice everywhere; he drinks his beer with salt; he mistakes the attentions of a predatory call girl for true love.

But De Niro invests all of these traits with a grounded realism, making them seem human and true, if not always dignified, and not in the least lampoonish. And because we know, virtually from the start, that Pearson is dying, and because his only friend takes his situation so seriously, there is no license to laugh at him. We watch him carefully for signs of illness, of weakening, and he allows us none. Even when he's been discovered, he tries to put on a brave face, and a real nobility emerges.[*]

There's actual gravity in the performance. De Niro has some difficult lines to play: "I got to develop brains," "Sometimes I don't know what's goin' on sometimes," "I know I got faults, I always did." Dialogue like this is, in the contemporary critical phrase, too on-the-nose, but the lines are plausible as played because De Niro makes it seem as if Pearson is revealing things about himself that he's discovered through a deep inner quest. They're confessions, sometimes grudging, and they're presented with sufficient naturalism that it doesn't matter that they're not profound.

Partway through the film, Pearson has a health scare, waking up with night sweats and calling out to Wiggen, "Something's happening." As they wait for a doctor, fearing the worst, Pearson lets down all pretenses of macho and beseeches his roommate, "I'm scared. Hold onta me." Wiggen responds to this wrenching and tender request with a brotherly embrace. It's a devastating moment, partly because the two actors play it so well, and perhaps even more so because the director doesn't try to milk even a drop of sentimentality out of it, respecting the intimacy, vulnerability, and sincerity of Pearson's fear and Wiggen's honorable friendship.

But for all this gravity, there is humor and playfulness in De Niro's performance. He's quite handy with that chewing tobacco, with a

---

[*] A detail of some interest here: Pearson is apparently a Vietnam veteran, extremely rare for a major-league player of the time. As this detail couldn't have been in the source novel, which was written fifteen years before the film was made, the question of whether Harris, John Hancock, or De Niro himself added it to Pearson's biography remains beguilingly open.

plum-sized bulge of the stuff always stretching a cheek and virtuosic spitting skills. He greets a coach (who doesn't care much for him) with a laddish "Oh, Joe, how's the shooooooooow . . . ?" When he's asked to join a few of his teammates who perform as a vocal group on TV (the Singing Mammoths, of course), he's stone-faced and almost pitifully unable to keep up with the extremely pedestrian choreography, only to break out into a dance solo that's charmingly goofy and several degrees defter than might be expected. And when his teammates, who have learned his secret but don't let him know it, throw a beer blast in his room, he beamingly approves of them all, assuring Wiggen, "They a great buncha boys!"

In two of the most important sequences in the film, De Niro acts wordlessly or nearly so, and wins us over entirely. In the first, Piney Woods, the yokel phenom catcher who is clearly the intended replacement for Pearson, picks up his guitar in the locker room and launches into "The Streets of Laredo," the song from which Mark Harris's novel takes its title. Everyone in the room knows it's a song about a dying cowboy, and they try to dissuade him from singing it, but, unaware of Pearson's condition, he carries on. The camera comes in slowly on De Niro, who tries to appear unconcerned and even appreciative, picking at the laces of his mitt and looking everywhere except at the singer. It's an exceedingly brave moment in the face of death, and, as with the rest, De Niro plays it with impeccable reserve.

Not long after, illness starts to take a real toll on Pearson, affecting his ability to catch and throw the ball. He's in the lineup for a crucial late-season game, and declares, "I just feel a little dipsy." But his walk becomes increasingly unsteady, and he has to brace himself a bit more each time to get in and out of his squat behind the plate. His teammates are protective of him, though. Then, in the ninth inning, they cover for him when a pop fly that ought to be called for by the catcher gives them the chance for the final out. As the first baseman runs in to make the catch and the celebration of the playoff spot launches, Pearson spins slowly by himself, still looking for the ball, lost, uncertain, beyond help. It's heartbreaking. Not even the sight of him in the hospital soon after, with his head hanging limp and his fingers not entirely able to button his shirt, is quite so affecting. In a physical gesture—a

Shawn Levy

dance, in effect—De Niro brings to vivid life the pitiable spectacle of the athlete dying young.

BANG THE DRUM SLOWLY was well received, with strong notices from such widely read critics as Judith Crist ("a beautiful film"), Hollis Alpert ("an absolute gem"), and Rex Reed ("the best film around this summer"), and from the *New York Times* ("close adaptation of a good book has resulted in possibly an even better movie"), *Playboy* ("projected with rough humor and sizzling conviction"), and *New York* ("a super movie"). Hancock's tact and taste were very widely praised, as were the performances of Michael Moriarty and Vincent Gardenia.

But the biggest praise, in most reviews, was for De Niro. "De Niro's doomed bumpkin is wonderfully exasperating, one of the most unsympathetic characters ever to win an audience's sympathy," said Richard Schickel in *Time*. "Bruce is plumb simple, but Robert De Niro's strong comic portrayal keeps him from being a straight man," wrote John Lahr in *Vogue*. And in *Esquire*, the often persnickety John Simon was rapturous:

> *The film profits immeasurably from the performance of Robert De Niro, a Northerner who completely transformed himself into the Georgia cracker with the fatal crack running through him. De Niro accomplished this partly through patient research, and partly through sheer inspired acting. The way Pearson wraps his knowledge that he must die in forgetfulness, so that life can go on while it can; how amid all those spurious kindnesses, he is saved not only by his insight but by his obtuseness; these things are beautifully conveyed by a certain slowness, tentativeness, or excessive alacrity—a rhythm that is always a bit off. And there is a half-comprehending gaze that remains a little clouded, but amiably so, like an overcast day about which one notices less the lack of sunshine than the merciful absence of rain.*

There were a few naysayers—Stanley Kauffmann, who hadn't yet enjoyed a De Niro performance, suggested in the *New Republic* that

"De Niro does all right in outline and design, but he doesn't fill it out with sufficient flavor and body." But in the main, this calling-card role was received with genuine enthusiasm, respect, and eagerness for more.

THEN, ON OCTOBER 2, *Mean Streets* premiered at the New York Film Festival, and the response of those present was ecstatic. De Niro had been universally admired in the likeable *Bang the Drum*, but in the explosive *Mean Streets*, with the flashiest role he'd had since *Glamour, Glory and Gold*, he was a thunderbolt. Keitel was appropriately acknowledged, and Scorsese was catapulted into the front tier of young directors. But De Niro received virtually unanimous acclaim; even those who didn't care for the picture praised him (in *Esquire*, John Simon called *Mean Streets* "this year's most overrated film" but acknowledged De Niro's "bravura performance").

From the first we see of Johnny Boy Civello, he's an unknowable conundrum. Walking along in his $25 Dobbs hat and neat red sweater, he tosses, for reasons only he kens, a firework into a U.S. postal box, destroying all the mail inside—an act of wanton anarchy played just for kicks, to which he responds with a gleeful giggle. (That the scene is clearly shot not in lower Manhattan but rather on a sunny, hilly Los Angeles street only adds to the air of incomprehension.) Is he a protester? A vandal? A psychotic? There is no point of reference, no backstory, no explanation of any sort.

He next appears making an entrance into the neighborhood bar owned by Tony Volpe (David Proval). Charlie has learned that Johnny Boy is ducking another friend, Michael, from whom he's borrowed money. Charlie, who's already in a state of soul-searching, asks God for a sign. In slow motion, in comes Johnny with two girls, chewing gum, grooving, joking, gazing around knowingly but with a feral quality, the Rolling Stones' "Jumpin' Jack Flash" capturing the spice of his audacity, volatility, ferocity. Johnny jokingly checks his pants along with his hat and coat, then, fully clothed once again, introduces the girls to Charlie and Tony ("He owns the jernt," De Niro explains in Brooklynese) and orders them drinks: "Have a 7 and 7: it's good for bothayuz." Charlie invites Johnny into a backroom to discuss a private matter; Johnny doesn't like it, but he and Charlie defuse the tension by turning the moment into an Alphonse/Gaston routine: "After you." "No, after you."

What follows is a throwaway conversation that makes little linear sense but introduces the two characters, their milieu, and their relationship through a series of misunderstandings, evasions, concessions, promises, and untruths, largely improvised (in rehearsal, then honed for the actual filming), much of it irrelevant to the story, a jokey tennis rally that plays a bit like an Abbott and Costello routine and a bit like an FBI wiretap transcript of a pair of mobsters trying to avoid being *too* precise in discussing their crimes.

Charlie wants to know what Johnny has been doing with the money he's earned on the crummy job that Charlie's uncle has secured for him, and Johnny—slick, slippery, jivey, a defiant liar—comes clean but only in ways that, if anything, further muddy matters. "I'm so depressed about other things that I can't worry about payments," he explains, and it's easy to see why: earning $110 a week, he owes $700 to Jimmy Sparks, $1,300 to Frankie Bones, an unspecified but larger sum to Michael, another unspecified debt to Joe Black, and two tabs at Tony's bar. De Niro plays it with a conspiratorial intimacy; Johnny knows that Charlie is buying the story sympathetically, and he milks it, biting his knuckle with frustration and focusing on irrelevant details. The sense imparted is that Johnny Boy is desperate, self-destructive, conniving—a real loose cannon—but that his bond with Charlie is sincere (it's based in part on a youthful incident in which Johnny Boy took a beating that Charlie managed to escape). What's more, De Niro is quite funny, tossing off Italian American slang and hand gestures with saucy verve, grinning broadly in that soon-to-be-world-famous fashion that makes his whole face pinch up like an asterisk. The viewer, like Charlie, is on his side.

But just as that exploding mailbox ought to have signaled, Johnny Boy is not to be trusted. He's dangerous. We see him next in a car headed to help collect a debt for a friend from a pool hall operator who refuses to pay. Right away, Johnny Boy is less a diplomat than an instigator. When the disagreement turns into a fight, Johnny Boy is the first of his group to dive in and the first to grab a pool cue as a weapon. Ultimately, he's beset by four of the other mob, and even the intervention of the police doesn't put a lid on his attitude. The matter seems settled, but then Johnny Boy threatens to set it off once again: "Don't fuckin' touch me, scumbag!" he snarls at the reluctant debt payer, as if he had some sort of moral high ground in the matter of welshing on a bet.

The pool hall fight is only the first episode in a massive, event-filled day that includes the unveiling of a caged tiger in the backroom of Tony's bar, a random revenge shooting, a mock gladiatorial battle with garbage can lids, and finally Johnny and Charlie crashing in Charlie's bed. Throughout, at play De Niro gives Johnny Boy an almost rubbery physicality—a huge gaping laugh as he ices a swollen eye, a belly-out gesture of macho authority, a compulsive lurch toward the suggestion of a card game. He's an unbridled id, subject to wild impulses, civilized only in appearance, and only barely.

When Johnny Boy falls out of the story, the film feels less energized, less likely to explode. When he comes back, he's once again in anarchic mode, up on a rooftop firing a pistol in the sky, at war with his very surroundings. His antics are designed, he says, to "wake up the neighborhood," and when an errant shot hits an apartment, he declares, "I hate that woman with a passion, a vengeance," as if personal animosity could excuse his recklessness. Soon he'll make a fuck-you gesture to the Empire State Building, a sawed-off King Kong in a final act of defiance before his fall.

And fall Johnny does. When all his lifelines are denied him, Johnny turns on his last friend. "I ain't smart," he says, taunting Charlie. "I'm stupid, remember? I'm a *strunz*. I'm so stupid you gotta look out for me. Right? Right?" He mocks Charlie's even-temperedness in singsong, until Charlie has had enough and slaps him.

There's a final act of self-immolation in Tony's bar, where Johnny Boy offers Michael a mere $10 toward his debt. Michael refuses the money, and Johnny Boy explicitly mocks him: "I fuck you right where you breathe, 'cause I don't give two shits for you, or nobody else. . . . Fuck face. Dunce-ski. Asshole." (This is the stuff that enraged Romanus.) He pulls out his pistol and is disarmed; when it's revealed that the gun has no bullets in it, Johnny, his pallor ghostly, flashes a bitter grin at Charlie and tells him, "You got what you wanted." Johnny Boy has become a sin-eater, devouring the misdeeds that Charlie has thus far assumed as part of his fraternal obligation to his friend, in a cack-handed effort to be a man of respect.

It's a remarkable performance: charismatic, unpredictable, street-wise, mercurial, appealing, appalling. De Niro is not, despite his name, a genuine Little Italy hoodlum, but he has alchemized his observations of them—their clothes, their slang, their mien—into a character that's indistinguishable from the genuine article. It's Charlie's movie in terms of weight, focus, and theme, and Keitel is very strong, but De Niro's Johnny Boy is easily the most memorable thing on the screen.

And the idea that you could leave a theater showing *Mean Streets* and walk into another showing *Bang the Drum Slowly* right afterward is simply staggering. As an actor's breakout, it's like a boxer throwing a combination of punches too fast for the eye to see: the result is a knock-out that there's simply no way of explaining. De Niro completely and credibly transformed himself into two utterly distinct people with virtually nothing in common and had done so simultaneously and without preliminary fanfare. It was simply dazzling.

IT WAS ALMOST as if film critics were in competition to discover and praise *Mean Streets*. Pauline Kael, in a famous review in the *New Yorker*, anticipated the puzzlement of the wide movie audience by declaring, "This picture is so original that some people will be dumb-founded. . . . By the end, you're likely to be open-mouthed." In the *New York Times*, Vincent Canby wrote, "Some films are so thoroughly, beautifully realized they have a kind of tonic effect that has no relation to the subject matter. Such a film is 'Mean Streets.'" And Jon Landau of *Rolling Stone* declared it "the most original American movie of the year." (This was the sort of thing that likely compelled John Simon's backlash.)

The acting was widely praised. "There have rarely been performances of the caliber of De Niro's and Keitel's," said Stuart Byron in the *Real Paper* of Boston. "They don't seem to act their roles but live and breathe them." In the *New York Times*, Frank Rich said that De

Niro was "rapidly becoming the movies' foremost embodiment of sub-lingual schleppiness." Paul Zimmerman of *Newsweek* opined, "Beauti-fully realized in all his self-destructive flamboyance by Robert De Niro, Johnny Boy is a parody of the cool mafioso." And *Variety* predicted that the performance "should finally move [De Niro] out of the 'promising' category into which he has been regrettably stuck for five years."

There was a dismissive second notice in the *New York Times* by freelance writer Foster Hirsch, who relentlessly chided both Scorsese and De Niro for a lack of originality: "Like the movie in which it's the glittering centerpiece, the performance is too studied, too influenced by too many movies." And Stanley Kauffmann in the *New Republic* found a decidedly left-handed way of complimenting the rising star:

> *In* Bang the Drum Slowly *De Niro understood what he wanted to do as the dumb, doomed Southern catcher; he simply couldn't summon up enough of the juices and flavors. Here he is wild and strong. It's a flash part, and every actor who sees it will gnash his teeth because he'll know that anyone with talent could score in it. The* part *is a success . . . ; De Niro happens to have it. He uses it very well, but, without putting him down, I note that he's had some good luck in casting lately: a sweet guy doomed to die and a loose, pathetic, obscene quasi-maniac. What actor could ask for more?*

THROUGHOUT THE FALL the two films played virtually side by side (quite literally so in New York, where for a time they were the chief attractions at the famed Upper East Side first-run houses Cinema I and Cinema II). *Bang* got the bigger release; *Mean Streets*, which Warner Bros. hadn't produced but merely acquired for distribution, was starved for attention from the studio, which had *The Exorcist* chasing down the box office records that *The Godfather* had set just the previous year. Nevertheless, De Niro's achievement was widely regarded as tremen-dous. It was astonishing to see someone do two such different things so well and at seemingly the very same time. His ability to portray such disparate characters became legend that autumn and remained one of the key signatures of his public image for the next few decades of his career. He became famous for doggedly researching his roles and rehearsing until he had internalized a character, until he had, in his phrase, "earned the right to play a person," after which he would disappear into that person's skin entirely. In that regard, he reminded *Bang the Drum* director John Hancock of Alec Guinness, famed for his ability to go so deeply into roles that you could forget it was him inside. "Guinness isn't a personality actor," Hancock said. "He's a character actor who is also a star—and that's Bobby." There was a difference, though, and a crucial one: De Niro, Hancock added, "has an eroticism Guinness never had." Young, gifted, sexy, fresh, and hot, he was emerging as an actor of the moment, maybe *the* actor of the moment.

The success that he was to accrue from this pair of performances didn't quite bloom immediately, at least not in business terms. In late summer, with his work in *The Godfather, Part II* still ahead of him, he, Scorsese, and Jonathan Taplin were pursuing another film idea, *Booster,* about a guy who makes his living by shoplifting from Bloomingdale's; a writer named Ken Friedman was working on the script, which, Scorsese said, told "the story of a guy who's coming apart. He's the best and the worst of the New York crazies." It didn't gel, and Scorsese went on to follow up his fantastic breakthrough in the ultrapersonal *Mean Streets* with, of all things, the work-for-hire project *Alice Doesn't Live Here Anymore.* The director and his star stayed connected, fully intending to find another project to work on together; De Niro mentioned to a reporter that there was a story they were toying with, a script by Paul Schrader that had something to do with a New York cabbie . . .

THERE WAS SOMETHING else that proved elusive for him: the ability to sit still for an interview, to cooperate with the press to help promote a film or himself. He lacked the patience required of a person who succeeds at a public job and must give at least a little bit of his time and, yes, his soul to appease the public and the media that make his success possible.

His first interviews with journalists appeared in the summer of 1973, after his landing the role of young Vito Corleone had been announced and before the double-barreled blast of *Drum* and *Streets* in theaters. At first he seemed willing enough, sitting for chats with reporters for the *Los Angeles Herald Examiner* and *New York Post* and discussing his preparations for *Drum* and *The Godfather* and his relationship with Martin Scorsese. But from the very start there was something hesitant and cagy about him when confronted with the press. Tom Topor of the *Post* described it thus: "He is not inarticulate but he is a) very shy; b) not used to interviews; c) secretive about how he works," and that was a generous assessment given that Topor's story included passages such as this response to the (admittedly banal) question of why he wanted to be an actor: " 'Well . . .' a long silence. 'It's complicated . . .' a long silence. 'Getting into it . . .' a long silence. 'It's a personal thing.' Silence. 'Is that okay?' "

By November, with two smash performances in theaters, he was already becoming downright elusive. *New York Times* reporter Guy Flatley knew De Niro a bit socially. "We were both at a party on Riverside Drive a few years before," the journalist remembered. "I recognized him from 'The Gang That Couldn't Shoot Straight' and his work in Shelley Winters' play. And when he saw me, he came right over toward me and I thought, 'Who does he think I am?' We shook hands and he told me how much he enjoyed the story I'd written about Lionel Stander, who was a friend and mentor to him." Once De Niro's career seemed on the precipice of blooming, Flatley asked his editor if he could write a feature story on the actor, a task that was easier to imagine than actually execute. "I went up to his apartment and we both sat down with a beer, and everything that I asked him about—his parents, his school, his friends—he would say 'Oh, I could never say anything about that.' And it was very difficult because he was so shy and nervous and *I* was so shy and nervous. We went out to a restaurant and had another beer, but he never really loosened up. He was polite and friendly, but he seemed almost guilty about not being willing to talk."

At a loss for material for his story, Flatley turned instead to his acquaintance Shelley Winters, and the story that he finally published was built chiefly of her voluble telephonic ramblings. That in itself would have mortified the taciturn De Niro, never mind the actual things she said, such as

Listen, let's put it this way—I had a bigger romance with Bobby than I did with any of my lovers. Better change that to read "any of my husbands." No, I guess lovers sounds all right. The truth is, I feel very close to Bobby—and don't you dare tell him I haven't seen "Bang the Drum Slowly" yet. God forbid that you should miss seeing Bobby act. . . . By the way, was Bobby's apartment clean when you interviewed him? It was? Then his girlfriend must have cleaned it up for him.

Later on, Flatley heard that De Niro was, indeed, upset with Winters for the free way in which she spoke and the sorts of things she shared. And, in time, his aversion to the press became part of his legend, and he would avoid reporters and interviews assiduously over the coming years. When he finally did open up, he had a series of explanations for his reticence:

Why do people want to know what I eat for breakfast? After my first movies I gave interviews. Then I thought, "What's so important about where I went to school, and hobbies? What does that have to do with acting, with my own head?" Nothing. (New York, *May 16, 1977*)

After I give an interview I spend all my time explaining to people what I meant—or not explaining. (Time, *July 25, 1977*)

It was to be, as those remarks would show, a decades-long dance of attraction (on the part of the press and the public) and repulsion (on De Niro's), and he was only just learning the steps, reluctantly, petulantly, a truant dragged by the ear into the principal's office.

IN JANUARY 1974 De Niro was on location as Vito Corleone when end-of-the-year accolades for *Mean Streets* started to accrue. The film appeared on the top-ten lists in the *New York Times, New York Post, Cue, Newsweek, Time,* and the syndicated Gannett chain. It was edged out by François Truffaut's *Day for Night* for the Best Film prize from both the

National Society of Film Critics and the New York Film Critics Circle, but De Niro was named Best Supporting Actor by both groups. In early March, when Oscar nominations were announced, the film and his performance were ignored completely by the Academy of Motion Picture Arts and Sciences, prompting a puzzled response from *New York Times* critic Vincent Canby—"What happened to 'Mean Streets'?"—and a personal letter to De Niro from director Martin Ritt, who told him, "The fact that your peer group chose not to nominate you is shocking."

Peer group wasn't necessarily an apt choice of phrase. Yes, De Niro ought to have been recognized by the actors' branch of the Academy (which, for the record, nominated his *Bang the Drum Slowly* co-star Vincent Gardenia alongside the eventual winner, John Houseman for *The Paper Chase*). But he wasn't really part of the peer group of Hollywood actors in any meaningful way, at least not entirely, not yet. His role as Vito Corleone marked only his second appearance (after Mario in *The Gang That Couldn't Shoot Straight*) in a film that was conceived and financed from the start at a major movie studio. And so in March, if he felt slighted by the Academy in any way, it wasn't like not being invited to a good friend's wedding. He was still an outsider to the party, looking in from a remove, with a puzzled aspect. At some level he didn't think of himself as a Hollywood actor, and his response to this first flush of fame and success showed it.

THERE WERE GIRLS. There were always girls, starting from the time that he'd left his mother's house to travel and continuing when he lived on his own (albeit nearby, and still attached to her purse strings).

Often they were actresses whom he met in classes, in productions, in the clubhouse atmosphere of showbiz hangouts like Billy Ray's Eighth Avenue saloon. Always, remembered Jonathan Taplin, they were gorgeous: "He picked these incredibly strong girls, top chicks."

And almost always there was drama. "He'd fight with them all the time," Taplin continued. "They would always be in tears the next morning, and he would buy them some perfume."

Larry Woiwode recalled little quarrels between De Niro and the girl(s) of the moment during their scrambling young actor days. Shelley Winters recalled De Niro being stood up by an actress he'd invited to a dinner party that Winters threw for her little cohort of starving young artists. As she said, "I gave a Thanksgiving party. Invited all my theatrical waifs, my babies. Bobby was there, waiting for his date, a young actress he had a crush on. She didn't show up until dessert. She sort of floated in: 'Oh, hi Bobby . . .' He went into the bedroom and pounded the headboard with his fist. He was crying. He never talked to her again." And recall that on the night he was introduced to Scorsese at Verna Bloom's place, De Niro had showed up with the girl he'd been seeing and spent the night not exchanging so much as a word with her.

It's not surprising that these relationships rarely lasted for very long, given his taciturnity, his complete commitment to his work, and the sense, as related by those who knew him as far back as his teens, that he had a thin skin and a quick temper. But one stood out. Her name was Diahnne Abbott, and she was, like so many of De Niro's girlfriends, African American—specifically, a blend of English, American, and Creole lineage (she believed her father's family was Haitian, but her paternal cousin, singer Gregory Abbott, understood them to be from Antigua). And she was gorgeous in a way that Gauguin would have appreciated, with sleepy, luxurious eyes, a full figure, a sassy ease, a magnetic and sweet air of melancholy. There was a touch of Billie Holiday to her, a sensual blend of dreaminess and earthiness. She seemed world-wise and pacific, with a husky voice and a languid manner.

She was born in Boston and raised in Harlem. She left home young: the only child of an estranged couple, she was eventually separated from her mother and lived in a series of disagreeable situations until, at seventeen, she went out on her own altogether. She had ambitions to sing, and perhaps to act, but mainly she was waitressing, first at the West Bank Café and then at the famed Mercer Arts Center in lower Manhattan.*

---

* The arts complex closed in 1974 when the building suffered a collapse, but one part of it, a renovated kitchen, would live on for decades as The Kitchen, a famed New York performance space.

They met in the late 1960s, perhaps 1967, when Abbott was around twenty-two years old (prone to fudging her age, which could some-times swing three or four years in either direction). She had a daughter, Drena, named for a river in Yugoslavia that Abbott had read a book about when she was pregnant. And she was on her own—so on her own, in fact, that Drena would never meet her biological father, nor would she ever take or even reveal his name. Abbott would occasionally sing in a club under the name Diahnne Dea. She was a young mom living amid the hustle and glamour of downtown New York, open, in the spirit of the day, to whatever might come next.

She and De Niro didn't get together at first—although, consider-ing his attraction to black women (which the *New York Times* noted in 1973 in its first interview with him), De Niro certainly noticed her and, given his habits, more than likely asked her out. In truth, he didn't seem like much of a catch to her: "When I met him he was on un-employment," she recalled. In the next few years, though, their paths continued to cross, and after a conversation at a party in the early 1970s they became an item, if not quite exactly a committed couple.

He continued to see other women—and, now and again, to make scenes with them at parties, at dinners, or once, memorably, at an ac-claimed restaurant above Cannes, where the producers, filmmakers, and cast were celebrating the sale of the foreign rights to *Mean Streets* during the film festival of 1974. (That one started when De Niro killed a bee that had been kibitzing at the table, prompting his date to scold him. They had words, and she walked out—not only of the restaurant but the town. De Niro and the others found her hoofing it along the road as they drove back to Cannes; they gave her a lift.)

He was gentler around Abbott, or at least more under control. "By temperament he's mostly Italian," she admitted to Andy Warhol. In fact, he could be very watchful and judgmental of her behavior around other men, despite the emotionally effusive nature of so many of the show folk they met, not to mention the fact that they seemed to have an on-again, off-again relationship. At another event for *Mean Streets*, held just after the rapturously received premiere at the New York Film Festival, Abbott was De Niro's date, and he got loudly upset when he felt that she was being attended to a little too closely by François Truffaut. Privately, friends confirmed that his hot-blooded qualities were never entirely put to rest in the relationship: "Bob is very Italian with Diahnne, very possessive and jealous," one told the *New York Times*.

For a few weeks in 1974, while staying at the Chateau Marmont, De Niro was involved with the actress, model, and writer Carole Mallory, who at the time was engaged to Pablo Picasso's son Claude and then later had a long affair with Norman Mailer; her relationship with De Niro was mostly sexual, according to her memoir, with no strings attached. Indeed, there were times when, on his own, working in LA or Italy or even New York, he behaved as if he was free to do as he pleased.

The bond between Abbott and De Niro continued to strengthen, though, and sometime during the period when he was playing Vito Corleone, he and Abbott moved in together, filling his household with Drena and with Abbott's menagerie of cats, birds, and dogs, including a St. Bernard and a German shepherd. Such was the casualness of the ménage, however, that some of De Niro's friends and associates didn't know they were living together until the arrangement had been going on for a couple of years. This makeshift family clearly was too big for the apartment in which De Niro had been raised and which his mother passed on to him when she moved further downtown. So De Niro bought 14 St. Luke's Place,* a staid brick Greenwich Village townhouse on a quiet street in what was still a rough-and-tumble bit of lower Manhattan, and Abbott set about renovating it from its former semicommercial use into a family home. De Niro kept the 14th Street apartment, though, as a storage space, as a crash pad for friends who needed a place to stay, and for times when he needed privacy and quiet.

WITH HIS WORK on *The Godfather* behind him, De Niro started making notes on a 108-page treatment (the prose description of a film, as opposed to a script, which is generally much longer) of an epic film by

---

* The poet Marianne Moore had lived in the downstairs apartment with her mother at that address (which was sometimes listed as 71 Leroy Street) for more than a decade in the days before De Niro was born.

Bernardo Bertolucci, the Italian writer-director who had become respected with such films as *The Spider's Stratagem* and *The Conformist* and then genuinely famous with 1973's *Last Tango in Paris,* the sexually and psychologically daring film built around a remarkably unguarded performance by Marlon Brando. Now Bertolucci had upward of $6 million at his disposal—the most ever spent in Italy on a homegrown production—for a film that would do nothing less than trace the previous seventy-five years of his country's history through the story of two men born on the same day in the year 1900. *Novecento,* as it would be known in his native tongue, followed the lives of Alfredo Berlinghieri, the heir to a landowner's riches, and Olmo Dalcò, a peasant born on the wealthy man's land. The two are youthful playmates, even into their twenties; they share girls, occasionally in the same bed at the same time. But politics, heritage, and the vagaries of fate drive them apart. When World War II arrives, the wealthy man is a committed Fascist and the other a dedicated fighter in the resistance. They both survive the bloody conflict and live on almost to the present day, giving Bertolucci and his co-writers the chance to project forward toward the new Italian culture and civilization for which they yearned.

On the strength of his work with Brando, Bertolucci stockpiled an impressive roster of international stars for his epic. As the grandfathers of the wealthy man and the peasant, he had cast Burt Lancaster and Sterling Hayden. Donald Sutherland would play a Fascist leader; Dominique Sanda, Alida Valli, and Stefania Sandrelli would play key women in the men's lives; the rising French leading man Gérard Depardieu would play the peasant Olmo; De Niro, when he finally consented to be cast, would play the landowner Alfredo, a role at one time intended for Jack Nicholson.

Shooting on the film was well under way by the time De Niro started digging through the pages, wondering whether his character would have taken dancing lessons and opining that the ménage à trois featuring him and Depardieu could be a "good scene, if done right." De Niro showed up in Parma, Italy, at the start of fall. And he would be there, as the script metastasized in front of his eyes, almost through the end of winter.

From the start he was unhappy. Bertolucci wanted to begin work with De Niro on the material from near the end of the mammoth script, meaning that he was playing the older Alfredo before getting his legs steady underneath him as the younger man. "We shot the old stuff on the first day," De Niro recalled, "and I realized there that that was a mistake—it just wouldn't work, nobody was into it. I didn't know what I was doing sitting in another country with this director who I like very much but it was like, 'Where are we?' If I had thought about it more, I would have said, 'Can we not do this scene later, not the first day?' I was sensible enough to know you don't do things so out of order. But I went along with it, I remember that, and it just didn't work."

Bertolucci, too, knew he had a problem on his hands. "The first few days were a nightmare," he admitted. "But I told myself that what I had felt about Bob when I met him was so strong I couldn't have been wrong. I began to try to help him build confidence, and slowly a fantastic actor emerged. The fact is that with Bob you mustn't judge by the first few days. He's a very sensitive and probably neurotic person, so a director can be fooled. But if one has patience, well, it's worth it."

The conflict, though, was deeper than they could ever work out. Bertolucci came from the Italian school in which the director was absolutely the autonomous power on a film; De Niro thrived on partnerly collaboration with his directors. As a result, rather than give his star the room and time to find his way into the role, Bertolucci instructed him outright how to behave, a tactic that completely rankled De Niro. "Bertolucci . . . would tell me what to do," he complained later. "As a person I liked him very much, but as a director he has another style that for me wasn't as good as it could have been."

As the months dragged on, the career that De Niro should have been enjoying in American films was left to idle. Martin Scorsese still wanted him for that cab driver project that he had sharpened together with screenwriter Paul Schrader, but De Niro's absence caused delays that threatened the financing. (Scorsese, to his credit, wouldn't budge when it was suggested he go with another actor: "I can't do it without Bobby. I gotta have him," he said.) And Harry Ufland, who should have been casting his hot young star in lucrative and high-profile works, kept deferring offers from studios and filmmakers until finally, in a sense, he threw up his hands and let De Niro carve his own path. "Bob will never be a movie star," the agent sighed. "He is just not seduced by glamour."

Then in December, while De Niro was still living in hotels in Italy, *The Godfather, Part II* arrived fully finished into the world, and the stardom that was rumbling in the background of his life became, inescapably, its dominant theme.

8

FRANCIS COPPOLA'S SECOND GODFATHER FILM IN LESS THAN three years opened in five Manhattan theaters on December 14, 1974, and the reception was absolutely rapturous, maybe better than that accorded the first film. And as for De Niro, whatever reservations the critics had (and they were few) about praising him for the double-barreled debut of *Bang the Drum Slowly* and *Mean Streets* were utterly obliterated. His performance was hailed instantly as a work of mastery, and overnight he went from being an actor's actor to being a star—in, of course, his tenth screen appearance (thirteenth, technically, if you counted walk-ons and unreleased films).

In a rapturous review in the *New Yorker*, Pauline Kael said that De Niro "amply convinces one that he had it in him to become the old man that Brando was. . . . It is much like seeing a photograph of one's own dead father when he was a strapping young man; the burning spirit we see in his face spooks us, because of our knowledge of what he was at the end . . . suggesting Brando not from the outside but from the inside." Similarly, Charles Champlin of the *Los Angeles Times* noted that "De Niro, hoarse-voiced and imperiously handsome as he grows in assurance, does an amazing job of preparing us for the Brando we remember."

To be fair, the *New York Times* actually panned *The Godfather, Part II*, Vincent Canby saying, "The only remarkable thing about [it] is the insistent manner in which it recalls how much better [the first] was. . . . It's a Frankenstein's monster stitched together from leftover parts. . . . The plot defies any rational synopsis." Accusing Coppola's film of "self-parody," Canby didn't spare the stars: "De Niro, one of our best young actors, is interesting as the young Vito until, toward the end of his section of the film, he starts giving a nightclub imitation of Mr. Brando's elderly Vito." But this was decidedly the minority view of what would come to be hailed as a classic performance.

MARLON BRANDO'S Vito Corleone was a lion: courtly, patient, slow-moving, wise, judicious, deadly. He made speeches, coined catch-phrases, cracked sly jokes, spoke in judiciously weighed words, flashed anger only when absolutely necessary, and did everything in cautious proportion. He was solid and authoritative, a man who lived his creed (however crooked it might be) and demanded a similar integrity of those around him. He treasured his family, stood resolutely by his word, and treated friends and enemies with just fairness.

The young Vito Corleone, whom De Niro would play, would effectively fill in the background of this titanic figure. He would embody a bridge connecting Sicily to New York, 1891 to 1955, the Old World to the New. He would be an immigrant without resources who fashioned himself into a man of respect: part hoodlum, part businessman, part king. He would kill with guns, knives, words, patrimony—whatever it took. He would demonstrate in nascent form the unforgettable qualities of the elder man who was still fresh in the minds of movie audiences. And he would do it all in minuscule portions, with very little dialogue.

De Niro would appear in less than 47 minutes of the 202-minute theatrical cut of *The Godfather, Part II*. He would speak a mere 122 sentences, many of them fragmentary, and most of them in the demotic Sicilian that De Niro had mastered, often paring away at his lines to achieve a more credible semblance of the silence and cunning of the mature character. Brando spoke in fluent, flowery English, but De Niro's Vito Corleone has but seven lines in his adopted language, forty-two words in all, many of them muttered, all of them heavily accented. The powerful impact he imparts comes not from his tongue but, indeed, from his entire being.

De Niro's Vito is a watcher, staring in silence at his children, at his wife, at a stage show, at a parcel of guns, at a looming threat. He absorbs everything around him and rarely projects any emotion whatever, and yet his thought process is somehow always apparent. Partly this is the effect of the audience's knowledge that he will become the character played by Brando. But partly it is because of De Niro's amazing ability to become, in effect, translucent, to allow himself to be inhabited by the character's inner life and use his body and especially his eyes to convey it. He creates intimacy or draws lines of enmity with a gesture, a posture, a gaze.

As a measure of De Niro's strength in the role, consider Vito's relationship with his wife, Carmella, played by Francesca De Sapio. By the time De Niro enters the film, in 1917, he is married with a son, and he relies on his wife to run their meager little household in a traditional, responsible, respectful manner. Returning home with some bad news, he places a pear, carefully unwrapped from its paper packaging, on the dinner table; as he watches, she expresses delight with the surprise, and he breaks into a smile. As they sit to eat, he puts his hand over hers and stretches across the table to kiss her cheek. Several times in the ensuing scenes Vito communes similarly with her: watching as she tends to the ailing Fredo, helping her serve dinner to his (literal) partners in crime, listening patiently as her friend complains about ill treatment at the hands of a slumlord. Now and again Vito communicates his feelings to his wife with a gaze, but never in words. It's astounding. The two actors (and Coppola) create an impression of a complete marriage, a loving partnership, an intimate understanding, and yet De Niro's Vito speaks not one word aloud to De Sapio's Carmella. It's uncanny.

Vito is almost equally taciturn with his enemy Don Fanucci (Gaston Moschin), a Black Hand big shot. Vito's friends Abbandando, Clemenza, and Tessio are all cowed by the gangster, but Vito regards him as someone to be tested for strength of character. The two have three encounters, and in each Fanucci does the majority of the talking and Vito is the observer, heeding each word and probing beneath it to feel whether it is supported by steel or air.

De Niro's Vito has three conversations that account for the majority of his dialogue in the film:* a brief talk when he loses his position in the grocery, a strategy session in which he convinces Clemenza and Tessio to trust him to handle Don Fanucci, and a meeting with a slumlord in which he tries to convince the man to change his mind about evicting Carmella's friend. Tellingly, all of these have to do with money and with relationships of power. Vito expresses or promises gratitude and loyalty in each case, assuring the others of his steadiness and attempting to convince them to go along with his wishes. In each case, along with his escalating power, his words carry real weight. Buying oranges at a fruit stand, he finds that the peddler won't accept his money. "If there's something I can do for you, you come, we talk," he tells the man. It's his longest line in English in the entire film, and it is the foundation of the life and career of Vito Corleone.

In the absence of words, De Niro creates his character out of gestures, poses, and gazes. The first three times the film fades from the tale of Michael Corleone in the late 1950s to Vito in the 1910s and '20s, De Niro is captured staring silently: at the playful Sonny, the ailing Fredo, the fruit seller's wares. The second is the most characteristic: in his undershirt and suspenders, standing outside the bedroom where the baby is being treated for pneumonia, he's as thin and edgy as a jackknife, unable to offer any assistance, beset by real anxiety, silent but revealing his fear in the way he shields his body and face from the scene. His empathy and helplessness are palpable.

In action, he is a man of calculation, resolve, and purpose. He kills Fanucci with three bullets, the last of which he delivers with cool calculation directly into his victim's mouth. He rifles the man's pockets for money, then moves swiftly but collectedly to the roof, smashing the murder weapon and scattering the pieces of it into various chimneys. Afterward, he walks determinedly against the flow of a crowd to the stoop where his family waits. He puts the toddler Michael on his lap and waves a tiny American flag with him, having,

---

* It's worth underscoring here not only that De Niro rewrote much of his dialogue per his understanding of Sicilian but also that he pared away at Vito's lines, giving himself, in a perverse reversal of actorly ego, *less* to say than the script indicated.

in a sense, arrived anew in the New World by eliminating an emblem of the old.

De Niro has also, in a sense, usurped Brando's place. He only slightly resembles the older man, but he has the rasp in the voice (which becomes more pronounced as the character ages) and much of the body language: the stiff-backed formality, the habit of stroking his face with his fingers when engaged in deep thought, the impeccable wardrobe, the slicked-back hair. He has hints of Brando's jowliness and one of Brando's most famous lines—"I make an offer he don't refuse"—but more than that he has Brando's bearing. In barely forty-five minutes of screen time, De Niro has suggested how one of the most memorable characters in film history rose from grocery clerk to Mafia lord, and he does it less by projecting forward than by finding the seeds of the older man in the younger and letting them germinate in a way the audience can see. When you recollect that this is the first that critics or moviegoers had seen of him since the stunning one-two of *Bang the Drum Slowly* and *Mean Streets*, there is little wonder that he was being hailed as potentially the most gifted actor the screen had ever seen.

WHEN THE OSCAR nominations came around, *The Godfather, Part II* was overwhelmingly acclaimed, with eleven nominations in all, including three for Best Supporting Actor: Michael V. Gazzo, Lee Strasberg, and De Niro.* Francis Coppola, nominated as director and screenwriter for *Godfather II*, as he had been for the first film, was also cited as the sequel's producer. In combination with the nominations of his other film *The Conversation* for Best Picture and Best Original Screenplay, it was a stupefying achievement. The other players in the Best Picture race were *Chinatown, Lenny,* and *The Towering Inferno,* but, esteemed as at least the first two may have been, *Godfather II* was easily the strongest candidate.

The nominations for Gazzo and Strasberg were particularly revealing, both of how well acted the *Godfather* films were and of how

---

* The other nominees in the category were Fred Astaire for *The Towering Inferno* and Jeff Bridges for *Thunderbolt and Lightfoot.*

the array of performances in them was related directly to the Stanislavskian system that Strasberg (and, of course, his rival Stella Adler)
had so long promulgated. The dean of the Actors Studio hadn't been
seen on-screen for more than twenty years, yet the first *Godfather* film
was built on the performances of two of his most celebrated students,
Marlon Brando and Al Pacino. The sequel would add both Strasberg
and Gazzo, the author of the play A *Hatful of Rain*, which had been
performed by Actors Studio students consistently for decades.* Either
of them could have been selected as a sentimental choice by the Academy, as could have Fred Astaire for his role in *The Towering Inferno*.
Although *Inferno* was a ludicrous nominee for Best Picture, it had eight
nominations altogether, and the producers of the Oscars telecast were
planning a tribute to the great dancer to be performed by one of the
evening's co-hosts, Sammy Davis Jr. It seemed entirely possible that
the three *Godfather II* actors could split the ballot for Best Supporting
Actor between them and allow Astaire to waltz off with his first Oscar.

De Niro was working on *1900* in Italy when the nominations were
announced, and he was still there on April 8, 1975, when the Oscar ceremony was held on a rainy night in Los Angeles. It would turn out to
be a tumultuous evening, going down in history for the remarks about
the Vietnam War that Bert Schneider, producer of Best Documentary
winner *Hearts and Minds*, made during his acceptance speech and for
the angry rebuttal penned backstage by co-hosts Bob Hope and Frank
Sinatra and read aloud on the broadcast by the latter. By the time those
fireworks had exploded, the Best Supporting Actor prize had already
been announced by the father-daughter team of Ryan and Tatum
O'Neal: Robert De Niro for *Godfather II*.

In the absence of his star, Coppola accepted the prize, as he would
three Oscars of his own that night for *Godfather II*, which took six prizes
altogether, including Best Picture. He declared, "Well, I'm happy that
one of my boys made it. I think this is a very richly deserved award. I
think Robert De Niro is an extraordinary actor, and he is going to enrich the films that are made for years to come, and I thank you on his
behalf."

---

* De Niro had a heavily annotated copy of the play among his papers.

De Niro didn't offer a statement immediately, but he was interviewed about the Oscar later that spring and tried delicately to dance around his feelings about a competitive prize that had been publicly shunned or denigrated in recent years by the likes of Brando, George C. Scott, and Dustin Hoffman. "Lots of people who win the award don't deserve it," he told W magazine, "so it makes you a little cynical about how much it means. Did it mean that much to me? Well, I don't know. It changes your life like anything like that will change your life. People react to it. I mean, it's not *bad* winning it." This ambivalence may have been at the heart of things a year or so later, when Coppola, interviewed for a profile of De Niro, opined, "I like him, but I don't know if he likes himself."*

As RECOGNITION FOR his impressive achievement of the past few years mounted, both inside and outside the business, De Niro felt something new: a pressure to choose roles well, rather than the automatic drive to go after every possible opportunity that presented itself, no matter how ill-suited or beyond his grasp. "I've got to decide what I want to do," he fretted to a reporter. "People now tell me if I will consent to a project, they can get the deal going. But what should I commit myself to? 'Godfather' took a year of my life. This one ('1900') will take another year. The years go by and what will be left?"

But, in fact, he knew what he was going to do. While making *1900* he would be granted regular hiatuses, and he usually used them to return to New York (though, in fact, he dallied in Italy at times, often with female companions). On September 11, 1974, in a municipal building on Beaver Street in lower Manhattan, he applied for a hack driver's license at the New York City Taxi and Limousine Commission. And now and then over the coming months he would arrange to drive a taxi through the streets of the city, hacking through the city at night and never refusing to go to the most dangerous neighborhoods, prepar-

---

* There was another honor in the wake of his Oscar. De Niro had never submitted to the Actors Studio's famous two-step audition process, but after winning his Academy Award, he was granted admission to the Studio by Lee Strasberg.

ing to make that movie about a cab driver that so captivated Martin Scorsese.

> *He seems to have wandered in from a land where it is always cold, a country where the inhabitants seldom speak. The head moves, the expression changes, but the eyes remain ever-fixed, unblinking, piercing empty space . . . Travis is now drifting in and out of the New York City night life, a dark shadow among darker shadows. Not noticed, no reason to be noticed. . . . Then one looks closer and sees the inevitable. The clock spring cannot be wound continually tighter. As the earth moves toward the sun, Travis Bickle moves toward violence.*

As those words from the shooting script convey, *Taxi Driver* would stand as the cinema's most lifelike and harrowing vision of the decay of New York City in the mid-1970s. But it had its origins in Los Angeles, in a hospital room and a dirty car and a rented room—and, even further back, in a suffocating Calvinist household in Grand Rapids, Michigan.

Paul Schrader was born in 1946 to deeply religious parents who regularly inflicted pain on their children—Paul and his older brother, Leonard—in order to give them a sense of what eternal damnation might feel like: whippings, pinpricks, belittling lectures, deprivation of comforts, real psychological torture. It almost goes without saying that the boys were permitted virtually no popular entertainment. There was no TV in the house, and they were not permitted to go to the movies. They were, though, permitted to have guns, and they both grew into the habit of sleeping with them, Leonard going so far as to stick the barrel into his mouth "like some infant's pacifier" to help him sleep. And so it wasn't until he had reached his late teens that Paul ever saw a film. He would later remember that he lost his cinematic virginity to *The Absent-Minded Professor,* which failed to ignite him in any way. The next was *Wild in the Country,* an Elvis Presley film co-starring Tuesday Weld in which the King plays, of all things, a budding writer. The combination of the girl and the plot got him: he had the movie bug.

Dutifully he attended a Calvinist college near home, but while studying theology formally, he began, as so many in his generation did, to devour movies—a local art house was showing the works of Ingmar Bergman, which struck a nerve—and he aspired to connect his talent for writing with his passion for the screen. He worked for a student film society and wrote reviews for a student newspaper, and he sent off some of them (including some of the germs of what became his 1972 book *Transcendental Style in Film: Ozu, Bresson, Dreyer*) to *New Yorker* critic Pauline Kael, who was deservedly earning a reputation for cultivating and helping young writers. She recommended he attend film school, and so he did, at UCLA, starting in 1968.

It must have been like being yanked out of a dark cellar and thrust into the noontime sun of a carnival midway. The atmosphere was like nothing he had imagined, not even in a movie theater seat, and it overwhelmed him. Short, schlubby, chubby, inexperienced, anxious, itchy, culturally naive, socially inept, and prone to fits of depression, Schrader was hopelessly, painfully out of his element. But he could write, and as he learned more about film he became a more confident critic. He got some assignments reviewing movies for the underground press in LA (he lost one of them for panning *Easy Rider*), and then, his rise abetted by a word from Kael in the right ear, he found himself editing the prestigious journal *Cinema*.

But writing about movies wasn't as sexy as making them, at least not in Los Angeles, and he was ambitious; he began to conceive that he could be a screenwriter. It would be another metamorphosis, and it was a traumatic one. Always tightly wound, Schrader began to drink heavily, to use pills, to turn his gun fetish into a threatening and dangerous habit, carrying a loaded pistol around and sometimes brandishing it for effect among the flowery Hollywood types with whom he'd begun to associate. He made some friends in the film business—Brian De Palma, with whom he played chess; John Milius, a fellow wordsmith and firearms enthusiast—and he found himself invited to parties where young filmmakers met, bonded, and networked. But he was still an outsider, and no one was interested in his scripts. He was, frankly, in crisis. A youthful marriage fell apart; his nights were consumed by insomnia; he would drink until he ran dry and then start again when the bars and liquor stores opened; he haunted pornographic theaters;

his money, never a grand sum, withered to near nothing; and he would sometimes sleep in his car. "I was," he later confessed, "very suicidal." Finally, in the spring of 1972, his body simply crashed: he was admitted to a Los Angeles hospital with a bleeding ulcer.

The ulcer, Schrader later realized, saved his life. He had experienced an epiphany while he was convalescing, and he felt that he had to pursue it before he said goodbye to the life and career he had apparently failed to build. In his mind, the wry, rueful wisdom of the song "Taxi" by Harry Chapin fused with the increasingly iconic image of the lone gunman, as embodied most recently by Arthur Bremer, who shot Alabama governor George Wallace. He realized that he had stumbled upon an astounding metaphor, and in the coming weeks he alchemized all of his anxiety, self-loathing, and hurt and poured it onto the page. "I wrote the script very quickly, in something like fifteen days. The script just jumped from my mind almost intact."

Called *Taxi Driver*, it concerned one Travis Bickle, a Vietnam veteran from the Midwest who finds himself living in Manhattan and taking the only work he can get: driving a cab through nighttime New York, the darkest, dirtiest, most degraded, and most dangerous environment conceivable, a Dantean nightmare of prostitutes, pimps, thieves, corruption, sin, and death. When normal human relationships prove impossible, Bickle's thoughts turn to murder, and he drives himself— literally and figuratively—toward a self-immolating holocaust of violence and purgation.

Even in the wild Hollywood of 1972, after *Midnight Cowboy* and *Easy Rider*, with *The Godfather* and *The Exorcist* combining elements of exploitation cinema and mainstream entertainment and achieving critical acclaim and mammoth box office such as nobody had ever seen, this was very, very strong stuff. Schrader sent the script to Kael, who was completely unnerved by it. "I was so upset when I finished it that I took it down the hall to my linen closet and put it face down under a pile of sheets," she recalled. "I didn't want to think about it at night. It was brilliant, but very frightening." (Later, she asked Schrader why he would write about such a distasteful character, which seemed, from her vantage, to have nothing to do with him. "It is me without any brains," he told her.)

He also gave a copy of it to Brian De Palma, who was making headway in Hollywood after migrating west. Despite a healthy macabre
streak of his own, De Palma couldn't imagine a film of the material—
"It was the strongest stuff I had ever read. I didn't think the movie
would ever be made," he said. But he passed it along to yet another
friend, the up-and-coming producer Michael Phillips, who with his
wife, Julia, and their partner, Tony Bill, was developing some juice
at a few studios, with a film called *Steelyard Blues* in the pipeline at
Warner Bros. and another, by the same screenwriter, David S. Ward,
in the works at Universal, a picture about con men called *The Sting*.
There was enough in *Taxi Driver* for Bill/Phillips Productions to offer
Schrader an option on it: $1,000 for six months, with a second optional
six-month period to follow at the same price. Schrader, broke and desperate to get out of LA, took the deal.

One more person had a chance to see the script in this very early
phase: De Palma had passed it along to Martin Scorsese, who was still
engaged in making *Mean Streets*. He, too, was stunned by what he
read: "I almost felt I wrote it myself," he told Schrader years later. "Not
that I could write that way, but I felt everything. I was burning inside
my fucking skin; I had to make it. And that's all there is to it." (After
the fact, he explained further, "I *had to make* that movie. Not so much
because of the social statement it makes but because of its *feeling* about
things, including things I don't like to admit about myself. It's like
when you're in therapy and the doctor takes a videotape of a session
and then shows it to you.") But, of course, it was a moot point: nobody
was going to make a film on this subject, and certainly not with the
Phillipses, who had no track record, nor with the creepy Schrader, nor
with Scorsese, who at that moment had only a student movie and a
Roger Corman film to his name.

Within a year of the option on *Taxi Driver* being signed, though, the
balance of the equation had changed. The Phillipses (who had ended
their marriage, as well as their partnership with Tony Bill) had delivered *The Sting*, which would go on to massive box office and a haul of
seven Oscars, including Best Picture; they parlayed the success into a
multiple-picture production deal at Columbia Pictures. And Schrader,
along with his brother Leonard, who had spent several years teaching

in Japan, had become a hot Hollywood commodity on the basis of *The Yakuza*, a screenplay about the Japanese gangster underworld that sold for more than $300,000, a record sum at the time; he was now being asked to write and rewrite scripts all over town (he marked his ascent with a blue Alfa Romeo with a license plate that read OZU, in honor of his favorite Japanese director).

With all that heat, it seemed suddenly that *Taxi Driver* could happen, but nobody knew exactly how. There was talk of Jeff Bridges playing the lead role for director Richard Mulligan; of Al Pacino playing the part; of other directors, such as Irvin Kirschner, Lamont Johnson, or John Milius, taking the reins. Nothing seemed right. And then the Phillipses and Schrader saw an early cut of *Mean Streets*, and they knew they had their director. Scorsese would be given the opportunity to deliver a cinematic version of the hellish New York of the script— but *only* if he could deliver Robert De Niro as Travis Bickle. And, of course, *only* if a studio would bite on financing it.

All of that, of course, was easier to imagine than to make happen. When the Phillipses and Scorsese bought the script (and at least one rewrite) from Schrader outright in January 1974, De Niro, still not a big enough name for anyone to hang a million-dollar-plus production on, was at work on *The Godfather, Part II* and on the verge of agreeing with Bernardo Bertolucci to appear in *1900*. Scorsese himself, also more of a succès d'estime than an actual hit, was engaged in the unlikely *Alice Doesn't Live Here Anymore*. Not only, in short, were they rather small fish by studio standards, but they weren't even available. If they were the perfect pair to make *Taxi Driver* and no one else would do, then it might be that the project would pass into legend as one of those great scripts that never got a chance to be the movies they might have been—like one of those what-if films that Orson Welles or Erich Von Stroheim never made.

By the end of the year, *Taxi Driver* was still not a go, in large part because the principals were suddenly so hot. Schrader had at least three scripts in some stage of development at various studios; Scorsese's so-called women's film, *Alice Doesn't Live Here Anymore*, had been a box office success, winning an Oscar for Ellen Burstyn in the lead and opening doors for its director; the Phillipses were following up *The*

Sting with a number of projects, including one with Steven Spielberg that would become *Close Encounters of the Third Kind*; and De Niro, as his hapless agent Harry Ufland well knew, was the subject of multiple offers to appear in multiple films. Any of them could have gone in any direction, really. But when De Niro, hack license in his wallet, was in New York on Christmas hiatus from *1900*, he met yet again with Scorsese and Schrader to go over the most recent draft of the script, and he effectively made up everybody's mind for them. "I don't know about anyone else," he said, "but the next film I'm doing is 'Taxi Driver.'"

UPON REFLECTION, it's a bit hard to see how the minds of Scorsese and De Niro should settle on material coming from such a radically different place than either *Mean Streets* or their own cultural backgrounds. Schrader acknowledged that the script was born from a moment "when I couldn't really distinguish between the pain in the work and the pain in my life," traumas that the actor and director didn't share.

There *was* a strain of severity and even self-hatred in the film, derived from Schrader's Calvinism, that harmonized with Scorsese's Catholicism. "It's kind of an exorcism for me," the director admitted once production had begun. He planned to surround the character with religious symbolism not in Schrader's original script: "There are a lot of Catholic references in the film," he said later, "even if they're only my own personal reference. Like the moment when he burns the flowers before he goes out to kill. And when he's buying the guns, the dealer lays them out one at a time on the velvet, like arranging the altar during Mass." (Scorsese revealed that they had even shot a scene of Bickle whipping himself with a towel—excoriating his flesh, in effect—before his murderous outing, but finally took it out "because it looked a little forced and unnatural.")

In effect, Schrader and Scorsese made a perfect, if unlikely, collaborative marriage. "My character wandered in from the snowy wastelands of Michigan to the fetid, overheated atmosphere of Marty's New York," Schrader said. "Travis Bickle is not a character that Marty Scorsese would ever think of or come up with; and that atmosphere is not one that I would come up with."

De Niro, though, had no particular religious upbringing and carried none of the anguished freight of his collaborators. For him, the script represented a chance to stretch beyond himself in a way that he was confident that he had sufficiently cultivated his craft to allow. There was an eerie coincidence, Schrader learned, in that De Niro had, during the period a few years prior when he considered writing material for himself to appear in, conceived of a script about a lonely man wandering New York City with guns and dreaming of an assassination. The script never came to be, but when De Niro told Schrader about it, the writer knew immediately what was going on: "I said to him, 'Do you know what the gun in your script represents?' I said it was obvious to me that it was his talent, which was like a loaded gun hidden in him that nobody would let him shoot, and that if somebody would just let him fire once, the whole world would see the enormous impact his talent would have." (It's easy to imagine De Niro hearing this analysis without offering any response at all.)

De Niro, Schrader saw, would bring an energy to the film that neither he nor Scorsese could provide. "De Niro's contribution," he said later, "was much of the schizophrenic quality of the character, which is not in the script. That quality in Travis of shooting the guy and then saying, 'Oh, I don't know what to do about this gun'—all those schizo elements come straight from his personality. The character I wrote was going crazy in a more linear fashion than the character Bobby acted; his characterization zigs and zags." If they could make it, if they could get onto film what they knew they were capable of when they sat around discussing it, they would rattle audiences to the core.

BUT THOSE WERE still big ifs. In order to make it work, in order to make a film of such explosive material under the imprimatur of a movie studio, every participant in *Taxi Driver* would have to take a pay cut. De Niro, who could easily have asked $250,000 after *Godfather II*, signed for $30,000. "Bobby was greatly pressured," Schrader remembered. "He was being offered a half a million for something else.

He was one of the strongest ones behind it all—absolutely adamant about doing it." Michael Phillips concurred that De Niro was the key to getting the film off the ground: "He could have demanded several hundred thousand . . . but he still agreed to honor his original deal. He was a saint."

And, in fact, nobody got rich on the film, not at first. Schrader had already sold the script for roughly 10 percent of what he'd been paid for *The Yakuza*. And the film's other main actors all worked for significantly less than they might otherwise: Cybill Shepherd, who was cast as the campaign worker of Bickle's dreams; Peter Boyle, as a fellow cabbie; Harvey Keitel, still not the star that, say, Al Pacino or Dustin Hoffman was or that De Niro was becoming, as the pimp; Jodie Foster, by some measures the most experienced actor of them all at age twelve, as the young prostitute whom Bickle wishes to rescue. Even the unions whose members would be involved in the production on the streets of New York made financial concessions.

The deal was struck regardless of money, as Michael Phillips explained, because the filmmakers "made a pact to do this movie." Schrader concurred: "It was an agreement made three years ago by friends when none of us were bankable. Even after we all got successful, we didn't give it up until finally we offered Columbia such a good deal they couldn't turn it down." As he later said, that they all worked for so little money was, in fact, a source of strength for them: "De Niro told me, when we were talking about whether the film could make any money, that he felt it was a film people would be watching fifty years from now, and that whether everybody watched it next year wasn't important. That's how we came to it, and that's why we didn't make any compromises; we figured if we were going to compromise on money, we're certainly not going to compromise on anything else." Finally, all of the important talent on the film was under contract for under $200,000, a budget of between $1.5 and $1.8 million was established, and production was scheduled for the summer of 1975.

THAT GAVE DE Niro time build his character, to do the sort of biographical background work that he had come to rely on, and to practice driving a taxi, which he was determined to do right. (What the hell: he'd been collecting unemployment only a few years before, so it couldn't hurt to learn a trade, right?) In the course of his work, he had occasion at least once to give a ride to a writer from a film magazine, who would later confess to stiffing him on the tip . . . en route to see *Alice Doesn't Live Here Anymore*. At other times De Niro let Scorsese ride around with him in the front seat. "We drove up and down 8th Avenue," the director remembered, "a bad neighborhood. The impression I had was that anything could happen. You have no control over what could happen. Your life doesn't belong to you anymore. That was exactly what the character had to feel. Believe me, anyone who drives a cab in New York at night will be like Travis sooner or later."

It was a foreboding atmosphere, Scorsese said, perfect for De Niro's preparation. "He got a strange feeling when he was hacking. He was totally anonymous. People would say anything, do anything in the backseat—it was like he didn't exist." But there was at least one light occasion. Not long after Oscar night, De Niro was putting in a shift in the taxi when, per Scorsese, "a guy gets in, a former actor, who recognizes his name on the license. 'Jesus,' he says, 'you won the Oscar and now you're driving a cab again!' De Niro said he was only doing research. 'Yeah, Bobby,' says the actor, 'I know. I been there, too.'"

He became so natural behind the wheel that New Yorkers accepted him as the real thing, even after production had begun. "One day when it was pouring rain," remembered Scorsese, "we were filming De Niro in the cab near Columbus Circle. Some businessman in a hurry spotted the cab, came rushing over and hopped right in. De Niro was so startled all he could do was point to his 'off duty' sign. The guy bounced right back out, cursing a blue streak all the way down the sidewalk. He never even saw the cameras."

Outside of the taxi, De Niro took his now standard step of seeking out authentic voices upon which to base his character's midwestern affect. Schrader, finally, was the best prototype he found, and he had the screenwriter read selections from the script into a tape recorder. He also borrowed some of Schrader's clothes for his character, until he finally arrived at a Travis Bickle who at least one observer thought was an uncanny likeness of Schrader himself. "Michael Phillips saw one scene in *Taxi Driver* and said to me, 'That's you. Bobby is doing you right to a T in there,'" said Schrader.*

He worked on the little physical details of the script: how to make dum-dum bullets, how a Marine would do calisthenics, how Travis would eat a cheeseburger. And he wrote up a little backstory about Travis's exit from the service (in a note, Scorsese indicated that it was via an honorable discharge in May 1971) and his arrival in New York, which, he reckoned, involved coming to see a girl, working in a series of menial jobs, getting introduced to amphetamines, and gradually going broke.

Mostly, though, he dove into the psyche of a character who was unlike any that he—or, truly, anyone else—had ever played. There was no ethnicity to Travis Bickle, no previous film character from which to triangulate, no real-life counterparts he could sit and observe from a bleacher seat or on TV. This was a role that had to be built of the raw materials of his imagination, his body, and his soul.

He began, oddly enough, under water. "I got the idea," he said, "of making Travis move like a crab. It's a hot sunny day. He's out of his cab, which is his protective shell—he's outside his element. He's all dry and hot, finally he breaks down. I got the image of a crab, moving awkwardly, sideways and back. It's not that you imitate a crab, but the image gives you something to work with. It gives you another kind of behavior." Years later he elaborated further on the conceit: "You know how a crab sort of walks sideways and has a gawky, awkward movement? Not devious in that sense. Crabs are very straightforward, but straightforward to them is going to the left and to the right. They turn sideways; that's the way they're built."

He remembered stories that he'd heard from a few Vietnam veterans he'd met over the years, including a fellow named Millard who had a small role in *Glamour, Glory and Gold*, and he spoke at some length about the experience of the war with Vic Magnotta, a stuntman whom Scorsese knew from his NYU days and who explained to De Niro that

---

* De Niro repaid Schrader for the clothes with the gift of a money clip. Decades later, the screenwriter auctioned off the clip for $10,000 on a crowd-funding website to help raise money for his film *The Canyons*.

Special Forces commandos would shave their hair into Mohawks to demonstrate their commitment to deadly missions. (Bickle's Mohawk, so startling in those days before punk rock, wasn't in Schrader's script, which simply says of his aspect at the film's climax, "Travis looks like the most suspicious human alive.") And De Niro remembered, too, little snatches of ordinary life that he had glimpsed over the years, and that helped him build a character: "Think of all the lonely people I see, like that girl that night on 15th St."

In April, Schrader visited De Niro in Italy as he was finishing the last of his work on *1900.* When De Niro was back in New York to stay, Schrader moved to town from Los Angeles to put the script through one last rewrite with Scorsese and the cast. Scorsese had taken a suite of rooms at the St. Regis Hotel—the Cecil Beaton Suite—as a base of operations, so Schrader moved into the hotel as well, and they worked at all kinds of odd hours, accepting suggestions from the actors who had been studying for their roles. Peter Boyle, cast as the older cabbie Wizard, who tries to reach out to Bickle as the younger man slides into his psychosis, made a few visits to the legendary Belmore Cafeteria on Fourth Avenue, an all-night spot frequented by taxi drivers, criminals, and street people, and heard some stories that he was allowed to incorporate into his dialogue. Harvey Keitel, who was appearing at the time on Broadway as Happy in a revival of *Death of a Salesman* starring George C. Scott, spent time talking with pimps and going so far as to have one of them look over his script to check his lines for authenticity. (He asked Michael Phillips if one particular pimp named Lucky could be hired on with the production so as to be handy for consultation during filming, maybe as an extra in street scenes. "Is he a SAG member?" the producer asked. "No man," Keitel said. "He's probably a fugitive from justice.")

Schrader, who'd been working on the script for three years, found new inspiration in the city. "I was feeling particularly blue in a bar at around three a.m.," he remembered. "I noticed a girl and ended up picking her up. I should have been forewarned when she was so easy to pick up; I'm very bad at it. The only reason I tried it that night is that I was so drunk. I was shocked by my success until we got back to my hotel and I realized that she was 1) a hooker; 2) under age; and 3) a junkie. Well, at the end of the night I sent Marty a note saying, 'Iris is in my room. We're having breakfast at nine. Will you please join us?' So we came down, Marty came down, and a lot of the character of Iris was rewritten from this girl who had a concentration span of about twenty seconds."

Even Cybill Shepherd, thought to be the weakest link in the cast, was given room to fill in her character during a rehearsal period. Shepherd was at a precarious moment in her career. After breaking into the business in a big way with her first two films, *The Last Picture Show* and *The Heartbreak Kid*, she had fallen in love with Peter Bogdanovich, who had directed her in the former and subsequently left his wife. The pair had comported themselves with some hauteur among the Hollywood crowd, both socially and professionally, and nobody was exactly weeping for them when they went on to create two critical and commercial flops in a row, *Daisy Miller* and *At Long Last Love*. With Shepherd's standing as a leading lady at a very low ebb, she was willing to take on the role in *Taxi Driver* for considerably less than her previous asking price. Scorsese and the Phillipses were looking at "Cybill Shepherd types," in fact, including a still-unknown Farrah Fawcett, when Sue Mengers, Shepherd's agent, contacted them and let them know that her client was interested in the role. "I told Sue we couldn't afford Cybill," Michael Phillips said, "but she said, 'Let's get together and we'll discuss money later.'"

Shepherd was a big name, but she was nobody's idea of a great actress. Once she arrived in New York, Scorsese and De Niro spent several days with her at the St. Regis working on her scenes, getting her comfortable with their methods and with the intense material of the script. As Scorsese filmed them with a 16 mm black-and-white camera, they spent hours, she remembered, "improvising all our scenes . . . [Scorsese] let his actors find the characters. His constant advice was 'Do even less than you're doing.' De Niro was a master of underplaying and a master of craft at every level. I learned more about acting on *Taxi Driver* than on any other film."

There was, she said, a current in the air. "There was an enormous amount of chemistry between De Niro and me. We didn't act on it. . . .

De Niro asked me out. It was a great compliment. Years later I said, 'Can you believe I turned him down?' But I was protective of what we were doing. . . . With actors you never know if too much familiarity really will breed contempt, so if you don't have that familiarity at least you have the freedom to act."

But Bogdanovich saw an uglier side to the rapport of the stars, claiming that De Niro translated his romantic rejection by Shepherd into a loathing for her: "He treated Cybill like a pile of dogshit. It was really hot. One of the grips or somebody gave her a little electric fan because she was in this really hot dress. De Niro would kind of like go 'the princess' kind of thing. It was horrendous to watch. The truth is, Bobby treated people badly if he decided they weren't up to snuff."

In fact, Shepherd, perhaps without knowing it, was mocked throughout the production. In LA, Julia Phillips would look at rushes of her scenes and cringe as Scorsese repeatedly gave her instructions for line readings and De Niro made his frustration obvious. Schrader, too, felt she wasn't up to snuff: "We always said we were looking for a Cybill Shepherd type. How much worse could she be than a Cybill Shepherd type? But she was always a Cybill Shepherd 'type.'"

On the other hand, Bogdanovich felt that Jodie Foster was favored by De Niro: "He treated [her] like a queen." And, to be fair, she did require special handling. Not quite thirteen, she had done scores of TV episodes and appeared in several films, including a few Disney hits and, most crucially, *Alice Doesn't Live Here Anymore*, in which she played the exceedingly worldly child of a hooker. But nothing in her experience prepared her for *Taxi Driver*: "When I first read the script, I thought, 'Wow, they've got to be kidding!' It was a great part for a 21-year-old, but I couldn't believe they were offering it to me."

As it happened, Foster (and, perhaps even more, her mother, Brandy) wanted the part, but there were significant hurdles to overcome to get a child actor involved in such material. She was examined by a Los Angeles psychiatrist to ascertain if she would be able to play Iris without doing herself any harm. ("I was determined to win," said Brandy Foster. "Here was some broad trying to tell me what was too adult for my daughter.") Eventually, Jodie was cast with some stipulations: the production also hired her older sister, Connie, to act as her double for the more explicit moments of sexuality and violence in the film, and every minute in which she appeared on the set was closely monitored by a child welfare worker. "She saw the daily rushes of all my scenes and made sure I wasn't on the set when Robert De Niro said a dirty word," Foster remembered.

She wasn't bothered by the gore. "It was really neat," she said. "It was red sugary stuff. And they used Styrofoam for bones. And a pump to make the blood gush out of a man's arm after his hand was shot off." And she wasn't bothered by the sexual aspects of the role. Far from it, in fact. "The memory I have is of [Scorsese] and Robert De Niro telling me how to unzip [De Niro's] pants," she said years later. "And Marty keeps bursting out laughing. He can't get a word out, and he tries to act serious, you know? He keeps smoothing down his face on both sides, but he just keeps laughing. And then De Niro decides he's going to take over because he can do it."

What *did* rattle her, she admitted, was that she learned in the course of working with De Niro how little she actually knew about the art of acting:

He kept picking me up from my hotel and taking me to different diners. The first time he basically didn't say anything. He would just, like, mumble. The second time he started to run lines with me, which was pretty boring because I already knew the lines. The third time, he ran lines with me again and now I was really bored. The fourth time, he ran lines with me, but then he started going off on these completely different ideas within the scene, talking about crazy things and asking me to follow in terms of improvisation. . . . We'd start with the original script and then he'd go off on some tangent and I'd have to follow, and then it was my job to eventually find the space to bring him back to the last three lines of the text we'd already learned. . . . There was this moment, in some diner somewhere, when I realized for the first time that it was me *who hadn't brought enough to the table. And I felt this excitement where you're all sweaty and you can't eat and you can't sleep. Changed my life.*

The film shot throughout June and July, entirely in Manhattan, which guaranteed stifling weather, uncontrollable crowds, and infinite unforeseeable little hassles. The air around the production—indeed, around the city—was shot through with a dark undercurrent; Scorsese and his location scouts witnessed a violent mugging outside Lincoln Center in broad daylight. And the weather was brutal. As Shepherd recalled, "New York was a fetid swamp. They couldn't turn on the air conditioning in the diner where we filmed our first scene because it disrupted the sound." To exacerbate the unpleasantness, the city, which was suffering an economic freefall, endured a brief but pungent garbage strike that affected not only the atmosphere on the set but the very look of the film. "I was accused, in *Mean Streets*, of just show-ing the garbage on the streets," Scorsese remembered. "When I was shooting *Taxi Driver* . . . everywhere I aimed the camera, there were mounds of garbage. I said, 'They are gonna kill me! Guys, take away some of the garbage.' Here I was trying to control reality, but that *was* the reality. In LA, with *Mean Streets*, we had to put garbage on the street to make it look like New York."

There were other aspects of the production that threatened to over-whelm the director: crowds at the staged campaign rallies, random people ruining shots by leaning out of windows or trying to sleep on fire escapes, visitors such as Brian De Palma, who helped Scorsese set up a complex tracking shot, or Scorsese's own mother, Catherine, who regularly brought homemade zeppoles to the set and ruined at least one shot by wandering into the camera's eye: "Cut!" her son hollered. "Ma, please, I'm directing a movie!"

In the middle of the shoot, Scorsese met Julia Cameron, a freelance writer who came to the set with the intention of doing a profile of De Niro that morphed into an assignment to write about Scorsese for *Play-boy* or *Oui*. After an initial luncheon meeting, lubricated liberally with booze, they talked for hours, and he gave her a copy of the *Taxi Driver* script with a promise to discuss it at a subsequent meeting, over din-ner. That meal wound up becoming a preamble to marriage. Cameron moved into Scorsese's suite at the St. Regis, and the two became an item. She had some knowledge of politics, and Scorsese allowed her to punch up some of the dialogue that took place in the campaign office.

The couple began appearing everywhere together, even dressing alike. Various voices around the film warned Scorsese that too much was happening too quickly, and Cameron wasn't very popular among his old friends, who saw her as opportunistic (Scorsese's assistant Amy Jones called her "a heat-seeking missile," and Julia Phillips dismissed her as someone "who came for an interview and never left"). But it was love, apparently. By the end of the year they were married, and before the following year was over they were parents.

Cameron's may have been the most dramatic visit, but she wasn't the only reporter welcomed to the set of *Taxi Driver*. The studio had arranged for a steady stream of writers to observe the production on various days, even during some of the most complex and sensitive sequences of the film, including the bloody climax. In those pre-Internet days, they all published stories on what they had seen—while the film was still in production—and most of them revealed the entire plot in their articles. Between the crowds, the reporters, the schedule, the heat, and the subject matter, Scorsese was almost completely overwhelmed, right from the outset, in fact. "The second week," he confessed, "I wanted to stop. I loved it so much, I wanted to kill it." Julia Phillips, who was working on *Close Encounters of the Third Kind* in Los Angeles, had her own ideas about what was happening as gleaned from the rushes she screened: " 'Taxi Driver' is a cokey movie. Big pressure, short schedule, and short money, New York in the summer. Night shooting. I have only visited the set once and they are all doing blow. I don't see it. I just know it." It was, in short, mayhem.

But in the center of it all, De Niro was remarkably silent, still, and inward-gazing, his ability to focus amid mayhem striking onlookers as a combination of diva-like affect and supernatural concentration. "When the camera isn't turning," observed Rex Reed, "he turns into Greta Garbo, shunning all communication." "Bobby chooses to stay in his trailer," Scorsese told Arthur Bell, "and that's it. I don't even bother him." And Shepherd remembered, "He stayed in character for the whole movie, so that disastrous date where Travis takes Betsy to see a porn film really did make me feel uncomfortable and turned off. When I turned him down in real life, it matched my character." Like his unwillingness to submit to interviews and the chameleonic variety of his roles, his monomaniacal immersion in his character during production was becoming the stuff of legend.

Indeed, during the shoot his agent, Harry Ufland, visited the set while De Niro, dedicating a little time to the selection of wardrobe for his next film, was decked out in a fashionable suit from the 1930s. As simple as it was, the transformation was so complete that, said Scorsese, "Harry didn't recognize him. For twenty minutes, Bob wasn't Travis anymore." Another visitor, Michael Moriarty, his *Bang the Drum Slowly* co-star, was about to approach De Niro during the setup of a luncheonette scene and then, getting a glimpse of his fellow actor, begged off. "No, don't bother," he told a production assistant who was about to announce his presence. "I don't know that guy at all. I knew Bruce Pearson. I don't know Travis Bickle or Robert De Niro."

De Niro went places nobody could imagine. His script was filled with reminders to keep himself on edge, to float through scenes in a dissociative haze, to stay still and stare blankly while churning inside, to strain toward an affect of formality and propriety while undergoing internal chaos, to cower meekly from the outside world when it rejects him and to smile coldly when he means to do harm. Gradually he was building toward what Schrader's script referred to as "the release of all that cumulative pressure . . . a reality unto itself . . . the psychopath's Second Coming."

What was perhaps the key moment in this descent, one that would live on for decades and haunt De Niro, sometimes amusingly and sometimes not, wasn't specifically scripted. After arming himself with a variety of handguns and knives, Bickle stood in his crummy apartment (which, like Iris's room, was constructed in an abandoned building at Columbus Avenue and West 88th Street) and addressed a mirror menacingly. Imagining himself in a conversation with someone mistreating him, he practiced drawing his weapons and turning the tables on his adversary. And he said it in words that he improvised on the spot:

Yeah? Huh? Huh? (he slides his gun into his hand) . . . Faster than you, fucking son of a . . . Saw you coming, you fucking . . .

Shitheel . . . I'm standing here; you make the move. You make the move. It's your move (he slides the gun out again) . . . Don't try it, you fuck.

You talkin' to me? You talkin' to me? You talkin' to me? Well then, who the hell else are you talking . . . You talking to me? Well, I'm the only one here . . . Who the fuck do you think you're talking to? Oh yeah? Huh? OK . . . Huh?

"It was the last week of shooting," Scorsese remembered. "I asked Bobby to talk to himself, and he improvised. I was sitting at his feet with my headphones on. Because the noises from the street were drowning his voice, I asked him to repeat it: 'Again! Again!' Gradually he found a rhythm."

The famous words were, apparently, stolen from Bruce Springsteen, who was about to burst into superstardom with his forthcoming album *Born to Run*, the release of which was preceded by a series of shows at the Bottom Line nightclub in Greenwich Village that De Niro had attended. Ever the master showman, Springsteen would do a bit in which he pretended not to realize that the audience's hoots of "Bruuuuuuuce" were for him. "You talkin' to me?" he would ask in mock humility. De Niro held on to that phrase and turned it into one of the most famous lines in all of American movies. "He just got into this wonderful paranoid monologue," Scorsese recalled. "He did this riff, like a jazz musician. He would just go." It was glorious. Even Schrader had to admit that it was a genius bit of improv: "To me, it's the best thing in the movie. And I didn't write it."

Technically, Scorsese did wondrous things, using his camera with piercing intelligence and taste to create an atmosphere that he likened to "a seeping virus." He shot many of De Niro's close-ups, especially those of his eyes, at forty-eight frames per second, twice the normal speed, conveying a hypersensitive effect to "draw out and exaggerate his reactions. What an actor, to look so great against a technique like that! I shot all those shots myself, to see for myself what kind of reaction we were getting." As a director, he was already becoming famous for an athletic ability to move the camera, but there were no handheld or freewheeling shots in the film: "I felt that it should be all tied down. Dollied or tied down, because the character is rigid." And, in a stroke of genius that kept the film from getting an X rating from the MPAA, he desaturated the blood in the scenes of gore to give them the timbre of what he liked to call "*Daily News* violence"—a lurid, otherworldly feeling. "It's sort of like tuning in a color TV where you get black-and-white at first," he said. "It's more what I wanted in the sense that it's more like a black-and-white daily tabloid newspaper. . . . I was going to do the whole picture that way but I couldn't afford it."

There was another bit of on-the-fly inspiration. One of Schrader's most disturbing inventions was a scene in which a man in the back of Bickle's taxi talks about the violence he wishes to wreak upon his unfaithful wife, a terrifying and explicit speech filled with misogyny, profanity, and hate. The part was to be played by George Memmoli, the rotund actor who debuted in *Mean Streets* in the pool room scene in which he refuses to pay a debt he owes to someone he considers "a mook." But Memmoli had injured his back while trying to perform a stunt on another film, and Scorsese, surprising everyone, elected himself to take his place.

Scorsese had appeared in *Mean Streets* himself, of course, also in a car, also with a gun. But that character had no lines. *This* character was nervously, horrifically chatty, and Schrader was one of many on the production who wasn't convinced that Scorsese could pull it off. "I think the director's or writer's job is behind the camera," he said, and "I think you should get a pro to do that stuff. . . . I knew his egotism was such that he wouldn't admit it if he was wrong, so we could very well have a bad scene on our hands." But Scorsese said, "I didn't trust anybody with it. So I just got in the back of the taxi and played the part myself."

Fortunately, he had an acting coach in the front seat who forced him into a real performance: namely, De Niro. "I learned a lot from Bob in that scene," he said. "I remember saying, 'Put down the flag, put down the flag' [referring to the taxi meter's on/off switch]. De Niro said, 'No, *make* me put it down.' And Bobby wasn't going to put down the flag until he was *convinced* that I meant it. And then I understood.

His move had to be a certain way and if he didn't feel it, the move wasn't going to be right."*

THAT TRANSACTION WAS indicative of the synergy that blossomed between director and star in the course of making the film. From that first formal meeting at Verna Bloom and Jay Cocks's house, De Niro and Scorsese had always felt simpatico, and that feeling had grown deeper during the making of *Mean Streets*. But during that fetid summer in which they made *Taxi Driver*, the two developed a rapport that would make their collaboration of the coming years one of the most justly celebrated in the history of cinema.

"The real stuff between Bob and me is private," Scorsese said. "Bob talks to me private [*sic*]. He needs a lot of time. We need a lot of time." Even during the shoot—*especially* during the shoot—the two would habitually convene in prolonged head-to-head talks, which irked another of Scorsese's actors sufficiently to complain about their process to the press (albeit anonymously): "Bobby hogs Marty on the set. Marty gives Bobby anything he wants. And what Bobby wants is constant attention— constant talk about his character." In fact, some of their interactions, perhaps the most important ones, were subverbal. "We understood each other perfectly," Scorsese said. "We don't need words to work together. The communication between us is like a form of sign language."

It could seem to outsiders—meaning everyone else, even Scorsese's wife—that they were uninterested in what the rest of the world thought or felt or had to say. "In Martin," sighed Julia Cameron, "Bobby has found the one person who will talk for 15 minutes on how a character would knot a tie. I've seen them go for 10 hours nonstop." And Scorsese admitted that the two of them were perhaps *too* fond of chewing over minutiae: "We have a shorthand. We have a longhand, too. We talk a great deal. Very often we talk about the same thing over and over."

---

* With his Luciferian beard and horrifyingly frank delivery of scalding dialogue, Scorsese was so good in the scene, according to De Niro, that "he was offered the Charles Manson character for the television movie *Helter Skelter*. But he was a little paranoid. He figured they were going to come after him, too."

But De Niro had some reasonable explanations for their intimacy and their lengthy parleys. After the pair had made a few more films together, he said, "I like sometimes to be very personal with the director. He can say whatever he wants to other actors, but when we talk, it's with each other and that's it. We've worked so much with each other now, we trust each other. Not that we didn't trust each other before, but I think now if there's another person around, we can still talk. I still like to just talk to him on the side so nobody hears. Maybe it's something I'm going to try, and I want to prepare him for it so he can cover it. It might get a reaction from the other actors, so he has to be ready for it."

And Scorsese equally valued their intimacy. Just as sports coaches relied upon certain players who could see a game with a managerial eye even while participating in the actual run of play, Scorsese found in De Niro someone who shared his vision of what the film was supposed to be and which details did and didn't aid them in achieving their aims. De Niro would, for instance, notice a prop or a bit of wardrobe that was out of sync with the rest and point it out to Scorsese: "It doesn't seem right." And the director would often agree: "Oh, absolutely, I didn't see it." This ability, according to Scorsese, derived from De Niro's astounding gift for concentrating within a character, a scene, a story. "His whole thing is concentration," he explained. "There could be a *war* going on, you know, he could be in the middle of the DMZ, and he'll be like this—[*in a trance*] 'Are you ready?' 'Huh?' 'Yeah, I'm ready.' 'I mean, go, now you go first.' 'No, no, after you.' 'Are you sure?' 'No, I'm fine.' Bobby. It's incredible." Or, as he put it later, "He *was* Travis. A piece of scenery could collapse behind him and he would react the way Travis would."

When production wrapped in late July, they parted knowing that it wouldn't be for long. De Niro had his next film lined up already, and he would be moving to Los Angeles to make it. And soon afterward Scorsese would join him there, to edit, score, and polish *Taxi Driver* and to begin pre-production on their next collaboration, a 1940s-style musical entitled *New York, New York* about the tormented marriage of a saxophonist, whom De Niro would play, and a big-band singer.

And De Niro had yet another project in mind. During the production of *Taxi Driver*, somebody had slipped him a copy of *Raging Bull:*

My Story, the autobiography of boxer Jake LaMotta, a middleweight from the Bronx famed for his ability to take a pounding, for his series of titanic fights with Sugar Ray Robinson, and for confessing to taking a dive to enrich mobsters he knew from his old neighborhood. De Niro had become chummy with LaMotta's boyhood friend and co-writer, Pete Savage, who had a cameo in *Taxi Driver* as a man who gets into Bickle's cab with a hooker. De Niro thought there might be a film in LaMotta's story, and he encouraged Scorsese to have a look at the book.

9

"WE'VE MISCAST IT."

In a Warner Bros. screening room in Burbank in August 1975, director Mike Nichols, screenwriter Neil Simon, and a pair of studio executives were watching rushes from the set of *Bogart Slept Here*, a comedy about an off-Broadway actor who finds himself overwhelmed by good fortune when his very first movie unexpectedly becomes a huge international success. The film had only been shooting for a week, but there were alarms indicating that something was going very wrong.

Marsha Mason, Simon's actress wife, was playing the actor's wife, a role written specifically for her. Playing the actor was De Niro. And it was De Niro whose work was worrying the filmmakers.

De Niro had arrived on the Hollywood set of *Bogart* only three days after wrapping *Taxi Driver*, and Simon and the other principals felt extremely lucky to have him. He was a rising star, a box office attraction, the hot new thing. Personally, Simon found him affable and approachable, if shy. "He didn't say very much," the writer recalled, "but what he said, you listened to. He spoke softly, nodded and shrugged a lot, and occasionally he gave you a quick smile that caused his eyes to squint."

But from the start there were troubling signs. De Niro had decided that his character should wear a single earring, and he spent, as Simon remembered, the better part of a day poring over a selection of earrings that the property master rustled up for him. Then there was the matter of acting styles. Mason had performed Simon's work onstage and was familiar with its blend of spritzing patter and warm sentiment. De Niro hadn't played such material since his dinner theater days, and scheduling the shoot so soon after *Taxi Driver* meant that he wouldn't be able to undertake his normal studying process or get to know the script in a proper rehearsal period. He would be finding his character, in effect, in front of the camera—a dicey prospect.

In fact, it was disastrous. He flailed at Simon's sensibility, unable to find a pry hole that would allow him to enter the world of the screenplay. And Mason was left to act opposite a cipher, forced to abandon her own instincts about how to play a part that had always been hers in order to find a way to engage with her co-star.

Simon, who'd seen enough theatrical work to know that it could take an actor a bit of time to get into the rhythm of a role, was willing at first to ride it out, to let De Niro find his sea legs. But he was growing concerned. "In the first few days of dailies," he remembered, "it was clear that any of the humor I had written was going to get lost. It's not that De Niro is not funny, but his humor comes mostly from his nuances." The script Simon had written was broader than that, and De Niro's subtlety was pushing it into a different tenor.

Nichols, who may not even have remembered that he had auditioned De Niro for *The Graduate* almost a decade prior, told Simon that it was going badly, that De Niro was misreading the part. "Well," said the writer, "maybe it shouldn't be funny. Maybe it *should* be a more serious picture."

"That's not what you wrote," Nichols replied, "and it's not what I saw when I read this script. If there's no humor in the first half of the film, we're dead."

So they ran the rushes for the Warner Bros. brass, who agreed that something was wrong. And when they asked Nichols what he thought should be done, he gave them a stunning answer: "Stop the picture."

"Reshoot what we have?" asked an executive.

"Yes," Nichols said. "But not with De Niro . . . We've miscast it." They sighed, they huddled, and the next day they called De Niro into an office and, in effect, fired him.

"He was, of course, livid," Simon recalled. "Luckily I was not in the room when he was told."[*]

---

[*] Coincidentally, Simon had been involved a few years prior in the firing of Harvey

The word hit the trade papers like a mortar shell; rumors circulated that Nichols had called De Niro "undirectable" and that De Niro had outright walked off the production when Nichols and Mason tried to tell him that he didn't know what comedy was. His friends, including Shelley Winters, spoke publicly to defend him, but there was sourness in the air. De Niro explained years later, "It didn't work, just didn't work out." But, he added, "then they tried not to pay me."

Everyone just wanted the whole sad episode to go away. Warner Bros. halfheartedly looked at a few other actors in the hope that there was a way to save the project, but nobody was deemed appropriate, for any number of reasons. Nichols went back to New York to the stage; he wouldn't direct another dramatic film until 1983. Simon continued to write smash hits for Broadway and the screen, arguably none bigger than one that grew out of the aborted *Bogart Slept Here.* Among the actors who tested to fill De Niro's shoes was Richard Dreyfuss, right on the heels of his titanic success in *Jaws;* Dreyfuss wasn't right for the part, according to Nichols, but Simon liked his rapport with Mason so much that he retooled the material for the pair, resulting two years later in *The Goodbye Girl,* for which Dreyfuss would win an Oscar.*

WHILE HIS STAR was getting himself fired from a Neil Simon comedy, Martin Scorsese had come to Hollywood to put the finishing touches on *Taxi Driver,* tweaking the edit to slide the violence past the censors, and adding a score by the legendary Bernard Herrmann, Alfred Hitchcock's favorite composer, the man who wrote the terrifying staccato chords of the shower scene of *Psycho,* among dozens of other works for film and orchestra, including the scores of *Citizen Kane, The Day the Earth Stood Still, Cape Fear,* and most recently Brian De Palma's *Sisters.* It was a new situation for Scorsese: *Mean Streets* and, to a lesser ex-

---

Keitel in almost identical circumstances from *The Sunshine Boys,* in which he'd been cast, inaptly, in the part ultimately played by Richard Benjamin. Small world.

* A few years later, Simon performed the inadvertent penance of buying a pair of paintings that caught his eye in a New York gallery and that turned out to be the work of Robert De Niro Sr.

tent, *Alice Doesn't Live Here Anymore,* were particularly celebrated for soundtracks built out of the sort of popular music that the characters in them would have listened to. But Travis Bickle, cipher that he was, didn't listen to music ("I don't follow music too much," he confesses on a date. "But I would like to, I really would"). Scorsese needed an original score, and he went for the best.

At first Herrmann wanted nothing to do with the project, based on the proletarian sound of its title alone. Then Scorsese got him to agree at least to read the script, and one thing seemed to sway Hermann to the film: "I like when he poured peach brandy on the cornflakes," he told Scorsese. "I'll do it."

He came to Los Angeles to do his work just before the Christmas holidays, and conducted the recording of the soundtrack himself, right up until the final session, which was held on December 23 and witnessed by Scorsese and Steven Spielberg, who'd been invited to meet the composer. Herrmann finished his work and went back to his hotel for the night. He never woke up, dying in his sleep of a heart condition on Christmas Eve. Not two months later, the first ominous notes of his remarkable score, which would go on to be recognized with an Oscar nomination, would be heard by audiences for the first time, as *Taxi Driver* made its way into the world.

To call the film a sensation would be an understatement. Critics and audiences had never seen anything like it, and the reviews and box office were beyond anything that Paul Schrader, the Phillipses, Scorsese, or De Niro had ever imagined.

HE IS A twenty-six-year-old midwesterner, honorably discharged from the Marine Corps two years before, alone in New York with no work, living on a steady diet of junk food, booze, pills, and porn, his life an eddying pool of loneliness, stasis, thoughts turned inward on themselves. He has received only a scattered education, yet he keeps a diary—a quaint affectation—and it reveals an intelligence, a sense of aspiration, an acquaintance with the Bible. You can see pain, fuzziness, skittishness in his eyes, which are often squinched defensively. But in the main he's a cipher—out of touch, by his own confession, with music, films, politics, social mores, and most every other aspect of ordinary life.

He drifts into a Manhattan taxi office seeking work, specifically overnight work. He doesn't make a brilliant first impression. He mutters a little, has trouble making eye contact, and doesn't understand what it means when he's asked if he's "moonlighting"; he makes a joke that lands with a thud, and he apologizes reflexively, though he doesn't like that he has to do it. Finally he wanders back into the street, sipping from a pint bottle tucked into his military-issue fatigue jacket, so ephemeral a presence that his mere walk along a city block is rendered in a dissociative jump cut.

Like Dostoyevsky's Underground Man, Ellison's Invisible Man, and Lennon's Nowhere Man, Travis Bickle is an emblem for alienation, disaffection, isolation, an existential antihero whose connection to our world is tenuous and yet who, in his alienation, is meant to be a symbol for the condition of us all. Until this film, De Niro has principally played southerners and Italians or Italian Americans. But there is no ethnicity to Travis Bickle, only the merest hint of a midwestern twang, and there is no backstory as singular as Johnny Boy's head injury or Vito Corleone's witnessing the death of his family. He is an invention of the imagination, of the page, of the movie camera, and of De Niro, relying on a foundation provided by Schrader and existing in a milieu created by Scorsese. He is a pure product of the cinema. It's even possible, given that the film both begins and ends with a close-up of his eyes, that he doesn't exist at all, that the events depicted in *Taxi Driver* are some lurid fantasy that has bubbled up in his sleepless mind.

He wants to be normal, but he's just slightly miswired. He swallows pills with a shake of his head like a snake ingesting its prey; he stretches after a long night behind the wheel with his elbows akimbo like a twisted scarecrow. Asked the simplest of questions—"How are you?"—he's stumped for an answer, seemingly distracted by something but, at the same time, apparently focused on nothing at all.

But of course he is sentient and, as we see as we stay with him, purposeful, if only in an effort to find a purpose for himself. He starts with a girl. He dons his one good jacket—burgundy, made of velvet or maybe suede—and proffers a surprisingly fluent line of palaver to a pretty girl. (He's not alone in admiring her: Martin Scorsese himself is depicted seated on a nearby stoop ogling her as she passes by.) Her name is Betsy, a golden, WASPy dream girl, and he takes Betsy on a proper date, for which he shows up in a tie and with a surprise: the movie that he'll take her to see is porn, *Sometimes Sweet Susan*, starring Harry Reems. Within minutes of their entering the theater, the courtship ends, and somehow Travis is confused that it has gone wrong.

Soon he picks up an apparently ordinary fare who turns out to be intent on doing harm to his cheating wife. Perversely inspired by this encounter, he arms himself with a small arsenal of pistols—$915 worth, including a Magnum that could take down an elephant—and hits upon a new way to connect with the world: through that staple of psychotic self-expression of America in the 1960s and '70s, a political assassination.

And then another girl catches his eye—a pubescent prostitute who works just a few blocks from the building where De Niro was raised. Her street name is Easy, but, as Travis learns, her real name, which she hates, is Iris. He had dreamed of rescuing Betsy from her loneliness, but Iris, "sweet Iris," really does need to be rescued. His plan is fixed: self-immolation via the murder of Betsy's preferred candidate, self-resurrection by leaving his life savings to Iris.

He devotes himself to a regimen of calisthenics, target range practice, working on a quick draw in the mirror ("You talkin' to me . . . ?"), making dum-dum bullets, fashioning a device that can deliver an automatic pistol to his hand with a jerk of his arm (and that transforms him, cyberpunkishly, into something that's half man, half weapon). In the gesture that marks his final intent to push through to his fiery demise, he shaves his hair into a Mohawk, fulfilling the script's direction: "Anyone scanning the crowd would immediately light upon Travis and think, '*There* is an assassin.'" Of course, he is spotted in the throng by the Secret Service and chased away, precipitating a rampage that leaves him, like Johnny Boy, bleeding from a neck wound, his connections to life and security and the future shredded beyond repair.

The story is singular enough, but what De Niro does with it is truly without precedent. The cinema has served up psychopaths and socio-paths and even sometimes assassins (the Frank Sinatra double bill of *Suddenly* and *The Manchurian Candidate* leaps to mind), but none of them has ever been drawn in the forefront of a film so purposefully, and no filmmaker and actor have ever before managed to bring an audience so intimately inside the mind, heart, and even metabolism of such a fellow.

Much of this effect is achieved through the eyes: we look into the abyss of Travis's gaze, and the abyss gazes back at us. De Niro's stare sometimes fastens on the lights and motion and, very often, the little outbursts of violence and sexuality in the world around him; just as often, though, it attaches itself to nothing, resulting in an almost bit-tersweet expression of wonder, confusion, and emptiness that makes you want to console him. His body, too, is a subject of fascination: early on, sleepless on his cot, almost sunken into the mattress, De Niro is a stick figure given shape only by his clothing; later, baptizing his fists in a flame on his stovetop in what he and Scorsese referred to jok-ingly as the Charles Atlas scene, his body is so sinewy and veined and gaunt that he looks like he has emerged from a POW camp. There's something repellent in his asceticism, but also something that elicits sympathy.

There's another effect, even more startling, that's achieved by zooming slightly out and seeing De Niro the actor playing Travis, a sense that the Oscar-winning chameleon has set a new standard not only for himself but for all actors. Was there anyone else who would so fully transform himself into a character so desperate, alienated, and wounded, someone who wouldn't rescue a single moment from such a harrowing film by giving the audience some sort of reassurance—a nod, a wink, a joke, the lift of an eyebrow—to indicate that this was a fictional depiction of an alternative reality and not a portrait of what was really going on all around them? Pauline Kael, horrified by the fi-nale of the film, is said to have gasped aloud, "He's still out there!" She meant Travis, of course, not De Niro, but at that moment it was impos-sible to tell the difference. When he first emerged as Johnny Boy, Bruce Pearson, and Vito Corleone, De Niro seemed like a chameleon. Now, playing a character without attachments, backstory, or explanation, he somehow seemed more like himself, as if the actor who created those amazing characters was nothing more than their hired driver, ferrying them to the movies, seething away in the front seat, ready to explode and to take them—and us—to hell along with him.

Taxi Driver hit the film public—and the reviewing press—like a thunderbolt or an avalanche. Nobody had seen anything like it before, and nobody seemed entirely sure what to make of it. Its power was undoubted, but for a great many viewers, including critics, its violence, darkness, and ambivalence were overwhelming.

To fill their superlatives, critics harked back to other films and, indeed, other media. "Imagine Hitchcock's 'Psycho' if it had been told from the point of view of *its* title character," explained Frank Rich in the *New York Post*. "*Taxi Driver* is a movie in heat," said Pauline Kael in the *New Yorker*, "a raw, tabloid version of *Notes from the Underground*."

The reviews—and, in many publications, re-reviews—waged a back-and-forth war about the morality of the film and its ultimate message (the coda *really* puzzled people). But very few even among the film's antagonists doubted Scorsese's energy or creativity, and nobody was anything less than floored by De Niro's work.

"Acting of this sort is rare in films," wrote Vincent Canby in the *New York Times*. "It is a display of talent, which one gets in the theater, as well as a demonstration of behavior, which is what movies usually offer." Frank Rich added, "You simply must see for yourself. He plays Travis . . . at an intimate human scale that makes even the better movie performances of the past few years look artificial and bombastic by comparison." In the *Wall Street Journal*, Joy Gould Boyum wrote, "De Niro creates a Travis who manages to evoke from us first a sympathy, then an empathy, and finally an understanding." Kael, invoking a metaphor that she would come to use again to describe De Niro's work, said, "Some actors are said to be empty vessels who are filled by the roles they play, but that's not what appears to be happening here with De Niro. He's gone the other way. He's used his emptiness—he's reached down into his own anomie. Only Brando has done this kind of plunging, and De Niro's performance has something of the undistanced intensity that Brando's had in *Last Tango*." Even more ecstatically, Jack Kroll of *Newsweek* declared De Niro

*the most remarkable young actor of the American screen. What
the film comes down to is a grotesque pas de deux between Travis
and the city, and De Niro has the dance quality that most great
film actors have had, whether it's allegro like Cagney or largo like
Brando. . . . De Niro has created a total behavioral system for his
underground man, much of which has a macabre comedy. Unlike
most actors, De Niro doesn't just express a personality, he creates
one.*

Taxi Driver would go on to reap more than $25 million in box office
in its initial release, against its $2 million budget—which Columbia
Pictures was initially reluctant to put up. (Schrader had been paid approximately $30,000 for the rights, but twenty years after the film's re-
lease his 5 percent share of its earnings had come to nearly $700,000.)
And Travis Bickle had become a metaphor for every lone gunman,
pent-up psychopath, and quiet-boy-next-door-who-went-bonkers for the
next forty years. (In 2001, for instance, when Crown Prince Dipendra
of Nepal unleashed an automatic weapon in the palace in Katmandu,
killing the king and queen and seven others and then trying to fire a
bullet into his own temple, a *New York Times* article on the massacre
called him "some Himalayan version of the Robert De Niro character
in 'Taxi Driver.'") Along with the "You talkin' to me?" business, the
character De Niro created seemed to seep off the screen and into the
real world: Julia Phillips and Paul Schrader drove past theaters in New
York where the film originally played and were at once thrilled and
sickened to see lines of young men dressed in Bickle's familiar outfit of
army fatigues and blue jeans, waiting to see the film for, presumably,
second and third go-rounds.*

---

* There was a chilling footnote to the film's release. In April 1976, a twenty-year-old
Chicago man, Perry Susral, drove over to a convent at three in the morning and fired
twenty-seven shots with a .22-caliber pistol at the building, harming no one but interrupting the sleep of the resident nuns, "who were too petrified to do anything except pray
their rosaries," according to police reports. Questioned, Susral explained that he was
imitating *Taxi Driver*: "I liked the shootout scene." A Chicago reporter tracked Scorsese
down in Los Angeles, where he said, "It is all wrong. We never intended anything like
that. If you look at the film, the whole thing is surrealism." True, but it wouldn't be the
last time the filmmakers would have to answer such questions about their creation.

For decades there was talk of reviving the character for a sequel, and De Niro, Scorsese, and Schrader talked seriously about it more than once. Schrader always contended that the characters he wrote in such films as *American Gigolo, Light Sleeper,* and even *The Last Temptation of Christ* were thematic variations on Travis Bickle, but he was rebuffed by De Niro each time he tried to interest him in appearing in one of those films. All three of the principals remained intrigued by the thought of exploring how Travis Bickle would have been treated by time. In 1998, after having lunch with De Niro and talking once more about reviving Travis, Schrader, again inspired by real-life events, thought he'd hit on it. "Theodore Kaczynski," he wrote to Scorsese, referring to the infamous Unabomber, who'd been arrested a year or so prior. "If the Travis Bickle character had survived, he probably could have ended up a violent, self-absorbed loner like Kaczynski." (Perhaps joking, he added, "Jodie [Foster] can play the Clarice Starling role.") The idea, for better or worse, never got further than that note.

AND WHILE THE world was greeting Travis Bickle, the man who embodied him was a continent—and several decades—removed from the fetid, menacing streets of New York. On the sound stages and backlot of Paramount Pictures, De Niro was playing Monroe Stahr, the hero of F. Scott Fitzgerald's *The Last Tycoon,* a roman à clef about the famed producer Irving Thalberg, the boy genius of MGM who died in 1936 at the age of thirty-seven having overseen literally hundreds of films, including the likes of *Ben-Hur, Grand Hotel, Mutiny on the Bounty, The Champ, A Night at the Opera,* and *The Good Earth*—almost none of which would, by his choice, bear his name. Fitzgerald found Thalberg a poignant and romantic character and had conceived of exorcising himself of the demons of working in Hollywood through the project—which, ironically, was left incomplete after the author's own early death, at age forty-four, in 1940.

The film had been proposed to De Niro as early as the fall of 1974, when Elia Kazan had sent him a copy of the script, which had been adapted by playwright Harold Pinter for producer Sam Spiegel. At the time, De Niro was booked back-to-back-to-back with *Taxi Driver,*

Bogart Slept Here, and *New York, New York*. But he was interested in working with Kazan, a scion of the Group Theatre and of Method acting, and a former director of his boyhood acting heroes Marlon Brando (*A Streetcar Named Desire, On the Waterfront*), Montgomery Clift (*Wild River*), and James Dean (*East of Eden*). The pedigree of the production was irresistible, and De Niro agreed to squeeze it in. (He was testing his wardrobe for the role when his agent, Harry Ufland, failed to recognize him on the set of *Taxi Driver*). Then, when *Bogart* imploded, he was able to step right into *The Last Tycoon*.

He felt, he said, immediate relief: "It was like going from the darkest depths to light and inspiration; from black to white; from total angst to being with Kazan and Sam Spiegel. . . . It was a whole other thing." Kazan especially was a godsend to him. Like Scorsese, he was willing to pore over the details of a character endlessly with his star, having long conversations, writing extensive letters and memos, prolonging the production to engage in quiet one-on-one sessions. Kazan, whose understanding of the Stanislavskian system was closer to Lee Strasberg's than to Stella Adler's, knew exactly how to coddle or confront an actor—even one of De Niro's caliber—to exact the performance he was seeking, a discipline to which De Niro was happy to submit himself.

They met first in London in the spring of 1975, when De Niro was commuting between New York and Rome while finishing *1900* and preparing to shoot *Taxi Driver*. After that, they kept in touch. Kazan sent De Niro a letter to bring to his attention a detail about Stahr: that he was a good dancer, specifically the fox-trot. De Niro responded on the back of the envelope in which Kazan's letter arrived, delighted with this detail about his character and promising to learn the dance.

When De Niro arrived in Hollywood in the fall of 1976 to work on *Bogart* and *Tycoon*, Kazan supplied him with a four-page, single-spaced précis of his impressions of Stahr: the character's attitudes toward art, business, work, women, colleagues, and his failing health, plus even some explanation of what would be going through the character's mind during and after sexual intercourse. The memo was a wormhole; De Niro loved it, annotating the pages extensively and working on his own copy of the script with fanatical attention to psychological detail.

In some ways all of this work was moot, as Spiegel, the producer of

Lawrence of Arabia, The Bridge on the River Kwai, The African Queen, and *On the Waterfront,* had contractually promised Harold Pinter that his adaptation would be treated like a stage play—that, in effect, it would be shot exactly as he wrote it, with no changes permitted to any of it, not even a single word of dialogue, without his approval. The script was locked as surely as if they'd already shot it; Kazan, describing this straitjacketing, liked to say that he was "realizing" the script, after the French fashion of referring to the director as the *réalisateur.* All De Niro could do was dive into the psychological and emotional subtleties in almost a theoretical way. But he loved that sort of thing, and Kazan encouraged and inspired him to dig in. On many of the screenplay's typewritten pages he would wind up writing more words than Pinter had, almost all of them for naught.

He did have control of some aspects of his character, though, and he took charge with his customary rigor. The wardrobe was bespoke, his suits tailored exactly as Irving Thalberg had worn them; he learned to write shorthand, as both the real Thalberg and the fictional Stahr could; he met with Paramount's founder, Adolph Zukor, who at age 103 still visited the studio regularly to kibitz; he spoke to doctors about the heart condition from which Stahr, like Thalberg, suffered, learning about the medications he would have taken in the 1930s and how his moods and energy would have been affected by them and by his illness. Dressed in his old-time wardrobe, with all three buttons of his suit jackets closed, he liked to parade silently around Paramount with an inner sense of ownership. "I spent time just walking around the studio dressed in those three-piece suits, thinking, 'This is all mine,'" he said.

Kazan knew he would have to mold De Niro to fit the material: "Bobby has never played an executive, he's never played an intellectual, he's never played a lover. I had to find that side of him; it was unexplored territory." He developed a novel technique to immerse his star in the character: having him don a suit and sit in an office, where he was besieged by phone calls, by interruptions from his "assistants" (played by actors), by manufactured crises to which he had to improvise responses and solutions. "I've impressed on Bobby that what he says is never a comment," Kazan explained. "Whatever he says is an instruction which someone has to do something about. . . . I've made him feel that his life is at the mercy of his anteroom, that he's a victim of the phone. I've now got him realizing what it means to be an executive."

De Niro ate it up. He adored working with Kazan. "He was an actor at one time," he reminded a reporter from *Rolling Stone.* "He's schooled. He's—as far as I'm concerned, the *best* schooling." And he appreciated the latitude that Kazan allowed him in finding and creating the character: "I sometimes see him as a parent who doesn't quite approve of his children or what they're doing," he said. "He can't relate to it, but he still loves them."

Kazan, for his part, was deeply impressed by De Niro's exactitude and commitment, noting, "He's very precise. He figures everything out both inside and outside. . . . Everything he does he calculates. In a good way, but he calculates, just how he sits, what his suits are, what ring is where. . . . Everything is very exact." And he was nearly overwhelmed by his star's work ethic: "He's the only actor I've ever known who called me on Friday night after we finished shooting and said, 'Let's work tomorrow and Sunday together.'" He did, however, notice that De Niro was prone to overdoing things: "He's getting thinner and thinner. I'm worried about him. Thalberg . . . had a rheumatic heart and was very frail. Bobby went to the greatest lengths to get that. I admire him for it." (At least one member of the cast thought it was an uncanny transformation. Ray Milland, who knew the real man, said, "De Niro *is* very much like Thalberg: very meek, very quiet, very thin.")

But not everyone involved with the production was similarly enamored. Spiegel, one of those old-school producers who worked independently of a studio and reckoned that every cent spent on a film was coming right out of his pocket, tried, according to De Niro, to shortchange him on his salary. "Sam pulled one on me," the actor remembered. "He tried to finagle paying me what he said he would. It was very simple. I don't understand why people do that. He was famous for it. And yet he had good taste and he was funny. . . . I still walked away from him, though. In the make-up trailer one night when we were shooting, Sam came over and said, 'Bobby . . . ,' and I said, 'Sam, you didn't do what you were supposed to do.' 'Well . . . ,' he said, and I just walked away from him. But I liked him."

The feeling wasn't necessarily mutual. Kazan had lobbied Spiegel to give De Niro the part—he had literally taken the actor by the arm and dragged him to a hotel suite, where he made the introduction—and Spiegel fought the casting even after the film was under way. Spiegel complained that De Niro brought "no nobility" to the role and that he insulted Spiegel behind his back around the studio. He denigrated De Niro's work while watching the daily rushes. He tried to scrimp on the wardrobe, complaining to Kazan that De Niro had asked for fourteen tailor-made suits. Once, as De Niro and Kazan ate lunch with him at the Paramount executive dining room, Spiegel excused himself and walked over to where Robert Evans, the young production executive who'd green-lit *Love Story, Chinatown,* and the two *Godfather* films, was eating. "Look at Irving Thalberg over there," Spiegel said quietly to Evans, indicating De Niro. "He doesn't even know how to pick up a knife and fork."

But De Niro stayed aboard, and Kazan finished the film, which would be his last. Compared to the protracted post-production De Niro's other recent films had been put through (*1900,* which wrapped before shooting began on *Taxi Driver,* was *still* being edited), *The Last Tycoon* made it from the sound stage to the screen in very quick order, and reactions were mixed to sour.

DE NIRO, if it's possible, is almost too true to the material and the character of Monroe Stahr. He captures the character's caution, reserve, reticence, prudence, and emotional stillness in such a way as to seem almost as if he's not in the film at all but rather a ghostly presence, as the dying Thalberg may well have been, pouring all his energy into the one thing he's incontestably best at—making movies. Excessively formal, perennially under wraps, pallid, with a flat affect and the hoping-to-please tenor of a boy being allowed to sit at the grown-ups' table, he sips water cautiously, gives orders in a soft voice, and floats elegantly but almost mistily through the film. It all feels played exactly as Kazan and De Niro had wished—and it's all lifeless and remote and tepid, as if De Niro were reading the part to himself rather than inhabiting it for an audience.

Stahr's milkiness is part of the story—his physical frailty, the incongruity of his talent and his manner, the longing of a young widower, the dreaminess of a man who can make up a beguiling film premise out of thin air or pinpoint the exact problem with someone else's story, the earthly disinterest of a man who works all day and leaves his beach house half finished partly because he's mournful and partly because he's other than (more than? less than?) human. Toward the end of the film he acquires a physical solidity, engaging in sex and boozing and even a fistfight (he doesn't get a single punch in and gets knocked on his ass with the first blow).

It's tough to fault De Niro's performance, as he appears to be doing exactly what was asked of him. He is meant to be vaporous, evanescent, vague, a ghost in the making. And that's precisely what he is. You're never magnetized by, compelled by, or even terribly interested in Stahr; the film's only red-blooded character, in fact, is the labor organizer, played by Jack Nicholson, who quarrels with Stahr and puts him down with that lone punch. De Niro manages to hint at an inner life, but that, too, is cloudy, couched, obscure. It's the imitative fallacy in action: an embodiment of wanness suggesting a wan character. It's no wonder at all that the picture and his role in it had so little impact.

If *Tycoon* was a setback, it was only a minor one. *Taxi Driver* was still dominating conversation about American movies when it premiered at the Cannes Film Festival—and, in the great tradition of the event, was booed not just once but twice: once upon screening, once again upon winning the festival's top prize, the Palme d'Or. And it was part of the mix on Oscar night 1977, when it was up for a mere four awards: Best Picture, Best Actor, Best Supporting Actress (Jodie Foster), and Best Original Score. (It would win nothing, as *Rocky* and *Network* dominated the evening.) Schrader and Scorsese may have been ignored by their peers in the Academy, but their film was clearly resonant in the culture. On Oscar night, Scorsese was under the cloud of a threat from an enraged fan of Jodie Foster, who said that if the actress won a prize for the things Scorsese had made her say and do, he'd pay for it with his life. The director was surrounded by FBI agents and was, not surprisingly, relieved when Beatrice Straight took home the Best Supporting Actress prize for *Network*. (Also swept aside in the evening's surge of recognition for *Network* was De Niro's performance; along with Giancarlo Giannini for *Seven Beauties*, William Holden for *Network*, and Sylvester Stallone for *Rocky*, he lost the Best Actor prize to Peter Finch, who had died that January of a sudden heart attack and was, with Bernard Herrmann, one of two prominent figures nominated posthumously that night.)

But his real trouble, Scorsese later confessed, was internal. "I was crazier when I finished *Taxi Driver* than when I began," he told Schrader. He was spiraling downward into a nightmare of drug use, adultery, hubris, paranoia, and anxiety. He was doing it all daily on the set of the most costly film he'd ever made. And De Niro was along for the ride.

SCORSESE FIRST ENCOUNTERED *New York, New York*, Earl Mac Rauch's screenplay about a love affair between a big-band singer and a saxophonist, in 1974 and thought it would be exciting to try an old-fashioned movie with a new-fashioned sensibility, to film a picture about New York on Hollywood sound stages, just as so many pictures he loved as a boy had been made, to infuse a film about the 1940s with the psychological depth that movies were permitting themselves in the 1970s. It was an ambitious project, entailing elaborate production numbers crammed with extras and filmed on huge sets filled with antique props and such. To do it properly would involve more time and money than Scorsese had ever spent on a film: twenty-two weeks (compared to the nine in which *Taxi Driver* was made) and at least $8 million, four times the biggest budget he'd ever worked with. It would star De Niro, who at that time had never played a truly romantic role, and Liza Minnelli, who had made only one movie in Hollywood—the expensive flop *Lucky Lady*—since winning an Oscar three years earlier for *Cabaret*.

And all of those obstacles, considerable as they were, paled in comparison to the real trouble the film was facing. Scorsese and De Niro decided that the film needed to be dark, lifelike, and probing, qualities they felt the script was lacking. And so they chose to rewrite it on the fly, like Butch Cassidy and the Sundance Kid leaping from a cliff into the unknown. "After winning the Cannes Golden Palm for *Taxi Driver*," Scorsese confessed, "we got big heads and felt that no script was good enough."

Scorsese hired his old friend Mardik Martin to rewrite the original script, first with Mac Rauch and later with his own wife, Julia Cameron, working alongside them. It was a combination guaranteed to result in conflict: the director's old friend and collaborator having to quarrel with his new wife, an aspiring screenwriter, over every passage in the script while the original writer shrank further and further back from the process. Cameron, pregnant with a honeymoon baby, clearly had the upper hand, but Martin had access to Scorsese and a shared history, and he risked their collaboration by warning his old friend that his wife was out of control and hurting the picture. Eventually, Mac Rauch just walked away and let the two of them have at it.

And have at it they did. As Cameron recalled, "We had a hard time agreeing on anything. 'I don't think she would do that, Mardik,' I would complain. 'Well, she certainly wouldn't do what you're having her do,'" he would reply. (As Martin recalled, it was even uglier: "She was insanely jealous of anybody who came next to Marty, very possessive. Marty was easily fooled by women.")

It would turn out that both of them were right to protect their points of view stubbornly, to be cynical about the viability of the work they were doing, and most of all to be afraid of where it was leading.

For starters, Scorsese somehow got it in his head that he could let his actors improvise, as they'd done so fruitfully on intimate, low-budget films such as *Mean Streets* and *Taxi Driver*, despite the fact that the scale of the production before him was massive. At first it worked. He began by shooting an intricate production number, "Happy Endings," which was meant to be the climax of the film. It was a ten-day job filled with color, music, elaborate camera movements, and artful cutting, and it so impressed studio executives when it was screened for them that they threw a party to celebrate the success of the film before they were even halfway through the shooting schedule. No less than Vincente Minnelli and George Cukor were among those invited to observe a day's filming, to watch the "Happy Endings" footage, and to toast Scorsese's achievement. For the movie-mad director, it was yet another crowning moment.

But there were few such golden days during the production. Right after shooting "Happy Endings," they spent seven or eight days on the beginning of the film, the encounter of up-and-coming saxophonist Jimmy Doyle and aspiring singer Francine Evans during the riotous celebration of VJ Day in Times Square and inside a jumpin' New York nightclub. As opposed to the carefully choreographed "Happy Endings" number, this crucial scene of the film was largely improvised by De Niro and Minnelli, who wasn't trained the way he was. "He would throw something at her," Scorsese said, "and she'd keep coming back. There was no stopping her." It was a risk, but it was one of those fortunate risks that proved successful in a way that doomed them: they made what everybody agreed was a great sequence: "That's when everything sort of fell to pieces and came together at the same time," Scorsese reflected. "It was beautiful."

In the wake of that lucky break, they began to believe that they could do the whole film as improv, despite the hugely expensive apparatus of the production. "We started to get cocky," Scorsese recalled. ("They went crazy," remembered Mardik Martin. "Everything got out of hand. Everyone was trying to improve it by improvisation.") Even De Niro, who loved to improvise within the confines of a character and a script, knew they were in trouble: "We'd all be trying to rectify things that just were not working," he remembered. "We were trying to shape it, but because of the improvisation we were always trying to build on what had been shot before or to fit a scene in if we shot out of sequence." In effect, each improvised scene had an impact on the scenes that surrounded it, and the problems that they initially saw in the script were multiplied, not lessened, by each change they made. The script ballooned into a crayon box of color-coded pages written and rewritten virtually the night before each day's shoot and then altered once again on the set. "It was a nightmare," said Mardik Martin. "I was writing up till the final frame. You don't make movies like that."

Later, wiser, Scorsese knew the truth of it: "It was a mess," he admitted. But at the time he couldn't see it, in part—in large part—because he was fueling himself on a combination of adrenaline, daring, hubris, and, by his own confession, drugs. Even though it's set in the big-band era, *New York, New York* was made under the influence of Hollywood's drug of choice circa 1976, cocaine. "I started taking drugs to explore," Scorsese admitted, "and got sidetracked." He had always used medication for his asthma and for some of his neurotic conditions—as a boy, he was known around Elizabeth Street as "Marty Pills." But now he was living the high life of success and hedonism, and little by little he became more lost in it.

He also wandered in another way, beginning an affair with Minnelli, who was at the time not only married (to Jack Haley Jr., whose father had played the Tin Man to Liza's mother's Dorothy) but already caught up in a dalliance with Mikhail Baryshnikov. What's more, not only were the star and her director engaged in an overwhelming movie production and a romantic liaison, but they began working on a stage musical entitled *Shine It On* (later renamed *The Act*) based on Minnelli's Francine Evans character.

And why not burn the candle in the middle as well as at both ends? So Scorsese agreed to make *another* film, a documentary about the final concert of the legendary rock group The Band, as soon as shooting on *New York, New York* was done. Jean-Luc Godard, one of Scorsese's heroes, famously declared, "I am cinema." Scorsese was pushing himself very near to a point where he could say truthfully, "Cinema killed me."

YET THROUGH IT ALL, while the cameras rolled for nearly six months, while the director strayed from his pregnant wife, while the female lead's private life fed the gossip columns, while the script metastasized into something its original writer no longer recognized and produced a film that not even three editors could make clear or smooth, De Niro bore an aspect of almost holy calm, dedicating himself to the details of the character and, in particular, losing himself in the study of the saxophone. Because it wouldn't be enough, of course, for Robert De Niro to play a musician; he was intent on becoming one—or, at least, on becoming indistinguishable from one.

Most actors who played musicians would be content to learn the postures and movements associated with an instrument, to do a dumb show of being an able player. But De Niro insisted that he actually be able to make music on the thing. He wouldn't ultimately be heard in the film—veteran big-band saxophonist Georgie Auld played the parts used in the soundtrack—but he was absolutely determined that nobody could tell that it wasn't him. "I wanted it to look like my horn," he explained, "that it belonged to me. I didn't want to look like some schmuck up there. You can do that, you can get away with that. But what's the point?"

De Niro started taking lessons from Auld, a tenor player who had been a member of orchestras led by Bunny Berrigan, Artie Shaw, and Benny Goodman during the big-band era and even had a group of his own in the 1940s, through which such future stars as Sarah Vaughan, Erroll Garner, and Dizzy Gillespie had passed. Auld, an old-time character who oozed jazz charisma, was cast as a big-band leader in the film and alternately marveled and bridled at his tutee's skill and dedication.

"It's incredible the way he learned," Auld said just before production began. "I'll teach him something on a Friday—a difficult passage—and by Monday morning, that son of a gun has learned it, he's got it down cold. He's got a little hideaway, and he practices until midnight. The kid plays a good tenor sax, and I mean it, and he learned it in three months." (In fact, De Niro practiced on an alto horn: "It's easier to carry around," he admitted.) Before long, though, De Niro's obsessive dedication found its way under Auld's skin. "He asked me ten million questions a day," Auld griped. "It got to be a pain in the ass." And: "He's about as much fun as the clap." Even Auld's wife, Diane, was overwhelmed: "We thought he was going to climb into bed with us with the horn."

Of course, De Niro had other things to do in order to create his character. "I thought of Jimmy Doyle as a fly stuck on flypaper," he explained, "trying to get himself free." In his copious annotations to the script and his research materials, he identified with the jazz musicians who were barred from improvising freely in the confines of the big-band sound and who had to join a union and obey a hierarchy of authority. He continually reminded himself to appear agitated and hyped up, to follow a beat or a melody that only he could hear, to tap his fingers on his knees or a table, to approach dialogue with musical rhythm. He fastened on such props of the jazz saxophonist's trade as reeds, tubes of ChapStick, handkerchiefs, and of course his horn. He made sure to remember that Doyle always had an eye peeled for the ladies, even when in the company of his wife. He devised a method of creating a drunken appearance by downing a shot of bourbon and spinning himself around in circles right before the camera rolled. And he repeatedly reminded himself that he wanted to convey in Doyle a combination of blunt directness and overweening ambition, whether it be for women, for music, or for money, regardless of whom else it affected or how. "I don't mind being a bastard," he told Minnelli, "as long as I'm an interesting bastard."

More than in any of his previous films, De Niro developed a aura of detachment and aloofness during the production of *New York, New York*. He had been installed, aptly enough, in Greta Garbo's former dressing room on the MGM lot, and he was extremely particular about the behavior around him on the set. At one point, he asked his lighting double, Jon Cutler, to replace another actor, who wasn't on camera, in a close-up shot of Doyle getting angry. "I can't get anything off that guy," he complained.

As on *Taxi Driver*, the producers had allowed a number of reporters to visit the set (this time with the proviso that they hold their stories until the film was actually released), and De Niro eluded them as long as possible and then gave them as little of his time as he could. "He didn't say it out loud," remembered Chris Hodenfield of *Rolling Stone*, "but he made it clear with his attitude that I was an annoyance to him by being there to interview him." The thick air and looming sense of dread that enveloped *Taxi Driver* seemed almost like a carnival in comparison to the tenor of the *New York, New York* set—and this one was a musical (or, as Scorsese continually insisted, "a film *with* music").

The darkness came shockingly to the surface late in the production, just around the time that, in real life, Scorsese's affair with Minnelli was discovered by his wife. While filming a scene in which Doyle flew into a rage and caused his pregnant wife to go into labor, De Niro worked himself into such a frenzy that he wound up needing medical attention. "I thought it would be funny to show, out of complete rage, an insane absurdity, where you get so nutty that you become funny, hopping mad," he said. "I saw that the roof of the car was low, and I hit it with my head, then I hit it with my hand." It was a hell of a thing, he admitted: "Liza got hurt, and I think I hurt my hand." The two of them, with Scorsese, raced from the studio to an emergency room. Drugs, adultery, hospital visits, miles of unusable film footage: *New York, New York* provided gossip pages with fodder for months. It would have to be a hell of a picture to make people forget all the whispers they'd heard.

But just as Scorsese let the film get away from him by turning it into a huge improvisatory exercise—"a $10 million home movie," as he called it—so did De Niro focus so much on the details of playing the saxophone that he let the characterization of Jimmy Doyle suffer. "I really worked on it very hard," he said of his saxophone playing. "But I wonder if I should have saved a little more energy for other things and just worried about what was going to be seen. I worked like hell on that thing."

THERE WERE OTHER distractions as well.

In the early part of 1976, De Niro and Diahnne Abbott visited Rome and stayed at the famed Raphael Hotel near the Piazza Navona. Some weeks after returning home from the trip, she discovered that she was pregnant. In April, in a rented meeting hall at the New York Society for Ethical Culture on Central Park West, they were married in a nonde-nominational service attended by, among others, Scorsese, Sally Kirkland, Elia Kazan, Harvey Keitel, Shelley Winters, Julie Bovasso, Joseph Papp, John Hancock, Sam Spiegel, Jay Cocks, Verna Bloom, and Paul Schrader, who, looking around the room, had the thought, "Everybody there was somebody who had helped Bobby to become a different person."

During the time he was shooting *The Last Tycoon*, De Niro rented a house in the Brentwood suburb of Los Angeles so that Diahnne Abbott and Drena, whom he had adopted, could join him there. "We would go to parties," Abbott recalled, "and people wouldn't be interested in me at all. They'd look at me as if to say 'Who *is* this woman?'

When they found out I was Bobby's wife, it was spooky to see how their attitudes would change."

De Niro, barely cut out for family life, was learning to negotiate a household that was already populated with nine-year-old Drena and the menagerie of dogs and cats that Abbott seemed always to have on hand. He found that he needed extra space around him, literally, and when it became clear that they would stay in Hollywood awhile, they moved from the Brentwood rental to a Bel Air estate where he really did have a hideaway—an outbuilding where he practiced the saxophone, studied scripts, and retreated into the silence that was a key to his concentration.

Even then, he was out of sorts. Accustomed to being able to flit in and out of scenes in the New York social world, he was entirely inept at the sort of socializing that was part of Hollywood life, where nights out often meant visiting friends and colleagues in their homes rather than, as in New York, meeting up at atmospheric actors' hangouts. Abbott loved to go out—she and De Niro were habitués of the Sunset Strip club On the Rox, where he liked to sit nursing Black Russians and watching the parade of celebrity flesh. But she also loved to entertain, which made her husband particularly ill at ease. "When De Niro is the host of a party," wrote a *New York Times* reporter who dined at his Bel Air house, "it has no center, no focal point."

They would invite the gang over—Scorsese and Cameron (whose pregnancy was just a month or two ahead of Abbott's), Brian De Palma, Paul Schrader, fellow actors such as Keitel, Peter Boyle, and Kathi McGinnis, chums from New York such as Steven Prince. But De Niro would stand apart, watching with the same stillness with which he'd carried himself as a boy and an acting student, becoming slightly ruffled when anything resembling excessive exuberance bubbled up in the house. At one dinner party, Boyle cracked up the guests by mooning a roasted turkey that Abbott placed on the dining table, and De Niro responded with a sheepish "Hey, hey guys, hey, that's too much." The life of the party he wasn't.

In October, huge with child, Abbott filmed a cameo appearance in *New York, New York,* playing a big-band singer performing a rendition of "Honeysuckle Rose," a brief moment that she infused with grace and glamour—even though she was hiding her very pregnant belly behind the artfully draped folds of her dress. (Told months later that her condition wasn't visible to the film's audience, she confessed that *she* could see it, though that might have been because she was "loaded" on pot on the night of the film's New York premiere.)

She went on to record the vocal track of the song at an LA studio in the presence of the film's stars. "I was standing in the box while they were getting ready," she remembered, "and I thought, 'What the fuck am I doing?' Liza Minnelli was there recording, and I felt it was going to be so embarrassing. My husband was there too, and I don't know if he thought I could sing. Liza was wonderful. She came into the box and said, 'Relax, you'll do all right.'"

On November 9, 1976, while the film was still shooting, the baby arrived at Cedars-Sinai Hospital: a boy whom they named Raphael, after the hotel in which he'd been conceived. De Niro was thirty-three, had an Oscar, was the magnetic center of the most talked-about movie of the year, was the star of a huge Hollywood production, and was already planning his next film, an epic story about the Vietnam War that would range from the mountains of western Pennsylvania to a prisoner-of-war camp on a fetid Southeast Asian river. He was married, and now he was a dad for the second time—once by adoption, once by blood. He had as full a life as he could ever have wished for.

And he had another iron in the fire: he was meeting a trainer regularly in a Los Angeles gym and taking boxing lessons. One way or another, he was determined to make a film about Jake LaMotta.

10

THERE WERE, OF COURSE, TWO ROBERT DE NIROS WITH public careers. De Niro the actor was becoming famous—which wasn't exactly the reason he had pursued an acting career to begin with, and certainly wasn't as delicious as a daily dish as it may have seemed at first. He was determined to keep the celebrity in check insofar as he could. (And, to be honest, insofar as he *chose*: being famous had been a great way to meet girls.) But even as his own work became known and praised and celebrated around the world, the younger De Niro remained as filially loyal to and boastful of the elder as ever.

In 1972, when the senior De Niro was granted a residency at the famed Yaddo art colony near Saratoga Springs, New York, he was driven up there by his son, who managed to squeeze his father's working materials and personal belongings into a sports car for the trip. Later on, when the younger De Niro became a magnet for news reporters and photographers, and maybe even art patrons, he made a point of showing up at his father's opening receptions, bringing much-appreciated attention to the work on display. (Once he showed up carrying the infant Raphael on his body in a baby sling, creating an even greater sensation than if he'd merely slipped in and smiled at people.)

Naturally, the elder De Niro was pleased with the higher profile granted his work by his son's reflected glory, but he was careful, too, to keep some space between himself and his art, on the one hand, and his son's work and fame, on the other. In 1976, he published a chapbook of poetry, in an extremely limited edition, entitled A *Fashionable Watering Place*—ninety-six pages of verse (revealing the influence of French Symbolists, Anglo-American Modernists, and, inevitably,

Greta Garbo) and drawings. At the beginning, where one might expect to find a dedication or some other note from the author, there was this: "These poems are by Robert DeNiro [*sic*], the painter, not to be confused with Robert DeNiro [*sic*], the actor, his son."

It wasn't a case of De Niro senior being jealous of or competitive with De Niro junior. There was real affection between them. Tom Mardirosian, a young actor newly arrived in New York at about the same time, knew the elder De Niro slightly from the artist's teaching stints at the State University of New York at Buffalo, which Mardirosian had attended as an undergrad. He recognized the painter one day at the YMCA and was charmed to learn how excited the older man was to share stories of Bobby's various successes, of which Mardirosian, like every other young actor on earth, was well aware.

Father and son saw each other regularly when they were in the same city. Usually that meant New York, but when Bobby started to spend more time in Hollywood, his father would visit him there (although he confessed to being overwhelmed by the tumult of Movieland socializing: "I ran to San Francisco to avoid the New Year's Eve parties"). And Bobby's paternal grandmother, Helen, was also part of the ménage, staying with her grandson and his family frequently after being widowed in 1976. (Young Raphael would later complain, as kids do, of having to sometimes share a room with his great-grandmother, only to have it explained to him by his father how lucky he was to be able to have visits from her; De Niro would always, but *always*, be loyal to his family and his oldest friends.) When Bobby acquired a beach house in Montauk, on the tip of Long Island, he petitioned the local council to allow him to build a studio on the property so that his dad could use the house as a place to retreat and paint.

For a while, the elder De Niro enjoyed the limelight that accrued to him through his son's success (his ex-wife, on the other hand, *never* did). But he admitted that there were limits to his appreciation. "I don't really like to talk about Bobby too much because he's very careful in talking about himself," he told one inquiring reporter. With another, he shared the view that his son's fame was a mixed blessing: "It creates a certain interest. But it can overshadow you. Anyway, the people he and I relate to are in two different worlds." Finally, he seemed happiest when he had nothing to do with it: "At first I was very excited about all the publicity Bobby was getting, but now we're kind of appalled by it. One of the nice things about a trip I took recently to Santa Cruz was to find students sketching from paintings I had done over 25 years ago, long before Hollywood became such a part of our life."

He was content to teach (throughout New York, as well as at various art schools and universities around the country), to live his life according to his own eccentric whims, and to make *his* art *his* way. His son might have to work within a market-driven field of expression, but the elder De Niro was never so constrained.

IF *New York, New York* had turned into a kamikaze mission for Martin Scorsese, *1900* had become the Hundred Years' War for Bernardo Bertolucci. The film wrapped in May 1975, after nearly a year of production, and the director was still editing it right up until the spring of 1976, when he finally brought it to the Cannes Film Festival in a cut that ran five hours and thirty minutes.

After Bertolucci trimmed twenty minutes, *1900* was released into several European markets as a two-part film. The sheer length of it overwhelmed audiences. Though business for part one was solid, part two saw a decline of more than 50 percent in ticket sales, meaning that fewer than half the people who saw the first part bothered with the second. With American distribution looming as one of the few remaining avenues to recoup costs that had metastasized from $3 million to more than $8 million, Bertolucci cut the film down to four and a half hours, but that wasn't enough to satisfy Paramount Pictures, which had contracted to pay him $1.75 million on the condition that he deliver a film of no more than three hours and fifteen minutes.

A battle was waged in studio offices and in the press—dozens of film critics and journalists, even those who weren't enamored of the movie they'd seen at Cannes, signed an open letter protesting such extensive cutting. Paramount finally agreed to distribute a cut of four hours and five minutes for a reduced sum. They debuted this version at the New York Film Festival in October 1977, and it moved into theaters a few weeks later, accompanied by mixed-to-hostile reviews.

—⁓—

THE WORLD DIDN'T receive *New York, New York* all that much better. United Artists banged the drum heroically, getting De Niro onto
the covers of *New York* and *Newsweek* on the very same day, with a
Rolling Stone cover and a *Time* feature appearing not long afterward.
Predictably, all of these pieces painted De Niro as an obsessive, reclusive, recalcitrant genius willing to go to extraordinary lengths to create
verisimilitude in his characterizations but equally stinting in personal
conversation and public revelation of private emotions, thoughts, and
information. Minnelli and Scorsese were trotted out for the press as
well, albeit far more cautiously, as rumors of their on-set romance had
circulated widely ("Do you think there's going to be a lot of that kind
of shit?" a concerned Scorsese asked a *Village Voice* reporter who in-
quired about their affair).

On June 21, the film had its Manhattan premiere in a benefit for
the Film Society of Lincoln Center, and patrons who paid $100 (in
addition to contributing at least $1,000 annually) were invited to a post-
screening dinner party at the Rainbow Room, atop Rockefeller Center,
and an after-party at Studio 54. As with *1900*, what they saw was a
lengthy but compromised film. At just over two and a half hours, *New
York, New York* was shorter than Scorsese's ideal version of the material
by about ten minutes—more or less the length of the "Happy Endings"
production number, which had been shot at the outset of the production as a mark of its bona fides and then cut at the last minute as being
out of tenor with the film that, gropingly, Scorsese and his collaborators had created.

The day after the benefit, the film opened to paying audiences. It
didn't help at all that *New York, New York* followed *Star Wars* into theaters by four weeks. Maybe movie audiences never would have wanted
what Scorsese had given them—a dark and furtive musical filled with
emotional trauma and feel-bad sentiment. But they certainly weren't
buying it in the summer of Luke Skywalker. And the movie press
wasn't much kinder.

Like almost everything else in *New York, New York,* De Niro's Jimmy
Doyle is too much, too much. Right from the get-go, with his garish

shirt and white slacks and saddle shoes and Juicy Fruit gum, he's like a snapped power cable whipping around menacingly and spitting out deadly sparks—a spectacle, for sure, but never warm or inviting, and in the main not sympathetic. In the opening scene, he throws himself again and again at the reluctant Francine Evans like a dog dropping a ball at the feet of a master who refuses to throw it. He tries smooth talk, charm, humor, frankness, practical reasoning, and even bare-assed honesty—"Do I look like a gentleman in this shirt and these pants?" And it's all bootless. She says no again and again, and she means it, even when she smiles on him and gives him a hint that there may be a yes in their future. You want to like him—his energy is fun, his patter is amusing, his smile is, as ever, a killer-diller—but he's exhausting.

As he woos her, he reveals even more tools. He can play the sax, of course, and he regards her with big, inviting eyes as he does so. When she finally succumbs, he smothers her in a wave of kisses that total more in number than all the screen kisses De Niro had engaged in up to that point combined. He expresses his affection as a suffocating need to control her. And his marriage proposal consists of a throw-away request and then a melodramatic mock suicide, lying behind the wheels of a taxi on a snowy road and imploring the driver to back up over him rather than have to endure her indecision.

Jimmy Doyle is like Johnny Boy with musical talent and a little less sociopathy, a creature of impulse and rock-headed certitude who will listen only to himself, even when he's demonstrably doing harm. He's summed up beautifully by the bandleader Frankie Hart (George Auld) in conversation with Francine: "He's not only good, baby; he's a bitch. He blows a barrelful of tenor. But he's some kind of a pain in the ass."

He's also an egoist who can't get comfortable with his wife's professional success or, when she breaks it to him, the news that she's having a baby. Learning he'll soon be a father, he stiffens and recedes into shadows, and when their professional trajectories split—she becomes a recording star, while he continues to push into new musical forms with his more adventuresome colleagues—the baby becomes the focus of his resentment, an external thing that he can point to as the cause of his frustration rather than seeking the root of the problem in himself. During an explosive argument in his car that looks like a genuine fight,

Jimmy finally shouts, "Did I tell you to have that . . . that . . . goddamn baby?" It's a savage indictment—of himself, really—that no subsequent words or deeds will ever be able to erase.

Like Francine, we're taken with and exhausted by Jimmy in equal measure, and we get frustrated with his ceaseless self-concern, to the point of wanting to be done with him for good. Even when the baby arrives—the birth triggered by that final violent argument—he cannot rouse an affectionate, fatherly response: "It's a him?" he asks, as if his child is an extraterrestrial. And when Francine becomes a movie star as well as a singing star, he can't resist taking little digs at her—with a smile on his face—for the sorts of films she makes, referring to "Happy Endings" as "Sappy Endings" just to let her know he feels superior to her and her work.

The film is clearly not intended to be a traditional love story, but the repeated inhumanity of the central character becomes punishing to watch, in part because De Niro is so committed to delivering it raw; none of Scorsese's often beautiful film craft—the sets, the costumes, the fluent camera work and editing—can make it go down smoothly. There's one beautifully sweet touch, though, provided by the pregnant Diahnne Abbott, who graces her sole scene with the languid air of Billie Holiday and a richly ironic line of dialogue. Presumably intimate with Jimmy, who's avoiding her clumsily because Francine is in the night-club in which they're performing, she lifts an eyebrow and asks him, "Family night?" If only the rest of the film were so amusing and light.

PERHAPS BECAUSE OF the mountain of ballyhoo the film accrued during its production, critics were poised to slash at it. And when it turned out to be at best a mixed success, the reviews were accordingly harsh, perhaps overly so. In the *New Republic*, Stanley Kauffmann referred to *New York, New York* as "one more of the current avalanche of disappointing US films," declaring it "occasionally repellent but mostly tedious and trite." Vincent Canby in the *New York Times* dismissed the film as "nervy and smug." Christopher Porterfield in *Time* accused the film of seeking "a dividend of unearned nostalgia," and Penelope Gilliatt's review in the *New Yorker* was simply entitled "Ho Hum, Ho Hum."

That said, De Niro was largely unscathed. Although Kauffmann declared him "a nuisance," Gilliatt called his work "the best thing about the film," praising his performance as "firm, rapid." In *Newsweek*, Jack Kroll agreed: "De Niro is astonishing, funny, crazy, angry, hurt, musical, and manly." But even in admiration, the critics cited flaws: Porterfield, commending De Niro, explains that "the reason such a character, as written, should interest us remains as elusive as the Lost Chord," while Canby compared De Niro to "a man running to catch a train, only to pass right by it."

To make the torture complete for Scorsese, *New York, New York* bombed at the box office, grossing less than $14 million. After a string of critical hits and a pair of commercial successes, the director felt slapped. The life he had been building for himself had crumbled to dust: after discovering the affair with Minnelli, Julia Cameron had moved out with their baby daughter, Domenica; he had been replaced as director of the Minnelli stage play by old pro Gower Champion; and his use of cocaine and pills was escalating perilously, particularly once he took Robbie Robertson, guitarist of The Band, as his Mulholland Drive housemate and began to live in a twilight world between rock-and-roll and the movies. His situation, professional and personal, caused him to slip into a slough of guilt, shame, and despair: "For a time after *New York, New York* I had really been thinking of going to live in Italy and making documentary pictures on the lives of saints for the rest of my life." He would, in fact, find his penance in the movies, but saints wouldn't have anything to do with it.

DE NIRO, in contrast, skated on virtually unharmed by the critical and commercial failure of three straight films. Ironically, his stock had actually risen. In the wake of *The Last Tycoon*, *1900*, and *New York, New York*, he was esteemed as much as ever, if not more, for demonstrating a desire to stretch himself, to test his abilities, to avoid repetition, to seek opportunities to work with the best directors. His next project was yet another important step in that vein.

Even though he had managed to avoid conscription during the 1960s, the Vietnam War hovered over De Niro's early career like an evil spell. In *Greetings,* he and his friends were intent on dodging the draft; in *Hi, Mom!* he was either a Vietnam veteran or someone who wanted for obscure reasons to pass as one; Bruce Pearson of *Bang the Drum Slowly* was a Vietnam veteran; *Mean Streets* included a scene in which a returning vet was feted by Johnny Boy and company; and *Taxi Driver*'s Travis Bickle had, of course, been honorably discharged from the Marines. But none of those films was truly a "Vietnam movie" of the sort that Hollywood became interested in making a few years after the fall of Saigon.

In the late 1970s, with the shooting war and the danger to American lives over, Hollywood sifted through the war in a number of significant films. In 1975, Francis Coppola chose to follow his triumphs of the two *Godfather* films and *The Conversation* with *Apocalypse Now,* a free adaptation of Joseph Conrad's *Heart of Darkness* co-written with Hollywood's favorite right-wing gun nut, John Milius. The film centers on a Special Forces officer sent upriver from Vietnam into Cambodia to kill an American colonel who has gone rogue. Coppola had wanted to make the film for years; the first drafts were written as early as 1969. With his standing in the industry unimaginably high (and, crucially, the shooting war and the danger to American lives over), he would be able to do it. In late 1975 he sent De Niro the script in the hope that he'd be interested in the role of the assassin, Captain Benjamin Willard. Coppola had already courted Steve McQueen, Gene Hackman, Jack Nicholson, and Al Pacino for the part; like them, De Niro passed.*

Hollywood had seemed assiduously determined *not* to mention the war while it was being fought—it was glanced on in some youth culture movies, it was explored in a few documentaries (including the controversial Oscar-winner *Hearts and Minds*), and it was celebrated as a necessary and patriotic enterprise in John Wayne's 1968 flop *The Green Berets.* Now, though, the culture seemed ready to grapple with the conflict, as well as its contradictions, cost, and aftermath, in the medium of feature films, and Hollywood's famously liberal creative community

---

* The role came down to a choice between Nick Nolte and Harvey Keitel, and the latter got it, but not for long: during production, he quarreled sufficiently with Coppola that he was replaced by Martin Sheen, and all of his footage was reshot.

was happy to do the job. By the time Coppola was preparing to go off to the Philippines to make his movie, there were several Vietnam films in the works. Hal Ashby was making a film about veterans adjusting to life back in the States that would eventually be called *Coming Home*; Robert Stone's *Dog Soldiers,* with a completely different spin on the experience of veterans, was being made by Karel Reisz;* Sidney Furie would soon be at work on *The Boys in Company C,* which would follow a Marine unit from basic training through to Vietnam; and no less than Burt Lancaster was set to appear in *Go Tell the Spartans,* which dealt with the earliest phases of American involvement in Southeast Asia.

As he continued with his insanely busy schedule and kept his eye on the Jake LaMotta film that he was determined to make, De Niro was offered a role in yet another Vietnam movie, which was written and would be directed by Michael Cimino. It was a big, sprawling film, following a group of steelworkers from their tiny western Pennsylvania hometown, with its old-time macho ways, to the unimaginable horror show of the war, during which three of them would be taken prisoner by the Viet Cong and forced to play Russian roulette against each other, and finally back home to the war's haunting aftermath. Cimino, who had written Clint Eastwood's *Magnum Force,* the second of the Dirty Harry series, and written and directed Eastwood and Jeff Bridges in the comic thriller *Thunderbolt and Lightfoot,* had a military background—he'd served six months as an Army medic in the early 1960s. But the film he wanted to make wasn't about the war so much as it was about the idea of the war and its impact, particularly on those who were touched immediately by it: young men who went into service under muddled assumptions and the friends and loved ones they left behind and, sometimes even more harrowingly, came home to.

The film was called *The Deer Hunter,* for a favored recreational pastime of its protagonists, and De Niro was asked to consider the role of Michael Vronsky, the most charismatic, exacting, and quietly heroic of the characters, a man of iron principles, determination, and inchoate, bottled-up emotions. He liked the script, particularly its focus on the

---

* And would star Nick Nolte.

ordinary lives of ordinary men thrust into extraordinary circumstances, and he was pleased to know that it would be shot on location in Pennsylvania and Thailand, which was subbing for Vietnam. Still, his initial response was nevertheless to beg off, explaining that *Raging Bull* was his focus. But neither that script nor his preferred director, Martin Scorsese, was in good enough shape to start work on that film, and so he agreed to go to war with Cimino.

It would in some ways be a homey shoot. At De Niro's suggestion, Cimino went on to cast a number of New York actors in key roles even though they didn't have much screen history: Christopher Walken and John Savage as Vronsky's fellow enlistees, Nick and Steven; Meryl Streep as the girl whom Vronsky loves but who has eyes only for Nick; and Streep's real-life beau, John Cazale, as Stan, one of the steelworking gang who *doesn't* enlist.* Cazale, who had appeared so memorably as Fredo Corleone in the *Godfather* films and the gunman Sal in *Dog Day Afternoon*, was being treated for stomach cancer and was considered too high a risk to cast. But De Niro made it possible for him to appear by offering a portion of his own salary to pay for insurance against the possibility that Cazale couldn't fulfill his part. Cazale did, in fact, finish the production, but he didn't live to see the film released or to make another picture. He died at age forty-two, a celebrated performer—and a footnote in film history as a man who made only five films (the two *Godfather* films, *The Conversation*, *Dog Day Afternoon*, and *Deer Hunter*), all of which were nominated for Oscars as Best Picture.

CAZALE APPEARED ONLY in the Pennsylvania parts of the film, which were shot in a number of small towns in the region and in the mountains of the Cascade Range in Washington state. The town in the film, Clairton, was a composite of some eight hardscrabble steel towns in four states along the Monongahela, Allegheny, and Ohio Rivers (not including, ironically, the actual Clairton, Pennsylvania). Before the

---

* At least one unnamed crew member told a national magazine that De Niro had, in fact, pulled rank on Cimino and cast many of these key roles himself.

production, De Niro, almost predictably, made his way to Mingo Junction, Ohio, just south of Steubenville, where he spent weeks "soaking up the environment. I talked to the mill workers, drank and ate with them, played pool . . . I studied how steelworkers talk and dress, how they relate to their job, their towns and their friends." He sought permission to put in a shift in the inferno of their workplace, but none of the mills would permit him (later, to shoot sequences on the factory floor, he and his fellow cast members were filmed among actual mill workers in asbestos suits and hoods within shouting distance of furnaces stoked to 3,000 degrees).

Also predictably, he did other sorts of research: reading about deer hunting, the war, the procedures of Special Forces, and the experiences of veterans, especially POWs. He spoke at some length with several former prisoners of war, tape-recording their testimony so he could study it. He put together lists of the things he would have as a hunter and sought ways to personalize his military uniform with graffiti on the helmet and custom-made patches. He immersed himself in military jargon and in the linguistic peculiarities of the Allegheny region: *gum bands* instead of *rubber bands*, *y'uns* instead of *you all*, and such mild oaths as *jagoff* and *jagging around*. He learned the words to Frankie Valli's "Can't Take My Eyes Off of You" for a barroom sequence and wrote choreographic notes to himself about how he wanted to move as the song played. During the homefront portions of the film, he lodged in a Holiday Inn in Pittsburgh and remained simultaneously visible and invisible as he devoted himself to the weeks of shooting. A *Time* reporter watched him pass through a lobby full of college students unnoticed, even though he was at that very moment on the covers of *New York* and *Newsweek* ("De Niro does not look like De Niro," the article noted).

It was a long shoot—Cimino was sufficiently obsessive about his vision for the film that, for instance, he had his crew turn summertime Mingo Junction into a winter scene by stripping the trees of their leaves, just one of the gestures that would lead to the film's budget to balloon from $8 to nearly $13 million. And the stateside portion was by far the easiest. When the crew went to western Thailand to shoot the Vietnam sequences along the Khwae Yai River—the famed River

Kwai of the Oscar-winning film's title—they were hit with almost the same nightmares of logistics, scarcity, and bad weather that had been plaguing Coppola's *Apocalypse Now* production in the Philippines for more than a year. The two months of work called for in the original production schedule extended to nearly double that, and a mood of gloom struck the cast and crew. "Everybody who was going to Thailand was worrying about that," De Niro said of the protracted shoot. "They heard about the monsoons and the jungle and being forced to shut down the filming. Subconsciously, it affected people. I know it did me. I said, 'I'm going to get stuck here.'"

He distracted himself by indulging in the local culture, sampling opium, peeking in on Thailand's infamous Patpong red light district, dining on dishes that he'd never tried before. But he maintained strict fitness, both to keep himself honed for the grueling scenes of combat, imprisonment, and escape and as part of his ongoing effort to make *Raging Bull*, which still didn't have a script or a bankroll. Along with Savage and Walken, he did his own stunts. Some were simple, at least on paper, such as shouting abuse at their captors or even at one another to keep themselves focused on survival, particularly as they were forced into games of Russian roulette. But even small things proved rigorous in the execution. "It's very hard to sustain that kind of intensity," De Niro recalled. "I mean, we were really slapping each other; you sort of get worked up into a frenzy. It's a very difficult thing to do. It took a long time." Walken's character was repeatedly slapped by one of his captors, and the sequence required take after take, pushing him beyond mere acting. As Walken recalled, "When somebody belts you 50 times, you don't have to fake a reaction. You don't have trouble shaking."

It was a genuine trial. "We spent a month in that river," De Niro remembered, and Cimino put the cast through real agonies. "The circumstances were genuine," Walken said. "We were up to here in water, it was hot, and we'd been doing it a long time. There were mosquitoes. There were rats."

And there was a near catastrophe. As part of their escape from the POW camp, the characters played by De Niro and Savage were to be lifted off a bridge by a passing helicopter that they'd managed to signal for help. Cimino and his cinematographer, Vilmos Zsigmond, were inside the helicopter, along with a pilot whom the Hungarian-born Zsigmond remembered "spoke very bad English." ("Perhaps that helped," he said rosily afterward. "Perhaps it gave an aura of confusion and frustration to the scene?") Whether as a result of a language barrier, weather conditions, or the sheer scale of the setting in which he had to operate, the pilot didn't want to bring the craft too low, but he somehow got the runners of the helicopter caught in the cables from which the bridge was suspended.

"Without knowing it," De Niro remembered, "the pilot lifted the whole bridge and twisted it around while John Savage and I were hanging from it. . . . I looked down and shouted 'Drop!' and we just dropped. We came up out of the water and saw one of the stunt guys standing on the bridge and lifting the cable off the runner of the helicopter. I thought that was it. I thought the helicopter would drop down on us." The irony, he reflected later, was that he was risking his life for no demonstrable purpose: "The thing is, sometimes the stunts don't even look like anything on film. Or the shot isn't even used. You could die doing one of those stunts, and when people look at it, they don't even know how dangerous it was." It was his first true action role, and he had to at least consider that some aspects of verisimilitude weren't worth pursuing.

THE PRODUCTION WRAPPED in early 1978, and Cimino went into an editing process that, like Bertolucci's on *1900* and Scorsese's on *New York, New York,* was not only protracted in itself but guaranteed to produce a protracted film. When he finally delivered a cut to Universal Pictures, which had paid for it, executives were chagrined to see that the opening sequences—the steel mills and bars and bowling alleys, a wedding and a hunting trip—lasted well over an hour. Audiences would have to sit through more than half the length of a standard feature film before the truly harrowing Vietnam sequences, the stuff they could sell, began. The whole picture ran beyond three hours, and although the studio wanted him to trim as much as an hour, Cimino was adamant that he needed every minute of it. There was a brief war between the director and the executives—at one point Cimino threatened to "kidnap" the negative of the film from the editing rooms. At great pains, he managed to put together a compromise edit of two hours and forty minutes, and, perversely, the studio didn't like the result. "We had every right to cut it," said Universal production boss Ned Tanen. "Instead, when the director took 20 minutes out, we told him to put it back."

But there were other pressures. Cimino and Universal knew that Francis Coppola was editing *Apocalypse Now* after almost a decade of development and production, and they felt that they had to beat that film into theaters or risk failure by comparison. What was more, the thinking around the studio was that *The Deer Hunter*, with its impressive length and punishing emotions, would need boosts from critics and awards to have a chance of succeeding in ticket-buying America. They decided to release the film in two stages: first, a one-week, nine-screening, reserved-seat engagement in New York at the end of the year, to qualify the film for Academy Award consideration, then a normal if slow rollout in February, just after Oscar nominations were announced. The unusual strategy prompted wags to start referring to *The Deer Hunter* as "Apocalypse First" and to encourage some of the most egoistic tendencies in Cimino, who told the *New York Times* that Coppola had visited his New York hotel suite to declare, "You beat me, baby." And his ego was, if anything, bolstered by the response the film got from critics and audiences.

Perhaps because he had been raised an only child, De Niro always seemed most at home playing loners. The only clubbish fellows in his canon to this point—Bruce Pearson and Johnny Boy Civello—stood markedly apart from their peers through the happenstance of health, in the former's case, and temperament, in the latter's. No character that De Niro had ever played was truly part of a crowd, laddish, one of the boys.

Michael Vronsky, though, is at least partly that sort of fellow, one of a close-knit group of friends who do virtually everything together: work, hunt, drink, chase girls. It's a small town they live in, which partly explains it, and there's a shared ethnic identity, which they all take seri-

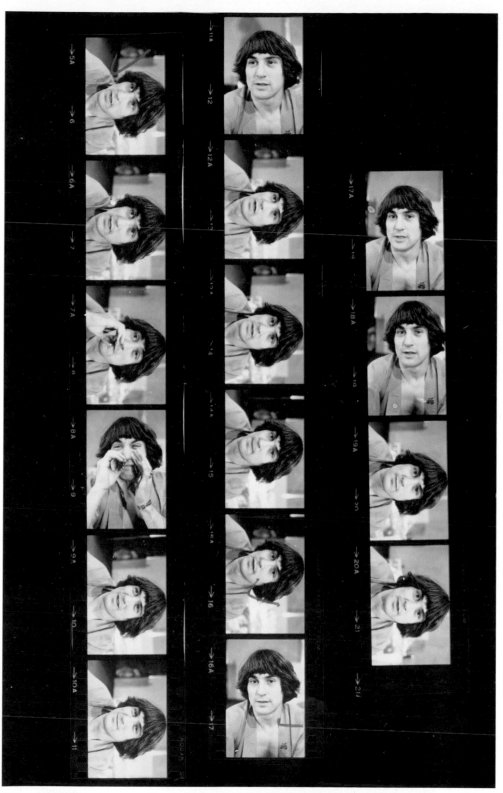

Circa 1970, the many moods of a *Noisy Passenger* (*New York Public Library*).

Prodigy: Robert De Niro Sr. seated with Josef Albers and standing with Hans Hofmann *(author's collection)*.

Kid actor: nineteen years old, with a crewcut, in *The Wedding Party*, filmed in 1963 *(Photofest)*.

Neighborhood guys: with Harvey Keitel on the set of *Mean Streets* (MPTV).

Film geek: Martin Scorsese at NYU *(Photofest)*.

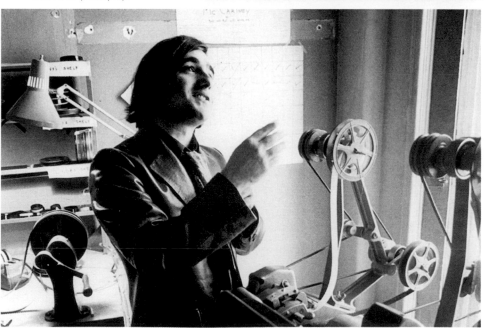

Men of respect: with Francis Ford Coppola on the set of *The Godfather, Part II* (*Photofest*).

The taste of victory: celebrating his *Godfather II* Oscar while filming *1900* in Italy (*author's collection*).

TAXICAB DRIVER'S LICENSE
EXPIRES: MAY 31, 1976

ROBERT A.

DENIRO

Hack Number

265216

See Other Side For Any Restrictions

NEW YORK CITY TAXI and LIMOUSINE COMMISSION
87 BEAVER STREET, N.Y., N.Y. 10005 - MOSES L. KOVE Chairman

03852

"I'll work anytime, anywhere." (*author's collection*).

Brain trust: with Martin Scorsese on the set of *Taxi Driver* (Kobal).

Old Hollywood: with Jeanne Moreau and Elia Kazan on the set of *The Last Tycoon* (Kobal).

Family man: with Diahnne Abbott on the *Mike Douglas Show* *(Photofest)*; and with Drena De Niro, Jack Nicholson, and Anjelica Huston at the New York Film Critics Circle Awards dinner *(Getty)*.

Beauty and the beasts: with Jake LaMotta and Meryl Streep *(ImageCollect)*.

Many happy returns: celebrating his birthday on the set of *The Deer Hunter* with Michael Cimino (in sunglasses) *(Photofest)*.

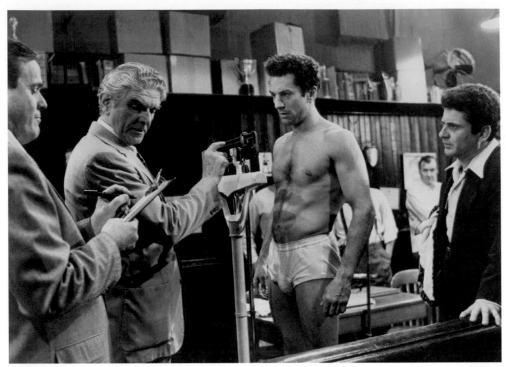

The two Jakes: before and after his weight gain in *Raging Bull* (Kobal).

ously (you could watch a hundred Slavic movies and not hear as many cries of "Na zdorovie!" as *The Deer Hunter* squeezes into three hours). But there's an anxious, clutching quality to their camaraderie: they *need* the reassurance of one another. Even Michael, the "weirdo" with the strange ideas, is part of a team, shaking hands with all of his work colleagues and even slapping their backs while they shower. For the first time in his acting career, De Niro felt truly knit into an ensemble.

Of course, top-billed and famous and, in truth, the title character, De Niro played a man who truly is first among equals. Michael's car, his house, his philosophy of hunting, his romantic longing, his military activity, his escape plan, his efforts to keep his friends alive, his determination to see his promises kept, his ferocious temper, his posttraumatic shock: it's all the centerpiece of the film. The picture is filled with fine acting, and Streep, Walken, and Cazale are especially memorable. But De Niro is in almost every sequence, and your gaze is drawn his way even when he's in a crowd. It's impossible to conceive of the film without him.

Fascinatingly, De Niro moves between his three chief co-stars in an embodiment of Michael's personality. With Streep's Linda he's courtly and moony, staring longingly, making a drunken pass, and watching with stoic reserve as she lights up around Walken's Nick. With Nick he's intimate and fraternal, going so far as to declare the unique sanctity of the bond he feels with him (and, ultimately, telling him explicitly that he loves him). With Cazale's Stan he's judgmental, scolding, and short-fused, and, in a gesture of hostility that threatens to rip apart the communal band, even dangerously violent.

There's a happy Michael who shoots pool as if he's fencing with his cue stick, sings along to the jukebox, leaps over cars, bear-hugs his buddies, and races naked through the wet, cold night in a drunken ritual of purification before the hunt. But mainly there's the Michael of stern ethics, opaque dicta, and calculated action. His philosophy that a deer must be brought down with a single shot, his impeccable preparation for the hunt, his strong belief that the only way to do things is the right way define him and keep him alive and semi-sane, and all of them are embodied by De Niro with a steely certitude.

Michael has weaknesses: Linda, of course, who continues to move him and serve as a shining star even though she belongs to his best friend; his war wound, particularly his right eye, which he soothes by pressing the heel of his hand to it; his post-combat anxiety, which he can quell only by crouching in what's almost a combat posture, with his back to a wall; and his short fuse when it comes to Stan, who despite his sloppiness, neurosis, and selfishness is an integral member of the makeshift family.

But chiefly he is a figure of strength: landing a massive buck with a single shot, just as he prefers; caught up so ferociously in battle that he doesn't recognize Nick and Steven when they stumble upon him; slamming the table in a firestorm of rage as he rouses to turn the table on his captors ("You're gonna die, you motherfucker!" he shouts in an otherworldly burst of fury. "You're gonna die!"); offering himself on the altar of blood sacrifice when Nick, dazed by heroin and his own trauma, tries to communicate with him through the medium of Russian roulette. De Niro was trimming his physique and learning boxing to play Jake LaMotta while shooting *The Deer Hunter*, and the single-minded purpose of that formidable undertaking informs his work as Michael.

In contrast to De Niro's steeliness and muscularity, Walken's Nick, so slender and delicate you can't imagine him surviving basic training, is a sympathetic and gentle spirit, gliding stylishly on the dance floor, insisting on fair treatment for Stan when he needs to borrow Michael's boots to hunt ("What's wrong wit'chou?" he asks Michael defiantly), describing his love of the wilderness in simple, poetic terms. He's got mettle in him; unlike Steven, he keeps his horror under wraps when awaiting his turn at the Russian roulette table. Ultimately, though, after months of putting a needle in his arm and a gun to his head, he's drained, barbed, ugly. Yet even then, at the climax of the film, with him spitting in death's eye yet again after who knows how many times, a glow slowly enters his eyes, an affection, a love. De Niro has the more powerful performance, but Walken's is by considerable measure the more lyrical.

Streep is wonderful in what amounts to, like Walken's, a coming-out role: pretty and simple and sad and giddy and earnest and vulnerable and grateful and mournful. Linda is infectiously happy dancing with Nick at the wedding and tumbling tipsily around the bowling alley. She's stoic to the point of grimness when dealing with her boozy, violent father. And she's incredibly touching when she offers her body to Michael. "Can't we just comfort each other?" she asks him, but he demurs, mumbling, "I feel a lot of distance; I feel far away." The Russian roulette is what people remember, but Michael's initial rejection of Linda may be the most hurtful moment in the film.

One last note worth remembering: Cazale, in his final role before succumbing to cancer, brings a remarkable frankness and lack of vanity to the role of a small-town Romeo without the inner resources to hunt properly or serve his country. Stan is something of a clown and, with his half-cocked pistol, a danger to himself and his chums; he deserves some of the scorn Michael heaps on him. But Cazale finds humanity and even nobility in Stan. In a remarkable moment—one the studio surely would have trimmed if they'd gotten their way with the film—he stares at himself in a car window before the wedding, fixing his hair and his tux and finally deeming himself, as he has just dubbed the bridesmaids, "beautiful." It's impossible to imagine the brutal, self-absorbed Michael or even the sweet-natured, ethereal Nick engaged in so bare a moment of self-regard.

THE DEER HUNTER gave rise to violent debate between those who felt it bore a muddled streak of jingoism, those who read condescension into its treatment of middle America, and those—by far the largest cadre of critics—who saw its depiction of the Vietnamese as crude, cartoonish, and even racist.

But nobody in any camp could deny the power of its impact. "It shoves the audience into hell and leaves it stranded without a map," said *Time*. "This movie has qualities that we almost never see anymore. . . . [It] leaves us exhausted and fully satisfied," said *New York*. "A film of great courage and overwhelming emotional power," said *Newsweek*.

And De Niro was, once again, praised to the heavens. "De Niro's acting is perhaps his purest yet . . . terrifying . . . poignant and gentle," said Jack Kroll in *Newsweek*. David Denby in *New York* wrote that he "establishes the singularity and strength of Michael through a hundred shadings of irony, mockery and courtly reserve." Even Pauline Kael, starting to turn on De Niro after a long period of unreserved kudos, found power in what she saw as his failings: "He's lean, wiry, strong. Physically, he's everything that one wants the hero to be. (The only thing that's unheroic about him is that he's still using the cretinous grin that he developed for *Bang the Drum Slowly*.) . . . We have come to expect a lot from De Niro: miracles. And he delivers them—he brings a bronze statue almost to life."

In December, after its Oscar-qualifying run had finished, *The Deer Hunter* was named best English-language film by the New York Film Critics' Circle after three rounds of balloting and against such other candidates as *Days of Heaven, An Unmarried Woman, Coming Home, Interiors,* and *Who'll Stop the Rain?* (De Niro finished third in the Best Actor balloting behind Gary Busey for *The Buddy Holly Story* and the winner, Jon Voight for *Coming Home.*) In February, just before its proper release, it was the leader in the Oscar race, landing nine nominations including Best Picture, Best Director, Best Original Screenplay, Best Cinematography, Best Actor (De Niro), Best Support- ing Actress (Streep), and Best Supporting Actor (Walken). (De Niro responded to the news of his nomination with a bland statement issued by a publicist, but his mother spoke up for him, uncharacteristically, in *People* magazine: "I'm sure he cares that he was nominated," she said, "I don't think there's much competition.") It wasn't just the critics; moviegoers were drawn powerfully to the film, and it grossed nearly $50 million, an impressive sum considering its length and darkness.

Added together with the eight nominations for *Coming Home*, the success of *The Deer Hunter* ensured that the talk around the Oscars would be dominated by Vietnam War themes. A blowback was start- ing to be heard against Cimino's film, with claims that it distorted the facts of the war, that it demonized the Vietnamese, that it was anti- American or somehow cruelly patronizing of the ordinary people it depicted. Cimino had always argued that the film wasn't meant to be taken literally—"it's not realistic, it's surrealistic." *Coming Home* star Jane Fonda, who of course had her own complex history with Vietnam, the war, and American veterans, denounced *The Deer Hunter* as rac- ist and actively campaigned against the film. "I hope it doesn't win," she told a Los Angeles newspaper. "I haven't seen it—I'm afraid to. My friends told me about it, though, and I just think it's amazing that good people can see the movie and not even consider the racism." As the awards approached, the critique of *The Deer Hunter* began to get louder; pickets were planned for Oscar night.

But the film continued to rack up accolades within the industry: a Golden Globe as Best Picture, and top prizes from the Directors Guild and American Cinema Editors. At the Academy Awards, no less a personage than John Wayne, gaunt from his second significant struggle with cancer, was called upon to open the evening's final envelope, in what would be his last-ever appearance on a telecast of the Oscars. Inside was the name *The Deer Hunter.* The film won five prizes altogether, including Best Director and Best Supporting Actor; both Cimino and Christopher Walken took time to thank De Niro in their acceptance speeches.

De Niro wouldn't get to make a speech of his own, however. Along with Warren Beatty (*Heaven Can Wait*), Gary Busey (*The Buddy Holly Story*), and Laurence Olivier (*The Boys from Brazil*), he watched as Jon Voight took the Best Actor trophy for *Coming Home*, duplicating the feat of his co-star, Fonda. Backstage, Fonda continued to rail against *The Deer Hunter* to the assembled journalists as Cimino, with his two Oscars, was led into the press area. Fonda chose not to sour the evening with debate, leaving Cimino once again to defend and explain a film that had just won the top prize in American cinema. "We're not trying to rewrite history," he said, "nor should we. We're moviemakers. We're not doing newsreels; that's what movies are about."

Besides, he had his mind on his next film, which looked to be even bigger, an epic based on an extraordinary episode of civil strife— indeed, near civil war—that had occurred in the American West. United Artists had contracted to spend nearly $8 million to produce the picture, which at the time was known by the name of the conflict it depicted, the Johnson County War. Eventually Cimino would entitle it *Heaven's Gate.* And he didn't offer De Niro a part in it, because after almost five years of development, *Raging Bull* was finally a go.

11

A FTER THE BARRAGE OF PRESS FOR NEW YORK, NEW YORK, De Niro wouldn't consent to a significant interview with a journalist for some four years. But on March 9, 1981, just three weeks before the Academy Awards for 1980's films would be handed out, he sat patiently and answered hours of questions about his work at great, careful length. His interrogators weren't members of the film press, however. They were attorneys representing Joseph LaMotta, brother of the boxer Jake, who was suing De Niro, Scorsese, and the Chartoff-Winkler production company over the way he was depicted in *Raging Bull*.

De Niro had finally, against significant obstacles, managed to realize his dream of seeing Jake LaMotta's story to the screen, inspiring Scorsese to create a film even more potent than *Taxi Driver* and delivering a performance that was recognized as an all-time classic the moment it appeared. But in the arduous process of wrenching a filmic narrative out of LaMotta's painful story, liberties were taken, corners were cut, and mistakes were made. Joey LaMotta had a legitimate beef and his lawsuit had merit, and all De Niro could do throughout his hours of legal deposition was explain how the film came to be and express regret for an unpleasant legal situation he could only bring himself to refer to as "this."

RAGING BULL HAD its genesis more than a decade earlier, when Jake LaMotta, his childhood friend Pete Savage (né Pete Petrella), and journalist Joseph Carter collaborated on the book of the same name, with an eye toward making it into a film. Savage was already something of a moviemaker, having written, produced, and directed about a half dozen independent films, including three—*The Runaways* (1965) and *Cauliflower Cupids* and *House in Naples* (both 1970)—that featured LaMotta in key acting roles.

As soon as the book appeared, Savage knocked together a screenplay and spent a few years trying to get somebody interested in making it. In 1974, when De Niro was still bouncing back and forth between the Italian set of *1900* and New York, where he was incubating new film projects, usually with Scorsese, Savage got a copy of the book and the script to him.

De Niro had no interest in the script, but the book genuinely compelled him. Written in the first person, but in an engaging combination of crude street talk and thoughtful reflection, *Raging Bull* was an astonishingly frank and disturbing account of a deeply flawed man's emotions, struggles, attitudes, and deeds.

LaMotta had been one of a generation of Italian American champion and near-champion boxers that included the likes of Rocky Marciano, Rocky Graziano, Two-Ton Tony Galento, Tony Janiro, and Carmen Basilio, among many others. He was a street kid—born in Philadelphia, raised in the Bronx—who was in trouble with the law from a young age and first learned the rudiments of boxing in reform school. Billed as "The Bronx Bull" and "The Raging Bull," he was known for an ability to take a beating from opponents and keep charging forward. He held the world middleweight title from June 1949 to February 1951, and he was famed especially for his six bouts with Sugar Ray Robinson, fought over nine years, the second of which marked the great Robinson's first professional loss (and the only one of the six bouts in which LaMotta was victorious). When he retired in 1954, just before turning thirty-three, LaMotta had a career record of eighty-three wins, nineteen losses, and four draws, scoring thirty knockouts in the process: an estimable record by any account.

But the story of a once notable boxer was hardly the stuff of a compelling movie or book. In fact, what fascinated De Niro about LaMotta wasn't his boxing record (De Niro never was much of a sports fan) but his astounding confessions and his fearless attitude toward physical punishment, which, the book indicated, he seemed to invite almost as a form of self-imposed justice, punishment for his bad deeds.

To wit: Jake LaMotta stole, sometimes using near-lethal violence in the act; he forced himself on women so violently that it would have been no exaggeration to call it rape; addled with jealousy and resentful at being domesticated, he beat his wives, causing one to miscarry; he went so far as to use his hands on Savage, his closest friend, who avoided him for decades after an especially grisly encounter; he defied the local gangsters who ran the boxing game until it became clear that he would get a shot at the title only if he cooperated with them, and then he threw a fight at Madison Square Garden to line their pockets and pave his way to the championship; after retiring and, naturally, squandering all his money, he served time in a Florida prison for the sexual corruption of a minor, an underage girl who worked as a prostitute from the harbor of a nightclub that he owned (albeit, he always maintained, without knowing what she was doing or how old she was); in total he was married seven times ("I hate the Jews so much I married three of them to make them miserable," he joked), most lately in 2013, not long before his ninety-second birthday.

In his book, LaMotta confessed bluntly to much of this, and *that* was the fellow who fascinated De Niro: brutal, self-lacerating, darkly driven, haunted by his misdeeds, painfully honest about his failings, funny and crude and sardonic and ugly and real. And he was a boxer, which meant a film about him would allow an actor to take his place in a great tradition of Method-acting pugilists, from John Garfield in *Body and Soul* through Paul Newman in *Somebody Up There Likes Me,* from such near-Method performers as Robert Ryan in *The Set-Up* and Kirk Douglas in *Champion* to, chief of all, Marlon Brando, who created such an ineradicable icon of Terry Malloy in *On the Waterfront* as to set the standard portrayal of the weary palooka without ever stepping into a ring or donning gloves. Playing LaMotta would allow De Niro to claim the championship of acting, if such a thing could be said to exist. It would be the role of a lifetime . . . *if* the character could be captured in a screenplay.

—◦◦◦—

As REVEALED IN the pages of the March 1981 deposition and the extensive production files of both De Niro and Paul Schrader, the process of forging LaMotta's autobiography into a screenplay took the better part of eight years, with at least a half dozen complete drafts, some radically different from the others, and a similar number of writers. And it also entailed gaining the trust, interest, and funding of a movie studio, which would naturally be loath to back a picture about such a disagreeable protagonist, and of a director, Martin Scorsese, who was struggling with demons, dark deeds, and destructive habits of his own.

At first it seemed a straightforward matter. De Niro had broached the subject of a film about LaMotta with Scorsese as early as 1974, when the director visited him in Parma during the production of *1900*. Scorsese wasn't interested at first—"A boxer? I don't like boxing," he said. But De Niro wasn't deterred. In 1976, while making *Taxi Driver*, he acquired the rights to the book from LaMotta and Savage during dinner at the famed Times Square Italian restaurant Patsy's.* Later on, while finishing *Taxi Driver*, Scorsese read the book and, his head turned by the darkness of the story and the themes of guilt, purgation, and redemption, agreed to at least pursue a film based not on the Savage-Clary screenplay but on the book itself. The job of adapting went to Mardik Martin, who was working for Chartoff-Winkler on a number of projects. Delayed by the chaos of *New York, New York* and his work on Ken Russell's *Valentino*, Martin didn't submit a draft until March 1978; then, with significant input from De Niro, he turned around another draft the following month.

At this moment, the project was known as *Prizefighter* and conceived of in a radical fashion: De Niro wanted to stage it as a play on Broadway, directed by Scorsese, and then film it simultaneously. "I had an idea to do a play to be done like a movie," he said, "and we almost did it in *Raging Bull*. We were gonna do it as a play and then we were

---

* Joseph Carter, who was not part of any phase of the movie deal, would later sue LaMotta and Savage for a percentage of the film rights. And decades later, Savage's daughter would sue MGM, which would eventually own the film, for her late father's portion of its total earnings, claiming copyright infringement on Savage's original work. In 2014, the U.S. Supreme Court agreed to adjudicate the matter.

gonna shoot it once we had mounted it. We were gonna shoot it in the day, and do it at night, and theatrically what we would get out of it during the day would apply to the scenes in the play at night, and I was just curious how it would have turned out, because on a movie it is looser. In a play you have cues and it's locked."

But Martin's scripts weren't, they felt, sharp enough for either the stage or the screen; in fact, they read like straightforward transcriptions of the book. And really, the whole thing was moot because Scorsese was a wreck. His woes made up a sobering list: *New York, New York* had flopped; he had been removed from the stage play that he had been working on with Liza Minnelli; his marriage to Julia Cameron was over and she and their daughter were living in Chicago; he had a new roommate in Robbie Robertson of The Band, whose rock-and-roll lifestyle and circle of friends unhealthily amplified Scorsese's increasing use of cocaine and pills; he had managed to make *The Last Waltz*, a great concert movie, but he was unable to focus on a new feature film; he was living in Southern California like a vampire, bouncing between superficial relationships with women, watching movies all night with a coterie of chums in a garage with blacked-out windows, drugging himself awake and asleep. It got so that the alcoholic John Cassavetes, still a mentor and a fan, upbraided him at a Hollywood party for wasting his talent.

De Niro kept trying to interest Scorsese in the film, but Scorsese was in no shape to work on it, and the inadequacy of the scripts gave him an easy out. Still, he didn't want to put De Niro off entirely. In the late spring of 1978, they decided between them that they would take the project away from Martin and give it to Paul Schrader, who had begun directing as well as writing films. De Niro visited Schrader on the set of his second film as director, *Hardcore*, and got him to agree to come to dinner with Scorsese to discuss the project. Schrader was doing his own thing, but agreed, reluctantly, at the price of $150,000 plus expenses, to have a look at the book and Martin's scripts and rewrite the film.

Right away, he knew that there *was* a good movie in *Raging Bull* but that Martin had been too faithful to the source material to find it. He began doing research of his own—he hired an assistant and did interviews with Jake LaMotta, his brother Joe, his ex-wife Vicki,* Pete Savage, and various other acquaintances, dug into newspaper clippings about LaMotta's career and post-boxing spiral, visited key sites in LaMotta's life, and watched kinescopes of LaMotta's fights. As he worked, Schrader came to believe that the problem with Martin's scripts—and with the film as it was being conceived—was that Savage had inserted himself overly into the Jake LaMotta story and was being granted a little too much input into the prospective film. As he explained to a Writers Guild arbitration board when the final credits for the film were disputed in 1980:

> *Mr. Savage had involved himself in the film project of "Raging Bull" just as he had in the book. In both cases, he had exaggerated his role in Jake LaMotta's life. It struck me that the true story of "Raging Bull" was not one of Jake, Peter and Joey but was a story of the "Fighting LaMotta Brothers." As young men, Jake and Joey were both better than average middleweights. Their personal and professional styles contrasted drastically. Joey was a dancer, Jake was a bull; Joey was a fast talker, Jake was painfully shy and inarticulate; Joey had a way with women, Jake did not. After two years of professional fights, Joey made the decision to give up boxing and manage his brother. Therefore, the drama of the LaMotta brothers: Joey had the freedom to give up boxing, Jake did not. Joey was able to establish a normal family life, preserve his body and mind—albeit from the sidelines. Jake, in some ways less of a fighter, could only go out and wear his opponent down. This sibling trade-off of roles and responsibilities I took to be the core and the theme of "Raging Bull."*

By the end of May, Schrader submitted a draft, which differed from Martin's in the use of key fight scenes to break up the domestic and psychological drama, and in framing the film with scenes of the older, retired, and out-of-shape LaMotta working in nightclubs. Then, after

---

* Her name would also be spelled "Vickie" and "Vikki" over the years in various publications and documents.

he finished post-production on *Hardcore*, Schrader spent five days in Palm Springs and Las Vegas working on a thorough rewrite, which he submitted to Scorsese and De Niro in early July. The character of Pete Savage was still in the film as part of a troika with the LaMotta brothers, but, Schrader felt, he had been whittled down to more appropriate dimensions.

Still, though, Scorsese remained elusive, unable to focus on a new film while his personal life whirled and deteriorated. Then, around Labor Day 1978 he hit rock bottom. At the Telluride Film Festival in Colorado, where he'd traveled with De Niro, Mardik Martin, and Isabella Rossellini, whom he'd started dating seriously and would soon marry, Scorsese collapsed. The whole group of them, Martin later claimed, were using some badly compromised cocaine on the trip, and Scorsese, his system almost entirely shattered by his unhealthy regimen, started coughing up blood and blacked out. He was rushed to New York and admitted to a hospital in grave condition, just in time for doctors to begin reversing the damage he'd been doing to himself. De Niro, who would prove over the years to be loyal and helpful to friends who hit health crises, particularly those involving drugs, came to see him in the hospital and put the idea of *Raging Bull* to him once again. Scorsese had originally been repelled because the character of Jake LaMotta seemed so dark and irredeemable to him. Now, though, at his own nadir, he could see the power of the project. "We could do a really great job on this film," De Niro said to him. "Do you want to make it?" Somewhere Scorsese found the resolve. "Yeah," he said.

They faced new problems, though, when they thought about shooting Schrader's script. For one thing, there was still the question of Pete Savage. Schrader had trimmed him down as much as possible but felt that the best thing to do was to remove him from the story altogether, a revision that De Niro, who had been working with Savage for almost four years, was loath to consider. Then, too, there was the brutality and frankness with which Schrader had imagined the film, culminating in a scene a couple of pages long in which the imprisoned LaMotta tries to masturbate by conjuring the women in his life, only to lose his erection when he recalls how cruelly he treated them all; add that to a scene depicting LaMotta becoming sexually active with Vicki before a fight but then dousing his erection with ice water to preserve his strength, and you had something that would be unimaginable to shoot or to screen—or, of course, to finance.

Money, pointedly, was the next obstacle to making *Raging Bull* at all. Chartoff-Winkler had a production deal with United Artists, where they had scored a tremendous success a few years prior with *Rocky* (which had beaten out *Taxi Driver* as Best Picture at the Oscars), and they were already engaged in *Rocky II* for the studio. With this kind of leverage, Irwin Winkler felt able to convince the studio to budget as much as $18 million for *Raging Bull*, even in the wake of *New York, New York* and the poor performance (which, to be fair, nobody blamed on De Niro) of *1900* and *The Last Tycoon*.

On a wintry day late in 1978, Winkler had Steven Bach and David Field, relatively new production executives at United Artists, accompany him to a meeting with Scorsese and De Niro at Scorsese's East 57th Street apartment. The pair had read Schrader's most recent script and had some legitimate concerns, and they wanted to at least pay the would-be star and director of the film the courtesy of having a meeting to discuss them. Bach, as he would later write, had significant issues with the script, which he called "brutally depressing and depressingly brutal." And he wasn't very comfortable in Scorsese's apartment, which, because the director had only just decided to move back to New York, had the bare-bones feel of a dorm room and was filled with mysterious and vaguely creepy friends and hangers-on.

Bach was further disquieted when he realized that one of these odd folks, a skinny guy in jeans and bare feet who wandered in from another room and greeted the executives in near silence, was in fact De Niro, who sank into a chair in the living room and contributed not one word to the ensuing conversation. After Winkler pitched the film to them, Bach allowed Field to take the lead in stating the studio's objections to and hesitancies about the project. For one thing, *Rocky* had created a new fad for boxing movies, and in addition to its sequel there were as many as a half dozen other fight films in some stage of production—a lot of competition, in other words.

There was also the matter of censorship, which Schrader's script would surely entail. United Artists would not put its name on an

X-rated film, as that designation had come to be associated with hard-core porn; they would find it impossible to book an X-rated film into normal theaters or, indeed, to advertise it in newspapers. *Raging Bull* would have to be delivered as an R, Field reminded them, and "this picture as written is an X."

"What makes you so sure this is an X?" asked Winkler.

"When I read in a script, 'CLOSE UP on Jake LaMotta's erection as he pours ice water over it prior to the fight,' then I think we're in the land of X," Field retorted.

Winkler explained that his team wasn't happy with the script yet, either. Field countered that UA's concerns went deeper than a few scenes. "It's the whole script. . . . We have a real question whether this story can ever be made as a movie any audience will want to see, whatever the rating."

"Why?" Scorsese asked.

"It's this *man*," Field replied. "The problem is will anyone want to see *any* movie about such Neanderthal behavior? Can any writer make him more than what he seems to be in the scripts we've seen?"

"Which is what?" Scorsese wondered.

"A cockroach."

The room went quiet. The deal was nearly dead.

Then De Niro spoke for the first time since his mumbled greetings: "He is not a cockroach. He is *not* a cockroach."

It all ended with the status quo in place: De Niro and Scorsese had a script that no one was ready to make.

BUT DE NIRO had made *Taxi Driver* happen because he determined that he wouldn't be dissuaded from doing it. Similarly, he had been focused on making *Raging Bull* for years, and he wasn't going to give up. He'd been working with the same boxing trainer who'd prepared Sylvester Stallone for *Rocky*, he'd maintained a strict diet and fitness regimen even while working on *The Deer Hunter*, and he had become increasingly involved with Jake LaMotta himself.

LaMotta had spoken with Mardik Martin and Paul Schrader, and of course with Pete Savage and his book- and screenplay-writing partners, but he and De Niro had developed an extremely intimate bond over the previous few years. And now that De Niro was focused exclusively on *Raging Bull,* the actor pushed the relationship even further, enlisting the old fighter to teach him to box in the exact style he had used; visiting the home LaMotta shared with his fifth wife so often that she mentioned De Niro in her 1979 divorce claim ("He was in the apartment constantly, for nearly two years"); probing him like a therapist about scenes from his past, about his emotions, fears, drives; trading admiration and understanding for the chance to dig into the very soul of the man. The movie, and LaMotta, had gotten under his skin.

De Niro was, LaMotta told a reporter as far back as 1977, "more qualified to be a psychiatrist than a psychiatrist. He goes very deep. He's telling me things about me that I never knew. I thought I was a pretty bad guy for a while, but he made me realize I'm not. I'm a pretty good guy." (He added, as if slightly unnerved: "Every once in a while I catch him looking at me. He studies me.")

In fact, De Niro relied on a combination of skills to comfort and probe LaMotta by turns. "I just kept repeating in his ear, 'You're not so bad, you're not so bad,'" he said. "People did not like him. Jake had done some low-life things that were supposed to be bad, but I felt that the drama in his life—with the brother and all that stuff—was real."

There was a limit to how far De Niro could get, even with great tact, sympathy, and sensitivity and a subject who was game to be mined. "I admired the fact that he was at least willing to question himself and his actions," De Niro said. "But what's he going to do? Should he be like a college professor and try to say, 'Well, I think the reason I did that was because . . . ?' He would talk that way sometimes, but he was more cunning. He'd look at you deadpan, or he'd laugh about certain things. He would protect himself sometimes, but then he would say, 'Aah, I was a son-of-a-bitch.'"

Finally the actor exhausted even himself: "I tried to ask him every kind of question," De Niro later admitted, "but it's hard to get somebody to be straight and honest about himself, because he is not even sure himself." Or, as he put it another time: "You can only go so far with people. Like I can only go so far with you here. There are things I can't tell you, I can't consciously or unconsciously give them up."

There was one thing, though, that LaMotta offered that gave De Niro and Scorsese the last impetus they needed to apply themselves successfully to the film. During one of their lengthy conversations, La-Motta stood up and started banging his head against a wall. As Scor-sese said, "De Niro saw this movement and suddenly he got the whole character from him, the whole movie. We knew we wanted to make a movie that would reach a man at the point of making that gesture with the line, 'I am not an animal.'"

WITH THEIR DEEP knowledge of LaMotta, and with Paul Schrad-er's suggestion that they jettison the Pete Savage character from the script, De Niro and Scorsese decided to make a retreat of sorts to the Caribbean island of St. Martin, where they planned to take one final stab at getting the thing right. They spent two to three weeks there— Scorsese suffering from the tropical climate, De Niro patiently taking care of him—working and reworking the pages. Somewhat reluctantly, because Savage was still connected to the project, they did as Schrader suggested: no trace of Pete was left in the final film.

Or, rather, no trace of a character named Pete was left. Fatefully, they took some of the actions, words, and situations involving the real Pete Savage and the character Pete Savage and ascribed them to the character (and, by implication, the real man) Joey LaMotta. Some of these were innocent things, but a few, including a beating given to a mobster acquaintance who was caught by Savage squiring Jake's wife to a nightclub when the fighter was out of town, amounted to defamation. To make matters worse, they had been so busy working with Savage, Jake, and Vicki that they somehow neglected to obtain Joey LaMotta's permission to use his name and likeness in the film. They had, in ef-fect, stolen his life rights and *then* defamed him, which was why De Niro wound up being deposed in a lawsuit.

But that, of course, was later, after the picture was made—which finally, on the basis of a new draft of the script delivered in early 1979, seemed likely to happen. This version, Steven Bach noted, bore no screenwriter's name and was accompanied by none of the usual paper-work the studio and the Writers Guild would normally rely on as they arbitrated credits and payments for the work. Rather, he remembered, the title page said, "in small type, tucked modestly in the lower-right-hand corner, 'RdN.'" De Niro had finally willed *Raging Bull* into life.

As EVER, his preparation took De Niro well beyond merely learning the script. There was the training, years of it, which put muscle on his eternally skinny frame and then taught him how to use it. He was in his mid-thirties and had never been athletic, but now he worked his body into something remarkable: rock-hard, sinewy, articulated. He had daily training sessions through long spans of 1977 and 1978, learning specifically from LaMotta about his idiosyncratic crouched style, his technique, his mentality; he took tutelage from Tony Mancuso, a journeyman fighter from Canada whose style sufficiently resembled LaMotta's that he was often hired by LaMotta's opponents as a sparring partner. And he kept extensive notes about what he learned: "*Don't* leap and lunge with wide punches which will ultimately miss . . . Be *constantly* aggressive and punch to the *body exclusively* . . . Try to rally when you have opponent on ropes or in the corner . . . Don't throw *one* punch at a time. *Combinations.*" Scorsese would meticulously storyboard and choreograph the fighting sequences like dance numbers (a nice carryover from *New York, New York* and *The Last Waltz*), but De Niro still felt he had to be able to improvise and create like an actual fighter in the heat of battle. Eventually his skill was such that he hurt LaMotta during sparring sessions and fought a few amateurs in competitive settings.

By early 1979 he was the spitting image of a younger professional fighter: he had scores of photos taken in traditional prizefight poses, and it's hard to believe that this was the same fellow who had played the gaunt Travis Bickle or the withered Monroe Stahr just a few years prior. He was toned and thick in the stomach, all muscle, without a cup of fat on his body. In and of itself it was a feat. And the transformation wasn't just in the body: he sat patiently for makeup that would provide him with a semblance of Jake LaMotta's mashed nose and ears and of the bruises, swellings, and other wounds accumulated in the ring, and he experimented with different ways of fixing his long, straight hair into something more like LaMotta's sloppy halo of ringlets. He watched home movies of the LaMotta family (some of these would be reproduced exactly for the film) and a rare film clip of LaMotta walking casually through his training camp ("It was only 25 seconds long," De Niro remembered, "but it was a big help"). And he worked on a bit of physical business that was never mentioned in the script but would be immediately familiar to anyone who knew the real man: Jake LaMotta was nearly deaf in one ear, so De Niro practiced leaning in to hear in such a fashion so as not to reveal the embarrassment of his hearing loss but still hear as much as possible.

In addition to his lengthy interviews with and observations of Jake, he spent time with Joey LaMotta, Vicki LaMotta (who had remarried but still often used her first husband's name), and Pete Savage, who had disappeared from the script but remained connected to the film— albeit at a remove—as a producer. (De Niro kept ongoing lists of questions to ask them all.) He took trips to the zoo to watch animals move; he listened to LaMotta's tape-recorded voice again and again to pick up its timbre and rhythm. He had every bit of spoken dialogue from the book *Raging Bull* transcribed so that he could acquire a full feel for Jake's idiom. (As proof of his mastery of LaMotta's argot, De Niro would take credit for a famous line in a scene in which LaMotta warns his first wife not to overcook his steak because "it defeats its own purpose." "I knew it didn't make sense," he said, "but in a way it did—it was like a double negative of some sort.")

As he always did, he annotated his script with monkish devotion, filling the margins with reminders about what to think, how to read a line, what gestures or facial expressions might create the effect he was after. Some of this work had begun before the final script was created. While making *The Deer Hunter*, he kept a notebook of thoughts, ideas, questions, and chores related to *Raging Bull*:

The way I talk is like poetry. The energy is what conveys this. I slur the words but the energy coming through is the important . . . Hated racket guys and tough guys . . . After I blew up [from drinking] I'd suffer a lot with remorse. "I don't know how I could do that." . . . My rage and frustration coming out through

the drink . . . Never lay around, always doing something: shop-
ping, golf, etc. . . . Never confided in people. Work it out myself.
Didn't want people to know my real problems.

But then, as each day's work presented itself, he kept up a running
account of his thoughts about the man he was playing and the scenes
he was filming:

I know I'm a fighter, I have a right to be a fighter and act like
one physically and in every way . . . Remember during all fights
you're not a fighter per se (or rather a fighter-fighter, style-wise).
You can only do so much. But you must have that intention, that
aggressiveness, and have fun with it and it will give you what you
need. Just concentrate on knocking the motherfucker out and keep
watching him, for any opening, and keep my block up . . . Re-
member, I just scare them looking at them . . . My humor doesn't
go over too well with these people—or people in general. Except
those who know me really well . . . I'm cold and distrustful with
people I don't know or am not close to but with family and friends
a little looser . . . Remember I'm paranoid. DON'T TRUST NOBODY!

While De Niro built this uncannily thorough physical and psychological portrait, Scorsese prepared to shoot the fight scenes with almost
heroic creativity and energy. The film may not have as much boxing
action in it as, say, *Rocky,* but it had more than a lot of fight films; as a
result, Scorsese planned to shoot inside the ring for ten weeks, a stretch
necessitated partly by the intricate motion and cutting he planned to
execute, partly by the exertions being asked of the actors in each take,
each of which would be repeated multiple times (De Niro got into
the habit of attacking a heavy bag just before the cameras were set to
roll so that he'd look appropriately sweaty and pumped), and partly
because he and his crew had to jerry-rig harnesses, dollies, and cranes
that would allow them to get the images he saw in his head.

It was grueling, sometimes comically so—at least to Scorsese, who
wasn't inside a boxing ring under hot lights pretending to fight all day
for months. "It was really funny," he said. "I was talking to Bob two

days in a row, and he said, 'What do I do in this shot?' I said, 'In this shot, you get hit.' And we went on to the next one. I got that one all worked out, and then he said, 'What about this one?' I said, 'In this one, you get hit!'" (Later Scorsese admitted, "It was excruciating for me to watch him because of the way we worked—every agonizing detail he'd go through, I'd feel for him.")

Throughout this period, Scorsese established a visual style for the picture: garish, close-in, unblinking. The prevailing metaphor came in the exaggeratedly loud and blinding pop of photographers' flashbulbs, which burst around LaMotta like firecrackers. There was frequent use of speed changes, with the imagery alternately slowing down ("I had to shoot the punches in slow motion or you wouldn't see them," Scorsese explained), and speeding up to give a sense of the adrenalized heat of battle. He had learned quite a bit of his arsenal of cinematic ideas by studying the films of the English director Michael Powell (especially *The Red Shoes* and *Tales of Hoffman*), and he shared some of the fight scenes he shot with the older filmmaker, who provided him with an artistic epiphany. Watching some early footage of De Niro in the ring, Powell remarked to Scorsese, "There's something wrong: the gloves shouldn't be red." In fact, he said, the scenes shouldn't be in color at all. At first Scorsese balked at the idea: "This from the man who had red all over his own films, which was where I'd got it from in the first place!" But after conferring with his cinematographer, Michael Chapman, who acknowledged that he felt that the color photography seemed drained of detail somehow, Scorsese got the permission of his producers to shoot the film in black and white.*

BEFORE THE SHOOT BEGAN, De Niro bided his time in New York, socializing with actors (along with Al Pacino, he attended a party at Lee Strasberg's house at which the Japanese Grand Kabuki troupe was feted), and he agreed to appear in Cambridge, Massachusetts, to ac-

---

* Given the raw scenes he was filming, this choice nicely mirrored that of Alfred Hitchcock, who shot *Psycho* in black and white during the greatest period of color photography in his career so as not to alienate audiences with garish displays of bloodshed.

cept the annual award of Harvard's Hasty Pudding Club ("I'm a little unhappy there's no pudding in this," he quipped while accepting his brass prize). In April he went to Los Angeles for nearly three months of shooting boxing sequences. By mid-June he was back in New York to spend a similar amount of time shooting scenes of life outside the ring during LaMotta's boxing years. In Los Angeles, LaMotta was an almost daily presence on the set, reminding De Niro about fighting strategy, attitude, posture. But when they went to New York, LaMotta was asked not to follow them. "When we did the acting stuff in New York, we didn't want him around," De Niro explained. "He understood, because you don't want the guy to come over and say, 'That's not the way I did it.' You feel his presence and all your energy is drained. You feel like you're doing it for the approval of someone else."

Instead, he had two other people to work with, actors who had been discovered for the film from almost literally out of nowhere and who would play the roles of Joey and Vicki. It was the Jake LaMotta story, but, following Schrader, Scorsese and De Niro had built the movie around three characters, and these actors would wind up sharing virtually every scene with De Niro that wasn't set in the ring.

At times it seemed like the roles would never get filled. Casting director Cis Corman was put on the hunt for likely types and found nothing. It was De Niro, in fact, who turned up an actor who might play Joey. Watching a little-seen mob movie from 1975 called *The Death Collector*, he was struck by a fiery actor playing the lead role. De Niro couldn't know it, but the fellow had actually been a child TV star in the 1950s, then a professional musician in the 1960s (he played guitar for Joey Dee and the Starlighters), and then, until appearing in *The Death Collector*, half of a Martin-and-Lewis-inspired comedy duo. He had only made the one film, it hadn't done anything, and he had finally quit showbiz altogether and was running an Italian restaurant in the Bronx. His name was Joe Pesci. Near the end of 1978, not very long before shooting commenced, De Niro and Scorsese called him to find out if he was interested in auditioning for the part of Joey LaMotta.

"How they found me in that restaurant, I don't know," Pesci said. He had truly given up chasing a career as an entertainer, he explained to De Niro in that first phone call, and he didn't feel that he was up to the job. "I told him I didn't think I wanted to do it, that I wasn't interested. He said he'd come and talk with me." They had dinner at Pesci's restaurant, Amici's, and De Niro brought along the script. "Robert told me, 'It's a good role, not a great role,'" Pesci recalled, "and I told him I didn't want to go back to acting unless I got a part that proved I was good." He was grateful for the opportunity, of course, but he was still reluctant: "I figured they should give it to a working actor who really wanted it."

But it turned out that they wanted him, and as soon as he was on board, Pesci began helping the production in ways nobody could have imagined. He helped them cast the role of Salvy, the wannabe neighborhood gangster charged by the local Mafia boss with putting the squeeze on the LaMotta brothers. Pesci persuaded Scorsese and De Niro to audition his old comedy sidekick, Frank Vincent, a pompadoured guy from Boston who was also a former lounge musician and who had also appeared in *The Death Collector*. In their nightclub act, which they performed as Vincent and Pesci between 1969 and 1975, "I would abuse the audience, and Joe would abuse me," Vincent remembered. And, in fact, *Raging Bull* depicted a brutal beating of Salvy by an enraged Joey LaMotta.* But real life lent a hand here: the former partners hadn't broken up amicably, so there was some genuine mistrust and sour emotion for them to draw upon in their scenes.

And then Pesci solved another problem for his new bosses. Cis Corman and her team had been working for long months to find someone to play Vicki LaMotta, who first met Jake when she was a neighborhood girl of fifteen and he was a married man some ten years her senior. Within a few short years they married, and she bore him three children during their time together, which coincided with his rise, his ascension to the title, his decline, and eventually his imprisonment. Vicki, who lived in Florida and was cooperating with the production, was still a bombshell in her late forties, and Corman had been charged with finding "a young Lana Turner" to play her. But she was getting nowhere.

One night Pesci walked into Hoops, a discotheque in Mount Ver-

---

* This scene was one of the reasons Joey LaMotta sued the production; in reality, it was Pete Savage who'd put the fellow represented by the Salvy character in a hospital.

non, New York, just north of the city, and he saw a picture of a girl on the wall that startled him: "a dead ringer for Vicki," he later said. He found out she was a nineteen-year-old Yonkers girl named Cathy Moriarty who was working as a model in the garment district, and he tracked her down.

"He wanted a picture of me for Marty for the film," Moriarty remembered, "and I said, 'Yeah, yeah, sure,' thinking it was one of those modeling jobs where all they really wanted was for you to take your clothes off." She agreed to meet the director and star at their midtown offices, and after she made a favorable impression, they asked her to continue coming in. "I would go down to the city and read for them," she recalled. "It was like taking private acting lessons. They never once said that I had the part or anything, and I know they were seeing other actresses, too."

It would be a huge risk, giving such a big part in a major studio production to someone who had never acted professionally, but De Niro was particularly struck with her. "She had a feeling and an aura you will seldom find in professionals," he said. "Sometimes amateurs are better to work with because of their instincts. . . . If you're doing a theatrical play, it gets difficult. But for a movie you can repeat the scenes." They tried all sorts of things to test her range and focus, and she never faltered. "She was totally natural even if we were doing nothing," De Niro remembered. "She was comfortable," Scorsese added. "She was so at ease it was incredible." They screen-tested her in February 1979 and hired her the next day.

COMBINED, THE BLACK-AND-WHITE cinematography, the post–World War II setting, the stifling lower-class milieu, and the unknown faces (which included even De Niro's, remade by his fitness regimen and the discreet prosthetics) imparted a neorealist quality to *Raging Bull*. The footage seemed almost to have been captured without the camera (and, of course, the audience) being noticed by the people on the screen. The craft that went into it was exquisite and exact, but there was a rawness and immediacy that made it feel almost like an invasion of the characters' privacy.

De Niro, taking advantage of the greenness of his co-stars, coaxed them into startling, unrehearsed displays of emotion. During a scene in which Jake, off-camera, confronts Joey with an accusation that he'd slept with Vicki, De Niro wasn't provoking the energy he sought from Pesci, so he came at him with a twist, changing the line "Did you fuck my wife?" to "Did you fuck my mother?" and startling Pesci into a genuinely confused and immediate response. ("When you see the film again," Scorsese laughed, "look at Joe's reaction!") He would get Pesci riled by repeatedly interrupting his takes with questions about trivial details until, Pesci remembered, "I'm hot, I'm ready to go."

Moriarty, too, confessed that "some of the scenes with Bobby actually made me nervous," particularly those in which Jake comes at Vicki with violence; De Niro would play them differently each time. "I began concentrating so much on not getting hit or how to go with punches that I thought, 'I'm never going to be able to say my lines,'" she said. The resultant fear and confusion she conveyed were, naturally, exactly what the moments called for. Scorsese and company also pointedly kept Moriarty from meeting Vicki LaMotta, who visited the set a few times, until after the production was done. "Marty didn't want us to get together," the actress explained. "He was afraid she'd influence me. . . . It was difficult to play a woman I had never met, and knew very little about, but even more difficult to play a character seen entirely through Jake's eyes"—which, of course, was just what De Niro and Scorsese wanted.

They shot the domestic scenes in New York from mid-June to mid-August, and then they stopped—not because they were done but because De Niro was about to undergo another radical physical and psychological change for the part. He had chiseled himself into an uncanny simulacrum of a boxer, and now, following LaMotta's story, he was going to let that exquisite body go to hell. The production would shut down for four months so that he could put on fifty to sixty pounds and portray the retired, slovenly, heedless older LaMotta.

"I just can't fake acting," De Niro said. "I know movies are an illusion, and maybe the first rule is to fake it, but not for me. I'm too curious. I want the experience. I want to deal with all the facts of the character, thin or fat." It was another stunning commitment to a role, another stupendous transformation, and it was an important aspect of his attraction to the material to begin with. "To see that deterioration and to capture it on film was really interesting to me," he said. But he wouldn't take Hollywood shortcuts such as using padding or fat suits or makeup; he would turn himself, in a matter of months, from an Adonis to a slob, just as LaMotta had, albeit over a span of years. "I needed to feel Jake's shame at getting fat," he said. "To feel my feet hurt with the extra weight, to know what it's like to be short of breath and not be able to bend down to tie your shoes."

He'd always been skinny, but not because he was a picky eater: he was just cut out that way, lucky bastard. But now he was going to have to make work out of eating, and eating specifically to gain weight fast. "At first it was fun," he admitted. "I ate ice cream and everything I wanted—it's like part of the fantasy that one has about eating *everything*. I took a tour through France, from Paris to the Riviera, stayed in inns and ate. And for two weeks I was miserable, because as good as the food was, it's rich—you could eat only one big meal a day and then lie there, digesting it." But before long he had to go beyond the limits of comfort and *force* himself to eat: "After 15, 20 pounds, it was hard work. I had to get up early to eat a full breakfast and digest that in order to eat a full lunch and digest that in order to eat a full dinner. And lots of Di-Gel or Tums."

Aside from the unpleasantness of feeling constantly overstuffed, there were aspects to his new size that he hadn't anticipated: "I began to realize what a fat man goes through," he said. "You get rashes on your legs. Your legs scrape together. You feel your weight on your heels when you stand up. It was like going to a foreign land." But, he said, the results could not have been achieved any other way: "The internal changes, how you feel and how it makes you behave—for me to play the character, it was the best thing I could have done. Just by having the weight on, it really made me feel a certain way and behave a certain way." (Ironically, as De Niro was bulking up to play the gone-to-pot Jake, Pesci, who would appear in a later-life reconciliation scene between the brothers, had to thin out a bit to play the older Joey. They shared a meal at Pesci's old stomping grounds, Amici's, during the production hiatus, and while De Niro gorged, Pesci skimped.)

Production resumed for one day in the autumn so that they could get some intermediate shots of De Niro's weight gain; then he went back to overeating until December, finally topping the 215-pound mark that he'd been aiming for. Scorsese had planned to shoot the later sequences in Los Angeles, doubling for Florida, and he quickly learned that he was no longer dealing with the same sort of actor he had had in front of the camera earlier in the year when they created the boxing sequences there. "Bobby's weight was so extreme that his breathing was like mine when I'm having an asthma attack," Scorsese said. "With the bulk he put on he wasn't doing forty takes, it was three or four takes. The body dictated. He just became that person."

The film wrapped just as the year ended. Scorsese took a break to energize for the six to eight months of editing, sound work, and scoring he would undertake for the film, and De Niro set about regaining his usual form—a daunting process. On a visit to Long Island, he put his son, Raphael, on a bathroom scale. "He was 30 pounds," De Niro said, "and I remember thinking that I had to lose two of him." He learned that he couldn't lose the weight as quickly as he put it on. "I couldn't go back to eating the way I normally did," he said, "because I would then feel sick. I had to let myself down gradually." When he showed up at the New York Film Critics Circle Awards at Sardi's that winter, he conspicuously ate but a small cube of steak for dinner; we know because the press were dutifully recording his diet, partly a testament to how much his personal commitment to the role captivated the world. For years, in fact, movie audiences would scrutinize each new photograph and film appearance to see if he had lost his *Raging Bull* fat, and it took him a decade and another severe physical transformation, this time for *Cape Fear*, to show the world that he'd done the trick fully.

As HARD AS De Niro had worked in making the film happen and in becoming—there really was no other word for it—Jake LaMotta, Scorsese would replicate his commitment and endurance in assembling the footage they'd shot into a film. Much of the editing was done by Scorsese and Thelma Schoonmaker—who had worked with him on his student film *Who's That Knocking at My Door?* and who would cut every one of his feature films after *Raging Bull*—in all-nighters in a cramped, makeshift editing room in Scorsese's apartment. They came up with certain aspects of the finished film's structure there, such as the slow-motion shots of De Niro dancing in the ring in a leopard-skin robe that ran over the title sequence and the concept of beginning the film with the older, fat LaMotta preparing to recite from, among other things, Budd Schulberg's script of *On the Waterfront* as part of a cabaret show ("De Niro playing Jake LaMotta playing Marlon Brando playing Terry Malloy," Scorsese noted)—revealing the end, or really the aftermath, of the story right at the outset.

United Artists executives had felt that surprising the audience with De Niro's weight gain would have more impact if it happened later in the film. But publicity about it had begun to leak out even while they were still shooting, and when the studio bosses finally got to see the film, in an unpolished but basically finished cut in July 1980, they saw the genius in the choice that Scorsese and Schoonmaker had made. "Scorsese," Steven Bach admitted, "had been right. He had feared that publicity about De Niro's weight gain would be too widespread and that audiences would sit through the film not seeing, not hearing, waiting only to see 'the fat man.' He undercut that voyeuristic fascination at the start, replacing it with curiosity not about an actor's stunt but about a man's life."[*]

That first screening of the finished film would become legendary for the reaction of Andy Albeck, the Russian-born (of Danish stock) film distributor who had made a personal fortune in the movie business in Asia before spending thirty years climbing the corporate hierarchy at United Artists, where he reigned as president at the time *Raging Bull* was made. He was a neat and punctilious fellow, a vigorous athlete, a stickler for protocol. If young, hip executives such as Bach and David Field had a hard time swallowing *Raging Bull*, even in a version tempered from Schrader's vision, they feared that Albeck would have a visceral reaction against it. When the film ended, Bach recalled, "the

---

[*] It was another echo, perhaps inadvertent, of Alfred Hitchcock, who had learned over time to put his famous surprise cameos near the beginning of his films so that audiences would stop looking for him and pay attention to the actual movie.

lights came up slowly in a room full of silence, as if the viewers had lost all power of speech." Bach saw Scorsese in the back of the room, cringing against a wall. "Then Andy Albeck rose from his seat, marched briskly to him, shook his hand just once, and said quietly, 'Mr. Scorsese, you are an Artist.'"

Indeed he was, but an exceedingly temperamental one, and ever more so as the long process of finishing the film dragged on. As the film's November debut approached, Scorsese was working day and night, literally, and becoming lost in the details of production. Near the very end, he threatened to remove his name from the film entirely because he didn't feel that the drink order of a background actor (played by the director's father, in fact) was audible enough. Irwin Winkler, who was deprived of the opportunity to throw a proper premiere for the film because Scorsese was taking so long to polish it, had had enough. "I said, 'People are going to look at this picture one hundred years from now and say that it's a great, great movie,'" he remembered. "Because you can't hear 'Cutty Sark,' which, by the way, everybody else says they can hear, you're taking your name off?' And he says, 'Yes, I'm taking my name off the picture.' I said, 'Okay, if you want to take your name off the picture, it's off, but meanwhile, the picture's going in to the lab.' And that was it. Obviously, he was a little emotional at the time."

In time, Scorsese would level out, and he would always feel that what he and De Niro had achieved in *Raging Bull* went beyond anything they'd ever done or ever seen in a film. "Look," he said soon after the release, "there's no way to do it unless you do it right. What other people might call 'honest,' we call 'right.' And that degree of honesty is highly painful. We had a similar idea in mind on *Raging Bull*, but I cannot verbalize that idea. The point is I'm standing there naked in this film, and that's all there is to it."

Raging Bull premiered on a single screen in New York, and the critical and public responses were an almost unanimous acknowledgment of the genius of it accompanied by widespread repulsion at the pith of it. (Among the viewers startled by the brutal tenor of the film was Jake LaMotta himself. After seeing *Raging Bull* for the first time, he said to his ex-wife Vicki, who was also at the premiere, "That wasn't me. I wasn't like that." "No," she replied. "You were worse.")

—◦◦◦—

T IME HAS LED us to believe that the foremost acting achievement in
Raging Bull is the fact that its leading man put on fifty or so pounds
to play the final portion of the film. But to be fair, putting on weight,
even in a binge, isn't as hard as what De Niro did with his body *before*
filming began, namely, building the scrawny frame of Travis Bickle
and Monroe Stahr into a body indistinguishable from that of a professional fighter fifteen years younger than himself. In his Everlast shorts
and old-timey gloves, the muscles in his belly, arms, and legs as hard
and sleek as marble, De Niro is every bit the picture of the prizefighter:
lithe, chiseled, not a cup of fat on his body, a thoroughly credible fighting machine.

When he moves in the ring—and Scorsese films the action in slow
and fast motion almost as often as at regular speed—De Niro doesn't
only move like a fighter (and, specifically, like Jake LaMotta) but *acts*
like a fighter: focusing like a laser on his opponent, trying to strate-
gize while engaged in combat, absorbing and meting out punishment
with a genuine sense of pleasure, relishing the challenge of the bout,
playing broadly to the crowd, too adrenalized and battered and in the
moment to absorb the things his cornermen are telling him. Not a decade before, De Niro played a baseball player of limited gifts and could
barely pass as a simulacrum of the real thing; in *Raging Bull*, he is one
of the most plausible movie-screen boxers ever filmed.

And yet, as ugly as things get in the ring—busted noses, eyes spinning after blows to the head, blood filling water pails and dripping
from the ropes—it is *outside* of it that LaMotta and his story are at their
most feral, ugly, and horrifying. Even when he tries to understand himself, LaMotta cannot separate one type of violence, one type of threat,
one type of fight from another (not for nothing, by the way, does the
film open with him staring at himself in a mirror, the first of several
such moments). In the first non-fighting sequence set in the 1940s, La-
Motta and his wife squabble viciously in an apartment no bigger than
a boxing ring, and he explodes, throwing over the table, dinner and
all, taking time to yell threats out the windows at the neighbor and his
dog. Soon he goads his brother into punching him in the face, hard,

without making any effort to defend himself. It's a remarkable, unblinking vision of masochism, a thirst for punishment and abuse made especially awful by the cockeyed grin De Niro sports throughout. He's proud that he can endure pain, even—maybe especially—outside of the professional setting in which it's expected.

Jake isn't entirely horrible. With his dapper 1940s wardrobe, gorgeous body, and killer grin, De Niro sells us on the fellow's appeal. LaMotta's "no Olivier," as he himself confesses in the film's brief opening scene, nor is he a Cary Grant. Among the local hoods there are several, including the unctuous Salvy, who have better manners, slicker clothes, more stylish miens. But Jake has panache, a sense of play, an occasional twinkle in his eye. On his first date with Vicki, when her ball disappears into an obstacle at a miniature golf course, he's positively endearing when he responds to her question "What does it mean?" by saying gently, "It means the game is over." You can see why, even if he weren't semi-famous, he'd catch a girl's eye.

But he is a haunted man, and the demons inside him will find a way out, whether in boxing or in some other medium. Often his behavior in and out of the ring seems identical. At times Scorsese slows down the action as the camera gets near to Jake's perception of things, so that Vicki and the men with whom she interacts seem as much of a threat to Jake as his opponents in the ring. De Niro indicates Jake's vigilance and predation with just a shade; he never *quite* reaches the verge of violence. But we know that there is hell brewing inside of him, and the slight churning behind his eyes is almost more frightening than anything he might unleash.

There is tenderness in him, as evinced by the remarkable scene in which he and the underage Vicki come close to having intercourse before his rematch with Robinson. Battered from the first fight (which was just a week or so prior), he insists that she get intimate with him: "C'mere, before I give you a beatin' . . . Touch my boo-boos." But then, aroused, he douses his passion by standing in front of a bathroom mirror and pouring ice water on his erection (which, *pace* United Artists brass, is never shown). The scene is a gripping blend of eroticism and denial, pleasure and punishment, classical beauty (both Moriarty in her lingerie and De Niro with his sculpted abs and chest) and grotesquerie.

But that one blissful idyll is wiped away by the things that happen when he succumbs to his worst impulses. Lost in a jealous rage, he beats his brother and then his wife, holding her face up before punching her, just as he had done to a recent opponent before destroying him. Even though he has thrown a fight and will later be convicted of procurement, this is the worst deed of his life, and it's no coincidence at all that he subsequently allows Robinson, in their final meeting, to beat him to a bloody pulp. "I done some bad things," he has told his brother, and at this moment we cannot imagine that he will be able to claw his way back into the good graces of his family, his God, or, most of all, himself.

The final space in which LaMotta's inchoate self-loathing is realized is the tiny isolation cell of a Florida lockup. There are no mirrors; there is no crowd; there is no opponent other than himself. Howling "I'm not that bad" like a beast, weeping (De Niro was never a good movie crier, but this is prime stuff), he beats his head at least a dozen times against a stone wall, as well as delivering literally scores of punches to it. (The wall, of course, was made of Styrofoam.) He has long sought to bring some sort of vengeance down upon himself, some sort of punishment for his perceived inner evil. Finally, he is left to do it himself. De Niro throws himself so fully into this moment, more violent than anything he's done to anyone else in the film, in or out of the ring, that we wince in sympathy for the pain in his hands, his head, and especially his heart.

Somehow, though, there is a path to salvation through this abyss. LaMotta emerges not so much a man intact as a survivor; life, like Robinson, has failed to knock him down. We leave him at the film's end just where we met him at the beginning, in a dressing room at the Barbizon Plaza Hotel, rehearsing his extremely dubious cabaret act in a mirror before donning his tux. Preparing for the stage, he recites some of the lines Brando spoke in the back of the car in the famous "It was you, Charlie," scene from *On the Waterfront*, an actor playing a washed-up fighter imitating an actor playing a washed-up fighter.[*]

---

[*] Even more vertiginous: for the second time in a half dozen years, De Niro will literally repeat dialogue first spoken by Brando in an Oscar-winning role in an Oscar-winning role of his own.

There's something strangely pacific in this bloated shell of a man finding a means to express something inside without resorting to violence, whether against a boxing opponent, a family member, or even (maybe especially) himself.

Despite the wishes of the studio executives who didn't want to green-light the film, we are not meant to empathize with LaMotta, not in the traditional sense in which a movie's lead character is an object of identification for the audience. Rather, his journey is emblematic of human struggle through pain, darkness, weakness, and temptation toward solace, strength, peace, and light. He *seems* to get there, heading off for the stage having pumped himself up with a few flurries of sparring jabs and the mantra "I'm the boss, I'm the boss, I'm the boss, I'm the boss." But he may be no more cured or healed than Travis Bickle, a cannon that has been strapped back into place but which might again get loose and threaten everything around it, including itself. As a character, he is not a warm figure or a figure of admiration. But he is so fully realized—and the frame in which he has been mounted so exquisitely wrought—that he has become an *immortal* character, and an astounding achievement by the men who conceived and created him.

It's hard to recollect a film so widely regarded as superb and so widely reviled at the same time. In *Sports Illustrated*, Frank DeFord put it this way: "Has any movie ever so utterly lacked soul and yet been so rewarding?" Like the executives at United Artists, critics were thoroughly repelled by Jake LaMotta and his story—and deeply puzzled about Scorsese's desire to bring them to the screen. In the *New Republic*, Stanley Kauffmann compared watching it to "visiting a human zoo," and in the *New Yorker*, Pauline Kael sounded a similar note, writing that De Niro and Scorsese "are trying to go deeper into the inarticulate types they have done before; this time they seem to go down to pre-human levels." (This was not proffered as praise.)

But even those who felt an almost visceral repulsion to the film acknowledged De Niro's power. "If you respond," Kael granted, "possibly it's not to LaMotta's integrity but to De Niro's; he buries the clichés that lesser actors might revel in. . . . With anyone but De Niro in the role, the picture would probably be a joke." Conceded Kauffmann, "Behind his false nose, he assaults us with force, engulfing force so sheer that it achieves a kind of aesthetic stature." In *Time*, Richard Corliss wrote, "When the film is moving on automatic pilot, De Niro is still sailing on animal energy." And David Denby in *New York* quite aptly captured the dichotomies the film presented to critics: "The truth is that De Niro doesn't want us to identify. His furious, cold, brilliant performances are a way of saying, 'Don't try to understand me, because you can't.' In *Raging Bull*, . . . he brings all his cruelly eloquent physicality . . . to a man with a soul like a cigarette butt. He is extraordinary and repellent."

For all these stellar notices, De Niro could be thin-skinned with anyone who didn't fully embrace the film. He annotated his copy of Pauline Kael's review, scribbling defensively in the margins, "That's the idea, that's right," and "So? That's right. That's him." And when he was told that the film was "a brutal portrait," he insisted otherwise: "*Raging Bull* is like a little domestic spat compared to what people can really do to one another."

DE NIRO RECEIVED an astounding array of letters from his peers congratulating him on his work in *Raging Bull*. Al Pacino joked that it was a bad precedent to write in admiration because he'd create the impression that he *wasn't* impressed henceforth if he *didn't* send a note. Jane Fonda described De Niro's work as "beyond any acting I've known about." Paul Newman wrote, "Dear Robert, I can't remember being humbled by an American actor for many a year. Well, you did that in spades. Can't add much to that."

But the public failed to respond, frankly staggering Scorsese, who was coming off a series of commercial disappointments. As was the practice at the time, the film received a slow rollout, starting with an exclusive run of several weeks in only four theaters and escalating gradually to a wider audience. While word of De Niro's performance clearly compelled some viewers to buy tickets, more people seemed to have been turned away by what they heard of the film's grim tone, foul language, open-eyed violence, and dark moral core. In a year in which such relatively breezy films as *The Empire Strikes Back*, *9 to 5*, and *Stir Crazy* dominated the box office, *Raging Bull* was a poor earner, grossing barely $23 million, placing it in twenty-seventh place among the year's releases, behind films such as *Popeye* and *The Jazz Singer*, which were widely seen as flops.

Money was never really the thing, of course. *Raging Bull* would surely find its redemption in the form of awards. Yet there, too, the film ran into rough seas. When the critics started polling themselves at year's end, De Niro walked away with almost every possible prize, being named Best Actor by the New York Film Critics Circle, the Los Angeles Film Critics Association, the Boston Society of Film Critics, the National Board of Review, and the Golden Globes (his only loss was in the polling of the National Society of Film Critics, which went instead for Peter O'Toole in *The Stunt Man*). Joe Pesci and cinematographer Michael Chapman also collected nice hauls of prizes. But Scorsese's sole accolade, for a film that in retrospect would be among the great masterpieces of a great director, received only the National Society of Film Critics award for Best Director; elsewhere, he lost out to the likes of Jonathan Demme for *Melvin and Howard*, Roman Polanski for *Tess*, and Robert Redford, who had made his directorial debut with *Ordinary People*.

And the Oscars turned out to be a mixed blessing for the *Raging Bull* team as well. In all, the film was in the running for eight Academy Awards: Best Picture, Best Actor, Best Supporting Actor, Best Supporting Actress, Best Director, Best Cinematography, Best Editing, and Best Sound, tying *The Elephant Man* for the most nominations that year. De Niro was the prohibitive favorite to win, in competition against O'Toole, Robert Duvall (*The Great Santini*), John Hurt (*The Elephant Man*), and Jack Lemmon (*Tribute*). But after the Golden Globes and the Directors Guild selected Robert Redford as Best Director of the year, Scorsese's chances looked dimmer and dimmer.

The Oscars were scheduled for March 30, 1981, but early that day a psychopathic loner named John Warnock Hinckley Jr. shot President Ronald Reagan and three other men outside the Hilton Hotel in Washington, D.C. There was no protocol for handling an awards show in the shadow of such a situation, and rather than risk celebrating themselves while the president fought for his life, Academy officials decided to postpone the telecast for twenty-four hours. Reagan, quite fortunately, would recover from his wounds. But the pall that the assassination attempt cast over the Academy Awards would only deepen the following day, when America would learn that Hinckley, in the sort of coincidence that wouldn't pass muster with anyone reviewing a script for a thriller, had been inspired to shoot the president by his obsession with *Taxi Driver* and, more specifically, his wish to impress Jodie Foster with a holocaust of violence like that depicted at the end of the 1976 film. As Scorsese, De Niro, and Schrader were waiting to hear if they'd been rewarded for the exceedingly bitter *Raging Bull*, it appeared as though their earlier collaboration had inspired someone to a wild act of real-world violence.

At the start of the telecast, though, almost nobody at the Dorothy Chandler Pavilion knew about the connection between Hinckley and *Taxi Driver*. In fact, when De Niro arrived, his attention was grabbed by a reminder of another sensational crime. Emerging from his limo, he noticed an ABC-TV page named Thomas Rogers wearing a green ribbon on the lapel of his suit. Curious as to the meaning of the symbol, De Niro learned that it was part of a nationwide effort to show solidarity with the citizens of Atlanta, Georgia, where a serial killer was preying on young black men. De Niro asked if Rogers had one that he could wear during the evening, and Rogers gave the star his own ribbon. Thus did De Niro inadvertently become the first celebrity to be seen sporting what became known as an "awards show ribbon" in support of some humanitarian cause.

Inside, as word of the Hinckley/*Taxi Driver* connection started to spread, the evening slowly slipped away from *Raging Bull*. Editor Thelma Schoonmaker and cinematographer Michael Chapman were awarded Oscars, but Pesci and Scorsese were overlooked. With only three awards left to be distributed, Sally Field, who'd won Best Actress the previous year for *Norma Rae*, came out to present the Best Actor award. To no one's surprise, the name in the envelope was De Niro's.

Six years earlier, his director, Francis Coppola, had accepted his Best Supporting Actor Oscar for him. But now De Niro was present to speak for himself, and he did so rather fumblingly, reaching into his tuxedo jacket for a slip of paper and joking, "I forgot my lines, so the director wrote them down for me."

"I want to thank everyone," he declared, and he more or less did, acknowledging the film's costumer, casting director, sound man, makeup artists, writers, and producers. He mentioned Pete Savage: "If Pete wasn't involved in the film he wouldn't have gotten it started . . . I'm a little nervous, excuse me . . . the film never would have gotten started." He thanked "Vicki LaMotta and all the other wives, and Joey LaMotta, even though he's suing us. I hope that settles soon enough so I can go over to his house and eat once in a while." After the audience laughed, he continued to a list of even more important thank-yous: "And of course, Jake LaMotta, whose life it's all about. And Marty Scorsese, who gave me and all the other actors and everyone on the film all the love and trust that anyone could give anyone and is just wonderful as a director. And I want to thank my mother and father for having me. And my grandmother and grandfather, for having them. And everyone else involved in the film. And I hope that I can share this with anyone that it means anything to and the rest of the world, and especially all the terrible things that are happening. I love everyone."

In the backstage press room, reporters tried to get De Niro to comment on the Hinckley business, but he was predictably reluctant. "I don't know about the story," he said. "I don't want to discuss the matter now." When the questions persisted, he put his foot down: "Look, I said what I wanted to say out there. You're all very nice, but that's it." He then left to pass the better part of the evening with the *Raging Bull* team at a Beverly Hills restaurant, where they had repaired to make sense of the day's events in privacy. He had been compelled by the law to answer the questions put to him by Joey LaMotta's attorneys. Hollywood reporters, as he well knew, had no such power over him.

12

W HEN HE AWOKE ON APRIL 1, 1981, IN POSSESSION OF HIS
second Oscar and a pile of congratulatory telegrams from,
among many others, Jack Nicholson, Mickey Rooney, California governor Edmund G. Brown, and Israeli politician Moshe
Dayan, Robert De Niro was by almost anyone's reckoning the greatest
screen actor on earth.

Just eight or nine years prior, he had been almost completely unknown, doggedly chasing small parts in independent films and appearing in off-off-Broadway plays, just as likely to be skipped over for work
as to have his name misspelled in the credits or be ignored in reviews
when he got a role.

Then came the remarkable one-two punch of *Bang the Drum
Slowly* and *Mean Streets*, followed by the revelation of *The Godfather,
Part II* (and the anointment of an Oscar) and the unimaginable explosion of *Taxi Driver*. In five years, he'd claimed a significant spot in the
upper tier of his profession. There followed three expensive and visible
flops (*The Last Tycoon*, *1900*, *New York, New York*), the blame for none
of which was hung on him. Rather, he was for the most part admired
for stretching his range and for choosing intriguing projects and, always, the best collaborators; if anything, his reputation was enhanced.
And then came another pair of back-to-back thunderbolts, *The Deer
Hunter* and *Raging Bull*.

His triumph was undeniable and complete. Nine films, including
several outright masterworks, and nine completely distinct performances. He had learned to speak in dialects and even in a foreign
language; he had learned to drive a taxi, to play the saxophone, to box;

he had literally rebuilt his physique twice; he had become other people again and again, and almost none of them resembled Bobby De Niro of Greenwich Village, whoever *he* was. He had taken the venerated standard of the actor as chameleon, as embodied by the likes of Marlon Brando during his first flush of glory and Laurence Olivier through his long and varied career, and infused it with a modern energy and freedom. There was no direct line, not of thought or gesture or intent or execution, that connected Bruce Pearson, Johnny Boy Civello, Vito Corleone, Travis Bickle, Monroe Stahr, Alfredo Berlinghieri, Jimmy Doyle, Michael Vronsky, and Jake LaMotta, only the tirelessness, self-lessness, talent, dedication, imagination, application, and will to power of the performer who had created them. He had been nominated for an Oscar four times and won twice; he'd gotten four Golden Globe nominations, winning once; and he had a trove of prizes from crit-ics' groups, including three from the New York Film Critics Circle, two each from the Los Angeles Film Critics Association and the Na-tional Society of Film Critics, and one each from the Boston Society of Film Critics and the National Board of Review. He had peers, yes—Hoffman, Pacino, Nicholson, Keitel, Voight, Hackman, movie stars and fine actors all—but he had no equals, not at that very moment, and everybody knew it.

His collaborators, even those with their own estimable accomplish-ments, spoke of him in terms of awe and respect. "Bobby De Niro's a perfectionist," Donald Sutherland said, "but he knows what's perfect; I don't." His technique left other actors agog: "De Niro once figured out what the guy he was playing would have had in his wallet," said Ryan O'Neal, admitting he didn't have the same tools. As Chris Hodenfield, virtually the last journalist De Niro had spoken to at any length at the time, put it: "A Dr. Jekyll who shifts into an endless number of Mr. Hydes, he doesn't imitate people, he stages an inquisition." His excel-lence was a given; his process was a legend. He had gone, in perhaps fifteen years' time, from sniffing inquisitively around the edge of the acting profession to, at age thirty-seven, standing indisputably on top of it.

But that remarkable rise—the struggle to get a foot in the door, to get those plum roles, to create those indelible performances, to maintain focus on the work, to avoid the distractions of the limelight, to keep from being bled by the press and the accoutrements of showbiz— came at a personal cost.

When he woke that morning, he was a man living apart from his wife and children. In 1979, with the hard work and travel of *The Deer Hunter* barely past and the *Raging Bull* preparation consuming him more than ever, he and Diahnne Abbott separated. She, Drena, and Raphael split their time between the home De Niro had leased in Brentwood and the townhouse he owned in lower Manhattan; he spent time between the New York building and a rented suite at the famed Chateau Marmont in Hollywood.

Their troubles were, per rumormongers, the result of their differing tastes and priorities. Their early days in California had been idyllic, Shelley Winters recalled. "We spent wonderful weekends together. I remember we used to lug big bags of cracked crab and iced white wine out to this funky beach—we called it Doggy Beach." But their differences had become vexations. De Niro had grown frustrated with the hassles and expense of maintaining the menagerie that Abbott insisted on living with. At first her cats had been the cause of problems when they were staying at the Beverly Hills Hotel. "I've heard they have hookers running all around the pool," De Niro remembered, "and yet when you have cats . . . I was told not to have cats, but I did and they locked us out. They put a padlock on the door and put the cats outside. I was furious. The manager threatened to call the police in front of me. . . . This was at night, we got home at midnight, and they had locked us out. I wanted to sue—he was a pig. It looked like he enjoyed being a son of a bitch." Then, after they vacated their first Los Angeles rental home, in Bel Air, they were sued by the owners for the extensive damage done by their "great number of cats" to the rugs, draperies, and furniture; the suit sought $10,000 in reparations. For a fellow as meticulous, parsimonious, and particular as De Niro, it was becoming an ongoing provocation.

But it went deeper than run-ins with obnoxious hoteliers or cats peeing on rugs. De Niro really was as quiet, self-contained, and sphinx-like in his private life as the press liked to depict him, while Abbott had more of a taste for partying and gadding about in a crowd. He had a handful of haunts he preferred—low-key spots limited only to A-list clientele, such as the ultra-private On the Rox nightclub on the Sunset Strip. She preferred to be in larger throngs, more visible and more varied: parties, premieres, awards shows.

De Niro told the press that their estrangement was simply "a cooling-off period" and that it was the fault of his celebrity, without which he "would have gone on being an ordinary guy, living a simple life, and nothing would have changed my marriage." But, of course, he had sought the life he now lived with single-minded purpose, and it was virtually inevitable that success would mean the sacrifice of "ordinary" and "simple." The marriage was still a work in progress; they were together more than they were apart during this period of difficulty, and Abbott continued to be presented and to give interviews as the wife of Robert De Niro. But he was rumored around Hollywood to be involved with several well-known women (gossips linked him to Bette Midler and Barbara Carrera), and there were many reports of him being on the town, in his furtive fashion, with female companionship. He could be obsessively secretive even in these liaisons, not acknowledging his actual identity and even asking dates to leave their own bedrooms so he could hide his wallet during trysts, but he was known to be comporting himself as if genuinely single.

In Italy on a publicity tour for *Raging Bull*, he reunited with Stefania Sandrelli, one of his co-stars from *1900*, who followed him after a while to New York, where they behaved affectionately toward each other in public. And in Los Angeles, he chased down—literally, while driving along in his convertible on San Vicente Blvd.—a beautiful young African American woman who turned out to be a singer named Helena Springs. Springs, who was approximately twenty-two at the time they met, remembered feeling frustrated by the behavior of the driver who seemed to be focused on her. "This guy is cutting me off," she said. "I'd go fast, he'd go fast. I'd slow down, he'd slow down. This asshole kept following me. I didn't even know him. Finally he put his hands in a prayer position and said, 'Pull over.' So I stopped and he said, 'Can we have lunch?'"

Springs, who had been a background singer for, among others, Bob Dylan, Bette Midler, and Elton John, finally realized who her pursuer

was, and she agreed to go to dinner with him, leading to their spending the night together. Over the span of a few years, they maintained
a non-exclusive relationship, during which, Springs later said, she became pregnant twice. She aborted the first pregnancy, she claimed,
without telling De Niro about it. But she said that when she found
herself pregnant again, in late 1981, she determined that she would
have the baby, and she told De Niro, setting him off on what she described as a series of ugly and intimidating conversations and encounters aimed at getting her to terminate the pregnancy. "It was mental
abuse," she concluded, but she held firm to her choice.

On July 1, 1982, she gave birth to a baby girl who was named—by
De Niro, Springs said—Nina. De Niro, Springs claimed, gave her
$50,000 to help with the care of the baby and even pitched in on set-
ting up a room for her. But he drew the line at providing her with his
medical history or a blood sample, fearing that she didn't merely want
to be able to fill in the gaps in the baby's medical records, as she said,
but rather that she was after more money. Springs dropped the matter,
she later explained, partly because of her own low self-esteem: "Black
women aren't used to being courted by handsome, famous, rich white
guys. So they don't say no to whatever the man wants." It would be
more than three years before De Niro would see Springs, or baby Nina,
again.

He had never liked to parley with the press. Now he was getting testy
with journalists and especially with photographers. In the summer of
1979 he got into a scuffle with a pair of photographers at the Stork
Club in New York, where one of them tried to snap him eating dinner
with Joe Pesci. Not long after, in Rome to do publicity for *Raging Bull*,
he found himself with Harvey Keitel riding in a taxi that was being
pursued by a carload of paparazzi. The cab driver came upon a policeman and told him that he and his passengers were being followed by
suspicious people. When the cop questioned the photographers, they
got their revenge by declaring that they were chasing a pair of terrorists
who were in the taxi. This was the height of Red Brigade revolutionary activity in Italy, and the charge was taken seriously; the taxi was

intercepted by the *carabinieri*, the state police, and De Niro and Keitel were forced out at gunpoint, their hands held high, and made to stand against a wall, the paparazzi photographing the entire episode.

When the police realized that they'd been duped into making a big mistake, they tried to disarm the situation, De Niro recalled. "The chief of police came over to me and said, 'I take all the cameras; put them over there. Don't worry, no problem.' And I said, 'Yeah, this I'll believe.'" After a talk at the police station—with the paparazzi present, claiming they were entitled to use any tactics whatsoever to get a picture—the actors were released. De Niro understood the cops' point of view, but he couldn't fathom the moxie of the paparazzi: "They were saying they had a right to take a picture. Those guys were actually arguing that—they're the slimiest people who ever lived."*

AS IT TURNED OUT, there were reasons other than thin skin or a heightened sense of privacy that made him chary of reporters. Increasingly he was living a lifestyle that he was keen never to have revealed. During the period in which he, Scorsese, and the crowd around them were using drugs, especially cocaine, De Niro became friendly with John Belushi, the gonzo comedian who'd risen to fame on *Saturday Night Live* and then segued into movies with the smash hit *Animal House*. They were an unlikely pair: De Niro so reticent in his private life and dogged and precise in his art, Belushi so voluble and voracious and heedless, both personally and professionally. But there was a common love of late night living, of Marlon Brando movies (Belushi, it was said, had seen *On the Waterfront* dozens of times), and, alas, of cocaine. Belushi clearly idolized De Niro, who was six years his elder, and De Niro surely saw in Belushi a form of comic release that he hadn't ever approached in his life or his work.

Belushi lived not far from De Niro in lower Manhattan, and De Niro would occasionally visit him at his home, where the comic had a private den that was the scene of many nights of conversation, movie

---

* Bizarrely, some of the first press reports about the incident to reach the United States claimed that De Niro's companion in the taxicab was Keith Carradine.

watching, partying, and the planning of yet further bacchanals. (One night in the late 1970s, De Niro cut his hand at Belushi's house and had to be taken for stitches.) They would similarly spend time together in Los Angeles, where both favored long-term stays at the Chateau Marmont, private dinners at the Imperial Gardens Chinese restaurant, and long boozy, cokey nights at On the Rox.

In February 1982 both were staying at the Chateau, and Belushi, always erratic, frequently living beyond reason in a fog of alcohol and drugs, was more out of control than usual, causing genuine concern among friends. Now and again De Niro would come down from his suite in the hotel's main building to visit Belushi in the bungalow in which he was living, to talk about a script idea that the comedian was developing with his *Saturday Night Live* chum, comic and writer Don Novello (aka Father Guido Sarducci). One afternoon De Niro, accompanied by his kids Drena and Raphael for a rare outing, ran into Belushi at a house party in Benedict Canyon at which the comedian, strung out on coke, was snorting heroin with some musicians and excusing himself to go off and vomit.

On a Thursday evening just a few weeks later, De Niro was out on the town with actor Harry Dean Stanton—they stopped in at Dan Tana's, the famed Italian restaurant to the stars, and then at On the Rox—and De Niro placed several calls to Belushi encouraging him to come out and join the escapades. Belushi didn't respond, so De Niro and Stanton made the short drive over to the Chateau Marmont to see if they could find him and entice him out into the world. It seemed to De Niro that the comedian had been on edge for days, apparently not sleeping or eating properly, certainly strung out.

They found Belushi in the company of Cathy Smith, a Canadian woman who had drifted in and out of the music business over the years, involved professionally and, often, romantically with the likes of Gordon Lightfoot, Hoyt Axton, various members of The Band, and of the Rolling Stones. Smith had a history of using heroin and cocaine and had turned to dealing to support her drug habit. She had recently met Belushi and was supplying him with heroin and hanging around his bungalow; her presence, according to those who saw her there, was vaguely sexual, vaguely drug-related.

De Niro didn't like Smith from first contact—he found her "trashy"—and he gladly agreed when Belushi suggested that he go back to On the Rox and return to the bungalow after the club closed. He took Stanton back to the club and then returned to the Chateau after two in the morning, not to Belushi's bungalow but to his own suite, with a small party including several women. Robin Williams, who was appearing at the Comedy Store, a stone's throw from the hotel, had gone to On the Rox looking for De Niro and Belushi and finally found De Niro, via phone, in his room; when Williams suggested they meet up at Belushi's, De Niro explained that he was occupied. Williams went by himself to Belushi's, where he, too, was creeped out by Smith and by the depressing and even sinister vibe in the air. After a while, sometime around three, he took his leave. Soon afterward, De Niro appeared at the back door of the bungalow, let himself in, helped himself to a little bit of the cocaine displayed on a table, and left again, saying barely a word.

The next day, March 5, De Niro woke late and tried to reach Belushi through the hotel switchboard. No luck. After failing several times, De Niro asked to speak to the hotel manager, who deflected his call. That agitated De Niro, who called back speaking in a much firmer tone of voice and demanding an explanation.

"Where's John?" he asked.

"There is a problem," the manager told him.

"What?"

"It's bad."

"Is he sick?"

"It's really bad."

De Niro started to cry and let the phone drop. John Belushi was dead.

At around noon that day, a friend of Belushi's had stopped in to help him work on a script and found the bungalow apparently empty. He called out for Belushi and then peeked into the comedian's bedroom, where he found him in bed, unresponsive to mouth-to-mouth resuscitation. By the time De Niro learned what had happened, word was beginning to spread and would soon hit the media like a bomb strike.

Naturally, De Niro was horrified. Not only because Belushi had been a genuine friend, not only because they had been together just hours before Belushi's death—which everyone immediately knew had to be by drug overdose—but because, as he learned in the coming days, Belushi had been experimenting with heroin in part because he wanted to play a punk rock musician in a movie and was imitating De Niro's famed technique of immersing himself completely in his roles.

Two days after Belushi's death, when the medical examiner was releasing a preliminary autopsy report, De Niro got a phone call from Richard Bear, a musician and scenester who'd known Belushi for years and had become acquainted with De Niro in the past few months. Bear had been present one day when Belushi and De Niro discussed the comedian's idea that he actually shoot up with real heroin on camera in the proposed film. He reminded De Niro about the conversation.

"Don't talk to anybody about that," De Niro told him. "I know John wanted to do that."

Bear was distraught: "Bobby, they rehearsed the scene. That's what killed him. . . . They were doing it!"

"Don't say a word to me," De Niro commanded. "Not to me. Don't say a word to anybody. . . . You, me . . . we'll put our heads together. But don't talk to anybody."

In the coming days, weeks, and months, De Niro would stay true to his own advice. When the Los Angeles district attorney investigated Smith for administering Belushi's fatal dose, a so-called speedball combining heroin and cocaine, De Niro was subpoenaed to appear before a grand jury. But he was out of the country, making a movie in Italy, and he was permitted to give his testimony over the telephone from Rome. It was the only official tie he would ever have to his friend's death or to the legal action taken against the woman who, however inadvertently, abetted it.

AND HE WAS MAKING that movie in Italy because, truly, he still had not slowed down. Nor had he even considered slowing down, despite his maniacal workload, the rigor with which he drove his body, the collapse of his marriage, his attraction to partying, and the human damage—both personal and professional—that he had witnessed over the past few years, often uncomfortably up close.

Raging Bull was still being edited when he began production on his next film, *True Confessions*, an adaptation of John Gregory Dunne's novel in which a brutal murder, based on the legendary unsolved "Black Dahlia" case, led to the unraveling of a culture of scandal and cover-up within the Archdiocese of Los Angeles in the 1940s. Along with his wife, Joan Didion, Dunne had adapted the book for Winkler-Chartoff, who had put the film in the hands of Ulu Grosbard, a Belgian-born director with a strong track record in the New York theater and such films to his credit as the critically acclaimed *The Subject Was Roses* (which he'd also directed on Broadway) and the cultishly admired crime story *Straight Time*.

De Niro was cast as Father Desmond Spellacy, a rising wheeler-dealer in the Catholic hierarchy whose brother, LAPD Detective Tom Spellacy, cannot be dissuaded from digging into the unsavory ties that connected a brutally murdered party girl with the wealthy laymen who form the Church's financial and civic power base. Robert Duvall, with whom De Niro had shared a credit but no screen time on *The Godfather, Part II*, would play Tom, and another familiar face, Charles Durning, would appear alongside the likes of Burgess Meredith, Kenneth McMillan, Dan Hedaya, and Cyril Cusack as a cardinal.

The book was atmospheric and powerful, an indictment of spiritual and institutional corruption written in a classical prose quite unlike the heated tenor that James Elroy would later become famous for bringing to bear on very similar themes. Catholicism was extremely important to the book and script, and De Niro was happy to immerse himself in the culture of the Church—the rituals, costumes, language, and daily lives of priests; the Latin liturgy; the intricacies of the profession of the priesthood as a way of life and as a career, with inducements to advancement and punishments for failures and insubordinations as in any career.

The film was shot in Los Angeles from January through April 1980, and De Niro cleverly employed the extra weight that he was still bearing from the previous year's fattening-up procedure for *Raging Bull* to give Father Spellacy an appropriately comfortable fullness of face and frame. He also did intensive research on the priesthood and the Church; his formal religious experience, after all, consisted of but a few fleeting encounters with Catholicism as a young child and, later, during his Bobby Milk days of running experimentally with the crowd from Little Italy. He was tutored for the film by Father Henry Fehren, who'd been hired by the production and endured the usual barrage of questions and requests from his pupil. "De Niro is a perfectionist," Fehren said later. "He wanted not only to master the fundamental routines of an ordained priest, but he wanted the sense, feeling and tradition of what the church was in 1948. He may be the most authentic priest ever seen on the screen."

In his files De Niro had annotated copies of books and articles about the rites and rituals of the Church; the education of priests; the duties of various members of the diocese; the proper way to don, wear, and remove vestments; the private lives of priests; the specific procedures of confession and communion; even the Latin liturgy, which he practiced daily as production approached, often by attending Mass. To mark the character of the social-climbing Des Spellacy more specifically, he took some golf lessons and had his fingernails manicured. He also added dandruff flakes to the shoulders of his costumes, a subtle hint of the character's human frailty, and did research into hyperventilation, the frightening condition to which Spellacy was prone ("NOTE OF CAUTION," a researcher told him, "be careful while doing this repeatedly. Maybe you should breathe into a paper bag between takes to restore your carbon dioxide equilibrium"). He conducted interviews, too. "I talked to tons of priests," he said. "But then I realized I don't want to complicate it and clog myself with wrong choices. *You can know too much.*"

That was interesting in and of itself: De Niro, the famed chameleon and free-diver who would learn and do anything in the name of accuracy, was suggesting that there was maybe a limit to that type of acting, that monomaniacal immersion in the role could become a problem for the performer, that there was a point beyond which the technique he had honed over the past decade, and which he had brought to a pinnacle with *Raging Bull,* was no longer efficacious.

Just a few years prior, while making *The Deer Hunter,* De Niro had declared, "You have to earn the right to play a character." In that same bit of publicity material, he was as explicit as he had ever been up to then in describing his aims in doing research and creating a sense of cocoonlike isolation: "I really don't like to be distracted when I'm working on these things. So maybe I sublimate my own personality in order to get the totality of the role . . . I try to make him appear as real as if I'd known him all my life. Therefore, it's not too easy for me to flip back out of character as I come off camera."

Just a few years earlier, while making *New York, New York*, he had told *Newsweek*: "Technique is concrete. . . . Acting isn't really respected enough as an art. Your body is an instrument, and you have to learn how to play an instrument. It's like knowing how to play the piano. There ought to be acting schools that take you in as children, the way it's done with musicians. You don't need experience to learn technique. You'd learn your technique, and as you got older and had experience you'd apply it to what you know."

In *Raging Bull* he had taken that technique as far as any screen actor ever had. But here on his very next project, De Niro seemed to be backing away from the thing he had just so recently mastered. He had pursued *Raging Bull* for the better part of a decade, but he had moved on to *True Confessions* with mere months of forethought. Following the style of the film as created by Grosbard, he played Des Spellacy, at least outwardly, as reserved, compact, efficient, unprepossessing. Where in *Raging Bull* he was all flame and heat and cataclysm, in *True Confessions* he was cool and still and calculating, a characterization more akin to Monroe Stahr or Alfredo Berlinghieri. It was as if he had taken the technique that he'd spent the 1970s perfecting, the Method of Constantin Stanislavski as distilled through Stella Adler and given life by Marlon Brando, brought it to its logical and practical extreme, and then, in a matter of months, weeks maybe, dropped it—not entirely, not by proclamation, but delicately, surely, and irreversibly. He would still be a significant actor and star, but he would never again chase the tiger of his muse and method so willfully and purposefully as he did in *Raging Bull*.

It wasn't a precipitous fall. Even as a follow-up to *Raging Bull*, *True Confessions* had substance and gave the public a De Niro once again working with quality material and first-rate collaborators. Like Monroe Stahr, Desmond Spellacy is a prince of an order and on the fast track to be something more: impeccable, sharp, exact, and sure. He keeps his own counsel, even when advising his superiors, and is certain of his decisions, even when they create collateral damage ("Looks like a leprechaun, thinks like an Arab," says one observer of his manner, not entirely disapprovingly). He is full of face, perfect in tailoring, steady of gaze and voice, as meticulous in play on the golf course as he is in the rituals of the Mass. He knows pride is a sin, but he has—perhaps in jest, perhaps not—already chosen his papal name.

Like *Raging Bull*, *True Confessions* is a tale of brothers, a responsible one (the monsignor) and a loose cannon (the detective), their public personae distinct from the way they interact with each other, which is warmer, jokier, less guarded, less actorly. With his brother, Des can tell a joke, do an Irish accent, allude to a shared past with a glance or a phrase. Around everyone else he embodies an idea and an ideal; with his brother, even when hearing his brother's confession, he's an ordinary man, prone to sentimental reminiscence, goofball humor, flashes of impolitic frustration, and even anger.

The most remarkable moments in the performance, though, are in the silences, as they so often are with De Niro. As the grisly murder case is connected more and more surely to the inner circle of Catholic laymen with whom he does business and threatens to soil the hem of the ambitious Monsignor Spellacy himself, De Niro slowly shifts from hauteur toward self-questioning and, finally, in a truly breathtaking moment, humility. Changing from his golf clothes to his priestly garb, he sits by himself, weary, determined, his doubts starting to outweigh his certainty. He is alone in a sparsely furnished room, but he could be orating a confession to a full auditorium; he is nearly naked with his thoughts, and De Niro conveys them without a sound. It's a fine, textured performance, and as unlike Jake LaMotta as can be imagined.

IN THE MONTHS after filming *True Confessions*, De Niro started working again with his *Bang the Drum Slowly* director John Hancock, who was developing a script for him based on the true-life story of Rick

Cluchey, who had been sentenced to death (and, later, life without parole) in 1957 under California's "Little Lindbergh" law, which added a mandatory death sentence to any crime that had a kidnapping component. During his time at San Quentin, Cluchey had become interested in writing and acting and composed a play about prison called *La Cage*. After his sentence was commuted in 1966 by California governor Pat Brown, he traveled the world with a troupe of ex-con actors, eventually making his way to Paris, where no less a personage than Samuel Beckett came to be an admirer of his work. Hancock was crafting this remarkable saga into a film.

Along with Robert Chartoff and Irwin Winkler, De Niro was interested in the project and worked closely with Hancock as he wrote the film, which had been entitled *Weeds*. He started to do his usual research thing—talking at length with Cluchey, observing his workshops, visiting a number of prisons, reading about the lives of convicts. That behavior was familiar to Hancock. But he also took note that De Niro was more demanding about a number of details of the film that Hancock felt ought to be the director's prerogative: casting, music, sets, and so on. In particular, Hancock was uncomfortable with De Niro's insistence that real convicts play major roles. The film had found a home at United Artists, with MGM distributing, but without an agreement on such a central issue, De Niro was never entirely ready to dive in, and the studio never green-lit the production.

Two years later, word of *Weeds* surfaced again, at EMI Films this time, with Universal distributing, again with Hancock and De Niro attached. Again De Niro went from apparent immersion in it to disagreement over how the material would be approached, and again it was shelved. In 1986, *Weeds* got yet a third life, this time with Nick Nolte in the lead role; it appeared the following year, to modestly favorable reviews and tepid box office, and Hancock and De Niro never came close to working together again.

BY 1981, DE NIRO had decided that he would live in Los Angeles only when work required it of him, and only in leased or rented housing, preferably at an entirely neutral and anonymous place—the Chateau Marmont being a favored destination, at least until John Belushi's death.

He still had his 14th Street apartment in Manhattan, and he still used it for storage and as a crash pad for friends—Meryl Streep and her baby daughter stayed there for a couple of nights in late 1980 when the heating in their own apartment was on the fritz. And he had the townhouse on St. Luke's Place in Greenwich Village, which he and Abbott had been renovating since they acquired it. It was a massive building— four floors plus a basement, with six bedrooms and four baths, and eventually a sauna, gym, and screening room. The detail work was meticulous, with upward of $200,000 going to, among other fine points, red oak in the entranceway, a redwood skylight in the master bedroom, and lots of teak, butternut, and cedar throughout.

Although the work on the house took more than two years and was estimated at some $3 million, De Niro was sued by a carpenter who claimed that he was given a check for $15,000 and then found that De Niro had put a stop order on it. When the matter finally came to court, the woodworker told the press he thought De Niro had misused him because "I treated him like just another customer, and he found that difficult because he's used to people kissing his butt." He made his case to the court's satisfaction, and De Niro had to pay him the disputed fee and pay another $5,000 in interest and court costs.

Undissuaded by the hassles of home ownership, De Niro was looking at acquiring places in Connecticut and on Long Island. If it seemed that he was becoming a land baron or real estate hoarder, it was, in fact, a family habit. His uncle, Jack De Niro, was a big-time real estate agent with thriving businesses in New York City and Florida, and his mother, Virginia Admiral, had been buying and leasing properties in lower Manhattan for some time. Under the umbrellas of a variety of corporate partnerships, formed sometimes just for a single deal, she acquired loft spaces in which the painters and bohemians she had known since the 1940s could live and work, and she was able to keep her ex-husband, who still couldn't be sure when or where his next paycheck would be, under a roof—a gesture of sisterly love, as it were, that endured throughout their lives. Admiral owned pieces of buildings all over Greenwich Village, SoHo, and other Manhattan neighborhoods that hadn't yet been branded with names or acquired trendy cachet. She even had a mantra for her wheelings and dealings: "All great fortunes were built on real estate." Her son might not have been after a fortune, but he clearly had heard the lesson.

AFTER WORKING for hire on *True Confessions*, he spent some time doing not much of anything. There were scripts to read, of course. Since *The Godfather, Part II*, his had been among the first names to come up in casting sessions, and he had scores of parts offered to him, some in films that were never made, some of which turned up on the screen with other actors in the roles De Niro had been offered. Among the former were such never-realized films as Brian De Palma's *Home Movie*, intended as yet a third go-round of the John Rubin persona from *Greetings* and *Hi, Mom!*; a script by John Cassavetes entitled *Knives*; and a Jean-Luc Godard film about Bugsy Siegel. The latter included Bob Fosse's *All That Jazz*, Paul Schrader's *American Gigolo* and *Blue Collar*, John Huston's *Wise Blood*, Wim Wenders's *Hammett* (originally intended as a Francis Coppola film), Martin Scorsese's dream project, *Gangs of New York*, and two films by Richard Attenborough: the World War II epic *A Bridge Too Far* and the psychological thriller *Magic*. A fellow might've made some pretty good films if he'd just stuck to that list, but De Niro was still chary about committing to projects: he'd rejected *A Bridge Too Far*, it was said, because Attenborough wouldn't agree to preliminary meetings with him to discuss his part.

His next director, though, showed more determination. In 1973, when De Niro was in Italy to play Vito Corleone, Sergio Leone, the great director of such westerns as *The Good, the Bad and the Ugly*, *A Fistful of Dollars*, and *Once Upon a Time in the West*, came to see him about a new project he was nursing along. Leone's films of the 1960s had enjoyed huge grosses around the world and had made an international star of Clint Eastwood, but they hadn't yet garnered the critical reputation they would enjoy decades later, and they were still derided as "spaghetti westerns."

Leone didn't wish to talk to De Niro about a western, though.* He had in mind a story based on a book he'd read some half dozen years earlier, an account of Jewish gangsters in New York by Harry Gray entitled *The Hoods*. The story, he later said, "attached itself to me like the malediction of the Mummy in the old movie with Boris Karloff. I wanted to make that film and no other." He had been going around Europe and the United States sharing his vision for an epic gangster picture for a number of years, and he told the story enthrallingly enough for De Niro, who didn't know Leone's work, to be at least politely interested. "He was a big guy," De Niro remembered, "and I liked him. . . . He was very Italian, very sympathetic, *simpatico*."

Years passed, and Leone continued to pursue the film, which he had come to call *Once Upon a Time in America*, chiefly as a producer, presenting it to a number of potential screenwriters, including Norman Mailer (who, Leone said, produced "a Mickey Mouse version" of a script) and journalist Pete Hamill, and such directors as Milos Forman and Peter Bogdanovich. Finally, Leone thought he'd simply direct the film himself, from a script of his own devising, and he wrote a treatment. Most movie treatments—prose descriptions of a story that will be expanded into script form—are perhaps a quarter as long as the completed screenplay. Leone's treatment for *Once Upon a Time in America* was 227 pages long, and the first script drafts were even longer: 260 and 290 pages. Given the usual calculation that a page of screenplay equaled a minute of screen time, those would be impossibly long.

Finally the problem was cracked, and Leone's epic was boiled down to a long but imaginable screenplay by two writers, the Italian Leonardo Benvenuti and the American Stuart Kaminsky, the latter focusing especially on dialogue. A new producer, the former art dealer (and, by his own admission, Israeli spy) Arnon Milchan, agreed to shepherd the project to the screen, and set about raising money. Leone came back to De Niro with the new script and a better pitch than the one of years before.

---

* And good thing: "I wouldn't want to touch a Western," De Niro said in 1980. "They've been done so often, and who wants to be out in the middle of the desert for three months?"

"Sergio told me the story in two installments over seven hours," De Niro remembered. "I sat and listened through a translator. He told the story almost shot by shot, with the flashbacks, and it was beautiful. I said, 'This is something that I'd like to be part of.'" The hook was in, and Leone offered De Niro his choice of the two principal roles—the flamboyant front man Max or his more circumspect boyhood friend and fellow gangster Noodles. De Niro agreed to give it serious thought.

There were some real obstacles to their collaboration, though. For one thing, the film was going to be shot entirely in Italy, even though it would be cast with American actors, and production would take the better part of a year, if not two. For another, De Niro was leery of putting himself in the hands of a director whose work he didn't have a real feel for. "Bobby made it clear to me," Leone later said, "that he has needs to be fulfilled, and one need is that he must feel he is completely understood by the director." He promised, De Niro remembered, not to be as officious and didactic as Bernardo Bertolucci had been during the making of *1900*. "Italian directors sometimes tell you how to do it," De Niro explained. "They say, 'You go over there, and you do this or that.' American actors don't like that, they want to find it for themselves, they don't want to be told where to go. But Sergio was very smart and clever and respectful enough not to do that in my case."

But then there was the matter of the urine.

As De Niro started warming up to the project, he visited Leone in New York at the Mayflower Hotel, where Milchan had booked a suite for meetings, allowing each of the principals some private space. As he always did, no matter who was stopping by, the portly Leone greeted De Niro and Milchan, who'd come along to smooth the process, wearing only a bathrobe and close-fitting underpants, a sight that rattled the fastidious actor. Milchan repaired to one of the unused bedrooms to wait for a phone call. After a bit, as he recalled, the phone rang. It was De Niro, calling from another bedroom in the suite and insisting Milchan come see him immediately.

The producer found De Niro agitated.

"I can't do the movie!"

"Why not?"

De Niro led him into the en suite bathroom of his bedroom and pointed to the commode. "Can't you see that he pissed all over my toilet seat?"

There was, in fact, urine on the toilet seat. A flummoxed Milchan improvised an answer: "Come on, Robert. He didn't do that on purpose. He's fat; he didn't see."

But De Niro insisted it was a power play, a marking of territory, a crude show of superiority, and he actually seemed ready to drop out of the film because of it.

Somehow the faux pas was forgiven, and De Niro, still undecided about the part, agreed to visit the sets that Leone was constructing in Rome. "They were gonna do it, with or without me," De Niro said, and that, in particular, appealed to him. "He didn't raise the money on me, so there was no pressure that way."

Finally selecting the role of Noodles, through whose aging eyes the epic narrative unfolds in retrospect, he agreed to make the film, and he went from reluctant involvement to active interest. James Woods had been cast as Max (after Gérard Depardieu had first agreed to learn English to play the part and then backed out), and De Niro would urge certain other performers on Leone: Joe Pesci, Burt Young, and Danny Aiello, whose screen test De Niro agreed to participate in just so the actor, who was touchy about having to audition at all, would agree to submit to one.*

De Niro took his usual rigorous steps in preparing for the role. He studied Jewish customs (there was a scene in a synagogue) and a bit of Yiddish, and in particular the speech patterns of old-time Jews and the special idioms used by the small set of Jewish gangsters of the Prohibition era. He packed extensively for his trip to Italy: toiletries such as Listerine, Maalox, Tylenol, and Kiehl's soap; videotapes of various movies he wanted to study; a Walkman and cassettes; a camera to take photos with his kids when they came to visit him in Rome (and on a side trip to London). To play the aged Noodles, he worked on a limp and a

---

* Leone auditioned scores of actors for the film, among them Val Kilmer, Sean Penn, Mandy Patinkin, Tom Beringer, Patrick Swayze, Michael Ontkean, Alex Rocco, Steve Guttenberg, David Paymer, and Peter Coyote, and, for the women's roles, Theresa Russell, Amanda Plummer, Joan Hackett, Sean Young, Candy Clark, Connie Sellecca, Stockard Channing, and Helen Hunt.

slow, raspy voice and submitted to extensive aging makeup. "It took so long to put the makeup on," he said, "that I was so tired that I *had* to look old." He had portraits taken of himself in the makeup chair, gesticulating like an *alter kocker* in full old-man guise. He seemed to love it.

Filming took place in Rome, Paris, Montreal, and New York over the span of fifteen months, and De Niro's presence was required for a great deal of it. During the shoot, Leone discovered a way to work with De Niro that brought the director outside his comfort zone in a way he found illuminating. "For better or worse," he remembered, "I had worked with actors like marionettes. But with Bobby you must work around him in a way, because the thing had to be explored through his eyes, too. So for the first time, in this film, I have had to follow an actor's ideas without destroying my own. Yes, Bobby will have his *interpretazione artistica*." Comparing De Niro to his frequent star Clint Eastwood, Leone added, "Bobby, first of all, is an actor. Clint, first of all, is a star. Bobby suffers; Clint yawns."

When shooting was done, Leone had to wrestle years of work into something like a releasable film, a task that in a real sense was never fully achieved. He arrived at an ideal cut of more than four hours, which he agreed couldn't be shown in theaters but only on TV or videotape. In May 1984, after cutting it mercilessly, he arrived at a version of three hours and forty minutes, which premiered out of competition at the Cannes Film Festival to mixed but respectful reviews. But that was still an hour longer than his American distributors had contracted for. Leone dreaded the thought that further cuts would be made without his input; "I hope the last version will be my own," he said at Cannes. But it was effectively out of his hands.

And, in fact, when *Once Upon a Time in America* arrived in America, it was butchered, compromised, unrecognizable, ruined. Gone were the flashbacks, replaced with a linear structure that robbed the film of its sense of poetry, nostalgia, and rue. Gone were expository scenes that made the plot coherent. Gone were charming bits of business and hair-raising bits of violence. The version released by Warner Bros. in June 1984 was half the length of Leone's preferred cut: two hours and fifteen minutes. It was a catastrophe, a crime. And it was a bomb: $5.3 million at the box office, a blip.

De Niro is but a piece of the epic swirl of Leone's massive, swoony, and altogether singular film, yet somehow his presence grounds and imparts resonance to the entire enterprise. Given his history of volatile, outsider characters, his ability to hold the audience with a quiet posture had rarely been the focus of one of his performances (the notable exceptions being *The Last Tycoon* and *True Confessions*, neither of which really loomed in his canon). But Leone saw in De Niro's eyes a capacity that could be put to use for something other than the expression of alienation, anger, or psychosis. He saw an ability to convey longing, melancholy, regret. And though his film begins in bloodshed and includes all manner of violence, sexual perversity, and human cruelty, his focus rarely strays from the mournful emotions carried in Ennio Morricone's score, and De Niro's eyes and silent glances are his chief visual vehicle for that mood.*

We first meet Noodles as a man at the height of his powers, his mind and gaze scrambled gently in an opium den. It's hard to see what's going on in there, but soon enough, without learning too many details, we know for sure. We see his pain and sorrow first—and perhaps best—in a long take about a half hour into the film, when the aged Noodles visits Fat Mo's, the restaurant and speakeasy where so many pivotal events of his life took place. He finds the peephole through which he used to spy on Mo's sister Deborah, and gazes through it as if at his own youth. Leone's camera stares into De Niro's eyes for a long, long while, and De Niro demonstrates his ability to become a transparent vessel for emotions. This is the sort of thing he loves best in film—acting without speaking, conveying an inner state through delicate physicality. His eyes—brown, moist, limpid, filled with pain and wistfulness—are the windows into the movie, and Leone holds focus on them for a daringly extended shot.

The irony, of course, is that those eyes belong to a thief, bootlegger, killer, rapist, and traitor. Somehow in the pantheon of bad guys that De Niro has played, Noodles is generally overlooked, but he commits

---

* *Once Upon a Time in America* would mark the start of a remarkable, if accidental, collaboration between De Niro and Morricone in the 1980s, followed by *The Mission* and *The Untouchables*.

some of the ugliest crimes of the actor's career: not one but two rapes, for starters, the second of which, of Mo's sister Deborah on the eve of her departure for Hollywood, is one of the most horrific things De Niro or Leone (or, for that matter, anyone) ever filmed.

Even though Leone spends more time in minutes with Noodles the high-living bootlegger, it's Noodles the broken, ponderous old man who sticks most with you. The hair and makeup work used to turn De Niro into a middle-aged version of himself is stunning—it would be decades before he would reach the age of the elder Noodles, and it would have been very smart money to bet that he'd look just as he does in the film. (As it happened, in real life he kept his enviable hair and regained his rail-thin physique.) Aging actors for roles in this way is a common Hollywood game, but it's played here with restraint, taste, and fine craft, like many other aspects of the film. If De Niro hadn't lived to see his own mature years, the old Noodles could have credibly substituted for the real thing.

And De Niro lends such internal weight that he sells us on the aging makeup completely. "You can always tell the winners at the starting gate," the aged Noodles tells Fat Mo, and he clearly doesn't include himself among them. The film's title suggests a fairy tale, and it's got its share of ogres, imperiled maidens, dangers, quests, and such. But more than anything else, it's got plangency and heartache and regret. And De Niro, it turns out, is as adept at conveying those aches as he is with fury or psychosis or wildness—even from under a haze of latex makeup, even with the weight of a four-hour film to bear. Leone's film is indeed some kind of masterpiece, and De Niro, particularly in his sorrowful aspect, is the heart of it.

WHEN IT WAS all over, when distributors had crippled and buried the film, De Niro felt sick for his director. "They tried to make it a linear picture, which never worked," he said. "I understand why Sergio didn't come back to the U.S. and deal with it, confront them, fight for it, say, 'Listen, this is the way it has to be. I'll give you this, but I want to take that.' That's really what you have to do. It's like having a child: you don't want somebody to come in and fool with it."

Leone was crushed, and he tried to rally himself to something positive, something forward-looking. He had been working on a new idea, a movie about the siege of Leningrad in World War II, and he tried to interest De Niro in taking a role. But the film was not to be. The director's health, never truly robust, declined after the catastrophic failure of *Once Upon a Time in America,* and he died in 1989, at the age of sixty, without directing another film.

Over the ensuing decades, various cuts of the film that were closer to Leone's vision would be released, and its reputation would grow substantially, until it was genuinely regarded as one of the best gangster films ever made and one of the best films of the 1980s. And it would be in support of the release of one of those restored versions that De Niro would, at the 2012 Cannes Film Festival, climb the stairs of the Grand Palais to the strains of Ennio Morricone's score and mist up at the thought of so much time, so much loss, more similar, in that moment, to the aged Noodles than ever before.

13

B EFORE SERGIO LEONE COULD BRING *ONCE UPON A TIME IN America* to the screen, in any form or at any length, De Niro appeared in yet another film that had undergone a protracted genesis. *The King of Comedy* first came to De Niro's attention in 1974, when he was sent the manuscript of an unpublished novel by Paul Zimmerman, formerly a film critic at *Newsweek*. The book, which began with an epigraph from Alexander Pope ("How quick Ambition hastes to Ridicule!") and another from baseball great Lefty O'Doul ("What's the use of doing something when nobody's looking?"), was a dark comedy about the age of celebrity, a frighteningly prescient vision of a world in which the cachet of fame trumped morality and the quest to place oneself in the center of the media spotlight drained people of their humanity.

Zimmerman had been inspired by an episode of David Susskind's talk show on which a group of autograph hounds explained themselves. "I was struck by the personal way they related to the stars," he recalled. "One said, 'Barbra is hard to work with.' Barbra Streisand had asked this guy not to bother her, but he turned that into 'Barbra is hard to work with.'" There was another fellow he learned of who kept a daily diary of his impressions of the Johnny Carson show. Finally, and perhaps inevitably given the times, he came to see a correlation between the celebrity stalker and the assassin: both, he said, "rise out of the crowd to make contact for an instant."

He combined the two notions to create Rupert Pupkin, an autograph hound and aspiring stand-up comedian who seeks the approval—and, indeed, the career—of Jerry Langford, a late-night TV show host in the

Johnny Carson mold. Pupkin insinuates himself into Langford's life and tries to get booked onto the star's show, but his unpolished material doesn't impress. He resorts to crime: with another autograph hound, the psychotic rich girl Masha, who has developed a sexual fantasy life around Langford, he kidnaps the star, ransoming him for a chance to perform on the show. At the same time, Pupkin courts Rita, a girl who ignored him in high school and who is trapped in a disappointing life from which he promises to rescue her.

His novel unpublished, Zimmerman adapted it into a screenplay and got it to Martin Scorsese, who passed it along to De Niro even before the production of *Taxi Driver*. It looked destined for the ever-growing pile of De Niro's maybe/what-if/not-in-this-form/no screenplays. But something in the story spoke to De Niro. "He understood the bravery of Rupert Pupkin," Zimmerman recalled, "his chutzpah, the simplicity of his motives. Bobby said he liked the single-minded sense of purpose. . . . I think Bobby understood Rupert because he's an obsessive person himself. . . . Bobby could see Rupert as someone who would rather die than live anonymously."

Another version of the script appeared in 1976, adapted from Zimmerman's still-unpublished book by screenwriter Buck Henry, who intended it as a project for Milos Forman. That project came back to De Niro, who mulled it over for a while and then told Forman and Henry flat out, "I really like the original. Do you mind if I take it and go to Marty with it?"

Of course, working with Scorsese would take a while, as the personal and professional ordeals and crises of 1976 through 1980 took their toll. What was more, Scorsese explained to De Niro that he really didn't have a feel for the material; he was more interested in another project he had in mind to make with De Niro, *Night Life*, a film about two brothers, one a cop, the other a comedian. But on the heels of *Raging Bull* and *True Confessions*, the theme of warring/loving brothers didn't appeal to De Niro very much. Brushing off *Night Life*, he kept pushing *The King of Comedy* on Scorsese.

In part it was because he was fascinated with Rupert Pupkin. De Niro had become a big enough star in the past half decade to acquire his own real-life cadre of Rupert Pupkins, hero-worshippers and semi-stalkers drawn to his aura of fame. As *King of Comedy* percolated in his head, he took the opportunity to accost his accosters, picking the brains of autograph hounds who approached him and scaring them by asking for their contact information; he wasn't trying to prosecute them, but rather to use them as research sources and even as extras. "Bobby developed a technique," Scorsese remembered. "Role reversal! He would set about chasing autograph-hunters, stalking them, terrifying them by asking them tons of questions." And, true to his word, De Niro threw some work at a few of them. "Some of the people I used to run into," he said, "I used in the film."

According to Scorsese, one semi-stalker in particular proved a font of insight. For years he had pestered De Niro to meet and talk with him, and with the new film in mind, De Niro finally agreed. As Scorsese said: "The guy was waiting for him with his wife, a shy suburban woman who was rather embarrassed by the situation. He wanted to take him to dinner at their house, a two-hour drive from New York. After he had persuaded him to stay in Manhattan, Bobby asked him, 'Why are you stalking me? What do you want?' He replied, 'To have dinner with you, have a drink, chat. My mom asked me to say hi.'" For De Niro, such an unaffected obsessive was pure gold.

Finally, not very long before *Raging Bull* premiered, Scorsese agreed to pursue *King of Comedy* with De Niro. He had been reluctant, he later explained, because "it was more Bob's project than mine. . . . The motives for making a film are very important for me. They have to be good motives. Mine weren't very clear when I started out on this picture."*

De Niro and Scorsese went out to Long Island with Zimmerman's still-unpublished novel and the two screenplays and worked out a new

---

* His motives may not have been clear when he initially joined the project, but surely Scorsese was struck by the similarities, revealed during the weeks leading up to the shoot, between Rupert Pupkin and John Hinckley Jr., who had become so confused by filmed media that he shot the president to impress a fictional character. Scorsese had agreed to make *The King of Comedy* months before Hinckley's attempt on the life of Ronald Reagan, but by the first day of production the delusional would-be assassin's fascination with *Taxi Driver* was known, and Scorsese could choose from a number of terrifying but relevant themes in the film—and in real life—as pry-holes for his creative process.

take on the material. The author later admitted to uncertainty about what the result might be, but when he saw the new version of the script he was delighted: "I literally jumped up and down. . . . They had synthesized the script and the book." (And, as with *Raging Bull*, they would neither take nor seek credit for their rewrite.)

Like *Raging Bull*, *King of Comedy* was a three-hander, meaning that the casting of the other two lead roles, Jerry Langford and Masha, would be vital. For the former, Zimmerman's original inspiration had been Dick Cavett, who didn't seem to have the proper gravitas to play the role (nor, six years after inspiring it, the career profile to qualify as a movie star). Johnny Carson was the obvious first choice, but he considered himself strictly a TV guy and told Scorsese he wouldn't enjoy the rigors of long days with multiple reshoots of scenes: "One take is good enough for me," he said. The next choice was Frank Sinatra, who was nearing the end of his screen acting days and demurred. Scorsese and casting director Cis Corman thought of Orson Welles, but they decided he "wasn't 'showbiz' enough." Then they circled back to the idea of, if not Sinatra, perhaps other members of his Rat Pack: Sammy Davis Jr., Joey Bishop, and especially Dean Martin, who was also virtually done with acting. And the thought of Dean Martin led them to consider his onetime partner, Jerry Lewis.

During his years with Martin (roughly 1946–56) and the decade thereafter, Jerry Lewis was one of the biggest stars in showbiz, with a sizable film audience, considerable drawing power as a live act in Vegas and elsewhere, and tremendous success on television with his annual muscular dystrophy telethon.* He hadn't enjoyed a favorable critical reputation in the United States since the 1950s, but he was celebrated in France and other foreign markets for his clowning; he had taught at the University of Southern California, where the likes of Steven Spielberg vouched for the quality of his instruction; and he had a cultish fol-

---

* Television had proved a hobgoblin for Lewis ever since the days when he and Martin regularly had the top-rated show as one of the rotating set of hosts of *The Colgate Comedy Hour.* In 1963, he received what was then the most lucrative television contract in history, for a live variety show on ABC that proved a jaw-droppingly large critical and commercial failure and was canceled by the network barely two months into its intended five-year run.

lowing among a new generation of comedians who had grown up with TV viewings of *The Nutty Professor, The Errand Boy, The Ladies' Man,* and other comedy hits that Lewis had written, produced, directed, and starred in decades earlier.

By 1980, Lewis had fallen on hard times: he hadn't made a film between 1972, when he was forced to abandon the star-crossed movie *The Day the Clown Cried,* about a clown held by the Nazis at Auschwitz, and 1979, when he made the ultra-low-budget *Hardly Working* in Florida, which wouldn't get released for two years and then proved a surprise hit. In his mid-fifties, Lewis was possessed of a darkness, a thin skin, and a quick temper that worked against him enjoying a late-life career, and he had only recently overcome an addiction to painkillers he'd developed after injuring himself in a pratfall on *The Andy Williams Show* in 1965. He was, in short, a risk in any number of ways.

But Scorsese was drawn to casting him as Langford almost because of all that. The telethon, in particular, fascinated him. As he explained, "With its combination of money pouring in for charity and its Vegas sensibility, [it] seems at times to verge on nervous breakdown. Also the thin line between reality and drama seems to be shattered constantly. . . . Anyone who could conjure up and sustain this atmosphere is quite extraordinary." He and Lewis took a couple of meetings, and Scorsese recalled, "I could see the man was *ripe* for it."

But the final call on the casting would belong to De Niro, who required that Lewis meet with him several times so that he could get a sense of Lewis as a collaborator—and, presumably, as a target for Rupert Pupkin's mania. "What we went through before we decided that we were gonna do it," Lewis recalled. "Bobby and I have five meetings, five separate meetings in six months." As he explained, "Bobby has to know the people that he's gonna work with. What he needs from them, I can't tell you—whether he has to know that they're genuine, whether he has to know that they're just goddamn good actors, that they'll commit—I'm not too sure, but he needs to know some stuff."

De Niro expressed his reservations about the casting choice in a note to Scorsese: "It's harder to imagine Jerry Lewis doing this as opposed to Johnny Carson. He (JL) has to do it straighter than he's ever done anything in his whole life." In conversation with Lewis, De Niro quizzed the comedian extensively about his years with Dean Martin, his ideas about filmmaking, the details of his personal life, even his relationship with his parents—things that had no immediate bearing on anything in the scripted role of Jerry Langford. Finally De Niro agreed to cast Lewis and the contracts were struck, whereupon he phoned Lewis and said, as Lewis remembered it, "'Jer—I need you to know that I really want to kill you on this picture. We can't socialize, we can't have dinner, we can't go out.' I said, 'Whatever turns you on, sweetheart. . . . Are there any ground rules about saying "Good morning"?'"

Scorsese and De Niro enlisted Lewis to sharpen Langford's character by bringing his longtime experience of oversized fame and celebrity to bear. "They don't know celebrity," Lewis said years later. "They only know anonymity. You could walk by Bobby De Niro today, you wouldn't know him. It's just the way he is. And for many of the films—*Taxi Driver, Mean Streets, Bang the Drum Slowly, Raging Bull, The Deer Hunter*: who the fuck knows who that is? They needed me to tell them about celebrity. And we wrote together—Paul Zimmerman and Marty and myself—we wrote the things that they had never heard about."

Among Lewis's contributions was an encounter on the streets of New York in which a passerby recognizes Langford and asks for an autograph. When Langford demurs, the woman turns hostile: "You should get cancer!" It was, Lewis claimed, something that had actually happened to him at a Las Vegas hotel. Further, following De Niro's practice, Scorsese encouraged Lewis to bring as much of his personal life to the character as possible. Lewis wound up wearing his own clothes in many scenes, Langford's apartment was decorated with some of Lewis's personal knickknacks, and the part of Langford's dog was played by Lewis's shih-tzu, Angel.

The casting of Masha proved another laborious process. It was a highly coveted role—the last young woman selected by De Niro and Scorsese for a big part, Cathy Moriarty, had been nominated for an Oscar, after all. The part called for a wild, almost psychotic energy, for comic chops, for someone who would play every scene with De Niro except for a long, excruciating one in which Masha would attempt to seduce the bound and gagged Langford.

De Niro promoted his *Deer Hunter* co-star and good friend Meryl Streep for the part. "I asked Meryl to come in and meet Marty and talk about it, because I thought she'd be terrific," he remembered. "She's very, very funny. She's a great comedienne. She came in, but I don't think she wanted to do it, obviously, for what reason I never really knew. But I knew that she *could* do it."*

Other young actresses met with Scorsese and De Niro, Ellen Barkin and Debra Winger among them. And then Cis Corman, who was combing through the ranks of stand-up comedians, got wind of a gangly young woman from Arizona named Sandra Bernhard. Bernhard was staying at the Chateau Marmont when she was summoned to meet Corman and read from the script for her. "She looked stunned," Bernhard said. "Maybe she was frightened. And she said, 'I think. You need. To meet Marty.'"

Bernhard auditioned for Scorsese and De Niro, and they came to see her act at the Comedy Store, just down the hill from the Chateau. After that she was flown to New York to meet Lewis, who was, she said later, "the most intimidating factor in the whole situation. Jerry Lewis was a large, looming figure. So I was scared to meet him, and he lived up to his reputation. He's one of the only showbiz people I've met who really has an aura." Her anxiety at meeting the grand star was exactly what the part of Masha called for; she was hired.

During this process, De Niro went about building Pupkin inside and out. Along with Scorsese and costumer Dick Bruno, he shopped in the sorts of old-school Times Square stores where magicians and other performers got their wardrobe: "There was one of these Broadway showbiz type stores, near the Stage Deli," De Niro remembered, "that had all these flashy clothes that you'd find in Vegas now. This little store with a mannequin, and the mannequin had the suit on and the hair and everything. We went in, took the clothes, I took the hairstyle, the mannequin hairstyle, I said it's all perfect. Marty said, great, let's just do that."

De Niro borrowed the swaying-while-standing-in-place behavior and the rat-a-tat speech pattern of Paul Zimmerman, who spoke even

---

* To date, Streep has never acted for Scorsese.

faster than the famously fast-talking Scorsese, and he mimicked the gait of a chicken. "Gawky. A bird whose neck goes out as he walks," as he recalled. He reminded himself to allow nervousness to show through, to add a whine to his voice, to hunch a little like an acquaintance who struggled with multiple sclerosis, to infuse his dialogue with what he called a "Jewish lilt." (In fact, Pupkin's ethnicity isn't made explicit in the film.) He picked the brain of a New York paparazzo named Barry Talesnick, looked up old gags in joke books, and bombarded Zimmerman with questions, prompting a frustrated letter from the screenwriter in which he declared, "I HAVE NOTHING LEFT. THIS IS IT. . . . This is all I know about Rupert. This is all you need to know about what I know about Rupert. Shit, you know more about him by now than I do, and I invented him."

And what did De Niro know about Pupkin? As he noted to himself, he was "very determined, no nonsense," but "basically ineffectual." He wanted to be careful, he told Scorsese, not to be "weird or creepy . . . there has to be something funny about me." He was a very keen observer of his prey, Jerry Langford: "*I watch him closely always!* Just to see what makes him great." He knew that Pupkin ironed his own clothes, kept an organized room (it would never be filmed or shown), had been an English major, was fast with a lighter with someone else's cigarette, stared without meaning to, and was polite to almost everyone he met for fear of being disliked if he wasn't. He knew that Pupkin would keep his comedy routine short so as not to overstay his welcome and that he would remain at all times "a gentleman . . . A little desperate perhaps but still a gentleman." Even when Pupkin turns dangerous, De Niro noted, he was "still so respectful. But a little tougher, a little harder. I learned."

THE FILM WAS scheduled to shoot in Manhattan in the summer of 1981, but Scorsese took ill that spring and sought to delay production. That wasn't possible, though, because of an impending strike by the Directors Guild of America; if a certain quota of key material on a film hadn't been shot by a specific date, the production would be shut down. Ill or not—and he was, per his own words, "coughing on the floor and sounding like a character from *The Magic Mountain*"—Scorsese would have to proceed.

Ironically, given that he was as thoroughly associated with New York as were Woody Allen and Sidney Lumet, this was only the second film that Scorsese would shoot entirely in the city since turning pro, and he found that the requirements of unions, permitting officials, and traffic control turned even the simplest procedure into an elaborate ritual. "It was like making a film with a dinosaur," he remembered. "The tail was so big it was wagging and slamming into everything, perhaps not intentionally, but destroying things as in a *Godzilla* movie." On top of his struggles with his health and De Niro's need for excessive retakes and reshoots, the filming schedule began to expand well beyond its original length—and all during the fetid heat of a Manhattan summer.

For Lewis, who had made dozens of films at the rapid-fire pace of the old Hollywood system, the protracted shoot was astounding. "When I saw Take 29 for a scene with no words," he remembered, "just walking from a theater mob to a limo, I said, 'We're in a mess.' I never saw the number 29 before in my career! When I saw we had four pages of dialogue the next day, I said to one of the crew, 'If this doesn't go to 136 takes, I'll buy you a car.'"

But Lewis knew he was in on a good thing, and from the very beginning he determined to keep his peace and do whatever was asked of him. As Scorsese recalled, Lewis told him at the outset, "I know I'm number two in this picture. I won't give you any difficulty and I'll do what you want. I'm a consummate professional. I know where I stand. If you want me to wait around, you're paying for my time, I'll do that." Lewis remembered the conversation with more or less the same gist but with a spicier tenor:

> *I went in with a very simple philosophy: If what they do got Rag-*
> *ing Bull up on the screen, then I'm prepared to do whatever's nec-*
> *essary. Bobby and Marty have eccentricities that I as a filmmaker*
> *had to adjust to because I wasn't there as a filmmaker. If they had*
> *hired me as a part of the filmmaking team, I'd have killed them*
> *both because it was against everything that I was taught. For ex-*
> *ample: I do my homework. When I come on the set I can tell you*

every shot that will be made on that picture that day, right up to wrap. Marty comes on the set and waits to see the temperature of De Niro before he really lays out in his mind what he's gonna do. Now, he's done his homework, but he's done it loose. If Bobby came on and was troubled, Marty would have a way to go to nurture that problem, or he'd go another way. Marty said, "Go with the flow." . . . So I kept my mouth shut and stayed in my trailer. When I am a passenger on the other captain's ship, I'm just a passenger. And if it means I see this ship going down because this fucker's pulling the cork out, he ain't gonna hear anything from me.

As Lewis came to see, Scorsese's indulgence of his star paid off in extraordinary bits of acting. "Bobby is no fool," he said. "He knows his craft. And that his craft needs his time, it needs his gut for it. Marty could tell him from now until next Tuesday that Take 5 was super. But De Niro knows fucking well that if he goes into Take 12 and 14 and 15, he'll find an 'if' and an 'and.' If he does Take 20, he'll pick up a quick turn, and on Take 28 he's got lips tightening, which he never had through the first 27 takes. I watched him feign poor retention just to work a scene. I watched him literally look like he couldn't remember dialogue. He knew the fucking dialogue. It was masterful. There's nothing he did that didn't stagger me."

LEWIS'S EQUANIMITY WAS tested repeatedly, however, not so much by the waiting around as by the actual material in which he was performing. In one of the most indelible scenes in the film, Rupert Pupkin shows up uninvited at Jerry Langford's Long Island estate and tries to wheedle the talk show host into letting him stay. Langford, predictably and understandably, takes a firm line and then explodes. The scene took two weeks to shoot, Scorsese said, and it was "extremely difficult for everyone. . . . It was just so painful because the scene itself was so excruciating."

Perhaps the length of time spent on the sequence was causing Lewis's energy to lag, because De Niro finally felt he had to prod his co-star into a more believable performance than he was giving. When it came time to shoot Langford's explosion, De Niro showed up agitated and mumbling invective, apparently upset with Lewis. The Jews, De Niro muttered, "turned this world into garbage for 5,000 years." Lewis, always quick to detect anti-Semitism, was truly staggered, and shot right back at him:

> I said, "You cocksucker, you're lucky you're alive. I'll rip your fucking head off." I didn't know he and Marty had met already, to go for it. "Do you realize you are close to my ripping your head off?" And the cameras are rolling. I know Marty is getting what he wants. I know Bobby is feeding me. But for me not to be aware of two cameras and an entire crew, and Bobby De Niro, throwing dialogue at me. "Maybe the Jews were motherfuckers in the first place." That didn't . . . But "If Hitler had lived, he'd have gotten all of you cocksuckers" was the fucking trigger. He knew . . . the son of a bitch knew. And he's doing this to me because he's just off camera. I pulled him into the scene by three feet, and I was on my way. Whew! He came into the dressing room. "Are you okay?" "Yes, I'm fine. I never want to work with you again."

(Questioned about this legendary bit of scene-building some time later, De Niro sidestepped it: "I don't know if I said anything anti-Semitic. I might have said something to really bust his balls.")

Lewis had a similarly volatile experience acting opposite Bernhard, with whom he had just the one long, difficult scene in which he has been kidnapped, bound and gagged, and subjected to her psychosexual ministrations. Bernhard, cast in large part for her ability to improvise in the scene, taunted, teased, and provoked Lewis, and he had to sit there in squelched silence, burning with rage underneath his bindings.

Bernhard adored working with De Niro and Scorsese—"When you work with great people it gives you a great sense of confidence, and it's a vote of confidence for your talents. You're like, 'How could I go wrong here?'" Propitiously, her first scene—Masha attacking Langford as he gets into his limo after a TV broadcast—was shot on the night of her birthday, June 6. But Lewis, she remembered, "didn't have anything to do with making things easier . . . I was just who I was, and that's who he was stuck with. I think he would've felt the same way about any actress who he had to play that role with. . . . I don't think he felt comfortable at all in the situation. Being intimidated by a young woman isn't really Jerry's forte." Lewis tried to improvise Langford's escape so as to physically humiliate Bernhard—"he wanted me, in my bra and panties and high heels, to spin into a large glass table lit with a hundred candles." But Scorsese devised a simpler, if similarly violent, bit of action. ("Marty told me later," Bernhard said, "that he had thought I really scared Jerry Lewis.")

Finally, Scorsese was happy with Lewis's participation. "Jerry is totally surreal," he said. "But he was very easy to direct. The role was difficult. He had to look as if nothing were going on—as if he were just walking along the street. He wasn't used to acting that way, and he had to keep his face less than elastic. That's hard to do." And Lewis, for his part, saved his highest praise for De Niro, with some reservations: "In order to work with Bobby, you have to make a deal with the Devil. He's one of the best actors I've ever seen in my fuckin' life when he's banging it out of the park. Bobby is very, very much like Babe Ruth in that he gets 60 out of that park. But remember, Ruth struck out 3,766* times. . . . I'm awestruck by Bobby's work, by his commitment. But he fears intellect. He fears anyone who can say anything other than 'Hi.'"

For De Niro, the difficulty in the film had nothing to do with getting along with Lewis or protecting Bernhard. He was interested in pushing Pupkin as far as he could, bringing the character to the edge of caricature but retaining a patent sense of his humanity. "What De Niro and I were trying for," Scorsese said, "was to see how far we could push that character—how far over the top Rupert could go and still remain within a realistic framework. How much could he get away with as an actor playing a character like that." Bernhard concurred that De Niro seemed vulnerable as Pupkin: "He didn't have that helmet on. He didn't have that shield, because somebody that intense and desperate, they don't even think about protecting themselves."

It all came to a head for De Niro when he shot the climactic com-

---

* Actually, only 1,330, but the point stands.

edy routine that Pupkin delivers on national TV as his payment for the safe release of the kidnapped Langford. The monologue—brutally self-lacerating and actually rather funny—was scripted carefully and built up by De Niro in exactly the way a stand-up comedian builds a set of jokes: the timing, the wording, the costume and posture. "The whole routine," he remembered, "was word-for-word—the whole timing and the way it builds." But shooting it, he confessed, was a trauma. As Scorsese recalled, when they finished the first take of it, De Niro told him, "I've never been as terrified, as humiliated in my life." Scorsese felt that De Niro had nailed it, but they went for another take. Again, it was grueling. After that they did one more take, and then they let it drop. "We reshot that monologue twice," De Niro remembered. "I wanted to do it again, but we let it go." They did make one change to it, at De Niro's suggestion. In the earliest versions of the script, the monologue appeared chronologically, at the moment in which it was performed live; De Niro urged Scorsese to show it later, when Rupert watches it on tape, along with the rest of the world, broadcast on the small TV in the tavern where his old high school crush tends bar. It was a savvy insight, adding both to the drama (is he any good?) and to the pathos of the climactic scene: Rupert may not be a king, we learn, but he's actually kind of funny and not at all bad at what he aspires to do.

Shooting on *King of Comedy* wrapped in early autumn, and Scorsese spent the rest of the fall and the better part of the winter editing. When he presented it to 20th Century Fox, they didn't know what to do with it. It fit no genre, its stars were either wildly out of their familiar métiers or completely unknown, and it had an ambiguous ending that seemed almost to mock the audience's credulity. They tested it in a few midwestern markets and it received horrible scores from preview audiences. They decided to release it in early February 1983, nearly two years after production had begun.

You start with the name, an impossible encumbrance: Rupert Pupkin. "Often misspelled and mispronounced," he repeatedly says, and before long we hear "Pipkin" and "Pumpkin" and "Pupnik."

There is the hair, combed to one side like a snowdrift, so big and thick and full that it almost looks like he snaps it on in the morning. The mustache is a dapper touch, and the wardrobe, well . . . On one hand, he's impeccable: three-piece suits, ties, polished shoes, always cleaned and pressed and straightened. But the colors can be a bit loud, the cuts a tad out of fashion, the shoes glaringly white beneath dark slacks: the whole thing is off, somehow, but never exactly objectionable. He's presentable, but within quotation marks, as it were. (Even dressed down to perform a kidnapping, he's a peacock, in a flame-red and orange aloha shirt, oversized sunglasses, and a Panama hat.) He's decorous, solicitous, polite. And yet somehow you feel it's a put-on. There's nobody *actually* like this guy, is there? Not in New York in 1982, not on planet Earth, not in real life.

In fact, Rupert Pupkin only *partly* exists in real life. He lives in New Jersey, commutes to Manhattan to work as the world's best-dressed messenger, hovers around stage doors to collect autographs (although he insists, "It's not my whole life"), drinks coffee at Howard Johnson's, has insane parleys with his frenemy Masha. He's *alive*, he's *here*, as far as that goes.

But he is truly and most completely alive when he's *not* here—when he's having imaginary conversations with Jerry Langford in his head, dreaming of himself as a guest on Langford's show, or sitting in his basement on a mock-up of the Langford show set, complete with full-sized cardboard cutouts of Langford and Liza Minnelli (just five years, mind, after *New York, New York*). In these moments, Rupert chats, schmoozes, argues, exchanges hugs, shares knee-slapping show-biz laughs, and genuinely seems to commune with his celebrity heroes. It's all in his head, but it's more real to him than Times Square.

If his ambition ended at reverie, he would be a simple soul—deluded, living at home with his mother, content to be, in his words, a "schmuck for a lifetime." But his desire for more, for a career in show-biz, for a *real* spot on the *real* couch on the *real* Langford show, leads him into conflicts: with his never-seen mother (voiced, almost inevitably, by Catherine Scorsese), who complains that he's too loud; with Masha, with whom he gets into wailing, siblinglike arguments in the street; with Langford's staff, from a receptionist who can't remember his name and an assistant program director who takes a pass on his material to a security guard who gives him the bum's rush and a butler who claims he's "having a heart attack" when Rupert touches things around Langford's house; and finally with Langford himself. Conflict, we're told, reveals the true inner person. If that is the case, the true Rupert Pupkin is a whining, wheedling brat who insists on getting his own way and will stop at nothing until he does.

But if his conversations with his mother and especially with Masha reveal the innermost man most clearly, the conversations with Langford reveal the full Rupert Pupkin in all his contradictory glory. There is the flustered Rupert, so eager to make a good impression on Langford in the back of a limousine that he can't get his words out and won't let the encounter end ("You don't know how many times I've had this conversation in my head," he confesses, almost innocently). There is the imaginary superstar Rupert who dotes on his own public image and makes the dream-world Langford beg him for a favor. There is the humble-ish Rupert who confesses, again in his own mind, that his comedy comes from his human pain ("I look at my whole life, and I see the awful, terrible things in my life, and I turn it into something funny"). There is the showbiz Rupert, appearing on the Langford show, where he is kowtowed to by his high school principal and then, on live TV, married to his high school crush. There is the determined Rupert who holds a (fake) gun to Langford's head and forces him to read cue cards about his own doom, but who is still sufficiently star-struck to help himself to one of the TV host's cough drops, like a saint's relic.

All of these Ruperts come together in the remarkable scene in which his weekend visit to Langford's Long Island estate is revealed to be a bizarre home invasion. Pupkin, per Langford's butler, "knows everything" about the house—the décor, the routines. He is helping himself piecemeal to the man's life: he even has the moxie to offer Langford a drink from his own bar when the man shows up, called away from his golf match to deal with the insane situation. For a long time Rupert tries to play the moment light, funny, flippant. But when he sees how angry Langford is, he drops the blithe act and chummy voice and returns to the supplicating tenor he had in their first encounter (and, until now, their only *real* one). He has called Langford "a prince" and he fancies himself "the king," but really he's a serf and he knows it. He's fortunate to be in the presence of royalty at all, and sometimes that fact becomes clear to him even in his perennial fog.

Watching De Niro through all this, it's impossible to conceive that we're looking at the man who, a mere two and a half years earlier, had been in credible fighting trim as Jake LaMotta—or had ballooned up like the older LaMotta, or, indeed, had looked or acted anything like LaMotta at all. In his fifth film with Scorsese in a decade, he looks, sounds, gestures, laughs, behaves, dresses, self-presents, and moves in a fashion unlike anything he's ever displayed before. Pumping up his image for secretaries whom he seeks to impress with his intimacy with Langford, he's haughty and slick. Told that his work is not quite ready for TV, he sinks into denial, his head bobbing like a chicken's, trying to be polite but nearing an edge. Goaded by Masha to insist on seeing Langford, he seems almost ready to explode, but he's still strangely decorous and in check, able to segue quickly into his veneer of civility when his humiliating ejection becomes public. De Niro had been in business against Marlon Brando all these years for the title of most in-depth and most committed actor in movies; here he seems more like Peter Sellers (or, indeed, Jerry Lewis) in his willingness to deflect vanity and even embrace shame for effect.

As complex as his relationships with Masha and Langford are, the most curious and beguiling encounters Rupert has are with Rita, the barmaid whom he had voted for as Most Beautiful when they were high school classmates ("Mr. Romance," she remembers). She's played by Diahnne Abbott with a knowing, world-weary air. "Do I know you?" she asks her estranged real-life husband when he sits at her bar. "I think you might," he replies. Rita is "a working girl," in her own words, who, in her mid-thirties, has clearly missed whatever train was going to take her to wherever she dreamed of going. For want of other prospects, she lets Rupert buy her a Chinese dinner and some fruity cocktails, and she endures his displays of childish ego during the meal, laughing along as the stranger behind Rupert mocks him to curry favor with her. Invited to a weekend on Long Island, she dolls herself up quite prettily, then helps herself to a drink, plays records to dance to, and—in a shocking, almost gratuitous little insert shot— steals a tchotchke from Langford's living room. She seems, in short, a bit graspy and desperate. But she knows with certainty that Rupert isn't the answer to her longing. "What do you want, Rupert?" she asks him, almost as if exhausted by the knowledge that he will answer, "You." It's a lovely performance.*

The other woman in Rupert's life, Masha, is played by Sandra Bernhard with an almost punk rock intensity, screaming and sneering and bedeviling and amping up to fury in her frustrated attempts to get close to Langford. She knows how to get almost immediately under Rupert's skin, and she uses that skill as surely as she does her parents' money (she dresses in a private-school blazer, throws cash around freely, and drives a Mercedes with her name on the license plate). With Langford she adopts a more balanced, even deferential air, appreciatively sizing up a sweater she's knitting for him like a doting aunt. And then, in a truly bizarre, stream-of-consciousness seduction scene, she reveals aspects of herself to him that, it would seem, only some well-paid therapists had ever seen before. It's a terrific performance, and also a dead end: see Bernhard in this role and you can't imagine her in anything else.

Jerry Lewis is superb as Langford, bringing his own celebrity aura to bear, as no one merely acting the role could, but also getting inside the character. He has the *real* Langford to play, the man whose limo is invaded, who must endure Rupert's desperate backseat pitch, whose dinner is interrupted by invasive phone calls, whose walk through Manhattan ends with a stranger wishing him cancer and Masha chasing him into his office, who becomes righteously furious when his home is beset by strangers, who is kidnapped and threatened with death. All of that is played with almost transparent naturalness: this isn't the Jerry Lewis from the movies or even from the TV telethon and talk shows, but it's something very like Jerry Lewis the flesh-and-blood man. But there's the *imaginary* Langford as well, the one who befriends Rupert and helps his career and even arranges a secret wedding for him. That kind of glad-handing showbiz Jerry is familiar from talk shows, includ-

---

* Up to now, Abbott had performed only once in a non-Scorsese film, Alan Rudolph's *Welcome to L.A.* (1976). But she'd soon work with John Cassavetes on *Love Streams*, take on a recurring role on TV's *Crime Story*, and continue pursuing other acting and singing opportunities.

ing his own briefly lived ones, but it's nothing that Scorsese or even De Niro could have brought to the film. Perhaps another celebrity could have brought the right energy, power, and vibe to the part, but Lewis is perfect in it.

The film climaxes on Rupert's monologue, a long, painful litany of self-hate, familial dysfunction, and almost masochistic confession—much of it truly funny, all done in a single excruciating take with De Niro mastering the body language, timing, and vocal inflections of a not-ready-for-prime-time-or-even-late-night stand-up. It's the big payoff we've been anticipating for more than an hour (Scorscsc fades into Rupert's reverie the first time he performs the act, for a tape recorder). The dark, dark inside joke of the whole enterprise is that there really is a germ of talent in the guy—with the emphasis, of course, on *germ*.

There are other inside jokes throughout the film: the casting of De Niro's wife and Scorsese's parents (his dad, Charlie, is watching TV at Rita's bar when Rupert changes channels on him); Margo Winkler, the wife of *Raging Bull* producer Irwin Winkler, as Langford's cheerful receptionist; various punk rock stars of the day (including most of the Clash) milling about on the streets of Times Square; De Niro's agent, Harry Ufland, playing Langford's agent; Shelley Winters announced as a guest on the Langford show the night of Rupert's appearance; and Scorsese himself playing the director of the Langford show (Tony Randall even tells him, "You're the director," in case anyone didn't recognize him). It's a regular old-home week.

But it's also chillingly new and prophetic and unsettled and unsettling. Rupert Pupkin is a clown, but how far removed is he from the likes of John W. Hinckley or Mark David Chapman, other disturbed loners whose guns were as real as their obsessions and who killed, or tried to, partly as a means of making their name? Like them, Rupert becomes famous (or, if you prefer, infamous), and he's rewarded for his audacity and psychosis with a real career. (Or is he? The final scene, in which Rupert presides over his own TV show, is so stylized and attenuated as to perhaps be another fantasy—much like the coda to *Taxi Driver*.) Throughout the film the subject of Rupert's name continually arises: how to pronounce it, whether it's real, how widely it will soon be known. In the end, even though the film wasn't a hit, it has become a synecdoche for a kind of undeserved celebrity, a figure for the power of the media to draw attention to freaks and outcasts and turn them into pop heroes. Rupert is more than famous and for more than fifteen minutes. He may not be a king, but he wears a crown of some kind, and he is finally impossible to ignore.

Reviewers didn't know what to think. Once again, Scorsese and De Niro polarized their critics. Some—like Pauline Kael, at great length—found the whole enterprise abhorrent and flawed. Some had mixed feelings but were willing to praise De Niro individually. A very few, such as Vincent Canby in the *New York Times*, appreciated it more or less without qualm ("It's not an absolute joy by a long shot," he wrote, "but, in the way of a film that uses all of its talents to their fullest, it's exhilarating").

The double edge of the film, and of De Niro's performance, made even experienced film watchers uneasy. "De Niro's Rupert has a cheerfully deranged imperviousness . . . that makes you laugh even as it makes you cringe," noted Richard Schickel in *Time*. "De Niro doesn't provide the key to the inner Pupkin," lamented Michael Sragow in *Rolling Stone*. "There's no fanatical gleam in his eye. His grin is shiftless." "He's not just mediocre," observed David Denby in *New York*, "he's *demonically* mediocre—a De Niro character after all."

Stanley Kauffmann of the *New Republic*, who had a long and troubled history with De Niro's work, found moments of brilliance in the performance, and in a notable turn called De Niro "one of our best film actors." But Kael was particularly enraged by the film and its star:

> *If De Niro, disfigured again here, has removed himself from comparison with other handsome young actors, it's not because what he does now is more than acting. It's less; it's anti-acting. . . . De Niro in disguise denies his characters a soul . . . he makes them hollow . . . and merges with the character's emptiness. . . . In most of De Niro's early performances . . . there was bravura in his acting. You could feel the actor's excitement shining through the character, and it made him exciting to watch. . . . And then he started turning himself into repugnant, flesh effigies. . . . De Niro cunningly puts in all the stupid little things that actors customarily*

leave out. It's a studied performance. De Niro has learned to be a total fool. Big accomplishment!

King of Comedy appeared in competition at the Cannes Film Festival that May, and De Niro, Abbott, Scorsese, Bernhard, and Lewis attended the premiere, De Niro honoring his host country by sporting a beret. As back home, it was shut out of prizes (the screenplay, credited to Zimmerman, did win a BAFTA award the following winter). But its legend grew considerably over the years, particularly as the idea of a media generating celebrities out of sheer self-reflection became less a matter of fictional hypothesis and increasingly the stuff of daily life. It was embraced by, among others, Marlon Brando, who had never met De Niro or Scorsese but invited them to his South Pacific island home after seeing the film; they finally made the trip in 1987, spending a couple of weeks lolling, reading, and talking—not so much about acting or the movie business as about life.

And, having done five films together in a decade, De Niro and Scorsese decided, after *King of Comedy*, to take a little break from working together. "We needed to go our separate ways," Scorsese said. "We needed to work with other people. We had worked so intensively for so many years." It wasn't, he insisted, a vote of no confidence in the film. "I think it's De Niro's best performance," he explained. It was just that "we couldn't go any further at that time."

In fact, despite the hundreds of offers fielded by De Niro's agents weekly, despite the director's intention to make a few films he'd already identified, Scorsese already had another collaboration in mind. He intended to follow *King of Comedy* with an adaptation of Nikos Kazantzakis's theologically challenging novel *The Last Temptation of Christ*, and he wanted De Niro for the role of Jesus.

SINCE BEING INTRODUCED to the novel by the actress Barbara Hershey on the set of *Boxcar Bertha*, Scorsese had harbored an ambition to film *Last Temptation*, a remarkable novel by the Greek novelist and philosopher Nikos Kazantzakis. Written in a kind of cerebral, abstract style that recalled Kafka more than it did Kazantzakis's worldwide bestseller *Zorba the Greek,* it tells the story of an adult Jesus who is trying to come to terms with the idea—which seems to emerge from inside his head like a demonic hallucination—that he is both mortal and divine, that he is the messiah, that he is *God.* It follows all the traditional episodes of the life of Christ, but it does so through the lens of his human side, imagining what it would be like to be an ordinary man of thirty-three years of age who embraced the call to leave home, evangelize, and die. Published in 1953 (and translated into English seven years later), it was such volatile material that it nearly got the writer excommunicated from the Greek Orthodox Church. And it would carry an air of controversy ever after.

Scorsese imagined a film that would reconcile the great biblical screen epics that had galvanized him as a boy—*The Robe, King of Kings, Ben-Hur*—with a vision of a world in which people behaved as they do in ours. It would depict the events of the gospels as real, but occurring on a recognizable earth and not in some golden Bible-story tableau. He got Paul Schrader—for whom the novel's themes and texture were beguiling, too—to begin adapting a screenplay, and he got Irwin Winkler interested in producing it. Together they constituted a sufficiently formidable force to convince Paramount Pictures to make it. Scorsese went off to Israel to scout locations. And in the spring of 1983, as he traveled between that work and the publicity duties attendant on the global release of *The King of Comedy,* he stopped in Paris, where De Niro was spending some time during a lull in production in *Once Upon a Time in America,* to ask him if he would be willing to play Jesus in the film—which, if he agreed, would have marked their sixth collaboration in a span of eleven years.

De Niro felt immediately that he was wrong for the part. He could never adequately immerse himself in the role using the methods he preferred. There was too much baggage associated with playing Jesus (he repeatedly compared it to playing Hamlet). And he felt that he was entirely ill-suited to a biblical drama. He repeatedly reminded Scorsese of *The Silver Chalice,* a film about early Christianity that was so badly received that it almost killed the career of its debuting leading man, Paul Newman, before it started.

He made light of it at that first discussion: "I had my head shaved because I was doing 'Once Upon a Time in America,' and I took my hat off, and I said to Marty, 'Do I look like I can play Jesus?'" But he knew that the subject matter was very close to Scorsese's heart: "He's very much into that," he said of the strong religious themes of the film. "I got my own problems. I had it, though, through some members of my family—like my grandmother—but not the way Marty must have had it." The gulf between their visions of the character was, he felt, impossible to cross: "Marty wanted to make him a person and all that, but I still saw him as a guy with long hair and a beard."

Finally he told Scorsese that he would do it only if he had to do it—that is, only if the film would not get made unless he was cast in the role: "If you really have a problem, if you really want to do it, and you need me, I'll do it. If you're up against the wall and you have no other way, I'll do it as a friend." As it happened, the timing was not right for the film with *anyone* in the lead: Paramount had gone through a change of management, and the new team was not terribly excited about making a film that could elicit backlash from the Christian right, the Catholic Church, and who knew who else. When Scorsese finally did make the film, half a decade later, De Niro wasn't considered for the role of Christ (which went to Willem Dafoe after a long period during which Aidan Quinn was Scorsese's first choice for the part). By then, De Niro had made *The Mission*, the Christlike themes of which satisfied his modest interest in religious storytelling ("It's different," he explained when asked why he was comfortable in that role, "it's not *Jesus*"). And when he was asked soon after *The Last Temptation of Christ* was released, to mixed reviews and over-the-top controversy, if he had any regrets about not making it, he answered succinctly, "No."

14

IN JANUARY 1984 DE NIRO STAYED AT THE DISCREETLY LUXURI-
ous Blakes Hotel in the Kensington district of London, where he
had gone to do something he'd never done before: play a cameo
role in a feature film.

The picture in question was *Brazil*, a mammoth, darkly comic
fantasy by Terry Gilliam, the American-born member of the Monty
Python troupe who'd gone from animating surreal short pieces for
the group's famed TV series to directing features, starting with the
beloved *Monty Python and the Holy Grail*. Since then, in such films
as *Jabberwocky* and *Time Bandits*, Gilliam's cinematic vision had become grander, more baroque, more mordant. He was making dazzling
pictures as big as Steven Spielberg's, with special effects and massive
sets and costumes, but with not one trace of Spielberg's sentiment or
warmth. They were funny, they were eye-popping, they were singular,
but they were cool and dark and strange and *very* expensive to make.

Brazil would be his most ambitious film yet. Based on a script co-
written by Gilliam with, among others, Tom Stoppard, it was a dys-
topian tale of a totalitarian bureaucracy run amok, with a lovelorn
functionary named Sam Lowry questioning his role as a cog in the
machinery and coming into contact with a group of subversive revolu-
tionaries, one of whom is (literally, in fact) his dream girl. Among the
producers of the film (which was first known as *1984-and-a-Half*, in
homage to George Orwell and Federico Fellini, both of whose influences can be felt everywhere in it) was Arnon Milchan, who seemed to
be everywhere in De Niro's working life of late. With Gilliam's blessing,
Milchan sent the script to De Niro with a note saying, "Pick your part."

De Niro loved what he read—"*That* will be remembered in years to come," he said later of the film, "no matter what you think of it." He responded to Gilliam and Milchan saying that he was interested in appearing in the film, specifically in the significant supporting role of Jack Lint, Lowry's old friend, fellow bureaucrat, and, though Lowry doesn't know it, a torturer for the regime. But that part had already been set aside for Gilliam's fellow Python Michael Palin, so Gilliam and Milchan steered De Niro the other way entirely, focusing his attention instead on the character of Harry Tuttle, the rogue state operative who leads the resistance and whose name is misspelled on an arrest order, setting off the plot. Tuttle would appear in only two scenes, but he constituted a crucial figure in the story line and in the psyche of Lowry, who sees him as a renegade hero and a father surrogate, a man's man whose determination to take action sharply contrasts with Lowry's milquetoast mien. Gilliam was somewhat surprised that De Niro agreed to such a small part: "He had to take what he could get," he joked. But he soon realized that De Niro "liked the idea of not having the burden of carrying the starring role in a film for a change."

In fact, it was the smallest role he'd played on-screen in nearly fifteen years, not that he saw it that way. The part of Tuttle called for just a week of shooting, but that didn't stop De Niro from preparing for it in his usual thorough fashion. He supplied his own prop tool belt and tools (Tuttle's rebellion takes the shape, in part, of a willingness to make repairs to the omnipresent government-owned heating ducts without following the protocols of paperwork). He toyed with adopting a British accent (and with constructing it so that it was clear it was a put-on). He determined to give his Tuttle a John Wayne–ish air of confidence, whistling and humming while he worked, even as he entered each encounter with prudent caution. He saw it, in short, as an acting job.

On the set, he drove Gilliam daft. Gilliam had been dealing in caricature, grotesquerie, and cartoonishness since before his Python days; there was to be humanity and pathos in *Brazil*, but it would be centered in Lowry (who was being played by Jonathan Pryce, for whom Gilliam had conceived the role). De Niro, however, prodded his director, as was his wont, for insight into his character, for take after take after take until, as Gilliam later said, he "wanted to strangle him." The week that had been blocked out for De Niro's work became two, adding to the film's overlong production schedule and helping to push it over its $15 million budget (contrary to its later reputation, *Brazil* wasn't nearly as costly as it looked).

Despite the brevity of his involvement and any on-set frustration that he may have caused, De Niro became a strong ally of Gilliam's in late 1985, when Universal Pictures refused to release the film in the United States in the director's cut, particularly with the downbeat ending that he'd written. Although *Brazil* had been playing profitably for months in Europe and elsewhere, although it was warmly received at the Cannes Film Festival, Universal, which had put up roughly two-thirds of the budget, refused to show it to the American film press or schedule a firm opening date. Gilliam bought full-page ads in the Hollywood trade papers, bordered in black like funeral notices, addressed to the Universal production chief who was his main antagonist: "Dear Sid Sheinberg, when are you going to release my film?" Gilliam showed the film at universities, which his contract permitted, and invited members of the Los Angeles Film Critics Association to see it. They rallied around him by naming *Brazil* the best film of 1985—even without a theatrical release.

Still Universal remained obdurate. In another gambit, Gilliam showed up on ABC's *Good Morning America* to state his case, and he achieved a considerable coup by bringing De Niro along with him as a star and advocate of the film. De Niro barely spoke, and only in niceties and commonplaces, but his heft as a respected megastar surely played some part in getting Universal to finally release Gilliam's cut of the film—albeit in the most cynical way possible, at once trying to capitalize on the Los Angeles Film Critics prize as a potential Oscar lure and keeping bookings and advertising to an absolute minimum. It didn't matter that Gilliam had produced a visionary classic; *Brazil*, and the battle to get it onto American screens, would mark him as a profligate and a nuisance for the rest of his career.

—◈◈◈—

IN THE SPRING, De Niro was in New York doing something else he hadn't ever done before: playing the leading role in a romance, *Falling in Love*. There were little love stories in *The Gang That Couldn't Shoot Straight*, *1900*, *The Last Tycoon*, *The Deer Hunter*, and *Raging Bull*, but none of those could truly be said to be romantic films, let alone full-fledged melodramas. (Told by Gene Siskel in an interview a few years later that he had never said "I love you" on-screen before, De Niro was taken aback: "Didn't I say 'I love you' to the girl in 'Once Upon a Time in America'? No, ah, I guess I didn't say it quite that way. I guess I've never said it before that directly. That's interesting.")

But, as indicated by the title of the new movie, which was written by Michael Cristofer, the Pulitzer Prize–winning playwright of *The Shadow Box*, this was first and foremost a love story. It would be something of an old-home week as well. It would pair De Niro with Meryl Streep for the first time since *The Deer Hunter*, and feature Harvey Keitel as his character's pal and confidante; Ulu Grosbard would direct. And it would be filmed in and around New York, which, increasingly, was a matter of genuine import in De Niro's choice of projects. "I was tired," he explained. "This script came along. It was a nice story, set here in New York."

That didn't exactly speak of an obsessive need to play the part. In fact, De Niro's notes for the film were scantier than any he had ever made in a film in which he had a significant role. (It's interesting, too, to note that on the two occasions he chose to work with Grosbard, he did so partly, by his own confession, so that he could commit himself less to his work than ordinarily.) His choice of props was minimal—a watch, a wallet, a ring, a shopping list. He wore the most workaday clothes as wardrobe. Remarkably, he didn't figure out what his character did for a living. "We weren't even sure if this guy was an engineer or a construction worker," he confessed. "I *still* don't know. That isn't what mattered."

To be fair, he did put effort into calculating the nuances of the progress his character, Frank Raftis, was making from an ordinary life to the verge of a passionate extramarital affair. In his first scenes, his notes reminded him to remain oblivious to the goings-on around him that had nothing to do with him, to adopt an air, as he put it, of a non-actor caught on the reality TV prank show series *Candid Camera*, "totally unaware of anyone watching me." He later indicates that he'll note his character's movement from interest in his new acquaintance to romantic feelings: *"There's got to be that look, that imperceptible look!"* And he spells out with precision his character's frame of mind during the climactic confession of his feelings: "Telling her is more important than anything, precedes and supersedes anything, and not only do I love her but she loves me and she knows it. She might not want to see me and might not think we ought to see each other, but she can't say she doesn't feel the same way about me."

He also finally shed almost all the extra weight he'd gained for *Raging Bull*, hiring a personal trainer named Dan Harvey to work with him at his own gym and whip those final twenty pounds off his stomach and legs, bringing his body fat down from an uncharacteristic 20 percent to a far more familiar 9 percent. His character was tweaked to include a fondness for exercising, and for the first time in years on-screen his famous cheekbones were once again clearly defined; when he smiled, the crinkles around his eyes were sharper and deeper than they had been since *The Deer Hunter*.

But the recovery of his fitness didn't translate into happy responses to the film. *Falling in Love* was released at Thanksgiving, as a kind of alternative at the multiplex for grown-ups, and it got swamped by its competition, finishing sixth at the box office in its opening weekend with $3.1 million in its first five days, well behind the ticket-selling champ of the week, *Supergirl*.

IF HE HAD CHOSEN to play a small role in *Brazil* and an easy-to-manage role in *Falling in Love*, at least in part because he was tired, De Niro soon found sufficient energy to tackle a series of new challenges and one of the most arduous projects in which he'd ever involve himself. *The Mission* was based on "a suggestion for an original screenplay" written in 1975 by Robert Bolt, the prize-winning playwright and screenwriter responsible for, among many things, *A Man for All Seasons*, *Lawrence of Arabia*, and *Doctor Zhivago*.

Asked by Italian producer Fernando Ghia to look into colonial South America as inspiration for a story, Bolt learned of the Guarani War, an eighteenth-century conflict between Amazonian natives and the forces of colonial Europe, which meant to impose slavery on the indigenous population despite the objections of the Jesuit order of Catholic priests, who made up a large portion of the missionary corps. He conflated that story with the life of Roque González de la Cruz, a Jesuit priest born of Spanish noble stock in 1576 in what is now Paraguay, who devoted himself to forging peaceful coexistence between colonists and natives and brought the ire of Spanish authorities down onto the Jesuit order.[*] Helping himself to bits of de la Cruz's story as raw material for one of his protagonists, the Jesuit Father Gabriel, Bolt created the other out of whole cloth. Rodrigo Mendoza is a savage Spanish mercenary, ex-military, who traffics in slaves. After a personal crisis, he forsakes his ways of anger and violence to follow the guidance of Gabriel, whose order he joins after a dramatic penance. Combined, the two men and their adherents try to create a small Eden of peaceful cooperative life in the remote jungle. But they have run afoul of political change, and they are attacked by a joint force of Spanish and Portuguese militaries.

After he wrote a screenplay for Ghia, who failed to find interest in it, Bolt poured the story into a novel, his first. But the idea of seeing it on-screen was never far from his mind. As he explained in his original eighteen-page "suggestion": "The visual background is spectacular and like the story little known to the world at large. All this affords the opportunity to make an artistically exceptional film of international appeal." In 1984, Ghia brought the material to London's Goldcrest Films and David Puttnam, the Oscar-winning producer of *Chariots of Fire*, *Midnight Express*, and most recently *The Killing Fields*. Puttnam, like Bolt, thought that big was the right size for this film, and he commissioned a revision of the screenplay with an eye toward making it the second theatrical film by Roland Joffé, who'd directed *The Killing Fields*. By late 1984 they were casting around for lead actors, and Joffé made the bold suggestion that they contact De Niro for the role of Mendoza.

---

[*] Beatified in 1934, he would be canonized by Pope John Paul II in 1988.

It was hardly an obvious choice. De Niro had almost never played a character who was born before 1900 (Vito Corleone and Monroe Stahr were the exceptions, born in the 1890s). For movie audiences, he was unvaryingly a figure of concrete and neon, of the New World and the American century; it was virtually impossible to picture him on horseback, wielding a sword, hacking his way through the jungle. But he was also an international star, somebody upon whom Puttnam and company could hang a $22 million budget and an epic running time and hope to recoup their investment. For Gabriel they had chosen Jeremy Irons, an accomplished actor but still not a movie star, having been seen principally on exports of British TV's *Brideshead Revisited* and in the screen version of *The French Lieutenant's Woman*. De Niro, or someone of similar stature, would be necessary to infuse the production with star power.

Joffé and Puttnam met De Niro at Blakes Hotel when he was in London to make *Brazil,* and it was something of a delicate dance of diplomacy. De Niro liked the material. "I thought it was really a wonderful, meaningful story," he later said, "and the idea of this man changing appealed to me a lot." It didn't seem to matter to him, somehow, that he would have to spend months in rugged and remote corners of Colombia or that he was playing a part almost as physically demanding as Jake LaMotta. The challenge was part of the appeal for him.

But Puttnam wasn't sure De Niro was the right man. He knew of the actor's penchant for multiple takes and on-camera rehearsal, and he expressed concerns about those habits right up front. De Niro sought to appease him: "I understand your problem," Puttnam recalled him saying, "and I will never delay your picture." Puttnam had other reservations about how well suited De Niro was for the part, but he was mollified by De Niro's collaborative assurances, and he eventually agreed to the actor's terms: $1.5 million, plus a percentage of the net profits, plus expenses. He did, however, have a backup plan: Liam Neeson, a strapping and little-known Irish actor, was hired to play a small part with the thought in the back of Puttnam's mind that he could use him as a substitute if, for any reason, De Niro couldn't do the film.

As so often in the past, De Niro treated the film as his own project. In addition to learning horsemanship (in Manhattan, naturally, at the

Claremont Riding Academy on the Upper West Side), swordsmanship, and a bit of Spanish, he pitched in on the production in material ways. "He spent eight weeks with Roland Joffé," recalled Puttnam, "reading every actor we cast." He dined with Robert Bolt, who had suffered a stroke since writing the script and struggled to communicate his thoughts about Mendoza, which De Niro dug for regardless. (He also, per Bolt's biographer, failed to pick up the bill for dinner.) When the producers hired the radical Jesuit priest Daniel Berrigan to accompany the crew to Colombia and serve as both an actor (in a cameo role) and a technical consultant, De Niro availed himself of access to the famed activist. (In his diary of the production, Berrigan admitted that he was of more use to Irons, whose character he understood more thoroughly. "Bob sees his role as someone who must make plausible an extraordinary change of heart, from murderer to Jesuit. *He* has to explain what would lead one to such a change. *I* can only outline the steps.")

De Niro arrived in Cartagena in the early spring of 1985 and was greeted with a box of Cuban cigars from Joffé and a cadre of bodyguards, two of whom would be with him at all times—outside his hotel room door, on the set, wherever. It was the height of Colombia's cocaine-fueled drug wars, in retrospect an absurd time to shoot a multimillion-dollar production there. Puttnam said that it was "sheer hell." Not only did nobody outside of the capital, Bogotá, care that the government wished the filmmakers to be shown all courtesies, but some fool of a functionary had decided to build crucial sets along a well-traveled drug courier route, meaning that there was a constant threat of genuine peril and a heavy-handed military presence. The weather proved oppressive. "There were floods," recalled Puttnam, "torrential rains, temperatures of 110 degrees." Worse, he said, "almost everybody fell ill with dysentery—except Bob. He takes terrific care of his body." Whether by virtue of his diet or his constitution, De Niro, who had the most arduous role in the film, never succumbed.

He built Mendoza with his characteristic exactness, adding such physical touches as a scar, reminding himself that the character ought constantly to be "tense like Mad Dog Kelly," and continually stressing that the transforming Mendoza must learn how to empathize with other human beings, whom he'd previously seen as objects: "Remember, always relate, always relate, the key, the key." Joffé was astounded to watch his star transform himself for the role: "Bobby De Niro actually *changed*," he said. "His look changed. In three days of walking about with Colombian men and observing their ways, the New York Italian began to disappear and a powerful Hispanic appeared." After meeting him in New York and spending time with him in Cartagena, Berrigan was fascinated by De Niro's absorption in the role and the process. "De Niro seems many light-years distant," he wrote in his diary. "Somewhat as though his existence and personality have passed into the film. As though, for the duration, his life will be available only to the camera and the director. This is a hard vocation; also, if the term makes any sense, a notable asceticism." (Imagine how the elder Robert De Niro would have appreciated that insight into the making of art!)

But even with the pressures of mass-scale filmmaking, angry weather, and a drug war just off camera, De Niro insisted, as ever, on working his scenes as he always had, take by take, piece by piece, despite the conditions, even despite the response of his co-star. As Puttnam remembered, "Jeremy [Irons] would come entirely prepared. He would be word perfect whereas De Niro was used to rehearsing on camera . . . by take three, it was probably as good as Jeremy would ever be. [But] on take three, De Niro was just limbering up. By take seven, when De Niro was beginning to get somewhere near a performance, Jeremy would get bored. By take 13, when De Niro was delivering a very, very good performance, Jeremy was glassy-eyed!" (To be fair, as difficult as this may have proven on the set, the film's editor, Jim Clark, saw the point of De Niro's craft: "With De Niro, you don't cut him, you mine him. You have to seek out the performance because it varies so.")

Nobody faulted De Niro's application to the tasks the film presented him. Patsy Puttnam, the producer's wife, was visiting the set when she noticed a ragamuffin figure bounding about the jungle barefooted. She asked associate producer Iain Smith, "Who on earth's that?" "It's Bobby De Niro," Smith answered. "He's got to do that in his scene tomorrow." She was appalled: "But his *feet* . . ."

Still, there were limits to what the producers would let their star do. At one point he questioned not only his dialogue in a certain scene but the very actions and thoughts behind it, suggesting that the script was flawed. Joffé tried to talk him into seeing through the pages as written, but he was stubborn. That night, dining at their hotel, De Niro discussed his reservations with Puttnam at length. When the producer realized that he wasn't making any progress in steering the actor back onto the task at hand, he took another tack: "Well, Bobby, you may be right, but if you're not, we stand to lose a lot of money. We're walking into a brick wall here. You know, if 'The Mission' only takes as much as *your last four films combined*, we'll lose a lot of money." De Niro, chastened by the reminder that moviemaking was a team sport and that his team had been on a poor streak of late, made no further protests.

After more than four months' work, shooting of *The Mission* wrapped in late 1984, and the completed film premiered in May 1986 at the Cannes Film Festival, where it was awarded the top prize, the Palme d'Or, marking the second time in a decade that De Niro was the star of a film to be so recognized.

PERSONALLY, DE NIRO seemed pleased with the film. He loved Colombia, calling it "an incredibly beautiful, mysterious place," and he was fond of Joffé: "He's a good director with a lot of heart." But there would be no denying that he was at the very least a curiosity in the finished picture. In his first-ever film set prior to the twentieth century, De Niro is, by and large, a man lost in time. He credibly conveys Mendoza's macho hauteur, his ruthlessness, his pride. He bears himself with a ramrod certitude, a fearless gaze, a beefy masculinity, a somehow credibly Latin air of nobility; he manages to look at home on a horse and plausible with a sword. But as soon as he opens his mouth and essays Bolt's stagey, old-timey dialogue, he's sunk. "So me you do not love?" he asks the woman he wishes to wed, sounding like he's translating his lines in real time, and badly. Only in the scene in which, having taken religious vows, he makes a grandiloquent and sarcastic display of apologizing to everyone in Asunción for an outburst of temper does he manage to wrestle the language into something that feels his own.

As it happens, the physical aspects of the role are more prominent, though that isn't always to the film's advantage. In the excruciating sequence in which Mendoza commits a personal penance by schlepping his battle armor over a mountain, up a waterfall, and through a jungle, De Niro seems entirely determined in what he's doing and entirely blind to how daffy he looks: a guy from Greenwich Village sent back to the eighteenth century to drag a bag of pots around Paraguay. But in the final going, when Mendoza forsakes his priestly vows and resumes his warlike ways, something of the character's earlier confidence returns to him, and his ferocious fight is credibly engaged. That spectacle is among the strengths of the film. But, like its star, whenever *The Mission* opens its mouth to say what it's thinking, it loses almost all of its power.

As it happened, David Puttnam had been right to be anxious about De Niro at the box office. Although the film had a certain middlebrow cachet and was widely admired for its epic craft, it grossed barely $17 million at the North American box office, not close to earning back its budget. (It did earn seven Academy Award nominations, including Best Picture and Best Director, though it won just one prize, for cinematography.)

BY THE 1980S, his marriage to Diahnne Abbott seemed less solid than ever, and De Niro's cat-on-the-town reputation grew. He was regularly seen in the company of attractive African American women, often in their twenties, always beautiful, always slender, and rarely with him more than once or twice. In New York and Los Angeles, restaurateurs and club-goers would often spot him in the company of these women, whom he met however he could: chasing them down in his car, approaching them in public places or at events, even spotting them on TV and in newspapers and contacting them through third parties. While he was making *Brazil* in London he got an eyeful of one of the *Sun*'s Page Three girls, a gorgeous South Londoner of Caribbean heritage named Gillian de Terville. Getting her phone number through the agency of one of his showbiz contacts, he rang her at her parents' house and began a now-and-then relationship that lasted longer than a year, seeing her whenever he was in the United Kingdom and inviting her occasionally to see him in New York.*

But of all the girls who drifted through his life when he was still legally married to Abbott, none would have the impact of Toukie Smith, a buoyant woman whom *Esquire* once called "a cyclone of dizzy charm." Smith was a well-known figure in the New York fashion and dance worlds, in the city's night life and charitable circles—in connection, it often seemed, with anything and everything to do with glamour, sparkle, and joie de vivre.

She was born in 1953 in Philadelphia, the youngest of three children of a butcher and a factory worker. Her parents split when she was four, and she and her older brothers, Willi and Norman, were raised by the combined energies of her mother's family. In that female-dominated household, Willi, the eldest, born five years before his sister, liked to joke that there was more clothing than food. He became interested in fashion and clothing design from a young age, winning a scholarship to the Parsons School of Design in New York. Soon after graduating, he entered the world of women's fashion with great energy, flair, and—for his age—success.

By the time he was twenty-five, Smith was one of the stars of a boom in African American fashion designers, with his clothing—mainly sports and evening wear for women of ordinary means—regularly featured in layouts in *Vogue, Glamour,* and the *New York Times.* And he had a favorite model, who sometimes gave him inspirations for specific designs: his sister, Doris, aka Toukie, thus dubbed for the way she pronounced the "toot-toot" of a choo-choo train in a favorite childhood song. "Toukie is my total inspiration," Willi once said. "She has enough energy to light up the World Trade Center." The fun that Toukie radiated in her modeling perfectly suited her brother's work; she smiled on the catwalk and actually seemed to mean it, which was just the sort of attitude that Willi's playful, trendy work embodied: "I don't design clothes for the Queen," as he put it, "but for the people who wave at her as she goes by."

---

* De Terville would go on to minor fame as a softcore porn model and actress.

At just twenty years old, Toukie hit New York like a ball of fire. She studied dance with the Alvin Ailey troupe, appeared in almost all of her brother's fashion shows, designed shoes, attended parties, got a contract to model for Issey Miyake, was named "Bloomingdale's Favorite Model" of 1978, and signed on with the powerful Wilhelmina modeling agency. She and Willi formed a clothing company that didn't last long, but he rebounded with a more stable firm, Williwear, that within a decade would grow to serve more than five hundred department stores and gross $25 million per year. And he was a critical as well as financial success. In 1983 he was awarded the Winnie, the top prize for women's fashion, at the annual Coty American Fashion Critics' Awards; two years later, he took the top prize at the Cutty Sark Menswear Awards.

Toukie met De Niro at a party after Williwear had become a thriving concern and her star had risen alongside her brother's. Physically, she was De Niro's type: bosomy, slender-waisted, very pretty. But she had more energy for socializing, party-going, and scene-making even than Abbott, which seemed to make it unlikely that she and De Niro could sustain a relationship. Yet somehow, because she doggedly maintained her independence from him—"I tell people, 'You deal with me as *Toukie Smith*,'" she insisted to a reporter—they kept seeing each other and formed a genuine bond that lasted for years. She would appear at premieres with him, at the public events that he rarely (and begrudgingly) attended, at private occasions such as dinner parties and birthdays and the like. But she maintained her own homes in New York and Paris; from his point of view, it was ideal.

As in all of his relationships, including his marriage, which would officially end with what his soon-to-be ex-wife Diahnne Abbott called a "reasonable . . . pleasant and friendly" divorce in 1989, De Niro was extremely circumspect and private. He had his pleasures, he had his preferences, he had his needs, he had his comforts, and he had his freedom, but he also managed to form genuine connections with formidable women. Soon after the divorce, the open secret of his relationship with Toukie was made public knowledge, and newspapers and such were referring to her as his "companion."

At the same time as her connection with De Niro was reaching this public level, Toukie began to suffer a series of personal losses. In 1986 her mother, June Harllee, died in New York of cirrhosis of the liver. In April of the following year came an even more devastating blow: Willi, age thirty-nine, died suddenly—"He went into the hospital on Wednesday and died on Friday," recalled a business partner—of what was at first reported to be pneumonia and was later acknowledged to be AIDS, which turned lethal very quickly when he contracted a parasite on a trip to India. He had always been frail and secretive, and apparently nobody around him knew how sick he was until it was too late for any of them to be of help or comfort. Toukie was still feeling those losses in June 1988 when she suffered more heartbreak, miscarrying De Niro's child. Characteristically, she rebounded from these losses with aplomb and vigor. She had been working on AIDS awareness programs and charity through the Smith Family Foundation, which she formed after Willi's death (De Niro joined her in hosting a Willi Smith Day fund-raiser in April 1990). She did some acting on television, danced and sang in benefits, and continued to make the scene not only on red carpets but, in effect, behind them, building a party-planning business, which grew to include catering, and yet another business as a beauty and fashion consultant, and continuing to model for fashion shows, charitable events, and catalogues. And even as she did all that, the losses continued to pile up. Patrick Kelly, another African American fashion designer close to both Willi and Toukie, died of AIDS in 1990, and Williwear spiraled financially, declaring bankruptcy in 1991, barely four years after its founder's demise.

DE NIRO HADN'T appeared onstage in any sort of dramatic production since the early 1970s, but his apparently total metamorphosis into a screen actor did not dissuade the indefatigable New York theatrical impresario Joe Papp from trying to coax him back to the stage. In early 1980, Papp, who ran the Public Theater in Greenwich Village and the New York Shakespeare Festival, famed for its summertime productions in Central Park, announced plans to mount a series of repertory plays with big stars, including Meryl Streep, Jill Clayburgh, Raul Julia, and De Niro. De Niro and Streep were said to be cast in three of them, one

being a production of Chekhov's *Three Sisters*, the other two, unan-
nounced, to be directed by Wilford Leach and Ulu Grosbard. De Niro
didn't really seem serious about the project at the time—"I told them
they can use my name," he explained to *Drama-Logue*—and by the
springtime Papp, millions of dollars shy of the funds the venture would
require, dropped it.*

But in February 1986 the news broke that Papp had finally landed
the big fish he'd had so long on his line: De Niro would be appearing onstage at the Public in April in *Cuba and His Teddy Bear*, the
world premiere of the first full-length work by a twenty-six-year-old
playwright named Reinaldo Povod. Povod's play had been developed
in playwriting workshops at the Public, but Papp didn't at first think
that it would become one of the star vehicles for which the theater was
noted. As he told a reporter: "I had no intention of casting it with stars,
but after I read it, I thought, I wonder if De Niro would be interested
in this? I had been after him for years to get back to the theater. So I
sent him the script." De Niro, Papp said, "was interested in it, but he
kept saying, 'I don't know. Well, maybe all right, but I still have these
movies to do.'"

The play concerned an illiterate Hispanic drug dealer, Cuba, raising his son Teddy in an unpromising and sometimes dangerous environment on the Lower East Side. The boy has aspirations to be a
writer, but he has chosen to emulate Che, a famed "playwright junkie"
celebrated in the New York media, and his father's concerns with the
protocols and particulars of his own chosen profession blind him to the
danger toward which his son is tending.† The pressures under which
the two men live build in the play's second act to an explosive climax
between father and son.

De Niro was vague when asked what drew him to the material: "I
always wanted to do a play, but I wanted to do a new play," he said.

---

* A few years later, Dustin Hoffman actually proposed to his producers that De Niro
play the role of Biff opposite his own Willy Loman in a Broadway production of *Death of
a Salesman*. Word got to De Niro. "You want me to be your son onstage?" De Niro asked
Hoffman incredulously. The role went to John Malkovich.

† Povod was an acolyte of the playwright and drug-and-booze addict Miguel Piñero.

"New plays are more interesting; you don't have all the stigma, the baggage you have with old plays. I just felt this one was very well written and very strong." He wouldn't commit, but he continued to respond to Papp's entreaties. "I introduced him to the playwright and his father," the producer remembered, "and we had two workshop readings with most of the same people who are in the cast with him now. But there was no commitment still, just wait and see. Finally I grabbed De Niro and asked, 'Are we going to do it?' and he said, 'We'll have to work it out.'"

The deal was struck: with a cast that included Burt Young and Ralph Macchio, who had taken part in the workshop readings, De Niro was scheduled to appear in *Cuba* from May 18 through June 14, with preview performances beginning in mid-April. The announcement proved to be lightning at the box office: the entire run of the show was sold out in three hours (impressive, but to be fair, the theater in which the show would be performed seated just over a hundred). Ever innovative, Papp found a way to sell even more tickets: petitioning Actors' Equity for a waiver of their policies against broadcasts of live plays, he was given permission to air closed-circuit television streams of the performances into another auditorium at the Public's complex; those seats went for $7 a pop.

The mounting of the play was the sort of work De Niro loved: real roll-up-the-sleeves acting, with lots of conversation about the characters and scenes. As Povod noted, "He trusted us entirely. He was willing to accept anything we would submit to him and give it a trial. He knew that a lot of the writing had to be examined or tested in rehearsal." The creators understood they had a rare opportunity at hand, and they were careful not to ask too much of their star; indeed, they gave him the latitude to perform the role as his instincts guided him. As Bill Hart, who was given *Cuba* as his directorial debut, noted, "With Bob De Niro, you'd just better be very careful about insisting on anything. Because you may insist on something that will be a lot less interesting than something he's going to come up with himself two weeks from now."

Young, who'd already appeared in three films with De Niro while sharing virtually no scenes with him, found him an engaged and accessible co-star. "After rehearsals," he recalled, "we'd rehearse some more in his loft. He had a floor plan laid out in his living room and everything. He was meticulous. And very patient with Ralph Macchio, who was his son in the show and had never been onstage before. I thought of Bob as our leader." In fact, De Niro fostered a variety of bonding efforts with the cast, going so far as to initiate the ritual of a football-team-style huddle before the opening curtain.

The show went through a month of previews before opening on May 18. De Niro was greeted with almost universally positive reviews. De Niro, per Mel Gussow of the *New York Times*, "amasses character detail, and . . . gives Cuba stage life . . . he reveals an earthy natural-ness and an ability to extinguish his own star charisma. Artfully, he subordinates himself within a company of actors." In the *Village Voice*, Michael Feingold declared, "Robert De Niro's an actor, a real actor, and a good one. . . . He has a lead actor's authority, which in the the-ater is a better asset than a star's mythical magic." The *New Yorker* de-clared the performance "stunning" and added that De Niro "couldn't be better." Jack Kroll of *Newsweek*, who'd written appreciatively of De Niro's last stage performance, in Shelley Winters's *One Night Stands of a Noisy Passenger*, said that the star gave his character "a riveting real-ity." And the hard-to-please John Simon of *New York* simply said: "As Cuba, Robert De Niro is every bit as effective and affecting as in his best movie roles—more than which I needn't say."

The reviews of the actual play were mixed, but commercially *Cuba* was review-proof. That month of previews had sold out in a snap, as had the four weeks of the official run, as had a $250-a-pop benefit performance, which included dinner. Tickets were nearly impossible to come by, even for stars: Tom Cruise, then dominating the movie screen in *Top Gun*, had to sit apart from his date on the night he caught the show, because neither Papp nor De Niro could get him a pair of seats together at the last minute. Powered by De Niro's presence, if not necessarily his work, the show was a massive hit for the always-underfunded Public Theater. It surprised exactly no one in New York, then, when Joe Papp announced, just as the production was winding down, that he was moving *Cuba and His Teddy Bear* to Broadway.

De Niro had committed to appear in fifty-five performances at the Longacre Theatre—a Broadway house with a capacity more than ten times that of the original Public Theater auditorium in which the play debuted. Tickets, with prices ranging from $10 to $37.50, went on sale on June 30, and by the end of business on July 1, more than $500,000 worth had been sold—more than 30 percent of the total potential gross. Considering that De Niro, Young, and Macchio, the stars of *Raging Bull, Rocky,* and *The Karate Kid,* were working for the Broadway minimum of $700, Papp and the Public were set to make a killing.

The Broadway production of *Cuba* opened on July 16. That night, De Niro received flowers from Diahnne Abbott and the kids, as well as from Sally Kirkland and Liza Minnelli, telegrams and letters from Harvey Keitel, Twyla Tharp, Michael Cristofer, Christopher Walken, and Tommy Lee Jones, and thank-you notes from Joe Papp and Ralph Macchio. The opening-night party was star-studded, but, as Mardirosian remembered, De Niro was more interested in family than celebrities. "Because I was an understudy," he said, "I was able to get to the party early. There were a lot of tables, and at one of them I saw Robert De Niro Sr., and I thought, 'I'll go sit with Bob,' and he beckoned me over, and I sat across from him. And we're chatting, mostly about tennis, and then the people start coming in from the theater. And when Bob, the actor, walks in, everybody's wondering where he's gonna sit, because that's gonna be the center of attention. And where does he sit? He sits next to his father! I had frankly had been hoping to stay in the background. Nobody had seen me in the show, nobody knew who I was, but as soon as Bob comes in, suddenly it was as if all the headlights in the room were pointing at us."

The engagement ran until late September, and once again it was a celebrity carnival; on one memorable night, the audience included Robin Williams, Richard Chamberlain, and Sylvester Stallone with his wife of the moment, Brigitte Nielsen. An even more intriguing crowd was treated to the play on August 18, when the cast performed it on Rikers Island before seven hundred inmates.

As Tom Mardirosian remembered, De Niro was always inclusive of his collaborators. Even though he was but an understudy in the show, Mardirosian was invited to De Niro's birthday party. "All these big celebrities were there," he said. "And I sat near Robert De Niro Sr., and he had a dog that he was petting. And when they brought out the cake and all these big celebrities were singing 'Happy Birthday' to Bobby, the dad said to me, 'Look at this: I remember when *nobody* came to his birthday party.'"

Onstage De Niro proved, once again, a willing collaborator. Mardirosian, among many others in the cast, was a more experienced stage actor than De Niro, and on the night that he understudied Young, he realized that De Niro didn't know how to, as theatrical actors call it, "hold for the laugh"—that is, wait for the audience to finish laughing at a funny line before resuming the dialogue. As Mardirosian recalled,

There was this one scene in the play that I always thought was funny and should have gotten laughs, but it never did, and I always thought that was odd. So when I went on for my one night, I was determined to have a good time . . . By the time the scene came on, I was real comfortable, and he says his line, and I say my line, and the audience laughs where they had never laughed before, and he talked over the laugh, because he's not used to them laughing there. And he stopped, and he kind of looked at me funny, like, "I don't understand that." And he said the next line, and I said the next line, and they laughed again. And again they topped him. So now he's thinking, "Hmmm . . . something's going on here." And by the time the scene was over, he had learned to hold for the laugh. I literally taught him how to do that onstage while we were performing in a Broadway house. At the end of the show, he came to my dressing room and knocked on the door and said, "You know, you're a funny guy." And I said, "Well, thank you . . ." And he said, "No: you're a funny guy." And I said, "No, really . . ." And he said, "No. I'm telling you: you're a funny guy." So I finally said, "Thanks, Bobby."

Cuba, sans De Niro, would be performed in London and Buenos Aires in the coming years, and a movie script, which De Niro didn't care for, appeared on his desk in 1988. There was talk in the fall, just after *Cuba* closed, of De Niro staying on Broadway to direct and star in a production of Bertolt Brecht's *Arturo Ui*, which came to naught, and the following year Joe Papp announced plans to mount a series consisting of every play by William Shakespeare featuring prominent stars, De Niro among them. But though he didn't specifically say no, it was clear soon afterward that De Niro had no plans to return to the stage anytime soon, and certainly not in a classical role. "I don't know that my way would be that special or interesting that I would want to put all that time in, to put myself on the line," he said. "There are other people with much better qualifications for doing it. I mean, Shakespeare is great, but I'd rather have the same problems in a contemporary situation where people can relate to it more directly."

15

WHILE HE WAS BUILDING AND PERFORMING HIS ROLE IN *Cuba*, De Niro was playing a different sort of heavy in a brief but crucial performance in *Angel Heart*, an atmospheric thriller that director Alan Parker was adapting from William Hjortsberg's novel *Falling Angel*. Parker, a onetime client of David Puttnam's when the producer was still an agent, had broken into feature directing with the very strange kids-as-gangsters picture *Bugsy Malone* and gone on to critical, commercial, and cult success with *Midnight Express*, *Fame*, *Pink Floyd—The Wall*, and, least seen but best, the domestic drama *Shoot the Moon*.

His new film was a mystery about a private detective, Harold Angel, hired by a shadowy client, named Louis Cyphre, to find a fellow named Johnny Favourite, with whom Cyphre has some sort of contract; Favourite, claiming amnesia, has reneged on his portion of the deal and disappeared, and Cyphre wants him found and brought to account. It was a lurid, sexy, overheated story steeped in blood and sex and the occult, set in the 1950s and moving between Harlem and New Orleans. Parker, a lush visualist and iconoclast, planned to push the material to a provocative edge, preparing to include an explicit sex scene between Angel and a voodoo priestess.* It was a picture designed to make waves.

At first Parker courted De Niro for the role of Angel. But De Niro

---

* These scenes, which featured extensive nudity by the young actress Lisa Bonet, from TV's *The Cosby Show*, wound up earning the film an initial rating of X from the Motion Picture Association of America. Parker and company appealed twice, losing both times. They finally cut ten seconds of footage so as to obtain an R rating.

had problems with the script. "I told Alan Parker that there were a lot of things wrong," he remembered. After a series of communications in which De Niro explained his reservations, Parker made him a different offer: what if he were to play Cyphre, who only had a handful of scenes? De Niro still objected to the structure of the screenplay, but he found himself engaged by the opportunity to build a memorable character without carrying a script. "It was what you'd call a cameo," he said. "But then it took me a lot of time to agree to that, too."

As Parker recalled, "He was lovely, only he wasn't definite. It took a lot of talking." But he understood the actor's trepidation. "De Niro has made very few errors in any of his choices. That burden weighs heavily on him each time he has to decide what to do. Certainly he's extremely careful with someone like Roland Joffé or myself, directors he hasn't worked with before." In the meantime, Parker had cast Mickey Rourke, then rising to the top tier of American screen acting, in the part of Harold Angel. De Niro, satisfied that the bulk of the heavy lifting would fall to someone else, agreed to play Cyphre. As he put it, "I thought it would be fun to do, not having to worry about doing the whole movie, you know, concentrating on four scenes, and that's it. It worked out schedulewise."

The film shot in Louisiana and New York through the spring of 1986, and De Niro was, as ever, punctilious about the appearance, emotional state, and background of his character. He had Polaroids taken of himself wearing dozens of different shades of contact lenses; he worked on specific looks for his eyebrows, hairline, facial hair, and fingernails; he practiced working with a cane and peeling a hard-boiled egg (this bit of business particularly absorbed and vexed him and wound up taking seven separate takes when it was finally shot); he sought out Hjortsberg to ask questions about Cyphre; and he read extensively in the background of the occult elements of the script, paying particular attention to historic illustrations of demons. (Ironically, he had a model close at hand for the eventual look of his character, perhaps without even knowing it. As he admitted in an interview, "You know, one morning I was looking at myself in the mirror, and I said to myself, 'Gee, you know, this looks a lot like Marty . . .'")

The connection between Scorsese and Cyphre ran deeper than the dark goatee and the provocative demeanor. As *Angel Heart* unfolds, it becomes clear that Louis Cyphre is not only an evil man but evil incarnate—Lucifer, in fact—and that Harold Angel is being led by the Prince of Darkness toward a revelation about himself in a fashion not unlike the process by which a film director might coax hidden truths out of a Method actor. But that subtlety was lost in the storm about the ratings board that preceded the film into theaters when it finally opened in March 1987.

DE NIRO APPEARS in only four scenes in *Angel Heart*, and they form little archipelagoes in the film, pauses for conversations that are somehow weighted and coded and only become entirely coherent in retrospect. Of course, Louis Cyphre (or, as Harold Angel pronounces it, "Sigh-fee-aire") knows exactly what he's up to, whom he's dealing with, and how it will all play out: it's his nature. But the audience, at least at the outset, is as clueless as the private eye.

De Niro playfully engages the macabre qualities of the script and the role: the long fingernails, the delicate fingering of his cane, the deliberately wispy, almost singsong voice, the dainty way in which he waggles his fingers when he describes something as a "fuss." He is at once cagily testing Angel to see if he really is ignorant of the truth of his situation and teasing him with all the clues he'd need to figure it out. Chief among these is the hard-boiled egg, which Cyphre says is believed to be a symbol of the soul; he cracks it open meticulously, salts it liberally, and bites the top off it purposefully, staring at Angel with unguarded intent as he does so.

Now and again De Niro flashes his eyes in response to something Angel says—particularly when he seems to implicate himself in someone's death—and the game is almost given away. Finally, when he reveals himself in their last meeting, he is resplendent: fingernails longer than ever, hair unfastened, eyes transformed with contact lenses into fiery amber lasers. He seems thicker of body, regal, a true demon king. It's not really a performance; it's more like a playful bit of hokum in the service of a punning riddle. But De Niro's pleasure in being the side dish and not the main course seems real. As a first real step in breaking away from having to bear the burden of an entire film, it shows promise.

WHILE STILL ON Broadway with *Cuba*, De Niro agreed to yet another smallish film appearance, with a completely different pedigree from *Angel Heart*. The new film was the brainchild of Art Linson, a Chicago native who'd amassed a track record of hits (*Car Wash, Fast Times at Ridgemont High*), critical successes (*Melvin and Howard*), and outright flops (*Where the Buffalo Roam*) as an independent Hollywood producer. Linson, like so many of his age, had grown up watching the adventures of federal lawman Eliot Ness in his battles against the bootleggers and mobsters led by Al Capone in TV's *The Untouchables*. In 1985, he learned that Paramount Pictures owned the rights to the series, and he was gladdened to discover that Ned Tanen, who was running the studio's film department, was also an *Untouchables* fan and had at one time tried to launch a film version of the story.

Encouraged at the possibility of bringing Ness and Capone to the big screen, Linson found himself dining one night in New York with yet another Chicago guy, David Mamet, who had just won a Pulitzer Prize for *Glengarry Glen Ross*. Linson rather audaciously proposed to the newly minted laureate that he consider adapting the story of *The Untouchables* as a screenplay, and to his surprise, Mamet answered almost immediately, "I'm in."

That agreement turned into a long process of script drafting. Mamet quickly realized that he had to throw away not only the fondly remembered *Untouchables* of his youth but the historical record as well. The story he crafted, over a series of first three and then ultimately seven drafts of the script, was a mythical tale of a white knight and a dark-hearted villain, with Chicago as a kind of fairy kingdom over which they struggled for control. Mamet envisioned Ness as a puritanical Treasury agent who has none of the street smarts needed for the battle. He acquires a mentor in Jimmy Malone, a weary veteran patrolman who is sick of corruption and relishes the chance to go head-to-head with Capone on something like equal terms. Mamet's Capone wasn't the drooling psychopath of some other film versions (in particular the Capone-inspired character played by Al Pacino in 1983's *Scarface*); rather, he was a man of slick words, political savvy, and even a kind of charm, utterly and irredeemably ruthless when he needed to be, but able to consort with journalists, celebrities, and elected officials on something like *their* own terms.

Linson brought the script to Brian De Palma, who had directed that recent hit version of *Scarface* but had become best known as a director of stylish gore with strong influences of Alfred Hitchcock and other masters, whose works he often cheekily quoted in films such as *Carrie*, *Dressed to Kill*, *Blow Out*, and *Obsession*. De Palma was in something of a low moment—he had just flopped with a goofball mob comedy, *Wise Guys*—when Linson approached him. He saw the potential for an *Untouchables* that combined elements of myth and even comic book morality with a traditional gangster picture and a stylish look and feel. He, too, was in.

But without a star, they would get nowhere in their quest for a $15–$20 million budget from Paramount. For the almost-too-good-to-be-true Ness, they were steered by the studio toward box office heavy-weights Harrison Ford, William Hurt, and Mel Gibson, and they were grateful, Linson said, to learn that they were all unavailable. Mamet's Ness wasn't as heavy a presence as those fellows, at least not at first. They needed someone whom the audience could see grow from a naive out-of-towner to a figure equivalent to the titanic Capone.

They found their man in Kevin Costner, a lean and handsome thirty-one-year-old actor from Southern California who'd broken into showbiz as a tour guide at Disneyland and who'd had only sporadic luck in movies thus far. He'd been offered the lead in the computer-themed adventure movie *War Games* and turned it down for a role in the ensemble film *The Big Chill*, only to have his part cut entirely out of the picture save for a shot of his wrist at the very outset. He appeared in a bicycling movie called *Fandango* and had a splashy role in the western *Silverado* (a makeup call, as it were, from *Big Chill* writer-director Lawrence Kasdan). But despite his good looks and all-American bearing, he hadn't really entered into the awareness of most moviegoers or, indeed, moviemakers. He was, however, fresh-faced and clean-seeming and carried a natural combination of grace and dignity that felt of a piece with the personae of Gary Cooper and James Stewart. He fit Mamet's vision of Ness perfectly.

As Ness's mentor, the streetwise Malone, they cast Sean Connery, whose raffish worldliness and thick brogue (Scottish, not Irish, yes, but still . . .) were ideal for the contours of Mamet's character. And as the slick, ferocious Capone they hit on the stocky, menacing English actor Bob Hoskins, who'd come to worldwide attention playing a gangster in 1980's *The Long Good Friday* and had recently played an American mobster in Francis Ford Coppola's ill-fated 1984 period crime-and-music film *The Cotton Club*. Not only was Hoskins happy to play the small but powerful part, he was willing to do it for the producers' budget line for the role: $200,000.

But Hoskins, Linson admitted later, wasn't their first choice. That was De Niro. When De Palma and De Niro first talked about Capone, the actor seemed loath to add a significant film role to his workload so soon after the arduous process of appearing live onstage. It was true that Capone made only a handful of appearances in Mamet's script. But it was a role that De Niro, who'd been playing a lean and hungry drug dealer onstage, would have to undergo another of his famed transformations to fill. "I didn't want to have to carry a movie," he said yet again when asked about his motives for taking on a relatively small role. "But doing *The Untouchables* was a lot like being a principal in the movie because of the preparation I had to do."

There would be a weight gain, and another episode of applied indulgence in rich foods. His hair, too, was all wrong: Cuba the gangster wore his long hair slicked back into a ponytail, while Capone had a thinning pate, and so De Niro would have wanted to alter his own hairline to play the part. And there was a long history of, in his view, bad screen Capones: he didn't like Paul Muni in the original *Scarface*, for instance, or Rod Steiger in 1959's *Capone*. What with the heavy lifting the role would entail, the hard work he'd just finished, and the relatively small fee the production would be able to offer him, it was easiest to tell De Palma thanks but no thanks.

Still, he was genuinely interested in the part. At the same time, Linson and De Palma were getting anxious about the actors they'd already signed. "Brian and I both worried," the producer recalled, "that with Connery being a Scot and Hoskins English, it was beginning to feel like a foreign cast. We needed De Niro." They knew the studio would balk at the additional expense of De Niro's salary, so they devised a plan that would allow them, in effect, to force the studio to hire him. They put off the Capone scenes until the end of the shoot, taking the chance that they would soon be able to demonstrate to Paramount executives the point of enhancing the film through the hiring of a real movie star.

In the fall, just as production began in Chicago, Paramount's Ned Tanen flew in to see how things were going. He was impressed by the preparation and the footage that had already been shot—the bombing of a speakeasy. Then Linson and De Palma sat him down and De Palma laid out his case to pursue De Niro: "We have the opportunity to get De Niro to play Capone. I believe if we stay with the cast we have, shorten the schedule [as the studio was hoping], and reduce the scale of the picture, that you will end up with a movie that at best will be suited for 'Masterpiece Theatre.' It is not the movie I want to direct. It will not work, and I cannot afford to make a movie that will not work." Linson added, "Ned, think of it, when Bob De Niro kills somebody with a baseball bat, with Brian directing, it will never be forgotten."

Tanen was hesitant, but he was mollified by word that De Niro would be willing to drop his fee by $1 million, taking $1.5 million and a piece of the gross of the film as his salary. He begrudgingly agreed to replace Hoskins, paying the actor his entire fee as a parting gift. Hoskins, for his part, had absolutely nothing bad to say. Asked if he was upset at being let go, he told a reporter, "Are you kidding? I got $200,000 for doing nothing and went on to my next project. De Niro has shown me only kindness. He's a real friend. He's helped me shop for my wife's and my kids' Christmas presents. He's invited me around to meet his granny, and he's come to my house for a pot-luck dinner. That really knocked my wife out. I think she was finally impressed with me. You can't do better than that for a friend."

Working with De Niro had been smooth thus far. His only demand had been that all his scenes be shot on continuous workdays, which actually made things easier for the production. But when he showed up in Chicago for rehearsals, some weeks before he was scheduled to begin shooting, Linson was alarmed. The producer went with De Palma to visit De Niro in a hotel suite and couldn't believe that the thin, sheepish fellow before him was the man he'd just hired to play Al Capone. "He was thin; his face was gaunt. He was quiet and he looked young. His hair was thick and low on his forehead and he wore a ponytail." As he later recalled, "If De Palma's introduction had not confirmed that this was Robert De Niro, I would've asked for some verification." When they left after their chat with the actor, Linson put his fears bluntly to De Palma: "If I didn't know that was Robert De Niro, I'd say we were doomed. Tell me we haven't made fools of ourselves."

Determined to go forward, De Niro told Linson about some problems he was having with the script. To De Niro's surprise, the producer indicated that Mamet had turned hostile toward the production and might not even be willing to answer any of his questions; he gave De Niro Mamet's phone number and wished him luck. Then he accompanied him to the wardrobe department, where De Niro looked at the costumes that had been prepared for him and declared them "great . . . good . . . nice . . . interesting . . ." Linson knew that what he was hearing was, in fact, the opposite of what the words said. "You have come to the conclusion that you hate the wardrobe," he said. "You would like me to start over and have it completely redesigned . . . under your supervision." De Niro smiled. Linson calculated another $50,000 had just been added to his budget, but he had passed the point at which he could say no.

De Niro took off for Italy, where he spent five or six weeks eating an obscenely rich diet like the one he'd indulged in during the production of *Raging Bull*. Linson, meanwhile, put in orders for ten bespoke suits, at $3,000 each, from a tailor whom De Niro recommended in lower Manhattan who'd actually made clothes for Al Capone. He also splurged on underwear: silk, from the famed Sulka haberdashery, which again was where the real Capone had shopped. Per De Niro's instructions, specific items of jewelry, hats, even cigars (Havanas, illegal, at $25 a pop) were obtained. Now all they needed was their Capone.

That winter, with production well under way, they got him. De

Niro returned to Chicago plumped out and with his hairline altered, unrecognizable as the quiet fellow from the previous visit. He sat for the makeup department to give him a prosthetic nose, then went into the wardrobe trailer, put on his silk drawers and bespoke suit, donned a fedora, lit a cigar, and stepped out onto the set. "It was like witnessing a grand magic trick performed by a maestro," Linson recalled. "Without uttering a word, by merely strolling to his position in front of the camera, Capone–De Niro suddenly became sly, dangerous, confident, and even witty. The entire crew felt the electricity. . . . The character had been created."

Of course, that magical transformation was the result of another of De Niro's deep exercises in mining and creating a character. He watched several of his old movies, particularly *Raging Bull* and *Once Upon a Time in America*, and compared his performances with images of Capone from newsreels; he read books by people who knew Capone, practiced working with a cigar, acquired a manicure and a suntan, listened to Capone's favorite operas, and looked at hundreds of photographs of Capone and other gangsters of the 1920s, paying particular attention to their clothing, haircuts, hats, and jewelry. (He sought, and failed to find, an audio recording of Capone's voice. "Getting the voice is *the* most difficult thing," he complained.) The hair was particularly vexing, he admitted: "It took a week, sitting in a barber's chair for seven hours at a stretch while they snipped and shaved and tweezed, checking with photographs of Capone. It was incredible; if just one hair was off it looked artificial."

He built his Capone as a man of words, of public relations, of political theater; larger than life, kingly, even godlike. He reminded himself in his script notes to move his head only barely, to speak clearly and forthrightly in expectation of deference, to make a show of candor when it seemed beneficial, to consider that Capone had acquired so much power and authority at a relatively young age, to always remember that he was a spectacle, that people were watching him, that even his most out-of-control moments had to have an element of restraint and dignity. He contrasted Capone's Neapolitan heritage with the Sicilian blood of Vito Corleone: "The Sicilian is a darker personality, closer to Africa," he opined. "The Neapolitans are more lively and flamboyant." The baseball bat scene, in which Capone hosts a banquet and then beats a pair of traitors to death in front of his tuxedo-clad minions, drove him to real depths of self-examination. "It's also personal what they did to me," he wrote in his script. "Just think of self, betrayals in life! . . . These men have betrayed me and I am now giving them a lesson to respect *loyalty! Loyalty!* . . . A little tighter and shorter cause I'm about to kill these motherfuckers right here."

In total, he spent eleven days filming as Capone—not even two weeks of work after putting on nearly thirty pounds. ("I promise you," he told a German interviewer, "I will never do it again.") He commanded a suite at the Ritz-Carlton Hotel, where he had a barber chair installed, having his hair and nails worked on every single day. In the final film he would be seen in only seven scenes, some quite fleeting, and yet, just as Linson hoped and De Palma knew, he was a dominant presence throughout. As Sean Connery put it, "He appears very little in the film, but you always know he's there."

He was there, too, in the spring of 1987, when the film was being test-screened (his grandmother Helen De Niro gave Linson, who didn't know who she was, a fit of anxiety by leaving the theater to use the bathroom repeatedly throughout an early screening). And he showed up at other screenings and even did a few interviews. Not only had Paramount gotten him for a lowered price, but they got more out of him, at least publicity-wise, than anybody had in years.

And it paid off.

WHEN WE FIRST see him, he is recumbent in a barber's chair, photographed from above, with a marble floor beneath him and his left arm extended into space: the Adam of Michelangelo's Sistine Chapel ceiling with no God reaching across the void to bring him to life. He is attended by a manicurist, a shoeshine boy, and a barber, who presently unveils his client's round, seal-like, hood-eyed face from beneath a hot towel. Three reporters and four bodyguards stand nearby, awaiting his word. "It is the time of Al Capone," we are told by introductory titles, and the truth of that blunt statement is patently clear from this initial glance.

It's Capone the charmer on display here—telling jokes, skirting unpleasant truths, making good newspaper copy. But when he's asked a question he doesn't appreciate—namely, whether he furthers his bootlegging business with violence—he reacts with a slight jerk of his head that reveals a flash of his volatile core. The sudden movement causes the barber to nick him with a straight razor, and the man rightly fears reprisal. But Capone, blood on his middle fingertip, assures the fellow that the accident will not have repercussions. Instead, he dismisses the interviewer's impudence with the assertion that he and his men don't engage in violence because, as he declares with dead eyes like a man lying on the witness stand, "it's not good business"—a claim that is shown to be an outright lie by the very next scene, in which a little girl is killed in an explosion triggered by Capone's henchmen.

The centerpiece scene, the moment that Art Linson and Brian De Palma knew that De Niro would make indelible, marks his next appearance, after which it is impossible for the audience to join the ranks of the press corps, manicurists, and bodyguards chuckling along at Capone's banter. Clad in a tux and white tie, squeaky clean and apparently fully self-possessed, he speaks to an assembled banquet table of his soldiers about his "ent'usiasms," chief of which, he says, is baseball. He's lecturing, playful, adapting an almost donnish mode.

But he shifts; his eyes narrow and start to lose their sparkle and take on that dead quality they had at the end of the barber chair scene. And then comes the point of his lecture: four deadly blows with a baseball bat, crushing the skull of a disloyal employee and leaving him—in another shot from the angle of the ceiling—facedown in a puddle of blood that seeps out sickeningly across the table. Now his chest is puffed with the strain of his effort, his lips are pursed, his chin is thrust out defiantly, and he gazes around to see that he has made his point. All along we've known that he's a psychopath and a killer, but he's kept it hidden underneath a civilized veneer of fine clothes and fancy décor. Now it has been unleashed, and the horror of who the man really is permeates the rest of the film.

Even with his violence and his outbursts, Capone's most chilling scene in the film may well be the most decorous: a trip to the Lyric Opera to see Enrico Caruso perform in *I Pagliacci*. Once again he courts the press from atop a staircase with a big toothy grin, a few bon mots, and a reminder that he is, in his view, "a peaceful man" being hounded unfairly by Ness. Then, as he teeters on the edge of tears at Caruso's virtuosity in performing "Vesti la Giubba," he learns that his henchman Frank Nitti (a deliciously unctuous Billy Drago) has killed Ness's colleague Jimmy Malone. While still dabbing at his eyes and choking back sobs, Capone smiles; De Niro somehow contrives to be laughing and crying at the same time, a living Janus mask, embodying comedy and tragedy, good and evil, at once.

There are a great many things that De Palma, Mamet, the cast, and the craftspeople do right in *The Untouchables*, but it's hard to imagine the film being so beautifully honed and so successful without De Niro's Capone in the middle of it. His airs of self-satisfaction, self-righteousness, and feral violence permeate even the scenes in which he takes no part. His confidence and power seem unassailable, and surely it won't be the skinny, boy-faced Ness who will bring him down. But by the end of the film Ness, pictured on a rooftop against a brilliant blue sky like a statue atop a plinth, has become as large a figure as Capone—with, of course, the mentorship of Malone. (There's an amusing subtext in which a leading man of a fading era, Connery, instructs a rising leading man, Costner, how to topple a reigning leading man, De Niro—a metaphor for the acting business that serves the film exquisitely.) *The Untouchables* plays like a comic book, like a fairy tale, like a western, like an opera. And like all of those, it requires a villain whom the audience truly fears. De Niro is all of that and more, translating his work, his ideas, and his experience into the most memorable Al Capone the screen has ever seen.

The film was well received by the press, and De Niro, especially, made a good impression. "De Niro is flamboyantly entertaining," said David Ansen in *Newsweek*. "He's always been a great actor," said David Denby in *New York*; "this is the first time he's seemed an exuberant one." And in the *New Yorker*, Pauline Kael, more disappointed in her onetime golden boy, De Palma, than exercised over her current whipping boy, De Niro, allowed, "De Niro isn't in many scenes, but his impact is so strong that we wouldn't want more of him. . . . He's ludicrous yet terrifying."

On top of that, *The Untouchables* was a hit, opening to a $10 million weekend en route to a $76.27 million domestic gross, sixth-best of the year. Behind box office like that, De Niro's gamble to take less money up front in exchange for a percentage of the gross had proved very smart business. Better still, it was his biggest commercial hit since *The Deer Hunter*, and its success was demonstrably related to his presence. As a result, when he and his agents were entertaining offers for new films, they had a new price: $5 million—or, roughly, a hundred thousand times what he had been paid the first time he worked in front of a movie camera with Brian De Palma in *The Wedding Party* twenty-four years prior.

IN MARCH 1986 the great Russian poet Yevgeny Yevtushenko was on a grand tour of the United States, and De Niro was honored with the opportunity to join him onstage and read translations from his epic "Babi Yar" at a gala evening at St. John the Divine Cathedral in Manhattan. The event was delayed by a series of phoned-in bomb scares, as De Niro's old student-acting chum Larry Woiwode recalled. Having become an author and poet of some note, Woiwode also was in attendance that evening, and he reunited with De Niro afterward, the two sitting opposite each other at a gala dinner and resuming, as if they'd just done it the night before, their youthful game of communicating whole conversations to each other using only their eyes and facial gestures.

It was the era of glasnost, with barriers against cultural exchange between the United States and Russia crumbling, and in the course of Yevtushenko's visit De Niro was introduced to a number of official representatives of Soviet arts organizations. That resulted in his being invited to the Moscow Film Festival the following year, and, even more, to serve as the first-ever American president of the festival jury. He had been to Havana in 1985, alongside Christopher Walken and Treat Williams, to attend the opening night of the International Festival of New Latin American Cinema; a true Manhattan lefty, he had enjoyed the opportunity to taste firsthand a culture that geopolitical conflict had made inaccessible to most Americans.

Moscow in the summer of 1987 would provide another such opportunity to see some otherwise shadowed sides of the world. He took to it as a once-in-a-lifetime trip, bringing along Drena and Raphael, nineteen and eleven years old, respectively, as well as a friend of Raphael's and his own personal trainer/assistant (who kept De Niro jogging and riding a stationary bike throughout the festival). The event featured such films as Federico Fellini's *Intervista* (which won the top prize), the English drama *84 Charing Cross Road*, and the fine American children's film *The Journey of Natty Gann*. And De Niro was hardly the only star power imported from the West by festival organizers: also on hand were Gérard Depardieu, Vanessa Redgrave, Marcello Mastroianni, Nastassja Kinski, and Quincy Jones.

He attended to his duties as jury chair, and he hobnobbed, but he also made time to visit the official Moscow, the burgeoning underground Moscow, and the homes of some famed Russian artists, activists, and cultural icons, including a faith healer who had known the recently deceased director Andrei Tarkovsky. He took the kids with him on almost all of these excursions, explaining to an East German journalist, "I took my children with me, because they should see how Moscow looks. I do the official program, but I like to see the other, unofficial culture, too. If young Russians would visit the USA they would see that there is an underground, too."

There were, of course, trips he didn't take them on, such as a jaunt to Argentina that same year, with Christopher Walken tagging along, to see a production of *Cuba and His Teddy Bear* and to party in Buenos Aires and then Rio de Janeiro. But he truly did believe in exposing his kids to finer things, and as Drena hit her late teens and twenties she would often accompany him to events around New York: film premieres, charitable galas, and the like. They developed a playful banter, she calling him out for being an oldster out of touch with contemporary culture, he trumping her by claiming personal acquaintance with many of the musicians and actors she admired. (Among his more unusual encounters were a visit to the set of Michael Jackson's *Moonwalker* film and a sit-down in a London bar with the members of the band Bananarama, who not long before had recorded a song called "Robert De Niro's Waiting"; they amused him by explaining that they'd originally titled the tune "Al Pacino's Waiting" but had come to realize that "De Niro" sounded better.) And he had to learn to keep his cool while witnessing such spectacles as Matt Dillon chatting Drena up at a movie premiere. In his forties, with growing children, he would have to evolve, at least a little, into an older lion.

ARGUABLY THE MOST significant aftereffect of the success of *The Untouchables* was summed up in an inauspicious six words in *Daily Variety* of June 5, 1987: "Robert De Niro signed with CAA." One of the most respected actors in movies was now a client of the most powerful talent agency in Hollywood.

When De Niro had signed on with agent Harry Ufland at the William Morris Agency some seventeen years prior, he was still touting his dinner theater experience on resumes and head shots that his mom printed for him. Ufland had been a patient proctor of De Niro's remarkable career—as well as that of Martin Scorsese—through the sorts of successes and opportunities that most agents can only dream of offering their clients. But the business of agenting had changed in the previous few years, and someone like Ufland, even with the might of WMA behind him, seemed old-school in the new environment of show business.

Creative Artists Agency, or CAA, was the new powerhouse agency, headed by the icy and relentless Michael Ovitz, who brought the most cutthroat business practices of Wall Street into show business, cloaked in a superficial veneer of Asian philosophy (for a time, everyone who wanted to be anyone in Hollywood was reading Sun Tzu). After breaking into the agenting biz via the traditional route of working in the mailroom at WMA, Ovitz had come to realize that the old movie studio model of production could be resurrected, with a twist that would put the talent agency at the center of the equation. In the golden age of the studios, all the creative talent had been under contract to a studio and worked on films as assignments. In the mid-1960s, power had shifted to actors (and, very rarely, directors), who signed on to studio films on a job-by-job basis or, often, developed projects on their own with their own production companies, partnering with studios for funding. Ovitz saw that a talent agency could put together a package—a script, a director, a cast—and then sell it as a turnkey project to a movie studio for a single price. The TV world had long depended on talent agencies to build new shows in just this fashion. CAA would transpose the technique to the movie business and, in effect, put together films in the way that MGM and Warner Bros. once had.

The keys to maximizing CAA's ability to force its projects on studios—and, of course, to maximizing the agency's profits—were getting as much top-flight talent on the books as possible and having CAA's agents work in strictly disciplined fashion, sharing the agency's wishes with studios and clients alike as if no negotiation or resistance were possible. To fulfill the first need, CAA had signed the likes of Paul Newman, Robert Redford, Dustin Hoffman, Julie Andrews, Sidney Poitier, and, from the ranks of television, the actor-directors Rob Reiner, Danny DeVito, Ron Howard, Penny Marshall, and Leonard Nimoy. To fulfill the second required steel and brass beyond any so far exhibited in the famously steely and brassy business of Hollywood. In just a few years' time, Ovitz became celebrated—and, more important, feared—as the most powerful man in Hollywood, in part because he was willing to use his power to crush competitors and even in some cases allies. (In a famed clash with the screenwriter Joe Eszterhas, who was planning to leave CAA for other representation, Ovitz declared, in a way that Vito—or at least Michael—Corleone would've appreciated, "My foot soldiers who go up and down Wilshire Boulevard each day will blow your brains out.") Compared to that ruthless, monolithic, and corporate frame of mind, Ufland was like an Old World shopkeeper who let his customers run up a tab. In fact, he left agenting altogether and began producing, working with both De Niro and Scorsese over the coming decades.

For the likes of De Niro and Scorsese, being represented by CAA was like having the Army, CIA, and IRS behind you. They themselves could focus on their art and leave the ugly business of money to Ovitz and his minions. Of course, they were just as deeply involved as ever in choosing their projects and their collaborators. But now they were partnering with CAA and its staff and client list in those processes, and then letting CAA agents hammer whatever projects or prices they came up with through the gates of the studios. It was an ideal situation for De Niro: he could let Ovitz and CAA play the heavy for him, driving his price to new heights and demanding that his ideas about new film projects be taken seriously, while he himself retreated into a more modest stance as the quietly committed artist. In some ways it was like having the fiery Virginia Admiral serving as a business negotiator for her relatively naive husband—with the crucial distinction that, unlike his dad, De Niro became rich.

16

THERE WAS MORE THAN A CHANGE IN PRICE WHEN HE TOOK on his next role: there was a change in genre, in tone, in commitment to the part. He was cast in a high-concept Hollywood buddy movie—a marketing-driven, studio-funded film of the cookie-cutter sort that he had never really made before. Not that the project didn't have quality. *Midnight Run*, as it was finally named on release, was based on a script by George Gallo, a rising screenwriting star whose sole credit thus far was Brian De Palma's goofball mob comedy *Wise Guys*. The story of a bounty hunter who nabs a fugitive mob accountant and tries to bring him cross-country to collect a reward, only to realize that he's saving the bad guys and endangering the good guy, it drew the attention of writer-director Martin Brest, who was red-hot after his 1984 smash hit *Beverly Hills Cop*.

With that pedigree, and with the marketplace bubbling with films of this tenor, Universal Pictures was willing to spend big, provided it got the right stars. A few years earlier, nobody would have thought of De Niro in such a picture—not only because he didn't do comedy-comedies, but also because he wasn't a significant box office draw. But on the back of *The Untouchables*, and with a taste for work that wasn't necessarily grueling or stone-serious, he was shopping around for lighter parts. He very nearly went to work for director Penny Marshall in the lead role in *Big*, a comedy about a boy who gets magically transported into the body of an adult while still retaining his childlike mentality. Marshall's first choice, Tom Hanks, had backed out of the picture; encouraged to think about casting a heavier-weight performer, she had several meetings with De Niro, who liked the idea of the part so much that he took skateboarding lessons in Marshall's Beverly Hills driveway in preparation. But the studio felt he was wrong for the film and repeatedly balked at his contractual demands—offered $3 million, he wanted $6 million. Eventually he walked away, and Hanks, impressed that the likes of De Niro would even consider the part, changed his mind and took it for himself—to career-changing results.

So, instead, De Niro did *Midnight Run*—for which he did, in fact, get a $6 million payday. With one major star involved, Universal wanted Brest to find another, and Eddie Murphy, Robin Williams, and even Cher were bandied about as real possibilities. Brest, though, liked Charles Grodin, dry, sardonic, chatty, subversive, and all but forgotten as a comedy star since not quite breaking through as a lead actor more than a decade before in *The Heartbreak Kid*. As Brest saw it, there was inherent comedy in De Niro playing a gruff tough guy who thinks he's doing good and isn't and Grodin playing a passive-aggressive fugitive from justice who's actually on the side of good. They were an odd couple in the Neil Simon vein, with De Niro as Oscar Madison with a gun and Grodin as Felix Unger with a price on his head. And by casting Grodin and not a huge name, the studio kept the film—which involved a lot of location shooting—to a budget just under $30 million.

Grodin, as he admitted later, was daunted by the challenge of going mano a mano with such a powerful and committed actor. "If we were going to do a movie in which we both play Aztecs," he said, "Bobby would go and live with the Aztecs. After three weeks he'd come back and I'd say, 'So what were the Aztecs like?' That's the difference between us. . . . He gains 50 pounds, he loses 50 pounds. If you have a scene on a bus, he's gonna drive the bus for five hours. You're worried it's going to be a depressing experience."

But this time De Niro didn't go all-in to play bounty hunter Jack Walsh. He read up on cops and bounty hunters and on searches for fugitives, he rode around with some New York City detectives, and he invented some emotional backstory for his character having to do with a sentimental and even neurotic attachment to a wristwatch. But chiefly he dedicated himself to getting the comedy straight, to preparing for the rigorous physical demands of the script, and to not pouring too much of himself into the character. The cameo roles he'd played in recent years, even the in-depth cameo as Al Capone, had worn away some of his mania for intense preparation. His personal notes on the various generations of the *Midnight Run* script were the scantiest he'd yet made for any film in which he had a lead role.

As he explained later, the special brand of comedy in the film was the chief attraction for him: "It's not a yuk-yuk comedy per se, with pratfalls in it. It's not that kind of buddy-buddy film. It's based in reality, which is the kind of comedy—if you can call it comedy—that I like." (He was quick to add, however, that the boy who loved Three Stooges movies was still inside him, however unlikely to emerge: "I even sorta like the pratfall kind of comedy if you can do it well and if the timing is right. It's an art in itself. I wouldn't mind being able to do it if I could take two years, maybe three years to work on it. Maybe longer.")

The film shot through late 1987 in various locations in California, Chicago, Arizona, Nevada, and even New Zealand, where the stars and key crew members flew to shoot a river scene in warmer water than was available to them in the Northern Hemisphere at that time of year. In December, De Niro flew from the Arizona location to Washington, D.C., where Mikhail Gorbachev was visiting for a summit and had requested the presence of the star, whom he'd met at the Moscow Film Festival earlier in the year. But even that didn't constitute an interruption: the studio chartered a jet to take him back and forth overnight.

Indeed, for all the tricky sequences of action that the film posed, the comedy was the hardest thing for De Niro to tackle—and not because he wasn't able to ratchet himself up into a funny character. In fact, it was quite the reverse: "Sometimes, when I do something that I think is really funny, I break up and start laughing, because it feels so good," he explained. "Then I get so mad at myself for breaking up, because the rhythm felt so right—I was right there—and if I'd held out just a little longer and not broken up, I wouldn't have ruined the take."

In *Midnight Run*, he felt, he finally learned to conquer that tendency. In a famed sequence in the film, Grodin's character is trying to get a rise out of De Niro's, and the words in the script weren't making it happen. Brest encouraged Grodin to improvise a line that got De Niro going, and he came up with a pip: "Have you ever had sex with an animal?" Flustered or not, De Niro managed to stay in the moment, racing through anger to a confession that revealed the human depths of his character.

Midnight Run was meant to be a big summer movie for Universal, but when it opened in July 1998, the studio got a nasty surprise: despite largely favorable reviews, and despite a publicity campaign that included De Niro appearing at a press conference at the Plaza Hotel in New York and sitting for a full-scale interview in *Rolling Stone*, the film sold only $5 million worth of tickets in its opening weekend, a pitiful result in a summer dominated by *Die Hard, Who Framed Roger Rabbit?, Coming to America,* and even *Cocktail.* Its final gross of a mere $39.4 million put it at twenty-ninth in the year's tally, right behind a rerelease of *Bambi,* and almost $140 million less than *Rain Man,* the year's winner as Best Picture at the Oscars and a film that in more than a few ways resembled *Midnight Run.*

De Niro always relished playing blue-collar roles; he would even see the criminals and gangsters in his filmography as ordinary working stiffs. So the role of Jack Walsh, honest ex-cop turned crafty bounty hunter, is a natural fit for him. He wears workingman's clothes—the same outfit through the entire film, in fact—and has a craftsman's way with burglar tools, surveillance equipment, false credentials, and so on. The man has become his job, just as Wizard explained to Travis Bickle more than a decade prior. Walsh has forged a hard shell around himself, a device of self-preservation forced on him by the loss of his position on the police force, the dissolution of his marriage, the near decade he has gone without seeing his daughter, and his constant exposure to the worst sides of humanity. "There's bad everywhere," he says. "Good I don't know about." He has stories that he tells himself to ease the pain: he'll get back together with his wife, he'll leave off bounty hunting and open a coffee shop. But the truth is he exists almost solely in and for his work.

This is a lot to bring to bear on a buddies-on-the-run comedy, one of the most cliché-ridden and routine of Hollywood genres. But De Niro respects the character enough to infuse him with credible humanity and realism. Walsh is smart, resourceful, brave, professional, and true. He lacks civilized polish, yes, but he is an honest man, and De Niro takes that quality almost as a challenge to give the character some depth. More than once, past and present, Walsh has turned down the chance to make himself financially secure in favor of keeping his integrity intact. And nothing said or done by the Duke (as Grodin's character is dubbed), the FBI, the mob, or a rival bounty hunter puts him off the completion, as it were, of his appointed rounds. He will get his man, and he will get him back to where he has to be by the time at which he has to be there.

But, of course, *Midnight Run* is a comedy, and although there were comic moments in many of De Niro's roles before now, ranging from the shocking insults of *Raging Bull* to the faux superhero antics of *Brazil*, the film marks the first time that he is deliberately playing a funny human being in a script written, at least in large part, to make people laugh. He threatens the Duke with a case of "fistophobia" if he doesn't comply with directions; he does a little jig with his fists, almost salivating, at the thought of "a little surf-and-turf action" as his in-flight meal; he tears into a duplicitous business acquaintance as a "slimeball in a sea of pus"; and he tries to end a contentious conversation with a malapropism: "Here are two words for you: 'Shut the fuck up.'" Grodin is nominally the comic actor of the pair, and he has plenty of good, droll moments. But De Niro is no mere straight man; he gets as many laughs as his co-star.

And yet there are grace notes that elevate the performance and the film. De Niro interacts beautifully with the young girl (Danielle Du-Clos) who plays his estranged daughter: a kind of embarrassed wonder at how much she has grown in the nine years since he's seen her, an almost sheepish refusal to accept her help when the girl, very dearly, offers him her babysitting savings to abet his getaway. He has another nice moment when reunited with another specter from his past: the Chicago mob boss (played by Dennis Farina) who cost him his position long ago. Enduring the man's insults, knowing he's a sitting duck for some sort of deadly double-cross, he stands erect and proud, unafraid of and even eager for a confrontation. Finally, in the film's dénouement, he makes the decision to sacrifice a big payday to do the *truly* proper thing. He checks his dodgy watch and sees that he would have succeeded in his mission with time to spare, a self-satisfaction that he can share with nobody. And when the script's final surprise is sprung on him, he greets it with a wonderful line reading: "I knew you had money, but I didn't know you *had* money"—a sadly ironic statement considering how poorly the film, which decades later would acquire a reputation for quality and entertainment, did at the box office.

De Niro's bold turn toward formula comedy was, somewhat unpredictably, welcomed by critics. "Like most fine actors," wrote Vincent Canby in the *New York Times*, "Mr. De Niro has never given a good performance that wasn't in some way illuminated by humor. . . . He brings to Jack Walsh's double-takes, slow burns, furtive smiles, and expressions of mock surprise the same degree of intensity with which he played Jake LaMotta in 'Raging Bull' and Travis Bickle in 'Taxi Driver.' Yet he's no Metropolitan Opera star trying to squeeze his tenor voice into the latest Michael Jackson hit. The laughter he prompts is big, open, and genuine." In the *Washington Post*, Desson Thomson wrote, "De Niro is one extended pleasure in 'Midnight Run'—a real actor putting his considerable talent to work in a well-scripted comedy." And in the *Chicago Sun-Times*, Roger Ebert opined, "Whoever cast De Niro and Grodin must have had a sixth sense for the chemistry they would have; they work together so smoothly, and with such an evident sense of fun, that even their silences are intriguing."

IF HE HAD COASTED through *Midnight Run* as a way of stretching to a role that *didn't* call for him to stretch—and to acquire his largest-yet payday in the process—his next film brought him right back to the sort of small, searching independent productions on which he had cut his teeth at the dawn of his career. *Jackknife*, adapted by screenwriter Stephen Metcalfe from his own play, *Strange Snow*, deals with the troubled friendship of Megs and Dave, a wild card and a troubled alcoholic, respectively, who first met as young men fighting in Vietnam. The film, shot on location in Connecticut on a minuscule budget (De Niro appeared for $1.2 million—20 percent of his *Midnight Run* price), was being directed by David Hugh Jones, who'd spent years in English theater and had made a ripple in movies with *Betrayal* and *84 Charing Cross Road*, a pair of high-minded (and well-received) adaptations from the stage. He seemed an odd choice for a piece of small-town

Americana having to do with the aftermath of the Vietnam War, but the presence of De Niro, Ed Harris, and Kathy Baker in the central roles indicated the sober tone of the project.

De Niro certainly took a serious tack. He spoke at length with veterans who were dealing with post-traumatic stress, read up on PTSD and the impact of Agent Orange, and, more mundanely, shopped for his own wardrobe in the sort of Main Street clothing store he felt his character would patronize. Having spent the first years of his film career playing a series of men who were in some way affected by the war, he felt the gravity of returning to see how they were faring a decade later: "When I was doing 'The Deer Hunter,'" he reflected, "I spent a lot of time with veterans, too. But that was like 11 years ago. They didn't talk about certain things then, the feelings. Now other things are coming to the surface. So in a sense, this movie is like a continuation of the other, like what might happen to the guy after he was home for a while. . . . They suffer in silence. But one thing I can tell you is that they don't like being portrayed as crazy all the time. And I have sympathy with that." In his publicity appearances for the film, which were relatively extensive, including a premiere to benefit children born with birth defects caused by their fathers' exposure to Agent Orange, he kept returning to the idea that a great deal of the emotional pain caused by Vietnam was only now becoming clear: "There's a feeling veterans have, and Americans have, that something happened, that they were involved in a failure or whatever. A lot of veterans were hurt, mentally or physically."

His character, Megs, was drawn as a live wire, and in his extensive script notes for the film—far exceeding the work he did for *Midnight Run*—he reminded himself to keep his energy up, to always act peppy, upbeat, even half-cocked ("think of Leonard Melfi," he wrote, referring to a famed underground playwright and boozer of 1960s New York, "always laughing, drunk, maybe fighting in bars"). As he described him in an interview, the character was "a dog. A stray dog. A kind of mangy dog mutt." The film was released to very little commercial impact and tepid, although never less than respectful, reviews.

And almost immediately after shooting a movie in Connecticut about Vietnam veterans, he found himself embroiled in a dispute with Vietnam veterans in Connecticut about another film that he was shooting, this one with Jane Fonda, the longtime bane of supporters of the war and, especially, of the men who fought it.

He and Fonda were making a film based on the novel *Union Street* by the British author Pat Barker. The script went by that title, then briefly by *Letters,* and finally, during production, was named after the lead characters, *Stanley and Iris.* Adapted by celebrated screenwriters Harriet Frank Jr. and Irving Ravetch, a married couple who'd broken into the movies in the 1940s and had worked together for almost all of that time, creating such films as *The Long Hot Summer, Hud,* and *Conrack,* it deals with the romance of a baker and would-be inventor who falls in love with a woman who comes to work at his cake shop a few years after the death of her husband. The baker is a mystery to the woman—affable but remote. Only after they start to become close does she learn the embarrassing secret that he has been hiding for years: he cannot read or write. What looked like a low-key love story about a pair of blue-collar lonelyhearts was, at another level, a film about the not-as-uncommon-as-one-might-think condition of adult illiteracy.

Directing would be Martin Ritt, a longtime member of the Actors Studio and a survivor of the Hollywood blacklist who had made such pictures as *Hud, The Long Hot Summer, Hombre, Norma Rae,* and *Sounder.* Ritt was known for getting big stars to give credible performances as ordinary people and for championing themes of social justice and responsibility in his films. He wasn't a big moneymaker, but he was respected.

None of that mattered, though, to veterans groups around Waterbury, Connecticut (which was standing in for western Massachusetts in the production), when word reached them that Fonda would be living and working in their midst for a few months. When a casting call for locals was held in April, a rally was organized to disrupt it, with more than one thousand protesters organized in opposition to Fonda by representatives of the American Legion (in this case, mostly World War II and Korean War veterans). Fonda met several times with veterans groups in the coming months, and she and De Niro participated in a fund-raising event in Middlebury, Connecticut, for Vets Who Care, an organization dedicated to helping the handicapped children of

Vietnam vets exposed to Agent Orange. The combination of apologies, conversations, and charitable efforts went a long way toward mollifying the hostility, but the production would be haunted by small clutches of protesters throughout the late summer and fall, when shooting took place.

De Niro was protected from the controversy because he'd had a long-standing association with Vietnam veterans. During the making of *Jackknife*, he involved himself in charitable efforts aimed at supporting their causes, and he was among the celebrities who read aloud the letters written home by servicepeople in the documentary *Dear America*, which was produced by the HBO cable network and was received well enough to get a theatrical release, a rarity. His continued association with veterans groups resulted in his receiving an honor from VETCO, a theatrical forum for actors who had served in Vietnam, and such was his respect for the group's cause that he showed up in person to accept, something he was generally loath to do.

So while Fonda dealt with controversy, De Niro was free to immerse himself in a part that, like those in *Midnight Run* and *Falling in Love*, required no external transformation. Instead, he dove into study of the phenomenon of adult illiteracy, watching hours of personal stories that were videotaped for him by a research assistant. He learned little tricks of hiding the condition—pretending to leave one's reading glasses at home; asking waiters to suggest items from the menu; taking extreme care with household chemicals; pretending to dislike board games, which often involve a lot of reading; being extremely careful about using public transportation and following road maps; and so on. (And he explained that videotape, as opposed to actual conversation, was now his preferred mode of research because it meant not only less work but less engagement with the work: "I could just play it back and pick up a lot of nuances that way," he said, "and it was at my leisure, and I didn't have to worry and extend so much of myself.")

The chief thing he took away, something he underscored more than once in his notes, was the sense of shame, of secretiveness, of having only partially grown up, of being always on the edge of making an embarrassing mistake or, worse, of being revealed. "There are many examples that I can think of for myself," he scribbled in his script (in

part he compared it to his very limited knowledge of Italian). He came
to realize that an adult hiding an inability to read was self-isolating,
both in the ordinary things of life and in the deepest emotions, and
that became the key to his character—a constant bluffing, defensive-
ness, and low-level anxiety.

The videotapes were also useful as a road map to the western Massachusetts accent he wanted to use for his character. Other than that, it
was simply a matter of finding the right clothes—he went to the same
shop in the town of Meriden, Connecticut, that he'd patronized while
making *Jackknife*—and working on the emotional truth of the scenes
with Fonda, because this was, in effect, only the second full-fledged
love story of his career.

Shooting finished in October 1988, but MGM didn't believe very
strongly in the film and held it for release until February 1990, when it
would be neglected not only by Oscar voters but by general audiences.

By the time *Stanley and Iris* made its way meekly through distribution, De Niro had already come and gone from theaters in yet another box office disappointment. *We're No Angels* was a project that
he himself had instigated back in 1987, when he and his new buddy
Sean Penn decided that they wanted to work together. "I like Sean," he
remembered. "I have a lot of respect for him, and I know he's a serious
actor. We were talking, and I said, 'Let's get together and try and do
something.' Then we got Art Linson."

Linson, demonstrating the classic producer's ability to forget past
slights if there's a new project in the air, discussed with David Mamet
an idea he had for a story about prison escapees hiding among holy
men at a monastery, based loosely on the largely forgotten 1955 Humphrey Bogart comedy *We're No Angels*. As in that film, the characters
in the tale Linson had in mind would turn from fugitives seeking only
to save their hides to Samaritans actually doing some good in the world
for others.

"When Art called I knew it could bode no good," Mamet half joked.
"But he's fairly persuasive." Mamet set the first draft of the screenplay
in the 1930s in a town on the U.S. side of the Canadian border, and

he forged two characters—hard-boiled Ned and simpleminded Jim—based on what he saw to be the comic personalities of De Niro and Penn, respectively. The script was revised in 1988 to a level that got Paramount Pictures, still tallying the take of *The Untouchables*, involved, and shooting was scheduled for February through April of the following year in British Columbia, which was becoming a go-to spot for Hollywood productions seeking to save money on wages, taxes, and other expenses.

The savings were important, as the film wound up being a more ambitious undertaking than its casual genesis might have foretold. The producers built an entire 1930s town in the woods: two dozen buildings, actual roads, and so forth, at a cost of U.S. $2.5 million—the largest set ever constructed in Canada. Orchestrating it all was the Irish novelist and screenwriter-director Neil Jordan, who'd broken out in the business with 1986's *Mona Lisa* but run into trouble with his follow-up, the expensive ghost story *High Spirits*, which had tanked at the box office. He was a little chary of American Method actors, but he loved the setting and he loved the script, the first he'd ever directed that he hadn't written. "The script has all the things I like—Madonnas, deaf children, a whore with a heart of gold, and low-grade characters who are redeemed," he said.

One of the key characters, as Jordan alluded to, was Molly, the town washerwoman and prostitute whose connection to Ned becomes a significant element in the story. Linson and company went through a copious list of possibilities in casting the role: Julia Roberts, Jennifer Jason Leigh, Amy Madigan, Kathleen Quinlan, Diane Lane, Rene Russo, Beverly D'Angelo, and Ann Magnuson, among others. The part finally went to Demi Moore, who possessed a toughness of voice and demeanor that, it was felt, suited the period of the film.

That sense of a bygone era, Linson argued, was one of the film's great assets, especially as embodied in its stars. "Sean and Bob," he said, "don't have faces, they have mugs. . . . These guys are not going to be modeling clothes in a department store when their careers are over." (De Niro, hearing of this description from a reporter, considered it for a while before declaring, "I can live with that.")

De Niro tried as much as was practical to get into the low-key energy of the production, forfeiting the right to stay at a five-star hotel near the set and instead traveling back and forth from more modest accommodations. He read extensively on what prison conditions had been like in Vermont in the 1930s, making contact with a former warden who wrote him a detailed account of the daily lives of his charges. And, he later confessed, he struggled a bit with the tempo of the comedy and the responsibility to play a tough guy of the 1930s as Mamet had written it. One scene in particular vexed him:

> *I was trying to find a line between what's funny and what's serious, because the scene was written in a serious manner and yet the style is funny. It took me many takes to get the right balance. . . . I didn't want to be too heavy . . . and bring it into the floor because there's a certain buoyancy about it. I never expected it to give me so much trouble. I wanted it to be real but also to have a slant. Plus I was in a position where I was lying down, which put me in a restful position in a moment where I'm supposed to be aggressive. Plus Mamet writes in such a specific way, in this case with a '30s-style Irish lilt that's not something natural for me. I never thought it would be such a problem. The whole scene is less than a page. But we kept going over and over it.*

In May, when filming ceased a few weeks later than it had been scheduled to, De Niro got a letter from Paramount president Sid Ganis: "Congrats on the wrap . . . From what I gather, it was a rough one— with all kinds of day-to-day stuff to deal with . . . but to me and the gang here at Paramount it feels and looks like something very special, very funny and very touching."

It wasn't, however, a feeling that they were able to convey to audiences. *We're No Angels* opened just before Christmas, a curious choice for such offbeat fare. If it proved, finally, too big a production for its intimate and often funny script, it's saved by the performances, particularly by Penn's as a street-flavored simpleton, a kind of Stan Laurel to De Niro's hard, cynical, and selfish Oliver Hardy.

De Niro's Ned truly does feel like he's been sharing a jail cell with Humphrey Bogart or George Raft—there's a distinctly old-time air to

his coarseness, his calculation, his energy. He gives a clever performance of a man giving a performance—a hardened convict attempting
to behave as he thinks a priest might, even when events around him
drive him to the sort of fury that got him into prison in the first place.
(In one of the film's little in-jokes, he must listen to the confession of
an adulterous sheriff's deputy, played by Bruno Kirby, who, of course,
was the young, carpet-stealing Clemenza in *The Godfather, Part II*.)
The film is, to borrow Andrew Sarris's useful rubric, lightly likeable, if
never quite profound, not as kinky as the best Neil Jordan, not as caustic as the best David Mamet, not as soul-baring as the best De Niro or
Penn. But it continually offers up small delights. It certainly deserved
better than its almost complete dismissal at the box office, where it
recouped only slightly half of its budget.

IF HIS WORK of the 1980s was spottier than his output of the previous
decade, you could mount a pretty good film festival with films that he
came close to making during this period but that reached the screen
without him or didn't get made at all. He was going to play a cameo
as impresario Sol Hurok in a film about the Russian ballerina Anna
Pavlova, and a key role in Michael Powell's never-realized production
about the Russian author Mikhail Lermontov; he was going to appear
in Sergio Leone's epic about the siege of Leningrad and to play Pancho
Villa opposite Tom Cruise in the role of Tom Mix. He was interested
in making films of two David Mamet plays—*Glengarry Glen Ross* and
Speed-the-Plow—and a film called *Waterfront* about the struggle to
make *On the Waterfront*. He was cast on paper, but never on film, opposite Danny DeVito in a comedy called *The Battling Spumonti Brothers*, in a cameo role in *Monty Python's The Meaning of Life*, in Elia
Kazan's adaptation of his own novel *Beyond the Aegean*, as Prospero in
a Cuban film version of *The Tempest*, and in Michael Cimino's never-
filmed life of gangster Frank Costello, *Proud Dreamer*. He came very
close, in 1988, to playing the role of Sal the pizzeria owner in Spike
Lee's *Do the Right Thing* (Lee's production diaries from the weeks
when De Niro was attached would include the director's reminders to
himself not to be cowed by an actor of De Niro's stature). And amid all

those unrealized projects, he very nearly debuted as a director with an adaptation of Haywood Gould's novel *Double Bang*, a cop story set in New York that he also would have starred in and produced.

HE'D STEERED CLEAR of the Chateau Marmont for a while after John Belushi's death, and in fact he barely worked in Hollywood throughout the 1980s, but by the end of the decade he began staying there regularly again—and, once again, it was a star-crossed experience. Twice in November 1988 his bungalow at the Chateau was burgled, once when he was asleep inside. The first theft was relatively minor—some clothes, some audio equipment. But the second, when De Niro was in bed, resulted in the disappearance of a rented Mercedes, which finally turned up a few days later in a hardscrabble neighborhood in Long Beach. At first De Niro claimed that the burglar had used keys to get into the bungalow, but he later confessed to police that he likely had left the sliding patio door unlocked and, he admitted, ajar. "I'm from New York," he explained. "New York people like fresh air."

A few months later he was a victim, in a sense, of an even more invasive crime. Robert Litchfield, a career bank robber from Florida, had escaped the federal penitentiary in Leavenworth, Kansas (becoming the first such escapee in a dozen years), and while in flight had undergone plastic surgery to accentuate an already close resemblance to De Niro. He was caught six weeks after his escape after robbing yet another bank in Florida, his eyes and ears still slightly swollen from his cosmetic operations. Turned out that being Robert De Niro wasn't as easy as the man himself made it look.

17

WHATEVER MIGHT BE MEANT BY THE PHRASE "CAREER criminal," it certainly was appropriate for James Burke, aka Jimmy the Gent, a hijacker, loan shark, gambler, extortionist, drug trafficker, and murderer who was born in New York in 1931 and had an adult arrest record from the time he was eligible for one. Burke was taken into custody by the NYPD four times in 1970, three times each in 1948, 1957, 1964, and 1966, twice each in 1961 and 1963, and once each in 1949, 1950, 1953, 1956, 1962, 1967, 1968, 1969, 1972, and 1973: thirty-three collars in twenty-five years, real archcriminal stuff.

That last bust—for beating a Florida man who owed money to some people in New York—wound up with Burke going to prison for six years, during which time a parole officer noted, with some understatement:

> This resident can be described as "The Model Inmate." . . . It is plain to see that this man knows how to "pull time." During interviews he was always courteous and cooperative and gave the appearance of being self-confident and mature. However, because of his lengthy criminal record he is considered to be street-wise and criminally oriented. . . . The prognosis for Mr. Burke to remain free of involvement in criminal activities is guarded.

Burke was aligned with the Lucchese crime family, which held sway over parts of Brooklyn and Queens, where Burke was born and committed most of his crimes. He was particularly keen on Kennedy Airport, which was near his base of operations, provided a rich source of cargo, cash, and valuables, and, in the days before 9/11, featured a loosey-goosey security infrastructure that could be easily exploited by a small and well-connected gang of thieves. Burke was famous in criminal and police circles for his ability to prey upon the airport; the most audacious heist of his audacious career, a $6 million haul of untraceable cash from a Lufthansa Airlines storage facility in 1978, became the stuff of legend, in part because in the years afterward Burke systematically killed so many of the people involved in the job.*

What Burke was *not* was Italian, and thus despite all his collaborations with mafiosi and all the money he made with and for them, he was never initiated into the mob. That was a privilege accorded to full-blooded Italians and never to Irishmen like Burke or even to the likes of Henry Hill, a half-Italian, half-Irish member of Burke's crew who grew up watching and emulating Jimmy the Gent and other gangsters from his neighborhood. Burke was a father figure to Hill and to the slightly younger Thomas DeSimone, both of whom he'd instructed in the ways of the mob from adolescence onward and who partnered with him on any number of crimes, including the Lufthansa heist. One of the lessons he repeatedly drilled into them was that they should never, under any circumstances, rat on a colleague or assist the police in any way. But when Hill was caught dealing cocaine in 1980—against the orders of Burke and their mutual bosses in the Lucchese family—he did what he'd been tutored never to do: he cooperated with law enforcement authorities against Burke and several others and vanished into the witness protection program. On the strength of Hill's testimony, Burke went to prison in 1982—not for the Lufthansa heist and all the murders that he'd committed or ordered others to cover up, but for fixing college basketball games as part of a 1978 gambling scheme. While he was incarcerated, though, he was convicted of the 1979 mur-

---

* As late as 2013, more than seventeen years after his death, Burke's home was excavated by authorities in search of human remains—which they discovered. In 2014, several of Burke's associates were arrested for, among other things, the Lufthansa heist.

der of a cocaine dealer, and any chance he had of being paroled disappeared. He died of stomach cancer in a prison hospital in 1996.

Burke's story came to the attention of Martin Scorsese in 1985 when
he read *Wiseguy: Life in a Mafia Family* by the New York journalist
Nicholas Pileggi. The book was an as-told-to account of Henry Hill's
life and deeds, recounted from the vantage of an unnamed safe harbor
and an assumed identity. Said Scorsese, "I was drawn to the book because of the details—life—stuff that I remembered friends saying when
I was growing up in Little Italy and that I had never seen written down
before." With Pileggi, Scorsese worked on adapting a script from the
book (the title of which could not be used because of a fear of confusion with the then-popular TV series of the same name). They focused
their work on the quotidiana of mob life that enthralled Scorsese, ending up with what Pileggi called "a mob home movie."

Before Scorsese could get around to it, though, he finally made *The
Last Temptation of Christ* and then the short film *Life Lessons*, which
was part of the *New York Stories* trilogy that also included pieces by
Woody Allen and Francis Ford Coppola. Finally, in the summer of
1989, he set about making *Goodfellas*, as the Henry Hill movie had
come to be entitled, with a $25 million budget from Warner Bros. Ray
Liotta, hot off successes in small but vital roles in *Something Wild* and
Field of Dreams, would play Hill; Lorraine Bracco, then married to
Harvey Keitel, would play Hill's wife, Karen; Paul Sorvino would play a
Lucchese family crime boss; Joe Pesci would take on a character based
on Tommy DeSimone, and De Niro would play the role of Jimmy the
Gent—or Jimmy Conway, as the script renamed him.

Whatever he was energized by—the story, the role, or the chance
to work with Scorsese for the first time since *The King of Comedy*—De
Niro dove into preparing for the part of Jimmy the Gent with a vigor
he hadn't demonstrated in years. In some ways it was a supporting role,
since Hill was the narrator and the protagonist. But De Niro treated
it with fanatical devotion. He never met with Burke—"It would have
been too complicated," he explained cryptically—but he spoke with
Henry and Karen Hill repeatedly (they joked about receiving seven or
eight phone calls from him a day), and his researchers helped track

down other people who could tell him about the mind, the heart, and the habits of the real guy.* And he heavily annotated his copy of Pileggi's book.

The result was a massive written portrait of Jimmy Burke, larger than the one Pileggi had written, teeming with insights and reflections that would shape De Niro's performance: an account of how Burke talked, walked, dressed, gambled, killed, ate, drank, moved, loved, hated, thought. In each scene in which he appeared, De Niro distilled his research into specific choices of actions, attitudes, and dialogue. It was the most work he'd done on a film role since *Raging Bull*.

Take, for example, these excerpts from his notes on the character:

Lots of bets . . . he liked to laugh . . . when drunk a little loud . . . tried to be a part of any situation . . . good at bullshitting people . . . bookmaker all the time . . . plays gin rummy . . . fabulous memory . . . dozen roses to mothers of guys in can . . . glide, little bounce . . . always shaking hands . . . Didn't like strangers . . . I'd go over in a restaurant if I knew them and say hello, buy drinks, send a bottle . . . big spender . . . likes to tell jokes, good company, a laugher . . . I created my own crew . . . I was contemporary . . . I networked very well. I was always working, my mind was working. Anybody and anything . . . I made myself known and I made myself feared. A rebel . . . I know that if I wanted to get it done right, anything, I had to do it . . . seemed to be everywhere, all the time . . . I have a set of values, set of rules . . . wonderful around children, respectful, a gentleman . . . hair short, clean . . . when had to do business, looked good. Good dresser. A rebel but respectful . . . expressive with eyes, looked right at you . . . intense smile you never knew how to take . . . could smile wide and be very angry . . . play one person against the other, egg a person . . . on power trips . . . never slept; once in a while took a cat nap . . . loved that he was Irish and when walked into place they'd play

---

* Somewhat coyly, De Niro wouldn't say whether he learned how to pistol-whip somebody from Hill. "Perhaps," he replied when asked point-blank if that had been something they'd discussed. "I would ask him how this might have been done, or that, y'know?"

*"Danny Boy" . . . a good sport; if someone needed, I'd give . . .
nice smile . . . normally laid back, take things in stride, always
in control . . . my mind was on making a score, not so much a
woman . . . when walked in the place glowed, but people didn't
like to see me get drunk.*

There are the makings of a complete performance in those observations, and De Niro's dossier would go on for pages and pages, noting
Burke's love of ketchup on his food, his preference for Chivas Regal or
J&B scotch neat with a glass of water on the side, his workaholism, his
inability to relate to women, his love of elevated diction, and especially
his singular status as an Irishman working for the Mafia: "Part of my
power was Italians needed me. They had the money but I had the connection with the Irish DA and politicians. I being Irish they could trust
me. So if I whacked guys from time to time they'd let it go, cause I was
too important to them and I knew that." He also cannily noted another
oddity of Jimmy's status vis-à-vis his Mafia connections: "I did all the
shit that the wiseguys wouldn't and couldn't do. I just *did* it! What*ever*
it was . . . I'm more of a wiseguy big shot than the actual wiseguy big
shots. I got more style than they do. . . . I act more Italian than the Italians to overcompensate."

In the course of the film, Jimmy the Gent would age twenty-four
years, and De Niro was, predictably, scrupulous in addressing the
changes in physique, diction, wardrobe, and especially hair color and
hair style that the character would undergo. (During production, he
went to a Manhattan nightclub to see the jazz singer Little Jimmy
Scott perform and was approached by a woman unknown to him who
wanted to know why he looked so gray. "That comes from the aggrava-
tion of being a star," he replied.)

He wasn't the only actor devoted to verisimilitude throughout the
production. Scorsese gave Joe Pesci the go-ahead to fill his prop pistol
with blanks for a scene in which he shot an errand boy in a fit of pique,
and the loud report of the gun genuinely took the other players in the
scene by surprise: "Everyone in the room was shocked," Pesci recalled.
"No one moved. I think they were really scared."

Pesci also remembered how carefully De Niro observed everything about the film, not just the details concerning Jimmy the Gent. When they filmed the famous body-in-the-car-trunk scene, he said, "I attacked Frank [Vincent] with the knife viciously. After the first take, Bob kept staring at me. I said, 'How was it? Was I ok?' Bob said, 'Yeah, it's fine.' But he kept staring like he wanted to tell me something. He said, 'Well, Joe, your emotions are great, but I don't see how you can get that knife in and out of the chest area that fast because of the bones and the tendons all around it. It's such a big butcher knife, it seems you'd have to force it in and force it out.' That's Bob. He really wants to help."

There were even true-to-life details that none of the filmmakers knew about. Cast as Fat Andy, one of the mobsters in the movie's slow-motion introduction of the Lucchese crew in their nightclub hangout, was Lou Eppolito, a Brooklyn detective who, it later emerged, was an active participant in as many as eight gangland murders, among a number of crimes for which he and a fellow officer were eventually tried and convicted—and sentenced to what was in effect life in prison.

That sort of thing helped infuse the film with the sort of spirit that Scorsese sought. *Goodfellas* would have a sexy patina that made mob life seem as attractive to the audience as it did to the young Henry Hill, but in the end the violence, disloyalty, and darkness of the life would emerge even more powerfully. "Anyone who wants to live that lifestyle after seeing this movie—it's beyond me," the director said. The film was designed to make clear, according to Pileggi, that "the honor code is a myth. . . . Once Henry's life is threatened, he has no qualms about testifying. He does no soul-searching because he has no soul."

DESPITE EVERYTHING THE actor had learned about the real-life Jimmy "the Gent" Burke, the sheer gorgeous style of *Goodfellas* is the most important determinant in De Niro's assured, breezy, and unimpeachable performance. The film belongs to Liotta, of course, and Pesci steals it (and was, properly, awarded an Oscar for the job), but De Niro's every appearance is memorably graced with savvy, showy, well-designed, and well-played moments. He's playing a fictionalized version of a real character rendered through the memories of another

based-on-truth character, and he plays with just the right degree of styl-
ization to fulfill that delicate charge and to enhance the film indisputably.

When he first arrives, in Henry's memory (which, of course, is the
vantage from which the entire film is seen), he is in his late twenties,
dark-haired, slick, and voluble, smiling deeply without baring his teeth,
sticking C-note tips in people's shirt pockets, and declaring, with his
head cocked at a jaunty angle, "The Irishman is here to take all you
[*sic*] guineas' money," the Cadillacs' boastful R&B hit "Speedoo" his
entry music. "It was a glorious time," Henry remembers; riding Jimmy's
infectious, energetic, and festive vibe, you have to agree.

From there, Jimmy takes on the role of mentoring Henry and
Tommy, telling them, like a good coach, when they've done well and
not and demonstrating with his professionalism and judicious meting
out of punishment how the game works. The three are grown men, but
Jimmy is the eldest, the most stable, the smartest, the most trustworthy
and emulable and wise. He's also deeply loyal, as he demonstrates by
joining in on the beating and murder of a gangster whose offense was
a verbal show of disrespect to Tommy ("You insulted him a little bit,"
as Jimmy famously points out to the fellow). De Niro leaps into the fray
with his patented kick to the body: arms outspread, knee lifted high to
bring his full weight to bear on a downward blow with the heel. When
next we see him, he's getting ready to tuck into the scrambled eggs that
Tommy's mother has cooked for the boys, and it's hard to say which
action has more engaged him: stomping a man to the edge of death or
spinning a ketchup bottle between his palms to get the contents flowing. He's got a zest, Jimmy does.

But he's also extremely vigilant and suspicious, to the point of paranoia and, eventually, murder. After the Lufthansa heist, one dope in
the crew after another shows up at a holiday party with an opulent new
toy: a fur, a floozy, a Cadillac. And Jimmy dresses them down in what
will become an iconic mode of late De Niro temper: "What did I tell
you? *What . . . did . . . I . . . tell . . . you?*" That face of Jimmy's cold-
ness is amusing; far less so is the one we see later, when he goes from
thinking that he has to whack his crew to save his own skin to *knowing*
that he'll do it. He's at the corner of the bar, chatting, smoking, his

eyes gelid, moving from the fellow he's talking to, to whom he smiles insincerely, to the blabbermouth Morrie, the ceaseless irritant of which he plans to relieve himself soon. The camera zooms slowly in on De Niro, Cream's "Sunshine of Your Love" on the soundtrack, and his expressions work on two levels: the superficial one of grins and chatter, the subtextual one of psychopathic intent declaring itself. It's one of the best things De Niro and Scorsese have ever done together.

He has two more standout scenes. Waiting at the diner with Henry for news of Tommy's initiation into the mob, Jimmy's all bubbly nerves, eating and laughing at once, clearly relishing life. When he receives bad news instead of good, he rages against the parking lot pay phone and struggles to keep from bursting into tears—one of the best such efforts in De Niro's career (he never was a very good crier). Later, behind the pair of cheaters he's taken to wearing in middle age, he seems kindly and caring when telling Karen how to find "some beautiful Dior dresses . . . down the corner." In fact, given the circumstances under which they're meeting—Henry has been busted by the feds and is being leaned on to turn against his friends—Jimmy's avuncular manner is terrifying. He *seems* not to have evil intent, but De Niro plays him on a delicate edge in a particularly quiet and attenuated scene, and he thus becomes unreadable. It's a marvelous trick: nothing in the scene suggests menace . . . except for everything.

As those reading glasses suggest, De Niro creates a character who spans a couple of decades credibly, graying, giving up a little bit of hairline, and becoming more cautious and more intent on survival with the passing of the years. The film is about Henry Hill, and secondarily about his wife. But Jimmy Conway is the principal third character in that his chronology runs almost as long—though never as deep—as Henry's. In a sense, De Niro gets to build an entire character as if he were carrying the film. Rather than mark the transitions, though (save that one from wondering about murder to committing to it), he simply makes them and appears in a slightly older guise: his hair, his clothes, his manner. It's a performance with flashes in it, and details, but it's mainly low-key ensemble work, and quite good. It's only the second time in a collaboration with Scorsese that he hasn't played the central character, and he's as engaged in it as in any of the major roles he crafted with the director.

And it was a hit. *Goodfellas* was released in September 1990 and led the North American box office on its opening weekend with $6.37 million. It wound up lasting five weeks in the top ten, grossing a total of $46.8 million—not a blockbuster but one of the best results its director and his longtime star had enjoyed to that point.

In AUGUST 1989, virtually as soon as he was done shooting *Goodfellas*, De Niro found himself in London's Highlands Hospital, observing and, when possible, interacting with a group of people who'd been living there for more than a half century: patients suffering from the aftereffects of an epidemic of encephalitis, a sickness that had left them immobilized, almost zombielike. He was there in the company of Dr. Oliver Sacks, the acclaimed British neurologist and author whose 1973 book *Awakenings* described his work with similar patients in the Bronx in the late 1960s. And he was preparing to play one of Sacks's patients in a screen adaptation of the book.

Sacks had observed the post-encephalitic patients and theorized that their physical catatonia could in fact be a form of Parkinson's disease—in effect, their bodily spasms had sped up to a point at which they froze. He experimented with the use of a new drug, L-dopa, which had been developed to slow the spasms of traditional Parkinson's patients. For a period the post-encephalitic patients responded, unfreezing, coming to life after decades, attempting to merge back into the world, sometimes with alarming results. In the course of time, though, they developed a tolerance for the drug treatment and regressed to their immobilized states.

Sacks's book had been warmly received in both scientific and literary circles; Harold Pinter had adapted a short play from it, and W. H. Auden had written a poem inspired by it. In 1983, a documentary made for British television told the story and showed Sacks and his actual patients, including some footage from their period of emergence. In 1989, screenwriter Steve Zaillian adapted Sacks's book as a project for director Penny Marshall, who was fresh off the massive success of *Big* (which, of course, had nearly starred De Niro). Now she was offering him the role of Leonard Lowe, loosely based on one of Sacks's patients who was among the earliest—and, when briefly "cured," the most volatile—of the L-dopa patients. Robin Williams would play Sacks, and shooting would begin in October, meaning De Niro had his work cut out for him in order to segue from the itchy Jimmy the Gent to Leonard, who'd been paralytic for decades.

In order to do so, according to Sacks, De Niro embarked on a serious study of Parkinson's, paralysis, catatonia, and similar medical conditions. He made particular use of a friend of friends in New York who had a severe case of Parkinson's. This fellow was responsive to L-dopa and very articulate about what it felt like to be in the throes of his condition and then freed by medication. De Niro interviewed him at length, as he did another Parkinson's patient, a man whose symptoms resembled those of Sacks's frozen patients; De Niro had a chance to accompany this fellow to an alternative therapist to see what it was like when his body was, in effect, thawed.

> *I'll never forget first meeting him in Penn Station—everyone rushing about at high speed, and there was this real-life, living statue of a man, just standing there still, quite frozen. When we picked our way down the stairs to the train so slowly, I could feel his terrible need for an impetus to move—as if he was flailing in some sort of fog we could both feel. We went to this healer on Long Island who could free him for a while by pressing parts of his body and nerves until Bang! All of a sudden he snapped out of it. He became wildly animated: "We mustn't miss the train back," he said, so there we were suddenly jogging along together to the station. He was able to explain to me, articulately, just how he was feeling, and what he was going through. He was a great artist in his own way.*

While De Niro observed Sacks's patients, Sacks observed De Niro, noting how eerily he could slip in and out of various moods—or, more accurately, the expressions of those moods. Watching him rehearse for a scene in which Leonard was particularly exercised, Sacks said, was "like overhearing a man thinking, but thinking with his body . . . thinking in action." At other times, watching De Niro play physical crises, Sacks became alarmed at the accuracy of the portrayal, his inner physician emerging from beneath the author visiting the film set: "I forgot he was an actor. I thought he *had* suddenly lost all his postural reflexes, that there had suddenly been a neurological catastrophe." He was amazed, too, to see that De Niro couldn't always turn it off at will; chatting with the actor in his dressing room between takes, Sacks noticed that De Niro's right foot was turned at a ninety-degree angle, just like the feet of his post-encephalitic patients. He pointed it out, and De Niro replied, "I didn't realize. I guess it's unconscious."

Sacks considered hooking up De Niro to his diagnostic machinery to see if he had actually created a post-encephalitic brain profile in himself, but he ultimately decided against it. Still, ever the neurologist, he developed a theory about De Niro's technique: "Bob's method, as far as I could see, was to take in everything he learned about Parkinsonism, absorb it silently, without any external sign, and then let the images sink down into his unconscious and ferment there, uniting with his own experiences, powers, imagination, feelings. Only then would they return so deeply infused with his own character as to be an integral part, an expression of himself"—as good a working definition of Stanislavskian acting as De Niro would have heard in Stella Adler's classroom or the Actors Studio.

What Sacks didn't see were the copious line-by-line notes that De Niro made in his script, reminders of virtually every bit of physical acting he wished to do: drooling, twisting his head, fidgeting, rocking, clutching the arms of a chair, shaking, speaking with subtle gradations of looseness and rigidity. De Niro wrote down dozens of questions for Sacks, and continually sought comparisons for the behavior he wished to embody: a sloth, the cartoon Road Runner, various of Sacks's patients, even Sacks himself.

During the production, De Niro impressed Marshall with his application, his imagination, his versatility: "You say, 'Bob, comb your hair,' and he does it several different ways, all amazing to watch." Even more eye-opening was the day on which Robin Williams accidentally broke De Niro's nose during a take of a scene in which Sacks was test-ing Leonard's reflexes. The blow was so severe, De Niro said, that "we heard a crack—you could hear it on the soundtrack at the rushes." As Marshall recalled, De Niro turned away immediately, staying in the scene, then turned back to reveal a stream of blood coming from his nose. *"Bobby went on with the scene,"* Marshall said, astonished. "We did nine more takes." The next day, after X-rays confirmed the break, swelling and discoloration caused the production to halt for a week so that he could recover. In fact, De Niro was almost grateful for the accident: "I had my nose broken first when I was a kid," he said, and Williams "straightened it out, knocked it back in the other direction."

SURELY THE CHIEF appeal for De Niro of playing the role of Leonard Lowe was the chance to perform with his body in a way that he might if he were cast as, say, the Elephant Man onstage: a series of stillnesses, contortions, and spasms that, almost without the need for dialogue, tells the character's fate. As it stands, Steve Zaillian's script is pain-fully pointed and overdetermined (and, almost without saying, Oscar-nominated), and wherever the writing manages to be naturalistic or at ease Penny Marshall imposes a heartless sentimentality, insisting al-most fascistically on specific emotional reactions, heavily underscoring her intent with pointed framing and cutting, with reaction shots that are meant to trigger mirrored responses in the viewer, and with a de-pressingly literal score by Randy Newman.

Still, De Niro is quite strong in the various phases of his role. Leon-ard is frozen; he thaws; he is restored to normal vitality; he becomes in-creasingly unable to control his body, first with facial tics and then with waves of spasms; he experiences short freezing spells; finally he returns to the "elsewhere" described by the elderly doctor (Max von Sydow) who first treated patients like him decades before. In all of it, you can see the depth of De Niro's study and effort, and you are physically un-comfortable with his struggle, just as you might be if you were in the room with him. At times the performance feels a little bit like some-thing whipped up for the workshop, but very often it's painfully lifelike, and you can't ignore De Niro for a second when he's on the screen.

Ironically, given that we know (from the movie poster or DVD jacket, if nothing else) that Leonard will eventually emerge from his catatonic state, De Niro is arguably most compelling in the moments when he cannot move at all and sits or lies, his gaze alertly fixed on Sayer. There are three or four such episodes in the early going, and you find yourself looking deeply into De Niro's eyes, in part because of the knowledge that he's awake and cognizant in there (a condition that von Sydow has rightly labeled "unthinkable"), in part because De Niro has always been able to infuse silence with a gaze in such a way as to convey as much meaning as any passage of dialogue.

Unfrozen, Leonard regains his muscularity and speech slowly, so there is a gradual escalation in his motor abilities and his verbal fluency—another challenge that De Niro seems to relish. Fully recovered, Leonard is a man of simple affect and appearance, his shirts tucked in boyishly and buttoned all the way up to his chubby neck, whether or not he's wearing his favored bowtie. He has old-fashioned ideas and a great store of knowledge (he has alerted Sayer that he's awake inside his frozen body by writing out the phrase "Rilke's panther" with a Ouija board); he's a model of the efficacy of clinical psychology and pharmacological therapy.

But when Leonard starts to lose control of his body once again, the performance begins to be painted with the same broad brush with which the film has been directed. A rabble-rousing speech in which Leonard enlists a ward of able-bodied patients to his side in rejecting the rule of the administrators is as heavy-handed in its acting as its writing. From then, the physicality of the character becomes more and more the focus of De Niro's efforts—and less and less easy to watch. Fully in the thrall of the sort of spasms you might see in someone with cerebral palsy, he gets so he can't fix his gaze long enough on a page to read. Your heart goes out to him, partly because, even with the showiness, De Niro imbues Leonard with simple, recognizable humanity, partly because he has been so sweet with his doctor, mother, and nurses—as well as a girl (Penelope Ann Miller) to whom he has attached himself. Finally, he is "elsewhere" once again, frozen, dependent, the faraway look in his eyes infinitely more meaningful and pointed than it was at the start of the film.

Awakenings debuted in New York and Los Angeles in December 1990, in time for Academy Award eligibility, with a nationwide roll-out planned for January. It outperformed *Goodfellas* at the box office, grossing more than $52 million and spending six weeks in the top ten—a second hit in a row. In fact, with *Goodfellas* still playing healthily, De Niro was enjoying his most successful combination of critical and commercial success since *The Untouchables*, maybe ever. In February, when Oscar nominations were announced, he was in the final running for the Best Actor prize, placing him in his first Academy Award race since *Raging Bull*. More impressive was that both *Awakenings* and *Goodfellas* were nominated for Best Picture, along with *Ghost*, *The Godfather: Part III* (which De Niro had lobbied Francis Coppola to play a role in) and the eventual winner, in one of the most often-cited instances of the Motion Picture Academy's bland taste, *Dances with Wolves*, for which Kevin Costner aced out Martin Scorsese as Best Director. De Niro lost, in what nobody considered an upset or miscarriage of aesthetic justice, to Jeremy Irons for *Reversal of Fortune*. (Oliver Sacks wrote De Niro from London to say, "Sorry you didn't get an Oscar—I was rooting for you." But another character in the De Niro saga felt differently: Pauline Kael, Virginia Admiral's onetime admirer and De Niro's early champion, had long since turned on the actor, and his work in *Awakenings* was one of the last things she commented on before her 1991 retirement from criticism, declaring in an interview, "He does the tics and jiggles well. It's in the quiet moments that he's particularly bad. People get the idea that somebody is a great actor and it takes them decades to shake it off.")

AFTER MAKING the move to CAA and acquiring the ability to command higher prices for his work and to have input into studio projects before the studio even acquired them, De Niro found himself wanting yet more control and earlier still in the process. He wanted to produce: to choose projects, select the creative team, pitch in on the script, cast actors, and help shape the PR campaign, even if he wasn't going to appear in the film at all.

In part, he came to it because it was smart business—movie stars had routinely taken this sort of creative control of their careers, often helping others along, since the 1960s. In part, though, he came to it because he viewed his art on a kind of continuum with the art he'd grown up around—painting and writing—and was frustrated that his fame and wealth still didn't bring him complete creative freedom: "A writer or a painter can control his work," he explained, "but in movies it's different. I see a tacky poster and I say, 'Why was it done that way?' Maybe I know a better way." At the time he made that comment, he was already doing at least some producing work on *We're No Angels*, and he had been actively working toward building a production company of his own, using the same meticulous practice with which he acted.

In part, he was driven by his new life. Upon divorcing Diahnne Abbott, De Niro bought a new apartment on Hudson Street, even further downtown than the Greenwich Village in which he'd lived almost his entire life. If the St. Luke's Place townhouse was a family home appropriate to an up-and-coming actor and his wife, children, and pets, the new place was more befitting a bachelor prince—or a king, even. De Niro acquired the top floor of 110 Hudson Street, a building marked by Greek-style columns at the street level and, from De Niro's 4,600-square-foot tenth-floor penthouse (complete with rooftop garden), expansive views of the Hudson River and the World Trade Center, mere blocks away. The neighborhood hadn't yet become popular with developers, but it would soon have a trendy name: Tribeca. The area was a mix of underused industrial spaces and, for lower Manhattan, inexpensive housing, in large part because so many of the amenities that people expect from the city were lacking in the community. De Niro may have moved to Tribeca for the quiet, or for the bargains to be had in real estate (he convinced Harvey Keitel to buy a unit in the same building at around the same time). Or he may have done it because he already had a vision, however unformed, for a new sort of control over his career, not only a production company but an actual production facility.

Tribeca wasn't an obvious choice for a home base for such a project. The film business per se had virtually no footprint in the area, despite the presence of adventuresome movie theaters and celebrity residents not very far away in more established neighborhoods. But in De Niro's mind there was an idea of an office that would house his production company and be part of larger infrastructure—a complex of offices, say, or even a movie studio. And his new neighborhood had room in which to build such a thing.

Before he could tackle that, though, he knew that he needed a strong partner beside him who could do the things that he wouldn't or couldn't: talk to the press, drive hard bargains, say no a lot. He hoped eventually to choose a project from his producing workload to make his debut as a director, possibly acting in it as well. And for that, too, he would need a partner whom he could trust, someone who knew the movie business and could handle the high profile that working with De Niro in New York would entail.

He was as thorough in his search for a producing partner as he was in digging into an important role. "There were 20 people I met with," he recalled. "I kept dragging it out." Eventually he settled on someone, and, as was often the case when major Hollywood stars hung out a producing shingle, the perfect man for the job turned out to be a woman: Jane Rosenthal, a tall, energetic thirtysomething NYU film grad from Rhode Island with an impressively diverse resume and sufficient polish and energy to serve as the public face of a boss who preferred to show himself to the world when wearing the mask of a character.

Rosenthal had fast-tracked through Brown and NYU, had served as the youngest-ever (and first female) page in the Rhode Island House of Representatives, and had worked as an assistant to the director of the original Broadway production of *The Best Little Whorehouse in Texas*. As a young hire at CBS television, she butted heads with Jimmy "the Greek" Snyder in the sports department, helped create *Sunday Morning with Charles Kuralt* in the news department, then produced TV movies and miniseries such as *The Burning Bed* and *Haywire* for the entertainment division. After that, she served as a production executive at Universal Pictures, at Disney (where she met Martin Scorsese while overseeing production on *The Color of Money* for the studio), and finally at Warner Bros., which was where she was working when De Niro first encountered her.

"Bob was shooting 'Midnight Run,'" she said. "We had a number of friends and acquaintances in common, so I wasn't that shaken [when we met]. I did become something of a motormouth, since he's so quiet." Rosenthal was flattered to be asked by De Niro if she'd consider going into business with him. But she was chary, too. They spoke on and off about the possibility for nearly a year; Scorsese even tried to convince her to take the gig, and she told him bluntly, "I'm not going to develop scripts for some actor, no matter who it is."

During their negotiations, De Niro's plans grew bolder and more substantial. The production company, named Tribeca after the neighborhood in which he lived and in which it would be based, was just part of a larger vision that included an office building designed to serve the New York filmmaking community, with a restaurant or maybe a nightclub on the ground floor. He wanted Rosenthal involved with all of it.

On one hand, she knew it was a crazy prospect: "People in LA thought I was cracked to even think about moving to New York. Also to work with an actor who wasn't known for producing or restaurants or real estate." But De Niro appealed to the world-beating drive he sensed in her. The chance to build a production company from the ground up was unlikely ever to present itself to her again—and certainly not in Hollywood. "He said, 'What do you want to be—a studio executive all your life?'" She took off to a desert spa to mull it over, and she came to a realization: "If I don't do something new and challenging, I will emotionally and creatively die." Besides, she missed New York. In her work developing films, she had come up with a trick designed to keep her visiting the city: hiring New York playwrights to work on scripts. "By hiring all these writers," she confessed, "I could come back for meetings. I'm not happy in any city where I can't hail a cab."

Finally she succumbed to De Niro's offers—"Look, if it doesn't work out, you can always hostess at the [restaurant]," he told her, only half joking—and took the job. (It was a nearer thing than she knew. "There was one guy I nearly hired," De Niro said, "and I feel like I got lucky because he didn't take the job. But Jane held in there, she kept up on it, she was always ready to go.")

Right from the start, their disparate working styles and personalities proved complementary. "I'm just the producer," Rosenthal remarked about her role in De Niro's working life. "Nobody's supposed to notice me." But De Niro, who could get lost in the details of a work project, appreciated that she had the same capacity and was willing to insist on it, not by mumbling to a director, as he so often did, but by presenting her wishes forcefully to collaborators. "She does all the real nuts and bolts," he said. "I'm just there, hovering. She's the one on the front lines."

They looked mismatched. "She is Miss Glam, the fund-raising, producing person," said film executive Stacey Snider. "She puts it all out there. He seems to keep it all inside and use his feelings for his profession." But they had a common impulse to get work done and get it done right: "Nobody is as meticulous as Bob," Rosenthal said, "but I like things to be perfect, too."

Tribeca Productions started on a modest scale. Upon launching in 1988, with the pair working at first out of De Niro's apartment, it owned the rights to a small clutch of projects. As Rosenthal described them, "One is an out-of-print novel and one a current novel. Another is a collection of home videotapes of a real person, and the others are original ideas from screenwriters." De Niro funded the early going out of his own pocket, but soon they had a two-year nonexclusive deal with Tri-Star to produce and distribute. The discretionary fund included in that deal allowed them to acquire more material: the Native American–themed crime story *Thunderheart*; William Least Heat Moon's *Blue Highways*; *The Battling Spumonti Brothers*, a comedy about Chicago politics; and a few other spec scripts, particularly crime stories. One of Rosenthal's concerns in accepting the job was that she wasn't sure there would be enough actual producing to do in New York; on that she was wrong.

That was plenty to deal with, but right from the start Rosenthal was wearing a construction worker's hard hat along with her movie producer clothes, because De Niro's notion of a physical space in which to house the production company was becoming a reality. De Niro bought a stake in a building at 375 Greenwich Street, on the corner of Franklin, one city block from his home on Hudson Street. It had long been the warehouse of the Martinson Coffee company, and it still bore painted advertisements on its brick exterior touting the fact, but

De Niro and his investment partners, Stewart Lane and Paul Wallace, were turning the eight-story building into an office block dedicated to film professionals, with a high-end restaurant as a key ground-floor tenant.

The warehouse offered 60,000 square feet of space and was an almost blank slate, so bare-bones that there were only two telephone lines in the entire building. De Niro and his partners acquired it for $7.2 million in 1988, three years after it had been purchased for $4.25 million—a sign of how quickly Tribeca, for many decades an industrial district of no particular commercial or residential appeal, was becoming a hot neighborhood. They hired the architect Lo-Yi Chan to reimagine it, and they set to work on renovations almost immediately.

Even though the building was entirely unsuited to the purposes for which he imagined it, De Niro was keen on it because of its proximity to his home. "When I started my own production offices, we worked out of my apartment. . . . [Back then] the only place for film people to work was midtown. But it's such a hassle getting there. I live down here, and the pace is so much quieter, more leisurely. I dreamt that I wouldn't have to leave the neighborhood to work. Then the building came up for sale, and it just seemed perfect. We could have production offices, and we could have a screening room, and we could have a restaurant. And I could work near home when I was in New York. Things sort of snowballed after that."

Throughout 1989, the entire building was remade, with Rosenthal overseeing the details that De Niro could be convinced not to oversee himself. Electrical, plumbing, and climate systems were rebuilt or installed; three hundred phone lines were put in; elevators and stairways were reconfigured; windows were carved out; a thirty-foot skylight was revealed beneath decades of paint and roofing. There were touches of luxury throughout, including solid oak doors, sandblasted exposed brick walls, and brownstone imported from China. On the top floor, of which De Niro would claim 6,900 square feet for his production offices, a deluxe bathroom, complete with Jacuzzi, steam shower, and bidet was installed. There was a THX-certified screening room, the first in New York, on the second floor, alongside a multipurpose party space.

The building was designed on the model of condominiums, with whole floors of it for sale outright and other portions available for rent. The first truly important buyer was Miramax Films, which was making a significant name as a producer and distributor of independent and foreign films; it took the entire third floor. De Niro's friend and producer Art Linson took offices, as did, on a rental basis in the earliest years, the productions of *New Jack City, Bonfire of the Vanities,* and *Awakenings.* After a period of courtship with the space, Martin Scorsese, who had long been based in the Brill Building in Times Square, chose to stay uptown. But for a variety of small production companies, talent agencies, and even solo writers who just needed a room with a door that they could close to the outside world, the Tribeca Film Center, as it was finally dubbed, was a perfect Hollywood-on-the-Hudson.

De Niro showed the place off proudly, explaining that he built it as a home for a New York film community that could often feel insignificant because it was so decentralized in a city with so many other priorities:

> *I haven't seen any film place in New York, or anywhere else, that's really "complete." Initially, the idea was to find a home where I could be and where filmmakers could be, to have offices and a restaurant where they could hang out and feel like a community— a creative center where you can get input and feedback from other people. . . . You just come up with ideas when you're around people. I always tell people I work with, if you just spend time together, an hour or so, you're bound to come up with something, especially if you have a problem you're trying to solve, but even if you're just trying to create. . . . With people just being around each other a lot, their presence is felt. So you say, "Let's talk to so-and-so about this idea." That would be a nice situation. The people are close; it's like a little community.*

The soft launch of the Film Center came in December 1989, and throughout early 1990 tenants kept rolling in as the work on their offices was finished. By the springtime, work was done, and, almost as if to cap it, De Niro hosted an evening in honor of Nelson Mandela, who was making his first-ever visit to New York. The guest of honor was asked to make a few comments in the course of the evening, and he did. "At the end of Mandela's speech," remembered Miramax boss Harvey Weinstein, "he talked about how, when he was in prison for 20 [sic] years, they would show a film every Thursday night. And he felt that those actors and actresses were his friends, and they kept his spirits up. I looked over and saw De Niro and Jane with tears in their eyes, and I realized that this was their dream; to build this building, to get people who love film involved, to create a community where this can happen. . . . I've already told De Niro that if he went on to buy more buildings, Miramax would keep expanding with him."

18

I n June 1990 De Niro stood on a street corner in Los Angeles that was covered with snow, staring at a newsstand that was selling New York newspapers from December 1951. His longtime friend and producer, Irwin Winkler, was doing something highly unusual for a producer to do on a movie set: giving direction. "Remember, it's freezing cold," Winkler told De Niro, and then he proclaimed "Action," and a film shot began.

After nearly twenty-five years as a producer, Winkler was making his directorial debut with a film titled, temporarily, *Fear No Evil*, a story about the impact of the Communist witch hunts and subsequent blacklist on the Hollywood filmmaking community of the late 1940s. De Niro was cast in the lead as David Merrill, a respected director whose brief dalliance with leftist causes more than a decade earlier was coming back to haunt him, crushing him professionally and personally. The script, which Winkler wrote after conversations with the onetime blacklistee Abraham Polonsky and extensive research on the period, dealt with the reactions of a number of filmmakers to the pressure imposed on them by the House Un-American Activities Committee (HUAC): some named names and saved their careers, some embraced their political beliefs and fled the country, and some, like Merrill, tried to defy the committee by keeping honorable silence and attempting to stay working in the movie business, the management of which was eager to ferret out anyone whom HUAC deemed undesirable. Merrill was a composite character, but the script involved a number of thinly veiled stories that anyone familiar with the period would recognize, including a director, based on Joseph Losey, who moves to

Europe because he's an avowed Communist, and an actor, based on Larry Parks, who caves in to the pressure to testify and is blacklisted despite the fact.

Winkler brought the script to De Niro when they were making *Goodfellas,* and De Niro's interest encouraged Warner Bros. to fund the $13 million budget ("A picture like this with a star like De Niro should cost $20 million," Winkler bragged/moaned in typical producer fashion). Annette Bening was cast as De Niro's ex-wife and principal confidante; Chris Cooper played the Parks character, and Patricia Wettig was cast as his wife, an actress based on Dorothy Comingore, whose blacklisting led to a complete collapse and early death. In a nifty twist, Sam Wanamaker, an actor who left Hollywood rather than succumb to HUAC, appeared as an attorney who tries to bully potential witnesses into cooperating.

De Niro expressed no particular concerns about working with a first-time director. "I had faith he could do it," he explained. "I have faith in myself, why shouldn't I have faith in somebody else?" Even though he regarded the film as "simple" dramatically, De Niro was engaged in the process of coming to seem genuinely like a director of the post–World War II era. He had worked with Elia Kazan, who was notorious for having named names in front of HUAC, and drew upon his memories of Kazan's on-set posture. And he studied photographs of directors at work to see how they dressed, where they positioned themselves in relation to the actors and the camera, what they held in their hands, and so forth. ("It was a question," he joked, "of whether I should wear a beret and use a bullhorn.") In the end, he focused on the look of John Huston, of whom he amassed a thick file of photographs, and the at-work personality of Kazan: "Think of involvement . . . For ex. the way Kazan does, that energy!" He watched film and read transcripts of HUAC hearings, he spoke with some survivors of the period, and he read several books on the subject. It was movie history, and he took it seriously.

The film, eventually entitled *Guilty by Suspicion,* shot through the spring of 1990 and debuted the following March. De Niro was in Florida working on another film, but he flew to New York to support the release by appearing at a press conference and giving select interviews.

The subject of Kazan came up, inevitably: many in the film world hadn't yet forgiven him, even four decades on, for cooperating with HUAC. As De Niro reflected, "It was really a no-win situation, and I feel sorry for people no matter what position they took. It was terrible for Kazan that he had to do what he did; I know him, he's a friend, and I have a great respect for him." At the same time, though, he acknowledged that he would at least like to think he would have handled himself differently. "I'd like to think I'd refuse to betray anyone and somehow survive like [Arthur] Miller did," he said, "but I honestly don't know." *Guilty by Suspicion* came and went with little impact, but in time De Niro would have occasion to consider further the history of Hollywood's blacklist era.

WHILE WORKING ON *Guilty by Suspicion*, he lined up his next two films. One was a pet project in which he was taking a producer's interest: a remake of the 1962 thriller *Cape Fear*, in which he would play an updated version of Robert Mitchum's role, an ex-con terrorizing the family of the lawyer who he believed perverted justice to put him away. Martin Scorsese would be directing in Florida and North Carolina in the winter. Before that, though, De Niro would go to Chicago for a chunk of the summer to play a feature role in *Backdraft*, a sprawling film about firefighters and arsonists written by Greg Widen and set to be directed by Ron Howard. Kurt Russell and Billy Baldwin were the stars, and De Niro would play an obsessive arson investigator named Rimgale, after a famed Chicago fireman who, at six feet six inches tall, cut an impressive figure around fire scenes.

De Niro was focused, it seemed, more on *Cape Fear*, for which he was whittling down his body to its slimmest form since the boxing sequences in *Raging Bull*, working out vigorously every day and observing a strict diet. As a result, he conducted most of his research work for *Backdraft* more or less on the job, latching on to Bill Cosgrove, a barrel-chested veteran of the Chicago fire department who was offered to De Niro as a technical advisor. Cosgrove had both fought fires and investigated them in his time on the force, and during De Niro's weeks in Chicago, he let the actor pick his brain, borrow (or, in some cases, outright buy) his equipment, and tag along to fires and fire investigations.

Just as Art Linson had upon initially meeting the star before shooting *The Untouchables*, Cosgrove found De Niro a shock at first: unshaven, his clothes slightly disheveled, his hair a mop, his feet sockless in his boat shoes. But he soon saw how De Niro dedicated himself to learning absolutely everything he could about the work he'd be portraying: the protocol, the tools, the language, the attitude. (He had to be admonished about the socks, though: on his first visit to a fire scene, De Niro wound up limping from blisters on his feet caused by wearing heavy boots without socks. When Cosgrove celebrated his birthday during the production, De Niro presented him with a signed script of the film, a bottle of Dom Perignon, a Dominican cigar, and a pair of socks to replace the ones Cosgrove had given him that first day.)

The two men bonded, De Niro appreciating Cosgrove's practicality and expertise. The movie star taught the firefighter to drink cappuccinos and, less successfully, Patrón tequila; introduced him to his kids, Drena and Raphael, and to Toukie Smith, all of whom visited Chicago in August for De Niro's birthday at the posh Chez Paul restaurant; and never stopped asking him questions, a tape recorder always at the ready to soak up more information about the job. De Niro was eager to meet a well-known Chicago arsonist named Fat Albert, and Cosgrove was willing to oblige, but his bosses in the fire department nixed it, fearing that any celebrity falling the fellow's way might encourage copycats. And De Niro was very respectful when introduced to a veteran fireman who had suffered burns, photographing the man's scars to serve as the basis of the make-believe scars he'd wear on his own back in a brief but compelling scene.

As Cosgrove remembered, De Niro liked best to drive to a quiet place along the Lake Michigan waterfront and pass away the summer night drinking a beer or two and chatting about the work of firemen. He read up on fire investigation techniques, firehouse life, and the causes of and motivations for arson; the subjects of Hollywood and movie stardom seemed never to be in his mind.

To others involved in the production, De Niro seemed a little more inscrutable. When Cosgrove had the opportunity to talk to Ron

Howard about the star, all the director could do was speak in platitudes about his "greatness." Greg Widen was a little more observant and revealing with a journalist later on, saying of De Niro, "He's always cordial, always polite, but I think, in daily life, he can be rattled by things and you can't be sure what those things are. He can be made uncomfortable. He's not weird and he never copped an attitude, but he's apart from the crowd. To know him as a person is grabbing at smoke. He came to the set an unknown quality and, on a personal level, he kind of left it that way."

The short prep time meant that a lot of De Niro's thinking about the character showed up in his script pages: lists of the steps a fire investigator would routinely take in the course of his work, reminders that Rimgale was "not a headline grabber" but rather a sincere and straight character who, like so many firemen, evinced a strain of black humor "*because* of the grimness of [the] situation." There was an oddness to him, De Niro surmised, but it wasn't very deep: "Maybe a beard. Or a moustache." When he probed deeper, he found some odd questions facing him: "I have a certain specific relationship with fire. What is it? Sexual? What? Fascination? Its power?" He introduced a single memorable line into the script, one borrowed from one of Cosgrove's real-life colleagues; asked by his superiors what had caused a fire, Rimgale, wanting to give away nothing of his thinking, replies, "Mice with matches." Apart from that, though, he poured very little of his own invention into the role.

THE TRIBECA FILM CENTER wasn't really a movie studio; there weren't production facilities such as editing rooms or sound stages or labs. But there was one thing that made it seem like something more than just an office building with a very heavy concentration of film biz tenants: the Tribeca Grill. De Niro had dreamed that the interactive energy of the film center would focus on a ground-floor restaurant, which would serve as a clubhouse, a commissary, a watering hole, a gathering place, a party spot. It wouldn't be a private club—it would have to pay its way just like any lessee. But it would be integral to creating a community space.

De Niro and Toukie Smith were regulars at Montrachet, a popular and critically esteemed French restaurant that had opened just a few blocks from the Film Center site in 1985. It was casual for a French spot, with no dress code, a menu in English, and a prix fixe dinner that cost as little as $16. It offered some of the best food in the neighborhood, and it was run with a real feel for combining the fine with the comfortable. In 1988, when the Film Center was coming together in his mind, De Niro approached the owner of Montrachet, a robust fellow named Drew Nieporent, and asked him if he'd be willing to consider opening a restaurant to anchor the building.

As it happened, Nieporent, who'd grown up wanting to be in the restaurant business, studying hospitality at Cornell and working his way up at some of Manhattan's best restaurants, was already considering opening another eatery of some sort in Tribeca. He liked the idea of having a little empire of restaurants within walking distance of one another. He agreed to consider it—provided it was funded adequately and built according to his standards.

The funding wasn't as tricky a matter as it may have seemed, as the late 1980s were a little heyday of showbiz celebrities attaching their names (and wallets) to fine dining establishments in New York and Los Angeles. De Niro had a plethora of friends and colleagues to call upon as potential investors. Some said no, including Madonna, Penny Marshall, Jeremy Irons, Danny DeVito, and Barbra Streisand; the last was all set to invest when she learned that she would have to be fingerprinted by the state liquor board if she were to become an owner of a place that sold booze, and she backed out.

But some two dozen investors fell into place, including Mikhail Baryshnikov, Christopher Walken, Sean Penn, Bill Murray, Ed Harris, Russell Simmons, Lou Diamond Phillips, the Miramax company, and the chairman of Elektra Records—and such non-showbiz types as a Newark poultry wholesaler. A total of $2.8 million was raised, half going to purchase the space, half for renovations. And then, as elsewhere in the building, everything about the place became more elaborate, more exacting, more detailed, more time-consuming, and more costly as they went along. Eventually, another $350,000 was needed, which was raised by refinancing the mortgage agreement.

Some of that money—estimates ranged from $15,000 to $50,000—went to the centerpiece of the restaurant: the mahogany bar that had once dominated Maxwell's Plum, the famed Upper East Side restaurant and singles bar where Nieporent once waited tables during its heyday in the 1970s. The bar was impeccably restored and placed smack in the middle of the room, creating a space, according to the restaurateur, "in which there really are no bad tables because the action is all around." (There was a private room in the back to which the truly famous would be directed, but by and large the 150-seat restaurant would mix the famous faces among the hoi polloi.) In other regards, the space was done up in downtown chic, with exposed brick and pipes alongside polished brass and woodwork, small islands of green carpeting (installed for sound control) dotting a tiled floor.

Besides the bar, the most noticeable design touch in the Tribeca Grill was the art on the walls: large canvases and sketches by Robert De Niro, selected and hung by the artist himself. As his son explained, it wasn't guaranteed at all that the elder De Niro would approve of such a use for his work. "When I approached him about placing them there," the younger De Niro said, "I wasn't sure he'd agree—he was very sensitive about giving paintings away. He'd say, 'You give it to someone, they put it in a closet.' But once they were up, he liked going to the restaurant to see them and to have them be seen. Larry Salander [then the senior De Niro's dealer] was worried about the odors and the food affecting the paintings, but I knew that their being there was something that my father had approved of, had blessed, and I didn't want to take them down, even for their own good." After the restaurant opened, in fact, the senior De Niro would occasionally hold court under one of his pieces, dining and drinking with friends, a sight that truly warmed his son's heart.

After a lengthy string of construction delays and an extended soft opening, the Tribeca Grill finally opened its doors properly for business in April 1990, and it was an immediate hit. Nieporent was doing two seatings a night—three hundred covers—and turning away almost as many diners virtually daily. Both Wall Street and Hollywood seemed to have designated the place as the hot spot of the moment; a partial list of diners in the first weeks included Dustin Hoffman, Gregory Peck, Tom Selleck, Cyndi Lauper, and New York Mets pitcher Ron Darling. Nieporent was concerned—"A scene can kill a restaurant," he repeatedly told the press—but the place was booming.

And it wasn't just celebrity that lured people. The food was praiseworthy as well. At first, just a week or two after the opening, *New York Times* restaurant critic Bryan Miller was dubious about the fare: "The kitchen will not win any Oscars for the food, nor does it strive to." But two months later, when he wrote a full assessment, his impression of executive chef Don Pintabona's work had improved. He summed up his two-star review thus: "It is a good thing for the wide-eyed crowd here that the food is very good. . . . TriBeCa [*sic*] Grill is one celebrity restaurant that needs very little editing. It should enjoy a long run."

THE IDEA TO REMAKE *Cape Fear*, director Lee Thompson's 1962 thriller about an ex-con seeking revenge against a lawyer who bent the rules to put him away, didn't originate with De Niro, who would come to fill Robert Mitchum's shoes as the terrifying vengeance seeker, or with Martin Scorsese, who would come to direct it. Rather, it came from, of all people, Steven Spielberg, who wasn't exactly noted for the sort of chilling psychosexual drama that made such a memorably disturbing experience of the original film.

But there was a theme of a family in danger in the original source material, the novel *The Executioners* by John D. MacDonald, that was well within Spielberg's wheelhouse. In 1989, he commissioned a new adaptation of the novel from screenwriter Wesley Strick, who'd been among the writers on the comic creature movie *Arachnophobia* for Spielberg's Amblin Entertainment. Thirty years after the original, Strick was free to make the villain of the piece, ex-con Max Cady, even more horrifying and threatening than he had been in the original. But there was a certain Spielbergian patina that would be required for it as well. "I wrote it as an Amblin thriller," Strick recalled later on. "It was big-budget and conventional, and it concentrated more on plot invention than it does now." At some point toward the end of the year, Spielberg realized that his directorial plate was full, with *Hook* in post-production and *Jurassic Park* in the planning stages, so he became open to finding someone else to make *Cape Fear.*

At the same time, he recognized that De Niro would be an exciting choice for Max Cady, and he sent him the script. De Niro liked what he saw well enough to agree to appear in it provided the right director and co-stars were found. The list of prospective directors proposed by Amblin was all over the place: Warren Beatty (who they hoped might also be willing to play Cady's target), Robert Redford (ditto), Ridley Scott, Jonathan Demme, Kathryn Bigelow, Mike Figgis, Harold Becker, Paul Verhoeven, Tony Scott, Peter Weir, Fred Schepisi, and more—a real smorgasbord of styles and talents with few obvious similarities. The suggestions about who might play the lawyer/father were equally diverse: besides Beatty and Redford, they included Mel Gibson, Gene Hackman, Jeremy Irons, Robin Williams, Michael Keaton, Clint Eastwood, Anthony Hopkins, Kevin Costner, Kevin Kline, Don Johnson, Jeff Goldblum, Bruce Dern, John Lithgow, Donald Sutherland, and Liam Neeson. At this point the film could have been anything.

But then De Niro had an idea: why not offer the film to Martin Scorsese? At first, as with *Raging Bull*, Scorsese didn't want to do it. He was a lifelong fan of the original film and he had never made a remake (though he had done well with a sequel, 1987's *The Color of Money*, which updated 1961's *The Hustler*). What was more, Scorsese had been working on an idea for his next film, an adaptation of Thomas Keneally's *Schindler's List*, a project about the Holocaust in which Spielberg had also shown interest. Urged by De Niro to consider *Cape Fear* ("We can do something with this guy," the actor told his longtime director), and with Spielberg willing to, in effect, swap it for *Schindler*, Scorsese softened. (According to Strick, De Niro and Spielberg "together sort of twisted Marty's arm—relentlessly, from what I gather.") In July 1990, a table reading of the script was held for Scorsese's benefit in New York, with De Niro as Cady, Kevin Kline as the attorney Sam Bowden, Patricia Clarkson as his wife, Leigh, and Moira Kelly as their daughter, Dany. Scorsese perked up. He agreed to go ahead with the film.

In the coming months, Scorsese and De Niro put Strick through extensive rewrites of the script, removing all traces of the sweetness and family focus with which Spielberg had sought to infuse his version, and the cast started to fill in. Nick Nolte, who'd worked with Scorsese on *Life Lessons*, would play Sam (after Redford nearly took the job), and Jessica Lange would play Leigh. Various actors from the original film, including Mitchum, Gregory Peck (the original Sam), Martin Balsam, and Telly Savalas, were offered cameo parts; all but Savalas appeared. But by the end of August, the role of the daughter hadn't yet been filled. Scorsese and De Niro spent several long days auditioning young actresses, including Moira Kelly, Fairuza Balk, Ileana Douglas, and Martha Plimpton. (Another hopeful, Reese Witherspoon, remembered her visit with De Niro and Scorsese as a disaster. She didn't know them by name when her agent prepared her for the meeting, she said, and then, "when I walked in, I did recognize De Niro, and I just lost it. My hand was shaking, and I was a blubbering idiot.") Finally they cast Juliette Lewis, a nearly unknown seventeen-year-old from Los Angeles, in the key role.

De Niro was making *Backdraft* while the casting, rewriting, and pre-production work was going on, but he had decided to take a producer's interest in *Cape Fear* and he kept abreast of all of the developments. He dove into the role with an energy not unlike that he'd expended on his research for *Goodfellas* or even *Raging Bull*—as if only working with Scorsese could get him to immerse himself at his fullest capacities.

Most impressive was that he completely remade his body. For *Raging Bull* he'd honed himself into the picture of youthful athleticism and then piled on abuse to embody a pathetic extreme of excess. For *Cape Fear*, he wanted to resemble a jailhouse hard case, a man who'd spent his time in prison sculpting himself into a weapon of vengeance. As De Niro noted on a piece of hotel stationery while in Chicago making *Backdraft*: "I [that is, Max Cady] worked out to keep from cracking up, going crazy." He stuck to a meticulous diet and exercised hard daily, building up the muscles in his chest, back, and arms. When he arrived on the *Cape Fear* set in Florida in the fall, he was carrying just 3 percent body fat. "He's probably the most focused person I've ever met," marveled his personal trainer, Dan Harvey. During production, De Niro would spend his nights working out for as much as five hours at a stretch, and he asked Scorsese to shoot his several bare-chested shots at the end of the film so that his body would be at its most jacked.

His application didn't stop with his physique, of course. He dedicated himself to a deep exploration of prison psychology, criminal insanity, and sociopathy, visiting and talking to convicts and mental patients who were suggested to him as subjects, reading books and medical articles about serial killers, rape, revenge, and torture, exploring the writings of Karen Horney, Frederick Nietzsche, and even Dante for their ideas about vindictiveness. He read up on prison life (especially the phenomenon of prison rape) and on legal ethics; he studied the Messiah complex, Pentecostal fundamentalism, revival meetings, snake handling, and speaking in tongues. He watched Barbara Koeppel's Oscar-winning documentary *Harlan County USA* and some episodes of Charles Kuralt's TV work (suggested to him by Jane Rosenthal) for the accents, Charles Laughton's baroque thriller *Night of the Hunter* for the dark themes, and his own work, especially *Taxi Driver, Bang the Drum Slowly, Jackknife,* and *Raging Bull,* to find things that he'd already done that might be of use. He made notes in a copy of the script of the first *Cape Fear* and, as they were prepared and sent to him, on Scorsese's storyboards for various scenes. He spent $5,000 on getting his teeth to look unhealthy (and then, after shooting, another $20,000 to have them restored to their usual luster). And he sat patiently for hours of makeup tests to help design his look for various moments in the film when Cady would be disfigured by the Bowdens, by police, or by other parties.

He was especially taken with the religious aspect of Cady's obsessions. He bought a Bible concordance and consulted it for ideas about revenge. He studied jailhouse tattoos and spent a lot of time and money designing the array of body art that Cady would wear, searching for just the right Bible verses, images and themes to convey the man's righteous, if twisted, fury.* "He was constantly looking to embellish his character with biblical quotations," Strick recalled. "Every scene of Bob's he would call me and say, 'Can Max say something

---

* The impressive array of body art he finally selected was imprinted on his skin with vegetable dye, which naturally faded over time.

else here about vengeance, from the Bible?'" And when he had his
scenes written to his liking, he had a researcher bring them to convicts and ask them to read them aloud for a video camera so he could
study how they spoke and behaved. "He's incessant," De Niro later said
about Cady. "He just keeps coming and coming. . . . He's like the Alien
or the Terminator." Indeed, so was De Niro: his preparation for Max
Cady was as thoroughgoing as any work he'd ever done.

The film was shot throughout Florida from November 1990 until
March of the following year. There was a hiccup at the end of December, when the actor originally cast as the private eye hired to protect
the family showed up on the set, changed his mind about being in the
film, and left, with Scorsese and the producers chasing after him; he
was replaced within days by Joe Don Baker.

But there were happy accidents, too, such as Juliette Lewis, who
was powerful and evocative in her scenes with De Niro. Scorsese was
worried that she might be too green to stand on her own, so he used
two cameras in the harrowing one-on-one scene between the two so
as not to miss anything good she happened to do. He got gold. "Bob
brought Juliette right up to his level," Strick said. "I remember Marty
told me after he shot it that there was such an embarrassment of good
footage that he was almost considering dividing the screen in half and
just running both of them the whole time."

BEFORE MAX CADY, Scorsese and De Niro had created several characters whose descents into evil were strains of self-hate and whose sociopathy was a means to redemption. Travis Bickle, Jake LaMotta, and
even Rupert Pupkin were, in a substantial sense, vehicles in which
Scorsese expressed a sense of himself as a soul-tormented sinner seeking to reclaim his humanity through some form of violence or, at least,
desperate behavior. The audience might not see itself reflected in these
characters, but their paths, however singular and disturbing, were
somehow plausible, emblematic, illustrative.

Max Cady is none of those things. He was purely and simply born
evil, has lived evilly, and looks certain to die in some sort of evil holocaust. His obsession with Sam Bowden has a strain of justice in it; the

lawyer truly did violate his professional creed in failing to defend Cady fully. But granting that Cady deserved a better lawyer, he also deserved to be punished. He is irredeemably vicious, base, and heartless, more so than any character De Niro had ever played (excepting, of course, *Angel Heart*'s Louis Cyphre—and even then it's kind of a close call).

De Niro makes a magnificent show of him, creating a grand and broad and grotesque and oversized character. De Niro's work on his accent, tattoos, reading habits, wardrobe, and especially physique marked his deepest commitment to a role in years, and in some ways Cady synthesizes much of De Niro's career until this point: the bodily transformation, the carefully constructed dialect, the methodical creation of a backstory (De Niro helped select the images taped to the wall of Cady's cell, which included Satan, Robert E. Lee, Dwight Eisenhower, and Alexander the Great). But he is well beyond anything De Niro has ever tried, almost inhuman, truly, in the vein of the Terminator or Freddy Krueger. With Scorsese, De Niro had created a powerful gallery of men at war with their demons; now he became those demons—all of them—with a rock-hard body, a bankroll, and an unquenchable desire to have every sort of vengeance he can.

Cady has a style—a kind of demented 1950s hepcat with slick hair, aloha shirts, a polished old convertible, and a cigar lighter decorated with a pair of boobs. He has mastered a sufficiently housebroken discourse to speak with civil clarity with legal authorities, to pick up Sam's (tipsy) mistress in a bar, to convince (naive) Dani that he's a faculty member at her high school. He has sufficient cheek to provoke incidents and sufficient smarts to turn the antagonistic actions of those he's goaded to his advantage. He's handsome, in a rugged, corn-pone way. And he's charming, serpent that he is. (In a brilliant bit of costume design, he's wearing a Lacoste cardigan with the iconic open-mouthed crocodile on it during the sequence in which he seduces Dani.)

But there are aspects of him that are so outré and outlandish as to make it seem that he doesn't exist at all, at least not on the same existential level as the rest of us: his insane, guttural laugh as he sits in the audience appreciating the knockabout comedy *Problem Child* (more specifically, a scene of John Ritter parodying Jack Nicholson in *The Shining*); his almost unnaturally taut and fat-free physique; his madman's tattoos; his appalling act of near-cannibalism as he prepares to beat and rape Sam's mistress; his diabolical scheme of increasingly cruel and intimate reprisals; his superhuman—indeed, literally monstrous, in terms of genre—physical resilience.*

The character is drawn in broad, almost cartoonish strokes: the tattoos ("I don't know whether to look at him or read him," scoffs Robert Mitchum as a cop witnessing Cady's full-body frisking); the ornate language and quotations; the astonishing shot that begins with Cady hanging upside down from a chinning bar while talking to Dani on the phone and then pivots so that the camera is upside down and Cady, twisted grin, hair standing on end and all, seems right-side up; the can't-be-killed indomitability in the final act; the speaking in tongues. This isn't a person; this is a living vision of movie evil, a creature from the black lagoon of the human soul.

And De Niro is exquisite in almost every single bit of it: the drawl, resurrected from his early films; the varied uses of his body; the black, black comedy; the fearlessness and immediacy and commitment; the forays into exotica; the absolute lack of movie star vanity. It's impossible to imagine Pacino, Hoffman, Hackman, or even Nicholson doing what De Niro does here: at nearly fifty years of age, with a cushy position in the movie business, he is ripped, ferocious, defiantly dislikeable, and frightening. There are aspects of *Cape Fear* that make it something of an art-house horror movie, a film of trip wires, sharp edges, and hurtful humor. And the most indelible of these is De Niro's performance, as large and as fully realized as any in his career and dedicated to the embodiment of vengeance, cruel irony, and hate. It's despicable. And it's delicious.

Almost inevitably, a De Niro–Scorsese project brought out the scold and moralist in critics. *Cape Fear* was admired but kept at arm's length by the likes of Stanley Kauffmann in the *New Republic*; calling the film "conventional fare," he backhandedly complimented its star, saying, "It's the kind of part that, for any actor of talent, let alone De Niro's talent, almost acts itself." In the *New Yorker*, Terrence Raf-

---

* The actress playing her, Illeana Douglas, was linked with Scorsese in gossip columns. Ahem.

ferty declared, "De Niro's frenetic but thoroughly uninteresting performance is emblematic of the movie's inadequacy." But Vincent Canby in the *New York Times* was full of praise for De Niro and Juliette Lewis, citing them for "two of the year's most accomplished performances," and Desson Thomson in the *Washington Post* declared De Niro's work "sterling."

If the material was brutally strong beer, it didn't turn away movie audiences. Opening at number one with a $10 million weekend, it went on to earn $79 million domestically and another $103 million abroad—easily the highest-grossing film that either De Niro or Scorsese had ever made. In many ways, they had confronted a darkness beyond any they'd ever contemplated, but the audience had somehow caught up to them and, indeed, may have gone further than they had dared.

And it wasn't only audiences who found merit in the film. *Cape Fear* was nobody's idea of a warm or noble movie, but it was obviously made—and especially acted—with great skill. When year-end award season arrived, De Niro and Lewis were cited by multiple critics' organizations for their remarkable work. And when nominations for the biggest awards, the Oscars, were announced, both were included in the mix: De Niro in the Best Actor category, Lewis as Best Supporting Actress. The horrifically caustic material might have seemed well beyond the tolerance of Oscar voters, who only the year before had passed up the opportunity to grant prizes to *Goodfellas* in favor of *Dances with Wolves*. But *Cape Fear* wasn't even the most grisly picture in the Oscar race in the spring of 1992. That honor would go to the film that dominated the awards by becoming only the second movie in history to win Oscars for Best Picture, Best Actor, Best Actress, Best Director, and Best Screenplay: *The Silence of the Lambs*. Maybe if Max Cady had chosen to swallow the chunk he'd bitten out of his rape victim's face rather than spit it out, De Niro's name would have been in the envelope instead of Anthony Hopkins's.

19

In 1991, Tribeca Productions finally put its first projects into production, almost simultaneously. One didn't involve De Niro directly—*Thunderheart*, a thriller about an FBI agent of Native American heritage (Val Kilmer) forced to grapple with his ethnic identity during the investigation of a murder on a Sioux reservation. De Niro had paid careful attention to the script development, annotating memos from TriStar Pictures, which was funding production and distribution, and telling the film's director, the Englishman Michael Apted, that the studio was correct in its assessment of the problems in the screenplay. "You're wrong," he wrote to Apted, "nothing works." The film shot on locations in South Dakota through the spring and summer of 1991, TriStar spending more than $17 million to make it and slightly more than that again to release it. It grossed less than $23 million at the box office when it was finally released to lukewarm reviews in April 1992.

By then, Tribeca's second production was in the can but not in the distribution pipeline. *Mistress* was the pet project of Barry Primus, a New York actor who'd been friendly with De Niro and Scorsese for years and had appeared in a key role in *New York, New York*. Primus, along with *Pretty Woman* screenwriter J. F. Lawton, had written a semiautobiographical script that satirized Hollywood, the story of a director so willing to find funding for an independent film that he promises key roles in the production to the girlfriends of various potential financiers, leading to a series of farcical misunderstandings and errors that threaten the viability of the movie and, potentially, the well-being of the director himself. In the mid-1980s, Primus showed the script to

De Niro, who expressed appreciation for it and even agreed to shepherd it in a fashion, bringing it to people who he thought might be interested in producing it. "I'm going to show this to people," De Niro told Primus, according to Primus. "[De Niro] would take it around. He would have a meeting, and he'd say, 'By the way, here's another movie somebody should make someday. I don't necessarily want to be in it. I'm not in the producing game, but maybe you'll do it.'" But nobody was interested. A few years later, Primus was still bemoaning his bum luck when he heard something promising from his old friend: "One day I was walking down Broadway with Bobby and he said, 'I'm going to start this company in a couple of years, and if you still haven't gotten this movie made, I'll do it.'"

When Tribeca was finally up and running, De Niro was at last in a position to help. It was, he said, a matter of principle: "I thought that someone like Barry Primus, who is a real artist, who really cares and is compassionate about people and has ideas, really should have more than the right to direct his own movie compared to some people who are hacks and who do movies time and time again, and they make money, enough money to keep moving from job to job and they have nothing to say." But his distribution partners at TriStar didn't agree, and they passed on the chance to make the picture. Tribeca found an angel in the project in Meir Teper, an Israeli financier who had previously done business with De Niro's sometime producer Arnon Milchan; Teper was able to raise $3.6 million for production, and the film was a go.

Primus started shooting in the spring of 1991, and he got a special delivery from De Niro to mark the occasion: "He sent me a telegram and a viewfinder the first day: 'Dear Barry, Good luck, and *please* don't fuck this up. Love, Bobby.'" Robert Wuhl was cast as the hopeful director, Martin Landau as his scrambling producer, and Eli Wallach, Danny Aiello, and De Niro as the would-be financiers with the starstruck girlfriends, played by Tuesday Knight, Jean Smart, and Sheryl Lee Ralph. Chris Walken had a bit part, as did Ernest Borgnine, who put in a day playing himself (for which kindness De Niro sent him a bottle of Dom Perignon as a thank-you gift).

Production wrapped by summer, and Primus edited and reedited with lots of input from De Niro. That would have to suffice, because nearly a year after filming, nobody had agreed to step in and distribute the film. "You've got to tell yourself it's one of those things," De Niro said, "not to take any of this personally. People wanted Barry Primus to make changes, but I said: 'Yeah, right. Barry wants to make it his way; it's his vision, so let's do it his way.'"

Without a studio to distribute the film, Tribeca finally found a partner in Rainbow Releasing, the boutique distribution company owned and operated by the filmmaker Henry Jaglom principally as a vehicle for his own work. With Harvey Weinstein (whose Miramax had passed on the film) advising from the sidelines, with De Niro willing to do publicity, and now with a novel story of how it made its way to the screen, *Mistress* was finally released in August 1992.* After all those years and all that work, it proved virtually stillborn, never playing on more than thirty-odd screens and grossing less than $600,000.

IN THE SUMMER of 1991, for the second year in a row, De Niro was in Chicago to shoot a film, but this time in one of the lead roles. *Mad Dog and Glory* was an original script by novelist Richard Price, whose books *The Wanderers* and *Blood Brothers* had been filmed in the 1970s and who had written original screenplays for Martin Scorsese (*The Color of Money*, the *Life Lessons* segment of *New York Stories*) and Al Pacino (*Sea of Love*). It involved a crime scene photographer who interrupts a holdup and thereby saves the life of a crime boss, who repays the photographer by sending a party girl to live with him as a thank-you gift. An uneasy friendship develops between the two men—the gangster wants to be a stand-up comedian and thinks the photographer has a gift for jokes—and then a rivalry over the girl's affections ensues.

The script had once been a project of the director Glenn Gordon Caron. But now it was being produced by Martin Scorsese, and in ad-

---

* Meir Teper wound up odd man out when it came to publicity for the film, and he resented the role, writing an angry memo to Primus (and cc'ing De Niro and Jaglom) when the first wave of feature stories about the film failed to name him at all. Eventually he'd find a happier way of collaborating with De Niro.

dition to choosing to shoot it in Chicago rather than New York, where Price had originally set it but where large-scale films were having a hard time getting made, Scorsese hired John McNaughton, a Chicago guy with a couple of fiery genre films to his credit, to direct it: the notorious *Henry: Portrait of a Serial Killer* and the sci-fi thriller *The Borrower*. The real novelty of the picture, though, and an indication of the sort of quirky tone the filmmakers were after, came in the casting. De Niro was playing not the hoodlum but rather the hapless milquetoast photographer; the gangster who thought he was a comedian would be played by . . . drumroll . . . Bill Murray.

That was a risk. Murray was a box office star, but his only dramatic role to date, an adaptation of *The Razor's Edge* by Somerset Maugham, had been loudly and widely deemed a catastrophe. Still, Price's script had an off-kilter quality that suggested that such an experiment could work (although at least one more straightforward choice, Stanley Tucci, was in the running for the gangster role for a while). Besides, Murray was a big star at the time, with *What About Bob?* raking in a huge gross and the *Ghostbuster* films not long in the past.

The casting of the female lead proved more elusive, though. A number of rising young actresses were considered, including Jennifer Jason Leigh, Mary Stuart Masterson, Annabella Sciorra, Kelly Lynch, Penelope Miller, and Melissa Leo. Finally Uma Thurman was selected, at a time when she and De Niro had been linked romantically in gossip columns.

De Niro skirted the drama of the casting situation by focusing on his role: Wayne "Mad Dog" Dobie, a punctilious stick-in-the-mud upon whom fortune had never smiled. "I feel like such a non-man," he wrote of the character. "Have to find movements that fit my character and make me feel awkward." Wardrobe would have been one way to achieve that sense of discomfort, but costumer Rita Ryack discovered that anything she brought in for De Niro to wear fit him beautifully, while the finest suits tended to look like crumpled messes on Murray. While she worked out a solution, De Niro went for ride-alongs with a crime scene photographer from the New York Police Department, noting how low on the ladder of authority the photographer stood, how his work would be scrutinized more carefully than even that of the supervising detectives, and how to use the most meticulous methods to generate unimpeachable work. Playing such a meek character, and gearing up for encounters with Murray's vaguely threatening gangster, De Niro reminded himself, "It's like me with tough guys *I* know. I take the passive role but give good advice and know how to regulate them. . . . I'm listening, and it's that thing where someone is taking themselves *very* seriously and I'm being attentive in a way to let them know I'm *that* attentive but giving them all the respect they deserve and think they deserve."

The shoot was a relative lark: Murray greeted De Niro on their joint first day with a gift and a card that read, "Thanks for this job. Let's both break our legs and live happily ever after." But in January 1992, when the film was tested on what happened to be the director's birthday, the ending was hammered by the screening audience. "It didn't go well," McNaughton remembered. "We had this saccharine, fantasy happy ending, and it just wasn't working." Scorsese and company realized they needed to write and shoot a new climax, but that would require not only reconvening the cast but also waiting for the weather in Chicago to return to a semblance of the previous summer. In July they worked another three days and got the ending they wanted, but then the studio, Universal, got balky, uncertain whether it had a summer movie, a Christmas movie, or neither on its hands. Too, there were scheduling conflicts with other films featuring the stars. Eventually they released it in March 1993, almost two years after shooting began.

GUILTY BY SUSPICION may not have lit the world on fire, but it launched Irwin Winkler as a director, and within months of its quick pass through the nation's theaters, Winkler was shooting a second film, also with its roots in the post–World War II era, also starring De Niro. *Night and the City* was a remake of a 1950 film noir based on a novel by Gerald Kersh, directed by Jules Dassin, and starring Richard Widmark as something of a con man living by the seat of his pants in London and trying to raise money to promote a wrestling exhibition. Almost a decade earlier, Richard Price had, at Martin Scorsese's request, updated the material into a tale of a shyster lawyer in contemporary New

York trying to rustle up funds to stage a boxing match; the project languished, but Winkler resurrected the script and Price touched it up to give it an early 1990s feel.

The film would be shot on location—no fake snow on Wilshire Boulevard this time—and it would reunite De Niro with Jessica Lange, this time as his love interest. Also in the cast were such evocative New York types as Alan King, Barry Primus, Eli Wallach, Cliff Gorman, and Regis Philbin. In shades of *Guilty by Suspicion*, Dassin himself, a blacklist survivor, would stop by the set for a visit at Winkler's behest. And Tribeca Productions would have a hand in the picture, though De Niro wouldn't claim a producing credit.

De Niro had a vision of his character, Harry Fabian, as a perpetual-motion machine, describing him alternately as "a chicken with his head cut off, or a rabbit darting through a maze" and "someone jumping across the street from rock to rock, just barely missing the piranha fish that are jumping up trying to get him." His script notes reminded him that Harry was "always moving, tapping knees, feet," and he directly asked Price, "What rhythm do you see Harry as?" He studied his own youthful performances, especially *Mean Streets*, and he and Winkler devised a scheme to keep his energy up in each shot: De Niro was outfitted with an earpiece that played Chris Montez's 1962 Latin pop hit "Let's Dance" for him on a loop ("We were going to blast it over Seventh Avenue," Winkler said, only half joking, "but it worked better in Bob's ear, and he got the rhythm, the cadence").

The cadence of De Niro and Lange working together wasn't so seamlessly achieved. Lange had reached a moment in her career at which she was ambivalent about working as an actress at all (although she had just agreed to play Blanche Dubois on Broadway opposite Alec Baldwin's Stanley Kowalski), and she didn't always agree with the actions and motives of her character as conceived by Price, Winkler, and De Niro. As a result, many of the most intimate scenes she had with De Niro were shot multiple times with different shadings of dialogue and action; De Niro, in a rare show of candor, not only allowed a reporter to watch some of these moments but spoke about them soon afterward. Asked why they'd shot a certain scene so many times and so differently, he replied, "Jessica was sensitive about it, and I was sensitive to her being sensitive. . . . Irwin wasn't sure, so he shot it both ways. One of them is right. When it gets down to the editing, he'll make a choice."

HE HAD BEEN working a brutal schedule, and he seemed hell-bent on continuing. In August 1991, when he had a short break in the shoot of *Mad Dog and Glory,* De Niro flew to Los Angeles to do a table reading of a script entitled *This Boy's Life,* based on a memoir of the same title by Tobias Wolff and dealing with the period in the 1950s when the author's mother was briefly married to a cruel and abusive man from rural Washington State. Wolff, who had been raised to harbor great aspirations for his education and career, was suffocated by the brutal small-mindedness of his mother's husband and the apparent hopelessness of the situation, and he fought openly with the man. But his mother often backed away and tacitly consented to her son being disciplined, afraid to lose the delicate handhold by which she was holding on to a means of support for herself and her son (actually, one of two sons: the other boy, Geoffrey, who would also grow up to be a memoirist, was with her ex-husband).

Producer Art Linson had commissioned a script of the memoir from screenwriter Robert Getchell and had landed on the Scottish-born Michael Caton-Jones, who had shown a flair for period filmmaking in *Scandal* and *Memphis Belle,* to direct it. De Niro had agreed to play the part of Dwight Hansen, the unlikeable stepdad, but would agree to make the picture only if he was comfortable with the choice of the lead character, Toby, who would be depicted between ages fourteen and seventeen and would essay a broad range of intense emotions throughout the film. Visiting Los Angeles, De Niro read with a number of rising young actors in a kind of marathon day of auditions: Tobey Maguire, Lukas Haas, Edward Furlong, and Leaf Phoenix (as Joaquin Phoenix was billing himself at the time). At the table reading of the script—during which actors read the material aloud informally to give the producers a sense of the dialogue and plotting as well as to help fine-tune casting—the role of Toby was read by Fred Savage.

Another young actor who had auditioned with De Niro previously was on hand at the table reading to handle the remainder of the juvenile parts. De Niro had already taken note of him, telling Linson after the day of one-on-one auditions. "I like the kid that was second-to-last," he said almost casually as he was leaving for the day. The sixteen-year-old kid had a long television career—sitcoms, mostly—but he'd never acted in a movie before. Linson and Caton-Jones had invited him back for the table reading, then kept looking at him, and finally chose him for the lead role. His name was Leonardo DiCaprio.

In the course of time, De Niro and DiCaprio would work together again, become real-life pals, and form creative bookends in the career of Martin Scorsese, who made five movies with the younger actor starting in 2002, seven years after the last (to date) of his eight films with De Niro.* But at the time De Niro noticed him, DiCaprio was unknown, and being cast opposite a big star in such a large, complex, and volatile role was a real challenge. It wasn't the only opportunity in front of him—he was set to go straight from shooting *This Boy's Life* to another dysfunctional family drama, *What's Eating Gilbert Grape*—but it could prove decisive one way or another in his career.

In fact, on one of his last days of shooting, the film's third crucial star made a point of telling DiCaprio that he might have reached the end of the best time of his life. Ellen Barkin, the brassy, sexy Bronx-born actress who'd appeared in *Diner, Switch,* and *Sea of Love,* was cast as Toby's mother (Beverly D'Angelo had filled the role at the table reading). Her last day of work with DiCaprio involved a scene of leave-taking, and DiCaprio had to rouse himself to tears. "That's hard to do, take after take," Barkin said later. "Of course, he had me whispering in his ear, 'This is the biggest experience of your career, you just finished a movie with Robert De Niro, it's all downhill from here. . . .'"

For his part, De Niro once again dove into his research. He visited Wolff at Syracuse University, showing up with a dog-eared copy of *This Boy's Life* and a notebook full of observations and questions. He meticulously selected his wardrobe from vintage Sears catalogues. He studied the idioms and accent of Washington's Skagit Valley on audiotapes and crafted a strange nasal vocal approach with dialect coach Sam Chwat.

---

* De Niro would, in fact, provide DiCaprio with his initial introduction to Scorsese.

He was, as ever, an obliging collaborator, and he was proud enough of his finished work to invite Elia Kazan to the New York premiere. But critics were divided on the picture, and audiences were repelled by De Niro's unpleasant character. In the end, only DiCaprio came out of the film with a boost.

DE NIRO HAD never been especially political, and never in public. Even, for instance, when he gave interviews in support of *The Deer Hunter* he used the vaguest terms possible in describing his opposition to the Vietnam War, which was already over. In fact, he almost never made reference to current events or political topics in interviews or even while inhabiting characters in films. But he had his preferences, of course, and given that he was a son of bohemian New York and an active member in the showbiz community, it's not surprising that his views were left-leaning. There were his visits to Moscow and Havana, of course, which were controversial in the mid-1980s, when he made them. In 1990, when Nelson Mandela made his triumphal tour of the United States, De Niro attended several of his speeches and private appearances, and hosted a $2,500-a-plate fund-raiser at the Tribeca Grill.

In the coming years, he would peek his head out a little more openly in political matters. He strongly supported Bill Clinton as a presidential candidate twice, and he joined a group of signatories in a published protest against Clinton's 1998 impeachment. At home, he had avidly backed David Dinkins in his successful 1989 campaign to become mayor of New York and then filmed and recorded ads and attended fund-raisers for his reelection bid four years later, when Dinkins lost to Rudolph Giuliani.* Mostly his touch in politics was light: he read stories to kids one year at the Clinton White House's Easter egg roll, and he appeared onstage at a New York City fund-raiser for Hillary Clinton's Senate run (again, against Giuliani) to teach Bill Clinton how to say "fuggedaboudit" properly by manipulating the

---

* He wasn't a stereotypical lefty, though: in 1992, the NYPD issued him a permit to carry a pistol. Asked why De Niro needed it, his spokesperson responded, "I don't want to ask him about that."

president's mouth and cheeks ("Don't shoot him!" Harvey Weinstein joked with the Secret Service). When the 2000 presidential election devolved into a turmoil of vote counting, De Niro was among the scores of celebrities who signed a petition published in the *New York Times* calling for a fair result (i.e., the election of Al Gore). Even when he visited troops overseas in 2003, during the Iraq War, he did it without any press coverage.

In fact, most of his activity in the public sphere was in assisting charitable efforts, only rarely embracing them so that his name and face became synonymous with them. Following through on his work with Toukie Smith, he continued raising money and awareness for AIDS research and care through the Willi Smith Foundation and Gay Men's Health Crisis, and he made himself similarly available to a few charities in New York, particularly those dedicated to improving the lives of kids or preserving cultural institutions in the city. Urged by Harvey Keitel, he even attended a Marine Corps anniversary dinner that Keitel, an old jarhead, was hosting as a fund-raiser.

In truth, though, he was far likelier to be visible at events having to do with the world of film, or the high-living adjuncts of it. He chaired a tribute to Martin Scorsese hosted by American Cinematheque, talked about film directing at Long Island University in a joint appearance with Spike Lee, gave a lecture at the Actors Studio West, and, starting with the Best Director prize in 1990, became an occasional presenter on Oscar telecasts, little knowing that his 1992 nomination for *Cape Fear* would be his last competitive entry at the Academy Awards until 2013. More commonly than any of those, he could be seen at cultural events in New York: a performance by the Alvin Ailey dance troupe, for instance, or an evening of readings by translators of Dante at the 92nd Street Y. More frequently still, he was seen at seats alongside the catwalk at fashion shows during New York's annual Fashion Week, where he frequently attended events displaying the latest work of Giorgio Armani, with whom he'd struck up a friendship. (Drena De Niro was unofficially the go-to DJ for Armani's shows, and in 1995, Armani sent her dad a leather jacket in which he had been dressed for a magazine photo shoot and for which he expressed appreciation.)

As often as he showed up to honor colleagues, share his insights on the movies, or look at fashion models in new outfits, he was even likelier to appear if he was himself the honoree. In March 1991 he was the centerpiece of a gala in support of the American Museum of the Moving Image, a $350-a-plate affair that drew more than eight hundred people to the Waldorf-Astoria to hear De Niro saluted and lightly ribbed by the likes of Martin Scorsese, Harvey Keitel, Jeremy Irons, Liza Minnelli, Charles Grodin, Penny Marshall, and Danny Aiello. De Niro, whose tablemates included both Toukie Smith and Diahnne Abbott, spoke at the end in support of the museum's mission and to gently tweak his peers. "I consider myself too young for awards like this," the forty-seven-year-old De Niro said. "They should have been given to guys like Al Pacino and Dustin Hoffman."

Just two months later, attending the Cannes Film Festival in support of the release of *Guilty by Suspicion*, he was decorated by Jack Lang, the culture minister of France, with that nation's Commander of Arts and Letters award, marking his life's work. A few years later, it was the Deauville Film Festival, which specialized in American cinema, that honored him. And then the citations, ribbons, and awards started coming faster: an honorary doctor of fine arts degree from New York University in 1996 (Steven Spielberg was also honored on the day), a New York State Governor's Arts Award later that same year, and, the following winter, the Jacqueline Kennedy Onassis Medal from the Municipal Art Society of New York for his work in preserving the architectural history of lower Manhattan.* This busy season of awards was capped in the spring of 1997 when he was in France once again, this time to be knighted as a Chevalier de la Légion d'Honneur, the highest cultural honor that the nation could accord a noncitizen.

As a citizen of New York City, meanwhile, he did things that only a movie star could do, such as appear in commercials promoting tourism

---

* The medal was presented by Onassis's children Caroline Kennedy Schlossberg and John Kennedy Jr., who had, just the previous year, featured a photograph of De Niro on the cover of his magazine, *George*, wearing a powdered wig and piercing a playing card with a sword.

in the city, and things that anyone might do, such as show up for jury duty when summoned, as he was in 1998.* He even, in a sense, raced at Belmont Park, where in the summers of 1994 and 1995 a colt named Robert De Niro ran several promising races for owner Peter Brant, a billionaire friend of the human Robert De Niro. The horse won a significant victory in the 1994 Tremont Breeders' Cup, coming from last to first and claiming a $53,240 stake, but he fared poorly at that summer's Saratoga Springs meet and in subsequent runs at Belmont, never fulfilling the promise of that earlier start. (A few years later, De Niro had a line in *Wag the Dog* that sounded the perfect final note on this curious episode: "If Kissinger could win the Peace Prize, I wouldn't be surprised to wake up and find out I'd won the Preakness.")

---

*   He wasn't empaneled, but he was asked back at year's end to pose for a photo on Juror Appreciation Day alongside another Manhattanite who'd been plucked at random for jury duty that year: the former courtroom stenographer Harvey Keitel.

20

WITH ALL THE YEARS HE'D SPENT IN FRONT OF THE CAM-
era, with all the red carpets and talk shows and press confer-
ences and galas and notepads and tape recorders stuck into
his face, he still hated interviews, still avoided them at any cost, still sat
through them in obvious discomfort, still answered questions tersely
and generically, as if being interrogated. As a result, not only was he a
difficult interview to get, he was a *lousy* interview: grudging, stammer-
ing, terse, evasive, sometimes adversarial, and almost always obviously
itchy to end it.

Virtually from the time journalists first started seeking him out,
he'd been hinky. In his very first interviews he was chary, reticent, almost suspicious. Now and again journalists would demonstrate how
uncomfortable he was with interviews by transliterating his pause-filled
responses, which could sometimes read like dialogue from a play about
stoners. He hated it, and in time he simply did whatever he could to
avoid the press altogether. He did almost no interviews in support of
Taxi Driver, The Deer Hunter, or *Raging Bull,* and the press began to
compare him to Greta Garbo and Marlon Brando, who were also well
known for their aversion to publicity. Asked by the *Chicago Tribune's*
Gene Siskel why he was so parsimonious with interviews, he replied,
"I know I'm right not to do them. Sometimes there's really nothing to
say." And not long after that, he sounded off in *Parade* on the same
topic: "I've never read anything that's completely correct. What we're
dealing with here is a one-dimensional portrait. If I say something, that
isn't *all* of what I said, or it isn't what I meant to say, or it isn't something compared to something else I said."

In 1987, *Vanity Fair* decided to profile him on its cover, and the job was assigned to the biographer Patricia Bosworth, like De Niro a life member of the Actors Studio. Through his publicist, Stan Rosenfield, his manager, Jay Julien, and his personal assistant/secretary, Trixie Bourne, De Niro repeatedly rebuffed her efforts to get a sit-down interview. She continued to ask. Finally Bourne broke the news to her bluntly: "Mr. De Niro will probably never talk to you, but he is giving you permission to talk to his friends."

Bosworth did just that, getting some time with unnamed acquaintances of his parents, colleagues from his early stage and theater days, collaborators on his film work, and such key names in De Niro's story as Martin Scorsese, Shelley Winters, Burt Young, Sally Kirkland, Brian De Palma, Barry Primus, and Art Linson. But, of course, not De Niro.

It was a thorough profile, and credible, but Bosworth's editors, perhaps peeved that their icon of the month should spurn them, splashed the headline "How Weirdo Is De Niro?" on the cover and entitled the story "The Shadow King" inside, asking in a subhead, "Is he pulling a Brando? Or is the secret that he has no secret?" No matter how even-handed the story, this was far from a flattering way to frame it.

Not coincidentally, De Niro fired back the following year, explaining in an interview in *Rolling Stone*, "There was a mixed signal. People were asking me if they should do it, and I said, 'Do what you want.'" As he saw it, "People were telling me that they liked the article—well, fine, that was okay. Certain things that people said were totally crazy. Not totally crazy, but just off." And he explained that his refusal to participate was based on principles, not on fear. "I didn't want to do it; I just sort of stayed out of it. I didn't want to be—not that they were doing that—but I didn't want to be shaken down: 'We're writing an article about you. If you talk to us, you'll only set the record straight.' Well, who cares about setting the record straight?"

But at the same time, almost as if dragged by the ear like a truant schoolboy, he was making a concerted effort to set the record straight. He consented to sit for a *Playboy* Q&A, one of the most thoroughgoing experiences in all of celebrity journalism. Lawrence Grobel, a contributing editor to the magazine, spoke with him throughout the year— eight sessions on two coasts over the span of seven months, resulting in a published article of nearly fifteen thousand words. It was the result of some real struggle: the published version recounts that De Niro turned off Grobel's tape recorder eleven times ("If I don't turn it off," he explained, "I may *say* it's off the record, but it's still on your tape"), looked at his watch in obvious impatience constantly, and outright declared that he wanted to leave five times.

And he wasn't shy about voicing his discomfort: "I'm feeling angry about this," he told Grobel. "I'm being pressured into doing an interview, and I resent that. I don't like the feeling. Why should I have to put myself in a position that makes me feel this way?" Prodded to explain his reluctance, he added, "I'm not good at editing how I feel. And those personal things that I feel . . . are not something that I care to let anybody know about. That's my own personal thing." Grobel, diplomatically, let the matter drop.

That wasn't enough, though. Whether counseled, coerced, or contractually obligated, he continued to meet, painfully, with the press. In 1989, he agreed to a major sit-down with *American Film* magazine, which, published under the aegis of the American Film Institute, had a more sedate, less tabloid vibe to it. The writer, Barry Paris, reported no incidents of tape recorders being turned off.

But by then, seeking an interview with De Niro and then writing up how frustrating the experience was had become its own trope of magazine journalism. And the tenor had shifted from amusement with a fellow who seemed to struggle with words offscreen to a mystery about a reclusive movie star to waves of thinly veiled hostility toward and superiority over someone whom most of the authors seemed to feel wasn't the great icon that fortune had made him out to be. "Don't talk about world politics, sports, fine wines or clothing. He doesn't know a lot about those things, which is why he comes off terribly in interviews," an "associate" told one such writer, who went on to quote a "friend" of De Niro's as saying, "His mother is quiet. His father is inarticulate. Bob is both of them."

Those comments came from a January 1991 cover story in *GQ*, which would inspire a small pile of imitators. Billed as "15 Mumbling Minutes with Robert De Niro," it "reported" what it was like for its author, Alan Richman, to prepare for a chat with De Niro, only to be left standing at the altar—in this case, a hotel bar in Manhattan. Their encounter wasn't technically an interview. It was rather an audition for the interview, a little tête-à-tête to see if De Niro would feel sufficiently comfortable with Richman to conduct a full-scale conversation at some other time. De Niro arrived late, and the pair had barely started conversing when Richman sensed De Niro starting to hold back. And then De Niro surprised Richman by asking him what his first five questions would be if they did in fact schedule a proper interview. Richman stammered, and De Niro changed the deal: the first two questions would do. So Richman, feeling the opportunity slip away, asked him flat out why he'd consented to the meeting if he didn't want to do it. "I guess . . . ummm . . . because . . . the ummm . . . the ummm . . . a lot of free clothes. It's GQ . . . umm, but I want it to be more interesting. Frankly, if there was no interview I'd be just as happy, but I have to justify getting the clothes. It's a way to justify the whole process and help the film to a degree, though I'd rather not do it, the movie will fly by itself whether I do an interview or not, not that it matters . . . No reason for me to do it except ultimately all the wrong reasons." And with that, the interview ended.[*]

BUT WITHIN A matter of years, the situation had reversed itself. De Niro suddenly found himself in need of publicity, seeking the press. In 1992, Tribeca Productions released its first home-grown picture, *Mistress*, and he did a fair number of interviews for it—albeit short and finely focused on the subject of the film. Then in the fall of 1993, he

---

[*]   This became a standard for reporting on De Niro. In 1997, *Esquire*'s Mike Sager got a half hour with the actor, found himself facing an iceberg, and left after twenty-five minutes of listening to De Niro harangue him on the subject of celebrity culture, gossip journalism, the paparazzi, and the like. Sager fleshed out the story with conversations from Tribeca shopkeepers and neighbors, who alternately plied him with misinformation about De Niro and cast aspersions on what they regarded as his prurient journalistic tactics. The apotheosis of this sort of grandstanding I-didn't-get-the-story story came, again in *GQ*, in 2007, when Chris Heath reported on his four conversations with De Niro, held over the span of three weeks, totaling two hours and twenty minutes, and resulting in 972 on-the-record words from the actor. It ended with a frank dismissal, De Niro telling Heath what the source of his difficulty in speaking with him was: "It's not me, it's *you*."

did even more, a veritable ocean of publicity by his stingy standards, and all of it with a more expansive attitude toward being interviewed, scrutinized, analyzed, and exposed. In the span of some six weeks, major profiles of him, written with his cooperation, appeared in *Interview*, *Vogue*, and the *New York Times Magazine*, and he sat down with journalists for perhaps a dozen or more shorter stories. He had directed a film, his first, and he was beating the drum for it as much and as loudly as he could stand to.

The film was called *A Bronx Tale*, and it had followed a roundabout path to the screen. It was adapted from a play—an elaborate monologue, really—written and performed by an actor named Chazz Palminteri who based it on the childhood experience of seeing a man shot to death right in front of his Bronx home. It was a gangland killing, and despite the horror of it, Palminteri (whose given name was Calogero) grew up looking upon the local gangsters as heroes, a fancy discouraged by his father, Lorenzo, who drove a city bus and consistently told his son, "The workingman is the tough guy, not the guy who pulls the trigger."

In his play, which started out as a brief reminiscence and then grew over time to a one-man show in which he acted all the parts, Palminteri explored the push-pull of his youthful self: the dazzlement with the gangster's style and aura and seeming nobility, the filial devotion to the honest, true, and caring father. An important subplot concerned an interracial romance between the adolescent Palminteri and a neighborhood girl of mixed heritage.

He mounted the show first in LA in 1989 with $6,000 given him by the actor Dan Lauria, who had gone to acting school with Palminteri and then hit stardom on the TV sitcom *The Wonder Years*. A slicker but still bare-bones production followed at Theatre West, financed by nightclub impresario Peter Gatien, for whom Palminteri had worked as a doorman. Word got around about the quality of the show, particularly the movielike tenor that Palminteri had achieved, and studio acquisitions people started showing up at performances, hoping to scoop up the rights from a hungry actor willing to make a quick deal.

But Palminteri, in his late thirties, was too savvy to go for the first big check that was dangled in front of him. Regarding the sale of his hot property, he remembered, "I had three conditions: I play Sonny [the gangster]; I write the script; and my friend Peter Gatien, who put up the money to produce the play, is the executive producer." The studios thought they needed a movie star as the gangster, though, and they were chary of dealing with a journeyman actor who sought to transform himself into a bigshot screenwriter and movie star. So they took what they assumed was the easiest way to get what they wanted. "In Hollywood," said Palminteri, "when you say 'No,' they think it means, 'He wants more money.' So they kept raising the money, until it got to seven figures and over." He held firm: "I wanted to write it and I wanted to star in it. So even though I only had $173 in the bank, I turned the offer down."

Among the people who saw A *Bronx Tale* onstage in LA was De Niro's personal trainer, Dan Harvey, who strongly recommended the show to De Niro, who in turn asked Jane Rosenthal to have a look at it. She, too, was favorably impressed and urged De Niro to see it. He did, more than once, and he believed that he could make a film of it that did justice to the material. "What I liked about it was, it was very specific," he recalled. "With that, you're ahead of the game right away. You're not doing somebody's idea about that world. You're doing the world."

He arranged to meet with Palminteri at the bar at the Bel-Air Hotel, where he put his own personal pitch to him. At first De Niro offered the idea that he would take on the role of Sonny, but when he saw how determined Palminteri was to play it, he backed off. In fact, he offered Palminteri everything he sought in a partner. As Palminteri recalled, "He looked me in the eye and said, 'You will play the part of Sonny, and no one else will touch the script.'"

Still, Palminteri didn't let go of his golden goose right away. He brought A *Bronx Tale* to New York, where it was staged at Playhouse 91 to yet more acclaim and yet more interest from movie people. But the promises De Niro had made stuck with him, and in July 1991 they reached a deal. Universal Pictures acquired the script for $1.5 million, with De Niro set to direct and to appear as the father of the protagonist, Palminteri writing the script and playing the role of the gangster, and Tribeca Productions on board to produce De Niro's directorial debut—one of the key reasons the company had been founded in the first place.

Initially, Universal imagined that the film would cost $15 million, but the budget soon spiraled upward, often because of De Niro's demands and preferences. He would be paid $4 million to appear, he would only make the movie in New York with a union crew, and he refused to guarantee cost overruns with his salary. Sensing the budget inching over $20 million, Universal agreed to let Tribeca go elsewhere to find new partners. ("We thought it would be an inexpensive movie," a studio executive said. "We were wrong. [De Niro] doesn't come from a guerilla filmmaking school.") Tribeca's white knight came in the form of the newly established Savoy Pictures, a production and distribution entity founded with $100 million of Wall Street money. Savoy bought the project with financial support from Penta International, an Italian-based company that would handle foreign distribution rights. They jointly agreed to a budget of $21 million, and an August 1992 start date was set for production.

De Niro finished work on *This Boy's Life* in May and immediately buckled down on *A Bronx Tale*. Only then did his obsession with the most minute details of the production emerge. Casting was always going to be an issue, and he'd charged his casting director, Ellen Chenoweth, with a mission long before he'd need his actors. "I said, 'It's not going to be the usual way of casting a movie. You have to hit the streets now, a year before we start shooting. You gotta get out there and look. I *know* the people we want are out there.'" Chenoweth scouted throughout New York, Philly, Chicago, and Boston for people with faces that didn't scream "movie actor" but who could still play the roles assigned them. She used local theater directors, such as Marco Greco of the Belmont Italian-American Playhouse in the Bronx, as scouts. De Niro was exacting. Insisting on approving every face on-screen, he looked at a pool of fifty potential extras and singled out one man who he felt didn't give off the proper vibe. It turned out that he had identified the only Irishman in a room full of Italian Americans.

They went to extraordinary lengths to fill the gaps in the cast. As De Niro remembered, "I read some actors to play [the character named] Eddie Mush. They were good, but then I said, 'This has got to be unique.' So then we looked at some neighborhood guys who weren't actors, and they were very interesting, so we were getting closer. Then I said to Chazz, 'Maybe Eddie's around. Where is he now? Can we find him?' And eventually Eddie came in. He read once. I said, 'We don't have to look any further. Where are we going to find someone else like that? Never in a million years.'"

The most crucial missing piece, though, was the adolescent protagonist, Calogero, the young Palminteri figure who would vacillate between fascination with Sonny the gangster and respect for Lorenzo, his bus-driving father. The summer was already upon them and they still hadn't identified the ideal actor to play their leading man. One day, one of Chenoweth's assistants was out at Jones Beach looking for faces when he saw a young man who he thought resembled De Niro. The kid responded, "You don't want me, you want my brother," and he ran toward the water shouting for his older brother to come and talk to the guy with the video camera. The boy, a sixteen-year-old from Yonkers named Lillo Brancato, mugged for the casting agent, doing impressions of De Niro from *Cape Fear* and *Raging Bull* and *Goodfellas*, and throwing in a little Joe Pesci for good measure. The guy with the camera fell into stitches. Brancato had grown up on De Niro, and the next day he got to meet his idol. Chenoweth called Brancato and asked him to visit De Niro's office in the Tribeca Film Center. A few meetings, a screen test, and, boom: he was hired, almost literally on the eve of production.

So: a first-time director, a first-time screenwriter, an absolutely untested lead actor, a cast full of nonprofessionals, shooting a period film set in the 1960s on streets in Queens and Brooklyn that people lived and worked and shopped on every day (the actual Bronx locations were too busy to shut down and, moreover, had lost their vintage appearance). What could possibly go wrong?

A lot, as it happened.

Just before shooting began, De Niro stumbled on the stairs and broke a bone in his foot, delaying production for a week. Then there was a long rainy spell that played havoc with the shooting schedule. Then Francis Capra, the young actor cast as the eight-year-old Calogero, lost a front tooth, delaying *his* scenes while he was fitted for a prosthesis. There was constant mechanical trouble with the two vintage buses being used as Lorenzo's work vehicles. (De Niro actually learned how to drive them, and had to take the DMV exam for the bus driver's license twice because his first effort was erroneously marked as failing.)

Too, De Niro's habitual meticulousness could be crippling to the schedule. A fair bit of the activity of the film was to be focused on the stoop outside Calogero's house, and De Niro and his crew dithered over the location for what seemed like ages. "We used to joke about it all the time with the production designer," De Niro explained. "Because he was waiting to know where to put the stoop. And we'd say, 'No, we changed our mind. We'll put the stoop back here.' Two weeks later, we said, 'Put it over here.'"

It may have made for amusing anecdotes, but it added up to money. After five days of shooting, the film was already two days behind schedule. By the time De Niro wrapped production in December, he had shot more than 200,000 feet—some twenty-nine to thirty hours of footage, fifteen times the length of the final film, a long but not excessively indulgent ratio for a major studio production, an absurdity for a small indie drama. The delays and slow pace meant that shooting ran several weeks late, and the budget had risen from $21 to $24 million; despite his earlier reluctance, De Niro covered the overage out of his own pocket. (The prolonged production also delayed the wrap party, which would have fallen in the middle of the holiday season; it was held in January instead.)

Post-production didn't go much faster. De Niro sought the advice of Francis Coppola and Martin Scorsese, going so far as to send two potential cuts of the entire film to the latter to get his opinion. ("It was almost like an exam," Scorsese said. "He knew the answer and he wanted to see if I had the same answer.") Finally, nearly a full year after he began shooting, *A Bronx Tale* was finished in time for a premiere at the Venice Film Festival, where it was received warmly. From there, De Niro brought the film to the Toronto Film Festival, pausing briefly in New York to do some press. In late September, a premiere was held in New York followed by a party at the Tribeca Grill, with a whole panoply of famous faces on hand: Uma Thurman, Dennis Leary, Steve

Buscemi, Donovan Leitch, Claudia Schiffer, and the odd couple of
the moment, Patricia Hearst and John Waters, with Waters saying of
the film, "It's my favorite interracial romance movie since 'West Side
Story.' It makes it look so appealing!"

GIVEN WHAT A huge, ungainly, mechanized, labor-intensive, rule-
bound, thankless, and unforgiving enterprise a feature film can be for
the person charged with making it, there's rich humor in the fact that
De Niro plays a bus driver in the movie that marks his first effort as
a director. It would be another year before Jan de Bont's *Speed* truly
delved into the metaphor of a racing bus as an action movie, but De
Niro surely tasted the irony of learning how to navigate a rolling be-
hemoth while finally being granted the power to start and stop the
cameras on a film set.

A *Bronx Tale*, with its focus on father-son bonding and Italian
American community life, is splendidly chosen as a debut script. Even
though the material is autobiographically Palminteri's, it could have
been written by De Niro—or, more aptly, by several of the characters
he played over the years. And while De Niro could have appeared as
either of the central character's mentors—Lorenzo, the bus-driving
father, or Sonny, the neighborhood kingpin—he made absolutely the
right choice in taking the role of the dogged, principled, watchful, earnest workingman.

Lorenzo has his passions: jazz, steak, the Yankees, the Friday night
fights. And those, along with his meticulous manner behind the wheel,
mark the man he is. De Niro loves characters of this sort: men of ethics, habits, tastes, and routines. His Lorenzo is a loving dad, a bit saucy,
proud, mindful of danger, and, when threatened, man enough to stand
up to those who he feels will do harm to his family. He's got a terrific
scene in which he rouses to anger with Sonny when he learns of the
gangster's interest in his son; heedless of peril, he reminds the mobster
that he himself has always been a standup guy, insisting, "This time
you're wrong." And he has other nicely drawn little moments with his
son, imparting life lessons and explaining away the frightening mys-
teries of the adult worlds of violence, criminality, hard work, even sex.

(It's always impressive to see how tender De Niro is with young actors, especially children.) It's not a major performance by any stretch, but it's solid and commendable.

As a director, De Niro shows an actor's affection for a variety of human types in working with so many unsung and, indeed, nonprofessional players. The kids Francis Capra and Lillo Brancato (as Calogero at ages nine and seventeen, respectively) and Taral Hicks (as the older Calogero's sweetie) are always at the heart of the film; we experience the story through Calogero's eyes and words, after all. And whether it's down to casting (in which De Niro took intense interest) or direction, there's not a misstruck note in any of their work. Brancato, especially, has a difficult part to play, and he does it with lightness, grace, and energy (and also looks the spitting image of a young De Niro, complete with a mole on his face, and especially when he frowns in a bathroom mirror when feeling the sting of aftershave). Many of the adults are also brand-new to film, if not to acting, and they play with more or less credible textures, even the famous Eddie Mush, who sticks out a little bit but in a fashion that actually serves the singular perversity of his character.

Still, even though it is well performed, *A Bronx Tale* can feel a bit leaden, in part because the staging, pacing, photography, and editing— the directorial film craft, in short—are so pedestrian. The film moves slowly, whether it's depicting intimate conversations, scenes of gang violence, moments of teen romance, a craps game, or a firebombing. It can feel like it has taken a particularly long route to get to someplace simple. It wants to bounce, but it feels like it's being kept under wraps. Even the soundtrack of pop hits tends to take you out of the picture when it ought to compel you.

Part of the issue is that so much of what De Niro is trying as a director in *A Bronx Tale* is taken from the Scorsese hornbook, and inevitably the film begs comparison to *Goodfellas*, which brings to mind the baseball career of Tommy Aaron, brother of Hank, or the music of Mike McGear, whose real name was McCartney and whose brother was, well . . . Making a movie set on the mean Italian American streets of 1960s New York, with colorful gangsters, a neighborhood boy who admires the bad guys, and a pop music score is like volunteering for a suicide mission. Given that, *A Bronx Tale* is surprisingly good, actually, with genuine heart, a brain, taste, some laughs, some drama, and solid acting.

If it's better than mere sawed-off Scorsese, that might be largely due to Palminteri, whose story and writing truly were worthy of a bidding war and whose screen presence is a disarming blend of dapper and ugly, genial and vicious. Give him the appropriate credit for auteurship of *A Bronx Tale* if you like, but give De Niro credit, then, as the producer and facilitator of the enterprise, the driver of the bus, as it were. He may not have been born a director, but the film reveals an eye for material and a talent for selecting collaborators, especially actors. To this day the history of Hollywood is choked with directors who have built lengthy careers out of far fewer skills and far less earnestness. If directing was truly to be a new phase of De Niro's life and career, this was a thoroughly persuasive first go. And, of course, it ends on the most tender and personal note that it can: a title card reading, "Dedicated to the memory of Robert De Niro Sr." It is an absolutely unquestionable sign that the maker of this film takes it as something truly and deeply near to his heart.

The critics were largely appreciative of the film, especially with De Niro's way with actors as a director, the self-effacing tenor of his own performance, and his ability to conjure the setting. "The first test of any film in which a star directs himself is whether the viewer can ever forget who is at the helm," wrote Janet Maslin in a positive notice in the *New York Times*. "Mr. De Niro's direction is generous and thoughtful enough to let that happen." "De Niro doesn't let arty camera angles sub for good storytelling," said Susan Wloszczyna in *USA Today*, "and he draws memorable performances from two amazing young, new actors." In *Variety*, Todd McCarthy adjudged it "a 'Goodfellas' with heart . . . a wonderfully vivid snapshot of a colorful place and time." Similarly, David Ansen of *Newsweek* deemed the film "wonderfully acted by a seamless mix of pros and amateurs . . . [It] lets us taste the flavors of a warm and dangerous place and time." And in the *New Yorker*, David Denby declared, "As a director, De Niro may not be a demon like his friend Scorsese, but he has humor and warmth of feeling, and that already puts him ahead of most of the competition."

Two Bobs: with Robert De Niro Sr. and his paintings *(MPTV)*.

A pair of kings: with Jerry Lewis on the set of *The King of Comedy* *(Photofest)*.

Reunited: with Brian De Palma on the set of *The Untouchables* (Photofest).

Uptown boys: with Burt Young and Ralph Macchio in *Cuba and His Teddy Bear* (Photofest).

Goodfellas: at an AIDS-awareness benefit with Sean Penn and Toukie Smith *(Corbis)*.

Diahnne Abbott with Drena and Raphael De Niro *(Getty)*.

The crew: with Ray Liotta,
Paul Sorvino, Martin
Scorsese, and Joe Pesci
publicizing *Goodfellas*
(Photofest).

Fighting trim: in *Cape Fear*
(Photofest).

Castle on Hudson Street: his penthouse home in TriBeCa *(ImageCollect)*.

Partners: announcing the first TriBeCa Film Festival with Jane Rosenthal *(ImageCollect)*.

Partners: opening the first Nobu Hotel with Nobu Matsuhisa and Meir Teper *(ImageCollect)*.

"You talkin' to me?": with Bruce Springsteen at the Kennedy Center Honors (*ImageCollect*).

Tears of age: with Grace Hightower at the restoration of *Once Upon a Time in America* at the Cannes Film Festival, 2012 *(Corbis)*.

Ringleader: with his family, including Grace Hightower (second from left); sons Elliot, Aaron, Julian, and Raphael (eyes closed); and cousin Jean De Niro (holding his hand) at the Kennedy Center Honors, 2009 *(ImageCollect)*.

Hands up: immortalized at Hollywood's famed Chinese Theater, 2013 *(Corbis)*.

Kings of old: with Jerry Lewis, Sandra Bernhard, and Martin Scorsese at a thirtieth-anniversary screening of *The King of Comedy* (*ImageCollect*).

Big night: at the 2013 Oscar ceremony with Grace Hightower (*ImageCollect*).

Despite this largely warm reception, A *Bronx Tale* did little to reassure the world that Tribeca Productions was a bona fide moneymaking enterprise. The film opened in seventh place at the nation's box office, with $3.7 million in ticket sales, behind *Malice* and *Cool Runnings*, among other new releases, and such holdovers as Martin Scorsese's period drama *The Age of Innocence*. That was the best it ever placed, en route to a final box office take of $17.3 million—well under what it needed to recoup its budget.* Its lackluster commercial performance aside, A *Bronx Tale* always had a good reputation, and Palminteri revived the stage production on Broadway in 2007; it was well received, and that success helped fuel talk a few years later that a musical version of the story would be written for the stage and that De Niro would, of all things, direct it.†

DE NIRO HAD enjoyed a modest success, but as the closing moments of A *Bronx Tale* indicate, he had a greater sorrow to deal with. While he was at work on the film that would mark his directorial debut, De Niro suffered the loss of his father, who died of cancer in New York on May 3, 1993, his seventy-first birthday.

It was a season of passings. In December 1992 Stella Adler, De

---

* Those mediocre earnings didn't stop Mark Travis, who directed and, by his claim, helped develop Palminteri's original stage production, from threatening a lawsuit against the production, seeking both credit and remuneration. The suit never materialized.

† There was tragedy attached to A *Bronx Tale* as well. In December 2005, on Arnow Place in the Bronx, Daniel Enchautegui, an off-duty New York police officer, was shot to death by one of a pair of burglars breaking into the house next door to his. One of the perpetrators—though not the gunman—turned out to be Lillo Brancato, whose acting career had briefly bloomed in the 1990s before collapsing into a series of increasingly minor film and TV roles (including one on *The Sopranos*) and frequent trouble with drugs. It turned out that he knew the street well: Officer Enchautegui was living in the basement apartment of the former home of Francis Capra, the youngster who played Brancato's *Bronx Tale* character as a child and whose older sister Brancato had dated during the production. Contacted by the press when news of the arrest broke, casting director Ellen Chenoweth, whose staff had discovered Brancato playing in the surf at Jones Beach, said, "I'm quite shocked. I'm just devastated." Three years after the crime, Brancato was convicted of the burglary but not the murder and was sentenced to ten years' imprisonment, finally being paroled in late 2013.

Niro's most important teacher, had died, and De Niro was among the many luminaries who spoke of her influence on his process of and respect for acting, issuing a statement citing, as he often did, her dogma that "Your talent lies in your choices."

At that moment, the elder De Niro was already beset by the sickness that would take his life. He had been diagnosed with prostate cancer a decade before and had been hospitalized at various times for treatment of the disease. He'd always been physically fit, but he'd been indifferent to certain aspects of his health care, as a bohemian artist of his era, age, and circumstances might have been expected to be, and by the time the disease was identified, it had already compromised his system. He continued to live on his own throughout most of the decade, painting, of course, and teaching and writing. He had solo shows throughout the 1980s in New York, Charleston, London, and New Hampshire, as well as a touring exhibition that was curated in Montana and traveled throughout the West. In 1991, he received an honorary degree from Briarwood College in Southington, Connecticut. He was, as ever, busy, playful, eccentric, elusive—that is, he was himself.

During the following year, though, his cancer progressed, and he weakened. Toward the end of 1992, he was forced to move out of the West Broadway studio that Virginia Admiral, his onetime wife and lifelong friend and advocate, had more or less given him permanently; he stayed instead in her Soho home, which was where he died. In addition to his ex-wife and only son, De Niro was survived by his mother, Helen (who would outlive him by six years, dying within sight of her hundredth birthday), his brother, Jack, and his sister Joan. In marking his passing, the *New York Times* noted, "Mr. De Niro's art was defined by an arresting physical confidence and a quality of natural talent that was widely acknowledged, even by critics who felt that his efforts could sometimes have an unfinished or impatient quality." Be that as it may, the work he left behind held real cultural and even monetary worth. Aside from works owned by the Metropolitan Museum of Art, the Whitney Museum, the Corcoran Gallery, and museums in Little Rock, Baltimore, Brooklyn, Youngstown, Denver, Syracuse, Charlotte, Helena, Oakland, Provincetown, New Haven, Tempe, and Billings, he left behind a collection that was valued initially at more than $2.5 million, all of it bequeathed to Admiral and De Niro.

Not long after his passing, a public memorial was held at the Fulcrum Gallery in SoHo, with a panel of artists remembering the man and his work. In the fall, the family held a private memorial, where De Niro himself spoke of his father in a rare display of personal emotion. "When De Niro finished reading this speech," said one witness, "he started to cry. After that, there was no holding back. Every woman in the place was in tears, too."

Approximately another year passed before De Niro made a more measured public statement about his father, in the form of an article signed with his name—but almost certainly not composed by him—in *Vogue*. "I look very much like him," it said, "and I have his name. To him I was Bobby; he was Dad. I also have his temper, his eccentricity, and his passion. And a strong connection to the smell of oil paints and cigarettes and musty old sweaters."

Those scents, and the atmosphere of his father's working and living space so associated with them, meant enough to him that, despite the high price that real estate in lower Manhattan was fetching, he kept his father's studio almost exactly as it had been at the time of the man's death, scattered about with the tools of his trade, his books and magazines, his clothes and household items, and even his bicycle. It was a time capsule of his father's days and deeds, and De Niro would maintain it for decades, visiting it as a kind of shrine and bringing his children to see it and get a sense of what their grandfather's life and work had been like. "For a long time," he told *Vogue*, "I didn't want to touch it, except to have it cleaned occasionally. I wanted to photograph it (I've done that) and videotape it (ditto), and now sometimes I just go there and sit. Everything is still the way he left it: the old chairs, the sketches tacked up, the big wire birdcage. There used to be a parakeet named Dimitrios, who's gone. Now there's a fake bird in his place."

In the coming years, De Niro would very carefully oversee the maintenance and promulgation of his father's legacy, working with Lawrence Salander, the artist's last dealer, to mount exhibitions throughout the United States and the world that burnished the senior De Niro's reputation—and, incidentally, increased the value of his estate. In a turn of fate that he likely would have appreciated, Robert Henry De Niro of Syracuse would ultimately become one of those legendary artists more appreciated in death than in life. And for the rest of his days his son would be the foremost champion of his father's memory and art.

21

IN AUGUST 1992 DE NIRO GOT THE WORST NEWS THAT ANY Hollywood personality could possibly receive: a missive from the law office of Marvin Mitchelson, the famed palimony attorney in Los Angeles, seeking money from him on the part of Helena Springs, then using her husband's surname, Lisandrello. The claim was based, of course, on the three years that De Niro and Lisandrello had been intimate and on the birth near the end of that time of her daughter, identified in the lawsuit as Nina Nadeja De Niro, in July 1982. The suit made reference to the romance, to De Niro's presence in Lisandrello's life during the baby's infancy, and to voluntary financial payments, as high as $8,000 to $10,000 a month, that De Niro had allegedly made to Lisandrello until not long before the suit was filed, when the payments simply stopped without explanation. The suit, seeking a total of $3,500 per month in child support, argued that De Niro had bonded with the child in the role of birth father and had established a long-standing relationship of financial and emotional support.

De Niro received the suit with cool aplomb, meeting the process server at the door to his Tribeca office and asking him quietly, "Is that all there is?" His attorneys tried to keep him from appearing in court in Los Angeles, the excuse being his hectic work schedule, but the California State Superior Court, which was handling the case, ordered him to appear, to resume payments for child support and tuition for private school (the Lycée Français in West Los Angeles, at $1,000 a month, *merci bien*), and to submit to a blood test to determine paternity. In October, he went to Los Angeles to comply.

Predictably, De Niro's side denied everything and called the case frivolous, so Lisandrello took to the gossip columns, claiming that she and De Niro had resumed their romance in the early 1990s when he had been longing to see more of Nina. She further claimed that he had refused any blood or DNA tests, that she had denied her current husband permission to adopt Nina, and that De Niro had tried to pay her outright for custody of the child—all of which De Niro's representatives denied.

In late October, the results of two separate blood tests came back: De Niro was *not*, as he had been told and always assumed, Nina's father. But that surprising turn didn't dissuade Lisandrello and Mitchelson from pursuing their suit, claiming, in effect, a kind of parental palimony. "We've always proceeded under the assumption that De Niro might not be the biological father," Mitchelson conceded, referring to another man "who could be the real father [who] was killed in a car accident years ago." The suit would continue, the attorney explained, because De Niro had voluntarily taken on the bulk of the financial responsibilities of fatherhood and at least some of the emotional ones, and that it was unfair to the child to simply drop them.

In November, without holding a hearing or taking testimony, the court ruled in De Niro's favor, declaring that he had no obligation to pay any sort of support to Lisandrello. Almost as if to mark his confidence in the outcome, De Niro had been seen out on the town in New York on two separate nights the weekend just before the court's declaration: once in the company of Toukie Smith and once in the company of Naomi Campbell, the twentyish British supermodel with whom he was now linked.

BY 1994, De Niro and Toukie Smith had more or less drifted apart, or at least could no longer be considered the steady item they once had seemed to be. Since her brother Willi Smith's death in 1987, De Niro had been supportive of Toukie's work on AIDS education and charity with the Smith Family Foundation, co-hosting and attending its galas and holding one of its biggest-ever events, a $250-per-plate dinner and auction, at the Tribeca Grill. But those ties had been tested by

De Niro's very public dalliances, particularly one with Campbell, who was barely twenty years old—nearly thirty years his junior—when they began an on-again, off-again relationship in 1990. Campbell, one of the highest-earning models in the world at the time, had recently split from heavyweight boxer Mike Tyson and was developing a reputation as a diva with lofty ambitions and a fiery temperament.

It was a volatile relationship. Even more than Toukie Smith, Campbell drew the limelight, and she was prone to getting into public contretemps such as scuffles at nightclubs. De Niro broke off with her more than once, but they kept reuniting for a few years, and Campbell's continued presence in his life caused Toukie at one point to threaten a palimony suit. That threat never materialized, even though De Niro and Campbell were spotted together in New York, Los Angeles, and the Caribbean island of Nevis over the span of nearly three years.

When Campbell learned that De Niro would be directing A Bronx Tale, which dealt in part with an interracial romance, she took it upon herself to begin acting lessons and to learn a plausible American accent from vocal coach Sam Chwat, with whom De Niro frequently worked. She didn't get the part, and by the time the film premiered her romance with De Niro had fizzled, but with no hard feelings, apparently: when they ran into each other at a New York tribute to Aretha Franklin, Campbell gave De Niro a friendly kiss, and in 2007, when she put her Park Avenue apartment on sale for an initial asking price of $5.5 million, her chosen broker was De Niro's son, Raphael, then working for a high-end Manhattan real estate firm.

Thus did Toukie outlast Campbell, as she also would such other dalliances of De Niro's as the singer Whitney Houston, the model Veronica Webb, and the actress Uma Thurman. By 1994, Toukie had reinvented herself yet again, opening a restaurant called—what else?— Toukie's on Houston Street in the West Village. Beneath a mural that depicted the owner among such divas as Marilyn Monroe and Dorothy Dandridge, Toukie's served home-style southern and soul food: fried chicken, short ribs, crazy corn, peach cobbler, black-bottom pie. A New York Times critic couldn't hide his delight with the big portions, the warm atmosphere, and especially the charm of the proprietor: "When you are greeted by Ms. Smith, you stay greeted. Expect kisses and hugs as if you are a long-lost friend. . . . Honey, this place makes me smile." It didn't, however, make money, closing in 1997.

By then, De Niro and Toukie were no longer together—at least not in any way that could be deemed traditional. In fact, though, in a certain sense they were more together than they ever had been. In early 1995, using their own sperm and eggs and the services of a surrogate, they conceived twin boys, who were born to them on October 20: Aaron Kendrick and Julian Henry. The news broke weeks after the birth, through an official announcement from De Niro's publicist, Stan Rosenfield, which explained that De Niro and Toukie would lead "separate personal and professional lives" and had agreed on "sharing the parenting of the children."

It seemed like a genteel enough agreement; De Niro and Toukie hadn't really been a couple for a few years, after all, and he was able to provide financially for the care and upbringing of the boys. But within a year they were battling in the gossip columns and then in Manhattan Family Court. It turned out that their agreement had been verbal only, reached at the beginning of the fertilization process, and that it had become untenable because each wanted to spend as much time as possible with the boys. In short, they were supposed to be Toukie's kids, but De Niro, who by all accounts was a loving and available father to Drena and Raphael, had bonded with them and wanted them half of the time. Their temporary arrangement—alternating custody of the twins in four-day blocks—was far more complex to execute than they had anticipated, and there were whispers from those close to Toukie that she needed more money than the maintenance sum to which they'd originally agreed. Complicating things even more, De Niro had a new and serious romantic interest: a model and former flight attendant named Grace Hightower.

HE HAD PLAYED a lot of variety in his roles of the previous decade— boldness and timidity, pride and fear, charisma and ugliness, good guys, bad guys, even the devil. But it would have been hard to say that he'd truly stretched. Not since he went to Colombia to shoot *The Mis-*

sion had he taken a part that seemed daring, incongruous, or, frankly, even intriguing. He was in a groove in selecting his roles, yes, and he was reliably good in them, but there is often an imperceptible moment at which a groove becomes a rut—and he hadn't had a significant box office hit since *The Untouchables*.

Well, whether he was feeling the weight of routine, seeking a potential smash hit, or simply wanting to invigorate himself and the movie audience with an off-kilter choice, he couldn't have chosen better than the part he tackled next: the monster in a new adaptation of Mary Shelley's *Frankenstein*. The film was being produced by Francis Ford Coppola, whose 1992 reimagining of *Dracula* had grossed more than $200 million worldwide against a budget of $40 million. With results like that, it was inevitable that *Frankenstein* would follow, as the two classic horror characters had been yoked together since being written and had always been linked in the movies as well. A script was commissioned akin to that for Coppola's version of the vampire classic, which had been entitled *Bram Stoker's Dracula*, with the idea being that the original novel—and not the decades of adulterated film versions—would be the source material. *Mary Shelley's Frankenstein*, it would be called. And De Niro's appearance as the monster wasn't the only eyebrow-raising aspect of it: although Coppola had originally planned to direct the film himself, that job, as well as the role of Dr. Victor Frankenstein, fell to the Northern Irish writer-director-actor Kenneth Branagh.

Branagh had come to fame on the English stage, and then achieved worldwide recognition for his films of *Henry V* and *Much Ado About Nothing*, the latter of which had also made a star of his wife, Emma Thompson. He had tried to crack Hollywood in 1991 with the noirish *Dead Again* and had been rebuffed. But this film, with a $44 million budget, would be a calling card that could not be ignored. It would shoot in England and Switzerland throughout the winter of 1993–94, it would also feature Helena Bonham Carter, Tom Hulce, Aidan Quinn, Ian Holm, and John Cleese, and it would surely prove as big a hit as Coppola's *Dracula* had.

After a lengthy transatlantic courtship, De Niro agreed to play the role in April 1993, and right away there was trouble. Coppola's

American Zoetrope studio took out an ad announcing that the film was a go and bearing the legend "It's alive." De Niro quickly shot off a letter to Coppola complaining that the ad made the film look "like a cheesy grade B movie. It's tacky and I'm deeply offended by it." (He had an associate producer credit on the picture—though Tribeca did not—so Coppola had at least to make a show of taking such notes seriously.)

Fortunately, in the coming months, De Niro busied himself with other aspects of the production—particularly the makeup. The makeup that Jack P. Pierce had devised for Boris Karloff in James Whale's 1931 version of *Frankenstein* had become synonymous with the creature but bore little resemblance to Shelley's description. De Niro—and Branagh and Coppola with him—was intent on creating a monster who was not only viscerally memorable and darkly hideous but also closer to the figure in the novel, in which the creature was created principally out of a single cadaver with various important bits added as needed: "a man made of other men," as Branagh saw it.

Over the course of several months De Niro traveled regularly to London for long sessions with makeup artist Daniel Parker, fussing over his hairline, his teeth, and a map of scars, burns, and disfigurements all over his body. There were, in essence, multiple characters to build: the original man, a thief who is hung and whose body is stolen for the experiment; the various stages of the creature's evolution; and the monster itself. De Niro sat patiently for it all, shaving his head, enduring a shower of latex poured all over his body, having prosthetic teeth and contact lenses and such fitted. He had hundreds of Polaroid photos taken of himself throughout the process, and he studied them carefully, sending back feedback to Branagh about what he felt worked and what didn't. ("The changes we talked about are underway," Branagh assured him in the summer, as shooting approached.) When the makeup tests finally ended, the snapshots he used as points of reference filled several photo albums as thick as Manhattan phone books.

De Niro got it into his head that he should play the creature as the victim of a cataclysm, and so he read up on survivors of shipwrecks, fires, natural disasters, and the Holocaust, as well as on prisoners of war and the homeless. He studied the bodies of strongmen of the nine-teenth and early twentieth centuries to give himself a notion of physi-cal bearing. He devised a speaking pattern (Shelley's monster was far more voluble than almost every film version) based on research into post-stroke speech disorders and other forms of dysphasia. And he pep-pered his scripts with exactingly phonetic transliterations of the way he wanted to say each line, each word, each syllable. (This was all in stark contrast to what Branagh did, buffing himself with weightlifting to almost comic proportions to play the romantic leading man—while, perhaps not coincidentally, beginning a romantic relationship with Bonham-Carter that would end his marriage to Thompson.)

During his visits to London before production began, and during the shoot, De Niro became friendly with Branagh and Thompson, din-ing at their home and exchanging Christmas gifts (she sent him fun and friendly notes after each visit, it seemed). He also became chummy with John Cleese, who was cast as Waldman, one of Frankenstein's fel-low doctors, a murder victim whose brain will eventually find new life inside the creature's skull. ("Remember," De Niro wrote in his script, "Waldman's brain.") He took the opportunity of a break in production to visit Paris and appear in a cameo role in Agnès Varda's *Les Cent et Une Nuits de Simon Cinéma*, a fairy tale celebrating the centennial of moviemaking; his role required him to laze in a swan boat on a lake with Catherine Deneuve.

He hadn't made a film in Europe in ten years, and he claimed later that despite the rigors of the shoot—the hours in the makeup trailer, the heavy wardrobe and thick-soled boots he wore—he had fun doing it: "I had some great times with Ken Branagh . . . particularly when my character of the Creature had to roll around on the floor. We used gal-lons of K-Y Jelly, and I could hardly focus. We just fell over laughing."

That wasn't how it played for other people. The initial previews went badly: audiences found it turgid, bloody, and strange. Coppola's *Dracula* was sexy and dark and thrilling. Branagh's *Frankenstein* wob-bled between tones. Coppola sent a lengthy memo to Branagh suggest-ing many changes to the film, but very few of them were heeded (near the end of his lengthy note, he confessed, "I once did this for Roman Polanski at his request and he never talked to me again").

The film premiered just *after* Halloween 1994 (that in itself seemed a misstep), and it disappointed commercially: grossing barely half of what *Dracula* had worldwide.

IN AUGUST 1993 De Niro was in New York, putting the finishing touches on *A Bronx Tale* and preparing for his upcoming role in *Frankenstein*, when he got a call from Irwin Winkler inviting him out to dinner at a hot new spot that folks were recommending. Winkler and his wife, Margo, picked him up and brought him to what looked like an unmarked restaurant, and when De Niro walked into the space (actually an empty loft known as the Prop Gallery), he was greeted with shouts of "Surprise!"

It was a fiftieth-birthday party, and even though invitations had gone out months before, everyone had managed to keep it a secret from the guest of honor. His family and near-family were there: Virginia Admiral, Diahnne Abbott, Drena and Raphael, Toukie Smith. Uma Thurman, whom he was dating, was on hand, as were such likely suspects as Martin Scorsese, Harvey Keitel, and Francis Coppola, along with others including Mike Ovitz, Penny Marshall, Robin Williams, Danny DeVito, Raul Julia, Gregory Hines, Kenneth Branagh, and Emma Thompson. Williams stood up to propose a toast and, inevitably, did fifteen minutes of standup, including various riffs on De Niro's squint-eyed, mumbling offscreen persona. Abbott got a laugh at least as good as any Williams managed by telling the crowd that De Niro was "a lousy husband but a wonderful father."

THE IDEA OF visiting a hot new restaurant was a perfect way to lure De Niro into a surprise. He had gotten everything he wanted out of the Tribeca Film Center and Tribeca Grill, but there was something that had eluded him from the start: sushi. He may have been associated in the popular imagination with pasta, but his favorite food was sashimi, and he was particularly fond of the fare at Matsuhisa, an exclusive and tiny Beverly Hills sushi bar in which he tried to make a point of dining whenever he was in Los Angeles.* When they were planning the Tribeca Grill, De Niro urged Drew Nieporent to consider installing a sushi bar, an anomaly considering that the kitchen would be serving American-style cuisine. Nieporent humored De Niro sufficiently to at least take a meeting with the owner of his favored Beverly Hills spot. The sushi master came to New York to inspect the still-under-construction restaurant, but other than handshakes and smiles, nothing was accomplished—in part because the visiting chef spoke almost no English.

Indeed, there really wasn't an appropriate space in the Tribeca Grill for sushi—either on the menu or in the actual restaurant. But De Niro and Nieporent never lost sight of the idea of importing that great Beverly Hills sushi bar to Manhattan. In 1994, on Hudson Street, just around the corner from their first location, they managed the trick, opening a restaurant that would forever change the image and status of sushi in New York City—and, eventually, around the globe. It was named for the master chef, Nobuyuki Matsuhisa, whom friends and family and regular customers knew as Nobu.

Nobu the man was a classic Japanese master sushi chef, albeit with an unusual pedigree. He had cooked in Lima, Peru, Buenos Aires, Argentina, and Anchorage, Alaska, before settling in Los Angeles, first working for other chefs and finally opening his own restaurant in 1987. When he agreed to come to New York, it was with considerable financial resources—as much as $1 million (much of it arranged by De Niro's former film producer partner, Meir Teper) went into opening Nobu, as the restaurant was named. And it paid off. From virtually the day it opened, Nobu was one of the most celebrated restaurants in New York ("a grand entertainment," raved Ruth Reichl in the *New York Times*; "something wonderful is always on the horizon"). With only seventy-five seats and a menu featuring items that no other spot in the

---

*   For the record, he was also partial to Italian food, French wine, Patrón tequila, and martinis, in which his tastes varied—sometimes with vermouth and lemon, sometimes with no vermouth but with muddled cucumber, always shaken far longer than usual until they were icy and frothy.

city offered, with the cachet of Matsuhisa preceding it and the imprimatur of De Niro and Nieporent on it, with a hip downtown location and imaginative décor by restaurant designer David Rockwell, it was a massive hit, grossing some $6 million per year and forcing ownership to open a second, more casual offshoot, Nobu Next Door, on the same block.

The bit firmly within their teeth, De Niro and Nieporent, under the aegis of the aptly named Myriad Restaurant Group, kept expanding around the neighborhood. In 1995 they opened Layla, a Middle Eastern spot, and TriBakery, which baked goods for various lower Manhattan restaurants and served them on-site. The following year, in the space adjacent to TriBakery, they opened Zeppole, a casual Italian restaurant. Locals began referring to the streets around the Tribeca Film Center as "Bob Row"; everything around them seemed to be owned by De Niro. And there was quality as well as éclat: in 1995, Nieporent's restaurants won four James Beard Awards, a phenomenal haul of the food world's equivalent of the Oscars.

They didn't have an infallibly golden touch: Zeppole lasted barely a year, and an effort by De Niro and Nieporent to restore Harlem's famed bebop bar Minton's Playhouse was announced in 1994 and abandoned five years later after they struggled in vain to find funding partners from the neighborhood to help them reach their projected $3.1 million budget. Later, they opened a saloon in Tribeca, Hudson Bar, which stayed open for less than two years. And in 1996, in a scene that seemed more like something out of De Niro's movies rather than his business affairs, gunmen burst into Nobu and shot the place up, wounding three employees and fleeing with $1,000 before one of them was apprehended hiding behind a nearby Dumpster.

But several of their other spots became staples, such as Rubicon, which they opened together in San Francisco with Francis Coppola and Robin Williams as fellow investors. And Nobu in particular became the seed of an impressive tree of restaurants. A London Nobu would open in 1997 and be awarded a Michelin star the following year; a San Francisco Nobu opened in 1998; by 2001 there were Nobus in Miami, Las Vegas, and Sydney; by 2004, there was one on 57th Street in midtown Manhattan. Eventually there would be more than two dozen of them, literally all over the world: North America, Central America, Asia, Australia, Europe, Africa, the Middle East. De Niro's fondness for Nobu's sashimi, his ceviche-inspired Japanese-Peruvian concoctions, and especially his black cod in miso broth had become a global taste.

22

AS RELUCTANT AS HE WAS TO BE INTERVIEWED, HE WAS TRULY loath to be photographed, particularly when doing the normal business of life, particularly when the paparazzi were involved. An antipathy borne of shyness and thin skin became, over the years, a really visceral hatred. Time and again paparazzi came away from encounters with him slightly the worse for wear.

In the summer of 1991, leaving a restaurant with Joe Pesci, he was alleged to have run up on a photographer, yelling repeatedly, "What do you want?," then grabbing the fellow's flash attachment. A criminal mischief/harassment charge was filed, and it was dealt with without fanfare. Three years later, again in Pesci's presence, he was photographed standing in line to use a pay phone at Elaine's on the Upper East Side. It was the premiere party for Pesci's new film, *Jimmy Hollywood,* but it was a low-key affair, and De Niro was surprised and of course annoyed to find flashbulbs popping when he arrived. He managed to sidle past the photographers unmolested, but once he was inside, someone snapped a shot of him, and he lit up: "Don't you *ever* take a picture of me waiting for the phone," he yelled. "Don't you sneak up on me and take a picture." (As it turned out, the target of his rage hadn't taken the offending shot.)

The encounters were getting worse—as, to be fair, were the paparazzi—and it finally came to a head in October 1994, when he was leaving the Bowery Bar in lower Manhattan at approximately one-thirty on a Sunday morning. Outside was a gaggle of photographers, including Joseph Ligier, a twenty-five-year-old paparazzo from Los Angeles. Ligier trained his lens on De Niro, and De Niro took it as a provocation. According to Ligier, De Niro hit his camera, grabbed him by the hair, and knocked him over the hood of a parked car, all the while yelling at him, "Give me the video." It was an eye-popping scene, according to witnesses, and Ligier got some of it on tape: "You can see De Niro wind up and—boom! The camera goes all over the place," said a photographer who saw the footage. Ligier and his attorney filed charges of assault, and De Niro was brought in for questioning, finger-printed, and photographed.

At first the paparazzo was hoping to make a big score with the foot-age—he claimed to have had a deal with the tabloid TV show *Hard Copy*, which a spokesman for the show denied. But he and his advisors came up with what they thought was an even better scheme: they would ask De Niro for $300,000 in exchange for the videotape and for Ligier's dropping the charges. Approached in this fashion, De Niro's attorneys Thomas Harvey and Edward Hayes smelled extortion, and they proceeded to negotiate a price with Ligier's lawyer, Anthony Amoscato, while surreptitiously recording the conversations. Over the span of two days, they agreed on a lump sum payment of $150,000: $20,000 for the videotape, $20,000 for release of civil claims, and $110,000 to drop the criminal charges.

On Friday, just five days after the original incident, De Niro withdrew $110,000 from the bank, bundled it with two checks from his lawyers' firm, and drove in a limousine (borrowed from billionaire investor Ronald Perelman) to meet Ligier and Amoscato. The limo took them to the DA's office, where the charges were, as agreed, dropped, and then took them away—and straight into the hands of detectives who grabbed up Ligier and his attorney and took them in for questioning. "We think it's extortion," a law enforcement source said. "At best it was a very sleazy approach." A grand jury was charged with evaluating the evidence against the photographer and his lawyer, and De Niro walked away from the matter unscathed, plus a scalp to show for his time.

IN THE WAKE of writing *Wiseguy* and seeing it turned into the masterpiece *Goodfellas*, Nick Pileggi had kept his eyes open for another mob saga that would complement and extend the story. Among the episodes that fascinated him was the way the mob had moved its opera-tions from East Coast cities to Las Vegas. Modern Vegas had begun, of course, with the inspiration of gangsters, and there had been mob in-volvement in many Vegas casinos from the start. But in the late 1960s, the mob had gone from a shadow group that funded and siphoned off casinos to nearly overt control of several of them, and in the 1970s, that control had been exposed by a series of sensational incidents centered on two Chicago guys who'd been sent to Vegas to run things.

Frank "Lefty" Rosenthal was a gambler who was considered one of the sharpest oddsmakers in all of sports betting. Being Jewish, and being essentially nonviolent, he could never become a made man in the Mafia. But he was a tremendous earner whom mob bosses trusted to make money and to keep up appearances of propriety. He was sent to Vegas in 1968 to run the sports books at a quartet of hotels, the Fre-mont, the Hacienda, the Marina, and the Stardust, and in time he was effectively managing them, running the casino, food and beverage, and hotel operations with the same acumen and attention to detail he brought to the handicapping of college basketball games.

To back him up with muscle, the bosses sent out Anthony "the Ant" Spilotro, a sociopathic hood from Chicago with a significant arrest rec-ord and a horrifying penchant for violence. Along with his brother, Mi-chael, Spilotro was charged with keeping order and making sure that Rosenthal was unimpinged in his moneymaking ventures. But Spilotro was, like many suspected mobsters, banned from the casinos because of his lengthy criminal record, and he resented the way that Rosenthal lorded it over him. He wound up setting up his own operation in the city, working outside of his portfolio, as it were, with his own little loan sharking, extortion, and robbery rackets, becoming a subject of interest to local police. Rosenthal, meanwhile, married a former showgirl and sometime prostitute named Geri, who bridled at the traditional role he expected her to fulfill as his wife. Among many other things that caused conflict in their marriage were her drug use, her spending, and her infidelity, which included a liaison with Spilotro—resulting in yet more friction, drama, and noise.

All of this wild behavior generated publicity and brought police attention—exactly what the eastern bosses *didn't* want. By the mid-1980s Geri had relapsed into drug abuse, been kicked out of the house by Rosenthal, and wandered off into a seamy haze, in which she died; Spilotro, banished from Vegas by the eastern bosses, was brutally murdered, along with his brother, in a midwestern cornfield; and Rosenthal, who survived the detonation of a bomb beneath his Cadillac, left Vegas altogether, setting up shop as a gambler in Florida, where he was living when Pileggi heard his story.

Pileggi spent more than two years trying to get Rosenthal to talk to him, and when he finally consented he provided the spine for a book that the writer was planning to call *Casino*. The new project picked up, in effect, where *Wiseguy* and *Goodfellas* had left off, taking the mob from the East Coast in the 1950s and 1960s and focusing on its doings in Las Vegas in the 1960s and 1970s. Martin Scorsese was keen on the subject matter—both the specific story of three desperate characters and the setting: "Any place that pushes people to the edge—and Las Vegas does that—creates great drama." And he got De Niro interested in playing Rosenthal and Joe Pesci in playing Spilotro.

Scorsese and Pileggi began collaborating on an adaptation of the book even before Pileggi had finished writing it. In early 1994 they broke the narrative down onto index cards, focusing, as Scorsese explained in a lengthy memo to De Niro, on "the emotional beats" of the characters and the story. That material would be structured into a screenplay that would then be put through several layers of revision. The pair would go to Florida to interview Rosenthal again; De Niro would read key scenes and prepare lists of questions for Rosenthal. All of that material would be sewn into the script, and then the process would be repeated at least twice more. *Then* Joe Pesci would be sent the script in order to let him shape the character of Spilotro, particularly with the dark humor that came so readily to him.

In that early memo, Scorsese repeated that the emphasis would always be on keeping the structure tight, on avoiding getting lost in the sexy details of Vegas life and mob legend, on shaping an emotionally coherent narrative out of a series of real-life events that often seemed chaotic. By August 1994, he and Pileggi had produced no fewer than sixteen drafts of the script, often after receiving notes from De Niro urging them to be clearer, deeper, more specific, more faithful to ac-tual events.

And De Niro knew what the actual events amounted to because Pileggi had made available to him all of the transcripts of interviews he had done in compiling material for the book project. (He admonished Pileggi more than once to be more thorough in reporting facts or to check again with Rosenthal to verify specific details.) He was an expe-rienced producer at this point, and the tenor of the notes he made on script drafts could sometimes be stern and demanding.

There was, of course, his own research. Taking seriously, as ever, the obligation to the real person he was portraying, he met Rosenthal several times for interviews, corresponded with him via telephone and mail for additional insight, talked with other of Pileggi's sources of infor-mation, made a visit to the Las Vegas offices of the FBI to study surveil-lance photos and tapes of Rosenthal and Spilotro, watched videotapes of Rosenthal's home movies and TV appearances (including his own late-night talk show, which actually happened), and read and watched anything that he could find about Vegas, the mob, and the Chicago crime milieu from which Rosenthal and Spilotro had emerged. Armed with the knowledge that Rosenthal was a clotheshorse, De Niro stud-ied magazine advertisements from the 1970s to get a sense of the colors and styles then in vogue, and he made an especial study of the fashions favored by MCA entertainment boss Lew Wasserman, a famously dap-per character who bore a slight air of mobbish mystery in his persona as a showbiz padrone. Working once again with costumer Rita Ryack, De Niro eventually had fifty-two complete outfits made—suits, shirts, ties, shoes, watches, jewelry. He posed for the most remarkable photos wearing each and every one of them, running full-color contact sheets of his costume tests past Rosenthal for his approval. When production finally began, each new scene required serious conversation among himself, Ryack, and Scorsese about what he should wear, down to the cufflinks.

Production was scheduled to begin in Las Vegas in September 1994, but the one accoutrement De Niro hadn't acquired as late as the summer was his Geri. A variety of actresses had read for the part—a short list included Jamie Lee Curtis, Lolita Davidovich, Patricia Arquette, Rene Russo, and Ashley Judd—and dozens more were up for consideration: Laura Dern, Sean Young, Melanie Griffith, Sarah Jessica Parker, Jennifer Tilly, Bridget Fonda, Joanne Whalley-Kilmer, Linda Hamilton, even Holly Hunter. Debra Messing showed up to audition, dressed in a way that De Niro found unusual. "What? Are you going to a prom?" he asked her. "Every part of my soul just withered," she recalled.

The process of finding the right Geri was well along when De Niro first heard from casting director Ellen Lewis that Sharon Stone was a possibility. "We are getting a lot of calls," Lewis told him. "There is interest in her for other things, so if we are at all interested we might want to do something sooner rather than later." The thirty-six-year-old Stone had been kicking around the business since 1980, when she appeared in a cameo in Woody Allen's *Stardust Memories*, and she had begun to emerge as a headline star in 1992 with her turn as a sexually voracious writer and murder suspect in Paul Verhoeven's *Basic Instinct*. She had become famous for her frankness with her body and her daring, if not necessarily for her acting, which would be seriously tested in the wide-ranging role of Geri. After her first meeting with Scorsese and De Niro she was unhappy with the way she'd presented herself. "It was uneven," she admitted. "I would start to extrovert into the character's rawness and then pull back." But she'd made a favorable impression nonetheless: "It was her presence and her look," Scorsese explained. "She has a tough-edged look that seemed perfect for Vegas at the time, the way her face is structured, something about her eyes. You can believe that she is what someone in the book called the real-life [Geri]: 'the most respected hustler in Vegas.' That's a matter of honor."

She got the part, and then her toughness nearly deserted her. "I started this movie in a state of abject terror," she admitted. "I could barely speak." But she found in De Niro an acting coach, ally, and friend. "De Niro really helped her through those scenes," Scorsese recalled. "He's very generous with her, and you can see how he's always helping. It's a scary role, a tough one." During production, De Niro sent Stone gifts (perfume, a bud vase) and encouraging notes.

The cast was filled out with a remarkable blend of old showbiz types (Alan King, Don Rickles, Frankie Avalon, and Steve Allen; Allen knew Lefty Rosenthal and wrote a lengthy memo for De Niro about his memories of the man and the era), Scorsese movie fixtures (Frank Vincent and Frank Adonis, as well as the director's parents, Catherine and Charles, and daughter, Cathy), and, in a key role as Geri's former pimp and drug connection, James Woods. The part of a Japanese gambler whom Rosenthal prevents from winning a fortune was played by De Niro's restaurant biz partner Nobu Matsuhisa, and the famed mob lawyer (and later mayor of Las Vegas) Oscar Goodman appeared as himself.

The Riviera hotel and casino on the Strip was the principal shooting location, renamed the Tangiers and standing as an amalgamation of all of Rosenthal's casinos. Rosenthal himself was redubbed Sam "Ace" Rothstein, Spilotro was rechristened Nicky Santoro, and Geri became Ginger. (This would all become slightly confusing when the film was released, as Pileggi's book, also bearing the title *Casino*, was published just a month prior, using the characters' real names.)

The shoot went as scheduled, from September 1994 through the following January; at Christmas time De Niro sent bottles of Chateau Lafite Rothschild to several of his co-stars, including Don Rickles, who sent a thank-you note saying that he and his wife, Barbara, had put it in a brown paper bag and drunk it up with winos on Hollywood Boulevard.

Throughout the spring and summer, Scorsese and his editor, Thelma Schoonmaker, worked on the final cut of the film, which included a great deal of voice-over by the three principals, much more than Scorsese had ever used in a movie. Such was the fluidity of the cut at various moments that De Niro was recording new passages well into July in advance of a November release. Too, Scorsese had to trim some of the film's terrifying violence when it became clear that he was courting an NC-17 rating, something that Universal Pictures wouldn't remotely entertain for a $52 million production. Even with those edits, *Casino* would turn out to be a particularly gory film, even by Scorsese's sanguinary standards. "The more greed," he explained, "the more blood. The more gold, the more blood. The more you show the money, you have to show the blood."

—⁓—

CASINO OPENED IN late November—on Thanksgiving weekend, in fact, a hand grenade stuffed inside the holiday turkey—opposite, of all movies, *Toy Story*. The picture starts with a bang: the aging Ace Rothstein exiting a restaurant, turning the key in the ignition of his Cadillac, and being launched, as if by an ejector seat, into a wall of flame. He has been talking about love and paradise; is he speaking from beyond the grave?

It's possible. For the next forty-five minutes or so, as Ace (De Niro) narrates in retrospective fashion, Scorsese sweeps us through the world of gambling, posh casinos, and Las Vegas morality with the same assurance with which Ray Liotta escorted Lorraine Bracco through the secret passageways of the Copacabana in *Goodfellas*. It's breathtaking. Ace explains the games, the systems, the skim, and the connections between the various wheelers and dealers and makers and shakers in the city. Partly he's being autobiographical, explaining who he is and where he's from and how he sees and weighs things; but partly he's offering a travelogue, or, in a way, a biography of the film's title character. Every human need—physical or spiritual—can be met inside a casino, he would have us believe. No wonder he thinks it's heaven.

Ace is a dude, a control freak, and a calculator, quick to anger, self-righteous, irritable, obsessive, dogged, cynical, and mean in the sense of being unkind as well as that of being parsimonious. He lives at a lavish rate, with dozens of gaudy but impeccably tailored suits (indeed, *outfits*), a tackily posh home, a big car, lots of deluxe accoutrements. But he can be roused to trickery, anger, even violence at the thought of a nickel escaping his grasp. He's chilly, he's selfish, he's brittle—and he's the *good guy* among the three principals.

Pesci's Nicky Santoro is a raw thug, by lifestyle closer to Tommy DeSimone than to Joey LaMotta, but kin to both in his temper, vulgarity, and brutality. Pesci lays a Chicago wiseguy accent onto his lines and has had something done to his eyes to, it seems, put space between them and give him almost a Eurasian cast. He's more playful than Ace, but it's also quickly clear that he's also uglier and much more dangerous—a psychopath who thinks nothing of putting another man's head in a vise and making good on the threat to use it.

Stone's Ginger is remarkably played, the fullest and best role in the film, essayed with real power, daring, and skill. (Deservedly, Stone received the film's only Oscar nomination, as Best Supporting Actress.) Ginger is a whore, a cheater, a boozehound, a junkie, a wretched wife, and a worse mother, and Stone dives into all those aspects of her with unadorned commitment. She is always, God bless, physically attractive—a golden girl despite everything we know about her. But in her own special ways she is as repugnant as the male leads.

That's the principal problem with the film. It's remarkably well made on every level of film craft—photography, editing, music, and, most of all, décor, costumes, and makeup; it's far more beautiful than *Goodfellas* or even *New York, New York*. But it's a long slog spent with people who you wish would simply go away, a litany of romantic and legal strife and moral and psychological disintegration, the most horrific bad marriage in Scorsese's long canon of such relationships, and some of the most nauseating violence that the director has ever put on film—which truly is saying something ("the more greed, the more blood").

De Niro brings a becoming substance and severity to his role, playing Ace as a ruthless hawk watching over the casino like it's his hunting ground, treating Nicky warily but firmly, pleading romantically and, in a few brief moments, openheartedly with Ginger, displaying deference to big-shot gamblers and out-of-town mob bosses, disdain to employees, defiance to Nevada politicians. There's always the wardrobe, a crayon box of astounding suits, shirts, ties, sportswear, and lounging apparel that practically deserves an acting credit of its own.

When he first ascends in Vegas, Ace is admirable and under control and cuts an appealing figure: "the golden Jew," as Nicky dubs him. As he loses himself—to Ginger, to Nicky, to gaming authorities—he becomes more desperate, whiny, demanding. There's nothing at all attractive about him, despite the wealthy trappings of his life. The bombing, meant to take his life, doesn't kill him; we finally learn that he's not narrating from beyond the grave, as is another of the film's characters. But he is a shell of what he was at his greatest glory. "Paradise," he repeats. "We managed to really fuck it up." He stares out from behind huge owlish glasses and mutters, "And that's that." Indeed.

And the idea of opening on a holiday weekend opposite what would turn out to be one of the most beloved animated franchises of all time? Not a good one. *Casino* debuted in fifth place and earned $42.4 million eventually—not close to paying back its cost.

As *CASINO* DEMONSTRATED, sometimes there are stories that seem to will their way into being told, as if the people who tell them are agents of some strange force. The story of Neil McCauley was one of them.

McCauley was a Chicago bank robber, thief, and murderer who spent more than half his life incarcerated (including a stint in Alcatraz) and was as dedicated to crime as the cops on his tail were to stopping him. One of those pursuers was Chuck Adamson, a Chicago detective who one day sat with McCauley over coffee in a luncheonette. Adamson tried to convince McCauley to go straight, to accept that he was on a course toward doom. "You realize," Adamson said, "that one day you're going to be taking down a score, and I'm going to be there." McCauley was unfazed. "Well, look at the other side of the coin," he responded. "I might have to eliminate you." The following year, McCauley and his gang robbed a supermarket, and Adamson was waiting outside. A shootout ensued, and Adamson brought McCauley down with a bullet, killing him.

Adamson left Chicago in the 1970s, heading west to Hollywood to break into screenwriting. He met Michael Mann, a writer of episodic TV police dramas such as *Starsky and Hutch*. Mann was also a Chicago guy, and the two began working together. When Mann created *Miami Vice*, he hired Adamson as a writer and technical consultant, and when he produced another cop show, *Police Story*, set in Chicago in the early 1960s, he further mined Adamson's experiences.

Adamson had shared the story of Neil McCauley with Mann, who was fascinated by it. In 1989, he wrote and directed a TV film based on the story, *L.A. Takedown*, with a cop named Vincent Hanna (Scott Plank) confronting a meticulous bad guy named Patrick McLaren (Alex McArthur) and then killing him in a blizzard of bullets. Then, in late 1993, he began work on the McCauley story yet again, envisioning a gangland epic about cops and robbers and their working and private lives and the people around them, especially their women and kids. Audaciously he sent the script to two of the greatest screen icons of the time, Robert De Niro and Al Pacino, imagining them as the characters Neil McCauley and Vincent Hanna. News that the pair were circling the film thrilled journalists, who recalled that while they'd both appeared in *The Godfather, Part II* they hadn't shared a scene in it. There had been many awards shows, galas, and parties at which both were present, of course; they were friends. But they had never been cast together in the way Mann was proposing.

What the press didn't know was that Mann had written the film in such a way that the two characters would have only two scenes together, the key one being in essence a re-creation of Chuck Adamson's encounter with the real Neil McCauley some thirty years prior. De Niro was especially taken with the idea that he and Pacino would share only one significant chunk of screen time and that it would be a strangely pacific moment of a cop and a crook having coffee and talking. "We have one terrific scene together," De Niro said, suggesting that anything more would almost be superfluous. With both stars happy, the deals were made, and the picture was a go.

Mann worked on the script extensively throughout 1994, changing the setting to Los Angeles and tailoring the material to his stars. For a time, he worked in the desert east of LA, where a crew of technical advisors taught the cast—which included Tom Sizemore, Val Kilmer, and Jon Voight as bad guys—how to use the high-powered assault weapons that they'd employ in the film's gigantic bank robbery sequence. By December, he'd put together a 154-page script—enough for an epic of two and a half hours—and had locked his cast in place.

Heat, as the film would be known, would shoot from February through July of 1995, and De Niro would be on hand for most of that time, barely a month after finishing work on *Casino*. During the break between the films, he joined Mann, Sizemore, and Kilmer on a visit to Folsom State Prison, where they spoke with inmates about their lives in crime and then behind bars; De Niro took home poetry and memoirs written by some of the convicts he'd met. Additional technical expertise was offered by Eddie Bunker, the career criminal turned author and movie actor upon whom De Niro relied for insights into McCauley's psyche; De Niro read and took notes on Bunker's book *No Beast So Fierce*, and Bunker invited De Niro, Sizemore, and Voight (whose character was loosely modeled on Bunker) to his home for dinner, cooking them chicken Kiev and regaling them with stories of his wayward times. Furthermore, some members of the white supremacist prison gang the Aryan Brotherhood were hired by the production to go over the script and confirm details of wardrobe, dialogue, jailhouse tattoos, and convict behavior. (As Ami Canaan Mann, the film's second unit director and the director's daughter, recalled, her father implored the crew, "Go as far as you can go. Talk to the most extreme people you can talk to, get as much information as you can.")

De Niro's chief research into McCauley, however, was conducted between himself and Mann. In January, just as production began, the two sat in Mann's office and spoke for hours about McCauley's state of mind, his prison experiences, his methodical mind, his sense of caution, his disconnection from the world. Mann spoke in lengthy paragraphs, throwing out literary references and allusions to psychology, sociology, and history, and De Niro took it all in, muttering agreement or acknowledging his understanding in brief replies. The conversation was transcribed by Mann's office and sent to De Niro, and he highlighted various passages of it to remind himself of Mann's thinking. A few weeks later, Mann sent De Niro a four-page memo detailing everything that could be known about the character: his upbringing as a ward of the state, his initiation to a life of crime, his adult imprisonment and jailhouse education (per Mann, McCauley had read Marx and Camus), and his relationships with his fellow inmates, his criminal associates, the women in his life, and his pursuer, Hanna. "Neil and Hanna are the smartest men in the movie," Mann reminded De Niro.

In June, the crew were ready to shoot the great scene between De Niro and Pacino. Mann and his production designer, Neil Spisak, chose as the setting Kate Mantellini, a Wilshire Boulevard restaurant that served as a kind of clubhouse for the movie world—not a fussy place at all. "The background is as monochromatic and as minimalist as I could get it," Mann said later, "because, boy, I did not want anything to take away from what was happening on Al's face and Bob's face." In his script notes, Mann compared the pair to "islands in the gathering storm of the picture"; he made a point of reminding Pacino that Hanna was "a hunter, rapid eye movement . . . aggressively going after data" and of telling De Niro to approach the encounter with the thought that "there's something for me in knowing the man, but I'll give him nothing." Reflecting later on the qualities of his two stars, he said that De Niro "sees the part as a construction, working incredibly hard, detail by detail, bit by bit, building character as if he were I. M. Pei." Conversely, he said, "Al . . . is more like Picasso, staring at an empty canvas for many hours in intense concentration. And then there's a series of brush strokes. And a piece of the character is alive."

Heat finished shooting in mid-July, and Mann, with the discipline of a veteran TV hand, had it ready for theatrical release before Christmas. In fact, it was out just three weeks after *Casino* was released, meaning that the nation's multiplexes were hosting almost six hours of new—and pretty darn good—De Niro films at the same time.

NEIL MCCAULEY's businesslike mien, appearance, and moral code are central to De Niro's approach to the character, which is professional, spare, and even muscular without ever succumbing to a show of strength, purpose, or emotionalism. Indeed, it's almost *too* clean a job of acting. It's not that De Niro doesn't indicate McCauley's inner life sufficiently; it's that he and Mann have determined that the character is so entirely focused on his work ethos that his life and personality are lost to it. He has buried all emotions save those that give him some kind of intuitive sense of the job he's working. De Niro's body, post–*Cape Fear*, is lean and sharp; his hair is slick; his goatee is impeccable; his home is spare; his gaze reveals nothing; he is a model of control. Even his furtive romance (with a sweet but thinly drawn girl played by Amy Brenneman) is more colored by his cold, appraising nature than by a need for affection, companionship, or lightness. The remoteness *suits* the character, mind, but it leaves the viewer cold.

If De Niro represents a cold heat, Pacino represents the hot kind. Divorced multiple times, and as defined by his work as by his relationships with women, he roars and preens and sasses. De Niro speaks his character's inner life in couched tones and undertones: "The last thing I am is married"; "I am never going back"; "I know life is short; whatever time you get is luck." On the other hand, when Pacino tears insanely into a line like "'Cause she's got a *great ass* . . . and you got your head all the way up it!!!" there's no need to weigh the words to get at their true meaning. In fact, the two characters aren't drawn nearly as differently by the script as the actors make them out to be. Indeed, in a way the two can even be said to be playing each other, much as Nicolas Cage and John Travolta soon would in John Woo's *Face/Off.* De Niro's McCauley is kin to Michael Corleone; Pacino's Hanna could be the cousin of Johnny Boy Civello.

When the pair finally sit down together, it's a mite anticlimactic. They're two dedicated professionals, two men cut from the same old-fashioned cloth, as true to themselves and their ethical codes as any of the heroes John Ford or Howard Hawks ever conceived, and if they'd met in other lives they could be best friends, colleagues, or, perversely, each other. They recognize as much. Hanna calls McCauley "brother" (as in "Brother, you are going down"), and McCauley sees something of a mirror image of himself in the cop who's chasing him ("There's a flip side to that coin" is how he phrases it). Each surveils the other, analyzes the other, stares the other down, respects the other, challenges the other to bring his best game, and, though neither would ever admit it, fears the other. Even if the scene is something of a letdown—if only because we've been waiting for it for a quarter century (how is it possible that that was allowed to happen, by the way?), there's still great resonance to it and pleasure in it.

You want the encounter to go on, but how could it possibly? This isn't a James Bond movie or a hostage drama; the antagonists don't parley at great, sporting length. This is a story about work, and even though the film is three hours long, work demands that these two truly meet only once, and briefly, however memorably. Particularly if you're susceptible to Mann's characteristically deliberate stylishness, elliptical storytelling technique, and fascination with male professionalism, the necessary brevity of their encounter is almost emotional. Almost.

And it similarly missed out on being lucrative. The film drew a lot of attention, both for the big shootout scene and for the big De Niro/ Pacino showdown, and it translated into $67 million in ticket sales. But Mann had spent nearly that much to make it. *Heat* would be remembered for its high level of craftsmanship and its macho vibe, but nobody was hurrying to get its stars back together anytime soon—not at those prices, anyhow.

23

WHEN HE SPLIT WITH TOUKIE SMITH, DE NIRO'S MIND was so far from thoughts of marriage that not even the birth of the twins changed it. However, a few years along into his fifties he did seem to be thinking about tying the knot again. At the time, he was seen around with Anne-Marie Fox, a onetime *Playboy* playmate who was just beginning a career as a publicity photographer on film sets; her first credited work along those lines, in fact, would be behind-the-scene shots from the making of *Frankenstein*, including many photos of De Niro at various stages of applying and removing his Creature makeup. In late 1995, New York newspapers reported that De Niro had bought a loft for Fox, who—younger than he, and African American—fit the profile of virtually every significant woman in his romantic life, and that marriage was in the air.

It wasn't, though, nor was it the following year when, once again, a New York paper said that he'd be getting married the following week at Don Rickles's house in Los Angeles. De Niro denied it and the paper retracted, but they insisted that De Niro had been discussing a wedding and had introduced people to a woman whom he'd identified as his fiancée. It wasn't Fox, though. It was Grace Hightower.

De Niro and Hightower didn't marry at the Rickles residence in 1996, but she did move into his Tribeca home with him—displacing Fox, in fact. De Niro and Hightower had known each other for nearly a decade at that point, since 1987, when he'd spotted her working at the New York restaurant Mr. Chow and passed a note to the owner asking if he could meet her.

She turned out to be an unlikely individual indeed. Born in 1955 as one of three girls in a family of ten children in Kilmichael, Missis-sippi ("a dot on the map 100 miles north of Jackson," she explained), she was of African American and Blackfoot Indian heritage, at a time and a place when being a girl with those bloodlines was to have three strikes against you. Her parents were hardworking and instilled in their children a powerful ethic of self-reliance, resourcefulness, duty, pride, and honor. "We lived on a farm," Hightower said years later, "of modest means, producing and eating nearly all that we ate. In fact, the only time we visited the supermarket was when we bought sugar. We worked the land, ate from the land, and became connected to the land." Her dad, she recalled, taught her a singularly important lesson: "Never go to bed without paying your debts."

But he also instilled in her a thirst to experience the world beyond the farm. She and her brothers used to thumb through an encyclope-dia, dreaming of travel, and as soon as she was able she got out into the world to work and make fulfilling that dream possible. "I did every-thing," she remembered. "I worked at S. S. Kresge, the five-and-dime. I worked in a mailroom. I worked processing insurance claims."

By 1980, in her mid-twenties, she had managed to land a job as a flight attendant for TWA, based in New York. In that capacity, she was noticed by a pair of public relations executives for Saks Fifth Avenue, who hired her as a model. In 1982, she was among a group of young black men and women working in the airline industry to be profiled in *Ebony*. Soon after that, she changed her home base to Paris, living at the Hôtel de Suez on the Left Bank, taking French lessons, and trying to get started as, among other things, a mutual funds trader. When that line of work didn't pan out, she came back to the States, winding up at Mr. Chow.

The first time she met De Niro, he didn't, unusually, try to make a move on her; in fact, she had to tell him that his reservation had been lost. The following year, though, he did ask her out, and they began to see each other as he passed through London to work. "It was an ease-in," Hightower explained. "It wasn't a whirlwind." Finally, in late 1995 she agreed to move back to New York and live with him.

The talk of De Niro and Hightower marrying came at almost the same time that he was quarreling in court with Toukie Smith over

the care and custody of their twin sons. In the ensuing gossip confla-
gration, it was rumored that De Niro and Hightower (who had taken
a hand in helping him parent the twins when they were in his care)
wanted to start a family of their own. She was a good candidate, said
De Niro's chum Chuck Low, who called her "the most stable of [Bob's]
girlfriends." But even though she was wearing a ten-carat emerald-cut
diamond that was said to cost six figures and there were whispers that
they had been working on a prenuptial agreement with their lawyers,
they didn't seem ready to pull the trigger.

Then in June 1997 Hightower phoned the Depuy Canal House
restaurant in High Falls, New York, and made reservations for a large
party on Tuesday the seventeenth. She ordered a five-course meal that
included wakame and lobster in rice paper and poussin breast with
cranberry quince stuffing, and she asked that the restaurant print up
special menus that would read "Love, Bob and Grace."

On the given day, De Niro and Hightower showed up at the restaurant at the appointed time, having been married a few hours earlier
in a civil ceremony "somewhere in New York State," according to his
spokesman. The party, numbering around a dozen, included Joe Pesci,
who had stood as best man, and Harvey Keitel. It was a week before
word of the wedding trickled into New York City, taking many of De
Niro's closest associates by surprise. "He's great at keeping details from
his best friends," Drew Nieporent told the New York *Daily News*.

Ten months later, almost as if it had been spelled out in their legal
agreement, they welcomed a baby boy, Elliot, on March 18, 1998. De
Niro was almost fifty-five; Hightower, who had taken the name De
Niro, was forty-four. He now had five children (one adopted) by three
women, and it looked for all the world as if his life and ways were finally settled.

MEANWHILE, PERHAPS INVESTED with a sense of urgency by a second marriage and growing brood of offspring, he ramped up his moviemaking work considerably—which was only possible, of course, if he
put concerns about quality aside.

In the winter of 1994–95, with *Casino* and *Heat* coming into theaters, he was in Los Angeles and the Bay Area to make a new film, *The Fan*, based on a novel by Peter Abrahams about a baseball fan whose connection to a star player for the San Francisco Giants becomes obsessive and, finally, deadly. De Niro played the title character, a traveling knife salesman named Gil Renard whose broken marriage has left him with only baseball as a means to connect with his son. When their favorite player, Bobby Rayburn (Wesley Snipes), falls into a slump that threatens his spot in the lineup, Renard executes Rayburn's would-be replacement (Benicio Del Toro) and then finally, completely psychotic, goes after Rayburn himself. On hand as well would be John Leguizamo as Rayburn's agent and Ellen Barkin as a sharp-tongued talk radio host whose criticism of Rayburn incurs Renard's wrath. Directing was Tony Scott, the hard-living, brassy visualist behind such commercial smashes as *Top Gun*, *The Last Boy Scout*, and *Crimson Tide*.

This was high-concept moviemaking, and De Niro was in it to get paid. Oh, he worked: he spent time going over the script carefully with Scott, recording their sessions, and suggesting changes to the character over a pile of transcriptions that ran to hundreds of pages; he interviewed cops and bodyguards about the phenomenon of stalkers; he spoke to a traveling knife salesman about the practices of his trade; he tapped his own experiences of being approached inappropriately by fans; he read up on Jeffrey Dahmer, David Berkowitz, Mark David Chapman, and various notorious celebrity stalkers; he even learned a little bit of knife throwing. But he was hardly stretching himself, merely reheating some bits of Travis Bickle and Max Cady.

There was a single memorable incident during production. A San Francisco cop stumbled across the set and, noticing the crew occupying a section of railroad line, interrupted shooting and ordered them off the tracks. De Niro, agitated, jumped behind the wheel of a Humvee that was part of the scene and gunned it around the traffic barricade, slamming to a stop just feet away from a passing train, then storming off to his trailer. When the cop declared that he was going to cite him for recklessness, De Niro sent his stunt double out to sign the ticket (the fine was $104), then emerged a few minutes later, shouting, "You don't know what the fuck you're doing!" at the officer.

Had anyone filmed that little bit of drama, it might've made for the most memorable thing in *The Fan*.

LORENZO CARCATERRA'S BOOK *Sleepers* seemed to many readers to be like a movie as soon as it was published in 1995. But that wasn't necessarily a compliment: they were comparing it to a film because it seemed, frankly, *fake*.

Carcaterra, a reporter for the New York *Daily News*, had written a memoir of a harrowing passage of his youth, when, he said, he and three friends from the Hell's Kitchen neighborhood of Manhattan were sentenced harshly for a prank gone bad and sent to an upstate New York reformatory, where they were brutalized and sexually abused by guards. Years later, Carcaterra and another of his chums had turned out well: a newspaperman and an assistant district attorney, respectively. But the other two had become criminals, and when they unexpectedly encountered the guard who'd been their chief tormentor in reform school, they killed him. The subsequent murder trial, Carcaterra said, had been manipulated by the defendants' friends—the writer and the prosecutor—with the help of a parish priest who willingly perjured himself to help acquit the killers.

Ballantine Books published *Sleepers* as nonfiction, and it was a best-seller, but virtually from the start its veracity was attacked by prison authorities, the Manhattan DA's office, the Catholic Church, and other reporters, who could find little or no evidence of any incidents that matched Carcaterra's story. Carcaterra and his editors stood behind the book, saying that many details of date, place, name, and even incident had been altered to protect people but that the story was true in its contours and its themes. That may have been the case, but such incidents deeply dented the book's credibility, and the author's reputation never fully recovered.

None of that, of course, meant a thing to Hollywood: *Sleepers* was a sensational tale with an ensemble full of meaty roles, and Warner Bros. paid $2 million for the film rights after a bidding war. Barry Levinson was brought in to adapt the book and direct, and his cast included Brad Pitt as the young prosecutor, Jason Patric as the writer, Billy Crudup and Ron Eldard as the killers, Kevin Bacon as their torturer/victim, Dustin Hoffman as a boozy defense attorney, and, as the priest willing to perjure himself because he had known the quartet of boys when they were young, De Niro.

He had only a few scenes, but he took them seriously, studiously comparing the script to the book and trying to create a character who was partly fun-loving but essentially sober and unimpeachably decent. As he knew, "priests are not supposed to violate certain rules or certain laws, even if they are unspoken. But that does not mean that they can't be broken if the priest feels it is morally right." He accepted that Carcaterra's account might have been fabricated: "It was hard to believe that the guards were so vile," he said. But it didn't finally matter. "I'm afraid I do believe it, because there are people like that. . . . If the abuse did not happen in this particular case, then it sure has elsewhere at some point."

The controversy over the story's veracity dogged *Sleepers* into theaters, and virtually every review took a stand on the question, usually scolding. Couple that with the deeply disquieting theme of child abuse, and no amount of star power could draw people into the theater. The one bright side: De Niro enjoyed working with both Levinson and Hoffman ("He really is terrific," he gushed to a reporter); it wouldn't be long before they tried it again.

SCOTT MCPHERSON'S 1991 play *Marvin's Room* was a cri de coeur from the first decade of the AIDS plague, even though AIDS wasn't explicitly a part of the story. It centers on two sisters whose father has been slowly dying after a stroke. One sister has cared for him for almost twenty years, but now she has leukemia, and she needs the help of her flighty sister, whose son has been institutionalized after deliberately burning down their house. McPherson wrote the play after caring for a partner who was dying of AIDS, and Tribeca Productions acquired the film rights in 1992, just as McPherson himself was dying of the disease. Jessica Lange was attached to play one of the sisters at that time, and De Niro was planning to produce it.

By the time it was made, in the late summer and fall of 1995, Lange was gone and De Niro had taken on a cameo as a physician with a goofball sense of humor and a contentious rapport with a colleague (Dan Hedaya). The sisters were played by Diane Keaton and Meryl Streep, the troubled son by Leonardo DiCaprio, and, in his final feature film performance, the dying man by Hume Cronyn. Jerry Zaks, best known for Broadway comedies and musicals, made his feature film debut as director.

The play had been dark (despite jagged bits of humor) and small, and it wasn't obviously film material, a sense that was borne out after Zaks finished shooting it. There seemed to be no appropriate distribution moment: it would get lost in the summer and wasn't quite powerful enough to be a serious awards season contender. It was released, finally, in February 1997, to modestly warm reviews and negligible box office.

IT WAS COMMONLY believed that De Niro and Martin Scorsese worked so well together because they understood each other's essence and background so well, but that wasn't entirely true. While De Niro had some firsthand knowledge of the Little Italy world of Scorsese's youth, Scorsese could only imagine what De Niro's childhood in the bohemia of the Greenwich Village art scene had been like. In 1996, though, De Niro met a director who, like him, had grown up in an artist's household.

James Mangold was the son of two artists—the painters Robert and Sylvia Plimack Mangold. He was raised in the Hudson River valley north of New York and had attended film school at CalArts and Columbia University, where, under the tutelage of Milos Forman, he developed two scripts: a story of a sad, overweight loner, entitled *Heavy*, and a loose remake of *High Noon* set in the world of contemporary police corruption. *Heavy* had been Mangold's debut and won him the Best Directing prize at the 1995 Sundance Film Festival. It brought Mangold to the attention of Miramax Films and Harvey Weinstein, and Mangold's other script, now entitled *Cop Land*, was put into production.

On the heels of the massive success of *Pulp Fiction*, and especially the resurrected career of John Travolta, the idea of an ensemble crime story from Miramax was exciting enough to attract a number of top stars to at least consider the film, including Travolta, Tom Cruise, Sean Penn, even Tom Hanks. However, none of them proved willing to work for what the studio was hoping to pay for the lead role, a hapless cop who finds that he has a nest of corrupt New York City detectives running his small Catskills town like their personal realm. Instead, seeking to bring back another star of the 1970s whose career had faded into self-parody, Weinstein landed Sylvester Stallone. Around him, as corrupt cops, were Harvey Keitel, Ray Liotta (with Cathy Moriarty as his wife), and Robert Patrick, while De Niro had a key role as an NYPD internal affairs investigator trying to convince the small-town cop to help him make his case against the bad guys.

"We feel overwhelmed and blessed that Robert De Niro has joined this project with his enormous talent, integrity and brilliance," Weinstein gushed to the press when it was announced that De Niro was in. He might later have wished that he'd tempered his words. Despite his association with De Niro and the Tribeca Film Center, Weinstein was the odd man out when De Niro and Mangold discovered the unusual coincidence of their parentage. "We both spent our childhoods at gallery openings," Mangold recalled. They bonded as well in wanting to see *Cop Land* made as Mangold intended it and not as Weinstein, who had earned a reputation as a heavy-handed producer in the old-time Hollywood style, wished to see it. Mangold was pressured by Weinstein in matters of casting and in shooting an alternative ending (which Weinstein himself wrote), and in both cases Mangold turned to De Niro, who, much to Weinstein's dismay, backed up the director's vision and authority. Both times—including the new ending, which De Niro simply refused to show up to shoot, no matter the fee dangled in front of him—Mangold won out.

De Niro didn't pour himself into the role. He'd played cops before, he knew the milieu, he trusted the director. He spent a little time boning up on the hierarchy of rank in the NYPD and on the off-duty lifestyle habits of cops, particularly the ones who chose to live outside the city. Otherwise, he knew he was merely a piece of the puzzle. The film shot throughout the summer and fall of 1996 and, after the typically protracted and painful Miramax editing process (not for nothing had Weinstein been nicknamed "Harvey Scissorhands"), it debuted the following summer to generally good notices and modest box office.

THE ONE INDISPUTABLY true thing to come out of *Sleepers* was the relationship that De Niro and Dustin Hoffman had forged in their few working days together. De Niro admired Hoffman's breezy personal style—"I always envy the way he can speak and be funny and smart"—and he liked to remind Hoffman of their very first encounter, back in 1968, when Hoffman was a rising star and De Niro, six years younger, was a struggling actor serving him drinks and canapés at a Eugene McCarthy presidential campaign event.

It was presidential politics that would bring them back together, in a fashion. In 1996, with *Sleepers* in theaters, Barry Levinson and New Line Cinema acquired the rights to *American Hero*, a 1993 novel by Larry Beinert that proposed, with tongue in cheek, that President George H. W. Bush had started the first Gulf War as a means of inflating his approval ratings and increasing his chances of reelection. "What we were interested in was the blurring of the line between Washington and Hollywood," Levinson explained. Screenwriter Hilary Henkin was called on to adapt the book, and then David Mamet was hired to punch up and energize her script. Late in the year, Levinson invited De Niro, Hoffman, and Anne Heche to a table reading of the most current draft, and they had a blast. As it happened, Warner Bros. was stalled on Levinson's pricey sci-fi film *Sphere*, which would star Hoffman, and a window of a couple of idle months lay ahead. With less than $20 million of New Line's money and a shooting schedule of less than thirty days, the three actors and Levinson agreed to go forward with the film, which had been retitled *Wag the Dog*.

De Niro was to play Conrad Brean, a political campaign strategist who has the luxury of a popular president running for reelection as a client. With a few short weeks to go before the election, however, and with the candidate abroad in China, a sex scandal breaks out involving the president and an underage girl whose youth group toured the White House. Called upon to distract the media from the ensuing firestorm, Brean hires Hollywood producer Stanley Motss (Hoffman) to stage a phony war in Eastern Europe, complete with fabricated atrocities and heroes, a theme song, a fad, and a logo. Heche was cast as the White House aide charged with riding herd on the pair of schemers, and Woody Harrelson, Dennis Leary, and Willie Nelson were among those with supporting roles.

De Niro was concerned that, despite the over-the-top nature of the story, there be an air of credibility throughout, and he sent the script to friends in the New York media, including Tom Brokaw of NBC and Judith Miller of the *New York Times,* to vet it for plausibility; he also asked for a review from veteran diplomat Richard Holbrooke. All three told him that the thing might be overly broad and was defiantly cynical but that there was a vein of realism in it. The film was shot in early 1997, just after the reelection of Bill Clinton, and, being a small movie with big stars, was released in late December, when film award talk was heating up—albeit on only three screens in New York and Los Angeles, to qualify for Oscar consideration.

It's hard to see how anyone thought of De Niro to play the WASPy, donnish Brean, but he seems to love the role: the shabby, vaguely academic mien and wardrobe, the slippery logic, the nonstop motion and rat-a-tat patter. He plays it low-key and, indeed, low-fi, not trying to create a character so much as slip into the role unnoticed, rather as he had in recent years in the likes of *Cop Land* and *Marvin's Room.* He carries much more of the film, though Hoffman is funnier by far and would be nominated for an Oscar (as, a bit curiously, Best Actor). There's an ease and likeability to Brean: he appreciates the skill and energy of his colleagues. He relates beautifully to Motss in the way they talk, the way they seem physically relaxed around each other, the way their minds and skill sets meld. In reality, Brean is a bad guy, intent on fooling the public and corrupting the government for the sake of political gain. But De Niro plays him so offhandedly and agreeably that the audience can't help but want him to succeed. Ultimately, *Wag the Dog* is remembered best for presaging eerily a real-life political drama, but it's still, in the main, a film dotted with pleasures, and De Niro's unaffected work serves it well.

The full release came a few weeks later, on January 11, and it made a respectable $7.8 million. And then, just one week later, a scandal involving Bill Clinton and a former White House intern, a young woman named Monica Lewinsky, stunned the world, leaking first on fledgling Internet-based news sites and then into the mainstream media, creating a long-running furor that ended in the impeachment of the president before the year was out.

It was a perfect instance of life catching up to art: among the commonly seen images of Lewinsky was one in which she wore a beret just like that sported by the underage girl in *Wag the Dog*. The tiny movie made on a lark had become synonymous with the juiciest presidential scandal since Watergate, and the film went on to play in theaters until spring, earning a healthy $43 million box office and Oscar nominations for Hoffman and the screenplay, and making the phrase "wag the dog" a kind of shorthand for the political use of media to distract the public from unpleasant realities.

DE NIRO CHOSE yet another ensemble role with his next picture, *Jackie Brown*, an adaptation of Elmore Leonard's novel *Rum Punch* by writer-director Quentin Tarantino. De Niro was cast as Louis Gara, a newly minted parolee who's back in business with his sometime partner in crime Ordell Robbie. Sloppy and out of sorts, Louis sits in quiet wonderment at the new world that has emerged during his years in prison: the technology, the sexual mores, the cat-and-mouse game with law enforcement. He was once sharp and dangerous, but incarceration has softened and neutered him, and even though Ordell wants to take him back on as a colleague, Louis needs more supervision than the services he can provide would seem to warrant.

Tarantino was an immense De Niro fan, both as a film buff and as an aspiring actor. "De Niro was it," he once said. "He was who everyone in my acting classes wanted to be." On British TV in 1994, not long before the release of *Pulp Fiction*, Tarantino provided introductions to a "Season of De Niro," including airings of *Mean Streets, Taxi Driver, Raging Bull, The Deer Hunter,* and *Once Upon a Time in America.* Getting a personal hero into the film was a coup for the director, but it may have paled in comparison to the fact that his producer, Harvey Weinstein, let him fill the principal roles in the film with two nearly forgotten stars of the 1970s: Pam Grier and Robert Forster.

The mammoth success of *Pulp Fiction* meant that the follow-up would be gobbled up by the film press and audiences alike. But Tarantino chose, cannily, not to push the wild tenor of his previous films any further. Rather, *Jackie Brown* would be closer to a character study, the story of an airline hostess (Grier) coerced by law enforcement into turning against Ordell (Samuel L. Jackson) and using her own wiles and the help of a friendly bail bondsman (Forster) to keep herself alive and free.

De Niro, like Bridget Fonda, Chris Tucker, and Michael Keaton, was but a minor player in this deadly roundelay. As a result, he did very little work to prepare for the role. He grew out his hair and a goatee, he made a very few character notes in his script ("Do I smoke? . . . I'm trying to be hip, black . . . High now! Feeling good"), and he concentrated mainly on wardrobe. Nothing about Louis is stylish, but he does carry a sort of cool old-school vibe. To that end, Tarantino dressed De Niro in bowling shirts and Hawaiian shirts, some designed for the production, some of them vintage items from the director's own closet. A few of those items were actually worn by De Niro in the film, but he and his director failed to bond over anything more substantial than shirts; rumors from the set indicated, in fact, that De Niro didn't care for Tarantino's manner and found the working environment uncomfortable.

That didn't affect his performance. There's humor and wistful sadness to Louis Gara. His post-prison manners are crude and simpleminded—one aspect of modern life after another causes him to revert to a watchful shell. He's glad of Ordell's solicitude, of the chance to get back on his feet, of the booze and weed and the minute or two of sex he's granted by Melanie (Bridget Fonda), but the world outside prison confuses and scares him. Asked to do something simple by Ordell—to accompany Melanie to pick up a stash of money—he is out of his element and flustered; it takes only a few verbal goads for him to turn on Melanie and do something truly stupid and, in fact, unforgivable. His weakness and incapacity finally come to define him, and he becomes another employee Ordell must, in his phrase, "let go." It's a measure of the man that Louis used to be that Ordell is practically on the verge of tears when he does so.

24

What the fuck happened to you, man? Shit, your ass used to be beautiful.

—Ordell Robbie,
giving Louis Gara his pink slip in *Jackie Brown*

In 1998, De Niro succumbed to an invitation to sit for a live interview as part of the popular *Inside the Actors Studio* television series, which took footage from a lengthy conversation between a notable actor and moderator James Lipton, with current acting students and members of the public in the audience.

What was curious about the event beyond anything said onstage was its timing in his career. For a few years, De Niro's acting choices—the actual roles and films and collaborators—had become the subject of cynicism in the critical community. Starting with a *Rolling Stone* review of *This Boy's Life* entitled "Is De Niro Slipping?" (it was a misleading headline: the gist of the article argued, "No, he's not, or at least not entirely"), there was a regular stream of articles questioning and even lambasting him for letting his status as "greatest actor since Brando" fade. Two antagonists in particular—Tom Carson of *Esquire* and *GQ* (the magazines most apt to bust De Niro's chops for not consenting to proper interviews) and David Thomson of London's *Independent*—each went after him more than once in articles entitled "Phoning It In," "Weight Problem," "The Buck Hunter," and so forth. The gist of their arguments was that De Niro was coasting on a well-earned but insufficiently sustained reputation, that his most recent projects weren't up to the caliber of his talents, and that his talent itself was rusting or withering from lack of proper use, like the muscles of a paralytic. "Robert De Niro is a hack," Carson wrote bluntly, while Thomson took a more expansive view, trying to put what he saw as De Niro's dubious choices in the context of his age, his family status, and his business activities.

It was true that De Niro had become more prolific over the years. He'd had thirteen films released in the 1970s, and the same number in the 1980s, but when the 1990s finally ended, he would have made twenty-four in those ten years alone. Granting that some of these represented fleeting appearances (as, to be fair, had been the case in previous decades as well, although less often), it was a significant increase in output. But it was true, too, that the 1990s saw him emerge as a director and producer, and he worked with such estimable collaborators as Scorsese (three times), Michael Mann, Barry Levinson (twice), Quentin Tarantino, John Frankenheimer, Alfonso Cuarón, Kenneth Branagh, Tony Scott, Harold Ramis and James Mangold. True, it wasn't equal to his stunning stretch of work from 1973 through 1984, which included two Oscar wins and perhaps nine classic performances. But it wasn't outright hackery, either, and almost every film in the period had something in it that made clear why De Niro had been attracted to it: a challenge in the characterization, an estimable set of colleagues, a story of weight or interest. There would come a time when he turned more toward comedy than to drama, when he seemed to be working for the experience of continuing to work rather than some greater artistic end. But it didn't come as early in his career as his detractors seemed to believe. Not every film he made was up to the level of *The Godfather, Part II* or *Raging Bull*—or even, maybe, *True Confessions* or *Midnight Run*. But he hadn't, as his detractors claimed, settled greedily into remunerative self-parody. The critical dismissals would keep coming, though, particularly as he turned to comedy and actually scored some box office hits. But the true depth of what he was choosing to do and what he was capable of doing continued, at least for a while longer, to be more complex and interesting than their authors would credit.

IN THE EARLY months of 1996, De Niro acquired a copy of the Cliffs Notes companion to Charles Dickens's *Great Expectations*. He wasn't taking adult ed courses or seeking self-betterment. He was considering a role in a version of the oft-filmed classic updated for contemporary sensibilities. Ethan Hawke was to play the lead role and Gwyneth Paltrow his dream girl, and De Niro was being courted by producer Art Linson to play the small but vital role of the escaped convict who is aided by the protagonist and goes on to return the favor.

The first drafts of the script came to De Niro while he was visiting London in February 1996, with the prompt to decide soon whether he was interested, as shooting was planned for Eastertime. It turned out that production didn't begin until the summer, under the eye of the Mexican director Alfonso Cuarón, then best known for his lovely children's film *A Little Princess*. By that time, De Niro had agreed to play the role of the prisoner Magwitch, renamed Lustig for the adaptation (Hawke's Pip had been similarly rechristened as Finn, a decision reached on the first day of shooting). It was another cameo—a few days of work, maybe a couple of weeks—and he was doing that sort of thing so often at that point that nobody blinked at it.

The script, by John Belushi's onetime writing partner Mitch Glazer, who had already modernized *A Christmas Carol* into *Scrooged*, was so different from the original that De Niro never did crack his Cliffs Notes. Rather, he focused on the physicality of the character: a hobbled walk, a cagy silence, and, especially, a beard. His production files were filled with scores of images of famous beardos from history: Fidel Castro, Rasputin, Lenin, Trotsky, Ulysses Grant, the Ayatollah Khomeini, and anonymous Orthodox Jews and Russian peasants. And he called in a small favor from Linson: his daughter Drena was cast in a tiny role as an art gallery assistant (Grazer's Pip/Finn had been reshaped into a painter).

The film appeared in the early part of 1998, to disappointing box office. Just fifteen months earlier, the same distributor, 20th Century Fox, had a massive hit with Baz Luhrmann's update of Shakespeare, *Romeo + Juliet*, but Cuarón's *Great Expectations* didn't spark nearly the same heat.

THE SHORT FORAY into the classics, even modernized, struck a chord in De Niro, however. As he was working on *Great Expectations*, he was producing an adaptation of *Moby Dick* written by the English novelist Philip Kerr and retitled *Ahab* to give a sense of its emphasis and the role De Niro saw himself as playing. This was the biggest thing that he and Tribeca had undertaken to date. So far the company had been content to put its name on a couple of De Niro's films and to work mainly on small, indie-scale movies and TV series, such as *TriBeCa* and *New York Undercover*, neither of which had succeeded in holding on to an audience for very long. *Ahab*, though, was to be a full-scale seafaring epic, with significant water work and special effects. On its own, Tribeca couldn't come up with anything near the more than $50 million that would be required to make it, so De Niro and Jane Rosenthal courted financial backers, eventually finding a partner in Shochiku, a Japanese film studio, which was willing to provide funds for three projects, including *Ahab*.

Even so, De Niro was never quite able to pull the trigger. He studied seafaring art from the nineteenth century and watched adaptations of *Mutiny on the Bounty*, Renny Harlin's *Cutthroat Island*, and the two epic films about Christopher Columbus released in 1992. Kerr's script bobbed around the Tribeca offices throughout 1996, and De Niro even sent it to Steven Spielberg, who knew from large-budget ocean-based movies, to get a reading on the material and the cost. "It's a very good project with exceptional writing," Spielberg replied. "I liked it a lot. I honestly don't know, with all my special effects expertise and experience on the water, whether $50 million is enough to put all of this up there." Eventually the project simply died.

Even with *Ahab* a no-go, and as busy as he was now that he had come to live with the idea that he was an actor for hire, he could have been much, much busier if he had had the time or the inclination. His name was attached to dozens of films throughout the 1990s. Some of the parts he rejected would go on to be filled by other actors: the Harvey Keitel role in Spike Lee's *Clockers*, the Jack Nicholson role in

Danny DeVito's *Hoffa*, the Kevin Spacey role in Curtis Hansen's *L.A. Confidential*, the Armand Assante role in Arne Glimcher's *The Mambo Kings*, the Al Pacino role in Oliver Stone's *Any Given Sunday*, the Jack Nicholson role in Rob Reiner's *A Few Good Men*, the Billy Bob Thornton role in *Monster's Ball* (Queen Latifah was rumored to be cast opposite him), the Joe Pesci role in Chris Columbus's *Home Alone*, the John Malkovich role in Jane Campion's *The Portrait of a Lady*, the Michael Douglas role in David Seltzer's *Shining Through*, the Paul Newman role in Marek Kanievska's *Where the Money Is*, the Nicolas Cage role in George Gallo's *Trapped in Paradise*, and the Liam Neeson role (opposite Meryl Streep) in Barbet Schroeder's *Before and After*.

The Hollywood trade papers carried word of him starring in biopics based on the lives of boxing trainer Angelo Dundee, Cuban leader Fidel Castro, painters Diego Rivera and Jackson Pollock (the latter, which actually seemed possible for a time, had Barbra Streisand penciled in as the artist's wife, Lee Krasner), financier Michael Milken, auto maker Enzo Ferrari (with Michael Mann directing), and, with Martin Scorsese, columnist Walter Winchell and Rat Pack icon Dean Martin.

There were rumors of De Niro appearing in another Scorsese film, *Silence*, based on a Shusaku Endo novel about Jesuit missionaries in Japan,* and yet another, a version of Arthur Miller's *View from the Bridge* that was to be staged as a play and then shot on film. There was a movie about the Red Scare called *33 Liberty St.*; a comedy opposite Dustin Hoffman entitled *Gold Dust*; *The Little Things*, a Danny DeVito–directed thriller about the search for a serial killer; Michael Cimino's adaptation of *The Fountainhead*; *Out on My Feet*, a Barry Primus film in which he would play the manager of boxer Mark Wahlberg; a film about espionage in the Middle East; and *Stagecoach Mary*, a western (!) with Whoopi Goldberg (!).

He even had at least one significant project of his own that went at least as far along as *Ahab: Stolen Flower*, an adaptation of Philip Carlo's novel about a Manhattan private eye hired to track down a girl who has

---

* It would finally go into production in 2014 with Liam Neeson in the role De Niro had once considered.

been kidnapped and used in a child pornography ring. For that one, he had scripts drafted and spent a while scouting locations in New York and Europe. But it never came together, joining a pile of unmade films that would have constituted a full career in itself.

HE HAD BARELY finished *Jackie Brown* when he jumped into another high-style crime film with an ensemble cast. He would spend the winter of 1997–98 primarily in France shooting *Ronin*, an espionage and heist film filled with stunning car chases and a cast of international faces including the French Jean Reno, the Swedish Stellan Skarsgård, the English Sean Bean, Natascha McElhone, and Jonathan Pryce, and even the German ice skater Katarina Witt. The script by J. D. Zeik, from his own story, had gone through at least six drafts, including a punch-up by David Mamet (writing under the pseudonym Richard Weisz). And the director was the legendary John Frankenheimer, who had been making pictures of this kind when De Niro was still sitting in a classroom bidding Stella Adler good morning.

It was a bit of a gamble, at least from the studio's point of view. The film involved several long action sequences that would take weeks upon weeks to shoot and push the budget over $60 million. Frankenheimer was in his late sixties, and his last film, the 1996 remake of *The Island of Dr. Moreau*, had been a widely ridiculed flop—albeit one that he had been hired mid-production to rescue from the original director, who'd been fired for being unable to rein in stars Marlon Brando and Val Kilmer, among other sins. But among his many stellar credits (*The Manchurian Candidate, The Birdman of Alcatraz, The Train, Seven Days in May*), Frankenheimer counted *Grand Prix*, the 1966 race car film, and *Black Sunday*, the 1977 film about international terrorism. He had lived in France for a period, and actors loved him. So in some ways he was a natural choice.

De Niro was brought in relatively late in the process, and his salary, a reported $14 million, was more than 20 percent of the whole budget. But his name gave the picture a global reach that the otherwise distinguished but low-wattage cast lacked. And he was a willing collaborator, boning up on his French and probing deeply into the logic and practice of espionage behind the script's details (Milt Bearden, a former CIA agent whom Frankenheimer had brought in as a consultant on what he hoped to be his next project, a history of the spying agency called *The Good Shepherd*, was De Niro's go-to source for questions about spies and their tradecraft). He even took some lessons in race car driving—although he would be filmed behind a dummy wheel, with a real auto racer driving from the right side of the cars.

He liked Frankenheimer—he gave him a custom-made chair for Christmas and a video camera to mark the end of shooting along with a note declaring "What a guy! . . . What a cineaste!" And he liked France—or at least he did until the morning of February 10, 1998, when, with a month still to go in the production, he was taken from his suite at the Hotel Bristol by as many as eight Parisian police officers and brought to the offices of judge Frédéric N'Guyen, where he was held for most of the day and questioned for more than three hours about his possible involvement in a high-end prostitution ring.

At issue was the case of Jean-Pierre Bourgeois, a soft-core porn photographer who was in custody pending trial as the operator of a high-class call girl ring. The charges against Bourgeois were sensational, involving the use of underage girls, $8,000-a-night escorts, Middle Eastern oil billionaires, shady middlemen, briefcases full of cash, and even an epic tryst involving an Arab prince, $1 million, and a well-known entertainment personality. De Niro's name was found in Bourgeois's address book, and there were at least three women involved in the prostitution ring who claimed to have met De Niro, one of whom, the English porn star Charmaine Sinclair, had told investigators that he had been her lover. Sinclair—shapely and dark-skinned, like almost all of the women in his life in the past twenty years—said she'd met De Niro in the early 1990s and would see him, on and off, until 1995. "He was attentive, very gentle and passionate," she told a London tabloid. "He left me totally satisfied. . . . I know I'll never make love like that again."

Confronted with Sinclair's story, De Niro didn't deny it, laying out the entire chain of events for N'Guyen. As he testified, he'd met Bourgeois through the Polish tennis star Wojtek Fibak, who *told me that Bourgeois was a fashion photographer and that he knew lots of beautiful girls. The first time Bourgeois showed me photos of girls, they were taken from mags like "Lui" and "Playboy." He said he could introduce me to them, in a friendly way, without any notion of money. It is possible that I chose one of these girls. And it seems that Charmaine Sinclair was the one. I said to [Bourgeois] that I was interested if he could introduce me to her. A few weeks later [he] contacted me and said that Charmaine was with him in St. Tropez.*

De Niro said he flew to Nice from Paris, took a helicopter to St. Tropez, and met Bourgeois and Sinclair in a villa. "I had sex with Charmaine in the villa. I left in the afternoon by helicopter, then took the plane to Paris. There had been no money transaction." Another girl who was on the scene said she'd seen Fibak and Bourgeois handling a bag full of cash while De Niro was at the villa, but the actor insisted, "I never had any attaché case full of dollars the day I met Charmaine in St. Tropez." As for any of the other girls involved in the prostitution ring who named him, he would say only that it was possible that he had "shaken hands" with them, and he insisted that nothing more had happened. He wasn't arrested, charged, or even given reason to believe that he would be, and he was let go at around 9:00 p.m.

The story of De Niro's testimony broke all over the world overnight, and he had paparazzi camped outside his hotel constantly (he received regular messages from the front desk about whether or not it was safe to emerge, and he generally did so through a back entrance). It was so bad that he actually called the New York *Daily News* gossip columnists George Rush and Joanna Molloy to deny any wrongdoing point-blank: "No matter how violent and defamatory the attacks on me are, it will all come out at the trial that I acted properly," he said, adding cryptically, "I have 20 years of experience. I am doing everything according to the law. I know what I am doing."

Privately, he fumed. The previous year he'd been named to the French Légion d'Honneur, a distinction that named him, in effect, an asset to the culture of France. He declared angrily that he'd send the medal back, and he also said that once *Ronin* was finished filming, he'd never work in or visit France again. With its treatment of him, he said, France had "betrayed its own motto of 'liberty, equality and fraternity.'"

Among the things he did was hire a prominent attorney, former French justice minister Georges Kiejman, who held a press conference to defend De Niro and denounce the investigator's tactics: "I was shocked and upset by the way in which [De Niro] was treated in a case in which his name came up only incidentally." He described his client as a ripe target for the attention of women: "He's a charming man. Young women are introduced to him all the time. . . . If you knew the number of women who are pretty and ravishing who have his phone number . . . He has a right to a private life." More specifically, Kiejman denounced the sensational tactics of N'Guyen, whom he called "another Kenneth Starr" and accused of seeking to create a "media circus" for his own glory.° "The name of Robert De Niro is like a jewel for a judge," he said. "He submitted voluntarily to be questioned on a matter that did not directly concern him. He in no way, shape or form is a subject of any investigation. . . . [But] they never let him free. He could phone me, he was not under formal arrest, but without freedom all day . . . He kept repeating the same answers to the same questions." After his angry conversation with reporters, Kiejman filed a complaint accusing the judge of "violation of secrecy in an investigation."

De Niro was guilty, prosecutors determined, of nothing more than having sex with a woman who, at other times, sold her favors for (lots of) money, but the whole ugly episode cost him at least one potential job: he had been among the actors invited to read English-language translations of the poetry of Pope John Paul II for a CD project that had been successful all over the world in the previous months. When news of this scandal broke, the invitation was rescinded. "De Niro's participation no longer seems such a good idea," said Father Giuseppe Moscati, who was coordinating the recording project. "It appears that the image we had of De Niro when we made the proposal is far from

---

° Starr, of course, was the special prosecutor who was, at the time, investigating President Bill Clinton's relationship with Monica Lewinsky, among other things.

the truth." For his part, De Niro sued the Parisian tabloid *France Soir* for defamation and violation of privacy for their coverage of his brush with the law, and he was eventually awarded more than $13,000 in damages by a court.

The whole matter had vanished from newspapers by the fall, when *Ronin* was released.* Producers might have worried that news of their big star in a sex scandal would hurt the film, but the star of *Ronin*, really, *is* the film *Ronin*: the construct of it, the execution of the driving sequences, the shootouts, the cat-and-mouse sequences, and especially the interplay between the very well-cast performers. De Niro's Sam is from the get-go presented as cagy, untrusting, and demanding, but he's also undoubtedly professional, possessed of a dab hand's tricks and insights and a sixth sense for danger, duplicity, and the likelihood of a scenario playing out a certain way. He forms bonds within the little cadre of players, principally a friendship with Reno's Vincent and a not-quite-romance with McElhone's Deirdre. But he's quick to smell a rat, to suss out a hopeless situation, and to deflect inquiries into his own past and motivation with black humor. "You worried about saving your skin?" he's asked, and he responds, almost without a glance, "Yeah, I am. It covers my whole body."

Sam is relentless in trying to get Deirdre to introduce him to her bosses, to get a heftier payment for his work, and, when the time for action comes, to see that he holds up his end and then some. He shoots, he drives, he fights, he connives, and in one of the film's most remarkable scenes, he even performs surgery on himself to remove a bullet. If he seemed at first a reluctant warrior, he proves himself a valuable one. And he has a code: "Whenever there is any doubt, there is no doubt." Stuff like that, played to low-key, hard-boiled perfection, is clearly what drew De Niro to the role, and he plays it just as he did Neil McCauley in *Heat*, giving himself over willingly to the larger enterprise, playing a part in a big, engaging cinematic machine. It's not a great movie, but

---

* Indeed, De Niro himself more or less forgot it, returning to Paris in May 1999 for the opening of an exhibition of Robert De Niro Sr.'s paintings at the Gerald Pitzer Gallery on the rue Matignon. Pointedly, perhaps, no figures of the French political establishment were present at the big party, though the paparazzi and mobs of star-gazers were camped outside to catch a glimpse of him.

it's a damn good genre film, and De Niro elevates it with the weight of his presence and his lack of showiness and vanity. (He didn't elevate it into a hit, though; the film grossed less than $42 million against a budget of around $55 million.)

EVEN BEFORE HE left for France and *Ronin*, De Niro was looking ahead to yet another film and another new direction: a script called *Analyze This*, about the relationship of a mob boss and the psychotherapist whom he starts to visit when he loses his confidence in himself. Billy Crystal had been attached to produce the picture and star as the shrink, and there was a director on board, Richard Loncraine, an Englishman with a resume that included period comedy (*The Missionary*) and Shakespeare (an updated *Richard III* with Ian McKellen).

De Niro had been courted for roles as a comic gangster since *Midnight Run*, but as Jane Rosenthal explained, "We weren't willing at the time to have Bob parody the one franchiseable character he has." In early 1997, though, he was willing to reconsider, and so he was game when he got a gander at the script, which had originally been written by playwright Kenneth Lonergan and had been put into the churning cycle of rewrites that so often plagued Hollywood comedies. During the next year and a half, writers Peter Tolan, George Gallo, and Phoef Sutton would all take cracks at the material, along with Crystal himself; in May 1997 Loncraine would be replaced by *Caddyshack* and *Groundhog Day* director Harold Ramis, who worked on yet another set of script revisions, along with colleagues Mort Nathan and Barry Fanaro.

Ramis was walking a tightrope of sorts: mixing genres, casting well-known actors against type, and having both of his stars as producers. "Bob was afraid Billy would turn it into a sentimental farce, a sitcom," Ramis said. "He was afraid it would be too pat, too unrealistic. And Billy was afraid it would turn into 'Goodfellas': too violent, too mean-spirited. I came in sort of to reconcile these points of view. I reassured Billy the film would be funny. And I told Bob this wouldn't be a send-up of 'The Godfather.' I said, 'Imagine you're watching 'Goodfellas,' and Woody Allen enters.'"

The script was finally shaped to everyone's satisfaction in the late spring of 1998, by which time De Niro had agreed to help produce the film and to join a cast that would include Lisa Kudrow, Chazz Palminteri, and the very credible Joe Viterelli, a shady character off the streets of Little Italy who liked to keep his background mysterious and had appeared memorably in Woody Allen's mob-and-theater comedy *Bullets over Broadway.* De Niro didn't dig very deep for his character; principally he made a detailed study of how contemporary mob bosses—particularly the famed "Dapper Don," John Gotti—dressed and wore their hair. But he did make the acquaintance of at least one bona fide made man, Anthony (Fat Andy) Ruggiano, a soldier in the Gambino crime family; another Gambino associate, Anthony Corozzo, had been cast in the film as an extra (he was a member of the Screen Actors Guild), and he brought Ruggiano to the set one day and made introductions, during which time a photo, which surfaced during a 2009 mob trial, was taken showing De Niro with his arm around Ruggiano. (Asked a few years earlier about running into mobsters, De Niro explained, "You know perfectly well who they are, but if I find them in front of me and they say, 'Hello,' I can't really turn away, can I?")

The film was shot quickly from May through July in New York and Florida, and Ramis turned it around in time for a March 1999 release. By then, though, they had competition. In January, HBO had premiered *The Sopranos,* an elaborate series about a mobster who begins to visit a psychotherapist, secretly, when he suffers a series of panic attacks. As it happened, Warner Bros., the studio that had produced *Analyze This,* was owned by the same conglomerate that owned HBO. There was some real concern that the immensely popular cable TV series was going to outshine the $30 million theatrical film. That turned out not to matter.

It must be made clear in any consideration of his performing career up to this point that De Niro was *always* funny. He was funny in *Hi, Mom!* and in that AMC car commercial, in *The Gang That Couldn't Shoot Straight* and *Bang the Drum Slowly* and *Mean Streets,* in *Raging Bull* and *Brazil* and *The King of Comedy* and *The Untouchables* and

Midnight Run (obviously) and *We're No Angels* and (yes) *Cape Fear* and *Mad Dog and Glory* and, most recently, in *Wag the Dog* and *Jackie Brown*. He has always been thought of as an actor's actor, a thespian most adept at playing heavies. But far more often than is commonly recollected, he had a breezy, winking lilt to him, a born comic's way with jokey dialogue, a killer grin that could sell you a pained laugh even in a picture like *Taxi Driver*. He never seemed exactly a joker, but he was, as Jerry Lewis used to say of Dean Martin, "funny in his bones." As Ramis, a comedian's comedian, said of De Niro, "It's not as if he has a shtick he does or some routine that he's worked up in clubs. He's funny because he'll grab on to a reality and just shake it and just milk it for everything. And he knows that excesses of behavior can be very funny. That's why we laugh sometimes at things that are excessively violent. It's part discomfort and part irony. But he knows that."

It's no surprise, then, that De Niro is so adept in *Analyze This*—far more so, indeed, than Billy Crystal, whose character, Dr. Ben Sobel, is essentially the straight man or interlocutor to De Niro's comically skewed mob boss, Paul Vitti. De Niro's Vitti always carries an air of menace—at any second he is apt to take a firm, even threatening, tone with his henchmen, his rivals, his psychoanalyst. But whether discussing his sex life, his family, his anxiety, his history of violence, or the ins and outs of his work, he's genuinely funny. "You don't hear the word *no* too much, do you," Sobel says to him, and Vitti insists that isn't true: "I hear it all the time, only it's more like, 'No! Please! No! No!'" Right there is the genius of the film: the shocking and straight-faced blend of mob movie and buddy comedy.

It works best in the early going, and better still when De Niro is on-screen and we're not caught up in any of the limp plotting having to do with Sobel's wedding or his inferiority complex vis-à-vis his own father. Vitti is cautious when entering Sobel's office for the first time, but he immediately comes to dominate it and to congratulate the doctor for having cured him even though they've only had a single vague conversation of a few minutes' duration. "The load? Gone," he says blithely about his troubles. "Where is it? Don't know." He insists that he's had a breakthrough, telling Sobel, "You got a gift, my friend." When the doctor demurs, Vitti is adamant: "Yes, you do" and then "Yes, you *do*."

But even in a happy fettle, he serves Sobel with a warning: "I go fag, you die."

He has a grand comic moment while trying to make love with a mistress whose chatter distracts him into impotence—"I'm trying to do this here!" he scolds her—and another when Sobel starts asking about his father and suggests he might have an Oedipal complex:

VITTI: "English! English!"
SOBEL: "Oedipus was a Greek king who killed his father and married his mother."
VITTI: "Fucking Greeks."
SOBEL: "It's an instinctual developmental drive. The young boy wants to replace his father so that he can totally possess his mother."
VITTI: "What are you saying? That I wanted to fuck my mother?"
SOBEL: "It's a primal fantasy. . . ."
VITTI: "Have you ever *seen* my mother? Are you out of your fucking mind?"
SOBEL: "It's Freud."
VITTI: "Well, then Freud's a sick fuck, and you are, too, for bringing it up."

(Later, when Sobel mentions Freud again, Vitti complains, "I can't even call my mother on the phone after that thing you told me.") At its best, the film rolls like that again and again, with De Niro effortlessly crafting a sleek, crude, ruthless mob boss aura and then digging into the rich dialogue with real gusto. Unfortunately, Ramis and company determined that they had to balance the Vitti story with a Sobel story, and the last act, in which Sobel becomes engaged in mob business, becomes increasingly inane, a tendency that became chronic and ultimately fatal in the awful sequel. But during that opening hour or so, when De Niro is diving into the chance to make light of his own tough-cookie persona, *Analyze This* is a genuine treat, and it truly deserved its success.

It was received well in the press. By now, critics had seen De Niro trying virtually everything that an actor could do, including—as far back as *Midnight Run*—straight comedy. But by and large they were impressed with his full-on comic turn in *Analyze This*. "Without betraying the genre that has handed him such choice opportunities," said Janet Maslin in the *New York Times* of the very notion of De Niro sending up a mob movie, "Mr. De Niro gives a performance that amounts to one long wink at the viewer." In the *San Francisco Chronicle*, Mick LaSalle wrote, "De Niro has figured out that his best strategy for playing comedy is to play it as he would a drama. He plays it straight and lets the situation determine whether it's funny." But there were some negative notices mixed in: "Playing tough is what made De Niro a star, and his reluctance—or inability—to send up his own clichés is understandable. Which is why he's especially awkward when he tries to be funny," said Manohla Dargis in the *LA Weekly*. "De Niro doesn't just seem uneasy—he seems lost."

In fact, it was a global smash, earning nearly $107 million at home and another $70 million or so abroad, spending two weeks at the very top of the North American box office and ten weeks altogether in the top ten. De Niro didn't get paid as much up front as he had on *Ronin*: his paycheck on *Analyze This* was a relatively modest $8 million. But Tribeca Productions owned a piece of the film, which provided the company with its first bona fide megahit. The success gave De Niro some ideas about what else he could be doing, ideas that would change his career, his life, even his legacy in ways nobody could have foreseen.

ELIA KAZAN WON ACADEMY AWARDS AS BEST DIRECTOR IN 1948 and 1955, for *Gentlemen's Agreement* and *On the Waterfront*, respectively, and he amassed five other Oscar nominations throughout his career for directing such films as *A Streetcar Named Desire* and *East of Eden*, as well as three Tony awards as best director. But his life's work had been mitigated, in the eyes of more than a few in the Hollywood community, by his 1952 testimony before the House Un-American Activities Committee, when he had been a friendly witness, providing the committee with names of people whom they had already identified as Communists or Communist sympathizers. Not only had Kazan never apologized for his decision, he staunchly defended himself in a full-page ad in the *New York Times* and in interviews and writings throughout his life. To many eyes, in fact, *On the Waterfront*, which was written by Budd Schulberg, another friendly HUAC witness, was an attempt to show how informing on one's former peers could be a sign of honor rather than a badge of shame.

In some circles, Kazan's cooperation with HUAC was overlooked; in 1983, he was named a Kennedy Center honoree, one of the highest civilian honors that can be bestowed in the United States, and in 1987 he was feted at a benefit for the American Museum of the Moving Image. But he was still considered a self-serving rat by others in Hollywood, a man who helped fuel the ruinous Hollywood blacklist of the McCarthy era, a cruelty that was still acutely felt decades later.

It was thus headline news when in early 1999 the Motion Picture Academy of Arts and Sciences announced that it would give the eighty-nine-year-old Kazan an honorary Oscar for lifetime achievement. Karl

Malden, who'd worked with Kazan before *and* after his testimony and who was a past president of the Academy, had proposed the award, and the thirty-nine-member board had voted its approval unanimously. The award would be presented during the Oscar telecast in late March by two of the contemporary cinema's most prominent heirs to Kazan's artistic legacy: Martin Scorsese and Robert De Niro.

In Hollywood, where various victims of the blacklist still lived and the business of sorting out which screenwriters should properly be credited for films they wrote pseudonymously while under the shadow of the blacklist was still being debated (witness the many feature stories about the era that had greeted the release of *Guilty by Suspicion*), the news of Kazan's honor was received with powerful emotions. A full-page ad in *Daily Variety* signed by, among others, Sean Penn and Ed Asner accused Kazan of having "validated the blacklisting of thousands" and doing "enormous damage to the motion picture industry." Survivors of the blacklist spoke out in the media and organized a demonstration for Oscar night. The award was meant to be a sentimental gesture, but it was shaping up to be a scrap.

De Niro had grown up enraptured by Kazan's work and had starred in the director's final film, *The Last Tycoon*, more than twenty years prior. The two had maintained contact and friendship over the years. Kazan had sent De Niro a letter after seeing him onstage in *Cuba and His Teddy Bear*, offering a few suggestions for the performance, and had written him again after having seen *A Bronx Tale*, declaring, "I don't know anyone who could have done it as you did." De Niro was among the five hundred people who turned out to honor the director at the American Museum of the Moving Image gala. So for De Niro the Oscar was a matter not only of artistic just deserts—Kazan's work clearly merited the recognition—but also of personal loyalty. Of course he would present it.

On the night of the awards, a frail Kazan entered the Dorothy Chandler Pavilion through a side entrance, meaning that he didn't have to walk past the couple of hundred people who were protesting his appearance peacefully across the street from the red carpet, where they were opposed, also peacefully, by a smaller group carrying placards in favor of Kazan. When the moment for his award came, highlights of Kazan's impressive career were shown and Scorsese and De Niro spoke from the podium, De Niro describing the honoree as "the master of a new kind of psychological and behavioral truth in acting."

Then, accompanied by his wife, Frances, Kazan came out from the wings to a mixed response. As TV cameras showed, some in the crowd stood immediately to applaud him, including Malden, Warren Beatty (who made his film debut in Kazan's *Splendor in the Grass*), Meryl Streep, Helen Hunt, and Kathy Bates; some, including Steven Spielberg, applauded but stayed in their seats; and some, including Nick Nolte, Ed Harris, and Amy Madigan, stayed seated and unresponsive, their hands still, their gazes accusatory.

Kazan did not make too much of the moment. "I want to thank the Academy for its courage, generosity," he said, noting his long and not always harmonious relationship to the institution. He looked around for Scorsese and De Niro and thanked and hugged them both. Then he declared, "I think I can just slip away," and Frances led him back off the stage.

THAT SUMMER, De Niro surprised Grace Hightower—and delighted gossip columnists—with the news that he wanted a divorce. The couple had always had lifestyle issues, according to whispers, and they were struggling as parents to Elliot, who was exhibiting some developmental difficulties. De Niro was happy to have nannies see to the boy, but Hightower wasn't, and he was said to be frustrated with having forfeited her, in effect, to the child. As per contingencies they'd ironed out before the marriage, they separated, and De Niro bought Hightower a twenty-fifth-floor condo at the Trump Palace on East 69th Street: three bedrooms, a living room with a balcony, a marble Jacuzzi in the master suite, custom built-ins everywhere, plus a set of four storage rooms in the basement. Elliot would live with his mother, and De Niro would be allowed to see him three times a week in the company of Hightower or a nanny.

They hadn't officially divorced, but they seemed to have reached a perfectly civilized entente, traveling and attending events together and seeing each other during holidays; Hightower and Elliot even visited the Montreal set of *The Score* in the summer of 2000. As he had during his separation from Diahnne Abbott, De Niro dated openly; tabloids connected him to Sharon Webb, a Philadelphia TV host, among others.

The following summer, however, the De Niros hit a truly acrimonious patch and made ugly headlines. De Niro filed suit in New York Supreme Court to have his visitation rights amended so that he could see Elliot on his own, including overnight visits at his Tribeca home; what was more, he wanted a legal guardian appointed for the boy. Hightower, he claimed, was unstable and had struck him during a violent outburst on a Florida cruise, fracturing a rib. Hightower's attorneys countered that De Niro had exaggerated, if not entirely fabricated, the attack and his injuries and that *he* was the unstable one, with a lifestyle that included indulgence in alcohol, drugs, and women; he should not be allowed to have Elliot without supervision under any circumstances, they argued.

The conflict spun out of events that occurred in June in Miami on a yacht owned by the actor/singer Marc Anthony and his wife, Dayanara Torres. According to both parties, De Niro and Hightower had brought along Elliot and his twin brothers and everyone was enjoying the day. At some point during the cruise, De Niro went belowdecks and was followed after a time by Hightower, who discovered her husband with the vessel's cook, who was also the wife of the captain. According to De Niro, she was showing him how to close and lock the bathroom door; according to Hightower, she was closing not a door but her blouse, and De Niro had "a frozen look on his face." Hightower stormed back up to the deck, announcing loudly what she'd seen and demanding to be taken back to shore; De Niro followed her, trying to talk to her, and she turned around and struck him, more than once.

In court in July, the pair and their lawyers were strongly encouraged by Judge Judith Gische to iron out their problems as best they could, and they managed to make some progress. But they were unable to reach an agreement on the visitation issues, and Gische ordered them all—De Niro, Hightower, and Elliot—to be evaluated by a court-approved psychologist. It was a situation that only a gossip columnist could enjoy.

—∽∾—

WITH *Analyze This* reaping rewards for him and his production company, De Niro could afford to take a job close to home that gave him a chance to noodle, and that turned out to be *Flawless*, an offbeat story about a retired cop who suffers a stroke and is nursed back to health by his Lower East Side neighbor, a drag queen whose very existence is anathema to the cop's way of thinking. The script was written by Joel Schumacher, the onetime Bloomingdale's window dresser who had directed such hits as *The Lost Boys*, *Falling Down*, and *The Client*. Philip Seymour Hoffman, rising to recognition on the back of his well-regarded stage work and such films as *Scent of a Woman*, *Boogie Nights*, and *Happiness*, was cast as the drag queen. Despite the bold-face names, the film would be made on the down-low and cheap, with a budget under $15 million.

De Niro hadn't truly researched a role in years, and the challenge of playing a stroke victim excited him. He brought the script to neurologists at the Rusk Institute of Rehabilitation Medicine in Manhattan to have them vet it for accuracy in depicting post-stroke recovery. He observed patients at various stages of recuperation and read up on dysarthria, aphasia, physical therapy, and other post-stroke phenomena. And, as with *Awakenings*, he visited his old friend Ed Weinberg to remind himself of how a body frozen by disease functioned.

He worked hard at the details of the role. "He designed weights for his arm so it would hang right," Schumacher said. "He designed four different prostheses for his mouth so it would show his progress over time. He had a therapist on the set, and if he didn't feel that what we were doing was . . . absolutely, totally correct, we did it over." His script was filled with notes about physical business such as "Let lips get rubbery" and "Bannister: cross over to right with left hand." He had specific instructions for himself about how to hold cards in a poker game, how to struggle with making a knot in a tie with one hand, and what to do with his cane.

But *Flawless* would be one of those films in which he would have been better served putting work in on the script, or at least supervising revisions. Schumacher hadn't written a movie since 1985's *St. Elmo's*

Fire, and his work on the page in *Flawless* was hammered when the film was released.

ON A WEEKEND night in late April 1999, in a chair at Gracie Mansion, the traditional home of New York City's mayors, De Niro sat patiently while the city's current chief executive, Rudolph Giuliani, the onetime United States attorney who famously had busted up the traditional Mafia in the 1980s, did impressions of Vito Corleone and Paul Vitti, the gangsters De Niro played in *The Godfather, Part II* and *Analyze This.*

De Niro hadn't come to the stately manor to be entertained. The mayor's sketch was a light moment in the context of a business conversation. De Niro was accompanied by Harvey Weinstein of Miramax Films and was discussing with Giuliani and his top aides a plan to invest $150 million in the Brooklyn Navy Yard, an industrial ghost town of fifteen acres between the Manhattan and Williamsburg Bridges, and build a 700,000-square-foot movie studio—twelve state-of-the-art soundstages just across the river from Manhattan.

De Niro and Weinstein, among many other New York–based filmmakers, had long lamented the dearth of adequate production space in the city. The two most prominent studios, in Astoria, Queens, and on the Chelsea Piers, were almost always being used for such TV series as *Sex and the City, The Sopranos,* and *Law & Order,* and even when empty they weren't quite large enough for big-money movies, which were inevitably filmed in Los Angeles, London, Toronto, or Vancouver. Although New York was becoming a popular filming location, there really wasn't a proper place to make movies there. The historic Navy Yard—built in 1801, birthplace of the USS *Maine* and many other ships, swollen at the height of World War II with seventy-one thousand workers, abandoned in 1966, and in 1970 acquired by the city, which had no pressing use for it—was in many ways a perfect site.

With the Tribeca Film Center an uncontested success a decade into its existence, De Niro was ready to think bigger, and Weinstein, always eager to build more and high off his recent Oscar victory for *Shakespeare in Love,* was if anything even more ambitious. The two had no intention of building a film studio, however, when in the early months of 1999 they were approached by a pair of real estate entrepreneurs, Cary Dean Hart and Louis Madigan, who just the previous year had signed a contract with the city to develop a film studio on the Navy Yard site and were seeking investors. De Niro and Weinstein discussed the possibility at dinner and ran with it. By April, they were able to propose a deal to the city that had almost half of the $150 million attached and would likely prove sexy enough to lure the rest without much effort.

On May 3, in a hastily assembled news conference, Giuliani, De Niro, Weinstein, Hart, Madigan, and others shared the contents of a press release snappily entitled "Mayor Giuliani Announces Major Film and Television Production Facility to Be Built at the Brooklyn Navy Yard—Facility to Serve as Pre-eminent East Coast Film and Television Production Studio and Create Thousands of Film, Television and Construction Jobs." It was a glitzy moment and a wonderful bit of news; De Niro muttered a few carefully noncommittal words to the press, and Giuliani refrained from his gangster movie impersonations. But in the background, Hart and Madigan were unhappy. They had birthed the idea and brought it to De Niro and Weinstein, and they felt that the small percentage they were being offered for their participation didn't reflect their importance to the deal. What's more, they had an ally in Giuliani's office: a deputy mayor who believed that there was a way to finance the deal without the $25 million from the city that the De Niro/Weinstein plan called for—and, perhaps, without De Niro and Weinstein at all.

By midsummer, the rifts between the various parties had widened, and word began leaking into the press that the film studio wouldn't be built as had been advertised on that hopeful May morning. The scale seemed out of whack, for one thing: there were perpetually empty soundstages in Los Angeles, and Miramax and Tribeca didn't generate enough production activity between them to fill a dozen such facilities in New York. Further, the way to make real money in the film biz wasn't to own the factory but to own the *product*—that is, the movies themselves. A huge investment in infrastructure would pay off only if it resulted in hit films, which nobody could promise would be the case.

And lastly, the two factions in City Hall continued to vie against each other, and Giuliani was privately fuming that he hadn't been sufficiently warned about the lack of cohesion among the principals behind the De Niro/Weinstein proposal.

It all came undone in October. Giuliani made another announcement: there would be a film studio at the Brooklyn Navy Yard, but the De Niro/Weinstein faction would not be part of it. Rather, Hart and Madigan would be backed by David S. Steiner, a New Jersey financier who so happened to be a strong supporter of Giuliani's bid to be a United States senator—in a race against Hillary Clinton, whom De Niro and Weinstein happened to endorse. True, the Steiner-backed bid was more favorable financially to the city, but no one who knew Giuliani could believe for a second that political one-upmanship wasn't involved in the calculations.

De Niro, Weinstein, and Jane Rosenthal issued a statement declaring themselves "shocked and perplexed" by the turn of events. Describing the conversations of the spring, they said, "The mayor told us we had a deal, all that remained to do was dot the I's and cross the T's." But a counsel for the city declared, "They had nothing. They had a press conference." And Giuliani, urged by reporters to explain what had happened, reminded them that he was a lawyer and that the announcement they'd seen back in May "says 'explore' at least three times, so it was explored. That's what the word means. It doesn't mean 'agreement.' It doesn't mean 'deal.'"

And it didn't mean "film studio." By the following spring, the Hart/Madigan/Steiner bid had collapsed, in part because Steiner was caught breaking into a judge's chambers to look into the contents of his wife's laptop computer during a divorce action. De Niro and Weinstein moved on to consider sites in New Jersey and Yonkers, neither of which seemed suitable or affordable, though they would have loved to have built outside of the city, according to one participant in their conversations, just to "stick it up Rudy's knickers." It may well have been true, as De Niro and Weinstein said when they were edged out of the deal, that "there is no question that our proposal, from the leading film producers on the East Coast, is better for Brooklyn and the needs of the city," but by 2014 there was still no new film studio in New York.

WHEN HE STOOD beside Elia Kazan on the stage that controversial night of the Oscars, De Niro gave the world at least one thing to think about beyond the morality of Kazan's HUAC testimony: his haircut. Throughout his life, just like his dad, De Niro maintained a full, flowing head of hair, which he could wear flopping into his eyes or back in a ponytail or in a leonine mane. For an actor so possessed by the external details of his characters, it was an immense asset. But that night in March 1999 he had it buzzed down to military length from the sideburns to near the top of his skull, where a thatch of full-grown hair stood untrimmed, neatly parted, like the green tops of a root vegetable. For those who watch the Academy Awards with an eye on fashion rather than film or politics, it was a puzzlement. Clearly he had cut his hair for a role, but was he playing an SS officer? A 1930s chain gang convict? A death row inmate facing the electric chair? No, none of those, but in retrospect, any of them would've been better than the truth.

De Niro had cropped his hair so eccentrically for the unimaginable role of Fearless Leader in the partly animated, partly live-action film *The Adventures of Rocky and Bullwinkle,* a big-screen adaptation of the absurdist, pun-drenched Jay Ward TV cartoon series that had been popular in the 1960s. Even in the age of *The Simpsons* and *Beavis and Butt-head* there was real salt and vinegar in Ward's parody of Cold War espionage, with his title characters, a flying squirrel and moose from rural Minnesota, pitched in constant struggle against their Eastern bloc nemeses, Boris Badenov and Natasha Fatale, and their ruthless master, the Pottsylvanian tyrant Fearless Leader. There had long been interest in developing a feature film of the property, but Ward and then his estate had always held the rights to the characters very closely, and nobody had succeeded.

And then came Jane Rosenthal. She had adored *Rocky and Bullwinkle* as a girl, and her husband, real estate investor Craig Hatkoff, had made a Valentine's Day present to her of the collected series on DVD. She, like others before her, thought there was a potential film in Ward's iconic characters and surreal sensibility, and in 1998 she negotiated a deal with Universal Pictures to acquire the rights and produce a $75 million film for the summer moviegoing season. A script was commissioned from Kenneth Lonergan, the playwright who'd had a hand in *Analyze This* and had some experience in TV animation; he came up with a story in which Ward's heroes and villains were alive in the modern day, after the end of the Cold War and the popular heyday of their TV show, surviving on memories and dwindling royalty checks but still pitted against one another in the final throes of their rivalry. Des McAnuff, a Tony-winning director with a distinguished stage pedigree and a bit of animation on his resume as well (he produced the fine but commercially unsuccessful adaptation of Ted Hughes's *The Iron Giant*), was hired to direct.

As Boris and Natasha, the unlikely pair of Jason Alexander and Rene Russo were cast. That left the matter of Fearless Leader, a role for which Rosenthal thought De Niro was perfect. When she asked him, she recalled, "he really laughed at me. . . . He didn't grow up watching it. It wasn't his thing." But she persisted. "I was always joking with him about it. Then I finally said, 'Okay, you've got to get serious here. It's a three-week role. Do you want it or not?'" Amazingly—perhaps because he knew the film was, as he called it, "Jane's baby"—he did.

Aside from the haircut and specific reminders on how he wished to play the role physically ("hands behind back . . . only mouth moves . . . pinkie out when holding cig holder . . . Von Stroheim collar"), De Niro spent a good deal of time ginning up a vocal approach to the character. Fearless Leader appeared on only a dozen or so pages of the script, but De Niro and a dialect coach worked out a plan for every line, every word, even every vowel and consonant, and transliterated them into an alternative text. The line "How would you like to produce the Rocky and Bullwinkle movie" was thus rendered in De Niro's script: *"Hah-oo woot yoo lyke ta pRa-dyooce dhe Rocky unt bull-wink'll moo-vee?"* And, depressingly, as the inside jokes included jabs at De Niro himself, the following also turned up in the pages: *"Ah yoo tawking to mee? Ah yoo tawking to mee? Ah yoo tawking to mee? Dhen hoo dhe hell elllce ah you tawking . . . Ah yoo tawking to mee? Well eye-eem dhe ohn-lee wahn hih-uh. Hoo dhe fahk doo yoo t'hink yoo-uh tawking too . . . ?"*

The film shot in the first half of 1999 and didn't make it into theaters until the July Fourth weekend of the following year, where it landed with a catastrophic thud. It had been programmed as family fare against two other blockbusters: Wolfgang Petersen's *The Perfect Storm* and Roland Emmerich's *The Patriot.* Both of them trounced *Rocky and Bullwinkle,* as did the previous week's premieres, Aardman's *Chicken Run* and the Farrelly brothers' *Me, Myself and Irene. Rocky and Bullwinkle* opened fifth, with only $6.8 million of box office in its opening weekend and $12 million total in its first full week of release. By the time the thing had lost all its steam, Universal's investment of more than $75 million had resulted in a mere $26 million in ticket sales.

"It was a big disappointment," De Niro reflected with detached understatement. Rosenthal took it much harder. "The failure felt so personal," she said. "I'm always worried about my career, but this wasn't 'I'll never work again,' it was 'I don't know if I *can* work again.'"

As IT TURNED out, *The Adventures of Rocky and Bullwinkle* limped along in theaters until the first days of October, and it was immediately replaced by a De Niro film that wiped all memories of its failure away for everyone involved—save, of course, those who'd endured it.

In some ways, the new film, entitled *Meet the Parents,* was among the least ambitious, least interesting, least challenging, and least accomplished movies De Niro had ever undertaken. But there was no mistake that it was also the most commercially successful film De Niro had ever made. In retrospect, it changed his life, his work, and his image forever.

Analyze This had reminded both critics and audiences that De Niro was a deft comic, but the role of a mafioso, however broadly pitched, was familiar, and the ground covered by the film was well trodden. In *Meet the Parents* and its sequels he would play a generic comic antagonist whose misdeeds and trespasses were somehow pitched as lovable and funny; it was as fake as *Raging Bull* was real, and it was a license to print money.

De Niro was cast as Jack (originally Ben) Byrnes, a retired Connecticut florist with an obsessive need to control things around him, particularly as they relate to his family, and even more particularly as they relate to his daughter, Pam, who is almost unhealthily the apple of his eye. What Jack doesn't know—what the women in his family have, in fact, hidden from him—is that Pam has a live-in boyfriend (strike one), named Gaylord Focker (strike two), a male nurse (strike three) who smokes (strike four) and is willing to do anything to convince Jack of his worthiness as a beau for his daughter (strikes five through infinity). And what nobody in the family knows about Jack is that he was never a florist but rather a CIA agent; when he meets—and takes an instant dislike to—Greg (as Gaylord understandably calls himself), he turns his experience as a spy and a doubter of humanity on him full force.

The broadly farcical script was brought to Tribeca by the indie producer Nancy Tenenbaum; Jane Rosenthal saw the possibilities and enlisted Jay Roach, who'd directed the first two *Austin Powers* films. Supervised by Roach, the script went through various revisions up to the time of shooting, which was done mostly around New York starting in November 1999. (At least one draft was by the team of Alexander Payne and Jim Taylor, who would soon be winning kudos and prizes for the likes of *Election, Sideways,* and *About Schmidt.*) Roach's involvement led to Ben Stiller coming aboard to play Greg. Teri Polo would play Pam, Stiller's chum and frequent co-star Owen Wilson would play Pam's former beau (and Jack's preferred prospective son-in-law), and Blythe Danner would play Jack's wife, Dina, replacing Beverly D'Angelo just a month or so before production.

There was almost nothing required of him in preparing to play the role. Not only was Jack Byrnes drawn thinly, but his one complex attribute—that he'd been a spy—drew upon De Niro's relatively recent experience making *Ronin,* in which he had profited from the technical advice of Milt Bearden, an espionage veteran who was still consulting with him about prospective film projects. De Niro's notes for the character and for bits of physical business and line readings were, by his standards, minimal. He was credited as a producer, yes, but Jane Rosenthal was doing the heavy lifting at Tribeca. In most regards, in short, it was a sleepwalk.

And it was an immense and instantaneous hit. *Meet the Parents* was released on October 6, 2000, to generally appreciative reviews and massive box office. Its opening weekend gross of $28.6 million accounted for more than half of its estimated $55 million budget and was more than one and a half times the earnings of its nearest competitor, the football story *Remember the Titans.* The film held the top slot at the North American box office for three more weekends, finally falling to second place behind *Charlie's Angels* en route to a total domestic gross of $166 million and a global box office of $164 million. De Niro's previous record box office, $107 million for *Analyze This*, couldn't compare, and his third-highest grosser, *Cape Fear*, with $79 million, represented less than half. After more than thirty years in the movies, he was well and truly a box office superstar. On the strength of the performance of *Analyze This*, he had been paid $13.5 million to star in *Meet the Parents*, and his potential earnings as the film's producer would equal or even surpass that impressive sum.

If De Niro was uniquely poised to play Paul Vitti in *Analyze This*, which capitalized on his decades of playing gangsters with real comic relish, the role of Jack Burns, the former CIA profiler (and, by the way, Vietnam POW), is so generic that anyone might have played him. Oh, De Niro's solidity and history of menacing roles definitely figure in the part, if only as a kind of residue that inevitably accrues to his screen persona. But there's no reason that, say, Gene Hackman or Harrison Ford or Tommy Lee Jones or Michael Douglas or Al Pacino couldn't have played the part, for instance. Jack Burns has no particular ethnicity, no eccentric tics, no dark obsessions, no unforgettable bits of business; any reasonably capable actor who generically fit the description of the character could have played him and, probably, had just as big a hit.

The film is really about the uncanny ability of Greg Focker to do the wrong thing—verbally, physically—in just the wrong spot at just the wrong time. In the film's most riotous sequence, a truly fine movie gag that Buster Keaton or Blake Edwards would have been proud to build, Focker opens a bottle of champagne, and the cork knocks over an urn containing Jack's mother's ashes, which, scattered on the floor, are immediately used as kitty litter by the precious Mr. Jinx. The uproarious moment is built of details laid carefully in the script up to that time—and having almost nothing to do with the human qualities of the characters. It's hilarious, but, like much of the film, it's mechanical.

De Niro is drolly funny, no doubt: "I have nipples, Greg. Could you milk me?"; "As long as you can keep your mouth shut for the rest of your life, you're in no immediate danger"; "A dog is very easy to break"; and a series of jibes about Focker's suspected drug use. But nothing of it seems organic or specific to him as an actor. He's a piece of a vehicle—a slick, breezy, and, as it happens, insanely popular vehicle, but a vehicle nonetheless. In time, generations of young moviegoers would come to him first as Jack Byrnes, knowing nothing about Johnny Boy Civello or Vito Corleone or Travis Bickle or Jake LaMotta or even Al Capone. Whether he had been aiming for it or not, he had finally achieved truly massive box office success, and all it cost him was the accrued aura built of his life's work.

THE MONEY THAT flowed from *Meet the Parents* helped Tribeca jump-start a number of ventures. The company had acquired the rights to Nick Hornby's novel *About a Boy* before it was published, and they went ahead to film it in London, quite well, with Hugh Grant in the lead and the Weitz brothers, Chris and Paul, who'd made the *American Pie* films, directing. Also in London, Tribeca backed a stage extravaganza (*play* didn't seem to be the right word) based on the music of Freddy Mercury and Queen, *We Will Rock You*, which proved a massive hit, being performed nonstop in London for more than a decade and traveling all over the world, in traditional theaters and sports arenas, well into the 2010s. De Niro was a classic rock guy himself, but there was nothing wrong with a little glam, particularly when audiences ate it up so appreciatively.

26

ON JULY 27, 2000, VIRGINIA ADMIRAL PASSED AWAY IN NEW York at age eighty-five, and in keeping with the silence in which she preferred to live—"I want to keep my life *my life*," she'd once told a reporter—the news didn't reach the *New York Times* until August 15. She had been a formidable woman, active in the arts (especially her own painting), a vocal participant in political issues, and busy with her various real estate deals. At various times she had owned buildings in several lower Manhattan neighborhoods, some quite well known in bohemian circles and some further beyond, such as the building that housed Gerdes Folk City up until the club was evicted for excessive noise in 1986. She had never remarried, but she had been present in the life of her only son, not quite a matron but a part of his circle. Near the end of her life, she had even gone door-to-door for him among his neighbors in Montauk, asking if they would mind if De Niro expanded his house (her efforts failed). De Niro never rhapsodized about her as he did his father, but he was filially respectful and, in his fashion, connected.

While Admiral passed away quietly, her onetime husband and life-long partner continued to be in the spotlight nearly a decade after his death, and not only because of his son's movie world fame. Through the 1990s and the first decade of the 2000s, the elder De Niro's work was exhibited in solo and group shows throughout the United States and in France, Italy, Spain, Portugal, and Japan. Along with these came catalogue publications, often with essays filled with reminiscences of the man and insights into his work, culminating in a large and handsome hardbound volume in 2004. The book included photographs of the painter, biographical and critical writings about his life and art, and reproductions of scores of his works in a variety of media, including his poetry and art criticism.

By then, the elder De Niro's reputation had taken on far more luster than it had at any time in his life after that first flush of glory in the 1940s—a classic instance of the stereotypical artist-neglected-in-his-lifetime. In 1995, the critic Peter Schjeldahl wrote, "I feel indebted to Robert De Niro Sr. . . . for many glancing hits of pleasure over the last 30 years. . . . He was a New York treasure." And a decade later, a critic of a completely opposed sensibility, Hilton Kramer, wrote:

> *Not only as a painter and a draftsman, but as a writer, too, he displayed a profligate talent that was designed to sweep us off our feet—and sometimes even succeeded in doing so. As a painter, De Niro aspired to nothing less than competition with the Old Masters . . . and as a writer on art he was often a more penetrating critic than many professionals.*

As HIS FATHER'S reputation continued to swell, De Niro's continued to ebb. For decades De Niro had been known as a chameleon, able to transform himself wholly into someone else, someone he'd never been before. He didn't do it as often as he used to; there was more mannerism and repetition in his work in his fifties than there had ever been before. He was still respected, although not so unconditionally as once. But his most daring transformations seemed to be well behind him, *Cape Fear* notwithstanding.

Now that he was doing comedies, in fact, his various screen personae became a ripe target of spoofs. Roles such as Travis Bickle, Michael Vronsky, Jake LaMotta, and Al Capone had become so enshrined as cultural icons that they were ripe for parody, or at least gentle comedy. The old, frighteningly immersive De Niro, apparently so at home in roles teetering on madness, was far enough in the past to have lost any sense of threat. And the new comic De Niro—softer, more domesticated, familiar—bore habits and tics that were endearing or at least comforting, rather than frightening or intimidating.

As a result, he was becoming a favorite subject of impressionists and others seeking to make a little bit of comic hay by imitating his physical and vocal manner. The most famous of these—and one of the earliest and best—was Frank Caliendo, an impersonator of genuine talent and range (he did John Madden *and* Charles Barkley, for instance). His De Niro, like so many others in its wake, began with the eyes and cheeks—an exaggerated squint and a tight, furtive smile, often rendered with the shoulders slightly hunched, the head slightly bobbing, the hands upraised in a "whattaya want from me" gesture. You could do De Niro by simply mugging with your face clenched and your head nodding, saying nothing, and people could still see it. But there were standard lines, too: "You talking to me?" of course, and "Never knocked me down, Ray," plus the baseball bat scene from *The Untouchables* and the "You insulted him a little bit" business from *Goodfellas*.

An apotheosis of sorts of this kind of thing came on MTV's *Celebrity Deathmatch*, a TV comedy series in which movie stars and their ilk engaged in professional wrestling bouts rendered in Claymation. In 1999, the show pitted De Niro against Al Pacino in a match refereed by the rotund Marlon Brando and following the rule that the combatants needed to talk and fight in the personae of characters they'd played. De Niro was the winner, fighting as Jake LaMotta and Travis Bickle before transforming into Al Capone and using Brando's minute sidekick from *The Island of Dr. Moreau* as a baseball bat with which to smash his rival's head clear off. (And it was done quite funnily and intelligently, in fact.)

An even stranger use of De Niro's manner and aura came to light in November 2001 when a fifty-one-year-old New Jersey man named Joseph Manuella, who bore a genuinely striking resemblance to his movie hero, was arrested on two counts of criminal impersonation after he posed as De Niro and convinced an upstate New York man who operated a private museum dedicated to Vietnam veterans to build sets on his property for a film about the war. Manuella, billing himself as De Niro, met with Vietnam vets in the region, asking them to share stories of their experiences, promising them considerations and payoffs when the movie got made; he got free meals and hotel rooms in exchange for autographs. His victim, who was living on a military pension, finally began to realize that the "star" wasn't who he said he was when he started griping about having to lay out $300 of his own money to purchase supplies.

A few years later, a short documentary about Manuella and a Joe Pesci impersonator named Mario Occhicone was actually submitted to the Tribeca Film Festival; in one scene, Manuella was shown carefully applying a mole to his right cheek to enhance his De Niro–ish appearance. De Niro and the festival had no comment about the film, but De Niro's lawyer, Tom Harvey, was happy to offer a comment on Manuella: "He's pathetic, and it's sad that he hasn't learned his lesson. I hope he seeks help."

THE STUNNING SUCCESS of *Meet the Parents* overshadowed De Niro's next picture, a rather by-the-book biopic of a significant but overlooked pioneer of racial equality, Carl Brashear, the first black sailor to attain the rank of master diver in the United States Navy. Born to a Kentucky dirt-farming family, Brashear had tried to join the army just before it was fully integrated in 1948; rebuffed, he entered the navy and was assigned to menial duties. But he was fascinated by the work of salvage divers and requested admission to diving school, an assignment that was denied him more than a hundred times, by his count, before he was finally admitted in 1954. He continued to run into racial barriers—both institutional and personal—in diving school and, after he graduated, in the active ranks. But he continued to rise, working at the requisite academic exercises and mastering deep sea diving techniques until in 1964 he achieved the rank of first-class diver.

Two years later, helping to recover a hydrogen bomb that had fallen to the bottom of the Mediterranean after a plane crash, he nearly died in an accident caused by equipment failure. He survived only by agreeing to have his left leg amputated. After being fitted with a prosthesis, he refused to leave the service, insisting that he could do the same work he'd done before his accident and just as well. He went through grueling tests to prove himself, including walking twelve steps unassisted while wearing three hundred pounds of diving equipment inside a naval courtroom, before being reinstated. His designation as a master diver followed in 1970.

Brashear's story came to De Niro and Tribeca in 1996 under the title *Navy Diver*, with the thought that De Niro would play a composite character built out of the bigoted senior officers who made Brashear's progress so difficult. But it wasn't until three years later that it became a tenable reality when Cuba Gooding Jr., an Oscar for *Jerry Maguire* on his mantle, agreed to play the lead. It was touch-and-go for a bit— Gooding was in and then he wasn't. But finally, in the summer of 1999, the film was shot in Oregon, Washington, and British Columbia under the eyes of director George Tillman Jr., who had a family-reunion film, *Soul Food*, as his best-known feature credit.

De Niro was cast as Master Chief Billy Sunday, a son of the South with a ferocious drinking problem married to a younger woman whose own boozy, flirtatious behavior brought out the worst in her husband. Charlize Theron, still better known for her beauty than her talent, was cast as his wife, Gwen, after the likes of Hope Davis, Kelly Lynch, Julia Ormond, Sheryl Lee, Mimi Rogers, Virginia Madsen, and Elizabeth Perkins read for the role.

De Niro was provided by Tillman and screenwriter Scott Marshall Smith with extensive notes comparing the script to the actual details of Brashear's life and with item-by-item comparisons of the lives of Brashear and the (fictional) Sunday. But he was chiefly interested in the character's Arkansas dialect, in the alcoholic codependency of Sunday and his wife, and in the details of diving. He took a course in commercial diving in Seattle and achieved a diploma in surface-supplied air and helium diving from the Divers Institute of Technology. He was put up in a rented private home while shooting in and around Portland, Oregon, and Vancouver, British Columbia, and Grace and Elliott came to stay with him, the baby's toys and crib and such shipped west at the production's expense.

As Gooding recalled, De Niro took to the role of a military taskmaster so seriously that the real servicemen hired to play extras were cowed by him. "He was walking in front of us," the actor said, "and there were some 25 soldiers in front of him, and a good majority were Navy SEALs—big, strong guys. He messed up one of his lines, and one of them laughed. But he stayed right in character and went up to him and demanded, 'What the fuck!' and scared the hell out of the guy. The next day, every single extra was performing just like he was in the military."

When the film, retitled *Men of Honor*, showed up in theaters in November 2000, it was recognized as earnest but unexceptional, doing a semirespectable $49 million at the box office, where *Meet the Parents* was still going strong.

BEFORE SPENDING ALL that time in the water on the West Coast to make *Men of Honor*, De Niro worked on a more or less routine police thriller shot mainly in New York and entitled *15 Minutes* after Andy Warhol's famous precept about the nature of celebrity in the modern world. The film was written in the early 1990s by its eventual director, John Herzfeld, as a caustic look at the phenomenon of instant celebrity that became increasingly common in the age of reality television. It focused on a pair of East European criminals who come to New York to film themselves committing heinous crimes. A cop (De Niro) and fire marshal (Edward Burns) combine forces to track the bad guys down as the crime spree grows increasingly awful.

At this point, De Niro had played enough roles of this sort in enough films of this type that he did very little in the way of extra preparation or research. Arguably, he was the least involved he'd been in any film role he'd undertaken up to this time. The hardest task he faced, in fact, was a chase scene, shot on Madison Avenue, in which he did his own stunt work despite the summertime heat soaring into the triple digits. ("He earned his money that day," Herzfeld said.) The film was shot and in the can for more than a year before being released by New Line Pictures in the slow season of late winter 2001; it grossed $24.4 million against a budget of nearly double that size.

MEET THE PARENTS was still atop the box office charts when De Niro's agents negotiated another pay raise for a film that promised to be many of the things that *Meet the Parents* never even tried to be. *The Score* was based on a script that was ultimately credited to the combined efforts of Lem Dobbs, Kario Salem, Scott Marshall Smith, and Daniel E. Taylor, although there would be several more hands involved in it along the way, including one of the principal stars. It centered on Nick, a Montreal jazz club owner and veteran thief who agrees to engage in one final heist as a favor to his old fence, Max. The two, along with Jack, a young upstart who has ambitions to be a master crook like the older men, have plans to steal a one-of-a-kind jewel-encrusted scepter. Nick doesn't want to undertake the job because he doesn't trust the kid and he has a girlfriend who wishes he would quit the life of crime.

Nobody was asking De Niro to quit his line of work. Mandelay Pictures gave him $15 million to play Nick and allowed him to revamp the script. Frank Oz, the former Muppeteer (and voice of Yoda) who had directed such popular comedies as *Bowfinger, Dirty Rotten Scoundrels, What About Bob?*, and *In and Out*, had Ben Affleck in mind to play Jack. But Affleck bowed out, penning a heartfelt letter to De Niro saying that he didn't feel he was up to the challenge ("If I'm going to work with an actor of your caliber, I'd better be great—and this is not a role I can be great in"). Affleck was soon replaced by Edward Norton, an exciting young actor with two Oscar nominations in his first five films. And then Mandelay scored a truly tremendous coup in casting the world-weary Max: Marlon Brando, who had barely made a film since 1996's risible *The Island of Dr. Moreau*, agreed, after a two-hour meeting with Oz, to join the party.

The film would shoot on location in Montreal between May, when rehearsals started, and September 2000. De Niro was committed to the longest spell—sixty-eight days before the cameras, compared to Norton's forty-one and Brando's twelve. But the producers made him comfortable, outfitting his rented home with gym equipment and vintage wines and flying Toukie Smith and the twins up to visit him. Montreal suited him—foreign yet familiar, Old World yet with a touch of New York.

Would that anyone had been able to make the director feel similarly content. From the get-go, Oz was under the cosh, with Brando leading the assault, Norton creating drama, and De Niro, a relative gentleman, standing to the side. The original script had a tongue-in-cheek tenor (Brando's Max, for instance, was depicted as a flamboyant old queen), and at De Niro's urging, the ensuing rewrites aimed at a grittier feel, not noir, exactly, but more realistic and character-driven. When the cast showed up for rehearsal, though, they weren't entirely satisfied that the transformation was complete. There were rewrites during the shoot. Norton was famous for insisting he be allowed to work on scripts, which he did with Smith throughout his time in Montreal, fixing not only his scenes but the overall structure and tone. De Niro, characteristically focused on the veracity of details, read up on thieves, safecrackers, and cat burglars and even hired an ex-burglar as a consultant to help write revisions of the robbery scenes. (As Norton put it later, "It was a studio affair and it did have the limitations of a lot of people standing around opining about it.") During the shoot, the three stars, famous for their love of actorly exploration on the set, for ignoring the pages, and for immersing themselves in the reality of the moment as it struck them, noodled to such an extent that two full weeks were added to the schedule.

And Brando? He made life merry hell for his director. Everyone knew the stories: how he wouldn't learn his lines but rather had himself cued by bits of paper with dialogue on them taped around the set or even on the actual bodies of his fellow actors; how he often didn't even know the plots of his films when he showed up to work, and frequently challenged the basic story line even when so much footage had been shot that no deep changes could be made; how he kept himself secluded and unavailable on days when he was on set, holed up in a trailer watching TV and, O brave new world, surfing the Internet; how he reviled the press and the movie business and, it would seem, his very collaborators. He was the most revolutionary—and arguably the greatest—American actor since World War II, yet he seemed contemptuous of acting, of filmmaking, of show business, of the people around him, of himself. Getting him to appear in the film was a coup, yes, but it was also a recipe for stress, crisis, and pain—and maybe, *maybe*, some flashes of genius in front of the camera.

Considering the strange ways in which their careers intertwined— in addition to growing up venerating Brando's movies and studying with his acting teacher, Stella Adler, De Niro literally quoted

Brando's two Oscar-winning performances in his own Oscar-winning performances—it must have felt like a kind of fulfillment for De Niro to get to work with the master. He knew him only slightly, and—judging by the way he talked about it—the visit he'd made to Brando's island with Scorsese some fifteen years prior hadn't been an entirely idyllic one. But they had a real bond, and Brando respected him and his work and treated him well. Too, both of the older stars felt sufficient kinship with Norton to treat him as a peer.

But Oz was made to suffer as if he had somehow personally been responsible for every inanity, injustice, and inconvenience Brando had ever suffered in the movie business. The two clashed immediately over tone: Brando appeared for his first scene almost campily attired, made up, and pitched, and Oz had to ask him, run-through after run-through, take after take, to be less froufy. Brando complied, to a point and never happily, frankly telling Oz, in front of the whole crew, "Fuck you," and referring to the director openly as "Miss Piggy" (one of the characters that Oz had invented and voiced for *Sesame Street*). "I bet you wish I was a puppet so you could stick your hand up my ass and make me do what you want," he declared. He insisted on playing some scenes pantsless (he was overcome by the heat and humidity of Montreal), forcing Oz to shoot him from the waist up. Finally he refused to work with Oz present in the room at all, forcing De Niro and an assistant director to act as go-betweens while Oz himself sat in another room watching the goings-on via monitors.

Time reported all of this sensational stuff just before the film's July 2001 release, and word spilled into the media everywhere (how could it not?), which meant that Paramount Pictures had to do some damage control. In statements from the producers, Norton, and Oz, the studio tried to make Brando's behavior seem like part of the creative process, the stress that turns coal into diamonds: "The assumption that conflict is bad is wrong," Norton said. "It's just creative wrestling." Even though he was clearly the aggrieved party, Oz more or less apologized to Brando in both *Time* and the *New York Times*: "I probably could have handled it better. I wish I had done things differently," and words to that effect.

There are a number of good reasons to lament the lost opportunity of *The Score*: the combination of Brando and De Niro promises some-thing titanic, even so long after Brando had effectively forsaken even the least hint of trying to be good at the work and when De Niro, too, seemed to see acting more as a paying gig than a form of personal ex-pression. They have a few scenes together: a breezy one near the start of the picture in which Brando's Max tries to cajole De Niro's Nick into taking the job, and a sweaty, desperate one near the end, when Nick comes to see how badly Max needs the caper to succeed. But there's nothing as crackling as the cup-of-coffee scene De Niro and Pacino shared in *Heat*, which, even in its elusive, low-wattage fashion, truly played like a confrontation-slash-meeting of acting styles and fleshed-out characters.

In fact, *The Score* is a much sketchier and more mechanical enter-prise than *Heat*, a talky variation of such caper films as *Rififi* and *The Asphalt Jungle*. The actual robbery isn't especially gripping, and the film gets distracted by Nick's romance (with a flight attendant played by Angela Bassett) and by his battle for supremacy with Norton's Jack. And if it's appropriate that Oz gives so much time over to Jack's mas-querade as the palsied janitor's assistant, Brian, it still feels like a cheat because the names of two of the greatest screen actors of all time are on the marquee. Once again, De Niro manages to impart a sense of weight with judicious reserve, probing gazes, and almost as much si-lence as chatter. But it's a role he could have performed in his sleep, and, given the *mishegoss* of the production, he may well have wished that he had.

And yet, despite mixed reviews, the conclave of acting giants drew audiences. *The Score* opened strongly and went on to earn $71 million domestically and more than $40 million abroad—an even more suc-cessful take than the heist it depicted.

27

H E WAS SPENDING TIME AT HOME, ENJOYING A RELATIVELY sedate year, his burning drive to work somewhat quenched by the global receipts for *Meet the Parents*, going about the daily routines he liked to observe when he wasn't off somewhere making or selling a film: jogging along the West Side Highway, walking to the office, dropping into one of the restaurants he owned for a bit of lunch, doing something with the kids, dining out or attending some sort of event in the evening with a date on his arm—often his estranged wife. The summer was just about over, and he wasn't using the beach house or the country house much. It was a crisp and clear Tuesday, and he had to be at the Film Center first thing in the morning.

And then he went home and watched the world change.

"I left a meeting right after they hit the World Trade Center," he remembered. "I went to my apartment, which looks south, and I watched it out my window. I could see the line of fire across the North Tower. I had my binoculars and a video camera—though I didn't want to video it. I saw a few people jump. Then I saw the South Tower go. It was so unreal. I had to confirm it by immediately looking at the television screen. CNN was on. That was the only way to make it real. Like my son said, 'It was like watching the moon fall.'"

The twin towers of the World Trade Center had dominated the view from his home for decades, and now they were gone. Like everyone else, he was uncomprehending, wounded, mystified, helpless. But he felt it a little more personally than many others. It was his neighborhood that had been hit—he lived only about eight blocks north of Ground Zero—and it was devastated.

He reacted well in a crisis. First thing was cleanup and recovery, and he and Drew Nieporent made a commitment to feed the rescue workers at the site of the attack, serving thousands of meals of sandwiches and hot soup and getting the food through the streets from the kitchen to Ground Zero by avoiding the streets altogether: they ferried it along the Hudson, installing a makeshift kitchen on one of the daytime cruise ships that in normal times offered tours of the city.

When fund-raising telethons and events took place, De Niro was present without hesitation: the *America: A Tribute to Heroes* program, broadcast on more than thirty TV and cable networks, and the Madison Square Garden concert and telethon honoring first responders. He appeared in a new round of "I Love New York" ads aimed at getting tourists to commence visiting the city anew. When a documentary commemorating the attacks was made for television, he served as its narrator.

The devastation appeared never to be far from his mind. In October, when he was presented with recognition for lifetime achievement at the Gotham Awards, an event hosted by the Independent Feature Project to celebrate New York moviemaking, he said tersely, "Proud as I am of this, it seems not as important after what has happened."

Quietly, he was crafting a bigger response. He and Rosenthal were planning an event that would focus positive attention on lower Manhattan, even as a wound lay gaping in what used to be its most visible point. It would be a means to bring people, money, and constructive energy to a neighborhood that still seemed like a tomb weeks after the attacks. "Bob felt personally insulted by what happened down here," reflected Harvey Weinstein, and De Niro and Rosenthal were determined to respond.

They had in mind a film festival to be held the following spring, focusing, like Robert Redford's Sundance Film Festival, on independent moviemaking. They discovered that the name Tribeca Film Festival was already being used, as a placeholder if nothing else; there was even a fledgling website dedicated to it. Through the aegis of the not-for-profit Tribeca Film Institute, they negotiated with the founder of that enterprise, the artist Nicole Bartelme, to buy the title, and in December, De Niro, Rosenthal, New York governor George Pataki, Martin

Scorsese, Meryl Streep, and others held a press event to announce the first Tribeca Film Festival for the following spring, with American Express stepping in as the chief sponsor to the tune of a couple of million dollars.

At first they said they'd program forty features and a similar number of shorts, but when they finally got around to announcing the full lineup in the spring of 2002, the festival boasted 150 titles, shorts and features combined, culled from more than 1,500 submissions. There were world premieres, including Tribeca's own production of *About a Boy*, featuring Hugh Grant in an adaptation of a bestselling novel by Nick Hornby, and *Insomnia*, a remake of a Swedish crime thriller starring Al Pacino and directed by Christopher Nolan. There were independent films from around the world. There were films with themes drawn from the experience of September 11, an entire block of children's films, and a restoration of Elia Kazan's *Viva Zapata* anchoring a selection of classic films curated by Scorsese. The judges for the awards included Helen Hunt, Kevin Spacey, Frances McDormand, Barry Levinson, Julian Schnabel, Isaac Mizrahi, and Richard Holbrooke; speakers on the various panels dotting the festival would include Susan Sarandon, Alan Alda, and Sidney Lumet. And the event was granted a massive boost when George Lucas agreed to a premiere screening of *Star Wars: Episode II—Attack of the Clones* as the centerpiece of a closing-night gala.

Rosenthal wasn't entirely sure they could pull it off. "I keep reminding myself I'm going to make mistakes," she said. "I know that no matter what I do, some important person will feel snubbed. I just hope people will understand we're only doing this to try to help downtown." Whether there were any bruised egos among the boldface names or not, the moviegoing public responded to the glitter, the hoopla, and the chance to reclaim lower Manhattan. More than 150,000 tickets were sold to the screenings, talks, and parties, a truly impressive number considering that the festival ran a mere five days. There were grumblings about "Hollywood East" and about how few films actually made in the neighborhood were included in the festival, but these were relatively few, and the thing was undeniably a hit.

They decided to make it a yearly event. "This neighborhood is my home," De Niro said. "I'm committed to it, and that's what this festival is about." In 2003, there were more than 200 films in the festival; the following year, they broke the 250-film barrier and augmented the springtime film festival with the first (and only) Tribeca Theater Festival in October, a fortnight of plays, readings, and discussions. By 2006, the total number of titles in the film festival had climbed to 274, which turned out to be the high-water mark. Over time, festival organizers pared back just slightly to an average of some 200 titles per year.

The trick for Tribeca was to distinguish itself from all the world's other film festivals, especially the biggies like Sundance (held in January in Park City, Utah), Berlin (February), Cannes (May on the French Riviera), Venice (August), and Toronto (September). Each had its own peculiar identity, history, savor. Tribeca seemed a mishmash in comparison: not curated to represent a small selection of high-quality work, like Venice or the venerable New York Film Festival (October at Lincoln Center); not a market for emerging talent or work available to purchase, like Sundance or Cannes; too early in the year to serve as a launching pad for awards season, like Toronto.

Jane Rosenthal liked to remind the press that there was a reason for the festival to exist beyond the movie screen. "It wasn't started as a traditional film festival," she said. "My sole goal was to bring people back downtown." But a decade on, downtown Manhattan was fully alive again, and the festival was moving along under its own momentum. De Niro came, rightly, to see it as part of his legacy, "part of the tradition of New York, part of the fabric, that I hope will be what it will be in years to come."*

—⁂—

---

* Some years later, the Tribeca Film Festival expanded well beyond walking distance of the Tribeca Film Center and Ground Zero. From 2009 to 2012, in partnership with the Qatar Museums Authority and the Doha Film Institute, there was a Doha Tribeca Film Festival, an effort to bridge the cultures of the Arab and Western worlds across the rupture that was defined in part by the September 11 attacks. The festival proved sufficiently successful that Tribeca pulled out of it in 2013, satisfied that it had helped launch a sustainable event that would continue to grow and to encourage filmmaking in the region.

AFTER MORE THAN thirty years in the movies, his became one of those names people thought of when they thought about giving awards. One of the most prestigious was the Life Achievement Award of the American Film Institute, which had been presented in a gala (filmed for television) since 1973 to such icons as John Ford, Orson Welles, Frank Capra, Alfred Hitchcock, Bette Davis, Barbara Stanwyck, Elizabeth Taylor, Jack Lemmon, Sidney Poitier, Gregory Peck, Kirk Douglas, and, in his own generation, Steven Spielberg, Jack Nicholson, Dustin Hoffman, Barbra Streisand, and Martin Scorsese. In late 2002, the AFI announced that De Niro would be presented with the honor the following spring, and the ensuing gala was as pomp-filled as could be hoped for.

De Niro was lauded by a range of his collaborators and friends, from Scorsese ("He has an extraordinary genius to be able to transform himself, to simply be, just *be* the person he's playing, not act but become and command and inhabit the character") to Jodie Foster, who remembered his transformative instruction on the set of *Taxi Driver* ("Although I had already been working for nine years, no one had ever trusted that I was capable of understanding what an actor really does. . . . I am grateful to you, Bob. You make a fine Henry Higgins"). There were Joe Pesci, Robin Williams, Leonardo DiCaprio, Billy Crystal, Harvey Keitel, Edward Norton, and James Woods, the last of whom brought down the house by describing *Once Upon a Time in America* as being about "an older man reviewing his life as a thug—not unlike tonight." The evening began on a solemn note with a filmed appearance by Gregory Peck, who had died earlier that day at age eighty-seven. And when De Niro finally spoke at night's end, he brought the affair full circle: "This isn't easy for me, but it isn't so bad as I look back on my life and all these movies. . . . Good night, and good night, Gregory Peck."

The following year, he accepted an award for his civic work from the Citizens Committee for New York and agreed to be toasted and lightly roasted at a dinner benefiting the American Museum of the Moving Image. You could do good things simply by putting on a tuxedo and saying a few words, he'd learned; though he never lost his reputations for reclusiveness and recalcitrance, he willingly attended such events as these and the many, many events to which Grace Hightower dragged him in her capacity as a philanthropist and socialite.

AND WHILE OTHERS were celebrating him, he came to celebrate himself. As he approached his sixties, with decades of moviemaking behind him, he confronted his lifelong pack-rat tendencies and discovered that he'd amassed a treasure. Since the days when he had first cluttered up his mother's 14th Street apartment with all those thrift store costumes, he had built, almost accidentally, a huge archive of materials to do with his acting career, his business ventures, and the simple stuff of life: not only written materials such as scripts and memos and research notes but trunkloads of costumes and props from his film career, from the baseball bat used by Al Capone in *The Untouchables* to the garish suits from *Casino*, boxing gloves from *Raging Bull*, and old makeup kits to which he ascribed some sentimental value.

It was an impressive collection—invaluable, truly—but what in the world to do with it? The first inkling he had that there was real worth in it came in 2001, when the American Museum of the Moving Image in Queens worked with him to mount an exhibit dedicated to his collection. *Robert De Niro: Costume and Character* opened in February 2002 and ran for the better part of a year, drawing tens of thousands of visitors through a truly unique tour of an actor's work as seen, in effect, from the inside out. De Niro may no longer have been making the epochal sorts of films that launched him, but it was clear that even his lesser roles had consumed him at the level of character creation. Costumer Rita Ryack, who dressed him for several films, remarked on the wardrobe he wore in *The Fan*, much of which came from J. C. Penney's: "He looked like a million bucks. He'd say, 'This suit looks too expensive,' and we'd say, 'But it cost $125 and it's made from Teflon!' He just looks really good in clothing; he just has the kind of shoulders that make him dress wonderfully. So you have to work very hard to dress him down—that's an interesting challenge."

The collection made curators around the country aware of what kind of treasure De Niro was sitting on, and they came courting. Finally, in 2005, he reached an agreement with the Harry Ransom Center of the University of Texas, Austin, a massive research facility filled with manuscripts, artifacts, and every imaginable sort of original material from significant figures in literature, art, politics, theater, and film. The Ransom Center's jewels included items from Stella Adler, David Mamet, and others whose lives and work touched on De Niro's (Paul Schrader's papers would eventually find a home there, too). And De Niro's bequest was one of the largest in the collection: two eighteen-wheelers delivered wardrobe cases, trunks, and literally hundreds of banker's boxes filled with notes, memos, letters, annotated scripts, photographs, sketches, and so forth, dating from his days in student theater and dinner theater in the 1960s through the films he made in 2005.

He was up for donating material, even very revealing material, but he could not be persuaded to tell his story on the page. In early 2004, word surfaced that De Niro and Scorsese would co-author a memoir about the eight films they'd made together and some of the issues that bonded them, such as growing up in Manhattan and losing their fathers (Charles Scorsese, a staple character in his son's films, died at age eighty just months after the senior Robert De Niro passed; they were in the same hospital at the same time during their final illnesses, and De Niro always made a point of dropping in on the elder Scorsese whenever he visited his own dad). The book never surfaced, though, and in 2013 De Niro declared that he simply wouldn't know where to begin his memoirs and that he couldn't imagine he'd ever write them.

IT WAS OFTEN remarked that De Niro had stopped working hard in the 1980s, perhaps with *Raging Bull*. But the films he made in that decade, which included some of his finest if less-recognized performances, simply didn't bear that out. He had done *The King of Comedy*, *The Untouchables*, *Once Upon a Time in America*, *True Confessions*, and so on: a film a year, more or less, of some palpable quality. Nor, in fact, did his work in the 1990s constitute sleepwalking: there were more films than ever, and if the roles were not as challenging, the productions were, in the main, ambitious and varied and nearly always had something of genuine interest either in the subject matter or, especially, the collaborators. In those ten years, he almost always worked with notable directors: three Scorseses, two Levinsons, a Mann, a Tarantino, a Frankenheimer, a Cuarón, a Branagh, and so on.

But after the success of *Meet the Parents*, the arithmetic he did in choosing roles changed, and he began making films out of dubious material with scripts and co-stars and directors that left audiences puzzling why De Niro was involved. He was accused of taking roles to support Tribeca, but *Meet the Parents* and *We Will Rock You* were hits, and the production company wasn't so big as to require constant cash infusions. He had multiple homes, children with three women, and a deluxe lifestyle to support, and that might explain some of the pace of his work. But it didn't necessarily explain the quality of the projects. His peers—Al Pacino, Dustin Hoffman, Gene Hackman, Jack Nicholson—also appeared often in films that seemed lesser than their talents could command. But De Niro outdid them all in frequency, and, alas, in the relatively low ambitions of the material he seemed again and again to select.

The first film to truly mark a dip in his interest in his work was *City by the Sea*, a potboiler by *This Boy's Life* director Michael Caton-Jones based on an *Esquire* magazine article by Mike McAlary about Vincent LaMarca, a homicide detective who learns that his son is wanted for murder. James Franco was cast as the younger LaMarca, which sounds like an exciting possibility until you realize that most of their scenes together are telephone conversations, with each actor standing on a set alone on what was probably the other fellow's day off.

The $60 million production was shot during the winter of 2000–2001 and held from release until September 2002, when it grossed a mere $22.4 million and scored the rare coup of angering the residents of two New York–area beach towns: Long Beach, Long Island, where the film was set and the real-life events actually took place, and Asbury Park, New Jersey, where it was filmed. People in both places felt their respective communities were made to seem more squalid and dangerous than they really were. They could take comfort in the knowledge, then, that very few moviegoers had bothered to leave themselves open to the possibility of acquiring that impression.

After just a few months off, De Niro was playing a cop again in *Showtime*, which shot in the spring of 2001 and was released just about a year later. It was a satire of the media, but far more strictly a comedy than *15 Minutes*, with De Niro as a crusty LAPD veteran forced to appear in a reality TV series in which he's partnered with a wacky patrolman, played by Eddie Murphy. The film was directed by Tom Dey, who had previously delivered the similar—and successful—buddy comedy *Shanghai Noon* with Jackie Chan and Owen Wilson. And Dey was sharp enough to see what he was working with in De Niro and Murphy: "Bob is very technical. He adheres to the script. Eddie improvises a lot. Eddie, who is a very physical comedian as well, may have the last word in a scene, but Bob usually has the last gesture, something economical, just a facial movement, perhaps."

Economical was an interesting word choice. In a deal finalized after the walloping success of *Meet the Parents*, De Niro was paid $17.5 million of *Showtime*'s $85 million budget. Which meant that he was paid more than the picture made in its opening weekend: $15 million, en route to an anemic $38 million gross.

HE STILL PROTECTED his privacy zealously. In 2002, for instance, he sued the Celebrity Vibe photo agency for circulating a photo in which he and Sean Penn blew out the candles on their joint birthday cake (they were both born on August 17) at a private party held in the rooftop garden of De Niro's penthouse. And yet, because of the line of work he'd chosen, his private life could sometimes become a matter of public record.

For instance, in September 2003 De Niro was visiting a Manhattan urologist whom he had been seeing regularly for more than twenty years. The visits had begun in 1980 when De Niro was experiencing trouble urinating freely, particularly after sexual activity. He was examined thoroughly, and he was diagnosed with inflammation of the prostate, a frequent and often harmless condition, particularly in a man of thirty-six years of age; De Niro left with a few prescriptions and no other treatment.

Three years later, when his father was diagnosed with prostate cancer, De Niro decided to become more vigilant about his health and told his doctor he wanted to be examined three or four times a year, a schedule he maintained regularly thereafter. At each visit his prostate was examined physically and blood tests were taken, and always he was deemed healthy. Over time he asked the doctor about a few discomforts to do with the urinary tract: a burning sensation upon urinating, hesitancy in the urine stream, and nocturia, the need to get out of bed to urinate several times throughout the night. Examinations found him healthy on all of these occasions, and he was so little troubled by the condition that he chose not to take the medication prescribed to curtail his nighttime visits to the bathroom.

Over the years, levels of the bloodborne protein PSA, which when elevated indicate prostate disease, had always been in the normal range, though they had risen over time, as happens in many men; an upward trend in the PSA doesn't necessarily indicate cancer. Still, in the later summer of 2003, the combination of his family history and the widely publicized prostate cancer episodes of Rudolph Giuliani, Joe Torre, and John Kerry inspired De Niro to get even more serious, to seek out a second urologist and to have a biopsy taken of his prostate, which was the most definitive way to identify or rule out cancer. "I decided to be even more proactive about monitoring my prostate health," he said. "I was concerned because of my age, and because [my PSA] was rising a bit. Although everybody was telling me there's no problem, I still was concerned because my father had died from it and I just wanted to be a little more proactive." On October 10, 2003, he had a biopsy taken.

Three days later, De Niro was in a Manhattan clothing store being fitted for costumes for a new film, *Hide and Seek*, which was set to begin shooting on October 27 and in which he would play a widowed New York psychiatrist whose daughter begins to have supernatural visions. As a routine part of the pre-production process, he was given a medical examination in the store by a doctor working for the producers and the insurance company that protected the production against delays and interruptions caused by health problems in essential members of the cast and crew. That exam raised no flags, and as a result, De Niro and the production were forthwith insured by Fireman's Fund Insurance Company to the tune of $2 million.

Two days after that, De Niro learned from his urologist that his biopsy had come back positive for prostate cancer.

It was, of course, staggering news. De Niro had just turned sixty, approximately the same age his father was at the time his cancer was diagnosed, and even though the thought of cancer had always loomed over him, he declared himself "shocked" in a statement his spokesperson revealed to the world a week later. In the years since the senior De Niro's cancer had been discovered, the survival rate of prostate cancer patients had dramatically increased from 67 percent to 97 percent, a trend attributed in large part to public awareness of the disease and an emphasis on screening and early treatment. The elder De Niro had struggled for a decade before succumbing, but his son was fortunate to have caught his condition earlier, almost without symptoms to prompt him to look for it. Given the very early detection and De Niro's overall fine health—he still worked out regularly to keep himself trim—his chance for a complete recovery was excellent.

On December 1, he went into Sloan-Kettering Memorial Hospital, Manhattan's premier cancer treatment facility, to have surgery to remove the cancerous tissue; there were no complications of any significance, and his recovery went well. And by late January, he began production on *Hide and Seek.*

In October 2006, long after the shoot had wrapped, Fireman's Fund sued De Niro for fraud and misrepresentation, claiming that he had bent the facts when he was examined on October 13 of the previous year and declared that he had never had cancer and had never been treated for prostate illness—both true on the day. The case went to trial, and in March 2008 a California court found in De Niro's favor, a decision upheld by the Court of Appeals of California in June 2009.

That was a gratifying result, though not nearly as gratifying, of course, as being free of a disease the fear of which had loomed over him for so long. And there was another positive outcome: during the time of his treatment, the person whom he could most rely on and who looked most vigilantly after him turned out to be his wife, Grace Hightower, who just a year or two before had been living apart from him and trading barbs with him in court and in gossip columns.

Somehow, despite the acrimony and the court visits and the splashy tabloid headlines of just a few years prior, the problems between them vanished. Not right away, not in so public a forum as their quarrels and split had been afforded. But by the summer of 2003, Hightower and Elliot were once again living in Tribeca with De Niro, she helped stage his sixtieth-birthday party at Le Cirque, and they traveled to Montecatini, Italy, where they were feted by restaurateur Sirio Maccioni at a gala dinner at which Andrea Bocelli sang.

Perhaps it was the counseling in which they took part, per the judge's orders. Or perhaps it was the growing recognition that Elliot was facing challenges greater than those that caused friction between his parents. Although no diagnosis would ever be made public, De Niro would occasionally allude to having a child who suffered from an emotional disorder, a description that didn't fit either the oldest kids, Drena and Raphael, who were adults embarking upon independent lives and careers, or the twins, who were attending school along with their peers.

Whatever the reason, the reunited couple seemed determined to make it last. In November 2004 they renewed their vows in a civil ceremony on the grounds of the farmhouse De Niro owned in Ulster County in the Hudson Valley. This time it was a bash, with 150 guests including Martin Scorsese, Meryl Streep, Harvey Keitel, Chazz Palminteri, Tom Brokaw, Ben Stiller, and all of De Niro's children. Guests gathered around an indoor pool while two justices of the peace ("So they can make sure this one sticks," De Niro joked) supervised an exchange of rings. A meal from Nobu, a raspberry napoleon cake baked by Daniel Boulud, and cases of Veuve Clicquot were served, and the newly recommitted couple danced to Tina Turner's rendition of "Simply the Best."

IN 2002, he made two pictures. *Analyze That*, the sequel to the 1999 film that changed his life and career, was another milestone for him: a $20 million payday. But it was a film that nobody involved with it seemed to want to make. "I don't know if I *hoped* it would go away or I *thought* it would go away," writer-director Harold Ramis said when it was released. As Ramis explained, De Niro was relatively enthusiastic to revisit the big hit, Billy Crystal was "reserved," and he himself was "skeptical . . . When I go to the movies, and when I feel people are just flogging the franchise, I resent it." (As proof, Ramis and his collaborators had, in fact, successfully resisted the pressure to make a third *Ghostbusters* film for more than a decade.)

Even with De Niro's salary more than doubling since the first film, when he was paid $8 million, *Analyze That* was made for a lower budget, $60 million compared to $80 million. All the more disappointing, then, that it should make only $32 million total, compared to the previous film's $107 million. It didn't help that the reviews were almost universally (and deservedly) condemnatory. But such notices didn't always put audiences off. Rather, it seemed as if moviegoers were beginning to smell out the quality of De Niro's recent films before they were released.

His next picture didn't reverse the trend: *Godsend*, a sci-fi-ish thriller about human cloning shot for approximately $25 million in the fall of 2002 by director Nick Hamm. De Niro's role was tiny—how else, at this point, could the budget stay so low?—and so was the film's impact: it earned back only $14.4 million when it was released in the spring of 2004.

That delay, in fact, meant that in 2003, despite all of the energy he was putting into work, De Niro failed to appear in a new release in North American theaters—the first time since 1982. He worked that year: he provided a voice for *Shark Tale*, an animated movie that combined *Finding Nemo* with *The Godfather*, and he appeared, even more randomly, as the Archbishop of Peru in an adaptation of Thornton Wilder's *The Bridge of San Luis Rey* that was shot in Spain and also featured Harvey Keitel, F. Murray Abraham, Kathy Bates, Geraldine Chaplin, and Gabriel Byrne.* Both pictures surfaced in American theaters long after they were shot: *Shark Tale* to robust business in October 2004 (with a gross of $161 million, it would be the third-largest box office in De Niro's career), *San Luis Rey* to puzzlement, obscurity, and $42,880 in ticket sales in June 2005.

IF IT SOUNDS crass to think so much about the cost and earnings of these films, it at least provides some sort of context to explain why they

---

* Marking, by the way, his first role as a pre-twentieth-century character since Frankenstein and, with *The Mission*, only his third ever.

were made. And no film would prove that point more obviously than *Meet the Fockers*, his second sequel to hit multiplexes at Christmastime in two years. As with *Analyze That*, he would command a $20 million fee and Tribeca Productions would be involved in the creation and the profits. But whereas *Analyze That* churned over old ground tiresomely, *Meet the Fockers* was enlivened by the addition of Barbra Streisand and Dustin Hoffman to the comic mix, which turned out to be a canny choice. Playing the parents of Ben Stiller's Gaylord/Greg, the pair were sex-mad, drug-friendly hippies utterly unlike either their son or his in-laws. De Niro would be asked to do the same things, more or less, as in the first picture, but the context would be significantly wilder.

There were several iterations of the script, including one by David O. Russell, the indie auteur whose *Flirting with Disaster* with Stiller had been a smart, if small, hit. But, really, none of that mattered. De Niro had almost nothing to do except show up on the Los Angeles sets, play happily with Hoffman and Stiller, and think about other projects. *Fockers* was an even bigger hit than the original, claiming the top slot in the box office charts for three weeks compared to *Meet the Parents's* four (a result of being released in the competitive Christmas season), but grossing $279 million in North America and $237 million abroad—nearly double the first film's earnings and easily the top-grossing film in De Niro's career.

Meet the Fockers was still holding its own at the box office in January when the delayed *Hide and Seek* debuted in the number one spot at the American box office. Another potboiler made by another little-known name (the Australian actor-turned-director John Polson), it echoed *The Shining* and *The Sixth Sense* in depicting a fractured man (a widower, De Niro) living in isolation with a child (his daughter, played by Dakota Fanning) with apparent extrasensory knowledge of some horrible secret. The reviews, as they seemed to be for all of De Niro's films now, were dismissive. But the film was a hit, grossing $51 million against its $25 million budget. When it finally dropped out of the box office top ten, the same week that *Meet the Fockers* did, De Niro had completed the most commercially successful two months of his career. Did it matter what anyone actually thought of the films and his work in them?

28

IT SEEMED LIKE A NICE BIT OF PUBLICITY WHEN THE ITALIAN government decided to bestow honorary citizenship on a couple of notables of Italian American descent: Robert De Niro and Martin Scorsese, two demi-sons of Italy who would be at the Venice Film Festival in August 2004 to present *Shark Tale*, the tongue-in-cheek animated movie about a blood feud between denizens of the deep, with De Niro and Scorsese providing the voices of Mafia-esque fishies.

But when the announcement was made before the festival, an outcry arose in the United States, where a heritage group known as the Order of the Sons of Italy objected to De Niro's career of portraying mobsters and belittling Italian Americans. "He has done nothing to promote the image of Italians," their spokesperson said, "and he has actually damaged their image by constantly playing criminal roles which tarnish the reputation of Italians." A De Niro spokesman immediately retorted by pointing out that "Robert De Niro has portrayed men of many nationalities. He has portrayed doctors, policemen, bus drivers, presidential advisors, CIA agents, prize fighters, military men and priests. That's what actors do—portray other people. He has brought nothing but pride and credit to his life, his profession, and his heritage. To suggest otherwise is irresponsible."

It was a silly spat—like housewives swinging handbags at one another in a Monty Python sketch—but it made for lurid headlines and genuinely hurt feelings. Italian authorities promised to take the protest seriously and look into the question more carefully, leading them to delay awarding De Niro his citizenship. De Niro defended himself personally in Venice: "The characters I play are real. They are real. So they have as much right to be portrayed as any other characters." But he felt sufficiently slighted by the whole business to skip a press event in Rome meant to celebrate a showcase of Italian movies at the Tribeca Film Festival, and he was a no-show at a film festival in Milan where he was to be awarded the city's highest civilian honor, the Gold Medal of St. Ambrose. It would be a full year before the wounds from this absurd slapfight fully healed.

MAYBE IT WAS because he was a secretive fellow at heart, but even though he might be the last actor in the world you could imagine starring in a spy story, De Niro had a fascination with the genre. Among the projects that seemed always to be simmering on a back burner at Tribeca Productions was an idea he had to make a film about the Cold War. When he visited Russia in 1997 to receive an award from the Moscow Film Festival, he arranged to stop by a former KGB social club and chat with some former agents in the sauna, just to size them up (one fellow half-jokingly challenged him to a boxing match, being as he was the star of *Raging Bull* and all, ha ha ha).

In 1997, when he was in France working for John Frankenheimer on *Ronin*—playing a spy for the first time in his career—he learned that there was already a well-regarded script about the CIA during the Cold War kicking around and that Frankenheimer was on board to direct it. Was he interested in maybe appearing in it? Yes; yes, he was.

The script, eventually known as *The Good Shepherd*, had been written by Eric Roth (*Forrest Gump*) for Francis Coppola, who found himself unable to pursue it. Director Wayne Wang briefly circled it with the intention of having Tom Cruise play the lead character, a man who joins the CIA after attending Yale and is involved in much of the clandestine spy-vs.-spy activity between World War II and the Bay of Pigs. That iteration of the film vanished, too, as did one with Philip Kaufman attached to direct. Then it fell to Frankenheimer.

Not long after, though, De Niro was in talks not to star in the film but to direct it. He even made a gentleman's agreement with Eric Roth, stating that if he got *Good Shepherd* made, then Roth would write a sequel, bringing the story forward from the 1960s to the present day. By the fall of 1999, talk of De Niro directing the film had gotten serious enough that the conversation turned to whom he would cast in the lead, as De Niro himself was clearly too old to play a Yale undergrad. In February 2000, De Niro held a table reading of Roth's script in New York, with Jude Law taking the lead and Winona Ryder, John Turturro, Christopher Plummer, Jake Gyllenhaal, Martin Scorsese, and De Niro himself reading along. Law never quite said yes, and in 2002 talk bubbled up that had Leonardo DiCaprio in the role. On the strength of that bit of casting, several financiers appeared ready to go through with funding the film's estimated $110 million budget.

DiCaprio, though, was proving trigger shy, with a strong commitment to Martin Scorsese to make *The Aviator* and a plan to follow up immediately with Scorsese's *The Departed*. De Niro grew frustrated with the young actor: "I said one night, 'You have to let me know now. Are you in or are you out?'" The combination of DiCaprio's time constraints and salary demands ultimately swamped the tenuous deal to make *The Good Shepherd*, and in November 2004 the film seemed to have been scuttled, with producer Graham King declaring, "I'd love to make this movie. It's one of the best scripts I've ever read. But you can't make this movie for any less than we have budgeted for. I certainly wouldn't disrespect Bob by getting him to cut the budget."

But a lifeline came in the form of DiCaprio's *Departed* co-star, Matt Damon, who (1) also loved the script, (2) would finish his work with Scorsese sooner than DiCaprio, and (3) was demanding less money. Suddenly, just a few weeks after DiCaprio's departure and the film's apparent demise, *The Good Shepherd* was back in business, at a budget of just under $90 million with a start date of March 2005. "Matt was crucial," De Niro later revealed. "He said, 'I love this script, I'd do it for nothing.' And he did. Not for nothing, but practically. It couldn't have been done otherwise."

Alongside Damon, an impressive roster of talent agreed to work for De Niro for a song: Angelina Jolie, Alec Baldwin, William Hurt, Timothy Hutton, Billy Crudup, Michael Gambon, John Turturro, and Keir Dullea among them (De Niro took a role for himself, and Joe Pesci showed up as well, as did such friends as Meryl Streep's son Henry Gummer and Lower Manhattan Development Corporation boss John

C. Whitehead). The production took place mainly in New York and Connecticut, with side trips to England and the Dominican Republic. Robert Richardson, who'd shot *Casino* (as well as a slew of other films for Scorsese and, especially, Oliver Stone), was along as director of photography, and Tariq Anwar would be the editor. Most important to De Niro, though, was Milt Bearden, the CIA operative who'd helped him research his roles in *Ronin* and, yes, the *Fockers* movies. "Milt is the real thing," De Niro always said, and the thirty-year CIA veteran helped impart notes of verisimilitude to the details of the story.

It had been more than a decade since De Niro had directed, though. The material wasn't nearly as close to him as *A Bronx Tale* had been, and he admitted that he wasn't always entirely steady in approaching the work. "I didn't have that much confidence," he said. "As you get older, you have more confidence, obviously. In certain areas. In others . . . still don't have much confidence. With this thing, every day I was worried."

In part, he overcame his trepidations by focusing not on the epic scale of the film but on his strength as a collaborative actor. He would, according to Richardson, direct his cast from within the scene, letting the camera run as he instructed them on nuances of their performances, even breaking into the scene to do so. "There were a number of sequences where Bob would walk in and out of the frame," Richardson recalled, "giving the actors notes on how the performances should shift on a particular line. . . . At some points we ran entire magazines [of film] simply on one line or as small as altering the gesture and position of an eye at a particular point."

Such attention to detail was, of course, a hallmark of De Niro's acting, but it also suited the material of *The Good Shepherd*, which was far more John Le Carré or Robert Littell than Ian Fleming or Robert Ludlum. "In movies where people are shooting at each other all the time, it just seems too much," De Niro said. "I like it when things happen for a reason. So I want to downplay the violence, depict it in a muted way. In those days, it was a gentleman's game." Similarly, he didn't mind that the film was steeped in ambiguity, which of course was an essential dimension of the world of espionage. "I'm always so used to seeing movies that to me have an obvious payoff that doesn't really follow logically," he said. "I felt this should be more restrained. . . . You want things to add up, and they must add up, but some things don't add up in life. So that's . . . that's what it is."

In October 2005 De Niro brought a short reel of scenes from *The Good Shepherd* to the Rome Film Festival, a new event that hoped to form ties with Tribeca. A crowd of some fifteen hundred people were on hand to watch the approximately fifteen minutes of footage and hear a few words from the director, who'd finally been granted his Italian passport that day from the mayor of Rome, a full year after the brouhaha about the negative impact of his portrayals of Italian American gangsters. In December, Universal Pictures released the film into theaters in the United States.

There's a stately dignity to *The Good Shepherd*, an intelligence, a clarity of intent, craft, and form. It's not as complex as a John Le Carré novel (or, indeed, some film adaptations of Le Carré's oeuvre), but it has grand scope, and it impressively blends delicate character observation and low-boil tension. You admire it, but you never quite warm up to it, and a good deal of that might be because it's impossible to understand what drew De Niro to make it, more than a dozen years after his notable and clearly personal directorial debut, *A Bronx Tale*.

There are tiny bits of the film that seem as if they would particularly resonate with De Niro. It depicts a tender but strained father/son relationship: Matt Damon's Edward Wilson has been abandoned by his own father and then raises a boy of his own, also named Edward, who's emotionally troubled (he wets himself on Santa's lap at a Christmas party, leading to a very sweet moment in which the father quietly and caringly cleans his son) and grows up to be skittish, earnest, and eager to follow his father's path into espionage. There's an interracial romance and a fascination with secrecy, betrayal, repressed emotion, and, naturally, the details of work. All of this seems suited to De Niro. But it's hard to see the film as a vehicle of self-expression in the way De Niro's previous directorial effort was.

Perhaps he nods toward that in his own string of brief appearances in the picture, playing Bill Sullivan, an obvious stand-in for William J. Donovan, the father of modern American espionage. He plays the role seated, because Sullivan suffers from gout, and when he's last seen, his legs have been amputated—perhaps a joking sign from De Niro that the making of the film took a particularly brutal toll on him. If that feels far-fetched, consider that Sullivan is the only person in *The Good Shepherd* who doesn't seem stricken with a crippling case of self-seriousness. It's a well-wrought movie, but overlong and too quiet and slow; ultimately, it lacks the spark of personal commitment and even obsession that made *A Bronx Tale*, let alone so many of De Niro's acting appearances, memorable.

The reviews of *The Good Shepherd* were by and large respectful, even when critics felt the film was dull or muddled. "For the film's first 50 minutes," wrote *Newsweek's* David Ansen in a typical response, "I thought De Niro might pull off the 'Godfather' of spy movies . . . but the unvarying solemn tone begins to wear. . . . Still, even if the movie's vast reach exceeds its grasp, it's a spellbinding history lesson." In the *Los Angeles Times*, Kenneth Turan praised the film's "smart, thoughtful, psychologically complicated script" and "De Niro's careful and methodical direction." David Denby of the *New Yorker* was nigh rapturous: "One of the most impressive movies ever made about espionage . . . long stretches of this [movie] are masterly; swift, terse, but never rushed." But Peter Travers of *Rolling Stone* felt that the film "has no pulse," Ella Taylor of the *LA Weekly* declared it "three slow, sincere and fitfully bamboozling hours," and Michael Sragow of the *Baltimore Sun* said of De Niro and his screenwriter, Eric Roth, "Despite their conviction and intelligence and their game, amazing cast, all they do is eke out a series of straight-faced dramatic reversals and personal betrayals that leave the dramatis personae, and the audience, numb."

The mostly favorable reviews helped buoy the dense and broody film to almost $60 million in ticket sales (with another $40 million coming overseas), which would have been a nice result had the picture not cost nearly that much to make. It would go down critically and commercially as a noble but ultimately insufficient effort—not enough, perhaps, to encourage De Niro to seek a third directorial project, at least not right away.

DURING THE YEARS that lower Manhattan struggled to recover from the attacks of September 11, 2001, De Niro never lost sight of the work that needed to be done. He had shored up his own financial, cultural, and personal interests, of course, but he had worked doggedly for the good of the greater community, investing his time and money and lending his name and face to any number of efforts large and small to revitalize Tribeca and the surrounding areas. In 2004, he accepted an invitation to join the board of the World Trade Center Memorial Foundation, a group dedicated to raising half a billion dollars to build a suitable memorial at the site of the new World Trade Center, including, it was said, a performing arts center and museum. The board was packed with heavy hitters from a wide spectrum of fields, including David Rockefeller, Barbara Walters, Michael Eisner, Robert Wood Johnson, and executives of American Express, AIG, the Blackstone Group, Bear Stearns, and other financial entities. De Niro was included for his visibility and as a magnet for fund-raising, as well as in the hope that the Tribeca Film Institute, the not-for-profit wing of his film business, would become active in the proposed arts center. There were a few high-profile meetings—controversially held outside public scrutiny— before Governor George Pataki derailed the process in late 2005 by declaring that the inclusion of a cultural component for the World Trade Center site opened the door to too much controversy. Suggesting that the emphasis should be on the memorial itself, he shut the door on further work, and the board De Niro served on, however briefly, dissolved.

De Niro continued to make himself a face of good works, taking part in telethons intended to raise money for the victims of the 2004 South Asian tsunami and 2005's Hurricane Katrina. But he remained on the lookout for ways to invest—in all senses—in the culture of New York City. A new such opportunity presented itself in May 2006, when the cheeky weekly newspaper the *New York Observer* was going through one of its periodical financial crises, and its owner, Arthur L. Carter, was looking for a buyer. De Niro, Jane Rosenthal, and her husband, venture capitalist Craig Hatkoff, considered putting on white hats and saving the paper. In fact, Tribeca Enterprises, the for-profit division of De Niro's empire, was one of as many as a couple of dozen entities approached by Carter to consider taking an 80 percent stake in the paper. A few weeks of due diligence ensued, generating a bit of buzz in the New York media terrarium. But in July, the Tribeca group backed away when a more substantial buyer, New York real estate heir Jared Kushner, stepped in and bought the *Observer*, leaving it free to join other New York papers in its seemingly endless exercise in cracking wise about De Niro, his films, his real estate holdings, and his private life, as had long been its practice.

HE CERTAINLY HELPED feed them fresh material, however unwillingly. On a June day in 2005, De Niro entered the Manhattan Criminal Court Building through a rear door usually used to deliver packages or to transport inmates and rode a judge's elevator to where a grand jury was convened. Wearing a ball cap, a blue blazer, jeans, and boat shoes with no socks, he spent a total of five minutes in front of a Manhattan district attorney, examining a pair of diamond earrings and confirming that they were a gift he'd given to his wife. Then he made his way out the back door of the courthouse.

A few hours later, the grand jury delivered an indictment of one Lucyna Turyk-Wawrynowicz, a thirty-five-year-old Polish immigrant who lived in Queens and had been employed by the De Niros for only a few weeks. In that time, the diamond earrings, valued at $95,000, a $1,000 pair of shoes, and a $500 belt all went missing, and Grace Hightower was certain that Turyk-Wawrynowicz, who was earning $1,000 a week to clean the house, was behind it. Hightower had retained the maid's impressive list of previous employers, which included the actresses Candice Bergen and Isabella Rossellini and the cultural trend guru Faith Popcorn, as well as a Rockefeller and a Rothschild, and she called them, asking if they had had any valuables go missing when Turyk-Wawrynowicz was in their employ. Several of them had, and Hightower immediately called the police to tell them about her suspicions and her discoveries.

When detectives arrived at her home to question her, Turyk-Wawrynowicz put on a brave front at first, claiming that a costly jacket they discovered in her closet was just some old thing: "Anybody can buy a jacket like this at Century 21," she said, referring to a popular discount store. Soon, though, she was casting aspersions on Hightower: "She is mean." After another couple of hours, she broke down and admitted to police that she had the earrings, telling the cops, "The diamonds are in the bathroom." Sipping a skim latte that had been fetched for her during the interrogation, she stopped defending herself and thought only of her husband, Jaroslaw, a construction worker who also was from Poland: "I am evil and guilty, but my husband did nothing. You can cut my hands and head off, but I can tell you he did nothing wrong." Explaining her theft from the De Niros, she initially suggested that she was encouraged by their butler, but then recanted that charge. Instead, she blamed her victims for her crimes: "If she [Hightower] had treated me better, with more respect, I probably wouldn't have done this. I didn't steal from Isabella Rossellini because she treated me well. I only stole from people who didn't treat me with respect."

Besides Hightower, Turyk-Wawrynowicz had stolen from Bergen, who confronted her about a jacket and a pair of cameras that went missing only to have the maid turn on her with a threat of blackmail: "If you have me arrested, I will go to the press and tell them the reason I was fired and accused of these crimes is because your husband sexually harassed me and I refused his advances." Another former employer had caught Turyk-Wawrynowicz using a stolen credit card to rack up $1,000 in purchases at Barney's and was told by the brazen maid, "I didn't think you would notice."

The victims had, in fact, noticed, and spurred by Hightower, they all agreed to cooperate with the district attorney's office, which initially filed charges of grand larceny, criminal possession of stolen property, coercion, and forgery against Turyk-Wawrynowicz. She had to forfeit her passport upon arrest, and bail was set at $150,000 bond or $75,000 cash; when Jaroslaw showed up with the cash, though, it was refused, as he was unable to prove that it wasn't the proceeds of criminal activity. As a result, Turyk-Wawrynowicz remained in a cell at Rikers Island for more than seven months, during which time prosecutors discovered that she had forged her Social Security and resident alien cards. In February 2006 she pled guilty to grand larceny and was sentenced to one to three years in prison, with credit for time served; it was reckoned she'd be free by the end of the year, at which point she would be handed over to the Department of Homeland Security for deportation to Poland—at her own expense, a banal dénouement to a banal crime.*

WITH *The Good Shepherd* behind him, De Niro resumed working at a hectic pace and making choices that didn't always pay off in either economic or aesthetic terms. But in most cases, the intent of the projects at least seemed pitched higher than had been the case in recent years.

He once again marched into a recording studio as a voice for hire, this time to dub the English-language dialogue for *Arthur and the Invisibles*, an animated feature by the French writer-director Luc Besson; De Niro, if anyone noticed, provided the voice of the king of an invisible race called the Minimoys.

Almost as if frustrated with what was in front of him, he next took on a completely surprising role in *Stardust*, director Matthew Vaughn's film of a fantasy novel by Neil Gaiman. De Niro played the small role of Captain Shakespeare, leader of a band of pirates whose ship floats through the air, and keeper of secret passions and predilections: the good captain is, in fact, a cross-dresser. (The part was barely a sketch in Gaiman's novel; Vaughn, who said he hoped the tenor of the film would recall that of *Midnight Run*, expanded the character with screenwriter Jane Goldman.) It was a charming film unjustly overlooked by the public, grossing a mere $38.6 million in its late-summer 2007 release even though the reviews were generally favorable.

Less of a leap was *What Just Happened?*, a movie about the movie business based on a book-length memoir by Art Linson, with whom De Niro hadn't worked in more than a decade, and directed by Barry Levinson, another collaborator of more than ten years prior. It was a

---

* The De Niros had rotten luck with domestics. In 2009 they were sued by a nanny who had been taking care of Elliot. The nanny claimed that she was owed $40,000 in back pay for more than 750 hours of overtime and ten days of vacation. The matter was settled out of court.

shaggy dog story about the life and works of an independent Holly-wood producer trying to launch a big-budget film starring Bruce Willis (as himself) and/or Sean Penn (also playing himself). It was droll stuff, with lots of in-jokes about the movie biz, celebrity, the expensive high life of Hollywood insiders, and those scratching and scrambling to claim a place among them. De Niro's character is always on the verge of either making it big or losing it big, and as the title indicates, he's not always entirely able to say which way he's headed.

As De Niro knew, the script had a lot of truth in it: "This is as close as it gets to what it can be like to be in the middle of this stuff," he told a reporter. "The fear factor is always there—everything from losing tens of millions of dollars on a film that doesn't work to not being able to get a good table in a top restaurant because your last movie flopped." (Asked if anyone had ever denied *him* a good table, De Niro demurred. "If they have, I haven't noticed," he said, then smiled and added, "I also bought my own restaurants.")

The film shot in Cannes, Connecticut, and Hollywood in the spring of 2007 and debuted the following year at the Sundance Film Festival to a relatively flat reception. Released into theaters in October 2008, it grossed barely $1 million.

By then, De Niro had appeared in a film that, at least on paper, marked an even more promising reunion: *Righteous Kill*, a dark and moderately bloody *policier* by director Jon Avnet that put De Niro alongside Al Pacino. It had been a dozen years since *Heat*, and in that film the pair had appeared in only two scenes together, which served at once to make the film feel special and to make the audience feel slightly bamboozled. *Righteous Kill*, on the other hand, would give the impression of a cheat for other reasons. De Niro and Pacino shared the screen plenty, yes, but *why?*

It wasn't that the script, by Russell Gewirtz, was *that* much easier to dismiss than those of other films recently starring De Niro or Pacino. It wasn't that the budget (some $60 million) was beneath them, or that their fellow cast members (who included Brian Dennehy, John Leguizamo, Carla Gugino, Melissa Leo, and the rapper Curtis Jackson, aka 50 Cent) weren't a good match. Rather, it was that the whole enterprise—a strictly by-the-numbers crime movie—was such an obvious comedown from *Heat*, not to mention *The Godfather, Part II*, the first film on which they'd shared billing.

The film was released by a small new independent distributor, Overture, in September 2008 without even being previewed by film critics in many American markets. There was once a time when the debut of a film with De Niro and Pacino in it was an event to be circled on a calendar. *Righteous Kill*, on the contrary, was escorted into the marketplace almost as if it were something shameful.

Frankly, it wasn't even that good. Built around the concept of cops chasing a serial killer who they suspect might be another cop, it presents the spectacle of a beefy De Niro and a spray-tanned Pacino playing scene after scene together with the energy you might expect of a gin rummy game. De Niro gets to disport himself sexually with Gugino, and Pacino has some nice moments in conversation with a psychiatrist. But there's nothing memorable about either of their performances or the combination of their auras or energies, and the garish and shallow film eventually devolves into a chain of plot twists that are neither engaging enough nor clever enough to ignite it. Watching it, you can't help but think that tens of millions of dollars could have been saved if someone had just filmed De Niro and Pacino having dinner together or going on a cruise around Manhattan—and that it would have made better entertainment to boot (and might even have grossed more than the $40 million that *Righteous Kill* managed).

And while he was doing this kind of thing, he passed on several films of much better quality. In the decade-plus after *Meet the Parents*, he was offered the roles of the chief villain in two Martin Scorsese films: 2002's *Gangs of New York* (which would have required him to work several months in Rome, where old-time Manhattan was rebuilt on stages at Cinecittà) and 2006's *The Departed*, which would have been his first appearance in a film nominated as Best Picture since 1990 (he skipped that one to make *The Good Shepherd*); the parts went instead to Daniel Day-Lewis and Jack Nicholson, and they delivered memorable performances. De Niro and Scorsese also talked about adapting the musical *Chicago* (De Niro would have played the role that Richard Gere eventually took on-screen) and the gangster picture *I Hear You Paint Houses.* But no go.

He turned down the role Denzel Washington played in Tony Scott's *Man on Fire,* the one Ray Winstone played in Martin Campbell's *Edge of Darkness,* and, before Tim Burton was involved, the one Johnny Depp played in *Willie Wonka and the Chocolate Factory.* He came close to working again with Michael Mann on the gangster film *The Winter of Frankie Machine.* And he was spoken about in connection with a number of other potentially engaging projects: biopics about Vince Lombardi, Bernie Madoff, and Enrico Caruso; a remake of the 1955 crime-and-show-biz story *Love Me or Leave Me,* with De Niro and Jennifer Lopez playing the roles originated by James Cagney and Doris Day; an adaptation of Robert Ferrigno's bestselling crime novel *Horse Latitudes*; a remake of the Japanese kidnapping drama *Chaos* for *Sexy Beast* director Jonathan Glazer; and reteamings with Sean Penn (*The Mitchell Brothers,* about the California pornography pioneers) and Meryl Streep (*First Man,* about the husband of the first female U.S. president).

It wasn't, of course, possible to say if any of these would have turned out worthwhile, but most of them carried at least a spark of promise that wasn't so readily apparent in, say, *Showtime* or *Hide and Seek.* He was immensely busy. Would that he had been equally selective.

29

BY THE MIDDLE OF THE 2000S, DE NIRO'S TRIBECA REAL ES-
tate empire had come to resemble a little fiefdom. There was
the Tribeca Film Center at 375 Greenwich Street, anchored by
the Tribeca Grill, which had long since been canonized as a classic
New York restaurant. There was TriBakery next door; on the same city
block were Nobu and Nobu Next Door on Hudson Street. He himself
lived on Hudson Street still, at number 110. At number 112, where his
longtime assistant Robin Chambers owned her own place, De Niro
owned a piece of the Fourth Estate newsstand and coffee shop, and he
owned or leased the vacant lot next door and the empty storefront on
the other side of it. And, of course, in establishing the neighborhood
as a celebrity redoubt, he had drawn a full contingent of restaurants,
clubs, boutiques, and goods-and-services businesses to what once had
been a moribund industrial neighborhood. Old-timers (the ones who
could still afford to live there, anyhow) griped about the limousines
and the late-night caterwauling in the street, but when they referred to
his portion of the district as "Bob Row" it wasn't entirely in hostility;
he really had created something out of nothing. (Still, there was often
an edge: "When something happens in the neighborhood, Bob gets
mentioned, pro or con," acknowledged Jane Rosenthal.)

Tribeca had been a neighborhood without a name when he showed
up there to set up a gym and learn how to box for *Raging Bull* more
than twenty years earlier, and now it was the center of an empire, a
place and a style—at once urbane and gritty, monied and low-key, hip
and old-school—known all around the world; De Niro and company
had even sued a restaurant in London for calling itself TriBeCa and

otherwise blatantly ripping off his brand. He was so protective of his manor, in fact, that he was known to surveil it actively via closed-circuit cameras, both as a bachelor with an eye on the ladies and as a family man with a mind toward security. It wasn't uncommon for acquaintances to learn that De Niro knew they'd been on the block—to dine or shop, say, without any intent to connect with him. He was always private and circumspect, and his zone of comfort had come to extend over a good-sized piece of lower Manhattan. And, truly, was anyone to say he hadn't earned it?

But, in fact, he owned properties all over the place. There was the Hudson Street penthouse he'd bought in 1988 for $857,000 and then augmented in 2001 with the purchase of the apartment immediately below, a 1,350-square-foot unit previously owned by Harvey Keitel, who had purchased it in 1988 also. There was the St. Luke's Place townhouse he had bought for himself and Diahnne Abbott in 1975 and had renovated extensively. There was a house on Long Island, which he'd never quite been able to renovate because of strict real estate codes, and a house in Roxbury, in upstate Ulster County. And there was the Upper East Side condo at the Trump Palace in which Grace Hightower had lived during their period of marital strife and which they still owned. (He had considered but then balked at the idea of buying a place in London a few years later.)

By 2005, the couple had their eyes on a new home—a new lifestyle, in fact. They wanted to move uptown, to Central Park West, specifically to the Brentmore, a posh and venerable building at West 68th Street, where they entered negotiations to buy a fourth-and-fifth-floor duplex for $20.9 million. That made Hudson Street superfluous, and they sold it that same year for $12.25 million—about $2 million under the initial asking price, but still a very nice return on his decades of residence. The following year, Hightower sold her Trump Palace unit and the extra storage spaces that she owned with it, for just over $2.5 million. And then, ensconced in the Brentmore, they put the St. Luke's Place home up for sale for $14 million in the summer of 2011; the following year, Raphael De Niro, who'd grown up in the building, sold it to De Niro's former CAA superagent, Mike Ovitz, for $9.5 million. Ovitz planned an extensive renovation and had architectural drawings made and city permitting hurdles surmounted, then decided to sell the building without doing any of the work; in the summer of 2013, it was once again for sale, this time for $12 million.

At the time, the De Niros might have wished they'd held on to it. In June 2012, in a clothes dryer in the laundry room of their unit at the Brentmore, which they'd expanded onto the building's sixth floor, a small fire broke out, causing significant damage and rendering the condo unlivable. It was speculated at the time that they'd need some-place else to live for as much as three years, and they wound up leasing on the Upper East Side.

HE HAD PLANS for that vacant lot next to the Tribeca Film Center. Way back in 1991, when the Film Center and Grill were new and clearly successful, he had thought about putting a hotel on the spot, a hundred rooms or so, something deluxe. The area, just a pleasant walk away from Wall Street and the World Trade Center, was an underused resource, in part because it lacked high-end accommodations for trav-elers. Talk started again in the summer of 2001, when he found an in-vestment partner, the hotel developer Richard Born, who had recently built a little chain of chic, high-end spots around the city. But the 9/11 attacks scuttled their plans.

Two years later, mere weeks after learning about his prostate cancer, De Niro sat in an audience listening to New York governor George Pataki talk about progress on rebuilding the area devastated by the terror attacks. Among the governor's announcements that day was the news that De Niro and a group of partners—including Born and one Raphael De Niro—would be receiving $38 million in tax-free Liberty Bonds, designated for development in lower Manhattan, to help them build a $43 million, eighty-three-room luxury hotel on that lot at 377 Greenwich Street. A design was approved by the city in 2004, and they hoped to open it the following year.

In fact, it wasn't until April 2008 that they finally got the job done. The Greenwich Hotel (so dubbed by De Niro, who thought the name "classic, elegant and simple") consisted of eighty-eight rooms starting at $525 a night, a restaurant, and a spa spread out over 75,000 square feet. It was high-end but spoke as well to traditional working-class New York. There were light fixtures from Horn and Hardart Automats and glass panels salvaged from the legendary Flatiron Building. The lobby sported furniture from a French flea market, and some Robert De Niro Sr. canvases were on the walls. The showcase was the Japanese-style Shibui Spa, which was built around a 250-year-old house from near Kyoto, dismantled, shipped, and reassembled inside the hotel.

It was a hit from the day it opened, but there were hiccups. The first restaurant to anchor the building, the high-end Italian spot Ago, failed within a year, to be replaced by the slightly lower-toned and smaller Locanda Verde, which hit the right note with hotel guests, neighborhood residents, and New York foodies upon opening in the spring of 2009. And De Niro and his partners had a fight on their hands from the very beginning with the city's Landmarks Preservation Commission, which objected to the size and appearance of the eighth-floor penthouse of the hotel, which was built differently from the initial plans. There was talk of actually tearing out the offending structure, and De Niro himself testified before the commission in June 2008, declaring, "We worked on this project a long time, to make it as good as we could make it and make a place that I want to stay in. It was a labor of love." As he explained, he would be among the first to object if the building had been built out of character with the neighborhood: "Anything that would be offensive would be offensive to me." The matter was finally settled when plans for a redesign were approved in November 2010.

THE IDEA THAT Raphael De Niro might have been considered a candidate to be his father's business partner would have been laughable only a decade before the doors of the Hotel Greenwich opened. Being the son of a movie star, the boy had enjoyed an unusually comfortable upbringing, but it had many of the same textures of partial abandonment and bohemian neglect that had characterized his father's youth.

Back in the mid-1980s, De Niro had decided that he wouldn't keep up a residence in Los Angeles, that he would simply rent homes when he was in town for work (twice in the mid-1990s, he rented Roger Moore's pile in Beverly Hills). And Diahnne Abbott finally chose to abandon LA as well, moving to New York and the St. Luke's Place townhouse permanently in 1986, when Raphael was about to turn ten. It wasn't a happy transition for the boy. He had been living in leafy, suburban Brentwood, and now he was riding a subway to go uptown to the Bank Street School and living in a West Village neighborhood that still hadn't quite tipped fully into gentrification. "It was dirty," Raphael remembered of the city of his youth. "It was loud. There was a lot of drug use. There were a lot of murders."

Fortunately, there was a safety net of family within walking distance of home: Virginia Admiral lived and worked and taught art classes in her renovated loft on Spring and Lafayette Streets; Robert De Niro Sr. painted and kept his menagerie on West Broadway (Raphael would remember playing with his G.I. Joe action figures on the floor of the cluttered studio); and De Niro himself lived in Tribeca, where, before long, he got busy building his little kingdom.

Neither of his parents had been a particularly avid student; nor, it turned out, was Raphael. But he did like to work, and he was willing to do it from the time he was in middle school, making a few dollars doing odd jobs at neighborhood street fairs or, later, as a shop assistant in a rug store on Bleecker Street. He got into trouble, almost exactly like his dad, getting pinched by the cops as a fifteen-year-old for spraying graffiti on a subway train in Chinatown. But he was, also almost exactly like his dad, scared straight and mostly out of trouble.

He didn't have his father's impulse toward a creative career. He worked on the set of *A Bronx Tale* and appeared as an extra in a couple of his dad's films, but it wasn't his thing.* He dabbled in college at NYU, but dropped out; he worked as a doorman at an Upper East Side building but left when his full identity was discovered. If he did

---

* His half sister Drena also dabbled in acting, after stints as a club DJ and as a fashion model (including some turns on the catwalk for Willi Smith), and she even popped up in tiny roles in a couple of De Niro's films. But she never quite built an acting career, and eventually she found herself more at home behind the camera, directing and producing films, doing charitable work in East Africa, and raising, as a single mother, her son Leandro, who was born in 2003—De Niro's first grandchild. In 2011, she hit the tabloids by getting into a public fistfight with a onetime fiancé. The man bore up stoically under a barrage of punches from his ex, who felt he'd scorned her.

the least thing out of the ordinary, the tabloid press hounded him for it: a fistfight outside a nightclub in 1998, another spat at a nightspot in 2002. Petty stuff, but not pretty.

In time, a different strain of the family's legacy started to emerge in him. Virginia Admiral had always had a little string of properties that she was developing, renovating, renting, flipping. "All great fortunes were built on real estate," she liked to say. The elder Robert De Niro's brother, Jack, had a nice business in commercial and residential real estate sales in New York and Florida. And, of course, De Niro was himself buying and developing properties in lower Manhattan. Raphael started to express interest in the real estate business, and De Niro decided to give him a boost by letting him be part of the team developing the Greenwich Hotel.

At first, De Niro's partner Richard Born didn't cotton to the idea. Raphael seemed to him to be "a little bit of a wild kid" and "our partner's son who initially wanted to sit in on meetings." But in time he proved his worth, pointing out ways in which the hotel could be made more amenable to a celebrity clientele.

Soon after that, Raphael decided to take classes toward obtaining a real estate license, which he did in late 2004. The following year, he was hired by Prudential Douglas Elliman, one of the largest residential real estate firms in New York, and he soon demonstrated a genuine knack for the business, selling two apartments in the $1.6 million range in his first year. He rose steadily at the firm, garnering a reputation for working well with famous clients and with moving expensive properties that sometimes had been sitting on the market for quite a while. In 2007 and 2008, when the New York real estate market started to sour on the eve of the financial crisis, he was able to pull off sales as rich as $14.8 million and to sell the lion's share of units in a few new condominium buildings in the Tribeca area.

It would have been easy to attribute his success to his famous surname, but as Raphael would retort, "No one is buying a $10 million apartment because my dad is Robert De Niro." Besides, he pointed out, "many of [his clients] have more money than my dad." (His dad concurred that the family name didn't mean much. "I put him in touch with people," he said. "Sometimes they don't even call him back.")

Rather, he was valued as an agent for his professional and personal habits of reliability and doggedness and for even downplaying his family name.

Raphael's magic touch continued after the financial crisis: his De Niro Group at Prudential sold more than $80 million in condos in 2009 and 2010 combined, bringing his total sales in his first six years as a broker past the $600 million mark. His grandmother would have been proud.

JUST AS RAPHAEL was rising to his own personal and professional glory, De Niro was still at work on maintaining the legacy of his own father. The decades after the senior De Niro's death continued to be filled with commemorations, retrospectives, and celebrations of the man and his work. In 2010, De Niro established the Robert De Niro Sr. Prize, intended to honor a midcareer American painter. Funded by De Niro through the Tribeca Film Institute, the prize granted its recipient $25,000 and the publicity attendant upon receiving such an honor from a movie star. Its first two recipients, Stanley Whitney (2011) and Joyce Pensato (2012), were selected for, in the terms established by the Robert De Niro Sr. Estate, "making a lifelong commitment to their art." De Niro explained the foundation of the annual prize thus: "It's a way of getting more involved, because I just never have been that much into the art scene, other than my father's work." In 2014 he continued to be involved, though, producing a documentary celebrating his father's life, art, and legacy, *Remembering the Artist: Robert De Niro Sr.*, a forty-minute film directed by Geeta Gandbhir and Perri Peltz, which premiered at Sundance and aired on HBO and for which De Niro submitted to on-camera interviews and did promotion in the press.

The one sour note in all of this posthumous glorification: the dealings involving Lawrence Salander, the Upper East Side art dealer who represented the senior De Niro's work at his Salander-O'Reilly Galleries during the last years of the painter's life and thereafter. In 2007, word started to circulate in the art world that Salander, whose lavish lifestyle included flying in private jets and hosting a party at the Frick Collection for his wife at an estimated cost of $60,000, was defrauding clients. Several investors gave him paintings only to learn that he had sold them without their permission; others, including tennis star John McEnroe, believed they were investing in masterworks with him but learned that he had never purchased the paintings or had sold them and neglected to share the proceeds. In 2007, it was discovered that Salander had settled a $5 million debt to an Italian art gallery by sending them a collection of paintings that included as many as a dozen works by the elder De Niro, and that was when De Niro put his lawyers on the case.

Salander was forced to shut his doors in October of that year, and soon after declared bankruptcy. In March 2009 he was arrested on an indictment charging that he'd stolen as much as $88 million from clients and investors; in announcing the arrest, Patrick Dugan, the chief investigator in the Manhattan district attorney's office, compared him to the character Max Bialystock from Mel Brooks's *The Producers*. In the coming months, more wronged parties emerged, and the total estimate of Salander's crimes was raised to some $93 million and then, a few months later, $120 million.

Cornered, Salander pled guilty to twenty-nine charges of grand larceny in March 2010 and was sentenced to six to eighteen years in prison and ordered to pay $114 million in fines and restitution. The following year, his associate, Leigh Morse, went on trial for her part in the fraud, including pocketing $77,000 from the sale of two works by the elder De Niro. His son was called upon to testify, which he did in March 2011 at the New York State Supreme Court in Manhattan. There wasn't much to it. He was sporting a beard he'd grown for a movie role, and wore an appropriate if somewhat wrinkled dark olive corduroy blazer and gray slacks. He answered questions from both the prosecutor and the defense attorney, suggesting that he had first become suspicious of Salander when he traveled with him to Portugal for an exhibition of the painter's work and discovered, to his surprise, that the art dealer had his own plane. The one dramatic flourish during his forty-minute testimony came when he was asked to identify Morse. He turned his right hand into a pistol, pointed it at the defendant, and let his hand recoil, as if he'd just fired a shot.[*]

IF *RIGHTEOUS KILL* wasn't what anyone wanted out of a De Niro/ Pacino crime movie, making it seemed to pique De Niro's interest in choosing projects. His next few films weren't all memorable, but they generally had ambitions, intentions, and/or collaborators of substance, especially compared to what he'd done in the past five or six years.

Everybody's Fine was a remake of a 1990 Giuseppe Tornatore film in which Marcello Mastroianni played a widower who travels to Italy after his wife's death to visit his grown children, only to find them all putting up false fronts of happiness and security so as not to reveal the painful truths about their lives to a father who had always seemed uninterested in them. It had been rewritten by the director Kirk Jones (*Waking Ned Devine*) for Miramax as a rather generic vehicle for an older male star and a trio of younger actors. De Niro was cast as the dad, Frank Goode, who traveled all across America with a tiny suitcase dropping in on his offspring, who were to be played by Kate Beckinsale, Drew Barry-more, and Sam Rockwell (genetic familial resemblances be damned). In a decision much more to do with money than with art, Connecticut would stand in for the entire United States, including Las Vegas.

It was a routine melodrama without much in the way of memorable writing or staging and a patently tacked-on happy ending (a homey Yuletide scene was clearly shot in the summer months, when the film was made). But De Niro took to it with a becoming seriousness, find-ing something empathetic in Goode's workaholism and disconnection. In a neat detail, Goode was said to have devoted his professional life to manufacturing insulation for telephone and fiber optic cables—a per-fect metaphor for De Niro's own isolated nature. And he knew he had done something special, if slight, in the film: "I never say this about myself," he told a reporter, "but I was very proud of that [performance], and Kirk is a terrific director. I certainly worked very hard on that one."

---

[*]   Morse was convicted at that trial of several of the counts against her, but *not* the charges having to do with the sale of the elder De Niro's work.

Considerably more interesting was his next picture, *Stone*, a small and intense story of crime, punishment, sin, and redemption. One of the chief appeals of the film, which shot around Detroit in the spring of 2009, was that it would reunite him with Edward Norton on something that might erase the memory of the sturm-und-drang that made the production of *The Score* such an ordeal. *Stone* was a pet project of writer-director John Curran, who'd previously worked with Norton on *The Painted Veil*. Based on a play by Angus MacLachlan, it deals with the relationship of a prison convict, his wife, and his parole officer, to whom the wife is willing to offer herself sexually in exchange for her husband's freedom. Curran had thought of Norton for the prisoner and De Niro for the parole officer, but they couldn't make their schedules mesh, and Norton dropped out. Not long afterward, Norton's calendar suddenly opened up. De Niro was still available and willing, and with the two stars aboard, a budget of $22 million became available.

The role of Lucetta, the prisoner's wife, was still unfilled. Curran wanted an African American actress in the part, which would mesh with the Detroit setting and with Norton's character's self-presentation as a street tough. As Norton recalled, "I was into that idea [and] Bob was into that idea." But there were some pressures from the international financial entities who put up the production budget to seek a name that carried some weight abroad. Then Norton remembered how good the Ukrainian actress Milla Jovovich had been as a street-smart New Yorker in Spike Lee's *He Got Game*, and when De Niro and Curran watched the film they agreed.

There was a long period of going over the script very carefully in New York, a kind of combination of rehearsal and revision between Curran and his stars, and Norton noticed that De Niro was more engaged in the process than he had been with *The Score*. "I think Bob was just switched on from the get-go," he recalled. "It was like weeks and weeks and weeks of kind of meeting with John in his office and going through stuff and all the best ways of working, talking, thinking, trying it out."

For all their careful planning, when they finally went to Michigan to shoot, Norton had a surprise to pop on De Niro. The younger actor had been having some trouble coming up with a characterization for his part, and he'd been interviewing prison inmates for inspiration when he met a fellow who he felt was perfect: a white man who wore his hair in cornrows and spoke in a raspy voice that bore a slight whistle on certain sounds. On the day they shot the convict's initial encounter with the parole officer, Norton sprang his persona on De Niro for the first time. De Niro, of course, relished the surprise and wove his astonishment into the scene.

Norton came away from the film impressed with De Niro's powerful sense of minimalism, the way in which he seemed almost to prefer *not* speaking dialogue, but to act from internal cues. "A lot of times actors want more lines," he said. "Both times I've worked with him he just takes a pen to it and kind of goes, I don't think I need to say that, I don't think I need to say that, I don't think I need to say that. Almost to a fault . . . I almost think a good director ends up having to persuade Bob . . . that certain text is actually needed."*

DE NIRO STARTED accepting awards again: from the Karlovy Vary Film Festival in the Czech Republic in 2008; from BAFTA-LA and from the Hollywood Film Festival in 2009; from the Taormina Film Festival in Italy in 2010. The biggest of these was the Kennedy Center Honors, the nation's highest cultural award, presented to him by Barack Obama alongside fellow honorees Mel Brooks, Bruce Springsteen, jazz musician Dave Brubeck, and opera singer Grace Bumbry. Meryl Streep introduced him (he returned the favor the following year, when she received the same honor), Ben Stiller and others offered their memories of working with him, and the whole evening had an air of dignity.

In early 2011 he accepted the Cecil B. DeMille Award from the Golden Globes for Outstanding Contributions to the World of Entertainment—but there was very little dignity in the air at all. Just the previous year, he had appeared at the same awards show to pre-

---

* In fact, every working script of De Niro's available for inspection would reveal that this tendency toward minimalism and silence had been part of his acting strategy since his first film roles.

sent Martin Scorsese with the same honor. On the night he accepted the award, though, De Niro's acceptance speech was a disaster of bad, even tasteless jokes (one suggested the service at the stars' tables was lousy because so many waiters had been deported, along with Javier Bardem), and he read it from a teleprompter ineptly, as if seeing it for the first time. He even took a lighthearted dig at his hosts, declaring, "We're all in this together: the filmmakers who make the movies and the Hollywood Foreign Press Association [which hands out the Golden Globes], who in turn pose for pictures with the movie stars." The responses to his speech—both in social media during the event and in the following day's newspapers—weren't kind.

The next year, he was honored by his hometown during the seventh Made in New York awards ceremony. Noting that Meryl Streep would be receiving an award later in the evening, he joked, "I'm proud I have the same number of these as Meryl. For now. By this time next year, she'll have seven. Last October, she beat me out for Italian-American man of the year."

And he gave as many awards as he got. In 2010, he presented an honorary Oscar to ninety-five-year-old Eli Wallach, quipping, "Now that we're going up for the same parts, I hope we can remain friends. . . . There's nothing I like to see more than an even older actor."

A few years later, accepting yet another acting prize, he went off on a rare comic spree about his status as an éminence grise in show business:

> What mostly gets me here is to present awards to other people. I've handed out Oscars to Sean Penn, Eli Wallach and Francis Coppola. I've honored Meryl Streep at the Kennedy Center. I've handed out about a half-dozen lifetime achievement awards to Marty Scorsese, from the BAFTA to the Golden Globes. So even though DiCaprio has taken my place in Marty's movies, I'm apparently the go-to guy in handing out the hardware. I've gotten pretty good at giving out awards, but frankly I've gotten out of practice accepting an award myself. It's been a while, except for getting that medal from the Irish American League when they couldn't get Liam Neeson.

As INTERESTING as *Stone* was, it satisfied neither his thirst to work nor his need to earn, and before the year was over he would address both of those with two more films, *Machete*, in which he played an evil-hearted southern politician with more than one dirty secret, and *Little Fockers*, yet a third go-round with Ben Stiller and Blythe Danner.

In *Machete* he seemed to have some fun, chewing up scenery in a way that suited writer-director Robert Rodriguez's overheated B-movie sensibility (the film had its origins in a mock trailer for a nonexistent film that appeared in *Grindhouse*, the portmanteau genre picture from 2007 that Rodriguez made with Quentin Tarantino). The script even gave him a little character twist—revealed in his final scenes—that allowed him to dig into the part with a bit of a wink and a spin.

Little Fockers, on the other hand, was about as subtle and nuanced as a steamroller leveling a fruit stand. There was a new director, Paul Weitz, who had made *About a Boy* for Tribeca, but virtually nothing else was added to the *Meet the Fockers* recipe save Harvey Keitel as a home-building contractor who's apparently milking his commission, leading to a shouting match with De Niro's Jack Byrnes staged, inelegantly, as an echo of the stairwell quarrel in which the actors had engaged in *Mean Streets* almost forty years prior. Everything about this third *Fockers* film was smaller, paler, and more strained, and audiences weren't nearly so charmed by it, resulting in $148 million domestically and $162 million abroad—the least any of the *Fockers* films had earned. That said, the three of them had a worldwide gross of $1.156 *billion*, and as De Niro and Tribeca were participants in the profits from the outset, they wound up constituting the most lucrative enterprise of his life.*

You'd think that would have slowed him down, but the late 2010 crop of films (*Machete, Stone, Little Fockers*) turned out to be the launch of quite literally the busiest phase of his career. In the coming three years, he would appear in no fewer than seventeen films, including one that never played in American theaters, one that played a single Times Square screen for a single week before appearing on

---

* The three *Focker* films and *Shark Tale* would, in fact, stand as the four highest-grossing movies in his entire career.

home media, and one that would earn him his first Oscar nomination in more than two decades.

In 2011 he appeared as a shadowy Wall Street tycoon in Neil Burger's *Limitless*, a thriller about a struggling novelist (Bradley Cooper) whose use of a drug to combat writer's block gives him superhuman abilities of concentration and application; as a bloodless mercenary (alongside Jason Statham and Clive Owen) in Gary McKendry's *Killer Elite*; and as a dying photojournalist whose last wish is to see the ball drop in Times Square at the stroke of midnight in Garry Marshall's *New Year's Eve*. (There was also Giovanni Veronesi's *The Ages of Love*, an Italian ensemble film in which he played a divorced art professor living in Rome and which never appeared in the United States either theatrically or for home viewing—a first for De Niro, not counting a few TV commercials he'd shot in Japan.) These pictures came and went almost unnoticed, often not screened for critics or only after virtually every print publication's deadlines for opening day reviews had passed. *New Year's Eve* made a small splash; buoyed by a cast that included Sarah Jessica Parker, Zac Efron, Michelle Pfeiffer, Halle Berry, Ashton Kutcher, Jessica Biel, and Jon Bon Jovi, it did $55.5 million in ticket sales against a budget of a similar sum. But that hardly excused it as a piece of work—nor did it make De Niro's appearance in it any less embarrassing.

He was similarly busy in 2012, with some wildly divergent results. In Rodrigo Cortés's *Red Lights* he had a sometimes amusing but ultimately grating role as Simon Silver, a blind psychic whose claims to paranormal abilities confound a team of scientists dedicated to debunking such phenomena. (A bit of levity was provided by director Eugenio Mira, Cortés's fellow Spaniard and an uncanny look-alike for De Niro, playing the young Silver in archival footage.) That picture came and went like a rumor, earning just over $50,000 at the American box office. But that was a massive hit compared to *Freelancers*, a film starring Curtis "50 Cent" Jackson as a rookie New York cop drawn into a culture of corruption by De Niro's senior officer; that film played just one New York screen for only one week—surely fulfilling a contractual mandate of some sort—before appearing for home viewing. It was as near to straight-to-video, to use the outdated phrase, as anything De Niro had ever done.

ONCE AGAIN, the murmurs rose: What had happened to Robert De Niro? Why was the man so widely regarded as the greatest American screen actor of the latter half of the twentieth century so willing to make so many movies of so little worth?

One obvious answer might be money, but how much could a fellow earn for an Italian film with no U.S. release, or in a direct-to-home-viewing thriller, or in films with entire budgets smaller than his individual paycheck for appearing in *Analyze That* or the *Fockers* sequels? No, not only was he working easy, he was apparently working cheap. He loved to quote Stella Adler's dictum "Your talent lies in your choices"; what did the choices he made in his sixties and beyond say about his own impression of his talent at that late moment in his life and career? Why was he working so much—and so seemingly indifferently?

The answer may have lain in the very word *work*. For De Niro, work seemed to be an end in itself—not so much something he liked to do as something he was fulfilled by doing and saw as a point of life. There were pleasures in the world—women, food, travel, exercise, booze (and, decades earlier, drugs)—and there was work, and it was almost as if he had some sense that one could not fully enjoy the former unless one had truly engaged with the latter. It was a product, perhaps, of a childhood spent watching two adults work hard at divergent fields of endeavor: Robert De Niro Sr. struggling to make art that satisfied his own high standards, even if the world wouldn't recognize or compensate him for it, and Virginia Admiral building a business and then a small real estate empire out of dogged determination.

In his earliest acting days, even before *Greetings* and *Hi, Mom!*, De Niro impressed student directors and fellow performers with his professionalism, his seriousness, his drive—not careerism, exactly, but complete application to the task of becoming an actor. This was the fellow who wrote letters to college newspapers to get tear sheets of their reviews of his work, who traveled on his own dime to learn accents and spent his own money on pieces of wardrobe even when he was working in films financed by major studios, who floored Elia Kazan with requests to work through the weekend, who learned to play the saxophone and to box at the same time. He poured himself wholly into his work in ways that almost no American actor of his stature ever had.

That determination to delve thoroughly into his own resources and into the contours of a character—whether wholly imagined or based on a real-life original—stuck with him well into the 1990s. His work on *Goodfellas, Awakenings, Backdraft, Cape Fear, This Boy's Life, Frankenstein, Casino, Heat,* and *Flawless* was, no matter what you thought of the films or even his performances, earnest and engaged. Sometime after making *Meet the Parents,* though, after achieving his greatest payday to date, his technique and especially his application slackened. He began to skim through roles more frequently than dive into them, to do minimal research if any, to repeat himself by rote. For the first time in his acting career, he seemed not to care what he was in, what he was playing, who was making it, what the truth underneath it all was, or how best to convey it.

He was not, however, lazy. As he ratcheted back on his effort in each film that he made, he still behaved as if the work-focused machinery inside him needed to achieve full expression. So, rather than pour himself wholly into individual roles as he so often had in the 1970s, '80s, and even '90s, digging deep and filling the spaces created by his excavations with the raw material of his talent and research, he began to expend the same amount of total energy, more or less, on a greater number of films, aiming for breadth rather than depth. It was almost as if he had a certain amount of time, strength, passion, and interest for his work, and instead of dedicating it to one film at a time he was meting it out widely all at once—and, far too often, less than discriminatingly.

Of course, once an actor decides that he will increase his workload, the paucity of worthy material becomes increasingly evident. The American movie industry has always been a factory, churning out products aimed chiefly at selling tickets, following fashions and trends, eyes always on the bottom line; only when attention is pointed its way and it is wearing its finest tuxedoes and gowns does it focus on art. Still, for all the wildcatting energy in the early days of the system, under the imperial powers of the movie studios, or in the renegade days of the 1970s or even the 1990s, there was no time when the sheer output of feature movies was greater than the twenty-first century. In the film exhibition capitals of America, New York and Los Angeles, it was possible to go to theaters and see nearly one thousand new films a year by 2010—and to watch perhaps that many premieres again, if not more, on home media. In such a climate, audiences weren't the only ones puzzled by the multiplicity of choices; filmmakers were as well. Which scripts to read, which to fund, which to distribute, and, in De Niro's case, which to appear in: none of it seemed terribly clear.

Somewhere in his brain—maybe even consciously—a switch had flipped, and he had begun to take a different attitude toward work. And he had chosen to do so at a ruinous time for his art and his legacy. Decades before, at the dawn of his career, when the sheer magnitude of his talent was beginning fully to emerge, he had said, "People now tell me if I will consent to a project, they can get the deal going. But what should I commit myself to?" Now that same conundrum faced him again: there were too many films to choose among, many of them needing only his approval to get made. And far too often after 2001 or so, for reasons that were genuinely unclear and even troubling, he chose wrongly. Once his talent had seemed like vintage wine, carefully decanted drop by painstaking drop into the finest crystal. Now he was pouring it sloppily into so many paper cups as if it were the cheapest, most indifferently made plonk. He couldn't even point to eye-popping box office or massive personal gains as excuses for his choices. His need to work had always bordered on a pathology, but whereas it once produced magical alchemy, now it left little spills that nobody could be bothered to mop up.*

ALONG WITH BECOMING a legitimate business force, Raphael De Niro had become a family man. In March 2008 he wed Claudine DeMatos,

---

* He had the grace to acknowledge that his working comportment had changed. At the 2014 White House Correspondents' Dinner, which De Niro attended, emcee Joel McHale made a joke about De Niro's career: "I don't do an impression of Robert De Niro, but I do one of his agent: 'Ring Ring!' (mimes answering phone) 'He'll do it!'" De Niro laughed.

the daughter of a Brazilian restaurateur and travel agent, whom he met when she was working for his dad's old squeeze Naomi Campbell, at the time that he was finding an apartment for the supermodel. Raphael convinced Claudine to come work with him at Prudential Douglas Elliman, and they dated and were finally married at a private home in the Bahamas. The two hundred guests included Harvey Keitel, Chazz Palminteri, magician David Blaine (a Raphael De Niro client, who performed some illusions at the party), and, in a detail that delighted tabloid gossips, all three women with whom De Niro had children: Diahnne Abbott, the mother of the groom, of course (by then married to the artist Noel Copeland); Toukie Smith; and Grace Hightower. Within three years, the young couple, who lived in a $3 million condo on Greenwich Street, just up the block from the Tribeca Film Center, had two children, a boy, Nicholas, born in May 2009, and a girl, Alexandria, born in March 2011.

Alexandria wasn't the only De Niro baby of the year. In December 2011 the world was briefly startled by the news that De Niro and Hightower, sixty-eight and fifty-six, respectively, were new parents. Helen Grace (her name a variation on that of her mother, Grace Helen, as well as a nod to De Niro's paternal grandmother, Helen O'Reilly De Niro, who died in 1999, just months shy of her hundredth birthday) was, like her twin half brothers Aaron and Julian, born to a surrogate. The couple's son, Elliot, was thirteen, and their marital difficulties were a decade or so behind them. The decision to bring a new baby into the family at their ages seemed puzzling, but it was a significant affirmation that their bond was strong and all of the fractures in it had fully healed.

The following year, with De Niro taking on a busier workload than ever before, Hightower started to make headlines with a business venture. Like most Americans, she was only partially informed about the effects of civil war and genocide on the people of Rwanda, but in 2011 she met the country's president, Paul Kagame, at an evening hosted by Jane Rosenthal. Inspired by the president's statement that his country needed "trade, not aid," Hightower, who had a history of working on the sort of charitable endeavors commonly supported by New York socialites, began to look into what sort of businesses she could help foster in the impoverished African nation, and she hit on coffee. In 2012 she started a business named, a mite inelegantly, Grace Hightower and Coffees of Rwanda, a fair-trade brand of gourmet coffee beans grown in Africa, roasted in Connecticut, and sold at upscale markets in New York City and online. The company was designed to funnel the profits back to local Rwandan coffee farmers, but by 2013 it was robust enough that Hightower was considering opening a storefront to sell the coffee—in bulk and to drink on the spot—in, where else, Tribeca.

30

I N THE SPRING OF 2011, DE NIRO JOURNEYED ONCE AGAIN TO the French Riviera, this time to serve as the president of the jury for the sixty-fourth edition of the Cannes Film Festival. He had been coming to the festival regularly since the 1970s, with films in and out of competition, and two of them had taken its top prize, the Palme d'Or: *Taxi Driver* in 1976 and *The Mission* ten years later. His fellow jurors included the actors Jude Law, Uma Thurman, and Linn Ullmann and the directors Olivier Assayas and Johnnie To, and the films they had to choose among included *The Skin I Live In, Once Upon a Time in Anatolia, The Artist, Melancholia, We Need to Talk About Kevin, Drive*, and the eventual winner, *The Tree of Life*. To enhance the De Niro–ness of the festival, there were events honoring two key directors from his past, Roger Corman and Bernardo Bertolucci, a retrospective screening of *A Bronx Tale*, and a gala dinner to fete De Niro himself, at which Gilles Jacob, the president of the festival, and Frédéric Mitterrand, France's minister of culture, spoke about De Niro's artistic and cultural achievements. De Niro, who had uttered a few words of fractured French at the opening festivities, responded to these accolades by declaring, "You're going to make me cry." But he muddled through, and he returned the following year to introduce a restored version of *Once Upon a Time in America*, the film that he, Sergio Leone, and James Woods had brought to Cannes almost three decades prior.

DURING NEGOTIATIONS TO direct *Little Fockers*, Paul Weitz told De Niro about another project he was interested in making, an adaptation of the 2004 memoir *Another Bullshit Night in Suck City* by the poet Nick Flynn. The book told the story of Flynn's struggle to become a writer and to live with the burden of the legacy of his father, Jonathan, an alcoholic, never-published novelist. The elder Flynn had always proclaimed his own literary greatness and his dedication to true art, and he lived on the margins of society, doing any kind of work to keep a roof over his head and even living on the streets at a time when his son was working as a nighttime attendant at a homeless shelter. Like his father, Flynn was prone to substance abuse, to failed relationships with women, to losing jobs and gigs because he was so antagonistic toward the people around him.

As the title would indicate, there was droll humor in the book, but Weitz, whose father, the fashion designer John Weitz, died in 2002, was interested in the darker material in it: the dysfunction and the horror of homelessness, the crippling legacies that so often pass from fathers to sons. Weitz described the script he distilled from the book as appropriate for a "Romanian arthouse film," but De Niro could easily identify with the theme of a young New York artist trying to make his way in the wake of a father who was also an artist—and isolated, slightly misanthropic, and maybe a little mad. When Weitz told him that studios had expressed interest in making the film only if he could brighten it up, emphasize the comedy, and otherwise coddle the audience, De Niro responded that Tribeca would be interested in helping to make the film properly and that he would be interested in playing the dad (a boon, per Nick Flynn, who claimed that De Niro carried just the combination of "grandeur and menace"). They finally got it green-lit by Focus Features for a budget of $8 million, with Paul Dano cast as Nick and Julianne Moore as his mother, who divorced Jonathan when Nick was just a kid.

It would be Dano's film, just as it was Nick Flynn's book and life, and it turned out that he was strong enough to play the part well in its best and its worst aspects. But the revelation in the film was De Niro, brushing against themes and situations from some of his earlier films and, more impressively, drawing on bits of his and his father's lives to build the most full-bodied and empathetic character he had played in years. *Stone* had shown that he could engage if he wished to; in *Being*

Flynn, De Niro brushed against autobiography and truly personal material in a way he hadn't done since *A Bronx Tale* almost twenty years prior.

For one thing, he took his research seriously for the first time in a while, learning about the day-to-day trauma of being homeless in lower Manhattan alongside Weitz and others in the cast.* He read the scattered writings of Jonathan Flynn and went to an assisted-care facility in Boston to meet him ("So, you do a little acting," the elder Flynn said to De Niro, to which he responded, "Yeah, I do a little acting"). De Niro picked Nick's brain about details of his father's behavior, habits, and comportment; he even hefted the club that the older Flynn carried around for protection, just to get a feel for it. The film was more or less shot in places where De Niro had grown up and lived his whole life, and a lot of it was shot in neorealist style, with the stars appearing in actual locations and blended in among non-actors.

There were outright allusions to De Niro's working persona: the elder Flynn worked, like Travis Bickle, as a Manhattan taxi driver; his outbursts at homeless shelters, including the one where Nick worked, echoed De Niro's explosive turns in *Awakenings*. And there was even a scene when Jonathan asks Nick to enlist some friends to help him move his belongings from the apartment that he's being evicted from into a storage facility, a re-creation of De Niro and his acting chum Larry Woiwode helping the senior De Niro fetch the belongings he'd had shipped back to him from France after returning to New York in the mid-1960s. The film didn't make much money, but De Niro showed some strength and spark in it.

DURING DE NIRO'S 1998 appearance on *Inside the Actors Studio*, the camera flashed, as it often did on that program, to show the audience of acting students, among whom one in particular stood out, with an intent gaze of appreciation, eyes wide, mouth slightly agape, as if being

---

* The film relocated the book's Boston setting to New York, meaning that De Niro spent a lot of time pretending to be homeless in a neighborhood where he owned millions of dollars' worth of properties.

shown by a magician how all those amazing tricks are really done. He was a twenty-two-year-old kid from Philadelphia who was enrolled at the Actors Studio school at the New School (where De Niro's dad had once taught painting) and who was just beginning to make his way from student stage productions to small parts in TV and film.

A few years later, when casting for *Everybody's Fine* was under way, that same kid was still building a career and hoping for a big break, and he took the bold step of sending a videotape of himself reading a scene as De Niro's son with his own mother, off-camera, reading the De Niro part. He didn't get the role, which went to Sam Rockwell, but he did get a nice response from De Niro, who encouraged him.

By the time *Everybody's Fine* made it into theaters, though, the kid had arrived, starring in a huge comedy hit and getting cast in leading roles regularly after a decade of toiling on TV and as part of an ensemble. In 2010, he finally got to work with De Niro, albeit not in very many scenes, in the surprise hit *Limitless*. His name was Bradley Cooper, and he and De Niro would, not long after *Limitless*, enjoy a high point in their respective careers by working together.

The two were cast as father and son—as senior and junior, in fact—in David O. Russell's *Silver Linings Playbook*, an adaptation of Matthew Quick's 2008 novel about a mentally unbalanced schoolteacher, Pat Solitano Jr., who is released from court-ordered institutionalization to the care of his parents, whose house is dominated by Pat senior's obsessive-compulsive disorder, gambling addiction, and hair-trigger temper. At first Pat junior's psychoses prove too much for his parents to handle, but he finds a path to normalcy and salvation in a relationship with Tiffany, a young widow of his family's acquaintance who has suffered a mental crisis of her own.

Russell, the father of a teenage son with a mood disorder, was taken with the book immediately and had hopes of filming it even before it was published. He had known De Niro since his work touching up *Meet the Fockers*, and he knew that De Niro, too, was the father of a son living with psychological challenges. He thought De Niro would make a perfect Pat senior, and he broached the idea with him in a meeting. "Robert and I have been speaking about these family matters for years," Russell said. "So I sat with him, and we discussed the script and personal matters, and he started to cry. I watched him cry for 10 minutes. . . . He told his agent, 'Make this happen.'"

Russell worked on adapting the book with Vince Vaughn and Zooey Deschanel in mind for Pat junior and Tiffany. When the script was done, it drew the attention of Mark Wahlberg, who was working with Russell on *The Fighter*, and Angelina Jolie. When they stepped back, the script fell to Cooper, and the producers landed on Jennifer Lawrence, the twenty-one-year-old Oscar nominee from 2010's *Winter's Bone*. De Niro, everyone's first choice for Pat senior no matter whom else the film starred, never budged and was ready to go when Russell was.

By the time the film was cast, it was mid-2011, and the Weinstein Company, which had budgeted the film at $22 million, was expecting shooting to be completed by Thanksgiving. That meant there would be almost no rehearsal, which suited Russell's technique. In such films as *Flirting with Disaster, Three Kings, I Heart Huckabees*, and *The Fighter* he had developed a style that employed multiple handheld cameras and improvised dialogue; he would literally throw lines at his actors to repeat or respond to in the middle of a take, with all the cameras running. "The actors are never given the release of cutting the camera," remarked the film's editor, Jay Cassidy. "David is consciously shooting variations because he's working out his script in the shooting and in the editing."

De Niro wasn't fazed by Russell's methods, which somewhat recalled the wildcatting style of *Mean Streets*. "You've got the camera moving around," he said, "he'll push the camera over to this character, to that character, he'll throw lines at you and you repeat them. And I don't mind that, it's all great. It's a particular way of working and gets right to it and it's spontaneous. You just have to go with it." In fact, he admitted, he wasn't always sure what shape the film was taking. Russell had reimagined the Pat senior he'd encountered in Quick's pages, De Niro said: "He kept to himself more in the book it was based on and was more angry, but he didn't have many other colors. I liked what David did: he kind of reversed him, pulled him inside-out." Couple that revision of the character with the improvisatory filming technique, De Niro said, and anything might have happened. "It had a certain chaotic, frenetic kind of energy, a spontaneity," De Niro recounted. "And people would say that they didn't know where it was going, which is a good thing."

A very good thing, in fact. When *Silver Linings Playbook* debuted at the 2012 Toronto International Film Festival, it was immediately projected as a significant Oscar contender, with fine performances in all the lead roles (including the Australian actress Jackie Weaver as Pat senior's wife, Dolores, and Chris Tucker as Pat junior's best chum from the mental hospital). If Russell had been the film's instigator, creator, and auteur, from the moment it left Toronto it belonged to Harvey Weinstein, a past master of turning Oscar buzz into box office and golden statuettes. Weinstein opened the film slowly, with New York and Los Angeles getting it just before Thanksgiving and the rest of the country on Christmas Day. The reviews were very strong, especially for De Niro, whose good work in *Stone* and *Being Flynn* had been overlooked but who was unignorable in what was turning out to be a crowd-pleasing smash; buoyed, in large part, by award-season eclat, *Silver Linings* went on to gross $132 million domestically and another $104 million abroad.

And De Niro could take some credit for that. His Pat Solitano Sr. is a jackknife of a man: slender, muscled, almost pompadoured, a natty dresser, with a quick temper, unbridled passions, and such a powerful need to control his environment that there could be ten of him in his small, neat Philadelphia home, straightening the remote controls near his TV-watching chair, counting the envelopes in his bookmaking business, carefully archiving his videocassettes of Eagles games. He loves his wife, Dolores, and his sons, Jake and Pat junior. But chiefly he loves his peace of mind and his routines and his football team, and anything that gets in the way of any of that is an issue for him.

When Pat junior comes home from a mental institution, his dad is dubious, and when Pat junior threatens to fall apart once again, the father's concerns spill out into a confused blend of self-protectiveness, anger, embarrassment, and worry. He loves his boy—he is moved to tears and a choked voice in an unsolicited confession of his wishes for him—but he has no clue how to handle Pat junior, perhaps because he has no clue how to handle himself.

Pat senior is a gambling addict, at the very least, running an illegal bookmaking business out of his home, and he can't attend Eagles games any longer because he's been banned from the stadium for fighting. (When he drops Pat junior at the parking lot before a game, his parting advice, "Don't drink too much, don't hit anybody, you'll be fine," seems equally directed at himself.) When he feels his territory is being invaded, altered, or even *touched*, his anxiety becomes palpable. His game-day superstitions are vividly real to him, and he truly believes there's some connection between a football team's performance and the posture in which people are sitting on the couch in his home or holding a lucky handkerchief.

Facing a real threat, though, he unleashes fury. When Pat junior finally loses the thread of his sanity and accidentally bloodies his mom's nose, Pat senior engages him in an actual fistfight that leaves both of them sporting shameful shiners. When a neighbor boy (played by David O. Russell's son) shows up on the doorstep during a loud family quarrel to ask if he can interview them for a school project about living with mental illness, Pat senior chases the kid back home and threatens him so terribly that the kid actually laughs (picture De Niro, bloody-nosed and pajama-clad, shouting, "I'm gonna take that fuckin' camera and I'm gonna break it over your fuckin' head and then I'm gonna come back and interview you about what it's like to get that camera broken over your head," and the source of the humor is clear).

But he's adaptable. When Pat junior's new love interest, Tiffany, makes the case that she is *not* a bad luck charm but rather *helps* Pat junior's pro-Eagles mojo, and she cites the statistics that prove it, Pat senior turns from lambasting her to endorsing her. "I gotta say I'm impressed," he declares with his face frowning in grudging appreciation. "I gotta rethink this whole thing." Soon enough, he's standing beside her and they're literally repeating each other's sentences.

Finally, in one of the most touching moments in the film, the older Pat tells the younger to chase after Tiffany and not let her get away. It's a truly memorable pep talk, delivered firmly and earnestly and with love: "I know you don't wanna listen to your father, I didn't wanna listen to mine . . . but it's a sin if you don't reach out. It's a sin. It could haunt you the rest of your days like a curse. . . . Don't fuck this up." They embrace. They're deeply flawed, but they're bonded just as deeply. It's a sweet, savvy capper to a quietly powerful performance.

IN JANUARY, WITH the film doing strong business on a relatively modest number of screens, Oscar nominations were announced and *Silver Linings Playbook* was a big story: eight nods in total, for Best Picture, Best Director, Best Adapted Screenplay, and Best Editing, and one each for Best Actor (Cooper), Best Actress (Lawrence), Best Supporting Actress (Weaver), and Best Supporting Actor (De Niro). It was the first film to earn nominations in all four acting categories since Warren Beatty's *Reds* more than thirty years prior. And it was De Niro's first Oscar nomination since 1992's *Cape Fear.*

Much had changed in the decades since he was last a contender in the Academy Awards sweepstakes, including the advent of Weinstein, who had turned the race for Oscar gold into a blood sport, first at Miramax and now at the Weinstein Company, and the rise of Oscarazzi, the hives of bloggers who spent as much as nine months of the year prognosticating the awards. Participating in this sort of exercise didn't seem like anything that the famously publicity-averse De Niro would dream of doing. Yet, perhaps bowing to the influence of his friend Harvey, perhaps acknowledging a special relationship to the material, perhaps grateful to be recognized for his work and not just by lousy impressionists or by people wondering what had happened to him, he plunged into the Oscar race, doing interviews and personal appearances, traveling and smiling and accommodating requests—behaving, in short, as he never had, not even when he was an eager up-and-comer.

He did interviews in *Vanity Fair* (to whose Proust Questionnaire query of "On what occasion do you lie?" he responded, "When I'm being polite. Like when *Vanity Fair* asked if I wanted to do the Proust Questionnaire and I said, 'Sure'") and two in the *New York Times*; he visited *CBS This Morning* and *The Tonight Show* and *The David Letterman Show.* In an appearance that made headlines, he broke down in tears on Katie Couric's syndicated talk show when he revealed, for the first time in public, that he had a son at home who struggled with emotional issues. After Russell described directing his own son in a scene,

Couric asked De Niro if he felt any special responsibility to bring the story to the screen because of the director's familial situation. De Niro was already on the verge of crying when he started to speak: "I understand what he . . ." He teared up and raised a finger as if to call a time-out, then wiped his eyes with a tissue that Couric handed him, while Cooper, his own eyes filling, patted him on the shoulder. De Niro continued, his voice choked, "I don't like to get emotional. But I know exactly what he goes through." A reaction shot of the audience showed much of it sobbing along with him. It was stunning.

He flew to Los Angeles, where in a single day he put his hands in the cement at Grauman's Chinese Theatre, attended the annual Oscar luncheon with his fellow nominees from all categories, and spoke at a screening of *Silver Linings* at the American Cinematheque. He attended the BAFTA awards show in London, the AACTA awards show in Sydney, the Screen Actors Guild awards in Los Angeles (he presented Jennifer Lawrence with her prize; "It's what I do," he joked), the Los Angeles Italia Fest, where he was himself honored, and the Weinstein Company's private Oscar weekend shindig. (He missed out on the Golden Globes, which failed to nominate him, staying in Nevada to work on a film and a business project.) He even showed up in person to receive a special proclamation from New York governor Andrew Cuomo acknowledging his New York heritage and all the work he'd done in and for his hometown.

And then, bless him, on Oscar night, he sat beside Grace Hightower applauding graciously as Christoph Waltz (*Django Unchained*) beat him (and Alan Arkin in *Argo*, Philip Seymour Hoffman in *The Master*, and Tommy Lee Jones in *Lincoln*) for the prize. The cliché says that it's an honor just to be nominated. Throughout the process, from the premiere in Toronto to Oscar night itself, De Niro comported himself as if it truly was.

YOU WOULD THINK that an Oscar nomination and a heartily waged awards season campaign might reignite his career, might make De Niro select roles more prudently or give him more top-shelf stuff from which to choose. But 2013 proved to be the single busiest year in his acting career, and a rather appalling one—six films in theaters from April to December, almost none of them worth leaving the house to see. There was *The Big Wedding*, a raunchy comedy by director Justin Zackham about a long-divorced couple (De Niro and Diane Keaton) reunited for the nuptials of their adopted son; *Killing Season*, Mark Steven Johnson's tepid thriller with John Travolta as a Serbian soldier going after the American officer (De Niro) who tripped him up during the Balkan War and has removed himself to isolation in the mountains to deal with his postwar stresses; *The Family*, a dark comedy by Luc Besson about a mobster (De Niro) and his family (including Michelle Pfeiffer as his wife) hidden in a small village in Normandy by the witness protection program; *Last Vegas*, a buddy movie by Jon Turteltaub, with De Niro, Morgan Freeman, and Kevin Kline joining their never-wed chum Michael Douglas for a bachelor weekend in the gambling mecca; *Grudge Match*, with De Niro and Sylvester Stallone directed by Peter Segal as boxers lured back into the ring to settle a beef born thirty years prior; and, the sole appetizing prospect in the bunch, *American Hustle*, a film about financial scams in the 1970s that reunited him—if only for a single powerful scene—with his *Silver Linings Playbook* writer-director David O. Russell and co-stars Bradley Cooper and Jennifer Lawrence.

It was, in the main, an appalling butcher's bill of make-work. The production cycle of filmmaking is such that most of these projects were under contract by the time *Silver Linings Playbook* proved a hit, but there was very little to recommend any of them in any context, much less as follow-ups to an Oscar nomination. Oh, there was some fun to be had in *The Family*, which allowed De Niro to indulge himself in bits of droll self-mockery akin to those practiced by Marlon Brando in *The Freshman*, which explicitly parodied his Don Corleone performance. And there was at least the potential for comic hay to result from such celebrity romps as *Last Vegas* and *Grudge Match*. But, like the overwhelming percentage of the films he had made in the preceding decade, his glut of work in 2013 consisted almost wholly of small movies—small, that is, in ambition, craft, budget, impact, and ultimately in public and critical esteem.

Offscreen, though, he maintained a defter touch. One of the original ideas for the Greenwich Hotel had been a Japanese-style oasis, a space of minimalism, quiet, clean lines, blank spaces. De Niro couldn't imagine it in the middle of Tribeca—"He doesn't like trendy, he doesn't like square lines. He likes curves, so to speak," said one of his Greenwich Hotel partners, Ira Drukier. But the idea still appealed to him, and he toyed with the notion of creating a residential hotel—a so-called condotel—with such an aesthetic in Manhattan. The post-crash economy scuttled that plan, but a few years later, with his first hotel running well in the black, he found the perfect setting for a second, built in a strongly Japanese style and carrying the cachet of the Nobu brand: Las Vegas, and specifically Caesar's Palace.

In February 2013 De Niro was in Nevada shooting *Last Vegas*, and he and Nobu Matsuhisa were on hand to cut the ribbon on the Hotel Nobu, the first of what they hoped would be a series of such hotels around the world. It opened properly in April, revealing itself to be at least as luxurious as the Greenwich and altogether otherworldly, a hotel within a hotel, costing $45 million, with 181 rooms and suites sitting on top of the largest of the twenty-five or so Nobu restaurants. In fact, the Asian-themed rooms featured the first-ever Nobu room service menu, with such breakfast staples as bagels and lox transformed by the chef into a crispy rice cake with salmon sashimi and tofu in lieu of cream cheese.

What on earth was a New York guy like De Niro doing opening a hotel on the Vegas Strip? "I kept seeing that people wanted Nobu to open restaurants in their hotels because it was a calling card," he explained. "So I asked, 'Why are we not doing our own?' Vegas is the place where things are always happening. It was the realization of a dream for me, too. I used to think about building [hotels] in a variety of places where you could have distinct experiences, from the tropics to a winter resort. I'd have fantasies that if I had enough money, I'd give it a shot." After only a few months of operation, the Nobu Hotel was such a success that it expanded its footprint at Caesar's Palace, and De Niro's fantasy of a global empire started to materialize as a distinct possibility, with talks beginning about opening branches of the hotel in London, Riyadh, and Bahrain. By year's end, he and some business partners, including his son Raphael, had signed an agreement to develop an 850,000-square-foot hotel, dining, and entertainment complex in Shanghai's famed Bund district. And yet another hotel site—Manila—was selected.

FOR A GUY pushing seventy who seemed shy about chatting, he could get in trouble with his mouth surprisingly often. In March 2012, at a fund-raiser to support the reelection of Barack Obama (whom he'd endorsed in 2008 against Hillary Clinton, despite his long, friendly history with her and her husband), De Niro noted Michelle Obama in the audience and quipped of the wives of the prospective Republican presidential nominees, "Calista Gingrich, Karen Santorum, Ann Romney. Now, do you think our country is ready for a white First Lady?"

It was a harmless if leaden joke, but it provided fuel for people who could get a few headlines out of a show of indignation, such as Newt Gingrich, who demanded an apology from both De Niro and the president. (Ann Romney, to her credit, dismissed the entire episode as trivial.) Michelle Obama's spokesperson expressed disapproval, De Niro's expressed contrition, and that was the end of it. (A year and a half later, he'd ruffle conservative feathers again by declaring that President Obama was a "good person" who was doing "the best job he can"—a bland sentiment for which he was pilloried in the right-wing chatterverse.)

In November of that same year, he attended a charitable fundraising party marking the birthday of Leonardo DiCaprio and got into a beef with the rapper Jay-Z. The hip-hop artist had noticed De Niro sitting at a table in a room filled with such boldface names as Martin Scorsese, Chris Rock, Emma Watson, Jamie Foxx, and Cameron Diaz, and he came over to say hello, only to find himself being chastised by De Niro for failing to return his phone calls. Jay tried to back out of the matter, and his wife, Beyoncé Knowles, even stepped in to try to mollify De Niro, but the actor, according to the sorts of people who whisper about such goings-on to gossip columnists, wouldn't relent. In the summer of 2013, promoting his new album, Jay was asked about the incident and declared indignantly that respect was something a person had to earn through his or her comportment, not by virtue of a name, an observation to which De Niro made no recorded retort.

—◦◦◦—

In August 2013 his seventieth birthday was marked with a private party at a Manhattan restaurant that was simply crawling with famous flesh. On hand were family members, old friends who might as well have been family (Scorsese, DiCaprio, Sean Penn, Harvey Weinstein), and other big names, Bradley Cooper and Keith Richards among them. The guests enjoyed a live performance by Lenny Kravitz, watched a filmed greeting from Kirk and Michael Douglas, and were treated to a couple of comical tributes, also on film, from Billy Crystal and Robin Williams. In the age of oversharing via social media, Samuel L. Jackson snapped a photo of De Niro, Harvey Keitel, and Chris Walken seated at a table, eating and laughing, and posted it on Instagram, where it enjoyed a day or two of viral heat.

The year found him everywhere: in Israel for the ninetieth birthday of Shimon Peres, in the Bay Area for the wedding of George Lucas, in Berlin and Tokyo and London and India to promote films. Along with fellow cast members from *Last Vegas* he appeared on *Sesame Street* to give a dramatic reading of a pop song (he was assigned Miley Cyrus's "Wrecking Ball") and co-hosted an hour of *Today*, including a cooking segment in which he prepared pumpkin casserole. He became the advertising face of a new checking service being offered by Santander Bank; his first commercial, in which he played himself chatting too much at a Robert De Niro film festival, was rather a hoot.

He signed on to more film projects: the crime story *The Bag Man*, the workplace comedy *The Intern*, the boxing biopic *Hands of Stone*, the police drama *Candy Store*. He talked often about working again with Martin Scorsese and Joe Pesci (and, why not, Al Pacino) on a mob picture called *The Irishman*.

He was relentless.

His schedule as a septuagenarian showed that he was, like his parents, defined in large part by his work. Yet there was something that seemed to drive him even more than the film performances, which piled up almost faster than anyone could watch them; the publicity campaigns, which seemed to become less onerous to him over time; the restaurant openings and the hotel deals, the awards given and received, the almost inexplicable ventures into advertising. And that something, almost inevitably, was his family.

He kept his father's memory alive by maintaining his studio and his artistic reputation. To a lesser extent, he tried to honor his mother's legacy—if only through pursuing her passion for Manhattan real estate. There had been lapses, he confessed, in his filial duties: "I always wanted to chronicle the family history with my mother. She was always interested in that. . . . But I wasn't forceful and I didn't make it happen. That's one regret I have."

He had, however, come to a place past regret with the family he had created. After all they had endured, he and Grace Hightower had finally become the committed couple they had twice vowed to be. At a birthday party he threw for her in the VIP room of his Locanda Verde restaurant, he toasted her briefly, warmly, and to much appreciation with "When she's happy, I'm happy." They traveled together on his various film and business obligations, and he supported her charitable work and her coffee venture. Standing side by side on red carpets all over the world, they seemed comfortable, connected, beyond the conflicts and upheavals that had once roiled them.

Too, his kids—six in all—were in the forefront of his mind, even after the eldest of them had become parents themselves. "I guess you could call it a fractionalized family of sorts," he said. "But I care deeply about all of them, and I have made a conscious effort to talk to and to listen to them."

He came to see himself as a paterfamilias, the graying man in the center of a teeming brood. It was a role unlike any he'd ever played onscreen, yet it suited him in real life. "I like my kids to be all around," he said. "I don't like them to be off here and there unless they really have a reason or a job that pulls them there. I think the Italian thing is good because the communities stay together. . . . You know, the whole family lives in different apartments in a building. That's nice stuff if you can do it."

His children must have agreed. From Drena in her forties to baby Helen in her diapers, they were all close to him, even when, as in the case of Raphael, they were entirely self-sufficient. When De Niro was young, it had seemed to some friends that he felt pressured by an obligation to keep a healthy bond between his parents. Over the decades, he had come to see that same intrafamilial responsibility from a different vantage: not as a son but as a father. An although his brood was somewhat motley in age and heritage, he worked to impart to it the tenor of a traditional family.

This wasn't easy as he entered his seventies. He knew there was an immense gap between the aging face he saw in the mirror and the young—some *very* young—people who were his children, and he somehow developed the equanimity to be a positive presence in their lives, or at least to have a philosophy about how he could do that. "I have young kids," he said, "and want to see them through a certain stage. I want to give them advice, but I know they're not going to listen. So I tell them, 'Ask me. Whatever you've been through, I'm sure I've been close to that.' I always want to be there for them. That's the most important thing in my life."

He was born bearing the name of a rising young star in the art world, and he had turned that name into a currency of its own, a legend built of decades of worthy and sometimes titanic artistic work, of unlikely and often quite successful business ventures, of rigorous adherence to an ethos of responsibility, loyalty, and hard work. He knew that he wasn't an ideal role model; "as I tell my kids," he said, " 'Everyone has their own *mishegoss.*'" But he had lived in such a way that he could remain optimistic about having created luck for himself and that his good fortune in life and work could be sustained through the power of his attitude, if nothing else: "I feel optimistic about things. You certainly don't want to think that the *worst* is yet to come. . . . We don't know what lies ahead. So I'm only going to think about the best."

Somehow, in all the work he was laying out in front of himself, he saw glimpses of the best.

And who could say that he was wrong to think that these glimpses, in and of themselves, were their own just reward?

Acknowledgments and Sources

Robert De Niro, through the offices of his publicist Stan Rosenfield, chose not to respond to perhaps a half dozen requests to be interviewed for this book, and a great many people who have known and/or worked with him over the decades followed suit, unwilling to participate in what is, technically, an unauthorized biography. However, as I often remind people, unauthorized doesn't mean salacious, and it is entirely possible to write a full and fair biography without ever speaking to the subject—as authors of books about, say, Abraham Lincoln and Napoleon prove every year. With work in archives and interviews with forty or so individuals who have had firsthand experience with De Niro, I have endeavored to produce a serious and reflective portrait balancing the private life of a man with his public work—which, of course, is what makes him interesting to begin with.

In very large part, I did this through many weeks of toil at the Harry Ransom Center at the University of Texas in Austin, where De Niro has stored his massive archives of scripts, research, production materials, costumes, props, and memorabilia. I pored over literally hundreds of boxes of materials, finding illuminating and delightful details at every turn, getting a real sense of De Niro's working methods as both an actor and a producer, discovering nuances of his thought that informed my deeper understanding of the man and the artist, and learning to decipher his rushed, crabbed, handwriting. I am grateful to the staff of the Ransom Center and to my friends in Austin for abiding my monomania on the subject of De Niro during my visits there.

That work in Texas was augmented by research elsewhere. In New York, I worked at the Humanities and Social Sciences Library of the

New York Public Library and, especially, the Billy Rose Theater Division of the New York Public Library for the Performing Arts. In Los Angeles, I worked at the Margaret Herrick Library of the Motion Picture Academy of Arts and Sciences. In Portland, as ever, I relied heavily on the good offices of the Multnomah County Library, as well as those of Powell's City of Books and Movie Madness—the best book store and video store, respectively, in America. Online, I was well served almost daily by such resources as Ancestry.com, Genealogy.com, Google News, the Internet Movie Database, Rootsweb, and Wikipedia, among many others.

As I say, I spoke and/or corresponded with perhaps four dozen people who have had firsthand acquaintance with De Niro and with events recounted in this book, some of whom wished to remain anonymous. Among those whom I can thank publicly are Verna Bloom, Christopher Cerrone, Norman Chaitin, John Curran, Paul Dano, Guy Flatley, William Friedkin, Charles Hirsch, Chris Hodenfield, Tom Kane, Sally Kirkland, Tom Mardirosian, Eugenio Mira, Merle Molofsky, Harold Ramis, Roberta Sklar, Jonathan Taplin, Dyanne Thorne, and Larry Woiwode. I wish in particular to cite the contributions of Sandra Bernhard, Jerry Lewis, and Martin Scorsese, all of whom spoke to me some years ago when I was writing *King of Comedy: The Life and Art of Jerry Lewis* and whose memories and impressions are as vital today as when they first shared them. Additional sources—or paths to them—were provided by Jay Cocks, Gerald Peary, Sheldon Renan, and Carrie Rickey. I'd like to acknowledge the help of Michael Millar in nosing through Manhattan real estate records. And I wish especially to thank Glenn Kenny for sharing an interview with Edward Norton that he conducted for his own book, "Robert De Niro: Anatomy of an Actor" (unpublished at the time of this writing).

When I began work on this project, I was in my last years of serving as film critic at the *Oregonian*, and I thank the newspaper and my editors and colleagues sincerely; for twenty-plus years I got to write about movies in a movie-mad city where people read the newspaper and took its content as the start of a (mostly civilized) conversation about film, art, and life; nobody ever had a better job than that. During the years I was working on *De Niro*—or should have been—I sustained my household coffers with projects edited by James Greenberg at *DGA Quarterly* and Tony Nourmand of Reel Arts Press; I thank them both.

At Crown I am grateful to John Glusman, who commissioned the book, and Dominick Anfuso, who has edited it. Likewise, I'm obliged to Sue Warga for careful copyediting and Amelia Zalcman for judicious legal oversight.

My deep, deep thanks go, as ever, to my agent, Richard Pine, and his staff at Inkwell Management, without whom I might well be asking you if you'd like to see a dessert menu rather than telling you all of this.

I have relied, often overly, on the brains, hearts, and shoulders of such friends and loved ones as Mary Bartholemy, Shannon Brazil, Chelsea Cain, Paul Carvelli, Marc Mohan, Lucretia Thornton, and Krista Walter, as well as untold numbers of the Timbers Army, and, as the dedication indicates, my sister, Jennifer, and her family, Jason, Harry, and Fanny Freeland. My mom, Mickie, left us while I was working on this book, but that doesn't necessarily mean she isn't its biggest fan.

For all that, nobody has done more to spur, inspire, and fulfill me than my children, Vincent, Anthony, and Paula, who mean far, far more than any book ever could.

Notes

Note: Citations marked "HRC" refer to materials from the Robert De Niro collection at the Harry Ransom Center at the University of Texas; citations marked "HRC Schrader" refer to materials from the Paul Schrader collection at the Harry Ransom Center.

Chapter 1

15   "He asked about": "Robert De Niro the Painter," Jerry Tallmer, *New York Post*, December 4, 1976.

17   "I was at an art school": "Same Name, Different Worlds," Sidney Fields, New York *Daily News*, December 16, 1976.

17   "Sometimes he seems major": "Student and Master," David Cohn, *New York Sun*, January 20, 2005.

18   "The whole lunatic fringe": Karen Christel Krahulik, *Provincetown: From Pilgrim Landing to Gay Resort* (New York: New York University Press, 2007), p. 134.

18   "Romping and bathing": Rivers with Weinstein, *What Did I Do?*, 125.

18   "We couldn't understand": Ibid., 78.

18   "He was handsome": "The Bohemian Life of Robert De Niro Senior," Christopher Turner, *Daily Telegraph*, March 19, 2009.

20   "A painting can't be": "Same Name, Different Worlds."

23   "This is our last nursery": *Robert Duncan: Drawings and Decorated Books* (Berkeley, CA: Rose Books, 1992), p. 11.

24   "Virginia and her friends": Nin, *Diary*, 2:247.

24   "The place is cold": Ibid., 2:72.

24   "My role": Bair, *Anaïs Nin*, 573.

25   "When I first met": Fitch, *Anaïs*, 228.

25   "Virginia tells me": Nin, *Diary*, 2:72.

26   "Virginia and De Niro": "It's Dilemma, It's Delimit, It's De Niro," Paul Gardner, *New York*, May 16, 1977.

27   "I was working in the fishery": "Robert De Niro the Painter."

27   "Every Friday night": Rivers with Weinstein, *What Did I Do?*, 126.

27   "I have been listening": Bair, *Anaïs Nin*, 271.

27   "Bob was completely": Nin, *Diary*, 2:128.

28   "Virginia stopped me": Nin, *Diary*, 3:72.

28   "What she was doing then": "Same Name, Different Worlds."

Chapter 2

30   "Our standards": "De Niro: A Star for the '70s," Jack Kroll, *New York*, May 16, 1977.

32   "important young artist": *The Nation*, Clement Greenberg, May 18, 1946.

33   "Contemporary abstract art": "Up from the Frenzy," *Newsweek*, July 9, 1956.

34   "He is lean": Ibid.

34   "He had these dank lofts": "De Niro on De Niro," *Vogue*, January 1995.

34   "When I was about five": "Robert De Niro on His Father's Art Studio," *Daily Beast*, July 9, 2012.

34   "As a kid": *Daily Telegraph*, March 19, 2009.

35   "*tall, saturnine*": "Warhol and De Niro: Modesty Is the Best Policy," Thomas B. Hess, *New York*, December 6, 1976.

35   "I didn't know much": "Robert De Niro on His Father's Art Studio."

36   "Anyone he knew": Kelly and Salander, eds., *Robert De Niro Sr.*, 27.

36   "He had a temper": "Robert De Niro on His Father's Art Studio."

36   "fiercely engaged": Hackett-Freedman Gallery, *Robert De Niro Sr.*, 9.

36   "loneliest person": Kelly and Salander, eds., *Robert De Niro Sr.*, p. 27.

36   "He had the air": Rivers with Weinstein, *What Did I Do?*, 127.

36   "a lonely soul": Kelly and Salander, eds., *Robert De Niro Sr.*, p. 27.

36   "Bob was a great dancer": Rivers with Weinstein, *What Did I Do?*, 127.

36   "De Niro did not spend": "Robert De Niro: The Painter's Painter," Sam Adams, *Flighttime*, January 1977.

37   "How nice": *Newsweek*, July 9, 1956.

37   "Book after book": "Robert De Niro Works on a Series of Pictures," Eleanor C. Munro, *ARTnews*, May 1958.

37   "He liked to work": Kelly and Salander, eds., *Robert De Niro Sr.*, 19.

37   "He was becoming somebody": Ibid.

38   "affectionate": *Daily Telegraph*, March 9, 2009.

38   "He did take me": "De Niro on De Niro."

38   "He even tried to paint me": "Robert De Niro on His Father's Art Studio."

39   "I want to keep my life": "It's Dilemma, It's Delimit, It's De Niro."

39   "Will": "The Shadow King," Patricia Bosworth, *Vanity Fair*, October 1987.

39   "He was never coddled": Ibid.

40   "Bobby was out": "It's Dilemma, It's Delimit, It's De Niro."

40   "Don't picture me": "Playboy Interview: Robert De Niro," Lawrence Grobel, *Playboy*, January 1989.

40   "I was very nervous": Ibid.

41   "We used to roller-skate": "What I've Learned: Robert De Niro," *Esquire*, January 2003.

41   "It wasn't anything serious": "Robert De Niro on Becoming the Quintessential Family Man," Chris Ayres, *Times* (London), February 2, 2010.

42   "You better not say": "Look—Bobby's Slipping into Brando's Shoes," Guy Flatley, *New York Times*, November 4, 1973.

42   "Some of them": "Robert De Niro on Becoming the Quintessential Family Man."

42   "I would see him": "Robert De Niro on His Father's Art Studio."

42   "Most people I knew": Ibid.

42   "Among the many who courted": Rivers with Weinstein, *What Did I Do?*, 126.

43   "Do you remember me": "What's Robert De Niro Hiding?," Marie Brenner, *Redbook*, May 1977.

43   "I had a bad high school scene": "Robert De Niro: He Had to Play Ball," Tom Topor, *New York Post*, August 25, 1973.

43   "His idea of high school": "The Quiet Chameleon," Richard Schickel, *Time*, January 27, 1975.

44   "I went in": "What I've Learned: Robert De Niro."

44   "They had so many students": "Playboy Interview: Robert De Niro."

44   "You figured the kids": "A Walk and a Talk with Robert De Niro," Peter Brant and Ingrid Sischy, *Interview*, November 1993.

45   "When I was around 18": "De Niro," A. O. Scott, *New York Times*, November 18, 2012.

Chapter 3

47   "He showed up": Hackett-Freedman Gallery, *Robert De Niro Sr.*

47   "there was a certain wall": "Robert De Niro on His Father's Art Studio."

47   "I hitchhiked from Dublin": "De Niro's Irish Hike," Debbie McGoldrick, *Cara*, September 2007.

48   "I made him a sign": "The De Niro 'Passione,'" Christopher Sharp, *Women's Wear Daily*, June 30, 1980.

51   "It was just a way": "Playboy Interview: Robert De Niro."

52   "It was an exciting time": "Robert De Niro Can Do No Wrong," Lee Child, *Parade*, November 8, 2009. Emphasis added.

53   "I think disciplined": "De Niro Talks!," Samir Hachem, *Hollywood Drama-Logue*, May 22, 1980.

53   "I was the star": "An Actor's Schedule Leaves No Time to Star," Robin Finn, *New York Times*, August 16, 2000.

53   "How she behaved": "Robert De Niro: 'I'm Prone to Overanalysis,'" Sheana Ochoa, *Salon*, March 16, 2012.

54   "I was afraid": "*New York, New York*: Martin Scorsese's Back-Lot Sonata," Chris Hodenfeld, *Rolling Stone*, June 16, 1977.

54   "I never expected": Kelly and Salander, eds., *Robert De Niro Sr.*, p. 42.

55   "his 'erratic' behavior": Ibid., 27.

55   "He didn't have a breakdown": "Robert De Niro on His Father's Art Studio."

56   "Larry was serious": Author interview.

57   "He seems oblivious": Woiwode, *What I Think I Did*, 197.

57   "He's out to please": Ibid.

59   "I had seen an advertisement": Wolfgang Wilke, "De Niro in Moscow," *The Face*, December 1987.

59   "He was very mild": "It's Dilemma, It's Delimit, It's De Niro."

60   "I thought I was getting": "De Niro in Moscow."

60   "There was a teacher": "Robert De Niro: 'I'm Prone to Overanalysis.'"

61   "Have certain things": HRC.

61   "I have a disrespect": HRC.

62   "Your dad gave it": Woiwode, *What I Think I Did*, 269.

63   "I eventually convinced him": "Robert De Niro on His Father's Art Studio."

64   "If they didn't fall": Woiwode, *What I Think I Did*, 298.

64   "tall and heavyset": Ibid., 299.

Chapter 4

65   "I had an optimistic": *Time*, unpublished background notes, June 2, 1977.
66   "He had a portfolio": "What's Robert De Niro Hiding?"
66   "I'm Bob De Niro": "The Shadow King."
66   "I remember a bunch": "Playboy Interview: Robert De Niro."
68   "The actors weren't paid": Author interview.
68   "They shot a scene of me": Author interview.
69   "I had years": "De Niro," Schruers.
71   "I did not have a Plan B": "Robert De Niro Can Do No Wrong."
71   "I got my first jobs": "It's Dilemma, It's Delimit, It's De Niro."
72   "The most expensive thing": "De Palma à la Mod," Geoff Beran, www.angelfire.com/de/palma/interviewparis.html, February 26, 2002.
73   "It was all ad-lib": "Maximum Expression," Barry Paris, *American Film*, October 1989.
73   "He showed up to shoot": "De Niro: A Star for the '70s."
77   "He was electrifying": "The Shadow King."
78   "When he moved": "It's Dilemma, It's Delimit, It's De Niro."
79   "I'm Bobby's *Italian* mama": "Look—Bobby's Slipping into Brando's Shoes."
82   "When walking always looking": HRC.

Chapter 5

85   "I don't even know all of you": "Look—Bobby's Slipping into Brando's Shoes."
85   "blow nose with finger": HRC.
86   "I thought he was concentrating": "The Shadow King."
86   "You have a marvelous": HRC.
86   "help the actors": "Playboy Interview: Robert De Niro."
86   "Roger is brief": HRC.
92   "As an actress": "Off Broadway Actors Go on Strike," Louis Calta, *New York Times*, November 17, 1970.
92   "I've been clobbered": "Shelley: 'I'm Bloody but Unbowed,'" Guy Flatley, *New York Times*, January 17, 1971.
93   "Bobby was acclaimed": Winters, *Shelley II*, 302.
93   "You're talking to the commission": HRC.
95   "Attitude: always cocky": HRC.

98   "I make believe I don't see": HRC.

99   "He told me, 'I'm casting' ": Author interview.

100 "I had a real problem": Author interview.

104 "They must've had a fight": Author interview.

Chapter 6

105 "I said to him": "The Shadow King."

106 "I didn't *really* know him": Kelly, *Martin Scorsese*, 72.

108 "I read for John Hancock": *Time,* unpublished background notes, June 2, 1977.

108 "I saw in every baseball game": "Dialogue on Film: Robert De Niro," *American Film,* March 1981.

108 "I used to think": "Stardom's Drums Banging for Robert De Niro," Richard Cuskelly, *Los Angeles Herald-Examiner,* August 12, 1973.

109 "I told him to read": "Jim Bouton Bangs the Drum Loudly," Jim Bouton, *New York Times,* September 30, 1973.

109 "I went down to Florida": "Robert De Niro: He Had to Play Ball."

109 "I wanted to listen": "Stardom's Drums Banging for Robert De Niro."

110 "I tried mixing": Ibid.

110 "to show what's unlikeable": HRC.

110 "I didn't try to play dumb": "Robert De Niro: He Had to Play Ball."

110 "He used stupid eyes": "De Niro: A Star for the '70s."

110 "I watched Bob": "Robert De Niro—The Return of the Silent Film Star," Susan Braudy, *New York Times,* March 6, 1977.

111 "He has death": HRC.

111 "He's an immigrant": "Colleagues Say De Niro Has No Peer," *New York Times,* March 11, 1991.

112 "You just spent a whole year": Thompson and Christie, eds., *Scorsese on Scorsese,* 38.

114 "For a long time": Ibid., 9.

114 "I always looked": Kelly, *Martin Scorsese,* 23.

116 "The first version of the script": Ibid., 71.

116 "Sandy had heard": "Spirit in the 'Streets,' " Stuart Byron, *Real Paper* (Boston), November 28, 1973.

117 "One is the guilt-ridden": *Rolling Stone,* June 16, 1977.

117 " 'If you want to make *Mean Streets*": Thompson and Christie, eds., *Scorsese on Scorsese,* 39.

119 "He'd already been cast": "A Walk and a Talk with Robert De Niro."

119 "I had never seen Bobby act": "Robert De Niro—Private, Professional, a Male Greta Garbo," *W*, July 11, 1975.

119 "Bobby and I were as close": "The Shadow King."

120 "Marty: I think (know)": HRC.

120 "I aspire to be": HRC.

121 "The neighborhood was just a sea": *Mean Streets* production notes.

122 "They had got on each other's nerves": Thompson and Christie, eds., *Scorsese on Scorsese*, 43.

122 "Literary reference": "Spirit in the 'Streets.'"

123 "immediately, he put him": Biskind, *Easy Riders, Raging Bulls*, 246.

Chapter 7

124 "Everybody tested": "A Walk and a Talk with Robert De Niro."

124 "I thought he was very magnetic": Lebo, *The Godfather Legacy*, 221.

124 "It kept rolling": Ibid.

125 "De Niro's assignment": *The Godfather, Part II* production notes.

125 "Sicilian is something else": "Actor," Bob Thomas, *Los Angeles Herald-Examiner*, March 2, 1975.

126 "I was always up front": *The Godfather, Part II* production notes.

126 "When I went into a bar": "Actor."

126 "If you'd asked me": *The Godfather, Part II* production notes.

127 "The people are very": *The Godfather, Part II* production notes.

127 "Never show how": HRC.

128 "There's a peasant": "Robert De Niro: He Had to Play Ball."

128 "lead a little": HRC.

128 "It's like being": *The Godfather, Part II* production notes.

128 "an attitude of just about": HRC.

129 "I watched the tape": "De Niro: A Star for the '70s."

129 "The slicked-down hair": "Actor."

130 "He wanted to do one scene": "De Niro: A Star for the '70s."

140 "earned the right": "Look—Bobby's Slipping into Brando's Shoes."

140 "Guinness isn't a personality": "It's Dilemma, It's Delimit, It's De Niro."

141 "'Well . . .' a long silence": "Robert De Niro: He Had to Play Ball."

141 "We were both at a party": author interview.

142 "Listen, let's put it this way": "Look—Bobby's Slipping into Brando's Shoes."

142 **"Why do people want to know"**: "It's Dilemma, It's Delimit, It's De Niro."

142 **"After I give an interview"**: "De Niro: The Phantom of the Cinema," *Time*, July 25, 1977.

143 **"He picked these incredibly"**: Biskind, *Easy Riders, Raging Bulls*, 248.

144 **"I gave a Thanksgiving"**: "De Niro: A Star for the '70s."

145 **"When I met him"**: "Amo, Amas, Abbott," Hilton Als, *Details*, November 1986.

145 **"By temperament"**: "Diahnne Abbott, Honeysuckle Rose," *Interview*, October, 1977.

146 **"Bob is very Italian"**: "Robert De Niro—The Return of the Silent Film Star."

148 **"We shot the old stuff"**: "De Niro," Scott.

148 **"The first few days were a nightmare"**: "De Niro: A Star for the '70s."

148 **"Bertolucci . . . would tell me"**: "Dialogue on Film: Robert De Niro."

148 **"I can't do it without"**: "It's Dilemma, It's Delimit, It's De Niro."

148 **"Bob will never be"**: "Robert De Niro—Private, Professional, a Male Greta Garbo."

Chapter 8

156 **"Lots of people who win"**: "Robert De Niro—Private, Professional, a Male Greta Garbo."

156 **"I like him"**: "De Niro: A Star for the '70s."

156 **"I've got to decide"**: "Actor."

157 **"like some infant's pacifier"**: Biskind, *Easy Riders, Raging Bulls*, 287.

159 **"I was . . . very suicidal"**: "A Fallen Calvinist Pursues His Vision of True Heroism," Samuel G. Freedman, *New York Times*, August 25, 1991.

159 **"I wrote the script very quickly"**: "Screen Writer: *Taxi Driver*'s Paul Schrader," Richard Thompson, *Film Comment*, March–April 1976.

159 **"I was so upset"**: "Creating a Landscape of Characters in Turmoil," Laura Winters, *New York Times*, January 3, 1999.

159 **"It is me without any brains"**: "Screen Writer: *Taxi Driver*'s Paul Schrader."

160 **"It was the strongest stuff"**: "The Shadow King."

160 **"I almost felt I wrote it"**: Paul Schrader, *Taxi Driver* [script] (London: Faber and Faber, 1990), xix.

160 "I *had to make*": "Martin Scorsese's Gamble," Guy Flatley, *New York Times*, February 8, 1976.

162 "I don't know about anyone else": "*Taxi Driver*: A Bargain for Tinsel Town," Nancy Collins, *Women's Wear Daily*, July 16, 1975.

162 "when I couldn't really distinguish": "Screen Writer: *Taxi Driver's* Paul Schrader."

162 "It's kind of an exorcism": "Making a Movie Here Is a Movie in Itself," Rex Reed, New York *Daily News*, August 3, 1975.

162 "There are a lot of Catholic": "*Taxi Driver* Is a Hit for Martin Scorsese," Roger Ebert, *Chicago Sun-Times*, February 22, 1976.

162 "My character wandered": "Screen Writer: *Taxi Driver's* Paul Schrader."

163 "I said to him, 'Do you know'": "Robert De Niro—Private, Professional, a Male Greta Garbo."

163 "De Niro's contribution": "Screen Writer: *Taxi Driver's* Paul Schrader."

163 "Bobby was greatly pressured": Ibid.

164 "It was an agreement": "*Taxi Driver*: A Bargain for Tinsel Town."

164 "De Niro told me": "Screen Writer: *Taxi Driver's* Paul Schrader."

165 "We drove up and down": Wilson, *Scorsese on Scorsese*, 51.

165 "He got a strange feeling": "*Taxi Driver* Is a Hit for Martin Scorsese."

165 "One day when it was pouring": "Making a Movie Here Is a Movie in Itself."

165 "Michael Phillips saw": "Screen Writer: *Taxi Driver's* Paul Schrader."

166 "I got the idea": "De Niro: A Star for the '70s."

166 "You know how a crab": "Playboy Interview: Robert De Niro."

167 "Is he a SAG member": "Night Shooting in NYC with Martin Scorsese," Patrick McGilligan, *Boston Globe*, August 17, 1975.

167 "I was feeling particularly blue": "Screen Writer: *Taxi Driver's* Paul Schrader."

168 "I told Sue": "*Taxi Driver*: A Bargain for Tinsel Town."

168 "improvising all our scenes": *Times* (London), April 23, 2011.

169 "He treated Cybill": Biskind, *Easy Riders, Raging Bulls*, 300.

169 "We always said we were looking": Ibid.

169 "When I first read the script": "Jodie Foster's Rise from Disney to Depravity," Judy Klemesrud, *New York Times*, March 7, 1976.

170 "The memory I have": "The Age of Scorsese," Laura Brown, *Harper's Bazaar*, November 2011.

170 "He kept picking me up": "What I've Learned: Robert De Niro," *Esquire*, January 2011.

171 "I was accused, in *Mean Streets*": Kelly, *Martin Scorsese*, 96.

172 "a heat-seeking missile": Phillips, *You'll Never Eat Lunch*, 249.

172 "The second week": Schrader, *Taxi Driver* [script], xiv.

172 "a cokey movie": Phillips, *You'll Never Eat Lunch*, 228.

172 "When the camera isn't turning": "Making a Movie Here Is a Movie in Itself."

172 "He stayed in character": *Times* (London), April 23, 2011.

173 "Harry didn't recognize": Kelly, *Martin Scorsese*, 93.

173 "No, don't bother": "Robert De Niro—The Return of the Silent Film Star."

174 "He just got into": "A Tribute to a Master of the Bravura Moment," Janet Maslin, *New York Times*, May 4, 1998.

174 "To me, it's the best": "Screen Writer: *Taxi Driver*'s Paul Schrader."

175 "I think the director's": Ibid.

175 "I didn't trust anybody with it": Kelly, *Martin Scorsese*, 95.

176 "The real stuff": "Robert De Niro—The Return of the Silent Film Star."

176 "Bobby hogs Marty": Ibid.

176 "In Martin . . . Bobby has": Ibid.

176 "We have a shorthand": *Rolling Stone*, June 16, 1977.

177 "His whole thing is": Ibid.

Chapter 9

179 "We've miscast it": Simon, *The Play Goes On*, 110.

181 "It didn't work, just didn't": "Playboy Interview: Robert De Niro."

185 "He's still out there": Kellow, *Pauline Kael*, 236.

188 "If the Travis Bickle character": HRC, Schrader.

189 "It was like going from the darkest": "Playboy Interview: Robert De Niro."

190 "I spent time just walking": "It's Dilemma, It's Delimit, It's De Niro."

190 "Bobby has never played": "Hollywood Takes on 'The Last Tycoon,'" Stephen Farber, *New York Times*, March 21, 1976.

191 "He was an actor": *Rolling Stone*, June 16, 1977.

191 "I sometimes see him": "De Niro: The Phantom of the Cinema."

191 "He's very precise": "Elia Kazan," Charles Silver and Mary Corliss, *Film Comment*, January–February 1977.

191 "Sam pulled one": "Playboy Interview: Robert De Niro."

192 "Look at Irving": "F. Scott Fitzgerald Gets a Second Act After All," Steve Chagollan, *New York Times*, August 21, 2005.

194 "I was crazier": Schrader, *Taxi Driver* [script], xxii.

195 "We had a hard time agreeing": Cameron, *Floor Sample*, 58.

195 "She was insanely jealous": Biskind, *Easy Riders, Raging Bulls*, 301.

196 "He would throw something": "Liza, Liza, Where You Been?," Cliff Jahr, *Village Voice*, June 27, 1977.

196 "That's when everything sort of fell": Kelly, *Martin Scorsese*, 106.

196 "We started to get cocky": Ibid., 106.

196 "It was a nightmare": Biskind, *Easy Riders, Raging Bulls*, 325.

197 "I started taking drugs": Ibid.

198 "I wanted it to look like my horn": "De Niro: The Phantom of the Cinema."

198 "It's incredible the way": "The Director of *Taxi Driver* Shifts Gears," Robert Lindsey, *New York Times*, August 8, 1976.

198 "He asked me ten million": "It's Dilemma, It's Delimit, It's De Niro."

199 "I don't mind being": *Village Voice*, June 27, 1977.

199 "He didn't say it": Author interview.

199 "I thought it would be funny": "Playboy Interview: Robert De Niro."

200 "a $10 million home movie": Cameron, *Floor Sample*, 59.

200 "I really worked on it": "Dialogue on Film: Robert De Niro."

200 "Everybody there was somebody": "What's Robert De Niro Hiding?"

200 "We would go to parties": "Amo, Amas, Abbott."

202 "loaded": "Diahnne Abbott, Honeysuckle Rose."

202 "I was standing": Ibid.

Chapter 10

204 "I ran to San Francisco": "Same Name, Different Worlds."

204 "I don't really like": "Robert De Niro the Painter."

204 "It creates a certain": "Same Name, Different Worlds."

205 "At first I was very excited": "EYEVIEW: The De Niro 'Passione,'" Christopher Sharp, *Women's Wear Daily*, June 23, 1980.

206 "Do you think there's going to be": *Village Voice*, June 27, 1977.

209 "For a time after *New York, New York*": Kelly, *Martin Scorsese*, 112.

213 "soaking up the environment": *The Deer Hunter*, production notes.

214 "Everybody who was going": "Playboy Interview: Robert De Niro."

214 "It's very hard to sustain": "Dialogue on Film: Robert De Niro."

214 "When somebody belts you": "Movies 'Discover' Christopher Walken," Janet Maslin, *New York Times*, December 26, 1978.

214 "The circumstances were genuine": Ibid.

215   "spoke very bad English": "The Men Who Work as Directors' Eyes," Shaun Considine, *New York Times*, April 8, 1979.

215   "Without knowing it . . . the pilot": "Playboy Interview: Robert De Niro."

216   "We had every right to cut": "Movie Angling for an Accolade," Aljean Harmetz, *New York Times*, November 23, 1978.

220   "I'm sure he cares": "In the Year the War Came Home, Beatty, De Niro, Voight, Olivier and Busey Are Gunning for Oscar," *People*, April 2, 1979.

220   "I hope it doesn't win": Wiley and Bona, *Inside Oscar*, 560.

Chapter 11

225   "I had an idea": "De Niro Talks!"

227   "Mr. Savage had involved": HRC, Schrader.

228   "We could do a really great job": Thompson and Christie, eds., *Scorsese on Scorsese*, 76.

229   "brutally depressing": Bach, *Final Cut*, 163.

230   "this picture as written": Ibid., 164.

231   "more qualified to be a psychiatrist": "De Niro: A Star for the '70s."

231   "I just kept reapeating": "Playboy Interview: Robert De Niro."

231   "I admired the fact": Kelly, *Martin Scorsese*, 126.

231   "I tried to ask him": "Playboy Interview: Robert De Niro."

231   "You can only go so far": "Method and the Man," Steve Grant, *Time Out*, May 22, 1991.

232   "De Niro saw this movement": Biskind, *Easy Riders, Raging Bulls*, 385.

233   "*Don't* leap and lunge": HRC.

234   "The way I talk": HRC.

235   "I know I'm a fighter": HRC.

235   "It was really funny": Kelly, *Martin Scorsese*, 133.

237   "When we did the acting stuff": "Dialogue on Film: Robert De Niro."

237   "How they found me": "The Delicate Art of Creating a Brutal Film Hero," Fred Ferretti, *New York Times*, November 23, 1980.

238   "I would abuse the audience": "Frank Vincent's Two-Limo Night," Edward Lewine, *New York Times*, February 18, 1996.

239   "He wanted a picture of me": Kelly, *Martin Scorsese*, 131.

239   "She had a feeling": "De Niro in Moscow."

240 "some of the scenes with Bobby": Kelly, *Martin Scorsese*, 139.

240 "I just can't fake": "De Niro's Method of Getting a Fat Part," New York *Daily News*, October 28, 1980.

241 "I needed to feel Jake's shame": "Untouchable World of De Niro the Godfather," Jean Rook, *Daily Express* (London), 1991.

241 "At first it was fun": "Playboy Interview: Robert De Niro."

241 "I began to realize": "The Delicate Art of Creating a Brutal Film Hero."

242 "Bobby's weight was so extreme": Kelly, *Martin Scorsese*, 143.

242 "He was 30 pounds": "The Delicate Art of Creating a Brutal Film Hero."

243 "Scorsese . . . had been right": Bach, *Final Cut*, 347.

244 "I said, 'People are going to look' ": Kelly, *Martin Scorsese*, 149.

244 "Look . . . there's no way to do it": "What's Black and White and Red All Over? Martin Scorsese," Hildy Johnson, *In Cinema*, December 1980.

249 "That's the idea": HRC.

249 "Dear Robert": HRC.

Chapter 12

254 "Bobby De Niro's a perfectionist": "Sutherland: No More Goofy Roles," Jordan Young, *New York Times*, September 23, 1979.

254 "De Niro once figured": " 'This Movie Is the Easiest Thing I've Ever Done': Ryan O'Neal," Robin Brantley, *New York Times*, May 21, 1978.

254 "A Dr. Jekyll": *Rolling Stone*, June 16, 1977.

255 "We spent wonderful": "The Shadow King."

255 "I've heard they have hookers": "Playboy Interview: Robert De Niro."

256 "a cooling-off period": "In the Year the War Came Home."

256 "This guy is cutting me off": "My Ugly Life with De Niro: Ex-Lover," Cindy Adams, *New York Post*, October 26, 1992.

258 "The chief of police": "Playboy Interview: Robert De Niro."

260 "Where's John?": Woodward, *Wired*, 405.

261 "Don't talk to anybody": Ibid., 412.

263 "De Niro is a perfectionist": *True Confessions* production notes.

263 "NOTE OF CAUTION": HRC.

263 "I talked to tons": "De Niro Talks!" (emphasis added).

264 "Technique is concrete": "De Niro: A Star for the '70s."

269 **"attached itself to me"**: "Once Upon a Time in America," Peter Hamill, *American Film*, June 1984.

269 **"He was a big guy"**: Ibid.

270 **"Sergio told me"**: "Playboy Interview: Robert De Niro."

270 **"Bobby made it clear"**: "Once Upon a Time in America," Hamill.

270 **"Italian directors"**: "Playboy Interview: Robert De Niro."

270 **"I can't do the movie"**: Doron and Gelmis, *Confidential*, 155.

272 **"For better or worse"**: "Once Upon a Time in America," Hamill.

Chapter 13

276 **"I was struck"**: Kelly, *Martin Scorsese*, 152.

277 **"He understood the bravery"**: Ibid., 153.

278 **"Bobby developed a technique"**: Wilson, *Scorsese on Scorsese*, n.p.

278 **"it was more Bob's"**: Kelly, *Martin Scorsese*, 153.

280 **"With its combination"**: Thompson and Christie, eds., *Scorsese on Scorsese*, 90.

280 **"I could see"**: Levy, *King of Comedy*, 419.

280 **"What we went through"**: Ibid.

280 **"Bobby has to know"**: "God's Biggest Goof," Michael Angeli, *Esquire*, February 1991.

280 **"It's harder to imagine"**: HRC.

281 **"Jer—I need you to know"**: "God's Biggest Goof."

281 **"They don't know celebrity"**: Levy, *King of Comedy*, 419.

282 **"I asked Meryl"**: "Maximum Expression."

282 **"She looked stunned"**: "Queen for a Day: Sandra Bernhard Looks Back on *The King of Comedy*," Dave Itzkoff, *New York Times*, April 17, 2013.

282 **"the most intimidating"**: Levy, *King of Comedy*, 423.

282 **"There was one of these"**: "De Niro," Scott.

283 **"I HAVE NOTHING LEFT"**: HRC.

283 **"very determined"**: HRC.

283 **"coughing on the floor"**: Thompson and Christie, eds., *Scorsese on Scorsese*, 87.

284 **"It was like making a film"**: Ibid.

284 **"When I saw Take 29"**: "After Open-Heart Surgery, King of Comedy Jerry Lewis Bounces Back with Bride-to-Be," Jim Jerome, *People*, February 7, 1983.

284 **"I know I'm number two"**: Ibid., 90.

284 "I went in with a very simple": "God's Biggest Goof."

285 "Bobby is no fool": "Penthouse Interview: Jerry Lewis," James Delson, *Penthouse*, May 1984.

285 "extremely difficult for everyone": Thompson and Christie, eds., *Scorsese on Scorsese*, 88.

286 "turned this world": "After Open-Heart Surgery."

286 "I said, 'You cocksucker' ": "Penthouse Interview: Jerry Lewis."

286 "I don't know if I said": "Playboy Interview: Robert De Niro."

286 "When you work with great people": "Queen for a Day."

286 "didn't have anything to do": Levy, *King of Comedy*, 423.

287 "Marty told me later": Kelly, *Martin Scorsese*, 156.

287 "Jerry is totally surreal": "What's So Funny About Jerry Lewis?," Lynn Hirschberg, *Rolling Stone*, October 28, 1982.

287 "In order to work with Bobby": "Penthouse Interview: Jerry Lewis."

287 "He didn't have that helmet": Kelly, *Martin Scorsese*, 157.

288 "The whole routine": "Maximum Expression."

295 "We needed to go": "The Shadow King."

296 "I had my head shaved": "De Niro," Schruers.

297 "If you really have a problem": Kelly, *Martin Scorsese*, 171.

Chapter 14

299 "liked the idea": Marilyn Beck, New York *Daily News*, January 7, 1986.

301 "We weren't even sure": "The Incredible Talent of Robert De Niro," Barbara Goldsmith, *Parade*, December 2, 1984.

302 *Candid Camera*: HRC.

303 "The visual background": HRC.

304 "I understand your problem": Yule, *Enigma*, 258.

305 "Bob sees his role": "*The Mission* Diary," Daniel Berrigan, *American Film*, November 1986.

305 "There were floods": "The Shadow King."

306 "Jeremy [Irons] would come": "A Master Class on Movies from Producer David Puttnam—a Child of Celluloid and Sprocket Holes," Geoffrey McNabb, *The Independent* (London), May 10, 2013.

307 "Well, Bobby, you may be right": Yule, *Enigma*, 272.

310 "I tell people, 'You deal with me' ": "Woman About Town," James Servin, *New York Times*, June 28, 1992.

312 "I always wanted to do a play": "An Unlikely Odyssey to Broadway," Leslie Bennetts, *New York Times*, July 17, 1986.

313 "He trusted us": "Povod's *Teddy Bear* Makes the Push to Broadway,"
     Michael Kuchwara, *New York Post*, July 19, 1986.
313 "With Bob De Niro": "An Unlikely Odyssey to Broadway."
313 "After rehearsals": "The Shadow King."
315 "Because I was an understudy": Author interview.
315 "All these big celebrities": Author interview.
316 "There was this one scene": Author interview.
317 "I don't know that my way": "De Niro," Schruers.

Chapter 15

319 "He was lovely": "Untouchable De Niro," Joan Goodman, *Observer*
     (London), September 30, 1987.
319 "You know, one morning": *Chicago Sun-Times*, March 12, 1989.
324 "Brian and I both worried": "Untouchable De Niro."
324 "We have the opportunity": Linson, *A Pound of Flesh*, 137.
324 "Are you kidding": "Untouchable De Niro."
325 "He was thin": Ibid.
325 "great . . . good . . . nice": Linson, *A Pound of Flesh*, 154.
326 "It was like witnessing": Ibid., 158.
326 "It took a week": "The Mob at the Movies," Tom Mathews, *Newsweek*,
     June 22, 1987.
326 "The Sicilian is a darker": Ibid.
327 "It's also personal": HRC.

Chapter 16

336 "If we were going": "Robert De Niro," Peter Williams, *Time Out*, Sep-
     tember 7, 1988.
337 "It's not a yuk-yuk": Ibid.
337 "Sometimes, when I do something": "Playboy Interview: Robert De
     Niro."
341 "When I was doing": "Reluctant Robert," Diana Maychick, *New York
     Post*, March 8, 1989.
341 "There's a feeling": "De Niro Talks About Acting," Marchall Fine,
     Gannett News Service, March 12, 1989.
341 "think of Leonard Melfi": HRC.
343 "I could just play it": "Maximum Expression."
344 "I like Sean": Ibid.

344 **"When Art called"**: *"Angels* Find Heaven in the Canadian Bush," Moira Farrow, *New York Times,* May 28, 1989.

345 **"The script has all"**: Ibid.

345 **"Sean and Bob"**: Ibid.

346 **"I was trying to find a line"**: "Coiled and Steady," Gene Siskel, *Chicago Tribune,* March 5, 1989.

Chapter 17

349 **"This resident can be described"**: HRC.

351 **"I was drawn to the book"**: "Fall Preview: Movies," David Denby, *New York,* September 10, 1990.

352 **"Lots of bets"**: HRC.

354 **"Anyone who wants to live"**: *"Goodfellas* Look at the Banality of Mob Life," Susan Linfield, *New York Times,* September 16, 1990.

358 **"I'll never forget first meeting"**: "Untouchable World of De Niro the Godfather."

359 **"like overhearing a man"**: "Into a Realm Where Time Stops," Oliver Sacks, *New York Times,* December 16, 1990.

359 **"Bob's method"**: Ibid.

359 **"You say, 'Bob'"**: "Miracles Happen in *Awakenings,"* Fred Schruers, *Premiere,* January 1991.

360 **"I had my nose broken"**: "Method and the Man."

363 **"A writer or a painter"**: "De Niro Is Trying Life Behind the Camera," William H. Honan, *New York Times,* August 23, 1989.

364 **"There were 20 people"**: "Wagging Tale," Merle Ginsberg, *W,* March 1998.

364 **"Bob was shooting"**: Ibid.

365 **"He said, 'What do you want"**: "Tribeca Titan," Amy Clyde, *Vogue,* August 1993.

365 **"Look, if it doesn't work out"**: "De Niro's Leading Lady," Joanna Molloy, *New York,* July 27, 1992.

365 **"There was one guy"**: *W,* March 1998.

366 **"She puts it all"**: "Jane of All Trades," Meryl Gordon, *New York,* May 6, 2002.

367 **"When I started my own"**: "Tribeca Stories," Martha Frankel, *American Film,* October 1990.

368 **"I haven't seen"**: "Maximum Expression."

369 **"At the end of Mandela's speech"**: "Tribeca Stories."

Chapter 18

371 **"I had faith"**: "De Niro Takes on Hollywood History," Candace Burke-Block, *Long Beach Press-Telegram*, March 15, 1991.

371 **"Think of involvement"**: HRC.

372 **"It was really a no-win"**: "Method and the Man."

372 **"I'd like to think"**: "Untouchable World of De Niro the Godfather."

374 **"He's always cordial"**: "'You Talkin' to Me?' 'No!,'" Alan Richman, *GQ*, January 1991.

374 **"not a headline grabber"**: HRC.

376 **"When I approached him"**: "De Niro on De Niro."

377 **"I wrote it as an Amblin thriller"**: "Martin Scorsese Ventures Back to *Cape Fear*," Janet Maslin, *New York Times*, November 10, 1991.

378 **"together sort of twisted"**: Kelly, *Martin Scorsese*, 283.

380 **"He was constantly looking"**: Ibid., 287.

381 **"He's incessant"**: "Are You Looking at Me?," Alexander Tresniowski, *Time*, August 19, 1991.

381 **"Bob brought Juliette"**: Kelly, *Martin Scorsese*, 290.

Chapter 19

385 **"You're wrong"**: HRC.

386 **"I'm going to show this"**: "How Primus' *Mistress* Found Its Way to Screen," Martin Grove, *Hollywood Reporter*, July 30, 1992.

386 **"One day I was walking"**: "Or Maybe He's Not the Big Bad Wolf," Caryn James, *New York Times*, August 2, 1992.

386 **"He sent me a telegram"**: "Barry Primus," Rosina Lita Rubin, *Premiere*, July 1992.

388 **"I feel like such a non-man"**: HRC.

389 **"It didn't go well"**: "Audiences Said, 'Try, Try Again,'" *New York Times*, April 11, 1993.

390 **"a chicken with his head"**: "*Night* Moves," Glenn Plaskin, New York *Daily News*, October 11, 1992.

390 **"someone jumping"**: "Night and the City and the '90s," John Culhane, *Los Angeles Times*, July 26, 1992.

390 **"Jessica was sensitive"**: Ibid.

392 **"That's hard to do"**: "Ellen Barkin: Is She Difficult or Just Straight Outta Queens?" Jan Hoffman, *New York Times*, April 4, 1993.

Chapter 20

398   **"Mr. De Niro will probably never"**: "The Shadow King."

398   **"There was a mixed signal"**: "De Niro," Schruers.

399   **"If I don't turn it off"**: "Playboy Interview: Robert De Niro."

399   **"I'm feeling angry"**: Ibid.

399   **"Don't talk about world politics"**: " 'You Talkin' to Me?' 'No!' " Richman.

400   **"I guess . . . ummm"**: Ibid.

402   **"I had three conditions"**: "De Niro Finds His Voice," Joseph Gelmis, *Newsday*, September 26, 1993.

402   **"In Hollywood . . . when you say"**: *Newsday*, September 26, 1993.

402   **"What I liked about it"**: *Newsday*, September 26, 1993.

402   **"He looked me in the eye"**: "De Niro Direct," Julia Reed, *Vogue*, March 1993.

403   **"I read some actors"**: "A Walk and a Talk with Robert De Niro."

405   **"It was almost like an exam"**: "Robert De Niro," Elizabeth Kaye, *New York Times*, November 14, 1993.

410   **"Mr. De Niro's art"**: "Robert De Niro, 71, a New York Painter and Actor's Father," Roberta Smith, *New York Times*, May 7, 1993.

411   **"When De Niro finished"**: "De Niro's Hushed Memorial for Dad," *Newsday*, October 19, 1993.

411   **"For a long time"**: "De Niro on De Niro."

Chapter 21

413   **"Is that all"**: "Self-service," Frank DiGiacomo and Joanna Molloy, *New York Post*, September 2, 1992.

414   **"We've always proceeded"**: "Pushing Till De Niro Cries Daddy," Richard Johnson, *New York Post*, November 4, 1992.

418   **"like a cheesy"**: HRC.

419   **"I had some great times"**: *Sunday Times* (London), January 19, 2004.

Chapter 22

427   **"Any place that pushes"**: "Martin Scorsese, Attracted to Excess, Still Taking Risks," Bernard Weinraub, *New York Times*, November 27, 1995.

429 **"It was uneven"**: "Holding Her Own with the Big Boys," William Grimes, *New York Times*, November 19, 1995.

435 **"Neil and Hanna"**: HRC.

435 **"The background is as monochromatic"**: "Michael Mann: Hot Again with *L.A. Vice*," Jamie Diamond, *New York Times*, December 24, 1995.

436 **"islands in the gathering"**: "Bob and Al in the Coffee Shop," *Sight and Sound*, March 1996.

436 **"sees the part"**: "De Niro and Pacino Star in a Film. Together," Bernard Weinraub, *New York Times*, July 27, 1995.

Chapter 23

440 **"We lived on a farm"**: "Grace Hightower's Coffee Journey," Laura Everage, *Coffee Universe*, March 24, 2013.

440 **"I did everything"**: "The TriBeCa-Rwanda Connection," Joshua David Stein, *New York Times*, July 18, 2013.

440 **"It was an ease-in"**: Ibid.

441 **"the most stable"**: "Raging Romance," *People*, July 7, 1997.

441 **"He's great at keeping"**: "Stealth Wedding for De Niro," George Rush, New York *Daily News*, June 24, 1997.

444 **"priests are not supposed"**: "Dark Star," Garth Pearce, *Time Out*, December 18, 1996.

450 **"Do I smoke"**: HRC.

Chapter 24

453 **"Robert De Niro is a hack"**: "Ten Things You Can't Say About the Movies," Tom Carson, *Esquire*, April 1999.

455 **"It's a very good project"**: HRC.

458 **"He was attentive"**: "'Call-Girl Leader' Set Up De Niro with Porn Queen: Tab," Bill Hoffman, *New York Post*, February 17, 1998.

459 **"told me that Bourgeois"**: Ibid.

459 **"I had sex"**: Ibid.

459 **"I never had any attaché case"**: Ibid.

459 **"I have 20 years"**: "Will Judge's 'Dog' Days Get a Collar?," George Rush and Joanna Molloy, New York *Daily News*, February 13, 1998.

460 **"I was shocked"**: "French Cops Quiz De Niro in Hooker Probe," Tracy Connor and Bill Hoffman, *New York Post*, February 11, 1998.

460 "He's a charming man": "Lawyer Insists De Niro Never Paid for Sex," *Times* (London), February 12, 1998.

460 "The name of Robert De Niro": "De Niro Fuming over French Diss," Tracy Connor, *New York Post*, February 12, 1998.

460 "De Niro's participation": "Police Probe Pushes De Niro off Pope's List," David Rooney, *Variety*, February 23, 1998.

462 "Bob was afraid": "Psychotherapy He Can't Refuse," Bernard Weinraub, *New York Times*, February 26, 1990.

464 "It's not as if he has a shtick": Author interview.

Chapter 25

474 "The mayor told us": "De Niro Group Replaced as Developers in Brooklyn," Terry Pristin, *New York Times*, October 14, 1999.

474 "stick it up": "De Niro and Weinstein Sticking It to Giuliani by Heading to Yonkers," Greg Sargent and Josh Benson, *New York Observer*, April 17, 2000.

476 "hands behind back": HRC.

477 "It was a big disappointment": "Jane of All Trades."

Chapter 26

482 "I feel indebted": Peter Schjeldahl, "Fruit and Turpentine," *Village Voice*, January 31, 1995.

482 "Not only as a painter": "Paint Brushes Full, Robert De Niro Sr. Really Thought Big," Hilton Kramer, *New York Observer*, March 7, 2005.

484 "He's pathetic": "Imposter Double-dares De Niro," Philip Recchia, *New York Post*, February 2, 2003.

489 "Fuck you": "How to Make a Score," Jess Cagle, *Time*, July 16, 2001.

489 "The assumption that conflict is bad": Ibid.

489 "I probably could have": "Tea and Reflection," Rick Lyman, *New York Times*, July 20, 2000.

Chapter 27

491 "I left a meeting": "What I've Learned: Robert De Niro."

492 "Bob felt personally": "Jane of All Trades."

493 "I keep reminding": Ibid.

493   "This neighborhood": "TriBeCa Film Fest, Take 2, Planned for May,"
      New York Times, February 21, 2003.

494   "part of the tradition": "Robert De Niro's Tribeca Mission," Ed Pilk-
      ington, *Guardian* (London), April 14, 2013.

500   "I decided to be even more": *Fireman's Fund Insurance Company v.
      Robert De Niro*, Court of Appeal of California, Second Appellate Dis-
      trict, Division Five, 2009 Cal. App. Unpub. LEXIS 4712, June 15, 2009.

502   "I don't know if I *hoped*": "The Patient Is a Don Named Paul," Dave
      Kehr, *New York Times*, December 6, 2002.

                              Chapter 28

505   "He has done nothing": "Uproar over Citizen De Niro," Paula Froe-
      lich and Christ Wilson, *New York Post*, August 14, 2004.

507   "I said one night": "Intelligence Design," John Horn, *Los Angeles
      Times*, November 5, 2006.

507   "I'd love to make this movie": "Spy Pic Coin Spooks King," Dana
      Harris, *Variety*, November 12, 2004.

507   "Matt was crucial": "Yeah, I'm Talkin' to You," Belinda Luscombe,
      Time, December 11, 2006.

508   "I didn't have that much confidence": "And Now, 972 Words from
      Robert De Niro," Chris Heath, *GQ*, January 2007.

508   "In movies where people": "Intelligence Design."

513   "If she [Hightower]": "Housekeeper to the Stars Admits Stealing from
      Her Least Favorites," Anemona Hartocollis, *New York Times*, February
      9, 2006.

513   "If you have me arrested": "'Maid' Out Like a Bandit vs. De Niro,"
      Laura Italian, Philip Messing and Lukas I. Alpert, *New York Post*, June
      22, 2005.

                              Chapter 29

521   "We worked on this": "De Niro Asks Commission to Spare Hotel's
      Penthouse," Michael Wilson, *New York Times*, June 18, 2008.

522   "It was dirty": "The Name Rings a Bell," Christine Haughney, *New
      York Times*, January 30, 2011.

523   "a little bit of a wild kid": Ibid.

527   "I was into that idea": Edward Norton interviewed in Kenny, *Robert
      De Niro*.

527 "I think Bob was just switched on": Ibid.
528 "A lot of times actors": Ibid.

Chapter 30

540 "Robert and I have been speaking": "Making of *Silver Linings Playbook*," Tatiana Siegel, *Hollywood Reporter*, December 14, 2012.

544 "When I'm being polite": "Proust Questionnaire: Robert De Niro," *Vanity Fair*, March 2013.

550 "I always wanted to chronicle": "What I've Learned: Robert De Niro."

550 "I guess you could call it": "Robert De Niro's Wife Grace Hightower Keeps Surrogate Daughter Undercover as She Steps Out with Bundle of Joy for First Time," Sarah Fitzmaurice, *Daily Mail* (London), March 2, 2012.

551 "I have young kids": "The Best Is Yet to Come," David Hochman, *AARP*, October–November, 2013.

551 "I feel optimistic": Ibid.

Bibliography

De Niro Biographies

Note: Of the following, those by Baxter and Dougan are the fullest works of biographical research and analysis.

Baxter, John. *De Niro: A Biography*. London: HarperCollins, 2002.

Brode, Douglas. *The Films of Robert De Niro*, 4th ed. New York: Citadel, 2001.

Cameron-Wilson, James. *The Cinema of Robert De Niro*. London: Zomba Books, 1986.

Dougan, Andy. *Untouchable: A Biography of Robert De Niro*. New York: Thunder's Mouth Press, 1996.

McKay, Keith. *Robert De Niro: The Hero Behind the Masks*. New York: St. Martin's Press, 1986.

Nisini, Giorgio. *Robert De Niro*. Rome: Gremese Editore, 2004.

Parker, John. *Robert De Niro: Portrait of a Legend*. London: John Blake, 2009.

Rauch, Andrew J. *The Films of Martin Scorsese and Robert De Niro*. Lanham, MD: Scarecrow Press, 2010.

Robert De Niro Sr. and Virginia Admiral:
Their Lives, Art, and Times

Bair, Deirdre. *Anaïs Nin: A Biography*. New York: Putnam, 1995.

D. C. Moore Gallery. *Robert De Niro Sr.: Paintings and Drawings, 1960–1993*. New York: D. C. Moore Gallery, 2012.

De Niro, Robert, Sr. *A Fashionable Watering Place: Poems*. New York: 1976.

Fitch, Noel Riley. *Anaïs: The Erotic Life of Anaïs Nin*. New York: Little, Brown, 1993.

Hackett-Freedman Gallery. *Robert De Niro Sr.: Selected Works*. San Francisco: Hackett-Freedman Gallery, 1998.

Harris, Mary Emma. *The Arts at Black Mountain College*. Cambridge, MA: MIT Press, 1987.

Jarnot, Lisa. *Robert Duncan: The Ambassador from Venus, a Biography*. Berkeley: University of California Press, 2012.

Kelly, Andrew, and Ivana Salander, eds. *Robert De Niro Sr.* New York: Salander-O'Reilly, 2004.

Nin, Anaïs. *The Diary of Anaïs Nin*, vol. 2, *1934–1939*. New York: Swallow Press, 1967.

———. *The Diary of Anaïs Nin*, vol. 3, *1939–1944*. New York: Mariner, 1971.

O'Hara, Frank. *Standing Still and Walking in New York*. San Francisco: Grey Fox, 1983.

Perl, Jed. *New Art City: Manhattan at Mid-Century*. New York: Knopf, 2005.

Rivers, Larry, with Arnold Weinstein. *What Did I Do? The Unauthorized Autobiography*. New York: HarperCollins, 1992.

Sandler, Irving. *The New York School: The Painters and Sculptors of the Fifties*. New York: Harper and Row, 1978.

Film Histories and Biographies Bearing on De Niro, His Films, His Career, and His Milieu

Abramowitz, Rachel. *Is That a Gun in Your Pocket? Women's Experience of Power in Hollywood*. New York: Random House, 2000.

Adams, Cindy. *Lee Strasberg*. Garden City, NY: Doubleday, 1980.

Bach, Steven. *Final Cut: Dreams and Disaster in the Making of "Heaven's Gate."* New York: William Morrow, 1985.

Baer, William, ed. *Elia Kazan Interviews*. Jackson: University Press of Mississippi, 2000.

Biskind, Peter. *Easy Riders, Raging Bulls: How the Sex-Drugs-and-Rock-'n'-Roll Generation Saved Hollywood*. New York: Simon & Schuster, 1998.

———. *Down and Dirty Pictures: Miramax, Sundance, and the Rise of Independent Film*. New York: Simon & Schuster, 2004.

Brenner, Marie. *Going Hollywood: An Insider's Look at Power and Pretense in the Movie Business*. New York: Delacorte Press, 1978.

Brunette, Peter. *Martin Scorsese Interviews*. Jackson: University Press of Mississippi, 1999.

Cameron, Julia. *Floor Sample: A Creative Memoir*. New York: Penguin, 2006.

Cosgrove, Bill. *Robert De Niro and the Fireman*. Bethel, CT: Rutledge, 1997.

Cowie, Peter. *Coppola: A Biography.* New York: Charles Scribner's Sons, 1990.

Doron, Meir, and Joseph Gelmis. *Confidential: The Life of Secret Agent Turned Hollywood Tycoon Arnon Milchan.* New York: Gefen, 2011.

Flynn, Nick. *The Reenactments: A Memoir.* New York: W. W. Norton, 2013.

Garfield, David. *A Player's Place: The Story of the Actors Studio.* New York: Macmillan, 1980.

Goodwin, Michael, and Naomi Wise. *On the Edge: The Life and Times of Francis Coppola.* New York: William Morrow, 1989.

Grobel, Lawrence. *Al Pacino in Conversation with Lawrence Grobel.* New York: Simon Spotlight Entertainment, 2006.

Harris, Mark. *Pictures at a Revolution: Five Movies and the Birth of the New Hollywood.* New York: Penguin, 2008.

Hirsch, Foster. *A Method to Their Madness: The History of the Actors Studio.* New York: Da Capo, 2002.

Hoberman, J. *Vulgar Modernism: Writing on Movies and Other Media.* Philadelphia: Temple University Press, 1991.

Kazan, Elia. *Kazan on Directing.* New York: Knopf, 2009.

Kellow, Brian. *Pauline Kael: A Life in the Dark.* New York: Viking, 2011.

Kelly, Mary Pat. *Martin Scorsese: A Journey.* New York: Thunder's Mouth Press, 1991.

LaMotta, Jake, with Joseph Carter and Pete Savage. *Raging Bull: My Story.* New York: Da Capo, 1997.

Lawrence, Mary Wells. *A Big Life in Advertising.* New York: Knopf, 2002.

Lebo, Harlan. *The Godfather Legacy.* New York: Fireside, 1997.

Levy, Shawn. *King of Comedy: The Life and Art of Jerry Lewis.* New York: St. Martin's Press, 1996.

Lewis, John. *Whom God Wishes to Destroy: Francis Coppola and the New Hollywood.* Durham, NC: Duke University Press, 1995.

Linson, Art. *A Pound of Flesh: Perilous Tales of How to Produce Movies in Hollywood.* New York: Grove Press, 1993.

LoBrutto, Vincent. *Martin Scorsese: A Biography.* Westport: Praeger, 2008.

Lourdeaux, Lee. *Italian and Irish Filmmakers in America: Ford, Capra, Coppola and Scorsese.* Philadelphia: Temple University Press, 1990.

Mardirosian, Tom. *Saved from Obscurity.* New York: Dramatists Play Service, 1989.

Navasky, Victor S. *Naming Names.* New York: Viking, 1980.

Phillips, Gene. *Godfather: The Intimate Francis Ford Coppola.* Lexington: University Press of Kentucky, 2004.

Phillips, Gene D., and Rodney Hill. *Francis Ford Coppola: Interviews*. Jackson: University Press of Mississippi, 2004.

Phillips, Julia. *You'll Never Eat Lunch in This Town Again*. New York: Signet, 1992.

Pileggi, Nicholas. *Casino: Love and Honor in Las Vegas*. New York: Simon & Schuster, 1995.

Schickel, Richard. *Elia Kazan: A Biography*. New York: HarperCollins, 2005.

———. *Conversations with Scorsese*. New York: Knopf, 2011.

Schumacher, Michael. *Francis Ford Coppola: A Filmmaker's Life*. New York: Crown, 1999.

Shales, Tom, and James Andrew Miller. *Live from New York: An Uncensored History of "Saturday Night Live" as Told by Its Stars, Writers and Guests*. New York: Little, Brown, 2002.

Simon, Neil. *The Play Goes On*. New York: Simon & Schuster, 1999.

Slater, Robert. *Ovitz*. New York: McGraw-Hill, 1997.

Stadiem, William. *Moneywood: Hollywood in Its Last Age of Excess*. New York: St. Martin's Press, 2012.

Stevens, George, Jr. *Conversations with the Great Moviemakers of Hollywood's Golden Age*. New York: Knopf, 2006.

Thompson, David, and Ian Christie, eds. *Scorsese on Scorsese*. Boston: Faber & Faber, 1989.

Tosches, Nick. *The Nick Tosches Reader*. New York: Da Capo, 2007.

Vineberg, Steve. *Method Actors: Three Generations of an American Acting Style*. New York: Schirmer, 1991.

Wiley, Mason, and Damien Bona. *Inside Oscar: The Unofficial History of the Academy Awards*. New York: Ballantine, 1987.

Wilson, Michael Henry. *Scorsese on Scorsese*. Paris: Cahiers du Cinema, 2011.

Winters, Shelley. *Shelley II: The Middle of My Century*. New York: Simon & Schuster, 1989.

Woiwode, Larry. *What I Think I Did: A Season of Survival in Two Acts*. New York: Basic Books, 2000.

Woodward, Bob. *Wired: The Short Life and Fast Times of John Belushi*. New York: Simon & Schuster, 1984.

Yule, Andrew. *Enigma: David Puttnam, the Story So Far . . .* London: Mainstream Publishing, 1988.

———. *Life on the Wire: The Life and Art of Al Pacino*. New York: Donald I. Fine, 1991.

Key Interviews with De Niro

Note: De Niro is famously reticent and chary of the press, but he has, in fact, given thousands of interviews over the years. The following, listed in chronological order, are the most thorough, revealing, and perspicacious interviews with him that I encountered.

"Stardom's Drums Banging for Robert De Niro." Richard Cuskelly. *Los Angeles Herald-Examiner.* August 12, 1973.

"Robert De Niro: He Had to Play Ball." Tom Topor. *New York Post.* August 25, 1973.

"Look—Bobby's Slipping into Brando's Shoes." Guy Flatley. *New York Times.* November 4, 1973.

"Robert De Niro—Private, Professional, a Male Greta Garbo." *W.* July 11, 1975.

"The Quiet Chameleon." Richard Schickel. *Time.* January 27, 1975.

"Actor." Bob Thomas. *Los Angeles Herald-Examiner,* March 2, 1975.

"Robert De Niro—The Return of the Silent Film Star." Susan Braudy. *New York Times.* March 6, 1977.

"What's Robert De Niro Hiding?" Marie Brenner. *Redbook.* May 1977.

"De Niro: A Star for the '70s." Jack Kroll. *Newsweek,* May 16, 1977.

"It's Dilemma, It's Delimit, It's De Niro." Paul Gardner. *New York.* May 16, 1977.

"*New York, New York*: Martin Scorsese's Backlot Sonata, in Which Robert De Niro Trades in His .44 for a New Axe." Chris Hodenfeld. *Rolling Stone.* June 16, 1977.

"De Niro: The Phantom of the Cinema." *Time.* July 25, 1977.

"De Niro Talks!" Samir Hachem. *Hollywood Drama-Logue.* May 22, 1980.

"Dialogue on Film: Robert De Niro." *American Film.* March 1981.

"The Incredible Talent of Robert De Niro." Barbara Goldsmith. *Parade.* December 2, 1984.

"The Shadow King." Patricia Bosworth. *Vanity Fair.* October 1987.

"De Niro in Moscow." Wolfgang Wilke. *The Face.* December, 1987.

"De Niro." Fred Schruers. *Rolling Stone.* August 25, 1988.

"Playboy Interview: Robert De Niro." Lawrence Grobel. *Playboy.* January 1989.

"Maximum Expression." Barry Paris. *American Film.* October 1989.

"'You Talkin' to Me?' 'No!'" Alan Richman. *GQ,* January 1991.

"Method and the Man." Steve Grant. *Time Out.* May 22, 1991.

"De Niro Direct." Julia Reed. *Vogue*. March 1993.

"A Walk and a Talk with Robert De Niro." Peter Brant and Ingrid Sischy. *Interview*. November 1993.

"Robert De Niro." Elizabeth Kaye. *New York Times*. November 14, 1993.

"De Niro on De Niro." *Vogue*. January 1995.

"The Man Who Acts Like God." Mike Sager. *Esquire*. December 1997.

"What I've Learned: Robert De Niro." *Esquire*. January 2003.

"Yeah, I'm Talkin' to You." Belinda Luscombe. *Time*. December 11, 2006.

"And Now, 972 Words from Robert De Niro." Chris Heath. *GQ*. January 2007.

"What I've Learned: Robert De Niro." *Esquire*. January 2011.

"Robert De Niro on His Father's Art Studio." *Daily Beast*. July 9, 2012.

"De Niro." A. O. Scott. *New York Times*. November 18, 2012.

"Proust Questionnaire: Robert De Niro." *Vanity Fair*. March 2013.

Index